73

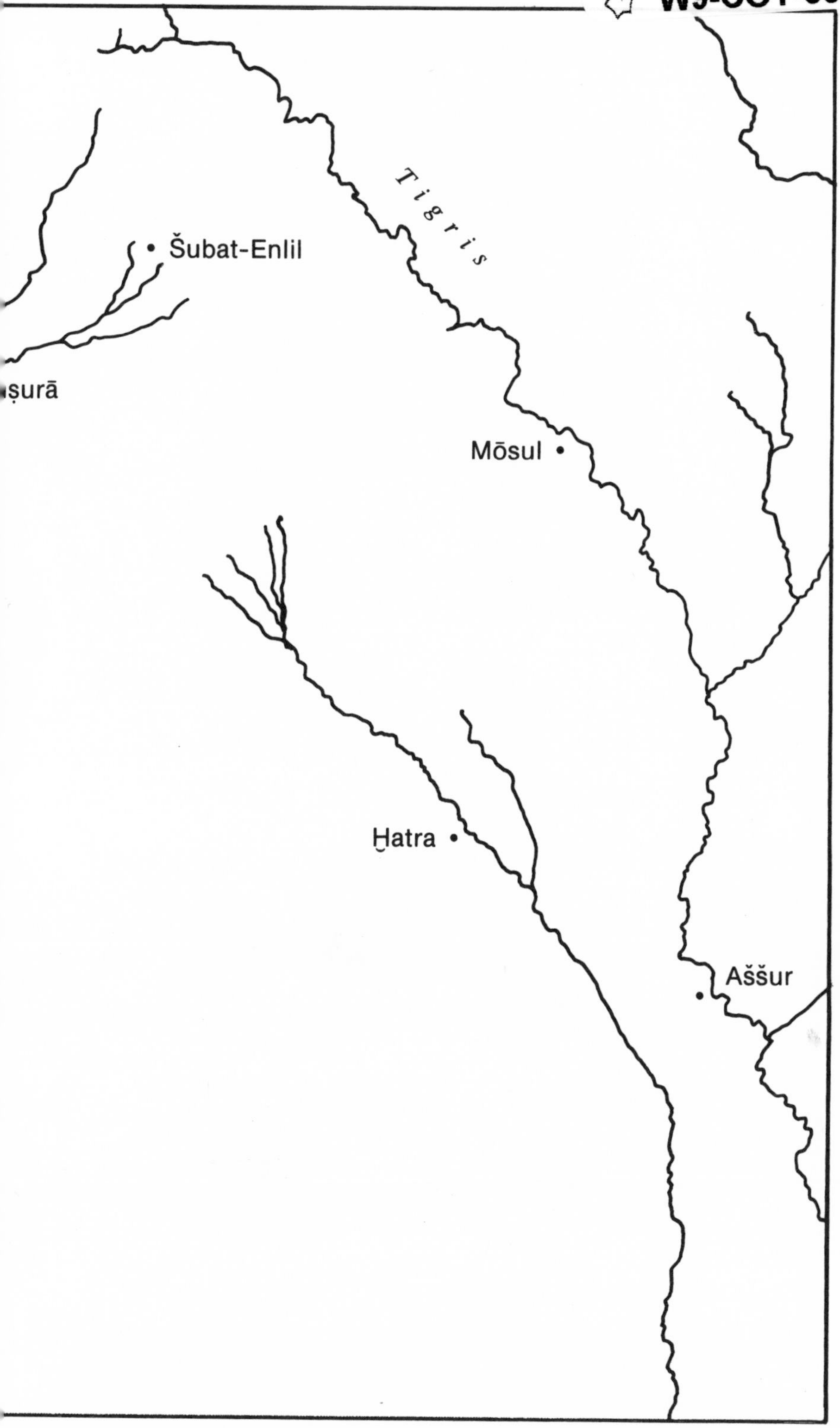

Mari in Retrospect

MARI IN RETROSPECT

FIFTY YEARS OF MARI AND MARI STUDIES

Edited by
Gordon D. Young

Eisenbrauns
Winona Lake, Indiana
1992

Printed in the United States of America.

Library of Congress Cataloging-in-Publication Data

Mari in retrospect : fifty years of Mari and Mari studies / edited by Gordon D. Young.
p. cm.
Essays originally presented at the joint annual meeting of the Middle West Branch of the American Oriental Society and the Midwest Region of the Society of Biblical Literature, held at the Oriental Institute of the University of Chicago in 1983.
Includes bibliographical references and indexes.
ISBN 0-931464-28-5
1. Mari (Extinct city)—Congresses. 2. Middle East—History—to 622—Congresses. I. Young, Gordon Douglas. II. American Oriental Society. Middle West Branch. III. Society of Biblical Literature. Mid-West Region.
DS99.M3M364 1992
93—dc20 91-37606

Mari in Retrospect

is dedicated to the memories of

André Parrot

brilliant discoverer and
excavator of Tell Hariri–Mari

and

I. J. Gelb

America's Assyriologist par excellence

While they can no longer carry the torch, their achievements still awe and inform those who have picked up the the torch. May their numbers multiply, and may their efforts keep the flame burning brightly.

Contents

Preface ix

Abbreviations xi

The North Mesopotamian Kingdom of Ilānṣurā 1
MICHAEL C. ASTOUR

The Old Assyrian Caravan Road in the Mari Royal Archives 35
B. J. BEITZEL

Les Legendes de Sceaux de Mari: Nouvelles Données 59
DOMINIQUE CHARPIN

Early Second Millennium Ceramic Parallels
between Tell Hadidi-Azu and Mari 77
RUDOLPH DORNEMANN

The *Mubassirū* Messengers at Mari 113
ROBERT W. FISHER

Mari and the Kish Civilization 121
I. J. GELB†

The *Nīšum* "Oath" in Mari 203
PAUL HOSKISSON

The Divine Nature of the Mediterranean Sea
in the Foundation Inscription of Yaḫdunlim 211
ABRAHAM MALAMAT

The 1979-1982 Excavations at Mari:
New Perspectives and Results 217
JEAN-CLAUDE MARGUERON

The Amorite Migrations 233
GEORGE E. MENDENHALL

Mari: The View from Ebla 243
PIOTR MICHALOWSKI

^{LÚ}*ebbum* as a Professional Title at Mari 249
M. DELOY PACK

"He Restoreth My Soul": A Biblical Expression
and Its Mari Counterpart 265
JONATHAN D. SAFREN

Bibliography 273

Indexes 309
General Index 309
Index of Names 314
Personal Names 314
Divine Names 319
Geographical Names 320
Index of Texts 329
Ancient Near Eastern Texts and Seals 329
Scripture 339
Language Index 340
Arabic 340
Aramaic (Including Syriac) 340
Akkadian (Including Eblaite, Kishite, and Amorite, Plus Semitic Words Found in Cuneiform Sources) 340
Early Northwest Semitic (Including Ugaritic and the Language of the Byblian Syllabic Texts) 343
Hebrew and Phoenician 343
Sumerian 344

Preface

The essays included in this book were originally presented at the joint annual meeting of the Middle West Branch of the American Oriental Society and the Midwest Region of the Society of Biblical Literature, held at the Oriental Institute of the University of Chicago in 1983. The authors have not had an opportunity to update their articles after submitting them in 1985; editor and publisher apologize to both readers and authors.

The Midwest AOS/SBL previously hosted a conference on the fiftieth anniversary of the discovery of Ugarit, and the papers presented there were published as *Ugarit in Retrospect: Fifty Years of Ugarit and Ugaritic*, edited by Gordon D. Young (Winona Lake, Indiana: Eisenbrauns, 1981). A subsequent centenary conference on the work at Tell el-Amarna, held at the Oriental Institute under the same sponsorship in 1987, will appear in the future.

After the untimely death of I. J. Gelb, his exceedingly complex article was proofread by the editor.

The Publisher

Abbreviations

(Bibliographic citations may be found in the bibliography, pp. 273–308 below.)

AAM	Archives administratives de Mari
	1 = Bardet *et al.* (1984) = ARM 23
AASOR	Annual of the American Schools of Oriental Research
AbB	Altbabylonische Briefe
	6 = Frankena (1974)
ADD	*Assyrian Deeds and Documents.* Johns (1898–1923)
	ADD 420 = 1: pl. 333, and 3: 47–48
	ADD 742 = 2: pls. 15–22, and 3: 489–91
AHw	*Akkadisches Handwörterbuch.* Von Soden (1965–81)
ANET^{3}	*Ancient Near Eastern Texts Relating to the Old Testament,* 3d edition with supplement. Pritchard (1969)
AnOr	Analecta Orientalia
	6 = Driver (1933)
	9 = Pohl (1934)
AOAT	Alter Orient und Altes Testament
ARAB	*Ancient Records of Assyria and Babylonia.* Luckenbill (1926–27)
ARET	Archivi Reali di Ebla, Testi
	2 = Edzard (1981a)
	3 = Archi and Biga (1982)
	4 = Biga and Milano (1984)
	5 = Edzard (1984)
ARI	*Assyrian Royal Inscriptions.* Grayson (1972–76)
ARM	Archives Royales de Mari
	1 = Dossin (1946) = TCL 22
	2 = Jean (1941) = TCL 23
	3 = Kupper (1948a) = TCL 24
	4 = Dossin (1951a) = TCL 25
	5 = Dossin (1951b) = TCL 26
	6 = Kupper (1953) = TCL 27
	7 = Bottéro (1956) = TCL 28
	8 = Boyer (1957) = TCL 29
	9 = Birot (1960a) = TCL 30
	10 = Dossin (1967a) = TCL 31
	14 = Birot (1976) = TCM 1
	18 = Rouault (1976) = TCM 2
	19 = Limet (1976a) = TCM 3

	20 = Dossin (in prep.)
	21 = Durand (1982a) = TCM 5
	23 = Bardet *et al.* (1984) = AAM 1
ARM HC	Archives Royale de Mari. Hors de Collection. Siglum for Mari tablets published in venues other than ARM or ARMT (see ARMT 17/1)
ARMT	Archives Royales de Mari Transcrites et Traduites
	1 = Dossin (1950a)
	2 = Jean (1950a)
	3 = Kupper (1950a)
	4 = Dossin (1951c)
	5 = Dossin (1952a)
	6 = Kupper (1954)
	7 = Bottéro (1957)
	8 = Boyer (1958)
	9 = Birot (1960b)
	10 = Dossin (1978)
	11 = Burke (1963)
	12 = Birot (1964a)
	13 = Dossin (1964a), Bottéro (1964), Birot (1964b), Burke (1964a), Kupper (1964a), and Finet (1964a)
	14 = Birot (1974)
	15 = Bottéro and Finet (1954)
	16/1 = Birot, Kupper, and Rouault (1979)
	16/2 = (in prep.)
	17/1 = Heintz, Marx, and Millot (1975)
	17/2 = (in prep.)
	18 = Rouault (1977)
	19 = Limet (1976b)
	20 = Dossin (in prep.)
	21 = Durand (1983a)
	22 = Kupper (1983)
AS	Assyriological Studies
	11 = Jacobsen (1939)
	16 = Güterbock and Jacobsen (1965)
	17 = Buccellati and Biggs (1969)
	18 = Gelb (1969)
	19 = Kaufman (1974)
	21 = Gelb (1980)
	23 = Whiting (1987)
AT	*The Alalakh Tablets.* Wiseman (1953)
BH	*Biblia Hebraica,* 3rd edition. Kittel (1937)
BHS	*Biblia Hebraica Stuttgartensia.* Elliger and Rudolph (1967–77)
BIN	Babylonian Inscriptions in the Collection of James B. Nies
	3 = Keiser/Kang (1971)
	4 = Clay (1927)
	6 = Stephens (1944)
	8 = Hackman (1958)

2BoTU	*Die Boghazköi-Texte in Umschrift* 2. Forrer (1922)
B.R. 513	B.R. 513 (Restricted). Geographical Handbook Series: Syria. April 1943
CAD	*Chicago Assyrian Dictionary*
CAH^3	*Cambridge Ancient History*, 3d edition
CCT	Cuneiform Texts from Cappadocian Tablets in the British Museum
	1 = Smith (1921)
	2 = Smith (1924)
	4 = Smith (1927)
	5 = Smith and Wiseman (1956)
CRAIBL	*Académie des Inscriptions et Belles Lettres: Compte Rendus*
CT	Cuneiform Texts from Babylonian Tablets . . . in the British Museum
	5 = King (1898)
	19 = Thompson (1904)
	50 = Sollberger (1972)
DeZ	Siglum for tablets from Deir ez-Zor
DN	Divine Name
EA	Siglum for tablets from Tell El-Amarna. Knudtzon (1908–15)
EL	Siglum for tablets published in Eisser and Lewy (1930–35)
GazSyr	Gazetteer No. 104: Syria: Official Standard Names, approved by the U.S. Board on Geographic Names. Department of Interior, Washington, D.C., December 1967
GazTurk	Gazetter No. 46: Turkey: Official Standard Names, approved by the U.S. Board on Geographic Names. Department of Interior, Washington, D.C., March 1960
GN	Geographical Name
HLC	Haverford Library of Cuneiform Tablets
	3 = Barton (1914)
HSS	Harvard Semitic Series
	10 = Meek (1935)
HT	Siglum for Hittite tablets in the British Museum
IM	Siglum for tablets in the Iraq Museum, Baghdad
Iraq 7	Siglum for Chagar Bazar and Tell Braq tablets published in Gadd (1940)
ITT	Inventaire des Tablettes de Tello
	1 = Thureau-Dangin (1910a)
K.	Siglum for tablets in the Kouyunjik collection of the British Museum
KAH 2	*Keilschrifttexte aus Assur historischen Inhalts* 2. Schroeder (1922)
KAV	*Keilschrifttexte aus Assur verschiedenen Inhalts*. Schroeder (1920)
KBL	Koehler and Baumgartner (1953)
KBo	Keilschrifttexte aus Boghazköi
	1 = Figulla, Forrer, and Weidner (1923)
	3 = Figulla (1923)
	4 = Forrer (1920a)
KTS	Keilschrifttexte in den Antiken-Museen Stamboul. J. Lewy (1926)

KTU	*Die keilalphabetischen Text aus Ugarit.* Dietrich, Loretz, and Sanmartín (1976)
KUB	Keilschrifturkunden aus Boghazköi
	8 = Weidner (1924)
	36 = Otten (1955)
MAD	Materials for the Assyrian Dictionary
	1 = Gelb (1952)
	2^2 = Gelb (1961^2)
	3 = Gelb (1957)
	4 = Gelb (1970a)
	5 = Gelb (1970b)
MAH	Siglum for tablets in the Musée d'Art et d'Histoire de Genève
	MAH 16158 = Garelli (1965) 41–43
MAM	Mission Archéologique de Mari
	1 = Parrot (1956)
	2/3 = Parrot (1959)
	3 = Parrot (1967)
	4 = Parrot and Dossin (1968)
MARI	*Mari–Annales de Recherches Interdisciplinaires*
MCS	Manchester Cuneiform Studies
	9/1 = Donald (1964)
MDP	Mémoires de la Délégation en Perse
	2 = Scheil (1900)
	14 = Legrain (1913)
ME	Mari empreinte. Siglum for Mari seal impressions
MEE	Materiali Epigraphici di Ebla
	1 = Pettinato (1979a)
	2 = Pettinato (1980a)
	3 = Pettinato (1981b)
	4 = Pettinato (1982)
Metr. Mus.	Metropolitan Museum, New York
MN	Month Name
MRS	Mission de Ras Shamra
	9 = Nougayrol (1956) = PRU 4
MSL	Materials for the Sumerian Lexicon
	9 = Landsberger (1967)
	11 = Landsberger, Reiner, and Civil (1973)
	12 = Civil (1969)
	14 = Civil (1979)
MVN	Materiali per il vocabolario neosumerico
	2 = Sauren (1975)
	3 = Owen (1975)
ND	Siglum for tablets excavated at Nimrud (Kalhu)
NEB	New English Bible
Not. Dig.	*Notitia Dignitatum.* Seeck (1876)
OBTR	*Old Babylonian Temple Records.* Lau (1906)
OBTTR	*The Old Babylonian Tablets from Tell al-Rimah.* Dalley, Walker, and Hawkins (1976)

OECT	Oxford Editions of Cuneiform Texts 2 = Langdon (1923)
OIP	Oriental Institute Publications 14 = Luckenbill (1930) 27 = Gelb (1935) 47 = Eisen (1940) 99 = Biggs (1974)
PBS	Publications of the Babylonian Section. University of Pennsylvania, the Museum 9/1 = Barton (1915) 13 = Legrain (1922)
PDTI	*Die Puzriš-Dagan Texte der Istanbuler Archäoligischen Museen.* Salonen *et al.* (1954)
PN	Personal Name
PRU	Le palais royale d'Ugarit 4 = Nougayrol (1956) = MRS 9
RGTC	Repertoire géographique des textes cunéiformes 1 = Edzard, Farber, and Sollberger (1977) = TAVO 7/1 2 = Edzard and Farber (1974) = TAVO 7/2 3 = Groneberg (1980) = TAVO 7/3 6 = del Monte and Tischler (1978) = TAVO 7/6
RLA	*Reallexikon der Assyriologie.* Ebeling and Meissner *et al.* (1932-)
RN	Royal Name
RS	Siglum for Ras Shamra (Ugarit) tablets
RSV	Revised Standard Version
RTC	*Recueil de tablettes chaldéennes.* Thureau-Dangin (1903)
SAKI	*Die sumerischen und akkadischen Königsinschriften.* Thureau-Dangin (1907)
SET	*Sumerian Economic Texts from the Third Ur Dynasty.* Jones and Snyder (1961)
SKL	*The Sumerian King List.* Jacobsen (1939)
T	Siglum for tablets in the Staatliche Museum, Berlin
TA	Siglum for tablets from Tell Asmar
TAVO	Tübinger Atlas des Vorderen Orients Beihefte 7 = RGTC 26 = Kessler (1980)
TC	Tablettes Cappadociennes 1 = Contenau (1920) = TCL 4 2 = Thureau-Dangin (1928) = TCL 14 3/1 = J. Lewy (1935) = TCL 19 3/2 = J. Lewy (1936) = TCL 20 3/3 = J. Lewy (1937) = TCL 21
TCL	Textes Cunéiformes. Musée de Louvre—Département des Antiquités Orientales 1 = Thureau-Dangin (1910b) 5 = de Genouillac (1922) 17 = Dossin (1933)

	For volumes 4, 14, 19–21, see TC
	For volumes 22–31, see ARM
TCM	Textes Cunéiformes de Mari
	1, 2, 3, and 5 = ARM 14, 18, 19, and 21, respectively
TLB	Tabulae cuneiformes a F. M. Th. de Liagre Böhl collectae
	1 = Leemans (1954)
	3 = Hallo (1963)
TM	Siglum for tablets from Tell Mardikh (Ebla)
TMH	Texte und Materialen der Frau Professor Hilprecht Collection of Babylonian Antiquities
	5 = Pohl (1935)
TRU	*Le temps des rois d'Ur.* Legrain (1912)
UE 2	*Ur Excavations II.* Woolley *et al.* (1934)
UET	*Ur Excavations, Texts*
	1 = Gadd, Legrain, and Smith (1928)
VAT	Siglum for tablets in the Vorderasiatischen Abteilung der Staatlichen Museen, Berlin
	VAT 9260 = J. Lewy (1952) 265

The North Mesopotamian Kingdom of Ilānṣurā

MICHAEL C. ASTOUR

Southern Illinois University
at Edwardsville

INTRODUCTORY REMARKS

Among the scores of petty states that existed in Upper Mesopotamia at the time of the Mari archives, the kingdom of Ilānṣurā was one of the more important.[1] Its king, Ḫāya-sūmû, though formally recognizing the overlordship of Zimri-Lim, king of Mari,[2] was in fact quite independent in his political and military actions. Over a century later, Ilānṣurā was the object of a Hittite expedition. In order to visualize the role of Ilānṣurā in the politico-geographical context of the Mari Age and the Hittite Old Kingdom, one must ascertain its location. This is closely connected with finding the positions of its subordinate towns, of the states that bordered on it, and with reconstructing the itinerary of the Old Hittite foray. This line of research will contribute to the recreation of the historical map of North Mesopotamia in the Middle Bronze Age by throwing light on one of its outlying districts.

As normal in this kind of investigation, the method used will be a combinatory one, utilizing all of the following data: (a) textual evidence about the relative positions of cities and states with respect to each other; (b) textual references to features of physical geography; (c) reference points that may be found by coordinating data of ancient itineraries with the presence of significant archaeological objects; (d) survival of certain Middle Bronze Age place names in the Neo-Assyrian, Roman-Byzantine, Medieval Arab, and modern periods. The criterion of correctness in locating ancient sites is simply whether all the pieces of the geographical jigsaw puzzle fall in place and form a consistent whole.

[1]The name is spelled *I-la-an-ṣu-ra-a*^{ki} (most frequently), [*I*]*-la-an-ṣú-ra*^{ki}, *I-la-an-ṣú-ur*^{ki}, [*I-l*]*a-an-ṣ*[*ú-u*]*r-a*^{ki}, and *I-la-ṣú-*[*ra-a*^{ki}] in Mari texts. See Kupper, ARMT 16/1 17. It is spelled ^{URU}*I-la-an-ṣú-ra*^{KI} in Hittite (KBo 3 60 iii: 14′). With Kupper, it will be here normalized as *Ilānṣurā*.

[2]Thus, in his letter to Zimri-Lim, ARM 2 62, he obsequiously calls himself "thy son," and declares that "these (Ḫāya-sūmû's) towns are thy towns."

Two remarks should be made before proceeding further:

1. Not all ancient settlements left their imprints in the Near Eastern landscape in the form of mounds. These can be found in the plains where houses were built of unbaked mud bricks. Mud brick constructions do not last very long, and once they collapse, their bricks cannot be put to new use. This results in the creation of large accumulations of debris, known locally as tells or hüyüks. In the mountains, however, wood and stone were used as building materials. Wooden houses burn down with virtually no trace. Stone houses stand for a very long time, and when they are destroyed, their stones are re-employed for new buildings, and sometimes transported to different sites.[3] One must not require the presence of a mound to confirm the antiquity of a mountainous site, because mounds do not arise in mountain areas.

2. Conversely, in the specific conditions of North Mesopotamia, ancient toponyms are apt to survive for considerable stretches of time in the mountains and their immediate piedmonts, where the continuity of settled life was seldom, if at all, interrupted, but not in the plains and steppes which were repeatedly abandoned to nomadic tribes for hundreds of years.[4] There is a difference in principle between trying to locate an ancient site in the middle of the Mesopotamian steppe on the basis of an apparent onomastic resemblance,[5] and doing the same in the massif of Ṭūr ᶜAbdīn, or the mountains of southern Armenia. Ancient cities whose names have been clearly revealed by excavated inscriptional evidence are still few and far between, and none of them, unfortunately, lies within the area of our present investigation.

THE HITTITE EXPEDITION AGAINST ILĀNṢURĀ

We shall begin with the Old Hittite material, even though it is later than the Mari texts, for it will provide us with our first bearings as to the general whereabouts of Ilānṣurā. This is the text KBo 3 60 = 2BoTU 21, an incompletely preserved literary composition which contains the legendary motif of cannibalism overlaid upon a description of military actions against real, historically attested cities.[6] The action of the story

[3]On this subject, see the remarks of Rostovtzeff (1932) 161–62, Goetze (1960) 47, and Mellink (1969) 291.

[4]This has been explained convincingly and demonstrated by Dillemann (1962) 69–71, and elsewhere in this book.

[5]Thus Falkner (1957–58) 36 identified Kasapā of the Mari tablets with modern Qṣēbah, which will be considered below because of its implications for the location of Ilānṣurā.

[6]Published in transliteration and translation with commentary by Güterbock (1938) 105–13. Only parts of columns ii and iii are extant. The motif of anthropophagy recurs in certain Greek myths which, interestingly enough, deal with the Pelopidai, a family of reputedly Anatolian origin. This motif does not concern us here. Laroche (1971) No. 17:1 lists KBo 3 60 as a fragment of an historical text relating to Hurrian wars.

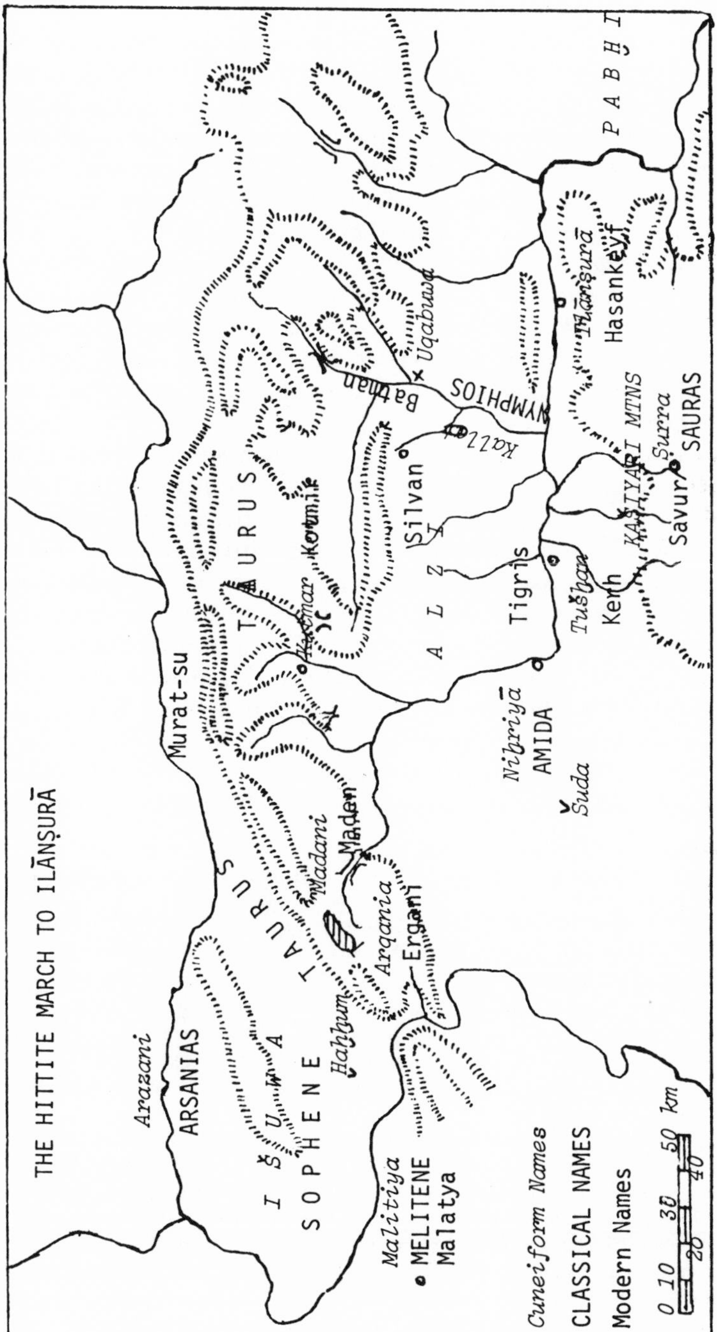
THE HITTITE MARCH TO ILĀNṢURĀ
Cuneiform Names
CLASSICAL NAMES
Modern Names
0 10 20 30 40 50 km
Arazani
ARSANIAS
Murat-su
Malitiya
MELITENE
Malatya
SOPHENE
TAURUS
Hahhum
Arqania
Ergani
Madani
Maden
Nihriya
AMIDA
Šuda
ALZI
Tigris
Tušhan
Kerh
Silvan
Batman
NYMPHIOS
Uqabuwa
Ilānṣurā
Hasankeyf
KAŠIYARI MTNS
Surra
Savur
SAURAS

Map 1.

doubtless takes place during the reign of Ḫattušiliš I: it is linked to the narrative of "The Siege of Uršu" (KBo 1 11)[7] by the person of Zuppa, the ruler of an unspecified state, who tried to relieve the beleaguered North Syrian city and, in the story under consideration, had his entire army, and his own mother, destroyed and eaten by the cannibals, leaving him as the only one to escape.[8] Since the man-eaters, led by a mysterious character whose name is spelled ideographically ᵐDUMU.MAḪ.LÍL,[9] had the same enemy as the Hittites, they must be taken as their allies.[10] The time of the action is later than the events of the first six years of Ḫattušiliš I's reign which are described in the bilingual *Res Gestae*, and end with the conquest and plunder of the city of Ḫaḫḫu, but do not yet include the siege of Uršu. The extant parts of the tablet deal with the man-eaters' attack on the city of Uqabuwa and the Hittites' advance from Nuḫuyana to Ilānṣurā. How are we to visualize the geographical arena of those operations?

Before the publication of Mari tablets mentioning Ilānṣurā, it was permissible to guess, as Albright did in 1940, that it was "somewhere in the region west of Harran . . . between Carchemish and Harran."[11] Such a location would be an easy goal of a short Hittite raid from Syria. But the Mari tablets disclosed that, wherever Ilānṣurā is to be placed, it was quite distant from Carchemish and Ḫarran. In order to reach it, the Hittites would have to march across much of Mesopotamia, that is, through the very heartland of the powerful kingdom of Ḫurri or Ḫanigalbat[12] with whom they were engaged in a bitter and protracted war since the third year of those recorded in the *Res Gestae*. One would expect to hear of immediate armed resistance on the part of the Hurrians, but we find instead that it was only after the Hittites began to plunder

[7]This text, written in Akkadian, can be consulted conveniently in the edition of Güterbock (1938) 114–38.

[8]Zuppa's mother (Güterbock [1938] 106, reads AMA rather than SILÁ, "sheep") was seized in ᵁᴿᵁ*Ti-ni-ši-pa*. Unfortunately, that place is otherwise unknown. The episode starts *ex abrupto* after a break.

[9]On this character, cf. Güterbock (1938) 111 n 1, with reference to Thureau-Dangin (1922) 175, where an epithet of the god Lillu is quoted: ᵈLil dumu Dingir-maḫ-gé, "Lillu, son of the Sublime Goddess." LÍL and GÉ are readings of the same sign.

[10]The narrative alternates between "they," the man-eaters, and "we," the Hittites, but both sides seem to act in concert.

[11]Albright (1940) 2 30. But one cannot excuse Giorgadze (1969) 78 for asserting, almost three decades and thirteen volumes of ARM later, that "the city of Ilānṣurā was located somewhere west of the Euphrates River, in the direction of the city of Ḫalpa."

[12]Scholars who did not want to admit that a state called Ḫanigalbat already existed at the time of Ḫattušiliš I claimed that *Ḫa-ni-kal-bat* in the Akkadian version of the *Res Gestae* was a modernizing term introduced into the text under the New Kingdom. But see Gelb (1968) 97, a quotation from an unpublished Old Babylonian tablet from the reign of Ammiṣaduqa, a contemporary of Ḫattušiliš I, which mentions *tu-ur-gu-ma-an-ni ša* ERIN *Ḫa-bi-in-gal-ba-ti-i*, "interpreters of the Ḫanigalbatean people."

and oppress the land of Ilānṣurā that its king sent golden vases to four Hurrian kings. They had to be paid for coming to the rescue of Ilānṣurā, which indicates that their own lands had not been encroached by the Hittite troops. This means that they took a different route to reach Ilānṣurā—one that would avoid the Hurrian territory.

Now, as we remember, the sixth and final year of those covered by Ḫattušiliš I's *Res Gestae* was marked by an outstanding double triumph—the capture of the Syrian royal city of Ḫaššu, crossing the Euphrates, and the conquest and burning of the rich royal city of Ḫaḫḫu. The location of Ḫaḫḫu—a city that occurs in Sumerian, Old Assyrian, Old Babylonian, Mariote, Hittite (from both Old and New Kingdoms), and Byzantine sources—has been much discussed in scholarly literature, and here is not the place to consider this controversial problem.[13] Let it be simply stated, for the time being, that the Old Assyrian data on one of the two principal routes by which Kaniš could be reached from North Mesopotamia firmly place Ḫaḫḫu(m) in the general area of present-day Elâziğ, classical Sophene: the land contained by the Taurus, the Euphrates, the lower Arsanias (Murat), and the uppermost Tigris.[14] All other inscriptional and toponymic testimonies concur with this location. It must also be taken into account that Ḫattušiliš I's capture of Ḫaḫḫu was not just a hit-and-run pillaging foray. The city's position on the main highway from the Hittite country to North Mesopotamia must have also been one of the king's motives. It was probably by that road that the Hurrians, three years earlier, had invaded central Anatolia. Now it became a Hittite outpost against the Hurrian lands. It still belonged to the Hittites in the early part of the fifteenth century, as shown by the mention of Ḫaḫḫu in a fragmentary text from the reign of Ammunaš (KUB 36 71 rev. iv: 15). Sophene was a convenient transit area for an army which, proceeding from Anatolia, invaded the region between the Armenian Taurus and the upper Tigris, as exemplified by the expeditions of Šuppiluliumaš I in 1366, and Lucullus in 69 B.C.[15] Let us assume, as a working hypothesis, that the military actions described in KBo 3 60 were launched from Ḫaḫḫu.

[13]This I hope to do in a separate study on the Old Assyrian roads to Cappadocia.

[14]The same conclusion was reached, or envisaged, through different approaches by Honigmann (1930) 302, (1935) 59–60 and n 2; Forbes (1950) 151; and Orlin (1970) 39 n 53.

[15]At the time of the Hittite Empire, Sophene was known as Išuwa. KBo 4 14 mentions an expedition to Niḫriyā by a Hittite king in alliance with the king of Išuwa. See Meriggi (1962) 84–90. [A new, important epigraphic disclosure on that campaign, published in Lackenbacher (1982), requires a separate study.] Niḫriyā occurs as Niḫriyā in Mariote, Old Assyrian, and Middle Assyrian records, and should be located at Amida-Diyarbakir, beyond the Ergani-Maden Pass from Išuwa. Urarṭian kings of the eighth century marched through Sophene on their way to Melid (Melitene). Cf. von der Osten (1930) 148–49 on the strategic role of the region.

ŠUDĀ AND ṢU[RRĀ]

According to KBo 3 60 ii: 6–21, DUMU.MAḪ.LÍL and his man-eating troops stood before the city of Uqabuwa, which was aided by the cities of Šudā and Zu[. . .].[16] The man of Šudā, Kaniu (^{m}*Ka-ni-u-uš*), who must have been the ruler of Zu[. . .], and the city of Uqabuwa marched against DUMU.MAḪ.LÍL. Kaniu tested DUMU.MAḪ.LÍL by offering him roasted pork to find out whether he was a god or a man: "if he is a man and a mortal, we shall fight." DUMU.MAḪ.LÍL ate the roasted pork and thus revealed himself as a man, but column iii breaks at this point and we do not know whether a combat took place, or how it ended.

Of the cities mentioned in this passage, Šudā is the easiest to recognize.[17] It had its own king at the time of Zimri-Lim's reign in Mari. According to certain Mari letters,[18] he was a neighbor of the king of Niḫriyā. The proximity of the two cities can also be deduced from ARM 1 19. Niḫriyā appears in the Cappadocian tablets as an important royal city on the Old Assyrian road to Kaniš via Ḫaḫḫum, and its position on that route, compared with its mention in other sources, points to Diyarbakir, on the right bank of the Tigris, as its most likely location.[19] On the other hand, Šudā could be reached from the steppe between the Balīḫ and Ḫabūr Rivers (ARM 1 28, 39, and 97), and its king, Sibkuna-Addu, proposed to Zimri-Lim that they jointly invade the land of Zalmaqum which lay in the northern part of the area.[20] Šuppililiumaš I, in 1366, marched from Išuwa to the land of Alše, which is on the left bank of the upper Tigris. He conquered the city of Kutmar,[21] invaded and devastated the district of Šudā,[22] and attacked the capital of Mitanni,

[16]^{URU}*U-qa-bu-wa*, l. 7; ^{URU}*U-qa-bu-ia*, l. 8; LÚ ^{URU}*Šu-tu-um-ma-na-aš* (ethnic), l. 6; LÚ ^{URU}*Šu-ú-da*, l. 7; and ^{URU}*Zu*-x x x, l. 6.

[17]Testimonies collected in Falkner (1957/58) 27–29, but with omission of KBo 3 60. The name is written *Šu-da-a*^{KI}, *Su-da-a*^{KI}, and *Su-da*^{KI} in Mari texts; ^{URU}*Šu-ú-ta*, var. ^{URU}*Sú-ú-ta* in KBo 1 1 obv.: 26–27; ^{URU}*Su-da* in Middle Assyrian; and ^{URU}*Šu-u-du* in Neo-Assyrian records.

[18]According to Dossin (1939d) 116–17.

[19]See n 13, above.

[20]Dossin (1939a) 991.

[21]$^{[U]RU}$*Ku-ut-ma-ar* (KBo 1 1 obv.: 26) was at first identified by Forrer (1920b) 20–21, 87 with Assyrian Kullimmeri, and the latter with Byzantine Chlomaron in southern Armenia, east of the Batman River. This equation was taken up by Weidner (1923) 8 n 2. But in Forrer (1932) 89, he stated that "Kutmar is the Neo-Assyrian Kullimmeri, and has survived as the 'ruin mound' Til-ḫarabe near the village Kunmar on the road from Palu to Hany (Hini), 18 km. from the latter." On the 1:200,000 map of Turkey, sheet E 14 (*Palu*), and in Gaz.Turk. 423, the village appears as Kotmir (38°30′N, 40°13′E), which is much closer to the ancient name than the form given by Forrer (probably due to the similarity of the Arabic letters *n* and *t* on an Ottoman map). Such a location of Kutmar fits perfectly the purpose of Šuppiluliumaš's march, but it does not agree with the much more eastern position of Assyrian Kullimari, Urarṭian Qulmēri, Byzantine Chlomaron, and Armenian Kᶜlmar. The two places must be disassociated from each other.

[22]*Ḫal-ṣí* ^{URU}*Šu-ú-ta/Sú-ú-ta*.

Waššukkanni, which stood near the headwaters of the Ḫabūr,[23] in all likelihood. In a Neo-Assyrian list of provinces, ^{URU}*Šu-ú-du* and ^{URU}*Tu-uš-ḫa-an* stand together.[24] The identity of Tušḫan with modern Kerh, near the right bank of the Tigris, ca. 28 km. to the ESE of Diyarbakir, has been ascertained by the discovery there of Assurnasirpal II's monolith inscription.[25] In the Mari Age, Tušḫum and Šinamum formed a single state.[26] Šinamum bordered on the city-state of Buru(n)dum, which was located on the great road to Cappadocia between Naḫur[27] and Niḫriyā, closer to the former, according to tablets from both Kültepe and Mari. These data narrow the area in which Šudā may be sought. It should be situated southwest of Diyarbakir, west of the great trade route, but astride a secondary road which passed through the gap between the massifs of Karaçok Dağ in the west and Ṭūr ᶜAbdīn in the east, and connected Diyarbakir with Viranşehir, from which an easy road leads to Rās el-ᶜAyn at the sources of the Ḫabūr.[28]

Such a general position of Šudā favors the restoration of the name of the other city which came to the relief of Uqabuwa as ^{URU}*Zu-*[*ur-ra*^{KI}], or rather, for etymological and onomastic reasons, ^{URU}*Ṣú-*[*ur-ra*^{KI}]. Ṣurrā, like Šudā, was a royal city in the Mari Age,[29] and an important

[23]Our reason for thinking so is not the often repeated (since Opitz [1926]), alleged onomastic connection between *Waššukkani* and *Sikani* (now confirmed as Tell Feḫerīyeh at the source of the Ḫabūr), but the place of Waššukkani in the itinerary of Piyyašiliš and Šattiwaza according to HT 21 + KUB 8 80, published by Friedrich (1924–25).

[24]K.4384 (II r.5 No. 1) obv. i: 18, transliterated in Forrer (1920b) 52.

[25]Translated in ARAB 1, §§ 496–502; ARI 2, §§ 629–43. In it, the city is called ^{URU}*Tu-uš-ḫa*. Elsewhere, in his annals (ARAB 1, § 466; ARI 2, § 550), Assurnasirpal states explicitly that he built a palace there, and "inscribed my stele (and) set it in the wall" of the city. Kerh was first identified with Tušḫa by Rawlinson (1863) 228. *Kerh* is the modern Turkish spelling for *Karḫ*, from Aramaic *karkʰā*, "fortified city," whence the Roman name of the city, Carcha or Charcha. See Dillemann (1962) 156–57, 238.

[26]*Ma-at Ši-na-mi-im*$^{KI.\{KI\}}$ *ù Tu-úš-ḫi-im*^{KI} in ARM HC A.49: 46 (= Dossin [1972b] 63). It is very probable that Šinamu(m), which still appears under that name in the Broken Obelisk of Aššur-bēl-kala, early in the eleventh century (ARI 2, § 241) is the same as Sinabu, associated with Tušḫa in Assurnasirpal II's records, as assumed by Streck (1898) 74–75.

[27]Naḫur was an important crossroads of the Old Assyrian caravans to Cappadocia, whence they could proceed either to the west (via Elaḫut, Uršu, and Mamma), or to the northwest (via Niḫriyā and Ḫaḫḫum). At the time of Zimri-Lim, it was a Mariote enclave in the middle of vassal kingdoms. Its probable location is the huge mound at Kiziltepe, formerly Tell Ermen, on which see Sachau (1883) 400–404; Dillemann (1962) 165–66, 170–73.

[28]The road from Amida (Diyarbakir) to Constantina (Viranşehir) was used in Byzantine times (cf. Dillemann [1962] 189 and n 5, 190) and in the nineteenth and early twentieth centuries (cf. Reclus [1895] 196–97; W. Schwenzer's map *apud* Meissner [1921–25] II). Goetze (1946) 167 placed Šudā "near modern Kurḫ," but in (1953b) 62 n 76 he thought of "a position near Derik," which puts Šudā too far south.

[29]The name is written *Ṣú-ur-ra-a*^{KI} in ARM 3 44: 9; *Ṣú-ur-ra*^{KI} elsewhere in the Mari tablets, and possibly *Ṣú-ra-a*[*m*]*-ma*^{KI} in ARM 2 62: 12 on which see pp. 17–18 below.

clue as to its location is contained in ARMT 14 109. Here Zimri-Lim is informed of a raid which his persistent adversary, Qarni-Lim, king of Andariq (a district on the right bank of the Tigris, in or south of the present day "duck bill" of Syrian territory),[30] had launched westward. He took Šubat-Enlil, the former capital of Šamši-Adad I's empire, and sent its grain back to Andariq. He then "reached Zunnanum and was crossing the heights, but Ḫammurapi, the 'man' of Kurdā, and Ḫatnu-rapi went together to meet him in battle, (saying to him) thus, 'Retreat from Ṣurrā, and let us make peace!' "[31] We do not know where Zunnanum lay, but the identity of Šubat-Enlil with the huge Tell Leylān, 30 km. southeast of Nusaybin,[32] indicated by the data of the Old Babylonian Yale Itinerary, and corroborated by an archaeological survey of the site,[33] can be considered as certain. The only heights in the vicinity of Tell Leylān are those pertaining to the long and wide massif of Ṭūr ᶜAbdīn which rises between the North Mesopotamian plain and the Tigris: a rugged but fertile terrain, well populated in all epochs.[34] We shall consider the location of Kurdā later on because of its direct connection with Ilānṣurā, but it may be noted in passing that it should be ascribed to the same region.

Since Ṣurrā was located in the Ṭūr ᶜAbdīn massif, it corresponds to the town which has preserved its ancient name throughout the ages. It

[30]For Qarni-Lim as king of Andariq, see Dossin (1972a) 111, and Birot (1973) 8 n 1. On its location, see pp. 18–19 below.

[31]In l. 16, as explained by Birot (ARMT 14 p. 239), "the term *gabaʾu* 'summit, crest, height' . . . is a rare word of West Semitic origin, unknown until now in texts of early periods." Ḫatnu-rapi is known as a king of Karanā (Tell el-Rimāḥ). His presence at the head of a military force in the area of the Ḫabūr Triangle and Ṭūr ᶜAbdīn was part of his vassal obligations to Zimri-Lim. The same is true for his predecessor Asqur-Addu (ARM 2 62, and ARM HC B.81 = Jean [1948b] 70–72).

[32]Nusaybin is the Turkish form of Syriac Niṣibīn, Roman-Byzantine Nisibis, and Neo-Assyrian Naṣibina. On its name in the Mari Age, see pp. 28–29 below.

[33]The location of Šubat-Enlil at Tell Leylān was tentatively suggested by Falkner (1957–58) 37 n 53; quoted as possible, but uncertain, by Hrouda (1958) 29–34; taken up by van Liere (1963) 119; and accepted and confirmed on the basis of the Yale Itinerary by Hallo (1964) 73–74, § 37. Tell Leylān has been the object of three seasons of excavations (directed by Harvey Weiss of Yale University) as of this writing. In his paper, "The 'Palace of Palms' at Tell Leilan," delivered at the annual meeting of the American Oriental Society at Baltimore, 20 March, 1983, Weiss adduced convincing archaeological and epigraphic facts supporting the site's identity with Šubat-Enlil.

[34]For a general description, see Streck (1934) 915–22; Dillemann (1962) 29–35 and map fig. II; Boulanger (1970) 714–16. For toponymy: Socin (1881). For travels: Sachau (1883) 393–422, and Bell (1911) 302–22. The population of Ṭūr ᶜAbdīn (Ottoman *sandjak* of Mardin) in 1890 (not a propitious period for the area) amounted to 194,072 according to Streck (1934) 918. In the Late Bronze and Neo-Assyrian ages, the ridges in the northern and western parts of the massif were known under the Hurrian name of Kašiyari. The upland as a whole was called Izalla in the Neo-Assyrian, Neo-Babylonian, Byzantine and Medieval Arab periods. *I-za-al-lu*^{KI} is already mentioned at Mari (ARM 9 259: 6 and the unpublished A.2145).

appears in Syriac sources as Ṣaura, the seat of a bishopric;[35] in early Byzantine sources as the fortress Sauras,[36] or Tzauras;[37] in Arabic sources as Ṣōr, or Ṣawr;[38] and as this last is rendered in modern Turkish, Savur.[39] It is now the chief town of a *kaza* which encompasses the western part of the upland. It stands on the right bank of a river which bears its name, and empties into the Tigris about 30 km. to the north.[40] The restoration of the incomplete toponym in KBo 3 60 ii: 6 as ^{URU}*Ṣú-*[*ur-ra*^{KI}] would harmonize with its association with Šudā, inasmuch as both of these royal cities occupied analogous positions in the northernmost marches of Mesopotamia, facing the Tigris.

UQABUWA

Continuing the same line of reasoning, one could expect that Uqabuwa was located in the same general region as Šudā and Ṣurrā, and within the plausible horizon of their interests. Unfortunately, no similar toponym recurs in cuneiform texts. Remembering the frequent persistence of ancient place names on both sides of the upper Tigris,[41] however, we may turn to Byzantine and Syriac sources from the sixth century for help. They tell about a fortress on a steep hill overlooking

[35]Peeters (1908) 169 and n 9. It should be noted that the Syriac dialect of North Mesopotamia (standardized as the language of the Jacobite literature) tended to use diphthongs where other Aramaic dialects had simple vowels: e.g., *ḥaurā* for *ḥōrā*, "cave"; *kaiphā* for *kēphā*, "cliff"; etc. This pronunciation is also reflected in Ptolemy's *Gauzanitis* compared with Assyrian *Guzana*, Hebrew *Gōzān*.

[36]Procopius, *De aedific.* II:4:1.

[37]Georgius Cyprius, *Descriptio*, No. 919.

[38]Honigmann (1935) 11 and map 1. The site does not appear in Neo-Assyrian records. Forrer (1920b) 21 was wrong in identifying Ṣaur with Assurnasirpal II's Sūra, or Šūra, near Mt. Kašiyari. The initial sibilants are of different nature. One may rather think of modern Ṣuri at 37°27′N, 40°52′E.

[39]37°33′N, 40°5′ E. Savur stands 30 km. to the north-northeast of Mardin in beeline: 50 km. by road. According to Boulanger (1970) 714, the population in the 1960s was 3400. Sachau (1883) 421 described the valley of Ṣaur as not very large, but with many trees, and all covered with vineyards, while "up the mountain, overlooking two valleys from its saddle, lies Ṣaur with its two picturesque castles."

[40]It may be noted that another town mentioned in the Mari records (ARM 4 51: 8, 19), and in the description of Assurnasirpal II's campaign in Ṭūr ᶜAbdīn, Madara (or Maṭara) stands on the same river, 18 km. north of Savur, and is still called Matar (not Mathra, as Forrer [1920b] 21 and Schwenzer on his map mentioned in n 28, above).

[41]Besides the already quoted Ḫaḫḫum, Kutmar, Ṣurrā, Madarā, and Izalla, one should mention the following place names from Neo-Assyrian sources pertaining to the region in question: *Abissa*, Byz. Pheison, Turk. Fis; *Amedi*, Rom.-Byz. and Arab. Amida; *Arbaki*, Byz. Aribachon; Mt. *Arqania*, Rom. *Arcania (miswritten Arsinia on the Peutinger map), Arab. Arġānah, Turk. Ergani; R. *Arzania*, Rom-Byz. Arsanias; R. *Kallat* (see next note); *Kullimmeri*, Urarṭ. Qulmeri, Byz. Chlomaron, Arm. Kᶜlimar; Mt. *Madani*. Turk. Maden (see n 62, below); *Mallani*, Turk. Mallan; *Uppumu*, Byz. Aphumon, Turk. Fum. Other onomastic survivals specifically in Ṭūr ᶜAbdīn will be met below.

the left bank of the river Kallat, or Nymphios,[42] now Batman, which formed the border between the Byzantine and Persian possessions in the corridor between the Armenian Taurus and the Tigris. It was the site of sieges and battles in 583 and 591. Its name was *ʾAqbā*[43] or *ʾOqbā*[44] in Syriac, *Akbas*[45] or *Okbas*[46] in Greek, which is quite close to Uqabuwa (minus its formative), and may have derived from an original **Uqab*- with the Syriac reduction of the second vowel when a noun was put in the emphatic state.[47] Its exact location on the Batman is not certain,[48] but its strategic role in the Perso-Byzantine wars of the sixth century seems to indicate that it controlled the principal crossing of the river, which then as now took place about 20 km. east of the ancient city Martyropolis (now Silvan).[49] After crossing the river, the road divides: one branch runs east, then northeast to the Bitlis Pass and Lake Van, and the other south, along the left bank of the Batman, then southeast, passes the Tigris, and crosses the Ṭūr ᶜAbdīn to its central town, Midyat, where it joins the longitudinal road Mardin—Savur—Midyat—Cizre. The latter road existed in the Middle Ages when it crossed the Tigris at Ḥiṣn Kayfā, to which we shall return.

Thus located, Uqabuwa was within an easy marching distance from both Šudā and Ṣurrā. An attack on it by an invading army must have been perceived as a threat to the northern fringe of Mesopotamia. The existence of a close connection between the plain of North Mesopotamia and the valley of the upper Tigris is attested by the statement of Ibal-

[42]It appears as ^{ÍD}*Kal-la-[a]t*, as emended by Forrer (1920b) 85, from *-ma*, a river of Urarṭu, in Tiglath-pileser III's annals. Syriac speakers perceived this name as meaning "bride," which was translated into Greek as *Nymphios*.

[43]John of Ephesos, *Comentarii de beatis Orientalibus* VI: 36, 37, quoted by Honigmann (1935) 24 and n 8.

[44]Michael Syrus, *Chronicle* X: 21. Edited by Chabot (1902/04).

[45]Theophylactus Simocatta, *Historia* I: 12; IV: 15. Edited by de Boor (1887).

[46]Evagrius, *Hist. eccles.* VI: 15. In Migne, *Patrologia Graeca*, vol. 86, col. 2868.

[47]Cf. Syriac *Ṭūrā de-ʾIzlā* from *Izala; g^{e}mal*, st. constr. *gamlā; šunar*, st. constr. *šunrā*, etc.

[48]Honigmann (1935) map I, tentatively placed it on the approximate latitude of Martyropolis-(Maya)farqin. Dillemann (1962) 236 fig. xxxiii, 237 placed it farther north, opposite the confluence of Lice Su.

[49]Before receiving the name Martyropolis, the city in all likelihood was called Tigranocerta, and briefly served as capital of Tigranus the Great's Armenian empire in the first century B.C. It should be mentioned, however, that the Spanish-Arab geographer Ibn Jubair, who travelled through North Mesopotamia in 1183/84, mentioned between Dunaysar (now Koçhisar-Kiziltepe) and Rās al-ᶜAyn "a large village, with a fort called Tell al-ᶜUqāb (the Hill of the Eagle) which belongs to Christians" (English translation by Broadhurst [1952] 251). Could the occurrence of this name be used in support of a Mesopotamian route of the Hittite march on Ilānṣurā? The village has not been located in the terrain, and does not recur in any other sources. Ibn Jubair's testimony belongs to a time when ancient place names in the North Mesopotamian steppe have already been largely replaced by Arabic names, of which *Tell al-ᶜUqāb* is one.

Addu, king of Ašlakkā (in the northwestern part of the Ḫabūr Triangle), in his letter to Zimri-Lim, king of Mari: "I am close to the Upper Land, and the news from *E-lu-ḫu-ut*^KI^, LÚ *Lu-ul-li-[e]*, *Ḫa-aḫ-ḫi-im*^KI^, *ma-a-at Za-al-ma-[q]í-im, Bu-ru-un-di-im*^K[I]^ *ù Ta-al-ḫa-yi-im*^KI^ are exposed before me."[50] Here the circle of interests of the king of Mari is understood to include Ḫaḫḫum.[51] Lullû, or Lulliu, cannot, in the given geographical context, refer to the well-known country in the Zagros mountains, but recurs in the variant form ^KUR^*Lu-lu-ta* in the annals of Assurnasirpal II as one of the districts north of Mount Kašiyari (Ṭūr ^c^Abdīn), and across the Tigris.[52] It is the "antimony country,"[53] and it is precisely in the region between the upper Tigris, the Batman, and the Taurus range that one of the two antimony mines in the upper Tigris-Euphrates area is located.[54]

NUḪAYANA

Another episode of the Hittite story (KBo 3 60 iii: 10′–13′) relates: "When we set out from Nuḫayana (^URU^*Nu-ḫa-ia-na-az*), we rose and rushed to Ilānṣurā. We took its cattle and sheep, we . . . its people." Nuḫayana does not recur in any other source, but Albright, long ago, suggested that "Nukhayana may plausibly be identified with the district of Nikhani in Subartu . . . listed by Tukulti-Ninurta I among his conquests."[55] This, of course, is incompatible with the location of Ilānṣurā "between Carchemish and Harran," made in the very same article,[56] but since that surmise has been refuted by the testimony of the Mari tablets, the hypothesis concerning Nuḫayana can be examined on its own, independently from the other one. The onomastic resemblance between *Nuḫayana* and *Niḫani* is not perfect, but the general location of the

[50]ARM HC B.308 (= Jean [1948a] 18–19): 26–30; cf. Finet (1966a) 19–21.

[51]This is of small wonder because sealings of Zimri-Lim have been found at Acem Hüyük in Central Anatolia, south of the Salt Lake (Tüz Gölü), probably the ancient Burušḫanta. Talḫayum, Burundum, and Ḫaḫḫum were stations on the great commercial road to Cappadocia. Anbar (1973) 20–33 assumed, probably correctly, that Šamši-Adad I's and his two sons' campaigns in northeast Mesopotamia aimed at protecting the road to Kaniš, and that Zimri-Lim's takeover of the region resulted in cutting the connections between Aššur and the Cappadocian cities.

[52]ARAB 1, § 502; ARI 2, § 642 (the Kerh Monolith).

[53]*Lullû* (or *Lulliu*) is a variant writing of Akkadian *lulû* (OA *luliu*), "antimony," while *Luluta* derives from *lulutu*, a variant designation of the same mineral. Antimony (*luliu*) is mentioned as an article of Assyrian trade in the Cappadocian tablet KTS 7a: 4, and was continuously imported into Babylonia for use in cosmetics, medicatments, bronze making, and manufacture of colored glass. Cf. the quotations in CAD L 243, and Oppenheim (1970) 19, 21, 54, and 79.

[54]Forbes (1958–64) v. 9, fig. 29.

[55]Albright (1940) 2 30.

[56]See n 11, above.

latter merits our attention. The relevant passage of Tukulti-Ninurta I's inscriptions refers to his first campaign (in 1244), and the enumeration of the conquered countries is always repeated in the same order, though in some versions with omissions or insertions of certain names.[57] The standard list runs as follows: "The lands of Pabḫi, Kudmuḫi, Bušši,[58] Mummi,[59] Alzi, Madani, Niḫani, Alaya, Tepurzi, Purulumzi,[60] the whole of the wide Šubaru land." The enumeration proceeds from the southeast to the northwest, and some of the mentioned toponyms can be put on the map rather accurately. Let us briefly survey them.[61]

Pabḫi (Hittite Papanḫi, Urarṭian Babanāḫi) is not just a "mountain land," as is the meaning of its Hurrian name, but a very definite area, the rugged terrain of Cudi Dağ east of the Tigris, between its tributaries Botan and Ḫabūr. Pabḫi was the northern neighbor of Assyria, and some of the Assyrian kings invaded it, but never succeeded in annexing it to their empire. The country is almost completely impassable, and there is small wonder that Tukulti-Ninurta, after raiding its outskirts, crossed the Tigris, and continued his march through the country on its right bank.

Kadmuḫi lay across the Tigris from Pabḫi, and included the present-day Syrian "duck bill," and the eastern part of Ṭūr ᶜAbdīn. Bušši (Pušši) is otherwise unknown. The ethnicon ^{URU}*Mu-ma-a-a* appears in a Neo-Assyrian letter in association with cities of the Cudi Dağ area. At that point, one version inserts "the whole of Mount Kašiyari," which was the Hurrian name, used by the Hittites and the Assyrians, of the western part of Ṭūr ᶜAbdīn. Now the itinerary recrosses the Tigris and enters the land of Alzi, called Alzi or Alše by the Hittites. This was an important country to the east and north of the upper Tigris, probably on both banks of the Batman.

Equally well known is the land of Madani. It lay around the strategically and commercially vital pass of the Taurus at the headwaters of the (western) Tigris, and its name has survived in that of the modern town, Maden.[62] The Assyrian expeditionary force must have entered it

[57]They are published in transliteration and translation in Weidner (1959) Nos. 1, 2, 5, 16, 17, 21, 22, and 26. English translations can be found in ARAB 1, §§ 143, 149, 164, 171, 205A (at the end of volume 2); instead of *Kurti,* read *Pabḫi,* instead of *Purukuzzi,* read *Purulumzi;* ARI 1, §§ 701, 715, 773, 803, 806, 819.

[58]Or Pušši.

[59]Two versions (ARI 1, §§ 783 and 819) omit "Bušši and Mummi;" one version (ARI 1, § 806) inserts "the whole of Mount Kašiyari" between "Mummi" and "Alzi."

[60]The reading *Pu-ru-lum-zi* is preferred epigraphically (the sign did not have the value *kús* in MA writing), as well as onomastically (Hurrian *purullu,* "house, temple").

[61]We shall not encumber this part of the study with detailed references. These may be easily found in Parpola (1970), in the published volumes of RLA and RGTC, and in Diakonoff (1968) according to the index of geographical names.

[62]I realize that Turkish *maden* (from Arabic *maᶜdīn*) means "mine," and that famous copper mines, exploited since remote antiquity, exist in the vicinity of the pass. Neverthe-

from Alzi through the gorge of the Tigris (here known as Ergani Su). This puts Niḫani north of the pass and of Lake Gölcük (Hazar Gölü), approximately in the area of Harput and Elâzig, and Alaya farther west, towards the Euphrates. Tukulti-Ninurta boasted that he had crossed the Euphrates and invaded the land of the Hittites.[63] Indeed the last but one in his list, Tepurzi, recurs as one of the countries that had rebelled against Ḫatti before the reign of Šuppiluliumaš (KBo 1 1 obv. i: 13, 22), and thus presumably lay west of the upper Euphrates.[64] Thus Albright's old and rather haphazard identification of Nuḫayana with Niḫani turns out, if correct, to agree with our premise that the expedition against Ilānṣurā started from the Hittite-occupied area of Ḫaḫḫu.[65]

KURDĀ AND KASAPĀ

Having thus arrived at the conclusion that Ilānṣurā was situated at the extreme northern edge of Mesopotamia, and was reachable from Anatolia via the countries which were known in the Late Bronze Age as Išuwa and Alzi, we shall turn to the geographical contexts in which it appears in the published Mari texts.

One of the city-states that bordered on Ilānṣurā and encroached on its territory was Kurdā. Its king, Ḫammurapi, a contemporary and at times a vassal of his more famous Babylonian namesake, was quite active, politically and militarily, at the time of the Mari archives. Besides Mari, Kurdā also appears in the contemporaneous tablets from Tell er-Rimāḥ (Karanā), and in Old Babylonian texts.[66] In the fourteenth

less, all indications of the pertinent Assyrian texts point unmistakenly to the identity of the mountain and country Madani (also Amadani and Madni) with the pass of Ergani-Maden—the more so since the name of the town at the southern entrance to the pass, Ergani (Arġanah in Arabic), perpetuates the Assyrian name of the mountain, Arqania (first proposed by Hommel [1885] 585; cf. Streck [1898] 98), and the town Mallan, a little way down the nascent Tigris (Ergani Su), the Assyrian Mallani.

[63]This has often been erroneously understood as an invasion of Northern Syria. See Astour (1981) 26–27.

[64]Tepurzi(ya) may correspond to Tapura, which Ptolemy V: 7 placed in Armenia Minor, or the region on the west bank of the upper Euphrates, north of Melitene (*-zi* is a frequent Hurrian formative).

[65]In an article published in the Armenian *Historico-Philological Journal*, 1958, No. 3, 59–74, and quoted in Diakonoff (1968) 224 n 89, 227 n 96, S. T. Yeremian "identified Niḫani with Nihan Dağ on the right bank of the Tigris," which Diakonoff considered "very probable." (Diakonoff [1968] 99, located "Madani and Niḫani in the mountains near the western sources of the Tigris River.") An ancient survival in Turkish oronymy is quite possible, but I have not found Nihan Dağ on the relevant sheets of the 1:200,000 map of Turkey, which are very detailed in matters of oronymy; nor does it figure in Gaz.Turk. Since I could not consult Yeremian's article, and check his sources, I must leave this question open.

[66]OBTTR 18: 5; 281: 10; AbB 6 30: 5–6; the Babylonian Dream Book (tablet from the Kassite period, but going back to an Old Babylonian original) in Oppenheim (1956) 313, l. 15, and cf. 259 and 268.

century, Kurdā figures in the treaties Šuppiluliumaš-Šattiwaza and Šattiwaza-Šuppiluliumaš as one of the seven Mitannian cities whose gods are cited as witnesses.[67] Then its name disappears from cuneiform records.[68] If Kurdā could be located on the map, Ilānṣurā would have to be assigned to the same general area. Can a toponymic survival provide a clue as to the whereabouts of Kurdā?

Margarete Falkner thought that the name of Kurdā may have been preserved until the Neo-Assyrian period as Gurête (URU*Gu-ri-e-te*), a station on Tukulti-Ninurta II's itinerary,[69] located between Magarisi and Tabite: that is, in general terms, in the steppe southeast of the Ḫabūr triangle.[70] Proceeding from this premise, she equated Kasapā (a town in which King Ḫammurapi of Kurdā is reported to have stayed) with el-Qṣēbah, a mound near the southern slopes of Ǧebel Ǧerībah, the western extension of Ǧebel Sinǧar.[71] Hence "Ilānṣurā, which must be placed between Kurdā in the north and Andariq in the south, should be located in the western part of Ǧebel Sinǧar."[72] This, of course, is utterly incompatible with our interpretation of the Hittite expedition to Ilānṣurā—a document which, incidentally, Miss Falkner did not include in her collection of ancient testimonies on Ilānṣurā.[73] But how close are her onomastic comparisons?

[67]KBo 1 1 rev.: 54 (URU*Gur-ta*); KBo 1 3 rev.: 41 (URU*Gur-da*). The other six cities are Ḫarrān, Kaḫat, Uḫuš(u)man, Waššukkanni, Irrite, and Šudā. The god of Kurdā was dGIR ("dagger"). The sign GUR also had the value *kùr* in Middle Babylonian writings of proper names. In Old Babylonian, the name was spelled *Kur-da*, rarely *Kur-da-a*, and once at Mari *Ku-ur-da*, which determines the reading of the sign KUR.

[68]The Neo-Assyrian letter, ND 2618 [Parker (1961) 37–38], lists URU*Gur-di-e* (or *Qur-de-e*) on l. 17′ among sixteen towns (or villages) and two landed estates, all of which are otherwise unknown except URU*Ka-ḫa-at*—a well-known city of the Mari, Middle Bronze, and Neo-Assyrian ages, securely identified with Tell Barri on the eastern bank of the Ǧaǧǧaġ (36°44′ N, 41°06′ E). See Dossin (1961/62). The extent of the territory covered by the list, and the relationship between Gurdê and Kurdā cannot be ascertained.

[69]The latest edition is Schramm (1970) 153 rev.: 34. See also ARAB 1 § 412; ARI 2 § 476; and cf. Falkner (1957/58) 19, 21 (map sketch).

[70]Magarisi, according to Assurnasirpal II (ARAB 1 § 159; ARI 2 § 577), stood on the bank of the Ḫarmiš River (med. Arab. Hirmās, now Ǧaǧǧaġ), or more exactly, on its lower reaches. It cannot be equated with "Tell Mitras, 5 km. northeast of Tell Tenēnir" (Falkner [1957–58] 19), which stands 17 km. south of that river.

[71]Falkner (1957–58) 36. The mound of el-Qṣēbah appears in Gaz.Syr. as al Qaṣaybah, 36°17′ N, 41°15′ E. This longitude should be reduced by a minute or two because it puts the mound on the Iraqi side of the border! Poidebard (1934) 153 noted a ruined castle there. See also his pl. CXL (map of the area around the bend of the Ḫabūr).

[72]Falkner (1957–58) 37.

[73]A Mari tablet which we shall consider below completely excludes the possibility of locating Ilānṣurā in Ǧebel Sinǧar, but it was published in the same year as Falkner's study, and was not known to her when she wrote it. I cannot tell what Finet's reasons were for advancing the guess about the location of Ilānṣurā "in the region of the Lower Zāb and the Tigris?" ARMT 14 p. 127, s.v.

Both the Old Babylonian and Neo-Assyrian scribes were generally very careful in distinguishing voiced and unvoiced consonants (unlike Hurrians and Hittites). The two names, Kurdā and Gurête, have different etymologies: the former going back to the root *KRD*, of which there are derivatives in Akkadian and Ugaritic;[74] the latter, to the stem *gur-*, which occurs, with different, but toponymically acceptable meanings, in Akkadian and West Semitic.[75] As for *Kasapā* and Qṣēbah, they do not have one single consonant in common, and in the steppe where Qṣēbah is located, the likelihood that a place name would be preserved from the Old Babylonian period until now is very small.

A Neo-Assyrian cadaster record presents a more convincing parallel to Kasapā, and in a region where toponymic survivals were more frequent than in the open plain. That lengthy tablet lists, among other places, eight settlements of the land Izalli (the Ṭūr ᶜAbdīn region): Anduli, Asiḫi, Kašpi, Yadaʾi, Barzanista, Til-Zanî (or Til-Ḫanî), Apsiyaya, and Ispallurê.[76] Unlike the Neo-Assyrian royal annals, which tried to follow standard Babylonian writing conventions, this text uses Assyrian phonetic spelling, in which *š* stood for *s*, and *s* stood for *š*.[77] Thus ^{URU}*A-si-ḫi* was pronounced *Ašiḫi* (to which we shall return later) and ^{URU}*Ka-áš-pi, Kaspi*. The latter name can be taken as a compressed form of **Kasapi*, with elision of the second vowel.[78] Such a location of Kasapā would agree perfectly with the defense of Ṣurrā (now Savur) by Ḫammurapi of Kurdā, against an attack by Qarni-Lim of Andariq, who entered the highland from Šubat-Enlil (Tell Leylān).[79] Ḫammurapi's stay at Kasapā (ARM 2 41, cf. ARM 2 69) was connected with the activity of another king of the same Andariq, Atamrum, who is reported to threaten Šubat-Enlil. This would put Kasapā in the southeastern part of Ṭūr ᶜAbdīn, overlooking the plain dominated by Tell Leylān.[80]

[74]See the Akkadian dictionaries for *karadû, kardû, kirâdu, kurādu*, and the Ugaritic place name *Ḫalbi-karradi* (*Ḫlb Krd*). In Arabic, *karada* means "to cut, hew, remove by cutting."

[75]Cf., e.g., Akkadian *gūru*, "reed" (the settlement was indeed located near the marshes of Wādī Radd), or Aramaic *guryetā*, "young lioness."

[76]ADD 742, republished by Fales (1973) No. 24: 18–33. The reading ^{URU}DU$_7$-*ḫa-ni-i* instead of Johns' *-za-ni-i* belongs to Fales.

[77]Compare ^{URU}*Bar-za-ni-is-ta* and ^{URU}*Is-pal-lu-re-e* of ADD 742: 28 and 32 with Assurnasirpal II's spellings of the same names: ^{URU}*Bar-za-ni-iš-tu-un* and ^{URU}*Iš-pi-li-ib-ri-a*.

[78]Such contractions are very frequent in Neo-Assyrian toponymy. To quote just a few: Ḫarabisina/Ḫarbisina; Ḫamarāni/Ḫamrāni; Ḫatarika/Ḫatrika; Labadudu/Labdudu. A city ^{URU}*Ka-sa-pa/Ka-sap-pa/Ka-sa-pi/Ka-sap-pi* also existed in the Neo-Assyrian period, but it was located in the Transtigris, in the district of Kalzu, according to the letter ND 2640 i: 34 (Parker [1961] 40, cf. 55). It corresponds, in all likelihood, to Tell Kešaf at the confluence of the Great Zab with the Tigris (Oates [1968] 14 fig. 2).

[79]See p. 8, above.

[80]Ḫammurapi's temporary presence at Kasapā does not necessarily mean that it was part of his possessions. More probably, he was there to defend the entire region against a

According to ARM 2 130 (a dispatch by Yassi-Dagan, a Mariote official at Šubat-Enlil), Qarni-Lim and his ally Būnu-Ištar intended to invade Šubat-Enlil, so Yassi-Dagan sent troops to Kasapā.

KURDĀ, ṢURRĀ, AND ILĀNṢURĀ

A special relationship between Kurdā and Ṣurrā is apparently implied in ARM 6 33. Baḫdi-Lim, the palace prefect of Mari, informed King Zimri-Lim that Ḫammurapi of Babylon sent letters "to Ḫammurapi, the 'man' of Kurdā, Zaziya, and Zimriya, the 'man' of Ṣurrā," reminding them that they have accepted his sovereignty, and demanding that they send troops. The letter does not state who Zaziya was. He is assumed to be identical with Zaziya, king of the Turukkû-people in the Transtigris—a region rather distant from the area we are dealing with now. But there is a reference to Zaziya in an unpublished letter from Yassi-Dagan (the high Mariote official at Šubat-Enlil) who was with Ḫatnu-rapi (whom we met as the king of Karanā, who, together with Ḫammurapi of Kurdā, barred the road to Qarni-Lim's attack on Ṣurrā) at that moment. They had already received a detachment from Ekallātum (on the left bank of the Tigris), and were expecting the arrival of Zaziya.[81] Ḫammurapi of Kurdā displayed a personal interest in Zaziya. The poorly preserved tablet ARM 10 168 is his letter to a woman at Mari, Šamaš-šunittum, whom he calls "my sister," and requests her assistance in hastening Zaziya's passage from Mari. Thus Zaziya, whether king of Turukkû, or simply a namesake, was indeed connected with the king of Kurdā, and the Ṭūr ᶜAbdīn area.[82]

This brings us to a surmise which A. Goetze made in passing, without elaboration. Having mentioned Kurdā, he noted (not quite accurately) that "there existed in Byzantine times a *Kordes* in the immediate vicinity of *Dara* (now Derik)."[83] Kordes was fortified by Justinian as an outpost of the big fortress Dara.[84] Both stood on the same

hostile invasion. Nor does the statement that Ḫammurapi intended to proceed from Kasapā to Mari (ARM 2 69) indicate that it was a station on the direct road from Kurda to Mari. If Kasapā lay far enough from Kurdā, Ḫammurapi may well have travelled to Mari by the shortest route, without returning to Kurdā.

[81]ARM HC S.115, No. 72–26 = Birot (1973) 5–6. He calls Zaziya "the Turukkean chief," but before the whole tablet is published, it cannot be ascertained whether this ethnonym actually appears in the text.

[82]Another area connected with Kurdā was *ma-a-at Ḫa-*[*a*]*t-na*[KI] (ARM 2 50:5) which rose against Ḫammurapi. *Ḫa-at-na*[KI] is also mentioned in OBTTR 202: 4. Since nothing is known about its whereabouts, its mention does not contribute to the location of Kurdā.

[83]Goetze (1953a) 59 n 49, with reference to Honigmann (1935) 11, but Honigmann never said that Dara corresponded to Derik, which is located some 65 km. in beeline ENE of the true site of Dara.

[84]Procopius, *De aedific.* (ed. Haury) II:2:2. The name should actually be normalized *Kordē*, of which *Kordēs* is the genitive. Procopius often used genitives of place names instead of nominatives.

little river (still called Wādī Dārā), and both have preserved their ancient names: one is Dārā (Arabic), or Dar (Turkish), the other, 7 km. farther north, is Kordis.[85] The latter is situated inside the Ṭūr ᶜAbdīn upland, about 12 km. from its abrupt southern edge. Kordis is relatively close to three other Byzantine fortresses which can be plausibly identified with royal cities of the Bronze Age. 16 km. to the south lies the site of Amudis, or Ammôdios,[86] now ᶜĀmūdā, ancient Urgiš.[87] To the west, at 15 km. distance, is the site of Horren,[88] Arabic Ḥurrīn,[89] Turkish (Gül)harrin,[90] which corresponds to the Ḫurrā of Mari and Middle Assyrian records in both name and position.[91] 37 km. north, in beeline, stands Savur, Byzantine Sauras, which we have identified with Ṣurrā. This configuration, conforming to what was noted above concerning the military and political connections between Kurdā and Ṣurrā, supports the equation of Kurdā with Kordis.

What topographical factors contributed to the importance of the site in the Mari Age? The fact that Justinian found it necessary to cover Dara from the north by fortifying Kordes, indicates that he feared an attack coming from Persian Armenia across the ridge of Ṭūr ᶜAbdīn. The disposition of certain Byzantine fortresses of the area in an almost straight north-south line—Sauras, Matzaron, Kordes, Dara, Amudis—finds its analogy in the Mari Age—Madarā, Ṣurrā, Kurdā, Urgiš—and both point to the existence, at times, of a transversal road from the North Mesopotamian plain to the upper Tigris: a rugged one to be sure, but one which provided a shortcut to the mineral resources of Armenia. Before the construction of Dara, Kurdā played the role of key to that route.

We now turn to the evidence of ARM 2 62, a letter of Ḫāya-sūmû, king of Ilānṣurā, to his theoretical suzerain, Zimri-Lim, concerning,

[85] 37°14′ N, 40°59′ E. Its distance from Dara is underestimated by both Procopius (2 Roman miles = 3 km.) and Honigmann (5 km.).

[86] Amudis: Ammianus Marcellinus XVIII:6:13; Ammôdios: Procopius, *De bello pers.* I:13:15; XXVIII:35; *De aedific.* II:1:26; Ammodion: Theophylactus Simocatta V:4.

[87] ᶜĀmūdā is located at 37°05′ N, 40°54′ E, on the Syrian side of the border. The tell south of the village was identified with Urgiš by van Liere (1957) 91 as the place of provenance of the bronze lions with the inscription of Tiš-atal, the *endan* of Urgiš. The Urbana Itinerary agrees with the position of Urgiš. See Hallo (1964) 83 § 70.

[88] Ammianus Marcellinus XVIII:10:1.

[89] Yāqūt II.287; Sachau (1883) 400: Ḥorrīn.

[90] 37°14′ N, 40°48′ E; a large village according to Dillemann (1962) 79 n 1.

[91] Ḫurrā bordered on Šinaḫ, and the two cities jointly undertook diplomatic actions (with Urgiš, ARM 2 38), or raids (against the territory of Ašnakkum (ARM 2 33). Šinaḫ bordered on Urgiš (ARM 4 40, ARM 10 121). Ḫurrā was within the visibility range of fire signals raised at Ašlakkā, ARM HC SIGN. (Dossin [1938b] 184–85), which was located in the northwestern corner of the Ḫabūr triangle (close to Naḫur, Talḫāyum, and Zalluḫān; cf. Birot [1973] 7 n 2). Adad-Narāri I counted Ḫurra among the principal cities of Ḫanigalbat (Weidner [1928–29] 90 l. 32; ARAB 1 § 73; ARI 1 § 381). In the twelfth century, under the variant name ^{URU}*A-ḫu-ur-ra*, it was an Assyrian district center. See Weidner (1935–36) 21.

among other things, the recovery of some of his towns. Ḫāya-sūmû complains that Ḫammurapi, king of Kurdā, has unjust claims to his towns, and that he attacked and plundered *a-li-ma-zu-ra-a*[*m*]-*ma*^{KI} and [. . .]-*ar-ri-ya*^{KI}.[92] The latter place name is too damaged to be restored, and the division of the former is not certain. As noted by Finet, "it could be divided *a-li-ma Zu-ra-am-ma*^{KI} (where *a-li*(*-ma*) means 'my town' and not 'the towns'). If this is the correct reading, Zuramma is perhaps only a different spelling of Zurrā, with the enclitic *-ma*."[93] In this case, we would have still another instance of the geographical connection between Kurdā and Ṣurrā, but also an indication that Ilānṣurā was close to both of these cities. It is true that Ṣurrā had a king of its own, but it is known from the Mari texts that some of the stronger kings who were nominally subject to the king of Mari, exercised or claimed a protectorate over their lesser neighbors.[94] If, on the other hand, one accepts the reading *a-li Ma-zu-ra-am-ma*^{KI} (in which *zu* may be read *ṣú*), we still remain within the same narrow area. A Byzantine fortress Massarôn, or Matzarôn[95] occupied the site of present-day Maserte,[96] 18 km. SSE of Savur, and 21 km. north of Kordis (Kurdā). Whichever division we choose, we are compelled to place the territory under the rule of Ilānṣurā, somewhere in the Ṭūr ᶜAbdīn east of the line Savur-Kordis.

ILĀNṢURĀ, ANDARIQ, AND TILLĀ

In the same letter, ARM 2 62, Ḫāya-sūmû also calls for Zimri-Lim's help in getting back his towns that have been surrendered to Atamrum, otherwise known as the king of Andariq, often an adversary, but at that particular moment, a friend of Mari. The numerous references to Andariq and its successive kings that appear in the Mari and Tell er-Rimāḥ tablets indicate for Andariq a location to the east, and not very far from Šubat-Enlil, on a road leading from Ešnunna, in the same general region as Karanā and Nurrugum, and (as we shall see presently) near

[92]Ll. 9–14.

[93]ARMT 15 130 and n 2. Cf. ARM 15 138; and the same possibility envisaged by Kupper, ARMT 16/1 23.

[94]E.g., ARM 2 109, where the king of Elaḫut declares, "The city of Amaz is mine, you know it," even though Amaz was a separate city-state, perhaps not even directly contiguous to the territory of Elaḫut; ARMT 14 94 which reports that Šarrāya (king of Elaḫut) conquered the land of Ḫuršānum, chased out its ruler, and appointed another man to its kingship; or OBTTR 1, in which Ḫatnu-rapi, king of Karanā, writes to Zimri-Lim, "And I here shall lead out all the kings my allies (lit., "brothers") who enjoy good relations with me." We shall also see below about Ilānṣurā's and Susā's protectorate over other city-states.

[95]Kastron Massarôn, Georgius Cyprius No. 931; Matzarôn, Theophylactus Simocatta II:18; (M)assara castellum, *Not. dign.* XXXVI Nos. 12 and 26 (emendation by Seeck [1876] 78).

[96]37°24′ N, 40°58′ E. Spelled Māṣertā in Sachau (1883) 408. It was a sizable village in 1930 according to Dillemann (1962) 230.

Tillā.[97] This points to the northeastern corner of Mesopotamia, west of the Tigris and south of the hills of Karaçok Dağ (Q̮arab Šūk Ṭaġ) in the Syrian "duck bill,"[98] an area of big springs and a cluster of mounds. Andariq cannot be placed much farther south along the Tigris, for the area between Tell ᶜAfar and the Tigris (including Apqu = Abū Marīya) belonged to Nurrugum,[99] and farther downstream began the domain of Aššur.[100] The suggested location of Andariq to the southeast of Ṭūr ᶜAbdīn explains the territorial conflicts between it and Ilānṣurā.

This location is corroborated by another passage of the same letter (rev.: 16′–21′): "Now, come up and let us attack the city of Tillā. . . . Write to Atamrum that your troops that are with him should join my troops and. . . . Let us attack the city of Tillā." Tillā is evidently situated in the proximity of the domains of both Andariq and Ilānṣurā. Can it be located on the map? Let us examine the often discussed letter of Šamši-Adad I (ARM 1 26) in which he informs Yasmaḫ-Addu that he will travel from Šubat-Enlil to Mari, via the following places: "from Šubat-Enlil to Tillā; from Tillā to Ašiḫum; from Ašiḫum to Iyati; from Iyati to Lakušir; from Lakušir to Sagarātum." Sagarātum, at the confluence of the Ḫabūr and the Euphrates,[101] was the obligatory transit point for

[97]The passages pertaining to Andariq in ARM 1–4 are conveniently summarized by Falkner (1957–58) 3–4. A more complete list of occurrences can be found in ARMT 16/1, 5, or Groneberg (1980) 17. ARM HC A.3093, published in Dossin (1972a) 128–30, presents a characteristic geographical context: Babylon, Andariq, Karanā, Andariq, Ešnunna, *A*[x x x] *tān* south of Karanā, Andariq, Andariq, *Ki-i*[d$^{?}$-x^{K}]^{I} (read *Ki-i*[*d*$^{?}$ -*uḫ*^{K}]^{I} = *Ki-du-uḫ-*{*uḫ*}^{KI}, on which see n 155, below). Cf. ARMT 14 50: Atamrum went up from Ešnunna and invaded Šubartum which here, as often, refers to Ṭūr ᶜAbdīn.

[98]Median point: 37°03′ N, 42°10′ E. Parrot (1974) 162 placed Andariq at Andivar (ᶜAyn Dīwār, 37°17′ N, 42°11′ E) on the Tigris just south of the Syrian-Turkish border. Rouault (1970) 109 thought that Ilānṣurā was probably situated to the east of Idamaraz (Ḫabūr Triangle) and Andariq, located close to it, and could hardly be sought much farther south than Ǧebel Sinǧar. In n 3, Rouault placed Kasapā on the road from Andariq to Šubat-Enlil, but at the same time "very probably near the Ḫabūr"—two incompatible statements.

[99]Cf. Dossin (1938b) 182 n 4: "The cities of Andariq and Nurrugum are to be sought in the Tigris Valley downstream from Ekallātum." In ARM HC AREP. = Dossin (1938a) 121, Q̮arni-Lim was ready to attack Ekallātum. Ekallātum has been identified with a site called Haikal, on the left bank of the Tigris, 25 km. upstream from Aššur. See Hallo (1964) 72 § 31, and Oates (1968) 38 n 5. Andariq and Nurrugum could have been located only upstream from Ekallātum, and on the right bank of the river. On Nurrugum, see also Falkner (1957/58) 22; Finet ARMT 15 231; Oates (1968) 31; and Birot (1973) 4, 5 n 3.

[100]It is true that according to ARM 2 120, Atamrum was seen at Yabliya, a city on the middle Euphrates, downstream from Ḫanat (now *ᶜĀna*), but he could have come there as an ally of Ešnunna, whose troops were precisely marching on Yabliya according to ARM 4 74 and 88. Atamrum's presence there is no reason for placing Andariq in the middle of the desert between Terqa and Aššur, as postulated by Falkner (1957–58) 21 (map) and 36. No cities or roads have ever been attested for that inhospitable region. On this and other, similar locations of Falkner, cf. the remark of Oates (1968) 39 n 5.

[101]Sagarātum is often wrongly placed on the Ḫabūr at a considerable distance from its mouth. See Kupper (1957) 2 n 1, for example. Its position at the confluence of the rivers

everybody travelling to Mari from the north and east. It was assumed that the points listed in the letter marked the shortest direct road from Šubat-Enlil to Sagarātum, and that Tillā was its first stage.[102] But it was Julius Lewy who, proceeding from the erroneous assumption that Šubat-Enlil was another name for Aššur, nevertheless came upon the correct answer.[103] He identified Tillā with the Neo-Assyrian Tillê (Tiluli)[104] in the land of Kadmuḫi, where Assurnasirpal II built a palace, and whence he ascended through the pass of Ištarāte to the cities Kibaki and Mat(i)yati, and into the Kašiyari mountains. Kibaki is modern Kivah,[105] and Mat(i)yati, a larger city, is the principal town of modern Ṭūr ᶜAbdīn, Midyat.[106] Shalmaneser III also entered the pass of Ištarāte,[107] and marched against the land of Iātu (^{KUR}*Ia-a-tu*, var. ^{KUR}*Ia-e-ti*.)[108] Hence it follows, as Sachau noted in 1897, that *Mat(i)yati* is a compound formed of *māt-(I)yāti*, "the land of Iyāti," and, moreover, that *I-ia-ti*^{KI}, Šamši-Adad's second stage after Tillā, is the very same site.[109] The intervening *A-ši-ḫi-im*^{KI} is the Neo-Assyrian ^{URU}*A-si-ḫi* (read *Ašiḫi*) which we have already met in a list of settlements of the land Izalli (Ṭūr

---

follows from these unambiguous testimonies: a) persons who travelled to Mari from Syria (i.e. on the Euphrates route) stopped at Sagarātum; b) there was one stage from Terqa to Sagarātum (ARMT 14 115: 5–8), and the actual distance from Tell ᶜAšāra to the confluence is 27.5 km. (cf. Birot [1964c] 37–38); c) according to the Middle Assyrian "Broken Obelisk" (ARAB 1 § 391; ARI 2 § 244), the city of Sangarite (cf. the variant *Sa-an-ga-ra-tim*^{KI} of ARM 4 5: 8) stood on the Euphrates, and the sequence of captured cities follows the Ḫabūr downwards.

[102]Finet, ARMT 15 136; Kupper, ARMT 16/1, 35 (in identical words); Goetze (1953) 58 n 41, where Tillā is placed near Ḥasakah (or Ḥaseče) at the confluence of the Ǧaġǧaġ with the Ḫabūr (he has confused the North Mesopotamian Ašiḫum with a homonymous city in Northern Syria, not far from Uršu); van Liere (1963) 120, where Tillā is located at either Tell Barri (see n 68, above), or Tell Brak.

[103]Lewy, J. (1952) 1–3, 7–9, 11; (1953) 301 n 5.

[104]Assurnasirpal II used the form ^{URU}*Til-u-li* or ^{URU}*Ti-lu-li*. It should not be normalized *Til-uli* (as in ARI 2 §§ 567, 634), but has to be understood as Aramaic *t^{e}lūlē*, "ruins, mounds," equivalent to Akkadian *tillê*, plural of *tillu*. Tillê was a provincial center, listed with Apqu, Raṣappa, and Isana—all of them in northeastern Mesopotamia. The identity of Tiluli and Tillê was assumed by Forrer (1920b) 17, and followed by J. Lewy, Falkner, and other authors.

[105]37°17′ N, 41°35′ E. Shown on the map *Midyat* 1:200,000. The location of Kuwaḫ on Schwenzer's map (see n 28, above) is incorrect. It should be read *Kudaḫ (cf. n 155, below). The modern name reflects the Syriac spirantized pronunciation of *b* as /v/ and of *k* as /ḫ/. The identification of Kivah with Kibaki is by Forrer (1920b) 18 (he wrote Kiwaḫ). Socin (1881) 259 has Kīvaḫ.

[106]Matiyati has been identified with Midyat by Sachau (1897) 51 n 1, followed by Forrer (1920b) 18.

[107]Written ^{d}INANNA.MEŠ, while in Assurnasirpal's records the name is spelled phonetically.

[108]The Bull Colossi Inscription, ll. 98–99 (ARAB 1 § 657). A shorter version, without the mention of the pass, is found in the Black Monolith, ll. 90–91 (ARAB 1 § 570).

[109]Sachau (1897) 51, and J. Lewy (1953) 301.

ᶜAbdīn).[110] Lewy identified it with Āzeḫ, ca. 30 km. ENE of Kivah, on the road from Cizre to Midyat. The modern place name appears on maps and in literature in a number of forms,[111] of which *Asaḫ* is phonetically the closest to the ancient name. In the Mari age, Ašiḫum had a king called Ḫazip-ulme who, as befitted a vassal, paid a visit to Mari (ARM 2 78).[112] We notice that Šamši-Adad's itinerary from Tillā to Iyati coincided with the route by which Assurnasirpal II and Shalmaneser III (and, we shall see presently, two earlier Assyrian kings) invaded Ṭūr ᶜAbdīn from the southeast.

Concerning Garelli's objection that "one cannot place a city called Ašiḫum . . . near Djezireh Ibn Omar [Cizre], for Šamši-Adad's journey (ARM 1 26) would then become totally unintelligible,"[113] one may recall M. Falkner's somewhat earlier statement, "It is by no means certain that [ARM 1 26] presents the shortest route from Šubat-Enlil to Mari. On the contrary, it is striking that, this time, Šamši-Adad explicitly mentions every station of his journey, while in all other letters that deal with dispatches from Mari to Šubat-Enlil, he finds it sufficient to refer, at best, to Šagarātum or Qatunan. . . . The conclusion that suggests itself is that, in this case, Šamši-Adad chose a route to Mari which was *not* the usual one."[114] For some reason, Šamši-Adad decided to inspect the eastern and central parts of Ṭūr ᶜAbdīn starting with Tillā. Lakušir (otherwise unknown) must have been located east of Iyati (Midyat). It marked the end of the eastbound leg of the journey, and the beginning of the southbound leg which followed the normal direct road to Sagāratum. It therefore needed no explanations.

Thus we see that J. Lewy was correct when he assumed that Tillā "was situated in the Sufan dere district, i.e., on the eastern approaches to

[110]See p. 15 and n 76, above. ^{URU}*A-si-ḫi* also occurs in the Neo-Assyrian tablet no. 69: 8 from Tell Ḥalaf (anc. Guzana), Friedrich, Meyer, Ungnad, and Weidner (1940).

[111]*Asach*: Petermann (1865) 2, 45; *Āzeḫ*: Socin (1881) 245, 259; *Azakh*: Bell (1911) 302; *Hezek* on the map of Syria in B. R. 513: *Syria*; *Hasak* on the map *Levant* 1:500,000, sheet 3: *Deir ez Zor*; *Hazak* on the map *Turkey* 1:200,000, sheet F 15: *Midyat*, in the *National Geographic Atlas of the World* (2nd ed., 1966) 127, and in Gaz.Turk. Its other modern name is Idil, coordinates 37°21′ N, 41°54′ E. It should be remembered that four languages are used in the Ṭūr ᶜAbdīn: Neo-Syriac, Arabic, Kurdish, and Turkish.

[112]According to the reading of Birot (1973) 8 and n 2 on the basis of the then unpublished tablet 72-14. Ḫazip-ulme travelled with Masum-adal, king of Alilānum. If this points to the proximity of the two cities, then Alilānum was also located in the Ṭūr ᶜAbdīn, and its name may have been preserved in modern Halilan, about 19 km. north of Hazak (37°28′ N, 41°48′ E). But the meeting of the two kings on the road to Mari could have been accidental, and there are three more Halilans in eastern Turkey: one east of Gercüş in the Ṭūr ᶜAbdīn; one in the upper basin of the Great Zab; and one in the basin of the Botan.

[113]Garelli (1963) 81 n 3.

[114]Falkner (1957/58) 30.

the interior of the Ṭūr ᶜAbdīn."[115] Sufan dere, more commonly called Sufan Çay, is a western tributary of the Tigris. Its name perpetuates the Assyrian *Supnat*.[116] In 886, Tukulti-Ninurta II marched from the river Supnat across Mount Kašiyari on his way to Bīt-Zamani (the district of Amedi-Diyarbakir).[117] Four years later, Assurnasirpal II came to the source of the river Supnat, and erected his image near the images of his forefathers, Tiglath-pileser I and Tukulti-Ninurta II. He received tribute from the land Izalla and crossed Mount Kašiyari.[118] In other words, he took the same route. At the beginning of our century, C. F. Lehmann-Haupt found important fragments of Assyrian inscribed steles at the village of Babil, which is located in the foothills of Ṭūr ᶜAbdīn very close to the headsprings of the Sufan Çay, and identified them with those mentioned by Assurnasirpal.[119] Three of these fragments were rediscovered in the Adana Museum, and published by J. D. Hawkins.[120] They belong to a stele of Assurnasirpal with the king's portrait in relief. Even though the extant parts of the inscription contain only invocations and royal titles, the discovery of Assurnasirpal's monument at Babil is of considerable geographic interest. It not only marks the route of Assyrian invasion into Ṭūr ᶜAbdīn, but also pinpoints the sites of Tiluli/Tillê/Tillā. The steles of Assurnasirpal and his two predecessors did not stand in an open field: the presence of a mound at Babil testifies to the existence there of an ancient town.[121] Later on, a Roman fortress was constructed at Babil.[122] It not only protected the Roman road from Nisibis to the Tigris (as seen by Poidebard), but also covered the approaches to the Ṭūr ᶜAbdīn upland. There is no reason whatever to separate Tiluli from the "source of the Supnat," and to locate the town farther west.[123] In the first

[115]J. Lewy (1953) 310 n 5.

[116]To be read this way rather than *Subnat.* That reading was influenced by a totally mistaken equation of that river with Zebenne (or Debenne) Su, the Turkish name of the eastern branch of the Tigris.

[117]Schramm (1970) 147, ll. 11–29; ARAB 1 § 405; ARI 2 § 467.

[118]ARAB 1 §§ 444–45; ARI 2 § 549. On the geographical names *Izalla* and *Kašiyari,* see n 34, above.

[119]Lehmann-Haupt (1907) 19–22 and pl. 1 no. 8 (an inadequate publication); Lehmann-Haupt (1910) 365, 442; cf. Dillemann (1962) 161, 213 n 2. Babil is located on the border between Turkey and Syria (on the Turkish side), ca. 23 km. to the southwest of Cizre. It is shown on the map *Deir ez Zor* (37°11′ N, 42°00′ E).

[120]Hawkins (1969); partial translation in ARI 2 §§ 644–46. Hawkins wondered what happened to a fourth fragment, described by Lehmann-Haupt and now missing. It may be the same about which Dillemann (1962) 213 n 2 wrote, "An important fragment of a cuneiform inscription, found in the surroundings [of the Babil village], was given by the author, in 1932, to the Aleppo Museum."

[121]Sachau (1883) 383 noted, "village and tell of Bâbil." Dillemann (1962) 161 spoke about "Assyrian ruins" at Babil, but without elaboration.

[122]Poidebard (1934) 159–60 and pl. XLIX 2.

[123]Falkner (1957–58) 30 contended that Tillā was located not near Sufan Çay, but much farther west, on a straight line between Apqu (Abū Marīyah) and Matiyati (Midyat). Her guess was either Tell Rumaylān, or Tell Tschilara (Gaz.Syr.: Šīlārḥā).

place, we have Assurnasirpal's testimony that Tiluli belonged to the land of Kadmuḫi, i.e., it lay not far from the Tigris, and in the second place, Ašiḫum (Hazak) and Kibaki (Kivah) on Šamši-Adad's and Assurnasirpal's routes from Tillā/Tiluli to Iyate/Matiyati, respectively, indicate that they both proceeded from Babil.[124]

We have seen in the preceeding section that Ilānṣurā lay to the east of the line Savur-Kordis. We can now determine that it must also be placed to the west of Tillā and Ašiḫum. This does not mean that its king, Ḫāya-sūmû, had no claims on those, and perhaps other cities and towns in the eastern part of Ṭūr ᶜAbdīn. Indeed, Tillā, which he proposed to recover, may have been one of them. It does indicate, however, that the city of Ilānṣurā, Ḫāya-sūmû's capital, must be sought in the middle part of the upland.

ŠURUŠUM AND YAḪMUMUM

Two towns, Šurušum and Yaḫmumum, are connected with Ilānṣurā in a Mari tablet,[125] and there are independent onomastic indications that they are located in the same area of Ṭūr ᶜAbdīn to which we have assigned Ilānṣurā itself.

Itūr-Asdu, the Mariote governor of Naḫur in the northwestern corner of the Ḫabūr triangle, wrote to Zimri-Lim, "Concerning the report from Aškur-Addu:[126] 'The Ḫapiru who had left the city of Šurusum (*Šu-ru-sí-im*ᴷᴵ) and remained before Ḫāya-sūmû, went at night and took the city of Yaḫmumum (*Ia-aḫ-mu-ma-am*)'—by now that city has returned into the power of Ḫāya-sūmû." It is not clear in what relationship these particular Ḫapiru stood with regard to Ḫāya-sūmû, but one may suppose, by analogy with the role of Ḫapiru in many other of the Mari letters that refer to them, that they were Ḫāya-sūmû's mercenaries.[127] Another Mari tablet[128] tells about Yaminites who assembled at Yaḫmumum. Was it from these Yaminites that the Ḫapiru, acting on Ḫāya-sūmû's behalf, took the city, or were the

[124]Schwenzer's map of Assyria (n 28, above) places Babil on a track leading from the Tigris crossing at Fēš Ḫabūr northwestwards into Ṭūr ᶜAbdīn, where it joins the road from Cizre to Midyat at 42°00′ E. Map *Deir ez Zor* shows a track that starts on the Syrian-Turkish border, 2.5 km. northeast of Babil, and joins the Cizre-Midyat road at Hasak (Hazak). The political division of Upper Mesopotamia between Turkey and Syria changed the outlay of the regional road network.

[125]ARM HC A.49 part of which was published by Dhorme (1938) 179, and again by Bottéro (1954a) 19, no. 20.

[126]Aškur (or Asqur)-Addu was a king of Karanā, and a contemporary of Zimri-Lim. We have already met him (as well as his predecessor, Ḫātnu-rapi) acting in the northern reaches of the Mari empire. On the sequence of the kings of Karanā in the Mari Age, see Dalley, *apud* OBTTR 4, 33.

[127]See Bottéro (1954a) nos. 18–24.

[128]Dossin (1939a) 986.

Yaminites themselves designated as Ḫapiru, as other tribesmen sometimes were?[129] Šurusum (spelled Šurušum) recurs in ARM 2 135, in which Šaknu, Zimri-Lim's representative at Ilānṣurā, after an assurance that Ilānṣurā, king Ḫāya-sūmû, and the Mariote troops were well, brought the news that General[130] Lawīla-Addu left Šubat-Enlil with three thousand soldiers: "perhaps toward Ašnakkum, perhaps toward Šurušum (*a-na Šu-ru-ši-im*^{KI}) his face is set. Who knows?"[131] Ašnakkum, if not necessarily identical with Chagar Bazar,[132] was at any rate located in the central part of the Ḫabūr triangle, roughly west of Šubat-Enlil. Šurušum, therefore, was situated in a different direction. We have already seen that Šubat-Enlil could be used as a base for invading the central and western parts of Ṭūr ᶜAbdīn.

E. Sachau, during his extensive journey over Syria and North Mesopotamia over a century ago, noted a small village in Ṭūr ᶜAbdīn whose name was transcribed Šâriš or Šíerš.[133] That village has long since disappeared from the map, but its name has survived as Şerşe, borne by a mound near Gersüş in the north-central part of the massif, the reputed provenience of a cylinder seal whose closest parallels are found in Level VII of Alalaḫ.[134] Since the name, location, and archaeological character of Şerşe perfectly agree with what is known of Šurušum, we may consider their identity as virtually certain.

For Yaḫmumum, we have a remarkably close toponymic parallel, which is, however, less solid geographically. Musil refers to the seventh century Syrian Arabic poet, al-Aḫṭal, who mentioned al-Yaḥmūm with aṣ-Ṣuwar.[135] Yaḥmum is a most accurate and etymologically correct

[129]Cf. Bottéro (1954a) nos. 17*, 19, perhaps 33, and Kupper (1961). See also my article "Habiru" in Astour (1976) 382 § 2.

[130]GAL.MAR.TU = *rāb Amurrim.* In the Old Babylonian period, the term designated a high military rank with no ethnic connotation. See Sasson (1969) 11–13.

[131]Quoted text, 11. 11–20. The beginning of 11. 14–15 is slightly damaged. I follow the interpretation on Kupper (1957) 8 n 1.

[132]As assumed by van Liere (1963) 120, mainly from the data of the Urbana Itinerary; followed by Hallo (1964) 74 § 39.

[133]Sachau (1883) 416. He defined its position as being north of Krmûte (map *Midyat*: Karmut), at the foot of the ridge which closes the Kefr Čōz (Gercüş) valley in the north, in the spot where the brook breaks through the ridge. This would put it at, or near, the present-day village of Bekes, or Bagas (37°34′ N, 41 °18′ E).

[134]Erkanal-Öktü (1979). Gercüş, one of the three principal towns of modern Ṭūr ᶜAbdīn, is located at 37°34′ N, 41°23′ E, about 18 km. north of Midyat, on a road that continues to the Tigris. It is also connected by road with Savur (ca. 45 km. in beeline). Unfortunately, Erkanal-Öktü did not specify the distance from Şerşe to Gercüş. Thus its identity with Sachau's Šéirš/Šāriš (which is not so very near Gercüş—11 km. in beeline) cannot be ascertained.

[135]Musil (1927) 86 n 48. The quoted passage is in al-Aḫṭal's *Diwān* (Ṣalḥani) 106 f. Al-Aḫṭal (ca. 640—ca. 710) was "the Umayyad poet laureate," see Hitti (1968) 196, 220, 252. I was unable to consult the original.

rendering of cuneiform Yaḫmumum, but if it is indeed associated with aṣ-Ṣuwar (a locality on the right bank of the lower Ḫabūr, about 43 km. from its confluence with the Euphrates,[136] this leads us much too far not only from Ṭūr ᶜAbdīn, but from any conceivable location of Ilānṣurā. But could not the poet, or more likely a copyist, have committed a slight error in punctuating the consonantal skeleton ṢWR as *Ṣuwar* instead of *Ṣawr* or *Ṣor*, the Semitic (Syriac and Arabic) name of Savur, ancient Ṣurrā? Such emendation, if justifiable by the context, would put al-Aḫṭal's al-Yaḫmūm, and its cuneiform counterpart, Yaḫmumum, right where we expect it to be found—between Şerşe and Savur. The retaking of Yaḫmumum by Ḫāya-sūmû appears, then, as an episode of that ruler's action to recover his towns that had fallen into the power of Kurdā.

THE LAWSUIT ABOUT ŠUNḪUM

We have dealt so far with Ḫāya-sūmû's actions in the western and southeastern directions. Two Mari tablets, which shed a bright light upon judicial practises of the period, provide interesting information about Ḫāya-sūmû's political interests in the south.[137] They deal with two successive phases of the same legal case of opposing territorial claims.

The first letter (ARM HC ORD2-A = Dossin [1958]) was addressed to Zimri-Lim by a high personnage called Šupram. He is known as the king of Susā, one of the city-states of the land of Idamaraz,[138] and he was also entrusted with the administration of Šubat-Enlil, which became a Mari enclave after the dissolution of Šamši-Adad's empire.[139] In the letter in question, Šupram acted as ruler of the land of Apum, which

[136]Located at 35°30′ N, 40°39′ E. Spelled aṣ-Ṣuwār in Gaz.Syr., Suwār on map *Deir ez Zor*. but (*aṣ-*) *Ṣuwar* or *Ṣuwwar* in Sarre and Herzfeld (1911) I 177–79; Musil (1927) *passim*; and Kupper (1957) 2, 121–22.

[137]The tablets have not yet been published in full, or in the original language. Dossin (1958) gave the translation of the first 42 lines (out of 65) of one of them, and the first 30 lines (out of 47) of the other. Their inventory numbers have not been given, but Kupper designates them as Ord. 2a and Ord. 2b in his index of geographical names in ARMT 16/1. [They are ARM HC ORD2-A and ARM HC ORD2-B as coded for the computerized index, ARMT 17/1—ED.]

[138]According to Dossin (1958) 388 and 390, Šupram reigned over the city of Kirdaḫat, but the Mari tablets published so far do not bear it out. For the extension of the land of Idamaraz, see the lists in ARM 9 298, and in the unpublished tablet A.1212, quoted (courtesy of G. Dossin) by Kupper (1978) 123 and n 39. It included the cities of Ilānṣurā, Ašnakkum, Susā, Šunā, Ašlakkā, Tarmani, Kaḫat, Apum, Qā, Šuduḫu, Nagar, Naḫur, Talḫāyum, Kirdaḫat, Zalluḫān, Ḫurrā, and several cities of whom only the names of the kings are known. It encompassed the western and central parts of the Ḫabūr triangle, and its northern extension into Ṭūr ᶜAbdīn.

[139]Birot, *apud* ARMT 16/1, 198, separates Šupram (or Šubram, as he spells the name), the king of Susā, from the homonymous governor (?) of Šubat-Enlil (ARM 2 109: 4, 6), but

suggests that the city of that name belonged to his domain, either directly or indirectly.[140] Šupram's letter is written in an elliptical language with too many pronouns used instead of the names of the persons involved in the case. Nevertheless, Dossin has succeeded, in our opinion, in explaining the affair, and in clarifying the relationship between its several participants.[141]

The gist of Šupram's letter is as follows. Earlier, when Zimri-Lim stayed at Tādum,[142] he received a complaint from Ili-Ištar, the "man" of Šunā, that Ili-Addu, the "man" of Kiduḫ, had taken his town, Šunḫum, by force. Zimri-Lim summoned Šupram, and ordered that Ili-Ištar and his elders, Ili-Addu and his elders, and Šupram, himself, together with the elders of the land of Apum, assemble in the residence of Ḫāya-sūmû, and receive and accept his judgment. Ḫāya-sūmû did not appear in person, nor did he send his elders, but he ordered, via his officials, that two men and two women from each side should undergo a judicial ordeal. One side is left unnamed, but clearly represents the "man" of Kiduḫ, while the other side is explicitly defined as that of the "man" of Apum. The two men and women from each side had to take some earth of the contested town in their hands, to declare solemnly that the town belonged by right to their master, and to plunge into the river. Whichever side won the ordeal would receive the town. But the culprit, Ili-Addu of Kiduḫ, refused to submit to Ḫāya-sūmû's judgment, continued to occupy the town, and plundered the inhabitants of the land of Apum. Šupram requested that Zimri-Lim write to Ḫāya-sūmû to settle the affair.

It seems that Zimri-Lim did, in fact, intervene. He commissioned a high official, Meptûm, to preside over the execution of the river ordeal, and we have Meptûm's report (ARM HC ORD2-B = Dossin [1958]). The

---

given the proximity of Šubat-Enlil to Šupram's domain, and the latter's firm allegiance to Zimri-Lim, one should consider them as one and the same man.

[140]Two kings of Apum are known by name, Ḫāya-abum and Zūzu, but Šupram may have ruled the city temporarily, e.g., during an interregnum, or Apum may have been one of his vassal cities (like Šunā).

[141]My own understanding of ARM HC ORD2-A agrees with its interpretation by Dossin, rather than with Sasson (1973) 72–73, who reverses the allegiances of Ili-Ištar and Ili-Addu with regard to Šupram and Ḫāya-sūmû.

[142]Tādum (*Ta-a-di-im*^{KI}, *Ta-a-da*^{KI}), or perhaps Taʾadum, should be considered an early form of the Late Bronze Age toponym Taʾidi (Hittite ^{URU}*Ta-i-ta*, Middle Assyrian ^{URU}*Ta-i-di*. That city, one of the principal centers of Mitanni-Ḫanigalbat, was located in the eastern part of North Mesopotamia, apparently not very far from Šubat-Enlil. Such a general location is corroborated by the Middle Assyrian itinerary DeZ 2521, reported by Röllig at the 27th Rencontre Assyriologique Internationale (Paris, 3 July, 1980). The equation of Taʾidi with the Neo-Assyrian ^{URU}*Ti-i-di*/*Ti-du* in the area of Tusḫa, Šinamu, and the Tigris bend (Weidner [1923] 26 n 2; Weidner [1935–36] 21; and Goetze [1953] 59 n 47) must be abandoned.

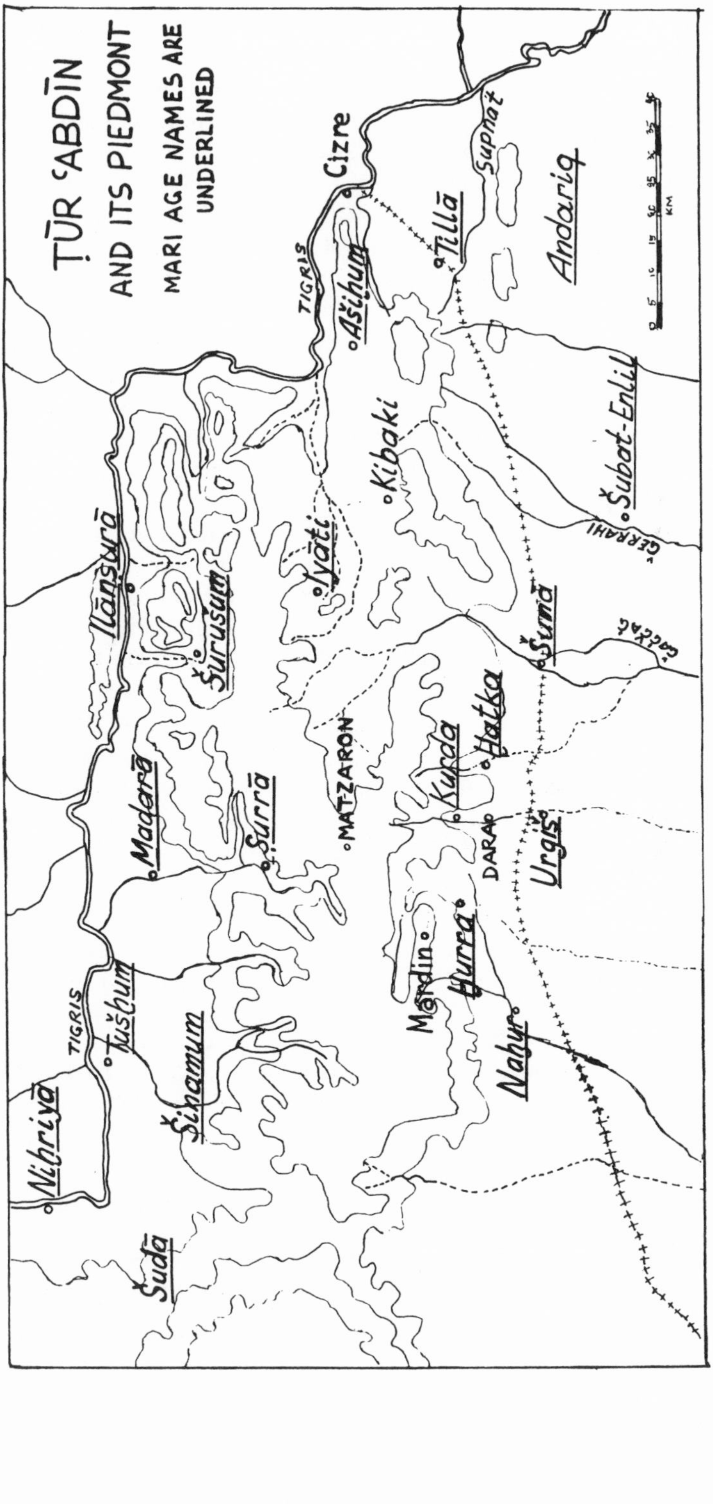
ṬŪR ʿABDĪN
AND ITS PIEDMONT
MARI AGE NAMES ARE UNDERLINED
Cizre
TIGRIS
Ašiḫum
Tillā
Supnat
Andariq
Kibaki
Šubat-Enlil
GERRAHI
Iyāti
Ilānṣurā
Šurušum
Šurnā
ÇAĞÇAĞ
Hatka
Kurda
MAT-ZARON
Surrā
Madarā
DARA
Urgiš
Mardin
Ḫurrā
Naḫur
TIGRIS
Tušḫum
Šinamum
Nihriyā
Šudā
KM

Map 2.

contest was now between representatives of Šupram and Ḫāya-sūmû, one elder and six women from each side.[143] When one of Ḫāya-sūmû's women drowned, his representatives admitted their defeat, implored Šupram not to have the remaining women thrown into the river, and volunteered to remit to him a tablet of non-revendication which confirmed Šupram's possession of the town and its territory. This was formalized on the spot by Meptûm.

The two tablets, besides their judicial interest, are highly instructive with regard to the political and geographical organization of the parts of Zimri-Lim's empire, which were not immediate provinces of the Mari kingdom. They were ruled by vassal kings, but the more powerful of them had their own vassals for whom they were responsible, and whose territories they regarded as part of their own domains. Thus Šupram was the overlord of Ili-Ištar of Šunā, and Ḫāya-sūmû, the overlord of Ili-Addu of Kiduḫ, and the zones of suzerainty of the two overlords abutted upon each other. Let us try to express this situation in terms of North Mesopotamian geography.

Of the localities that appear in ARM HC ORD2-A, the easiest to put on the map is Šunā, which is also the most relevant for our present subject. The Old Babylonian Itinerary from Larsa to Emar has the sequence Šubat-Enlil—Šunā—Ašnakki on the outbound journey, and Ašnakkum—Urgiš—Šunā—Ḫarsi (var. Ḫarrusi)—Šubat-Enlil on the inbound one.[144] The equations of Šubat-Enlil with Tell Leylān, and of Urgiš with Tell ᶜAmūdeh can be regarded as certain.[145] The average length of a day's march of the caravan (25–30 km.) is also known. Van Liere proposed to equate Šunā with the large mound at Nusaybin,[146] which is 30 km. distant from Leylān, and 26 km. from ᶜAmūdeh. Hallo preferred to identify Nusaybin with Ḫarsi.[147] But the impressive size of Nusaybin's mound reveals it as an ancient royal capital,[148] which Šunā was,[149] while Ḫarsi, which is never mentioned in the Mari tablets, must have been a small town or village on or slightly off the road from Šunā to Šubat-Enlil.[150] Nusaybin is located very near the southern edge of Ṭūr

[143]The technical side of the ordeal will be discussed in the next section, below.

[144]Outbound leg: Urbana Itinerary obv. ii: 5–8; Yale Itinerary 24–26. Inbound leg: Urbana Itinerary rev. iii: 21–25. See Goetze (1953) 51, 54, and Hallo (1964) 63. ARM 10 121 confirms that Šunā bordered on Urgiš, and ARM HC AREP., the letter quoted in Dossin (1938a) 119, that it bordered on Ašnakkum.

[145]See nn 33 and 87, above.

[146]Van Liere (1963) 120. Its coordinates are 37° 03′ N, 41°12′ E. Cf. n 32, above.

[147]Hallo (1964) 78 § 38.

[148]Van Liere (1963) 114.

[149]According to ARM 10 98, its king, Ili-Ištar, whom we just met in the Šunḫum affair, was married to Tispatum, a daughter of Zimri-Lim.

[150]Van Liere (1963) 120 tentatively identified Ḫarsi with Tell Ḥamīdī (36°48′ N, 41°10′ E) on the eastern bank of the Ǧaġǧaġ, 30 km. south of Nusaybin, and 35 km.

ᶜAbdīn, which agrees with the position of Šunā near the zone of domination of Ilānṣurā.

The approximate whereabouts of the contested town of Šunḫum may be deduced from ARM 1 131. Išme-Dagan announced to his brother, Yasmaḫ-Addu, that after having taken Tarrum, Ḫatka, and Šunḫum, he proceeded to Ḫurarā and conquered it after a seven-day siege.[151] Ḫatka probably corresponds to the Byzantine fortress Attachas,[152] Arabic al-Ḥattaḫ,[153] modern Turkish Hatik,[154] a site in Ṭūr ᶜAbdīn, about 17 km. north of Nusaybin. Tarrum and Ḫurarā are otherwise unknown. Šunḫum, which follows Ḫatka in Išme-Dagan's enumeration, must have been located in southern Ṭūr ᶜAbdīn, north or northeast of Nusaybin. Nothing is known about *Š*[*a*]-*b*[*a*]-*si-im*[KI], to which Šunḫum originally belonged, according to the people of Kiduḫ.

But we may be better informed on the location of Kiduḫ. Socin, who travelled to Midyat from Cizre, and Gertrude Bell, who proceeded to Midyat from the Tigris crossing at Finik, both passed through a village east of Āzeḫ (which we encountered earlier), whose name they transcribed Kōdaḫ (Socin), or Kôdakh (Bell).[155] The similarity of that name to that of Kiduḫ, combined with the location of the site in Ṭūr ᶜAbdīn, is too close to be considered accidental. True, the position of Kōdaḫ in the far eastern corner of Ṭūr ᶜAbdīn does not make it a direct neighbor of Šunā and the area of its influence. But the king of Kiduḫ, since he was a protégé of the powerful king of Ilānṣurā could well have seized Šunḫum,

---

southwest of Leylān. But Tell Ḥamīdī is a fairly large mound, of the same class as Chagar Bazar (Van Liere [1963] 114). On p. 93, Van Liere wrote that it "was well fortified, with enormous walls and a moat at a certain distance." This points to its role as a royal capital, perhaps to be eqated with Šupram's capital Susā, while the powerfully fortified Tell ᶜArbīd (36°52′ N, 41°10′ E) would correspond to Apum, which the Old Assyrian itineraries located approximately in that emplacement. On Tell ᶜArbīd, see Mallowan (1937) 117.

151(5) [*iš*]-*tu Ta-ar-ra-am*[KI] (6) *Ḫ*[*a-a*]*t-ka*[KI] (7) *ù Šu-un-ḫa-am*[KI] (8) *aṣ-ba-tu a-na Ḫu-ra-ra*[KI] (9) *ás-ni-iq-ma*, etc.

152Procopius, *De aedif*. II:4:14: *Atachas*; Georgius Cyprius No. 938: *Kastron Attachas*. The Greek and Arabic spelling reflect the Syriac spirantized *k*.

153Canard (1951) 799 quotes a passage from the medieval Arabic chronicler, Ibn Azraq, *Tariḫ Mayafariqin*, 114, V, where al-Ḥattaḫ appears among the North Mesopotamian fortresses that were destroyed by the Byzantine emperor John Zimiskes in 959. According to Sachau (1883) 394, the site was still called Melik Ḥateḫ when he passed it. Cf. Dillemann (1962) 228.

15437°11′ N, 41°05′ E.

155Socin (1881) 244–45; Bell (1911) 302 n 3. Socin's *ḏ* probably renders Syriac spirantization of *d*. Between Finik (now Finiki Geli, 37°26′ N, 42°04′ E) and Kōdaḫ, Bell passed through Thelailah (Gaz.Turk.: Telilâ, 37°23′ N, 42°04′ E). A name resembling Kōdaḫ does not appear on modern maps. The village was obviously renamed Garis Ağa (thus on the map of Turkey 1:200,000, sheet F 15: *Midyat*, and on the British quarter-inch map of Iraq, sheet J-38 M: *Jazīrat ibn Omar*), or Harisğa (Gaz.Turk., 37°22′ N, 42°00′ E). Schwenzer's map (n 28, above) erroneously spells the name Kuwaḫ, by confusion with Kiwaḫ (now Kivah, cf. n 105 above).

even if it was not contiguous to his domain. Fragmentation of territorial holdings, normal in the kingdom of Yamḫad of the same general period, was not unknown in the North Mesopotamia of the Mari Age, and military operations conducted by local rulers at often considerable distances from their homes were quite common there.

THE RIVER ORDEAL AT ILĀNṢURĀ

It follows from Šupram's letter (ARM HC ORD2-A) that the ordeal was to have taken place at Ḫāya-sūmû's residence, i.e., at Ilānṣurā, and from Meptûm's report (ARM HC ORD2-B), that it was performed in a big and deep river. The man and women who underwent the ordeal had to float for eighty cubits (ca. 40 m.),[156] and one woman drowned in the process. This means that the depth of the river exceeded the height of an adult man. Meptûm did not name the river, but it is evident that the ordeal could only be performed in a body of water of sufficient depth. The Euphrates served that purpose in Babylon, Mari, and Carchemish.[157] Ilānṣurā was far from the Euphrates, nor was it near the Ḫabūr, the only other river of North Mesopotamia that could be taken into account. But the Ṭūr ᶜAbdīn upland, to which all previously considered testimonies to the texts point for the emplacement of Ilānṣurā, is limited on the north and east by the Tigris, which having received several tributaries, has already become a wide, deep, and swift river. We have to conclude that Ilānṣurā stood on the right bank of the Tigris where it washes the northern edge of the massif.

ILĀNṢURĀ = ḤIṢN KAYFĀ (HASANKEYF)

Among the Ṭūr ᶜAbdīn localities on the Tigris, there is one that immediately attracts our attention as the most fitting site for a local capital. This is Hasankeyf, whose present-day name is a playful distortion of medieval Arabic Ḥiṣn Kayfā (or Ḥiṣn Kīfā), which in turn derives from Syriac Ḥisnā de-Kīphā (or Kēphā), "Fortress of the Rock."[158] It is mentioned in early Byzantine sources as a fortress called Cephae (Cefae),[159] Kiphas,[160] and Kastron Rhiskêphas.[161] The latter name renders

[156] I do not know the reason for Dossin's (1958) 392 computation of 80 cubits as "about 24 meters." Sasson (1973) 73 n 72 has the correct figure.

[157] Codex Hammurabi §§ 2, 132, ARM HC ORD1, the letter of Yatar-Ami, king of Carchemish, to Zimri-Lim, published in Dossin (1939d), proves that river ordeal was practiced at both Carchemish and Mari. It is also attested in Assyria, Nuzi, and Elam—countries washed by the Tigris and its major tributaries.

[158] 37°43′ N, 41°25′ E. On the present-day Hasankeyf and its ruins, see Boulanger (1970) 715. A picturesque description of Hasankeyf, seen from a raft floating down the Tigris, is given by Soan (1912) 78–79.

[159] *Not. dig.* XXXVI:15, 30.

[160] Procopius, *De aedif.* II:4:14.

[161] Georgius Cyprius No. 913 (cod. R).

the Syriac *rēš kēphā*, "Summit of the Rock."[162] These names reflect the position of the site upon a precipitous crag high over the Tigris. Ḥiṣn Kayfā, according to Arab geographers, and as evidenced by the extensive ruins of its citadel, palace, mosques, and the extant piers of a remarkable stone bridge across the Tigris, was an important place in the Middle Ages.[163] "Its strategic importance consisted in its fortified castle, its commercial importance in its serving as an emporium of the trade between Diyār Bekr and Ǧazīrāt Ibn ᶜOmar," noted Streck, adding that the Tigris crossing at that site was probably used for centuries before the construction of the bridge.[164] Authors familiar with the town and its ancient cave dwellings are certain that Ḥiṣn Kayfā was inhabited long before its name appeared in Byzantine records.[165]

These topographical factors support the equation of Ilānṣurā with Ḥiṣn Kayfā, and so does the itinerary of Hattušiliš I's expedition against Ilānṣurā which was examined at the beginning of this study. There is also an interesting semantic parallelism between the successive names of the city. *Ilānṣurā* is a composite name. Its first element, *ilān,* has an uncertain meaning. It might mean "tree" (Hebrew *ᵓēlōn,* Aramaic *ᵓīlān*), or "god" (Ugaritic *iln,* Phoenician *ᵓln*). The latter would explain the variant *I-la-ṣú-*[*ra-a*]. But the second element, *ṣurā* (with the West Semitic formative *-ā*) or *ṣūr* (in the variant *I-la-an-ṣú-ur*), which is also a component of several Amorite names in Mari texts, corresponds to Hebrew *ṣūr,* "rock, cliff,"[166] equivalent to Aramaic-Syriac *kēph*(*ā*).

CONCLUSION

This study in historical geography, which centered on the problem of Ilānṣurā, succeeded, as its author would like to believe, in ascertaining the site of that city (which has hitherto been placed in divergent and insufficiently substantiated locations), and the approximate extent of its kingdom and zone of influence. In the process of inquiry, the study also helped to clarify certain concommitant questions.

It reconstructed the route of the bold Old Hittite march from the upper Euphrates to the northern confines of Ṭūr ᶜAbdīn, with the probable intention of attacking the Hurrian lands in North Mesopotamia from an unexpected direction—an anticipation of Šuppiluliumaš I's military action in 1366, as it were.

[162]On Kēphā/Riskêpha in Byzantine and Syriac sources, see Dillemann (1962) 218, 228.

[163]The information by Muqadassi (10th century), the anonymous annotator of Ibn Ḥauqal, and Yāqūt (both 12th century) are summarized in Le Strange (1905) 113. See also the articles on Ḥisn Kayfā by Streck (1927) 340–41, and Ory (1971) 524–26, and the detailed description of the site by Gabriel (1940) 55–82.

[164]Streck (1927) 340. Similarly, Ory (1971).

[165]Streck (1927) 340: the dwellings "prove that an establishment existed at the site about 800 B.C." Ory (1971) 524: "The region had been inhabited from very early time."

[166]See Jean (1950b) 90, and Huffmon (1965) 258.

It adduced new data in support of certain previously proposed locations of ancient cities, refuted certain other hypothetical locations, and introduced a few topographical equations of its own.

It widened the extension of the region called Idamaraz (or Idamaraṣ) in the Mari texts, which was hitherto restricted to the Ḫabūr triangle. Now we know that it also included Ṭūr ᶜAbdīn, since Ilānṣurā was listed as one of the principal cities of the Idamaraz region.[167]

It placed the vast and well-populated Ṭūr ᶜAbdīn massif into the geographical and political horizon of the Mari texts, filling thereby a large blank spot on the historical map of the period. It also showed that, far from being an isolated cul-de-sac, remote from the main roads and power contests of the ancient Near East, it was, on the contrary, an arena of intense political and military rivalry, and a goal of repeated invasions by distant powers: Mari, Assyria, Ešnunna, and Ḫatti in the Middle Bronze Age; Mitanni, Ḫatti, and Assyria in the Late Bronze Age, and under Tiglath-pileser I; the Neo-Assyrian Empire under Tukulti-Ninurta II, Assurnasirpal II, and Šalmaneser III; and the Byzantines and Sassanids of the sixth century A.D.

POSTSCRIPT

Van Liere's location of Urkiš at Tell ᶜĀmūdā at Nusaybin, accepted in this study, may be subject to revision.

(1) According to the comparative chart of north Syrian and north Mesopotamian mounds, presented by Harvey Weiss in his paper "The Origins of Tell Leilan" at the annual meeting of ASOR, Chicago, December 9, 1984, a possible site for Urkiš may be Mozan, a mound with an area of 48 ha. Mozan (or Tell Mūzān, 37°03′ N, 40°54′ E) stands at a distance of 8 km. southeast of ᶜĀmūdā and of 23 km. north–northeast of Chagar Bazar. In his letter of February 10, 1985, Prof. Weiss kindly informed me that his survey of Tell ᶜĀmūdā did not find there any third and early second millennia sherds, while Tell Mūzān has that material.

(2) ADD 950, a list of *šakinte* (MÍ.GAR.MEŠ, female managers of high rank), enumerates (obv. 8–10) those of ᵘʳᵘ*Šu-u-du,* ᵘʳᵘ*Te-ʾ-di,* ᵘʳᵘ*Ka-ḫat,* ᵘʳᵘ*Su-né-e.* Since the former three cities are attested as district centers in North Mesopotamia, the same is probably true for the last one. K. Kessler, *Untersuchungen zur historischen Topographie Nordmesopotamiens* (TAVO, Reihe B, Beiheft 9, Wiesbaden 1980), 93, noted that Sunê "may possibly be identical with the Old Babylonian city Šuna." If *Sunê* is the Assyrian spelling of *Šunā,* which is plausible, the city cannot

[167]In the enumerations of kings of Idamaraz, Ḫāya-sūmû stands in the first place in A.1212 (unpublished, see n 138), and in the second place in ARM 9 298.

be equated with Nusaybin which frequently appears in Neo-Assyrian records as Naṣibina or Naṣipina. Šunā, then, should be sought somewhere else in the same area, perhaps at Tūlūl Muḥammad, 18 km. south of Nusaybin, 30 km. from Tell Leylān, 23 km. from Tell Mūzān, and 20–22 km. from Chagar Bazar—a position which fits the Old Babylonian itinerary even better than Nusaybin. This would leave the mound at Nusaybin (which may owe its large size to its development in the Roman and Sassanian periods) for the site of Šunḫum.

The Old Assyrian Caravan Road in the Mari Royal Archives

B. J. BEITZEL

Trinity Evangelical Divinity School

I. INTRODUCTION

Near the end of the first quarter of the eighteenth century B.C., as the political fortunes of the Lim dynasty began to revive at Mari under the genius of Zimri-Lim, certain Assyrian merchants were engaged in an extensive commercial enterprise, shipping tin and textiles to a number of markets across North Mesopotamia and Cappadocia, including Kaniš itself. Numerous facets of this trade are described in Old Assyrian literature, and have been the object of several noteworthy studies. Previous investigation into the actual route employed by these caravaneers, however, has not led to decisive conclusions, owing primarily to the fact that an actual itinerary has not yet been discovered, though presently a repertoire of some thirty intermediate sites is associated, in one way or another, with traffic along the course of the journey. One must infer from diverse geographic and documentary sources the location of the route; and in this regard, the Mari archive is of paramount importance, attesting as it does to some twenty of these stations. This essay represents an attempt to evaluate the Mari literature, together with pertinent Old Assyrian data, as it endeavors to plot the caravan route.

II. PRIMARY TEXTUAL DATA

TC 3/2 163		*BIN 4 193 + 124*	
E	*Saduatum	E	*Saduatum
	*Razamā		*Razamā
	Abi-tiban		Abi-tiban
	*Qaṭarā		*Qaṭarā
	*Razamā		*Razamā
	Tarakum		Tarakum
W	*Apum	W	*Apum

CCT 1 42a
E *Razamā ša Burama[x]
*Qaṭarā
*Razamā ša Uḫakim
Kaluzanum
W Abudazum

CCT 1 26b
E *Uzuḫinum
W Tarakum

VAT 9260
W #*Atmum
[Marda]man?
[. . .]
*Ḫabura
*Burallum
E *Širun

ARM 1 26
*Šubat-Enlil
*Tillā
*Ašiḫum
*Iyati
*Lakušir
*Sagarātum
(Mari)

CCT 5 44c
E *Qaṭarā
Tarakum
Ḫaqa
*Apum
*Amaz
*Naḫur
*Luḫayum
W Abrum

CCT 1 27a
W Abrum
E *Ašiḫum

TC 2 57
E *Apum
W Abrum

Other Pertinent OA Sites
Balīḫum
*Burullum
*Ḫaḫḫum
*Ḫaššum
*Niḫriyā
*Talḫāyum
*Uršum

* Site attested in Mari literature
# Common point in OA caravan and OB Itinerary

III. ANALYSIS OF EARLIER RESEARCH

Lewy.[1] Though the inquiry of Bilgiç had sought to address specific features of Anatolian geography, had broadly sketched out possible locations of five towns along the trade route (Abrum, Ašiḫum, Ḫaḫḫum, Niḫriyā, and Uršum), and had ventured to chart two highways from the Euphrates to Kaniš,[2] it was the research of Julius Lewy which constituted the first rather comprehensive investigation into the subject of Old Assyrian geography. His was a seminal work with enduring influence, but alas, with all due respect, we believe that current data render many

[1] J. Lewy (1952) and (1953).
[2] Bilgiç (1945–51).

of his conclusions unconvincing, and even somewhat confusing because of three fatal flaws.

1. Lewy interpreted the lexeme *massû* to mean "deep-drawing ship," and was obliged accordingly to locate any geographic name found in the expression, *ana massû ša* GN, along a river. For this reason, Niḫriyā was placed on the Tigris (MAH 16158: 12, 20),[3] Ašiḫum and Azuḫinum were located on the Ḫabur (CCT 1 27a: 12–13; CCT 1 26b: 1–2),[4] and Abrum was situated along the Euphrates (CCT 1 27a: 6–7).[5] He attempted to bolster his contention, in the latter instance, with an alleged West Semitic etymology that would have necessitated locating Abrum west of the Euphrates.[6]

Even on the surface, this interpretation of *massû* created an impossible situation for Lewy; for how could Ašiḫum have been located along the Ḫabur, if, according to the itinerary of Šamši-Adad (ARM 1 26), this site was situated a distance of only two days travel from Šubat-Enlil, which Lewy staunchly identified with Aššur?[7] He could circumvent this dilemma only by resorting to the theory of homonymy.[8] At issue, however, is the word *massû*, interpreted now by both AHw[9] and CAD[10] to refer to a ruler, or local official. Hence, it is not imperative that these sites, or any other associated with the vocable *massû*, be located along a river.

2. Lewy became convinced of the equation Terakum = Terqa (modern Tell ᶜAšāra).[11] Consequently, he proposed that the Old Assyrian route followed the course of the Ḫabur to its confluence with the Euphrates, and then downstream to Terqa.

3. In a detailed linguistic discussion, Lewy postulated the equation Elaḫut/Luḫaya = Liḫšu/Nuḫašše.[12] Therefore, he plotted the caravan route along the Euphrates from Terqa to Thapsakos (Abrum for Lewy), westward past Nuḫašše, and on to Rhosus (Uršum for Lewy).[13] This was despite the fact that in CCT 5 44c, as in Lewy's own translation,[14] Luḫayum was placed *between* Naḫur and Abrum. At any rate, a logical entailment of this equation was that the intermediate stations of Apum, Amaz, and Naḫur had to be positioned along the mid-Euphrates. His

[3] J. Lewy (1961) 66 n 201.
[4] J. Lewy (1952) 274.
[5] J. Lewy (1952) 275–76 n 1.
[6] J. Lewy (1952) 286–87.
[7] J. Lewy (1953) 293–321.
[8] J. Lewy (1952) 1–12 and (1953) 321 [map].
[9] AHw 619a.
[10] CAD M/1 328.
[11] J. Lewy (1952) 271, 274–76.
[12] J. Lewy (1952) 403–13.
[13] J. Lewy (1952) 287–90.
[14] J. Lewy (1952) 271–72 n 4; 393.

localization of Naḫur, in particular, has generated confusion, although he relied here upon the discussion of Sachau,[15] and the map of Kiepert,[16] from whom the confusion seems ultimately to have risen. These scholars described two tells referred to as el-Menâkhir, situated some twelve miles ENE of the Balīḫ-Euphrates confluence. Lewy advanced their discussion by equating these tells both with Old Assyrian Naḫur, and with the Neo-Assyrian site of Tell Naḫiri, listed in the so-called "Ḫarrān census."[17] These, however, are mountains, actually volcanic craters, which are so listed in the investigations of Sarre and Herzfeld, Musil, Müller, as well as the map of the British War Office and Air Ministry.[18] And evidence available today suggests that Tell Naḫiri should most likely be sought in the immediate vicinity of Ḫarrān itself.[19]

One further observation in respect to Lewy's work seems felicitous. Predicated in part upon a Mari text which contained the same toponym (ARM 2 63), Lewy proposed the restoration [Marda]man in VAT 9260, and then proceeded to hypothesize that this city might have been located at Mardin.[20] While his restoration has been widely accepted,[21] of those discussing Old Assyrian caravan geography, only Garelli has adopted the equation.[22] Later, however, based precisely upon this hypothesis, Lewy attempted to locate the station Atmum just north of Nisibin,[23] a placement that becomes additionally confusing because it dictates a *westward* movement in VAT 9260.

On the other hand, Birot has supplied a resume of a yet unpublished Mari text in which the king of Mardaman is described as having had warm relations with the king of Ḫaburātum.[24] In the time of Šamši-Adad, Ḫaburātum, together with Razamā and Burullum, was administered by a single official (ARM 1 109; cf. ARM 5 67). In Rimāḥ documents, Mardaman and Ḫaburātum are presented as towns within the domain of Karanā, and dependent upon its king. And, interestingly enough, one of these texts (OBTTR 251) goes on to list the town of Širwun as a dependent municipality. This town is also listed in the royal archives, and in all likelihood is identical to Širun in VAT 9260. As a consequence, it seems highly probable that Mardaman should be sought in the area of the

[15]Sachau (1883) 250.

[16]Kiepert (1882) [map in Sachau (1883)].

[17]J. Lewy (1952) 281–82. The "Ḫarrān Census" was published by Johns (1901). The Tell Naḫiri reference may be found on p. 71 (#21.2). Cf. Johns (1898–1923) I 333 (#420.3).

[18]Sarre and Herzfeld (1911) [map]; Musil (1927) 90–91; Müller (1931) 72(*bis*); War Office and Air Ministry, Survey D: Series 1404 (1:500,000) s.v. Deir ez Zor (1962).

[19]Bilgiç (1951) 23 and de Vaux (1978) 195.

[20]J. Lewy (1952) 265 n 2.

[21]Goetze (1953) 65, 67; Falkner (1957/58) 21, 35; Garelli (1963) 90; Kessler (1980) 64.

[22]Garelli (1963) 90. This equation was also adopted by Civil (1967) 36.

[23]J. Lewy (1953) 298–99.

[24]Birot (1973) 9 n 2.

Sinjār, or near the lower Ḫabur, where Ḫaburātum and Burullum are commonly positioned,[25] and a location at or near Mardin becomes altogether unconvincing.

Goetze.[26] Albrecht Goetze published a version of the Old Babylonian Itinerary to which he appended an analysis of the Old Assyrian caravan route. He plotted the journey from Aššur and Ḫatra to the lower Ḫabur, near Tell ᶜArbān. Here he located Azuḫinum and Ašiḫum, suggesting that they might have represented alternate places to cross the river, possibly being led at this point by Lewy's interpretation of *massû*. In any event, he rightly rejected Lewy's proposal to consolidate these two sites into one,[27] and extended the route westward from ᶜArbān, skirting the southern edge of Jebel ᶜAbd el-Azīz, and on towards Ḫarrān and an eventual Euphrates crossing, most likely at Bireçik.[28] This represents a problematic sector in Goetze's reconstruction, because, despite the existence of a modern road which follows this line, and connects the Ḫabur basin with Ḫarrān, it runs adjacent to very few ancient ruins, and I can locate only two widely scattered tells near its course, which show evidence of second millennium occupation.[29]

On the other hand, Goetze asserted that the itinerary station, Atmi, should be related to the Old Assyrian caravan stop, Atmum, a site manifested also in the ARM. We believe that the testimony of the Mari texts which cite Atmum sustains Goetze's assertion, and that this represents a capital contribution with far-reaching geographical consequences, a point to which we shall return.

Falkner. Margarete Falkner traced an Old Assyrian route that closely resembled that of Goetze, though it differed in two important respects.

1. She extended the route from Tell ᶜArbān upstream along the course of the upper Ḫabur valley as far as Tell Faḫḫārīya (Naḫur for her), where it veered north in the direction of Derik, before turning west towards Viranşehir and Urfa.[30]

2. She clearly delineated two routes proceeding from Urfa: one crossing the Euphrates at Bireçik, between the stations of Abrum and Uršum (area of Gaziantep for her); and the other crossing at Samsat,

[25] J. Lewy (1952) 260; Goetze (1953) 66–67; Falkner (1957–58) 35; Civil (1967) 36; Kupper (1979) 8, 13.

[26] Goetze (1953).

[27] Goetze (1953) 67. Cf. J. Lewy (1952) 274.

[28] Goetze (1953) 64–70.

[29] Those two tells are T. Mouazar and T. Dalhīs. The former is located approximately 21 miles west of Tell ᶜArbān, while the latter is positioned about 5 miles southwest of Tell Chūēra. For evidence which discloses second millennium occupation at T. Mouazar, see Van Liere and Lauffray (1954–55) map; Van Liere (1963) 114. Evidence for T. Dalhīs was collected by Mallowan (1946) 119.

[30] Falkner (1957–58) 21, 35.

between the caravan stops of Niḫriyā and Ḫaḫḫum (area of Adiyamān for her).[31] On the other hand, like Goetze, she rejected Lewy's Elaḫut = Luḫayum equation.[32]

One of the foundational questions in Old Assyrian caravan research, this equation has been embraced by Lewy, Kupper, Tocci, Garelli, Veenhof, and Larsen,[33] and repudiated by Bilgiç, Goetze, Falkner, and Finet.[34] The question arises principally because there is a paucity of Old Assyrian documentation that spells out successive caravan stations west of Abrum. Falkner was convinced that Old Assyrian Luḫayum had to be located near Abrum, which on other grounds, was placed near Bireçik. But her interpretation of Mari literature obliged her to locate the district of Elaḫut between Derik and Viranşehir. Thus she rejected the equation. A necessary consequence of her schema was that the sites of Naḫur and Luḫayum would have been separated by more than 160 airline miles, so she interposed the stations of Burundum, Atmum, Mardaman, and Niḫriyā.[35]

Now uncertainties remain regarding this equation, but we offer an alternative series of suggestions as a working hypothesis.

1. If one rejects Falkner's proposal to locate Abrum on the Euphrates, which, in the first place, was anchored entirely on Lewy's *massû* hypothesis,[36] the only reason to seek Luḫayum near Bireçik is eliminated.

2. If one accepts the equation and locates Elaḫut = Luḫayum in the region of Viranşehir, where she had sought Elaḫut, the whole of CCT 5 44c may be interpreted in an essentially sequential manner, and the kind of intrusion occasioned by Falkner's version is completely avoided.

3. Veenhof's study of *dātum* texts (see below) demonstrates that more miles separated Abrum and Kaniš than separated Zalpa and Kaniš.[37] If present evidence justifies localizing Zalpa somewhere between the great bend in the Euphrates and the Balīḫ,[38] Abrum should most likely be placed nearer the Balīḫ than the Euphrates.

[31]Falkner (1957–58) 2, 6–7, 21, 35–36.

[32]Falkner (1957–58) 8–10, 21, 35.

[33]J. Lewy (1952) 403–13. There are really two issues here: the equation itself, and the association of possible Elaḫut = Luḫayum with the city-state of Nuḫašše. It is only the equation which these writers embrace. Cf. Kupper (1957) 254; Tocci (1960) 35; Garelli (1963) 92–94; Veenhof (1972) 242 n 375; Larsen (1976a) 242 n 50.

[34]Bilgiç (1945–51) 24 n 174; Goetze (1953) 68 n 114; Falkner (1957–58) 8–10, 21, 35; Finet (1964b) 138 and n 2.

[35]Falkner (1957–58) 21, 35. Goetze (1953) 65-68 was faced with the same dilemma because he sought to locate Luḫayum near the Euphrates.

[36]Faulker (1957–58) 2, 36.

[37]Veenhof (1972) 240–44.

[38]Goetze (1953) 68; (1964) 116–17; Veenhof (1972) 423; Larsen (1976a) 237–39.

Taking into account the *dātum* texts, the probable location of Atmum in the Old Babylonian Itinerary and the Old Assyrian caravan route, as well as the Mari texts containing references to Elaḫut and Niḫriyā, it seems neither rash to affirm the Elaḫut = Luḫayum equation, nor imprudent to propose a likely sequence of caravan stations between Naḫur and the Euphrates: Naḫur, Elaḫut = Luḫayum, Abrum, Atmum, Niḫriyā, Zalpa, and on to the Euphrates.

Garelli. Professor Garelli was favorably disposed towards Lewy's [Marda]man = Mardin equation and localization.[39] Consequently, he charted a route from Aššur which arrived at the Ḫabur. Here its course was altered northward, presumably via the Wadî Aᶜwej, to the foothills of Ṭūr ᶜAbdīn (Mardin), where it turned west towards Atmum and Ḫarrān.

Orlin.[40] Convinced by the writings of Bilgiç, Smith, and Klengel that Uršum must have been situated immediately west of the Euphrates, between Bireçik and Carchemiš, Louis Orlin embraced a somewhat traditional, southern (i.e., Uršum) route, suggesting that the Assyrian merchants would have journeyed from the region of the headwaters of the Ḫabur triangle westward in the direction of Bireçik, and on to Kaniš via Maraş and Elbistan.

On the other hand, Professor Orlin proposed an innovative scheme for the northern (i.e., Ḫaḫḫum) route. This latter route, he asserted, extended from Diyarbekir to Elazij via Maden, west to Malatya, and on to Kaniš by way of Darendi and Gürün.[41] Orlin made this assertion on the strength of two texts which, he felt, required one to locate Ḫaḫḫum in the neighborhood of modern Ḫarput, some 63 miles northeast of Malatya. In the first of these, Gudea boasted that he had imported to Lagaš gold from the mountains of Ḫaḫḫum. Now Forbes's metallurgical research had disclosed the fact that gold was conspicuously absent from eastern Asia Minor, existing in antiquity only in Armenia (Taljun River), the mountains surrounding Lake Van (Kedabekbegh, Karabegh) and near Ḫarput.[42] From this, Orlin reasoned that since Ḫarput was the only one of these deposits located in reasonably close proximity to the Old Assyrian route, Ḫaḫḫum must be sought in the same region.[43] His argument, however, seems to be freighted with an obvious circularism, and it rests ultimately upon a text that is notoriously devoid of precise geographic data. One recalls that it was largely on the basis of this

[39]Garelli (1963) 90–92.
[40]Orlin (1970).
[41]Orlin (1970) 39–43.
[42]Forbes (1950) 151. See now (1971) 166, 163 [map].
[43]Orlin (1970) 39–40 n 53.

document that Matthiae's equation Ebla = Tell Mardīḫ was initially called into question.[44]

Secondly, Orlin contended that a text of Hattušiliš III required locating Ḫaḫḫum near the city Pitiyarik. The text recorded how the Hittite monarch, sent on an expedition to liberate the people of Pitiyarik, engaged and defeated their enemy at Ḫaḫḫaš (= Ḫaḫḫum). Since Pitiyarik, for other reasons, had been sought in the region to the north or east of Malatya,[45] Orlin felt the feasibility of looking for Ḫaḫḫum in the vicinity of Ḫarput had been additionally strengthened. Such optimism was not shared by I. J. Gelb, however, who concluded that the text in question offered no data at all upon which Ḫaḫḫum could be located.[46]

As we hope to demonstrate below, Old Assyrian and Mari records place Ḫaḫḫum along the same road with sites which must be located either in the Ḫabur triangle (Luḫayum, Burundum, Talḫāyum), or near the Balīḫ valley (Niḫriyā, Zalmaqum).[47] This evidence, we believe, is fatal to the contention that the caravan route to Ḫaḫḫum was linked in some way with the town of Diyarbekir, as this would seem to entail an impossibly circuitous route. Moreover, Orlin's delineation of a route between Diyarbekir and Aššur is sketchy, and rather confusing. On the one hand, he describes a route which would have skirted the Ḫabur headwaters, hugged the Sinjar, and proceeded down the Tigris to Aššur.[48] Presumably, then, Orlin would chart this segment of the route from Diyarbekir to Mardin, and on to Nisibin, where it would have followed the course of the modern road which parallels the railroad that links Nisibin and Mōsul. On the other hand, his discussion of certain sites and his map imply that the road would have passed from Mardin to Hasseke, and on to Mōsul.[49]

Veenhof. Veenhof's volume introduced a new dimension into Old Assyrian caravan geography. He observed that Assyrian merchants were obliged to pay a *dātum,* "caravan tariff," to local authorities through whose territories the caravan passed. He noted also that the total *dātum* routinely paid by merchants who journeyed along the entire route amounted to approximately 10% of the value of the given shipment.[50] From this, he deduced that there must have been a correlation between the percentage of *dātum* paid, and the actual distance travelled. Accord-

[44]Astour (1971) 12–14.

[45]Orlin (1970) 39–40 n 53, following Garstang (1942) 452, and Bilgiç (1945–51) 27–28.

[46]Gelb (1938) 76. Orlin (1970) 43 charted a third route which crossed the Euphrates at Samsat.

[47]CCT 2 22; ARM HC B.308 = Jean (1948a) and Finet (1966a) 19–21.

[48]Orlin (1970) 43 and n 62.

[49]Orlin (1970) 83–85 [map 1].

[50]Veenhof (1972) 233–38.

ingly, by calculating the percentage of *dātum* paid at any given point, one can ascertain the approximate location of this point along the route.[51] By comparing percentages, one can discover relative sequences of towns. This has been a most helpful insight that is presently limited only by the relatively few number of sites found in *dātum* texts.

IV. PRESENT HYPOTHESIS

The balance of this essay represents a delineation of the geographic and documentary evidence to support what I perceive to have been the most likely course followed by Old Assyrian caravaneers in their tin and textile commerce. At the outset, certain methodological considerations must be expressed.

1. The principle of geographic determinism is embraced.[52] By this, we mean that in ancient Near Eastern geographic research, there are largely unchanging physiographic and/or hydrologic factors which determine, except where temporarily or partially contravened by geopolitics, that routes followed by caravans, migrants, or armies remained relatively unaltered throughout extended periods. When this tenet is applied to the Old Assyrian route, one discovers that the hydrologic element would have been significantly operational across North Mesopotamia, as the merchants were confronted at some places with water barriers to be forded, while at others with the need to travel near a sufficient supply of fresh water. But the force of physiography would have been felt acutely as they arrived at the frontier of the Anatolian plateau, faced as they were with the barrier of the Taurus mountains—a range of densely forested slopes rising nearly 10,000 feet, with tortuous defiles, and only three main passes.[53]

2. One must establish a priority of documentary sources. Itineraries and texts of military campaigns which are clearly annalistic should be assigned the highest priority. Preferential status should be conferred on archival testimony, especially when this encompasses epistolary, diplomatic, and administrative components. Such a combination enables one to develop a site profile synchronistically and coherently to a degree of accuracy not possible with an isolated source or passing reference, particularly if the latter does not emerge, in this case, from the Old Assyrian period. Further, the fact that the circumference of a particular town or district was not the same at all times, and that one and the same stretch of geography frequently carried dissimilar names in different eras must be given due consideration. But when more than one

[51] Veenhof (1972) 238–40.

[52] Lattimore (1979) 35–40 applies this term to Chinese society and environment in a slightly different manner.

[53] One recalls the proverb of the Semites' inability to cross the Taurus mountains.

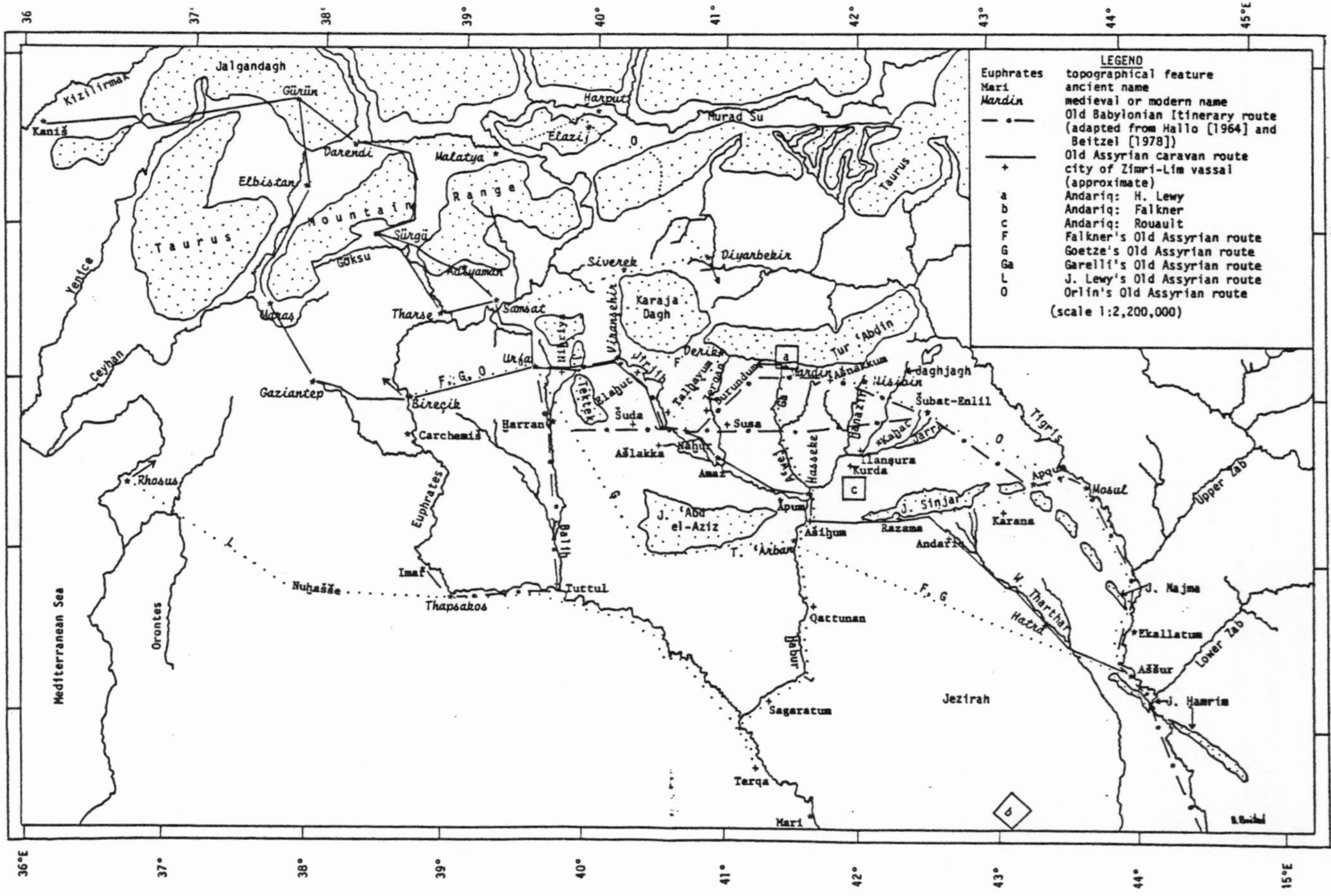
LEGEND
Euphrates topographical feature
Mari ancient name
Mardin medieval or modern name
Old Babylonian Itinerary route (adapted from Hallo [1964] and Beitzel [1978])
Old Assyrian caravan route
city of Zimri-Lim vassal (approximate)
a Andariq: H. Lewy
b Andariq: Falkner
c Andariq: Rouault
F Falkner's Old Assyrian route
G Goetze's Old Assyrian route
Ga Garelli's Old Assyrian route
L J. Lewy's Old Assyrian route
O Orlin's Old Assyrian route
(scale 1:2,200,000)
Jalgandagh
Kizilirmak
Kaniš
Gürün
Darendi
Elbistan
Taurus
Mountain
Range
Malatya
Harput
Elazij
Murad Su
Taurus
Sürgü
Göksu
Adiyaman
Yenice
Maraş
Tharse
Samsat
Siverek
Diyarbekir
Karaja Dagh
Tur 'Abdin
Ceyhan
Gaziantep
Birecik
Urfa
Viranşehir
Derik
Mardin
Ašnakkum
Nisibin
Daghjagh
Šubat-Enlil
Carchemiš
Harran
Tektek
Šuda
Susa
Burundum
Talhayum
Ašlakka
Nahur
Amaz
Ilanşura
Kurda
Hasseke
Apum
J. 'Abd el-Aziz
Ašihum
Razama
Andariq
J. Sinjar
Karana
Tigris
Apqum
Mosul
Upper Zab
Rhosus
Euphrates
Balih
Tuttul
Imar
Nuhašše
Thapsakos
Mediterranean Sea
Orontes
Qattunan
Habur
Sagaratum
Terqa
Mari
Jezirah
W. Tharthar
Hatra
J. Majma
Ekallatum
Aššur
Lower Zab
J. Hamrim
39°N
38°
37°
36°
35°N
36°E
37°
38°
39°
40°
41°
42°
43°
44°
45°E
15°E

contemporaneous archive contributes to the site profile, as is often the case with toponyms found in the literature from Kültepe, Chāgar Bāzār, Tell Ḥarīri, and Tell Rimāḥ, a refined accuracy and enhanced clarity should result, while the danger of circular argument should diminish.

Taken as a whole, geographic and documentary evidence suggests that the caravan voyage proceeded west from Aššur to the upper Tharthār. From here, it essentially followed the contour of the wadi as far as the southern edge of the Jebel Sinjār. The route veered west towards the Ḫabur at this point, probably sweeping past a number of second millennium tells which flank the Sinjār, on a line similar to that of the modern highway from Mōsul. At the brink of the lower Ḫabur valley, the road would have been altered to follow the northward course of the valley to Hasseke, where it would have begun to maneuver through the upper Ḫabur valley past Rās el-ᶜAin, thus traversing what in antiquity was an important transportation artery. Continuing in a northwestern direction, the route most likely extended up the Wadi Jirjib as far as the vicinity of Viranşehir, where it turned west toward Urfa, perhaps following the course of a modern road through the only pass in the Tektek range. From Urfa, a road past Ḫaḫḫum to Kaniš probably crossed the Euphrates at Samsat, and made its way to the Elbistan plain, via the pass at Sürgü. Alternatively, a road from Urfa past Uršum probably crossed the Euphrates at Bireçik en route through the pass commanded by Maraṣ.[54]

Admittedly, circumstances could arise which forced the merchants to take a detour—text TC 1 18 is such an example. And other texts seem to be concerned with roundabout ways taken by traders who engaged in smuggling. Moreover, one need not doubt that Aššur and Kaniš were alternately linked by a tributary of that transportation artery later known as the Persian Royal Road.[55] In fact, Assyrian "copper trade" texts may be referring to this latter road, and, in any event, are describing a separate itinerary. Nevertheless, since a number of those intermediate sites associated with Old Assyrian tin trade can be located with relative precision, one is enabled to configure the route as described above. Most especially, documentation from the Mari archives permits this theory to be tested at five critical points: the Karanā corridor; the Idamaraz district; the intersection point of the Old Babylonian Itinerary and Old Assyrian caravan trade; the Balīḫ River sites; and the Euphrates crossing point.

[54]For studies on the road system in Cappadocia, see Anderson (1897); Gelb (1935); Woodbury (1941); Garstang (1943); Goetze (1957); Garelli (1963) and Winfield (1977).

[55]Refer to Larsen (1967) 161; (1976) 248–49, 258 n 27, 263.

1. *The Karanā Corridor: Karanā, Andariq, Qaṭarā, and Razamā*

By this expression, I mean to denote that 37-mile plain bordered on the north and east by hills stretching between the Sinjār massif and Jebel Najma, and on the south and west by Jebel Ḥamrim, and the Wadi Tharthār, and dominated in the Old Babylonian period by the city of Karanā (= Tell Rimāḥ). Though this city is not yet found among the intermediate stations of Old Assyrian trade, it is clear from a Mari text that the king of Karanā exercised control over a caravan destined for Kaniš,[56] and a Rimāḥ tablet speaks of caravans from Aššur travelling to Karanā.[57]

But it is the localization of Andariq which forms the datum point for a Karanā corridor discussion, because it is precisely in relationship to this city that one can attempt to locate the caravan stations of Qaṭarā, Razamā, and, to a lesser degree, Azuḫinum.[58] The problem of the localization of Andariq is perhaps as complex as that of any site mentioned in Mari literature. The city has been sought in the environs of Mardin, in the area of the western Jezīrah near Ḫarbē, and in the region between the Sinjār and the Ḫabur triangle.

Predicated upon two assumptions, Hildegarde Lewy averred that Andariq should be located in the vicinity of Mardin.[59] She began by assuming that there were identical circumstances being described in two texts in which Zimri-Lim was attempting to conscript Babylonian soldiers in preparation for launching an expedition. But in these texts, Zimri-Lim was employing different agents (Ibal-pī-El, Yaqqim-Addu), and was preparing his offensive against different enemies (Andariq and Kurdā, Šubartum). Lewy's first assumption is not necessarily borne out by the texts.[60]

Her second assumption, we would argue, is totally erroneous. Inclined to believe that Andariq was a city in the land of Šubartum, Lewy conjectured that the latter name had survived in the modern name Saur, which designated both a town and a river in the region of Mardin.

In ARM 1 132, Yasmaḫ-Addu was informed by his older brother that mules and donkeys from the land of Andariq and the land of Ḫarbē were about to arrive (at Mari). Later in the text, Išme-Dagan remarked that although there were mules and dogs in the land of Andariq and

[56]ARM HC HATT. = Dossin (1939e) 73–74.

[57]OBTTR 122. This text is also discussed in Dalley (1976) 158–59.

[58]See Dalley (1968) 93–96 for a discussion of the way Andariq is described in Rimāḥ documentation.

[59]H. Lewy (1956) 331–32 n 2; (1967) 24–25. The texts involved were ARM 2 23 and ARM HC TEXT. = Thureau-Dangin (1936) 171–76.

[60]As pointed out by Rouault (1970) 108 n 1. Later discussion in this essay makes evident that I find H. Lewy's (1956) 348 n 4 restoration of ARM 2 34: 3 unconvincing.

Ḫarbē, she-asses from the upper country were small of stature. Largely on the basis of this text, Falkner argued that Andariq must have been located in the western Jezīrah, adjacent to Ḫarbē.[61] Context, however, does not demand that the two towns be located in the same region. In point of fact, that the semantic indicator *mātum* is repeated before both towns (ll. 6–7) might lead to the suspicion that the mules and donkeys came ultimately from different places.[62] In any event, no other Mari texts can be marshalled to support this localization, and there does not appear to be evidence of ancient ruins in this sector of the Jezīrah.[63] Nor does present evidence warrant positing a case of homonymy for Andariq or Ḫarbē.

Olivier Rouault has recently published an article in which he maintained that Andariq was to be sought in the region northwest of the Jebel Sinjār, and east of the Ḫabur triangle, in close proximity to the cities of Šubat-Enlil,[64] Ilānṣurā,[65] and Kurdā.[66] This viewpoint has been endorsed by Kupper.[67]

There are certain geographic data, however, which seem to be poised against such a localization. Yasmaḫ-Addu received a memorandum (ARM 5 67) in which one of his functionaries was rehearsing problems having to do with the plucking of sheep at the town of Ašima. It seems that, despite Šamši-Adad's directive to Karanā officials, an insufficient number of wool pluckers had arrived at Ašima, and so the sheep remained unplucked. Yasmaḫ-Addu was entreated to send a protest letter to Ḫasidānum at Karanā, demanding that a large contingent of wool pluckers be given travel provisions for two days, and dispatched to Ašima, where, on the third day, plucking could commence. This obviously indicates that Ašima was located at a distance of not greater than two days travel from Karanā. But the correspondent went on to specify that Yasmaḫ-Addu, staying at Andariq en route to Karanā, was himself only two *bērū* (or 15 miles) from Ašima (ll. 23–26).[68] If we are correctly interpreting this text, it necessarily follows that Andariq should not have been separated from Karanā by a distance greater than 55–60 airline miles (i.e., two days travel—ca. 40–45 miles—plus *šina bērū* = 15

[61]Falkner (1957–58) 3–4. Her conclusion seems to have been adopted by Luke (1965) 316 [map].

[62]My argument is informed at this point by Rouault (1970) 107–8 and Dalley (1976) 4 n 25.

[63]Hrouda (1957) map; Oates (1965) 64.

[64]Rouault (1970); ARM 2 41, 130.

[65]ARM 2 62; ARM 10 32; ARM HC A.479 = ARMT 14 50.

[66]ARM 10 165; ARMT 14 109.

[67]Kupper (1979) 5.

[68]See CAD B 208b for this translation of *šina bērū*. For the approximation *šina bērū* = fifteen miles, see Mallowan (1946) 8; Smith (1957) 168 n 4; H. Lewy (1958) 6; Anbar (1973) 12 n 37; During Caspers and Govindankutty (1978) 134.

miles), thereby automatically ruling out the locations sought by Lewy or Falkner, and, more importantly, restricting the possibility of Rouault's view essentially to territory north of the eastern section of the Sinjār mountain, placing Andariq at a point north or northwest of Karanā.

On the other hand, while it is undeniable that various political figures from Andariq were associated at times with Šubat-Enlil, Ilānṣurā, and Kurdā, to place Andariq north or northwest of Karanā appears to collide with still other geographic data. A military dispatch from Iddiyatum, ARM 2 43, whose activities concerned Karanā, informed Zimri-Lim that the allied forces of Išme-Dagan were inside Razamā (Hatra?), were making overtures to Karanā's king Aškur-Addu in order to gain his defection from Zimri-Lim's ranks, and were preparing to launch an attack against Andariq.[69] To meet this challenge, three of Zimri-Lim's loyal generals (Yanṣibum, Yasīm-El, and Bēlšunu) led their armies to Andariq (from Karanā?) to start out towards Babylon (i.e., towards Išme-Dagan's forces at Razamā in the direction of Babylon—ll. 24–29; OBTTR 68: 4–9). The intimation of the text, therefore, is that Andariq lay between Karanā and the oncoming Assyrian-Babylonian coalition, or at a point east, west, south, but not north of Karanā.[70]

Such an assumption appears to be justifiable on the basis of text ARM HC A.3093, undoubtedly related to the same set of events.[71] Here we learn that Yasīm-El and Bēlšunu had led their troops from Andariq to Karanā. There, however, they received an urgent message from Iddiyatum, who ordered them to return to Andariq because Išme-Dagan and his forces had taken control of the town A[x x]tan, south of Karanā (*šaplānim Karanā*); whereupon they returned immediately to Andariq (ll. 8–22). The clear implication of this passage is that Andariq lay in grave and immediate danger from Išme-Dagan's troops. Hence the loyalists' forces returned from Karanā to Andariq with alacrity (*qātam ana qātima*). But the strategy dictated by Iddiyatum also implies that Andariq should not have been situated north or northwest of Karanā. Were that the case, the army of Yasīm-El and Bēlšunu simply could have remained at Karanā, and intercepted Išme-Dagan's northward advance from A[x x]tan.

If one could ascertain the northward course taken by Išme-Dagan from Razamā and A[x x]tan, still greater specificity could be assigned Andariq's placement. J. E. Reade has charted what are, in effect, three possible routes of travel between Babylonia and Assyria (Jezīrah, Tigris,

[69]ARM 6 26 speaks of Aškur-Addu's vassalage.

[70]Jean (1939) 64; Kupper (1948b) 39–40 and Dalley *apud* OBTTR 4–5 n 25 had earlier placed Andariq in the vicinity of Karanā, while Dossin (1938b) 182, (1939a) 106 and Gaebelein (1976) 246 had sought the city along the mid-Tigris. My understanding of the context of ARM 2 43 is radically different from that espoused by Gadd (1973) 181.

[71]Text published in Dossin (1972a) 128–30.

and trans-Tigris). If on this occasion Išme-Dagan had used the Jezīrah route, one would be obliged to search for Andariq at a location to the west or south of Rimāḥ. In this regard, it is pertinent to note Reade's remark concerning the aversion of the more difficult Tigris route (cf. Itinerary of Tukulti-Ninurta II).[72] Alternatively, Išme-Dagan's use of the Tigris route would argue for a location more to the southeast of Rimāḥ.

A geographical notice contained in a Yaqqim-Addu text, ARM 14 109, appears to be consistent with this interpretation. In the document, one discovers that Qarni-Lim was endeavoring to transport some grain from Šubat-Enlil to Andariq. He had proceeded as far as the town of Zunnanum, where, attempting to cross over mountainous heights (*gabʾu*),[73] he was attacked by the kings of Kurdā and Karanā. Now Šubat-Enlil was certainly located in the eastern sector of the Ḫabur triangle, and quite possibly at Leylān. From this area, the only mountain chain in the general direction of Kurdā and Karanā is the Jebel Sinjār. If, then, as seems reasonable, Qarni-Lim was attempting to surmount the Sinjār *en route* to his capital city, Andariq must have been situated south of this mountain range.

There are, in the area west or south of Rimāḥ, a number of tells that exhibit second millennium occupation, but none compares to the walled ruins of Tell Hadhail (22 miles southwest of Rimāḥ), or Tell Huwaish (11 miles northwest of Hadhail). One ventures to suggest, therefore, that Andariq should be sought in this section of the Karanā corridor, and perhaps at one of these tells.[74]

Consequently, Qaṭarā must also be located in this part of the corridor, since it was near to Andariq (ARM 2 39; OBTTR 216), and, like Andariq (OBTTR 100, 202, 216), was subject to Karanā's jurisdiction (ARM 5 36, 40; OBTTR 79, 200, 278, 319). One arrives at the same conclusion, moreover, from an Išme-Dagan letter, ARM 4 29, in which Qaṭarā was described as having been located a distance of two days travel from Ekallātum (or Aššur) in the direction of Šubat-Enlil. A walled city

[72]Reade (1968) 237 n 5. For the Itinerary of Tukulti-Ninurta II, see most recently Grayson (1976) 101 § 469.

[73]So CAD G 6–7, though cited there with Middle Assyrian texts only. Cf. Finet (1954) 239.

[74]This conclusion is obviously predicated upon Išme-Dagan's use of the Jezīrah route. ARM 2 130 and 10 165 seem to suggest that Andariq may have been located between Mari and Karanā. For a description of T. Hadhail or T. Huwaish, consult Lloyd (1938) 126; Oates (1968) 35–36 n 3, 55; Reade (1968) 236; (1978) 175–76. If, on the other hand, Išme-Dagan's advance followed the course of the Tigris more closely, approaching Karanā from the southeast, the walled ruins of Tell Kamira, located some 13 miles east-southeast of Rimāḥ, suggest themselves as a possible location for Andariq. In any event, it follows from my interpretation that Zimri-Lim could not have gone into exile at Andariq (*contra* H. Lewy [1959] 449). Šamši-Addu would never have tolerated a pocket of resistance so near and accessible to his capital.

(ARM 5 37), Qaṭarā was an important center for military (ARM HC S.115 = Birot [1973] 5, #72–32) and commercial (OBTTR 196–98, 213, 215) operations, and would therefore have been selected quite naturally as an Assyrian caravan station.[75]

Andariq's location also aids in the placement of Razamā. I have elsewhere presented argumentation in favor of situating Razamā (*ša* Burama[x]) in the vicinity of Ḫatra, and of localizing Razamā (*ša* Uḫakim) at Tell Ḥayal.[76]

2. *Idamaraz District: Ašnakkum, Talḫāyum, Amaz, Apum, Naḫur, and Azuḫinum*

The dimensions of this district may be largely determined by identifying and locating the cities of which it was comprised. Kupper recently referred to an unpublished ARM text which cites the names of ten Idamaraz monarchs, among whom are the kings of Ilānṣurā, Ašnakkum, Susā, Ašlakkā, Tarmani, Qā, and Zalluḫān.[77] Published materials identify other cities which were part of the province. These include Amaz (ARM 7 219), Ḫurrā (ARM 2 37), Šinaḫ (ARM 2 38), Siḫaratā (ARM 2 33), and Šarmaneḫ (ARM HC AREP. = Dossin [1938a] 117, translation). Another tablet specifies that Idamaraz was contiguous on its western border to the land of Zalmaqum (ARM 2 35). But ARM 5 51 is perhaps the most important document in the context of Old Assyrian geography, for it explicitly refers to four cities of the upper Idamaraz district (*ina ḫalaṣ* GN *elîm wašbū*): Naḫur, Talḫāyum, Ašnakkum, and Kirdaḫat.

Now the relative locations of Ašnakkum and Kirdaḫat are firmly established in the heart of the Ḫabur triangle. According to the Urbana Itinerary, Ašnakkum was the station visited two days west of Šubat-Enlil.[78] Similarly, Kirdaḫat was an important administrative center which functioned under the aegis of the king of Chāgar Bāzār. Residents of Kirdaḫat travelled to Chāgar Bāzār to register in a census on one occasion (*Iraq* 7 48, and Pl. I: text A.926), and animals receiving food allotments from Chāgar Bāzār's cadre were fed in the district of Kirdaḫat (*Iraq* 7 48, summary of text A.929; and cf. Dossin [1958] 390).

The location of Talḫāyum is well defined in Old Babylonian literature. It was located a distance of not more than one day's journey

[75]Oates (1968) 35–36 n 3 suggests T. Ḥayal or T. Huwaish as possible locations of Qaṭarā.

[76]Beitzel (1984).

[77]Kupper (1978) 123 n 39 (ARM HC A.1212), Cf. ARM 7 199 and 11 198.

[78]Van Liere (1963) 120, Hallo (1964) 74–75, Luke (1965) 178 n 93 and Aro (1966) 142–43 all identify Ašnakkum with Chāgar Bāzār, whereas Anbar (1971) 199 n 44, 202 n 66 and (1973) 14 n 46 equates the site with Tell Ailoun. My research leads me to search in the vicinity of ᶜAmouda, located some 17 miles west of Nisibin.

from Tillā (*Iraq* 7 51, summary of text A.952): each of thirty oxen was given rations for one day and dispatched on a trip from Tillā to Talḫāyum.[79] The location of Tillā, for its part, is also fixed inasmuch as it represented the first station along Šamši-Adad's Itinerary from Šubat-Enlil to Mari (ARM 1 26).[80] Talḫāyum is likewise recognized to have been situated in close proximity to the well-known towns of Mammagira and Šapanazum (ARM 1 53), Burundum (ARM HC B.308; d. 1 = Jean [1948a] 21), and Naḫur (ARMT 13 144), and it was juxtaposed to the land of Yapturum (ARMT 13 144; and cf. Yawi-ilā's concerns in ARMT 13 139–50). These combined factors lead to the hypothesis that the upper Idamaraz district was wholly contained within the Ḫabur triangle, and somewhere between the Zergān-Jirjib tributaries. From this it follows that the Old Assyrian route transected the same region, as merchants are known to have purchased supplies there.[81]

A survey of the texts which mention Amaz leads as well to the conclusion that it most likely was located in the Ḫabur triangle, probably on its western frontier. Ibnatum reports to her father, Zimri-Lim, that her husband, Ḫimdiya, king of Andariq, had reclaimed the city of Amaz in the name of the throne (ARM 10 84). Another text, ARM 2 109, which is difficult to interpret because of its fragmentary condition, combined with the fact that in it, two men bear the same name, is a report received by Zimri-Lim from one of his ambassadors to Šubartum (Yasīm-El). The ambassador, in turn, was transmitting a message from one Šukrum-Teššub, king of Elaḫut, to Šubram, governor[82] of Šubat-Enlil. The Elaḫut monarch was disturbed because Šubram, king of Susā, had attacked and seized the city of Amaz, which, Šukrum-Teššub claimed, belonged to the sovereignty of Elaḫut (ll. 6–14).[83] If this interpretation is reasonably accurate, Amaz should then be sought towards the western

[79]Therefore we understand the Mari and Chāgar Bāzār literature to be referring here to identical sites. *Cf.* Groneberg (1980) 232–33, 236–37.

[80]On the strength of *nubattū* (l. 13), we infer that this is an actual, and not a selective itinerary, though certain stations may not have represented customary stops. The overall distance separating Tell Leylān and Tell Ḥarīri is 190 miles if one followed the somewhat circuitous course of the Ḫabur to its confluence with the Euphrates, thus yielding a daily average of some 31 miles, or a distance slightly higher than normal daily downstream travel. But a more direct route, especially by following the course of Naḫr Darwîn—on which see Kupper (1952) 168–69 and Spender (1976) 159–63—from Sejer to Tell Ḥarīri, permits an overall daily average of 25 miles to obtain. Note that Stol (1979) 81–82 takes ARM 1 26 to be a description of an unusual route, and locates Tillā within the Ḫabur triangle.

[81]See Bilgiç (1945–51) 12 n 89 and Veenhof (1972) 191 for documentation.

[82]Birot (1979) 198 suggests reading line 4b: *š*[*a*?]-*p*[*í*?-*ṭ*]*ì-im*. Note the contexts of ARM 14 98, 112. Cf. ARM 1 62, 2 98 and ARM 14 81.

[83]My interpretation of ll. 11–12 is informed by AHw 762b, "*bittend,*" as against CAD N/2 85a, "threaten bodily harm."

edge of the Ḫabur triangle, close to Susā and Elaḫut (cf. ARM 7 219). Accordingly, it appears certain that the site mentioned in the Assyrian text CCT 5 44c, listed between Apum and Naḫur, should be equated with the Marian Amaz. And, by employing the *dātum* criterion, Veenhof argued that Old Assyrian Amaz was situated a little less than twice as far from Kaniš as from Aššur,[84] or in the southwestern division of the Ḫabur triangle.

It is from the contexts of Talḫāyum and Amaz that a study of Naḫur is presently best undertaken. Such a study might appear premature prior to the publication of ARM 20; nevertheless, in addition to those arguments for Talḫāyum and Amaz already adduced, certain other observations concerning Naḫur can be made. (1) Naḫur had a Mari governor under Zimri-Lim's sphere of control. (2) This governor bore a name that was Akkadian, not Hurrian. (3) Beyond forming a part of upper Idamaraz, Naḫur is described as being near the Ḫabur river (ARM 2 112–13), and the cities of Kawala (ARM 4 35; cf. ARM 1 107), Yapturum (ARMT 13 144), Burundum and Ašlakka (ARM HC B.308 = Finet [1966a] and Jean [1948a]; ARM 2 112–13). I submit that a combination of all these factors renders probable the hypothesis that Naḫur was located in the environs of Rās el-ᶜAin. Poidebard has shown that the upper Ḫabur from Hasseke to Rās el-ᶜAin represented a vital transportation artery in antiquity, manifesting an alignment of tells spaced at regular intervals in proximity to either bank.[85] Subsequent archaeological survey has disclosed that a number of these tells were occupied in the second millennium.

From this location proposed for Naḫur, one would have reason to search along the caravan route towards Aššur a distance of approximately twenty miles in pursuit of Amaz, and another twenty or so miles in search of Apum. Flanking the left bank of the Ḫabur some 22.5 miles from Rās el-ᶜAin is the site Tell Aasāfīr, from which Mallowan's survey uncovered second millennium ceramic remains.[86] Bordering the right bank of the Ḫabur another 21 miles downstream is Tell Majdal, described by Van Liere as a second millennium citadel,[87] a description which may be eloquent in light of two military encounters that are said to have occurred at Apum (ARM HC S.115 = Birot [1973] #72–14; ARM HC EXCE. = Thureau-Dangin [1939] 119–20 #1.105). While Amaz and Apum may or may not be actually pinpointed to these respective tells, to seek them in this immediate vicinity comports with all geographic and textual indicators.

[84]Veenhof (1972) 240–41. He is attempting to locate Apum, Amaz, and Naḫur.
[85]Poidebard (1927) 60–61.
[86]Mallowan (1946) 119.
[87]Van Liere (1963) 114. Cf. Beitzel (1984).

Azuḫinum also formed part of the Idamarz district, listed in an administrative inventory dealing with Idamaraz sites (ARM 7 219; cf. ARM 7 104, 113). In ARMT 14 108, its forces were allied with those of Burullum, a city which must be located, according to the *dātum* criterion,[88] in the eastern sector of the Ḫabur triangle (cf. VAT 9260). Azuḫinum's king responded on one occasion to a military threat in the Jebel Sinjār region (ARMT 14 106), and the city came under the jurisdiction of Karanā at times (OBTTR 145). The balance of probability, therefore, favors equating this city with the caravan stop attested in CCT 1 26b, and situating A/Uzuḫinum near modern Hasseke.[89]

3. *The Intersection Point in the Old Babylonian Itinerary and the Old Assyrian Route: Atmum*

Two ARM texts which refer to Atmum leave no doubt regarding its location. From ARMT 13 139, one infers that the town was subject to Yawi-ilā, king of Talḫāyum. It was *to him* that a report was sent regarding the gathering of barley at Atmum. ARM 1 103 discloses Atmum's close association with Niḫriyā. Perhaps the towns were separated by a distance of one day's travel or less. It seems that Šamši-Adad was concerned about an impending insurrection at the town of Ḫurmiš—possibly part of the Zalmaqum territory.[90] So he reported to Yasmaḫ-Addu that he would travel from Niḫriyā to Atmum, where, at dawn, he would send a reconnaissance report. As a result, Goetze's desire to equate this town with the Old Babylonian Itinerary station, cited as the third stop along a ten-day detour from Ḫarrān to Tell Ḥalāf, bears a reasonable degree of certainty.[91] Based on the probable course of this detour (Ḫarrān-Urfa, 27 miles; Urfa-Viranşehir, 66 miles; Viranşehir-Tell Ḥalāf, 37 miles), Atmum should have been situated a short distance east of Urfa, along the road to Viranşehir. And this coincides with the eastward trek of VAT 9260, which required Old Assyrian Atmum to be located west of the Ḫabur triangle.

4. *Balīḫ Locations: Niḫriyā, Balīḫum*

The city of Niḫriyā obviously played a pivotal role in Old Assyrian tin trade: it is attested as a caravan station (CCT 2 22; CCT 4 36b; KTS 12 33); it maintained a *kārum* (EL 210a–b), an *eširtum* (AnOr 6: 15), and a *kaššum*-official (Garelli [1965] 42, #17: 17–18); and it is closely

[88]Veenhof (1972) 241–42.

[89]This is actually very near to where Goetze (1953) 67 had placed Azuḫinum. His localization, however, was based on the *massû* argument. For the A/U interchange, see Astour (1973) 33.

[90]So Anbar (1973) 28.

[91]Goetze (1953) 61–62, 67.

connected in Old Assyrian literature with other important stations (e.g., Ḫaḫḫum, CCT 2 22).[92] Documentary evidence from Mari indicates that Niḫriyā was situated in or near the Balīḫ valley. Two men from Niḫriyā are called "Zalmaqum citizens" in one text (ARMT 14 77), and in another (ARM 3 57), Būnuma-Addu is said to have been governor over Niḫriyā and Zalmaqum. The latter district must be sought along the western edge of the Balīḫ, between Ḫarrān and Zalpaḫ. This same Būnuma-Addu meddled in the affairs of the town of Irrid (ARM HC ORD1 = Dossin [1939d] 113), located on other grounds between Ḫarrān and Carchemiš.

BIN 6 176 specifies that an Assyrian merchant obtained a large quantity of wool *ina Balīḫum*, "in (the town of) Balīḫum."[93] This town was certainly situated along the homonymous river,[94] and may plausibly be related to the site Balīḫu of the "Ḫarrān census,"[95] tentatively located by Goetze near the Balīḫ headwaters.[96] And because the transactions of this document include the well-known entrepreneur, Šū-Ištar, one must assume that it is concerned with towns customarily involved in tin/textile trade, and, accordingly, that the standard Assyrian route intersected the Balīḫ valley.[97] We submit that this evidence for the localization of Niḫriyā and Balīḫum is fatal to the contention that the caravan route was somehow linked with the town of Diyarbekir. Such a reconstruction would create an unnecessarily ambigious route.

5. *The Euphrates Crossing Point*

Aššur-nādā was a well-known and important Assyrian caravaneer. Some thirty-five letters between himself and his father, Aššur-īdī, are attested in Old Assyrian literature.[98] In one of these, TC 1 18, which we assume was received while in transit along the route to Kaniš, Aššur-nādā was told if he feared travelling by way of the station, Ḫaḫḫum, he should go via Uršum instead, but he should not enter Maʾama. Since the

[92]Bilgiç (1945–51) 23 n 167 and Larsen (1976a) 269–71. One must underscore the point already made by Larsen (1976) 241 that *kārū* were clustered along main caravan routes. On the other hand, one need not seek a station with a *kārum* along a river. Cf. Larsen (1976a) 230–31 and CAD K 231–37. It is clear then that I cannot agree with Astour (1979) 5, who localized Niḫriyā at Diyarbekir. Professor Mellaart has indicated (personal letter, 22 March 1983) that the copius springs at Urfa could very well elicit a town named Niḫriyā.

[93]So translated by J. Lewy (1952) 395; Veenhof (1972) 143–45. Refer to Veenhof (1972) 130–39 for Old Assyrian wool trade.

[94]So J. Lewy (1953) 298 n 5.

[95]Johns (1901) 47 (#4 ii:6, iii:19), 62 (#8 i:12) and 69 (#15 i:4).

[96]Goetze (1953) 61.

[97]It is important in this regard to point out the presence of another Balīḫ site. There was a *wabartum* settlement at Badna, commonly located in the vicinity of modern Sürüç: so Goetze (1953) 68; Orlin (1970) 43; Veenhof (1972) 293–95; and Larsen (1976a) 240.

[98]Larsen (1967) 106–9, 163–66; (1976a) 55 n 26.

Uršum-Maʾama route was not without additional risk, the caravan was to be divided into three companies, each proceeding separately, when word was received of the safe passage of an earlier company. We infer, therefore, that Ḫaḫḫum and Uršum-Maʾama lay along separate routes.[99] Moreover, since Aššur-nādā seems otherwise to have been on a direct route, and since he originally intended to pass Ḫaḫḫum, the main caravan route passed through Ḫaḫḫum, and an alternative route passed Uršum-Maʾama.[100] Ḫaḫḫum's connection with Niḫriyā (CCT 2 22), Luḫayum, Zalmaqum, Talḫāyum (ARM HC B.308 = Jean [1948a] and Finet [1966a] 20), Timilkia (CCT 4 28b), and Qaṭarā (TC 3/1 24), strongly supports this inference.

Though the city has been sought near the Mediterranean at the modern town of ʿArsūz,[101] or at Urfa (Edessa),[102] Uršum had to be located near Ḫaššum, Carchemiš, and Yamḫad, according to Mari texts (ARM 1 1, 24, and 43). In another letter, ARM 2 131, which is clearly the most eloquent testimony regarding its location, the land of Uršum was west of the Euphrates, but in close proximity to the river, and to the city of Carchemiš.[103] Such geographic definition comports well with the theory, most recently advanced by Larsen[104] and Astour,[105] that Uršum should be sought at Gaziantep.

The precise localization of Ḫaḫḫum has long been a controversial matter. The city is attested but once in ARM literature (ARM HC B.308 = Jean [1948a] and Finet [1966a]). Ibal-Addu, the king of Ašlakkā, reports to Zimri-Lim the most recent allegiance of the king of Burundum: from now on the king of Mari will hold Burundum under his sovereignty, just as he holds Naḫur. Then Ibal-Addu continues that since he resides at Ašlakkā, he is in a better position than anyone to observe what goes on in the *mātum elītum*, "upper country," for the greatest profit of Zimri-Lim. And so he entreats his sovereign for permission to be the one to send regular news flashes concerning Elaḫut, Lullû, Ḫaḫḫum, Zalmaqum, Burundum, and Talḫāyum. This geographical

[99]BIN 4 219 also specifies that Uršum and Maʾama were in close proximity and directly connected by a road, apparently a mountainous one (CCT 2 11a).

[100]Following Bilgiç (1945–51) 27–28; Goetze (1953) 69 (by implication); Falkner (1957–58) 35 and Kupper (1979) 37. Garelli (1963) 106–11 argued that Uršum and Ḫaḫḫum were along the same route.

[101]So Forrer (1920) 57; Albright (1925) 197 n 7; J. Lewy (1952) 188–90 and (1950–51) 371–72 n 46. Later, having examined the remains of ʿArsūz, Albright (1933) 30 repudiated this equation.

[102]Goetze (1949) 43; Kupper (1949) 79–87; Landsberger (1924) 235–38; Albright (1940) 28.

[103]This is the position cogently argued by Bilgiç (1945–51) 25. He was followed by Falkner (1957–58) 31, Klengel (1965) 1:19, and Gurney (1973) 241–42, among others.

[104]Larsen (1976a) 237.

[105]Astour (1978) 11 n 67. Cf. Falkner (1957–58) 31.

notice, when taken together with evidence from *dātum* texts which suggest that Ḫaḫḫum was located near the Euphrates, indicates that the city most likely should be sought at a point along the upper Euphrates, north of Carchemiš.[106] Based largely on Hittite documentation, this road station has been positioned at numerous spots, from east Cilicia to the mountains of central Anatolia near Divrik.[107]

Now the upper Euphrates possesses four direct fords of significance. From north to south, they are Kemah, Malatya, Samsat, and Bireçik. The course of the route already charted through the Ḫabur triangle and Balīḫ headwaters itself eliminates Kemah from contention, and renders Malatya extremely doubtful. Further, the Euphrates is non-navigable directly below Malatya,[108] and though barely navigable immediately above the city, the merchants would have faced turbulent waters, and would have been hemmed in by rock cliff walls.[109] Since Uršum seems to have been situated near Carchemiš (ARM 2 131), I suggest that the main route (Ḫaḫḫum) crossed the Euphrates at Samsat, but that an alternative route (Uršum) crossed at Bireçik.

V. CONCLUSION

This essay has aimed at geographic questions, and has advanced geographic conclusions: these are what we wish to underscore. They may have impact, however, upon an important historical question. During the two generations of *kārum* Ib (= Šamši-Adad, Išme-Dagan), North Mesopotamia was considered a political entity, as the caravaneers travelled with relative ease over a route that was generally secure. And at the same time, the distribution of "Ḫabur ware" throughout North Mesopotamia suggests that this region was a homogeneous cultural entity.[110] But then the apparently lucrative trade between Aššur and Kaniš suddenly came to a halt (ca. 1775–55),[111] after which a modest reoccupation of the *kārum* was soon aborted.

Most attempts to explain this mystery focus upon Cappadocian politics, suggesting either a dynastic move to a more strategic location,[112] or a total collapse of the local political system.[113] Now while it is clear that Kaniš was visited by a destruction at the end of level Ib, if we

[106]Refer to Veenhof (1972) 243 for the *dātum* text.

[107]See del Monte and Tischler (1978) 61–62 for a summary of locations.

[108]Woodbury (1941) 32.

[109]Garstang (1942) 457; (1943) 48, 57.

[110]See Hamlin (1971) 268–78, 291, 295. Cf. Orlin (1970) 171, 183, and RlA 4 30, s.v. "Ḫābūr-Ware."

[111]So Orlin (1970) 246.

[112]So Gurney (1973) 236, 240–41.

[113]So Orlin (1970) 246.

assume with Orlin[114] that the chief aim of the trading colonies, in the first place, was to procure copper for the Assyrian government, would it not follow that the Assyrians should have found it economically expedient to establish colonies with a new government, or to relocate with the former government, in an effort to satisfy their partisan objective? Could it be that we have to look at the other end of the trade route for an answer to this mystery, especially since we know that military sovereignty along the route belonged to Aššur, and that it was the Assyrian government that executed authority over the colonies?[115]

I have attempted to demonstrate elsewhere[116] that Išme-Dagan's hold on the Ḫabur triangle was broken by Zimri-Lim in the first battle of Razamā, which Birot has now dated conclusively between Hammurapi's 27th and 29th regnal years, or between 1768–63.[117] This bears, of course, a striking correspondence to the moment when Old Assyrian tin trade was discontinued. Moreover, among the vassals added at that time to Zimri-Lim's dominion were princes from every sector of the Ḫabur triangle. Cities which had served as stations along the Assyrian route—Luḫayum, Naḫur, and Talḫāyum, in addition to Niḫriyā—were now wrested from Assyrian hands, and became a secure part of Zimri-Lim's hegemony. Nor must we forget that Zimri-Lim at this time inaugurated his own tin trade with a number of western markets (ARM HC A.1270 = Dossin [1970], 97–101, for example). Accordingly, there seems to be sufficient chronologic, geographic, and economic evidence to render possible the hypothesis that the kingdom of Zimri-Lim stood in the way, and, in part, prevented a revival of Old Assyrian colonization. At the very least, his burgeoning, if short-lived, monarchy, would have necessitated the establishment of a different caravan route.

[114]Orlin (1970) 56.
[115]Orlin (1970) 61–65 and Larsen (1976b) 119–20.
[116]Beitzel (1984).
[117]Birot (1978b) 185–86.

Les Legendes de Sceaux de Mari: Nouvelles Données

DOMINIQUE CHARPIN

Université de Paris I

0. Depuis trois ans, un projet a été entrepris par J.-M. Durand et moi-même, visant à établir un corpus général des empreintes de sceaux de Mari à l'époque amorite (règnes de Yaḫdun-Lim, Samsi-Addu, Yasmaḫ-Addu et Zimri-Lim). Ce projet s'attache essentiellement aux légendes des sceaux;[1] l'iconographie fera par ailleurs l'objet d'une étude par D. Beyer.

0.1 On doit rappeler que fort peu de sceaux ont été retrouvés lors des fouilles à Mari:[2] ce que nous connaissons des sceaux, ce sont essentiellement des empreintes, dont il existe trois types principaux. Tout d'abord, des *scellements d'objets*: non pas tant des "bouchons de jarres" comme on l'a longtemps cru, que des scellements de pommeaux de portes,[3] ainsi qu'un certain nombre d'étiquettes (surtout de paniers à tablettes). Les empreintes sont également présentes sur des *tablettes*, contrats ou textes administratifs. On trouve enfin des empreintes sur des *enveloppes*, qu'il s'agisse de textes juridiques ou de lettres. Cette situation a pour l'archéologue l'avantage de permettre une datation très fine. Elle a en revanche un inconvénient majeur: à l'exception des enveloppes de lettres, les empreintes sont généralement partielles, et le plus souvent limitées à la légende du sceau. Le phénomène est tellement systématique qu'il ne saurait être dû au hasard: ce qui semble avant tout avoir compté aux yeux des Anciens, c'est l'apparition du nom du propriétaire du sceau. Cela prive évidemment l'archéologue d'une bonne partie de sa documentation potentielle.

[1]Il sera publié comme deuxième partie du "Répertoire analytique" sous le titre: *Les légendes de sceaux* (ARMT 16/2). On y trouvera la copie de toutes les empreintes inédites citées en transcription dans le présent rapport préliminaire qui n'est nullement exhaustif. Je tiens à remercier J.-M. Durand de m'avoir permis d'exposer à ce symposium les résultats de notre travail commun.

[2]Cf. MAM 2/3 146 et 247. Pour le cylindre de Ana-Sîn-taklāku, retrouvé en Iran, voir Parrot (1966) 335.

[3]Les derniers exemples connus viennent d'être publiés par D. Beyer (1983) 52–55, où l'on trouvera les références aux travaux fondamentaux sur ce sujet de E. Fiandra.

0.2 Quant à l'épigraphiste, s'il a la chance que les sceaux anépigraphes soient assez rares, il ne faut pas croire sa tâche aisée. Les empreintes sont en effet souvent partielles et dans bien des cas assez effacées. Il faut donc comparer soigneusement toutes les empreintes différentes d'un même sceau afin d'en reconstituer la légende dans sa totalité. Il a donc fallu collationner tous les documents déjà publiés, que ce soit dans MAM 2/3 ou dans les ARM parus jusqu'à présent, ce qui a permis d'améliorer un certain nombre de lectures.[4] D'autre part, on a entrepris de déchiffrer les empreintes présentes sur toutes les tablettes encore inédites, ce qui a permis de doubler le corpus déjà connu.

0.3 Un tel travail, inspiré par une préoccupation tout autre que celle de collectionneurs, présente un triple intérêt. Dans le domaine administratif et juridique, il s'agit d'étudier les pratiques du scellement et leur signification: engagement du débiteur, du vendeur ou des témoins, sphère de responsabilité des fonctionnaires etc. Le colloque "Seals and Sealing" organisé à l'Oriental Institute en 1976 par McGuire Gibson et R. Biggs a montré le chemin à suivre,[5] mais Mari était jusqu'à présent resté en dehors de ce type d'investigation.[6] Le deuxième intérêt d'un tel corpus est d'ordre prosopographique: les légendes, lorsqu'elles indiquent le nom du père (ce qui est très souvent le cas) ou le titre du propriétaire du sceau, ou les deux, sont à cet égard très importantes. Enfin, l'étude des légendes de sceaux n'est pas sans retombées dans le domaine de l'histoire politique, qu'il s'agisse de mentions de rois sur les sceaux de leurs serviteurs ou des sceaux des rois eux-mêmes.

0.4 J'ai choisi de vous présenter trois aspects de ce projet:

a— l'étude d'une famille grâce aux légendes des sceaux de ses différents membres: il s'agit de la famille du devin Asqudum;

b— les sceaux des fonctionnaires mentionnant le nom, et parfois aussi un titre ou une épithète, du roi au service duquel ils étaient;

c— quelques sceaux royaux: présentation du sceau de Samsi-Addu, enfin complètement connu; problème de la multiplicité des sceaux de Zimri-Lim et présentation d'un nouveau sceau de Zimri-Lim; enfin, présentation du sceau, jusqu'à présent inconnu, du roi Yarīm-Lim I d'Alep.

* * *

[4]Voir déjà les articles de J.-M. Durand et moi-même à propos des textes juridiques de ARM 8: Durand (1982b and 1983b); Charpin (1983a).

[5]Voir Gibson and Biggs (1976), et, tout récemment, Leemans (1982).

[6]On trouvera des remarques relatives aux empreintes de sceau figurant sur les tablettes dans ARMT 7, pp. 22 (§ 40) et 227 n 2; ARMT 8, p. 161 (§ 7); ARMT 9, pp. 250–52 (§§ 10–12) et 353–54, addendum *d*; et ARMT 11, pp. 125–27 (§ 7).

1. La famille du devin Asqudum.

1.1 Le bâtiment fouillé au "chantier A" de Mari en 1979, 80 et 82 a livré jusqu'à présent environ 120 tablettes. Parmi celles-ci, on note quelques textes scolaires, dont une grande liste de dieux.[7] La majorité des documents est cependant d'ordre administratif. Les tablettes ont été retrouvées pour l'essentiel en trois endroits:

a— un premier lot contient des listes de rations, toutes datées de l'époque assyrienne (éponymat d'Ibni-Addu, à une exception près);

b— un deuxième lot concerne des activités textiles (reçus de laine, fabrication et distribution d'habits), ainsi que la gestion du personnel (états nominatifs, listes de morts ou de fuyards, etc.);

c— le troisième ensemble est constitué par des comptes d'aliments destinés aux "repas de l'homme" (NÌ.GUB LÚ) ou aux rations de ses domestiques et de son écurie.

Les lots b et c datent des premières années du règne de Zimri-Lim (dont trois textes de l'année "accession au trône"). Toutes ces tablettes permettent de décrire la gestion d'une maison, qui fonctionne comme une sorte de palais en réduction: ainsi les "repas de l'homme" font-ils évidemment songer aux innombrables "repas du roi" (NÌ.GUB LUGAL) retrouvés dans le palais de Zimri-Lim.

1.2 Le problème est donc d'identifier l'occupant de cette résidence, au demeurant d'assez grande taille; il s'agit manifestement de quelqu'un d'important. Or, parmi les gens mentionnés, figure en bonne place un certain Asqudum: il est question de tablettes scellées par lui, de vêtements qui lui ont été envoyés lorsqu'il était en voyage. On possède également un fragment d'enveloppe de lettre adressée "à Asqudum."

Or il existe dans la documentation du palais de nombreuses références à la "maison d'Asqudum" (*bīt Asqudim*). S'il est possible d'identifier désormais cette maison d'Asqudum avec le bâtiment du "chantier A," c'est grâce aux empreintes du sceau d'Asqudum figurant sur plusieurs tablettes qu'on y a découvertes. On y lit:

zi-im-ri-li-im	Zimri-Lim,
ša-ki-in ^{d}*da-gan*	préfet de Dagan;
às-qú-du-um	Asqudum,
MÁŠ.ŠU.SÙ.SÙ	devin.

Il s'agit du même cylindre que celui dont G. Dossin a publié l'empreinte figurant sur le soi-disant "Panthéon de Mari,"[8] et dont de nombreux autres exemplaires figurent sur des tablettes du même dossier publiées par J.-M. Durand dans ARM 21 (pp. 16–31).

[7]Les textes scolaires seront publiés par J.-M. Durand dans MARI 3.

[8]Dossin (1950b) 42 et pl. III.

1.3 Un autre personnage se trouve cité dans les tablettes de la maison d'Asqudum: il s'agit d'un certain Kabi-Addu. Or l'empreinte de son sceau a été retrouvée sur une étiquette de panier à tablettes, dont le libellé indique qu'il s'agissait de comptes de laine et d'habits. Ce cylindre, au très beau décor,[9] comportait la légende suivante:

ka-bi-^{d}IŠKUR	Kabi-Addu,
DUMU *às-qú-di-im*	fils d'Asqudum,
IR_{11} *zi-im-ri-li-im*	serviteur de Zimri-Lim.

Qu'il existe d'autres empreintes de ce cylindre sur des tablettes (inédites) du Palais permet selon toute vraisemblance d'identifier le Kabi-Addu fils d'Asqudum avec le haut fonctionnaire du temps de Zimri-Lim, mentionné en particulier en ARM 7 106: 10 et ARMT 13 1 xiv: 64.

1.4 Mais la personne dont le nom revient le plus souvent dans les archives de la maison d'Asqudum est une certaine Yamama. Nous ignorerions ses relations avec Asqudum sans une empreinte (unique!) de son sceau, ainsi libellé:

^{MÍ}*ia-ma-ma*	Yamama,
DUMU.MÍ *ia-aḫ-du-li* (*sic*)	fille de Yaḫdun-Lim,
DAM.A.NI *às-qú-di-im*	épouse d'Asqudum.[10]

Il apparaît dès lors que le devin Asqudum, père de Kabi-Addu, avait épousé une princesse fille de Yaḫdun-Lim; il était par là-même beau-frère du roi Zimri-Lim! On ignore quand ce mariage eut lieu, mais il se peut que le rôle très important tenu par Asqudum dès l'époque assyrienne s'explique par un tel mariage.[11] Le cas du devin Asqudum, uni par des liens matrimoniaux à la famille du roi, doit être rapproché de celui de son collègue Aqba-ḫammû, révélé par les textes de tell Rimah: ce dernier avait en effet épousé Iltani, fille de Samu-Addu et soeur du roi Aškur-Addu.[12] Dès lors, les activités militaires d'Asqudum et de Aqba-ḫammû pourraient peut-être s'expliquer davantage par leur appartenance (par alliance) à la famille royale, que par leur statut de devin.

[9]Publié par Beyer (1983) 50–51. J'ai pu identifier depuis trois autres empreintes du même sceau sur des tablettes inédites du palais.

[10]Comparer DAM-A-NI, "épouse de," avec DUMU-A-NI, "fils de," dans les trois passages de Chagar-Bazar cités par Walker (1970), addendum p. 30 (mais pour l'inscription de Šarrum-kīma-kalima, voir OBTTR 277). Voir aussi dans ARM HC A.3151 rev. 5: 20, 3 DAM-A-NI LÚ SIMUG* *ša ka-ḫa-at* (Dossin [1971] 62) ainsi que ARM 7 226: 51 et 234: 11, collations et commentaires dans Charpin and Durand (1983) 93–94.

[11]Sur le rôle du devin Asqudum, voir Finet (1966b) 92.

[12]Dalley *apud* OBTTR, p. 33.

On voit comment, grâce à trois empreintes de sceaux, un problème capital d'histoire politique et sociale, tel que celui de la nature des liens unissant les principaux personnages de l'Etat au souverain, peut désormais être posé.

* * *

2. Les fonctionnaires "serviteurs" du roi.

2.1 Dans l'ensemble du corpus, il existe très peu d'individus dont le sceau ait eu comme troisième ligne de sa légende "serviteur de tel dieu." De tels cas sont limités à deux types de contexte. Il s'agit d'une part de textes juridiques, où bien des témoins sont des personnes privées n'appartenant pas à l'administration palatiale.[13] On trouve également de tels sceaux imprimés sur des textes administratifs du palais, mais il s'agit en général de reçus scellés par des habitants du royaume extérieurs à Mari.[14] La rareté de tels sceaux nous interdit toute étude statistique sur les divinités personnelles des habitants du royaume de Mari.[15]

2.2 Il ne fait pas de doute que la mention "serviteur de NP," où NP est un nom de roi, indique que le possesseur du sceau fait partie de l'administration royale. On notera toutefois quelques sceaux où le nom mentionné sur un sceau de ce genre, présent sur une tablette de Mari, n'est pas celui d'un roi de Mari. Il s'agit alors de cylindres appartenant à des étrangers, dont le statut, que rien dans le texte n'indique par ailleurs, peut ainsi être repéré.

2.2.1 On connait ainsi quatre empreintes de sceaux ayant appartenu à des fonctionnaires des rois d'Ešnunna, Daduša,[16] et son successeur, Ibāl-pî-El.[17]

2.2.2 De même, un reçu de poissons livrés au roi d'Ilân-ṣurā, Ḫāya-sūmû, a été scellé par un serviteur de ce dernier.[18]

[13]Voir les textes publiés dans ARM 8 et les collations des sceaux de ces tablettes dans Durand (1982b) et Charpin (1983a).

[14]Ainsi en M.8884 trouve-t-on le sceau suivant: *ú-ra-nu-um* [DU]MU *mu-tu-^{d}da-*[*gan*] [ÌR]^{d}*da-*[*gan*]. Le texte de la tablette permet de savoir que cet Urānum est un habitant de Dabiš, ce qu'indiquait déjà ARM 7 225: 3//226: 3, comme me le fait remarquer M. Birot.

[15]Pour ce genre d'étude, voir Charpin (1980) 288–91, et mon article "Les divinités personnelles des Babyloniens anciens d'après les légendes de leur sceaux," à paraître.

[16]Voir cette empreinte sur ARM 7 292, d'après la collation publiée dans Charpin and Durand (1983) 99.

[17]Deux de ces empreintes figurent sur ARM 8 52. Cf. Charpin (1983a) 65. Une troisième est inédite.

[18]ARM 21 88. Le Louvre possède par ailleurs un cylindre dont le propriétaire était un "serviteur de Ḫāya-sūmû." Cf. Kupper (1959) 98.

2.2.3 Il faut enfin mentionner une empreinte unique d'un serviteur d'Ḫammurapi:

^{d}AMAR.UTU-*mu-ša-lim*	Marduk-mušallim,
DUB.SAR	scribe,
DUMU *sí-ia-tum*	fils de Siyyatum,
IR$_{11}$ *ḫa-am-mu-ra-pí*	serviteur d'Ḫammurapi.[19]

2.2.4 Les sceaux les plus fréquents sont naturellement ceux des serviteurs de Yaḫdun-Lim, Samsi-Addu, Yasmaḫ-Addu et Zimri-Lim.

2.3 Il existe toutefois un autre type de légende, dans lequel figure d'abord le nom du roi, suivi d'un ou plusieurs titres ou épithètes, puis le nom du propriétaire du sceau, accompagné le plus souvent du nom de son père ou de l'indication de sa fonction, et enfin (mais assez rarement) la mention "son serviteur."[20]

2.3.1 On sait que ce type de légende était le seul à exister à l'époque des *Šakkanakku*;[21] la légende était alors parfois répartie en deux colonnes, celle de gauche étant réservée au nom et au titre du *šakkanakku*, celle de droite au propriétaire du sceau. Dans le cas (fréquent) où l'empreinte n'est pas complète, on peut croire qu'on a affaire au sceau du souverain, alors qu'il s'agit en fait de celui d'un de ses serviteurs.[22]

2.3.2 Il existe sous Samsi-Addu quatre légendes de ce type, dont deux seulement sont publiées. La première est connue par une empreinte sur la tablette ARM 21 91:

[^{d}]UTU-*ši*-[^{d}IŠKUR]	Samsi-Addu,
[*ša*]-*ki-in* [^{d}EN.LÍL]	préfet d'Enlil,
ENSI$_2$ ^{d}[*a-šur*$_4$]	vicaire d'Aššur;
[*ia*]-*ma-ti*-[*el*]	Yamatti-El
[Ì]R - [ZU]	(est) son serviteur.

Le second cylindre est connu par de nombreuses empreintes; les collations ont permis d'en vérifier la lecture:

^{d}UTU-*ši*-^{d}[IŠKUR]	Samsi-Addu
ša-ki-in ^{d}E[N*.LÍL]	préfet d'Enlil,

[19]Cette empreinte, qui figur sur ME 193, avait été mal lue par Dossin dans MAM 2/3 257). La légende qu'on trouve en ME 225 appartient en fait à un autre cylindre.

[20]Pour ÌR-ZU à traduire par "son serviteur" (akkadien *warassu*) et non "ton serviteur" (sumérien ìr-zu), cf. Zettler (1976) 38 n 1.

[21]Voir MAM 2/3 156–60 et 251–52, et les collations publiées par Durand (1981a) 180.

[22]Voir en ce sens les remarques de Durand (1981a) 180, et notes 6 et 8.

ENSI$_2$ ^{d}a*-[šur$_4$]	vicaire d'Aššur;
AMA.DU$_{10}$.GA GEME$_2$*.Z[U*]	Amaduga (est) sa servante.[23]

On remarquera l'identité de la titulature de Samsi-Addu dans les deux cas.

2.3.3 Jusqu'à présent, aucun sceau de ce type n'était connu pour Yasmaḫ-Addu. Deux empreintes peuvent maintenant être citées. La première se trouve sur deux inédits, datés de Nīmer-Sin et de *warki* Ṭāb-ṣilli-Aššur:

[*ia*]-*ás-ma-aḫ*-[^{d}IŠKUR]	Yasmaḫ-Addu,
ša-ki-in ^{d}*da*[-*gan*]	préfet de Dagan;
a-na-ku-DINGIR-*ma* Ì[R.ZU]	Anāku-ilumma (est) son serviteur.

La seconde empreinte figure sur un fragment de scellement de coffre ou de porte.[24] On y lit:

[*ia-ás*]-*ma-aḫ*-^{d}IŠKUR	Yasmaḫ-Addu,
[*da*] - *núm*	le fort,
[*na*]-*ra-am* *eš*$_4$-*tár*	bien-aimé d'Eštar;
[^{d}]EN.ZU-*mu-ba-li-*/[*iṭ*]	Sin-muballiṭ
[ÌR] - ZU	(est) son serviteur.

Dannum employé seul est un titre typique de l'époque d'Agadé;[25] il a été porté à Mari par Apil-kēn, contemporain d'Ur-Nammu[26] et par Samsi-Addu.[27] *Narām Eštar* est de même une épithète portée par Samsi-Addu.[28]

2.3.4 C'est toutefois sous Zimri-Lim que ce genre de sceau est le plus abondant.[29] Selon l'épithète du roi, on peut répartir les légendes en quatre sous-types:

a— "Zimri-Lim, roi fort" (LUGAL KAL.GA): sceaux de Abum-El,[30] Sammêtar et Šunuḫraḫalu. Ce dernier a été publié comme étant le

[23]D'après un nouvel examen de toutes les empreintes de ce sceau. Le début de E[N] est clair in ARMT 11 87; le *a* de *Aššur* et le début de Z[U] visibles en ARMT 11 69.

[24]ARM HC S.115 #72-15 = Birot (1973).

[25]Voir Michalowski (1980) 235.

[26]Cf. Civil (1962) 213.

[27]Seux (1967) 69.

[28]Seux (1967) 192.

[29]Voir précédemment la remarque à ce sujet de Birot *apud* ARMT 9, p. 251 n 5.

[30]Voir la photo publiée dans MAM 2/3 241, fig. 129 (ME 272). La légende n'a pas été transcrite dans l'ouvrage.

sceau IV de Zimri-Lim.[31] D'après collation de J.-M. Durand, il faut lire en réalité:[32]

zi-im-ri-li-im	Zimri-Lim,
LUGAL KAL.G[A]	roi fort;
šu-nu-uḫ-ra-ḫa-lu	Šunuḫraḫalu.

Sunuḫraḫalu, secrétaire personnel du roi, possédait donc deux sceaux, puisqu'on connaissait déjà un autre sceau à son nom:

šu-nu-uḫ-ra-ḫa[*-lu*]	Šunuḫraḫalu,
IR$_{11}$ *zi-im-ri-li-*[*im*]	serviteur de Zimri-Lim.[33]

Il en va de même pour Šūbnalû. L'un de ses cylindres a déjà été publié, quoique sa légende n'ait pas été transcrite (MAM 2/3 212, fig. 114, ME 290):

[*šu*]*-ub-na-lu-ú*	Šūbnalû,
(image)	
[ÌR] *zi-im-ri-li-im*	serviteur de Zimri-Lim.

On trouve en revanche sur l'inédit M.13185 l'empreinte d'un autre cylindre, dont la légende appartient au type ici étudié:

zi-im-ri-l[*i-im*]	Zimri-Lim,
LUGAL *da-*[*núm*]	roi fort;
šu-ub-na-lu-ú [ÌR.ZU]	Šūbnalû (est) [son serviteur].

b— "Zimri-Lim, bien aimé de Dagan" (*narām Dagan*): sceaux de l'échanson Puzur-Šamaš,[34] de Ripʾi-Dagan et de Yaḫad-maraṣ.

c— "Zimri-Lim, préfet de Dagan" (*šakin Dagan*): sceau du devin Asqudum.

d— "Zimri-Lim, préfet d'Adad" (*šakin Adad*): sceau de l'engraisseur Dabi'um. On remarquera le très haut statut de la plupart des personnes

[31]MAM 2/3 253; Noter toutefois le doute émis p. 166 n 2.

[32]Comme on peut d'ailleurs s'en rendre compte sur les photos publiées dans MAM 2/3: pour ME 165, pl. XLV, et pour ME 220, p. 167, fig. 103 et pl. XLVI.

[33]Voir MAM 2/3 194, 256 et pl. XLIX (ME 18).

[34]Ici encore, le sceau a été pris par l'éditeur pour celui du roi Zimri-Lim. L'erreur de Bottéro (ARMT 7, p. 139, 219 n 1, 222 et 227 n 2) a déjà été corrigée par Birot, ARMT 9, p. 251. Voir maintenant Charpin and Durand (1983) 96.

qui ont possédé de tels sceaux, comme Sammêtar, Asqudum ou Šunuḫ-raḫalu: se pourrait-il que ces sceaux leur aient été offerts par le souverain?[35]

2.4 Que le sceau ait comporté simplement la mention "serviteur de NR" ou que la légende ait débuté par le nom et une épithète du roi, dans les deux cas se pose le problème de savoir ce qui se passait lors d'un changement de règne: tous les fonctionnaires—à supposer qu'ils soient restés en poste—devaient-ils changer de sceau? Cela pourrait paraître peu probable, vu le coût de l'opération. Il semble toutefois que tel était le cas.

2.4.1 Ainsi Asqudum, dont on sait qu'il était déjà en poste à l'époque assyrienne, se fit-il faire un nouveau sceau mentionnant le roi Zimri-Lim (cf. supra § 1.2).

2.4.2 De même, Amaduga, qui possédait un cylindre au nom de Samsi-Addu (cf. § 2.3.2), se fit-elle graver un nouveau cylindre ainsi libellé:

AMA.DU$_{10}$*.[GA]	Amaduga
GEME$_2$ *š*[*a**]	servante de
zi-im-ri-li-im	Zimri-Lim.[36]

L'empreinte de ce cylindre figure sur des tablettes datées des années 3′ à 7′ de Zimri-Lim. Ce que le cas d'Amaduga a de particulier, c'est qu'elle a continué à utiliser son ancien sceau, dont on trouve les empreintes sur des tablettes datant des années 3′ à 5′ de Zimri-Lim. On voit même qu'à deux jours d'intervalle, on utilisa tantôt son ancien, et tantôt son nouveau sceau.[37] P. Steinkeller a signalé deux cas identiques à l'époque d'Ur III, où un sceau "périmé" continue à être utilisé concurremment avec le nouveau.[38]

2.4.3 Le seul autre exemple d'emploi d'un sceau périmé à Mari est fourni par la maison d'Asqudum. Sur une dizaine de tablettes qu'on y a découvertes, on trouve l'empreinte du sceau de Yašūb-Dagan, serviteur de Yasmaḫ-Addu. Aucune de ces tablettes n'est datée, mais elles

[35]Comme Zettler (1977) 36 en a fait l'hypothèse à propos de sceaux analogues datant de l'époque sargonique.

[36]Quatre empreintes publiées jusqu'à présent: ARM 9 58, ARMT 11 93, ARMT 12 108 et 723. Elles ont toutes été collationnées, d'où la difference de lecture avec les éditions princeps.

[37]Ancien cylindre en ARM 9 43 (8 IGI-KUR Trône de Šamaš); nouveau cylindre en ARMT 11 93 (10 IGI-KUR Trône de Šamaš).

[38]Steinkeller (1976) 47.

appartiennent au lot d'archives qui remonte aux premières années du règne de Zimri-Lim. Il semble donc que Yašūb-Dagan ne s'était alors pas encore procuré de nouveau sceau, bien qu'à ce moment là son patron Asqudum disposât déjà du sien. On peut donc penser que l'avènement de Zimri-Lim a été une période faste pour les lapicides!

* * *

3. Quelques sceaux royaux.

3.0 La dernière partie de cette communication sera consacrée aux sceaux possédés, non plus par leurs fonctionnaires, mais par les rois eux-mêmes.

3.1 Jusqu'à présent, le sceau de Samsi-Addu n'est connu que par quelques empreintes très partielles figurant sur des bulles découvertes à Acem Höyük. N. Özgüç en a publié l'iconographie,[39] mais on attend toujours la publication de sa légende par K. Balkan.[40] Les empreintes de Mari permettront d'abréger cette attente.

3.1.1 Il s'agit de trois fragments d'enveloppe de lettre, découverts en 1972 dans la salle 115 du palais par M. Birot.[41] Sur le plus petit de ces fragments (n° 72-132), la légende du sceau a été partiellement effacée par l'inscription dans l'argile d'une mention: *a-na i*-[. . .]. L'usage étant qu'une enveloppe de lettre comporte l'indication du destinataire, il y a lieu de restaurer: *a-na i*[*a-ás-ma-aḫ*-^{d}IŠKUR]. Il s'agirait alors d'une des très nombreuses lettres adressées par Samsi-Addu à son fils Yasmaḫ-Addu, et dont l'enveloppe portait l'empreinte du sceau de son royal expéditeur. Les deux autres fragments (M.5148 et surtout M.5151) fournissent le déroulement presque complet de la vignette, et permettent également de compléter la légende, qu'on peut restaurer ainsi:

^{d}UTU-*ši*-^{d}[IŠKUR]	Samsi-Addu,
[*n*]*a-ra-am* ^{d}[*a*]-*šu*[*r*$_4$]	bien aimé d'Aššur,[42]
[P]A . TE . S[I]	vicaire

[39]Özgüç (1980) est essentiellement la traduction par M. Mellink de l'article précédemment paru en turc dans *Belleten*, Özgüç (1977). Cf. Mellink (1978) 319a.

[40]Özgüç a simplement indiqué: "on Shamshi-Adad's bullae it is the impression of the legend of the seal: his name, his titles, and his father's name, which is done with care, rather than the design"—Özgüç (1980) 65. Noter que les photos publiées sont celles des trois meilleures empreintes *pour l'iconographie* (comme il est spécifié, p. 65). On ne peut y lire des cinq lignes de la légende que: ^{d}UTU-*ši*-[. . .] [*n*]*a-ra-am* ^{d}[. . .] [P]A.TE.[SI] ^{d}*a*-[. . .] [. . .].

[41]Cf. Birot (1973) 9 n 1. Les trois fragments ici publiés ne sont pas jointifs, en sorte qu'il n'est pas possible de savoir s'ils appartenaient à une même enveloppe.

[42]Pour la graphie ^{d}*a-šur*$_4$ (^{d}A.LÁL.SAR), voir Tadmor (1958) 92 n 303.

d *a* - *šur*$_4$	d'Aššur,
[DUMU] *i-la-kab-ka-bu-ú*	fils d'Ilā-kabkabû.

3.1.2 Cette légende est intéressante à plusieurs points de vue. On notera d'abord qu'à la différence de ses inscriptions, Samsi-Addu n'y prend pas le titre de "roi" (LUGAL),[43] mais seulement celui de "vicaire d'Aššur" (*išši'ak Aššur*). De plus, on sait que l'une des innovations introduites par Šamši-Addu dans sa titulature est d'avoir fait précéder ce titre de "vicaire d'Aššur" par celui de "préfet d'Enlil" (*šakin Enlil*).[44] De fait, c'est le couple *šakin Enlil/išši'ak Aššur* qu'on a trouvé plus haut sur le sceau de deux de ses serviteurs (§ 2.3.2). Or, sur le propre sceau de Samsi-Addu, "vicaire d'Aššur" est précédé par "bien aimé d'Aššur." Cette épithète ne figure dans aucune de ses inscriptions, mais rappelle bien évidemment l'épithète "bien aimé d'Aššur et d'Eštar" (*narām Aššur u Eštar*) portée par Ilušuma et Erišum I,[45] qui est d'ailleurs la seule épithète utilisée par les rois paléo-assyriens.[46] On aurait pu s'attendre à voir plutôt figurer l'épithète "bien aimé de Dagan," comme sur une inscription toujours inédite[47] où Samsi-Addu est qualifié de "vicaire d'Assur, bien aimé de Dagan." Or cette épithète, liée à la possession du moyen Euphrate,[48] n'apparaît pas ici.

3.1.3 La conclusion me paraît claire: cette légende montre, de façon assez inattendue, en Samsi-Addu un roi paléo-assyrien respectueux de la tradition.[49] Dès lors, la mention de son père Ilā-kabkabû n'en prend que plus d'importance; sa rareté dans les titulatures connues jusqu'à présent avait été en effet interprétée comme due à un sentiment d'illégitimité, ce qui ne semble pas avoir été le cas.[50] Ce sceau permet également d'envisager de façon renouvelée la transformation de l'idéologie royale

[43]Cf. Grayson (1971) 312 "Suddenly with Shamshi-Adad I both the internal structure of the society is transformed and externally the Assyrian state becomes a leading power. It is with Shamshi-Adad that the idea of Assyrian monarchy is born, and the word 'king' first appears."

[44]Cf. Seux (1967) 112 n 29.

[45]Cf. Seux (1967) 191.

[46]Cf. Larsen (1976) 110.

[47]Dossin (1939c) 98.

[48]Seux (1967) 125 n 12.

[49]Même si l'inscription de son sceau diffère notablement de celle des trois sceaux de rois paléo-assyriens que nous possédons [réf. dans ARI 1 §§ 28 (Ṣilulu), 97 (Irišum I), 115 (Sargon)]. Pour ces deux derniers, la schéma de la légende est: NP$_2$ *išši*ʾ*ak Aššur* DUMU NP$_2$ *išši*ʾ*ak Aššur*.

[50]"Note that with one exception, Shamshi-Adad I never gives his genealogy. This phenomenon, so unlike the practice of other early Assyrian monarchs, was due to the fact that Shamshi-Adad was not of Assyrian lineage." Grayson (1971) 313 n 15, après Landsberger (1954) 31–36.

en Assyrie sous Samsi-Addu.[51] Le caractère "traditionnel" de la titulature de Samsi-Addu dans ce sceau s'explique en effet au mieux si l'on suppose que celui-ci a été gravé peu de temps après la conquête d'Aššur par Samsi-Addu. Ce n'est qu'après l'extension de sa domination jusqu'à l'Euphrate, grâce à la conquête du royaume de Mari,[52] que prit naissance la nouvelle idéologie impériale, qui se manifesta en particulier par une titulature beaucoup plus développée et triomphale que celle qui figure sur ce sceau, témoin de plus humbles débuts.

3.2 Si l'on manquait jusqu'à présent d'informations sur le sceau de Samsi-Addu, la situation s'inverse lorsqu'on aborde le cas de Zimri-Lim; en effet, pas moins de quatre cylindres différents sont actuellement réputés avoir appartenu à ce roi.[53]

3.2.1 La collation par J.-M. Durand des empreintes publiées dans MAM 2/3 a permis de simplifier le problème: les cylindres III et IV n'appartiennent pas en réalité à Zimri-Lim. Le cylindre III est en fait celui d'un serviteur de Yaḫdun-Lim. On lit:

[*x*]-*ma*-AN
[Ì]R *ia-aḫ-du-un-l*[*i-im*][54]

Quant au cylindre IV, on a vu précédemment qu'il commençait bien par le nom de Zimri-Lim et l'épithète "roi fort," mais que figurait sur la troisième ligne le nom de son propriétaire, Šunuḫraḫalu (cf. § 2.3.4).

3.2.2 Dès lors, seuls restent en lice les cylindres I et II. Leur légende est identique, à ceci près que le cylindre I possède l'épithète "qui rassemble le bord de l'Euphrate" (*gāmir aḫ Purattim*), absente du cylindre II. Cette différence correspondrait-elle à un décalage chronologique, Zimri-Lim s'étant fait graver un premier sceau (II) lors de son avènement, puis un nouveau (I) après avoir affermi son pouvoir sur les rives de l'Euphrate (cf. le nom de l'an 1')? Il ne semble pas: l'étude de la distribution des empreintes montre en effet entre les deux cylindres une différence d'emploi.

3.2.3 Le cylindre I était ce qu'on pourrait appeler le sceau de chancellerie. Avec lui étaient scellées les enveloppes de lettres expédiées

[51]Même chez Larsen (1976) 221, cette transformation est présentée "en bloc: "Šamši-Adad retained the old titulary and accepted the position as Aššur's steward, but this was a secondary title which came after such titles as *šakin Enlil*, 'Enlil's prefect,' and *pāliḫ Dagān*, 'who fears Dagan.' "

[52]Pour l'antériorité de la conquête d'Aššur sur celle de Mari, voir Charpin (1983b).

[53]Voir MAM 2/3 162–67 et 253.

[54]Sur la photo de l'empreinte ME 166, publiée dans MAM 2/3 pl. XLVI, on voit clairement le clou vertical terminant le signe ÌR, qui ne saurait être confondu avec la fin du signe DUMU.

par Zimri-Lim.[55] On notera d'ailleurs que le fragment d'enveloppe de lettre retrouvé à tell Rimah portait l'empreinte du cylindre I.[56]

3.2.4 En revanche, le cylindre II apparaît imprimé sur des scellements ou sur des documents administratifs. Toutefois, un examen très attentif de toutes ces empreintes a montré certaines différences, minimes, entre elles: il semble que les empreintes du "cylindre II" aient en fait été produites avec au moins deux matrices différentes. Cela s'explique aisément, si l'on admet que plusieurs services du palais pouvaient avoir besoin du sceau royal.[57] Ce phénomène est d'ailleurs connu par d'autres exemples.[58]

3.2.5 L'autorité du sceau royal était manifestement considérable. Un seul exemple suffira. Zimri-Lim, en déplacement, avait demandé à Mukannišum l'envoi de vases en argent. L'échanson Appūḫ-illassunu indiqua à Mukannišum que ceux-ci se trouvaient dans le magasin de dame Man[nu-kīma/balum-]Eštar, et qu'il n'avait qu'à les y prendre. Dans son rapport au roi, Mukannišum indique alors: "j'ai regardé ce magasin: il était scellé au sceau de mon seigneur. Plein de révérence, je n'ai pas ouvert le magasin et je suis allé trouver la reine. La reine m'a répondu: 'le voyage du roi [n'est pas fini]. Que ce soit donc dame Man[nu-kīma/balum-]Eštar (elle-même) qui fasse sortir le coffre (où sont stockés) les vases-*uridū*, et qu'elle scelle (à nouveau) ce magasin'!"[59] Il semble bien que si le magasin avait été scellé avec un autre sceau que celui du roi, Mukannišum l'aurait ouvert et se serait servi directement, et il est probable qu'il aurait ensuite scellé la porte avec son sceau.[60] La présence du sceau royal fournissait donc une garantie supplémentaire d'inviolabilité.[61]

[55]Les 13 empreintes publiées dans MAM 2/3 (ME 3, 16a et b, 20, 21, 27, 29, 31, 35, 36, 40, 48 et 49) figurent sur des fragments d'enveloppes, comme il est indiqué dans la publication. On peut préciser qu'il s'agit d'enveloppes de lettres, comme le montre l'adresse conservée sur trois de ces fragments: E.20 (*a-na mu-ka-an-ni-*[*ši-im*]); E.40 (*a*-[*na* . . .]); E.45 ([*a-n*]*a mu-ka-an-ni-š*[*i-im*]).

[56]Voir Hawkins *apud* OBTTR p. 250 n° 5. On remarquera que sur le dessin de C. Postgate (pl. 107), la 8° ligne de l'inscription apparaît séparée par une "déesse Lama" des 7 lignes précédentes. Ce fait n'avait pas été signalé dans le publication des empreintes de Mari (MAM 2/3), mais un nouvel examen de celles-ci m'a permis de confirmer l'exactitude de l'observation faite sur l'empreinte retrouvée à tell Rimah.

[57]Cf. Birot, ARMT 9, p. 250 § 10.

[58]Le plus célèbre étant celui d'Ini-Tešub de Karkémiš. Voir dernièrement Beyer (1980) 276 n 38. Voir aussi le cas d'Abban d'Alep dans Collon (1975) 7 n 1.

[59]ARMT 13 22: 24–33. Je reprends ici pour l'essentiel la traduction proposée par Durand dans les collations de la correspondence de Mukannišum qu'il a publiées dans Durand (1983c) 145.

[60]Selon la procédure illustrée par ARM 10 12: le sceau d'Igmilum, brisé, est remplacé par un autre, celui de la reine en l'occurrence.

[61]Il n'est pas certain que la femme qui scelle à nouveau le magasin ait détenu un exemplaire du sceau royal; c'est toutefois assez probable.

3.2.6 Si certains services du palais disposaient d'un exemplaire du sceau royal, on doit cependant noter un cas où Zimri-Lim, absent de Mari, fit porter son sceau à la reine, afin de sceller dix jarres de vin destinées au roi de Babylone. Ce sceau est décrit comme ^{NA_4}KIŠIB *ma-ar-pí-qa-tim* (ARM 10 133: 5, 21). M. Birot avait proposé de voir dans ce terme une parure féminine, sans doute une sorte d'agrafe (ARMT 9 p. 318). Le CAD a songé à "a piece of jewelry, probably a necklace": on aurait alors affaire à un sceau inclus dans un collier. Récemment, J.-M. Durand a proposé une interprétation plus satisfaisante, en y voyant une formation *ma-PRiS-at* sur RPQ "enclore, enfermer":[62] le terme désignerait alors la monture métallique[63] d'un sceau-cylindre. On sait que ce genre de monture à capsule débordante laisse souvent sur l'argile un profond sillon de chaque côté de l'empreinte du cylindre proprement dit: les empreintes d'une des matrices du "cylindre II" de Zimri-Lim se caractérisent par un tel sillon, orné de petits trous à effet décoratif.[64] Il pourrait donc s'agir du sceau personnel du roi, puisque celui-ci en réclame le retour dès que les jarres de vin destinées à Hammurapi auront été scellées.

3.2.7 La situation, jusqu'à présent éclaircie, va toutefois se compliquer avec l'apparition d'un nouveau cylindre de Zimri-Lim.[65] Celui-ci a été déroulé sur l'enveloppe d'une lettre adressée par Zimri-Lim à Tiš-Ulme, le roi de Mardaman. L'enveloppe a été retrouvée intacte, indice que la lettre n'a vraisemblablement jamais été envoyée à son destinataire.[66] La légende est la suivante:

zi-im-ri-li-i[*m*]	Zimri-Lim,
[*n*]*a-ra-am* ^{d}*da-gan*	bien aimé de Dagan,
[*š*]*a-ki-in* ^{d}[. . .]	préfet de [. . .],
LUGAL *ma-ri*$^{[ki]}$	roi de Mari
ù ma-at ḫ[*a-na*]	et du pays de Ḫana,
DUMU *ḫa-at-ni-*^{d}[*x*]	fils de Ḫatni-[. . .].

[62]Voir Durand (1983b) 134 n 37 sur le travail du métal à Mari.

[63]Cf. la mention de *marpiqatum* en or. Limet publie dans MARI 3 un texte mentionnant un *narpiqatum* (noter *na-* au lieu de *ma-*) en fer.

[64]Cela avait été observé, mais mal interprété, dans MAM 2/3 où il est indiqué que "le cylindre II avait les bords creusés et dentelés" (p. 165). Voir la photo de ME 54 (p. 163, g. 102).

[65]L'annonce de la présence, sur des bulles trouvées à Acem Höyük, d'empreintes d'une nouveau sceau de Zimri-Lim dans Mellink (1972) 170b était prématurée. Il s'agit en fait du sceau d'une fille de Yaḫdun-Lim, et non de Zimri-Lim comme il a été indiqué par erreur également dans Mellink (1976) 266. Cf. Özgüç (1980) 66.

[66]Cf. ARM HC S.115 #72–15 = Birot (1973) 8–9. Si la chancellerie avait voulu garder un double, comme le suggère Birot p. 9, n 1, il est peu vraisemblable que celui-ci ait été conservé dans une enveloppe scellée.

Cette légende est presque identique à celle du cylindre II, à ceci près que les lignes 2 et 3 sont en chiasme (II: *šakin Dagan/narām Enlil*), et qu'on a ligne 4 la graphie défective *ma-at* au lieu de *ma-a-at*. Mais c'est surtout la ligne 6 qui diffère, puisque le père de Zimri-Lim n'est pas, comme on s'y attendrait, Yaḫdun-Lim, mais un certain Ḫatni-[. . .]. Comment expliquer cette filiation? Il paraît peu raisonnable d'admettre qu'on a affaire à *un autre Zimri-Lim*. Plusieurs hypothèses sont alors possibles. On pourrait envisager que Zimri-Lim n'ait pas été en fait le fils de Yaḫdun-Lim, mais seulement un membre de la famille royale, et qu'il se soit paré du titre de "fils de Yaḫdun-Lim" pour légitimer sa montée sur le trône de la dynastie: "le trône de son père" ne serait pas à prendre au sens strict. Mais une autre explication paraît préférable. En effet, on ne peut manquer de rapprocher ce sceau de celui d'Addu-dūri:

^{MÍ} ^{d}IŠKUR-*du-ri*	Addu-dūri,
GEME$_2$ *ḫa-at-ni*-^{d}IŠ[KUR]	servante de Ḫatni-Addu.[67]

Dans ce genre de sceau, la mention "servante de NP" semble qualifier une épouse de second rang. En effet, le sceau de la reine de Mari, épouse principale, est ainsi libellé:

^{MÍ}*ši-ip-*[*tu*]	Šiptu
DUMU.MÍ *ia-ri-im-li-im*	fille de Yarīm-Lim
DAM *zi-im-ri-li-im*	épouse de Zimri-Lim.[68]

En revanche, J.-M. Durand a pu identifier le sceau d'une des épouses secondaires de Zimri-Lim, Yataraya, qui est ainsi rédigé:

^{MÍ}*ia-ta-ra-i*[*a*]	Yataraya
GEME$_2$ *zi-im-ri-li-im*	servante de Zimri-Lim.[69]

Addu-dūri serait donc, d'après le type de son sceau, une épouse secondaire de Ḫatni-Addu. Or, à partir des textes d'ARM 21, J.-M. Durand a suggéré qu'Addu-dūri était peut-être une soeur de Zimri-Lim (ARM 21 p. 19 n 9). S'il faut identifier le Ḫatni-[. . .] du sceau de Zimri-Lim avec ce Ḫatni-Addu, Zimri-Lim se dirait donc fils de mari de sa soeur.

[67]Pour ce sceau, cf. dernièrement Durand (1981b) 188. Sa collation de ME 227 est confirmée par une autre empreinte sur l'inédit M.13161. On possède également un cylindre d'un serviteur de Ḫatni-Addu. Voir Kupper (1959) 99.

[68]Empreinte sur l'inédit M.18025, beaucoup plus complète que ME 181 publiée dans MAM 2/3 254. C'est ce sceau qui est décrit dans ARM 10 119 (où on notera toutefois *aš-ša-at* au lieu de DAM!).

[69]Il s'agit de ME 170, faussement attribué à un serviteur de Zimri-Lim dans MAM 2/3 255.

Pour expliquer ce phénomène, on ne peut à nouveau qu'émettre des hypothèses. La reconstitution traditionnelle des évènements veut que Zimri-Lim, contraint à l'exil par suite de la conquête de Mari par Samsi-Addu, ait choisi refuge à la cour d'Alep, où il aurait épousé Šiptu, la fille du roi Yarīm-Lim.[70] En réalité, nos certitudes se bornent au fait que Yarīm-Lim a aidé Zimri-Lim à conquérir le trône de Mari.[71] Cela ne veut pas dire que Zimri-Lim ait vécu en exil à Alep. En outre, nous ignorons quand Zimri-Lim épousa Šiptu. Des lors, on peut très bien admettre que Zimri-Lim se serait réfugié chez le mari de sa soeur, Ḫatni-Addu, dont il serait devenu en quelque sorte le fils.[72] Il ne s'agit toutefois nullement d'une certitude!

3.3 Pour ne pas terminer sur trop d'hypothèses, je voudrais achever cette communication en présentant la plus récente découverte qu'il m'a été donné de faire, le 30 décembre dernier. Il s'agit d'un minuscule fragment d'enveloppe,[73] mesurant 2,5 × 2 cm, mais qui nous donne l'essentiel de la légende du sceau du roi Yarīm-Lim d'Alep. On lit:

ia-ri-im-[*li-im*]	Yarīm-Lim,
DUMU *su-mu-ẹ*[*-pu-uḫ*]	fils de Sūmu-e[puḫ],
[LU]GAL *ia-*[*am-ḫa-ad*]	roi du Ya[mḫad],
[*n*]*a-ra-*[*am* ᵈIŠKUR]	bien aimé d'[Adad].

Du point de vue typologique, on remarquera que cette légende s'insère parfaitement dans la série des sceaux des rois du Yamḫad dont l'empreinte nous a été conservée sur les tablettes d'Alalaḫ.[74] Leur légende comporte quatre éléments: le nom du roi, celui de son père, le titre de "roi du Yamḫad," et l'épithète "bien aimé d'Adad." Aussi les lacunes de la

[70]Cf. Dossin (1952) 236.

[71]Cf. ARM HC A.1153 = Dossin (1973) 179 ss., et le fameux oracle d'Adad de Kallassu, ARM HC A.1121 [= Dossin (1950c) 103–7]. On doit noter dès maintenant que de toute façon, Yarīm-Lim n'était pas encore roi d'Alep au moment où Samsi-Addu s'empara de Mari: son père Sūmu-epuḫ (cf. *infra*) mourut en effet pendant l' "interrègne assyrien" (cf. ARM 1 91: 5).

[72]Dans la lettre ARM HC A.1153 = Dossin (1973) (cf. n 71), adressée à Yarīm-Lim, Zimri-Lim se dit également son "fils" (*umma Zimri-Lim māruka-ma*), mais il s'agit là de la formule habituelle par laquelle un roi se reconnait comme le protégé d'un souverain plus puissant.

[73]Ce fragment (n° 8090) devait appartenir à l'enveloppe d'une lettre écrite par Yarīm-Lim. Jusqu'à présent, cette correspondance comprend deux lettres, l'une adressée à Zimri-Lim [ARM HC S.115, n° 72–39 = Birot (1973) 11], et l'autre à sa fille Šiptu (ARM 10 151). (Je mets de côté la lettre de Yarīm-Lim à Yašūb-Yaḫad publiée dans Dossin [1956] 63–69 [ARM HC A.1314], qui a dû être interceptée à Mari [p. 64]). Le fragment ne comporte malheureusement pas au revers l'empreinte en négatif du texte de la tablette, en sorte qu'il n'est pas possible de la rapprocher de la lettre qu'il servait à envelopper.

[74]Cf. Collon (1975): sceaux de Abban (n° 3 et 4), Yarīm-Lim II (n° 5), Niqmepuḫ (n° 6), Irkabtum (n° 8) et Yarīm-Lim III (n° 10).

présente empreinte peuvent-elles être restaurée avec certitude.[75] Mais il faut évidemment du point de vue historique renverser la perspective: le sceau de Yarīm-Lim I apparaît comme le modèle qu'ont imité ses descendants.

L'information historique essentielle fournie par ce sceau concerne évidemment le nom du père de Yarīm-Lim. Les deux premiers signes sont entièrement conservés: *su-mu-*, et le début du troisème fait songer à *e-*, en sorte qu'une restauration *su-mu-ẹ[pu-uḫ]* ne fait guère de doute. Sūmu-epuḫ est en effet connu pour avoir aidé les rois de Samānum, Tuttul et Abattum dans leur attaque contre Yaḫdun-Lim: "les troupes de *Sumu-epuḫ du pays de Yamḫad* vinrent à leur secours."[76] Dans son commentaire, G. Dossin décrivait Sūmu-epuḫ comme "un chef de bande qui loue ses services au plus offrant."[77] S. Smith, comparant l'inscription de Yaḫdun-Lim avec la lettre ARM 1 1 (qui mentionne l' "homme du Yamḫad" l. 6′), concluait en revanche: "the king of Yamḫad at that time can only have been Sumu-epuḫ."[78] Il a été suivi par Fr. M. Tocci[79] et H. Klengel. Ce dernier indique, toujours à propos de ARM 1 1: "dieser au̯īl I̯amḫad zur Zeit des Abīsamar und I̯aḫdunlim kann jedoch kaum ein anderer gewesen sein als Sumuēpuḫ. Sumuēpuḫ dürfte somit mit eine Zwischenstellung zwischen einem Schēch und einem sesshaften König eingenommen haben. Er gehört an die Spitze der Dynastie der I̯amḫad-Könige, wobei allerdings sein Verwandschaftsverhältnis zu I̯arimlim I. von I̯amḫad/Ḫalap noch ungeklärt bleiben muss."[80] Si l'empreinte ici publiée ne nous éclaire pas davantage sur le statut exact de Sūmu-epuḫ, elle permet du moins d'établir définitivement celui-ci à l'origine de la dynastie des rois du Yamḫad, en tant que père de Yarīm-Lim I. Une fois encore, c'est à un sceau que nous devons une information historique aussi importante.

* * *

ADDENDUM

Plus de trois ans se sont écoulés entre la rédaction de cet article (janvier 1983) et la correction des épreuves (avril 1986). On voudra bien noter quelques compléments bibliographiques:

[75]L. 3, le nom de *ia-am-ḫa-ad* est entièrement conservé sur les sceaux n° 3 et 5; (au n° 3, corriger *ia-am-ḫa-dum* en *ia-am-ḫa-a[d]*; l. 4, le nom du dieu (^{d}IŠKUR) est conservé sur les sceaux n° 3, 4 et 5. On sait que Yarīm-Lim considérait Adad comme sa divinité poliade, et Sin comme son dieu personnel. Cf. ARM HC A.1314: 27–28 = Dossin (1956) 67.

[76]ARM HC M.2802 iii: 12–15 (inscription de fondation du temple de Šamaš), Dossin (1955) 14.

[77]*Loc. cit.* 27. Voir depuis Dossin (1970) 101 n 1.

[78]Smith (1956) 38.

[79]Tocci (1960) 45–46.

[80]Klengel (1965) 113.

0.1 note 3: voir désormais Beyer (1985) 375–84.

1 Voir Charpin (1985) 453–62.

1.1 note 7: un de ces textes scolaires a été publié par W. G. Lambert dans Durand and Kupper (1985). Voir W. G. Lambert (1985) 181–90.

1.3 Voir Beyer (1984) 255–56.

2.2.3 Il est intéressant de noter que le sceau de Marduk-mušallim ne se trouve pas imprimé sur un «bouchon de jarre» ou sur une étiquette, mais sur un scellement de porte (Beyer [1985] 380); il fournit un témoignage de plus de l'occupation du palais de Mari par les Babyloniens.

2.3.2 Aux sceaux de Yamatti-El et d'Amaduga, il faut désormais ajouter ceux de Yaḫuzanum et de Ammi-iluna: cf. Charpin (1984) 51.

2.4 On notera que, jusqu'à présent, aucun sceau d'un serviteur de Sumu-Yamam n'est attesté.

3.1 Voir Charpin (1984) 51 (avec photo p. 70 et copie p. 81).

3.2.7 L'interprétation ici proposée est à abandonner. Voir maintenant Charpin and Durand (1985) 336–38.

3.3 note 73: J. Sasson (1980) 134 a montré de façon convaincante que le Yarim-Lim auteur de ARM 10 151 ne pouvait être le roi du Yamḫad; voir aussi Durand (1984a) 137 n 58.

Early Second Millennium Ceramic Parallels between Tell Hadidi-Azu and Mari

Rudolph Dornemann

Milwaukee Public Museum

Any comparisons we try to make between the ancient sites of Mari and Azu have to be made on the basis of incomplete and uneven evidence, though a considerable amount of evidence exists. In antiquity, there was clearly a great difference in the reputation, influence and importance of the two sites. The roughly 280-acre area of Tell Hariri is approximately twice the size of the 145 acres of Tell Hadidi. The royal residences and temples at Mari can only be compared to the non-royal, domestic areas of Azu. The massive archival material of not one, but now several, major chronological periods at Mari can only be compared to a small personal archive at Azu of the Late Bronze Age, hundreds of years after the destruction of Mari. The wealth of royal inscriptional material from Mari clearly attests to the major role played by the city of Mari in the history of the ancient world and provides insights into an almost endless variety of customs and practices of its citizens, dependents, and the people with whom they had contact. The importance of the city of Mari is well documented in the cuneiform evidence from many Mesopotamian sites, as well as the Syrian sites of Ebla and Ugarit, and also from the city of Alalakh. At Azu, the cuneiform texts provide a very narrow focus which barely reflects the world beyond a few kilometers' stretch along the Euphrates' banks, and external mention of Azu is very limited (Dornemann [1979] 146). Contemporary reference at Alalakh is the most significant, but not very enlightening, and an apparent reference in the archives of Early Bronze Age Ebla (Pettinato [1981a] 223) indicates a long continuity in the name of the site at Hadidi.

When artifactual materials are compared, a greater amount of comparable material is available at the two sites, but a great disparity is still evident in the types of artifacts and their wealth. We will focus our attention on two categories of objects for which good evidence exists at both sites. First, the ceramic repertoire of the Zimri Lim palace at Mari and the other second millennium pottery from Mari will be examined in the context of what we are designating the Middle Bronze Age II A and B pottery sequence at Tell Hadidi. Second, we will briefly compare a selection of clay figurines from the two sites and make a few observations on similarities in artistic details and style.

For many years, our evidence for the pottery sequence at the beginning of the Middle Bronze Age in Syria has been very limited and difficult to date with precision. Despite the rich architectural, epigraphic and other artifactual materials found in the Middle Bronze Palace at Mari, very little has been published of the pottery from the Palace. Baghouz, not far from Mari, provides a large ceramic corpus, and we have a basic representation from Khabur sites eastward to the Assyrian heartland with Tepe Gawra, Nuzi, and Ashur. On or near the coast, we have a small amount of material from Alalakh, and a similarly small amount from Ugarit. There is a limited amount from Tell Khazel and other coastal sites, a few tombs scattered through central Syria, and a stratified sequence at Hama.

In the past decade, reports of recent excavations have begun to appear from Tell Ashara in the southeast to Tell Mardikh in Central Syria, and particularly from sites in the big bend area of the Euphrates. The new material provides a basis upon which we can begin to restructure the ceramic sequences of the Middle Bronze Age. In 1979 we provided a basic overview of the MB II material excavated at Tell Hadidi (Dornemann [1979] 132–41), but then temporarily turned our attention to earlier (Dornemann [1982]) and later (Dornemann [1981]) Bronze Age materials. In the past year we have again worked in greater detail on our Middle Bronze materials with a view toward our final publication. We have been able to reconstruct a considerable amount of pottery from the main MB IIB floors of the buildings in Area B (fig. 1), and have begun to review the materials beneath these floors.

We have dates on nine C-14 samples from the floors of the MB rooms in Area B, but publication of the latest CRD-82 (Calibration of Radiocarbon Dates) corrections for C-14 makes us wonder if corrected dates will, for many years to come, provide any additional precision to a stratified pottery sequence, particularly when second millennium B.C. samples with plus or minus 50 to 70 year ranges are corrected to year ranges between 305 and 465 years. Unfortunately, before we can hope to understand the broader cultural picture of the early second millennium B.C., we must firmly establish the basic sequences and detailed correspondences. It is for this reason that we will concentrate here primarily on these considerations.

Large groups of pottery were found on the stone pavements shown on the plan published in 1979 (Dornemann [1979] fig. 25, and after additional clearance, fig. 1). The stratigraphy of Area B is quite complicated, and the area supervisor, Joanna McClellan, has been working out the detailed sequence starting with the earliest EB III materials in the earliest occupation remains of this area. She has completed that portion of the analysis, and is now working through the equally complicated MB stratigraphy. The pavements all date to the MB IIB period, and though our recent efforts have provided more complete forms, they have basically duplicated rather than added to the previously existing corpus.

A number of distinctive forms stand out as the basic components of the MB IIB assemblage. (1) There are a variety of carinated cup forms (Dornemann [1979] figs. 20:45–49; 22:19, 20; and fig. 3:10, 11, 16, here) which occur in similar proportions on small- and medium-sized vessels. Variations occur in the rims from simple out-turned rims to more complicated profiled forms, occasionally with a rib beneath the rim. The carination can be gracefully curved or quite sharp and angular. The stratigraphic development of such forms is not simple and straightforward, but a matter of popularity in usage at a given time. The rounded profiles occur throughout, as do the angular forms, though a general tendency toward angularity increases and seems most common late in the Middle Bronze Age. (2) A related series of primarily neckless bowls, deep bowls, and kraters occurs (Dornemann [1979] figs. 21:1–3; 22:25–29; and figs. 4:13–15; 5:1–7; 8:6, 7; 9:2–10, 12, 13; 10:1, here). The variety and complication of rim profiles are a distinguishing feature, though there is some gradation between types, and the use of incised decoration occurs regularly. (3) The rim types, body proportions, and body shapes of the globular bowls just mentioned are separated with additional variations in larger vessels ranging in size to meter-tall storage jars (Dornemann [1979] fig. 21:26, 30, and figs. 6:1, 3–5; 10:3, 5, 6, here). Ribbed rims, ledge rims, and the feature of ribs beneath the rim are basic to the vessels. Decorative nicked ribs are more common than incised decoration.

(4) Open bowl forms are less frequent than the forms mentioned so far but there are isolated examples of a great variety of forms (Dornemann [1979] figs. 20:38–44; 22:12–18, 22; and fig. 3:1–7, here). The most common of these bowl forms is a medium-sized, open bowl which normally has a vertical side and rim, and often is also decorated with ribbed bands. (5) Tall elongated (oval in vertical cross-section), almost neckless jars (figs. 4:1–7; 8:4 and 9:1, here) with rounded or flattened bases occur, often with a hole pierced through the center. The rims can be simple, ribbed, or collared, but seldom with much in the way of overhang or projection. Both combed bands and ribbing on the shoulders are used as decoration. (6) Closed jar forms are common primarily as standard globular, often irregular or ovoid, large vessels with narrow necks (Dornemann [1979] fig. 22:7–11, 15; and figs. 3:19–29; 7; 8:1–3, 5, here) and flaring, folded-over rims (fig. 3:23, 25–29, and fig. 7, here). Toward the end of the Middle Bronze Age, after the tradition is well established, the rim often

shows a quite elaborate profile. Decoration is normally restricted to the area beneath the neck and occurs as single or multiple ribs or as incised decoration.

(7) Cooking pots occur primarily in two forms (a. Dornemann [1979] figs. 21:19, 23, 28; 22:37, 38; 23:1, and figs. 4:7–10, here; and b. Dornemann [1979] fig. 21:22, and fig. 4:11, here) in wares which are normally medium to lighter shades of brown. A simple, graceful, out-turned, usually thickened and rounded rim continues a tradition that was present from the beginning of the third millennium B.C. at Tell Hadidi. The folded-over form occurs infrequently in MB IIB and becomes more common later, but never as a predominant form. A third cooking pot type occurs in a cream-colored ware with shorter, out-turned rim, but is found primarily late in the Middle Bronze Age.

Two particularly distinctive forms occur only infrequently, but provide clear links with other sites. (8) Fenestrated, low heavy stands (fig. 11), and (9) tall heavy, decorated vases (figs. 3:9 and 12) seem to be among the most characteristic of the earliest Middle Bronze Age materials. Ribbed decoration, nicked-ring bases, and the feature of pierced bases are also distinctive (figs. 3:8; 4:3; 6:1–5, and 4:1, 2). Incised decoration is common on many of the vessels above, and we have included a selection of examples to illustrate the variety which exists throughout the Middle Bronze Age (fig. 13). The use of single or parallel bands of comb-incised decoration is clearly most common, and some forms utilize little other decoration. Three of the forms mentioned will, with equal frequency, be decorated with wavy incised lines alternating with or framed by such parallel lines. It is difficult, so far, to find a chronological significance to the occurrence of variations within the Middle Bronze Age.

The assemblage which we have defined above as characteristic of Middle Bronze IIB at Tell Hadidi is, in our estimation, contemporary with that of the Zimri Lim palace at Mari. The pottery published from the Mari palace seems to fall better within the MB IIB phase at Hadidi and may represent both close political and cultural connections in contrast to the more restricted parallels in the following periods between our Middle Bronze IIC and the "Khana Period" materials at Tell Ashara (partially presented in Dornemann [1979] fig. 23:9–46, and Kelley-Buccellati and Shelby [1977]). Though infrequent, specific parallels can be found at Tell Hadidi for all of the examples of burnished-neck jars (Parrot [1959] fig. 88, nos. 874, 908, 909, and our fig. 3:17, here) and the bowls with black-painted decoration and clear Old Babylonian, Mesopotamian associations (Parrot [1959] fig. 90). In general, the medium to large jars provide many features with excellent parallels at Hadidi in the stated time range: folded over, out-turned jar rims; simple, short rims; ribs beneath the rim; incised decoration; and disk bases. The combinations of features, however, resemble only some of the vessels found at Hadidi, and not the common forms. Of the vessels illustrated by Parrot (1959) fig. 87, no. 897 would be the closest to any of the Hadidi forms. Nos. 893 and 894 can be paralleled at Hadidi, but without the ring bases. The rims on nos. 895 and 886 have good parallels, but on vessels with more globular bodies. Body forms like 895 are usually neckless at Hadidi. No. 885 provides an illustration of a third-millennium form at both Mari and Hadidi.

All of the bowl forms illustrated by Parrot (1959: fig. 89) can be paralleled at Hadidi. No. 926 is a good early second millennium Hadidi form, while nos. 924, 925, and 927 are infrequent forms at Hadidi, but fit well at this point and do have very close parallels. No. 882 would be unusual for Hadidi on present evidence, so far as its proportions and base are concerned, but the form and rim have good parallels. The last three bowls with incurved rims have good parallels as well, but are most common in late Middle Bronze contexts, specifically MB IIC and continuing into LB I.

It is difficult to indicate a significance for the absence of certain vessel categories such as the carinated cups, globular jars, and globular deep bowls. This is even more the case with the category of storage jars, since excavation photographs indicate many such vessels were excavated, but none have been illustrated in profile drawing. Clearly the picture is incomplete, and it would seem that, despite the similarities, the variations define a local inventory with clear geographical and cultural boundaries.

The material published so far from Tell Asharah, only 70 kilometers north of Mari, illustrates the same specific and general conclusions. The tomb material from Baghouz, again not very far from Mari on the opposite bank, has been known for a long time, and has also been placed in the first half of the second millennium B.C. Though some vessels may belong toward the end of the Middle Bronze Age, the majority seem typologically earlier than the Hadidi materials mentioned so far.

As was the case at Hadidi, very little painted pottery, apparently, was found at Mari. Few pieces of the painted Khabur wares of Northeast Syria and Northern Iraq were found at Mari, and similarly, only a few sherds which could be related to these were found at Hadidi. Many parallels to the forms mentioned above from Mari and Hadidi were found at Nuzi, Tepe Gawra, and Ashur in the Assyrian heartland, indicating closer similarities between these areas than the northeast Syrian–Khabur area. The few painted sherds from Hadidi would seem, with one possible exception, to have their best parallels in the Amuq and on the Mediterranean coast.

Relatively little painted pottery was found at Hama or Tell Mardikh. The painted jug of the "Tomb of the Princess" at Mardikh is probably an import from the north Syrian coast (Matthiae [1980] 13). Most of the Hadidi painted sherds, the simple lattice painting on jugs, have better parallels at Ugarit than elsewhere (Schaeffer [1949] fig. 100) but like

Hama and Mardikh, the "Cilician" painted wares very common in the Amuq (Woolley [1955] pls. 84–85; 90–91; 97–98) are apparently not a component of the assemblages of other Syrian areas. Tell Atchana and Tell Judeideh have an extensive array of painted pottery which duplicates the materials from Tarsus, Mersin, and other Cilician-southeastern Anatolian sites. Though some of the simple decoration overlaps with the "Khabur ware" decoration, the "Cilician" painted decoration occurs on a wider variety of forms and has a higher percentage of vessels with finer and more elaborate decoration. These painted pottery traditions help define regional assemblages, but since similar painted decoration is not a part of the central Syrian or the Syrian Euphrates Valley tradition, we cannot take the time to explore them further here.

The basic central Syrian pottery assemblage is still best illustrated by the materials from Level H at Hama, and recently from the IIIA phase at Tell Mardikh, which Matthiae dates to the first half of the second millennium B.C. (Matthiae [1981] 111–12). Similarities with the Hadidi pottery, of course, are much greater, but significant differences also exist, even between Hama and Mardikh. Short, heavy, solid stands occur in H_3 at Hama (Fugmann [1958] fig. 120), as well as the tall, narrow, decorated stands in H_4 through H_1 (Fugmann [1958] figs. 117, 120, 124, 127), but are not yet illustrated among the Mardikh pottery forms. The carinated cups/bowls are common at all sites, but the preference in rim forms is not consistent between sites. Neckless or short-necked ovoid jars with incised decoration are rare at Hama (Fugmann [1958] figs. 110 and 120), and a few are illustrated at Mardikh (Matthiae [1981] fig. 35:15, 16). Mardikh provides a large number of jar rims like those on the Hadidi large globular jars (Fugmann [1958] fig. 35:1–14), but this form seems to be rare at Hama (Fugmann [1958] fig. 110). Hadidi deep bowls have better parallels at Mardikh (Matthiae [1981] figs. 34:8, and 36:2, 3, 6). Similarly, krater forms at Mardikh, though also very common at Hama, have their closest parallels in form and particularly in rim profiles at Hadidi (Matthiae [1981] figs. 36:4, 37:1–6, and 38:3). The krater rims illustrated at Mardikh are types which seem to occur both early and late in the Middle Bronze Age at Hadidi, though as at Hama, the later Hadidi forms seem to be more common (Fugmann [1958] figs. 110, 127, 132 and 139). Inturned bowl rims occur at Mardikh and from H_4 on at Hama. A distinctive low, carinated bowl with rounded C-profile rim is common at Mardikh (Matthiae [1981] figs. 33:1–8, and 34:4, 5 and 7) and occurs in the H silos and H_4 at Hama (Fugmann [1958] 109, 110, and 124). Such rims are not attested at Hadidi, and only a few examples occur at Tell Judeideh.

Our evidence for the Middle Bronze Age pottery tradition of the seacoast is extremely limited. Only Tell Judeideh, somewhat farther inland, provides a basic sequence. We have already mentioned the "Cilician" painted pottery of the Amuq, and the range of pottery forms is restricted. The larger forms are primarily kraters and smaller storage jars. Ribbed rims and incised decoration are common and are the closest to the decorative practice at Hadidi of any of the sites mentioned so far. A development can be seen on the rims of these vessels, where ribbing is very common, which basically divides with the step divisions for TT-20 at Judeideh. The general appearance and proportions of MB pottery consistently stand out in contrast to Early Bronze Age and Late Bronze Age wares as a broad-ranging phenomenon, but each assemblage is stamped with such local individuality that the sequence of periods must be seen primarily on the basis of parallel developments rather than continuous, consistent, "universal" changes. A quick glance at a selection of Early Bronze Age pottery vessels from Mari (Parrot [1956] figs. 100, 101, 106, and 107) and Tell Hadidi (Dornemann [1979] figs. 12–19:6) demonstrates the great changes which occurred between the Early Bronze Age and the Middle Bronze Age, when these vessels are compared with the Middle Bronze Age materials we are discussing.

A search for transitional phases between the Early Bronze Age and Middle Bronze Age traditions has yielded limited evidence, either in central or coastal Syria, or in the south Syrian Euphrates area at Mari. We anxiously await ceramic materials from the post-Ur III through Yaḫdun Lim levels at Mari to illuminate this problem and to help to fix the position of the earliest Middle Bronze materials at Hadidi and other Euphrates Valley sites such as Halawa, Sweihat, Habuba, and Mumbaqat. Early Bronze Age carry-over forms are not common at Hama or Mardikh. A few distinctive bowl rim and narrow-necked jar rim profiles provide the majority of these forms, and if transitional layers from the beginning of the Middle Bronze Age exist at these sites, the evidence is not available in published form.

Though our discussion has ranged to many sites, we have confined it primarily to materials contemporary with our MB IIB phase at Hadidi with the characteristic components outlined at the beginning of the paper. We would now like to turn briefly to those materials which were found in earlier MB layers at Hadidi and nearby sites. Pottery from the earliest floors, clay platforms, and associated with the lowest Middle Bronze wall foundations (fig. 2) clearly show earlier stages in the MB tradition. Many of the changes are quite subtle or changes of degree, but, as more material has become available, it has taken on a specific character of its own, and we feel more confident in assigning a specific designation of MB IIA to this material. Winfried Orthmann's recent publication of the Halawa excavations (Orthmann [1983]) provides excellent parallel material to the Hadidi MB IIB, and we need not repeat his citations of our 1979 AASOR article. Orthmann indicates that the Halawa level 2b–c materials are somewhat earlier than those illustrated in our AASOR report. The pottery mentioned earlier, from the stone pavements in Area B, represents an earlier phase of MB IIB. We would consider it as more closely parallel to the Halawa 2b–c pottery, and tentatively date it to the beginning of MB IIB.

Little new seems to have been produced in MB IIB which had not been present earlier, and most forms occurred already in the earliest MB layers. There are noticeable variations in the rims, but it is not clear how significant all of these variations are. As an example, grooves on the rim were formed differently on most of the early rims (figs. 18:14–16; 19:1–3, compared to figs. 5:1, 3, 5, 11; 6:2–5), possibly with a sharper tool than later, and the later rims are decorated so that the profile shows freer, more evenly modeled curves. In general, the rims are more block-like than later, the angles and curves more restricted, and the ribs and depressions create minimal relief. With the developments into the MB IIB tradition, the potters demonstrate an increasing confidence in their medium. The shape of the rims can be quite delicate and the vessel thickness increasingly thin and refined for larger vessels. In this respect, the Halawa materials provide basically developed stages for particular forms and provide a bridge between the MB IIA and MB IIB periods. It seems that the developments between layers at the Euphrates Valley sites, as well as at Mardikh, Hama, and Judeideh, are not parallel and consistent.

There is no indication that any of the sites mentioned so far were first occupied at precisely the same time as part of a massive event. Rather, changes from level to level do not seem to coincide. Each site had its own history, and though the general period developments follow pretty well from site to site, they are not necessarily contemporary. Local factors determine the temporal duration of specific features, whether they are preserved for any length of time or die quickly.

Some of the forms at Halawa are clearly a continuation of Early Bronze Age forms. Such forms do not occur with the Hadidi MB IIB pottery assemblage described from the start, but they do occur with our MB IIA. The same is true at Hama, where ribbed, vertical-rim bowls and cup forms in particular continue (Fugmann [1956] fig. 109:3B964, 3C710, and 3B988), possibly as "fossil" forms in a basically new Middle Bronze tradition. It seems that in the lowest Middle Bronze layers in Areas B and F at Hadidi and Areas I, III, and IV at Tell Sweihat we have a still earlier, poorly documented, and possibly quite brief phase, which we are tentatively designating MB I for the sake of discussion (Holland [1977] figs. 2, 3, 5–7). The characteristics are a mixture of Early Bronze and Middle Bronze features. Early Bronze Age rim forms occur in non-typical varieties on wares which are new and either in the Middle Bronze tradition or developing toward it, as the illustrations on fig. 20 show: variations of the common Early Bronze folded-over, incurved bowl rims, interior beveled and pointed cup rims on short cup forms, ribbed rims on vertical-sided bowls, ribbed shoulders on narrow-necked jars, specific developments on the larger Early Bronze jar rims, etc. The first vessels made in the Middle Bronze tradition begin to appear: ribbed rims on the horizontal tops of medium-sized, open bowls with sides curved up to a vertical stance, ribbed jar rims, and neck-ridged, globular jars with simple out-turned, rounded rims.

Much needs to be done to articulate these early phases of the Middle Bronze tradition fully, and we have only tried to highlight some of the features and problems. Hopefully, the important sequence of cultural materials at Mari will come to our aid in articulating the features of the formative phases of the Middle Bronze Age. Our preliminary comparisons indicate that, though some details differ, the basic features demonstrate closer contacts for the pottery tradition in the Euphrates Valley, stretching at least from Mari to Azu during the first quarter of the second millennium B.C., than for contacts with the pottery traditions of other adjacent cultural spheres.

In conclusion, we want to shift briefly from pottery profiles to something of greater general interest because it provides a glimpse into the artistic styles of the areas under discussion. Though Mari provides a good selection of plaque-made clay figurines, they are clearly minor to the great monuments of artistic achievement which were excavated on the site. At Hadidi we have to be content with the former as the best we can illustrate for the artistic production available at the site (Dornemann [1979] fig. 28).

The most elaborate Middle Bronze Age plaque found at Hadidi (Dornemann [1978]: 25 and fig. 21 here) is a ceremonial scene which has so many stylistic features in common with the famous investiture scene from Room 106 of Zimri Lim's palace at Mari (Parrot [1958] pls. VIII–XIII and A), that it must be attributed to the same period and be contemporary with the MB IIB pottery we have been discussing. A quick glance at the stance of the figures, their robes, hats, and beards reveals a striking similarity. The ceremonies are different, but Mari plaques provide parallels to the Hadidi ceremony. Actually, the Hadidi scene seems to be a conflation of two distinct themes at Mari. Unfortunately the lower half of the Hadidi plaque is missing so we cannot tell how the two themes were integrated on that part of the plaque.

In one scene (Parrot [1958] fig. 57 and pl. XXX), two divinities (called a divine couple in the Mari publication) wearing horned headdresses stand in profile on *podia*. They both hold a standard in two hands. The standard is identical with the one on the Hadidi plaque, with a crescent supporting a sun disk. The shaft of the symbol is different, but the depiction of the disk as an eight-spoked wheel with dots interspersed between the spokes seems to be identical. The Mari symbol rests on the back of a lion, but the Hadidi symbol probably did not. Instead, the remainder of the central portion of the scene is illustrated on another group of Mari plaques (Parrot [1958] fig. 58 and pl. XXIX:1506), a beer-drinking scene. The opposing figures wear long robes and hold drinking straws in one hand. The straws extend down into a small jar on a stand. From this point, the details differ. The faces in the Mari plaque are in front view and not well represented either in the impressions or in the care taken while making the mold. At Mari, the hands cross the bodies to grasp the straws, while at Hadidi the hands on the inside grasp the straws, and the other hands, though this is not very clear in the impression, are apparently raised in an attitude of salute or swearing an oath with palms vertical and toward the other person. The hats or helmets do not look the same but may have been intended to be more similar than they look. The Hadidi drinking vessel seems to be more of a storage jar in size, though only a portion of the top of the rim is preserved. It would seem that two long heads of grain flank the standard shaft at the rim of the storage jar. It is possible that the edge of the garment is represented, rather than ears of grain, but we tentatively favor the interpretation of grain, possibly representing the barley used to brew beer.

It is hard to tell from the Hadidi impression whether the garments of the two men were identical, but they seem to represent fringed shawls such as the ones represented in the investiture scene, rather than the garments represented on the Mari plaques. The shawl seems to be wound around the body and held in one hand, as it is in the investiture scene. The tassel at the back in both scenes may come down from the headdress. The headdresses are identical in proportions; the width of the border at the base and the use of a doubled edging line over the top are similar.

Comparing a number of nearly similar headdresses shown on the Mari murals, the proportions of the Hadidi headdresses most resemble the ones worn by the main royal figures. A simple hat of similar proportions is common on Mari plaques (Parrot [1958] fig. 54 and pl. XXVIII) and may illustrate a long tradition represented by hand-made figurines in the Early Bronze Age at both Mari and Hadidi. Bracelets are shown on all the figures mentioned, but how similar the necklaces are is uncertain because only a portion are represented on the Hadidi figures.

It seems that the small plaque from Hadidi represents a royal ceremony which is performed before the symbol of a god and solemnized by sharing a drink from the same vessel. Though the medium is prosaic and the depiction on a small scale, the artistic style seems quite polished and a reflection of the artistic tradition which produced the palace murals at Mari. I will close with a question to the philologists: Is there evidence in the rich textual materials from Mari which would document and explain a ritual which includes the communal drinking of beer?

Figure 1. General view of Middle Bronze II architectural remains in Area B at end of 1976 season (photo taken from southwest).

Figure 2. Removing earliest second millennium floors, walls, and foundations in Area BII in 1977 season (photo taken from northeast).

Figure 3

Figure	Area Locus.Basket	Size Ht/Dia	Clay Firing	Inclusions			Ware Color	Surface Color In	Surface Color Out
3:1	BI	20/129	m	sand	m	F M	5YR7/6	2.5Y7/4	2.5Y7/4
	40C.140			straw	lt	F	r y	p y	p y
3:2	BI	31/262	m	sand	m	F M	5YR6/6	10YR8/3	7.5YR7/4
	48.113			straw	lt	F	r y	v p b	pk
3:3	BIV	38/310	m	sand	m	F M	7.5YR6/4	10YR7/3	10YR7/4
	105.207			straw	lt	F	lt b	v p b	v p b
3:4	BIV	30/195	m	sand	lt	F MF	5YR6/6	10YR8/4	10YR8/3
	105.207			straw	lt	F	r y	v p b	v p b
3:5	BI	17/250	m	sand	lt	F MF	10YR8/3	10YR8/3	10YR8/3
	48.113			straw	lt	M	v p b	v p b	v p b
3:6	BI	35/230	m	sand	m	F MF	7.5YR7/4	7.5YR7/4	10YR7/3
	48.113			straw	lt	F	pk	pk	v p b
				limestone	v	L			
3:7	BI	70/420	m	sand	lt	F	5YR6/6	5YR6/6	5YR7/4
	48.113			straw	lt	F	r y	r y	pk
3:8[a]	BI	46/114	m	sand	lt	F M	2.5Y7/4	10YR8/3	5Y8/3
	48.113			quartz	lt	L	p y	v p b	p y
				straw	lt	F M			
				chalk	v	L			
3:9	BXV	76/144	m	sand	m	F MF	2.5YR6/8	10YR7/3	2.5Y8/2
	49.113			straw	lt	F	lt r	v p b	w
3:10	BI	143/76	m	sand	m	F M	5Y7/3	5Y7/3	5Y7/3
	47.105			straw	m	F	p y	p y	p y
3:11	BI	45/80	m	sand	m	F	7.5YR7/4	10YR8/3	10YR7/3
	40C.148			straw	lt	F	pk	v p b	v p b
3:12	BIV	28/186	m	sand	h	F	7.5YR7/4	10YR8/3	2.5Y8/2
	105.207			straw	m	F M	pk	v p b	w
				chalk	v	L			
				limestone	v	L			
3:13	BIV	21/100	m	sand	m	F MF	5YR7/6	5YR7/6	7.5YR7/4
	105.207			straw	m	F	r y	r y	pk
3:14	BI	38/80	m	sand	h	F MF	2.5Y8/2	2.5Y7/4	2.5Y8/2
	49.106			straw	lt	F	w	p y	w
3:15	BIV	20/40	m	sand	lt	MF	7.5YR6/4	7/5YR7/4	2.5Y8/2
	105.207			straw	lt	F	lt b	pk	w
3:16	BI	67/140	m	sand	h	F	10YR8/4	10YR8/4	10YR8/4
	46.100			straw	lt	F M	v p b	v p b	v p b
3:17[b]	BX	170/84	m	sand	h	F	2.5Y7/2	2.5Y7/2	2.5Y7/2
	16.48						lt gy	lt gy	lt gy
3:18	BI	120/200	m	sand	m	MF	10YR7/3	2.5Y8/2	5Y7/3
	48.113			straw	lt	F	v p b	w	p y
				limestone	v	L			

[*Caption continued on p. 94*]

Surface Treatment: [a]nicked ring base; [b]neck (out) burnished

Abbreviations used in figure captions

		Inclusions			
Firing	Concentration	Size	Color		
m=medium	h=high	F=fine	b=brown	ol=olive	v=very
mh=medium-high	m=medium	MF=medium-fine	d=dark	p=pale	w=white
h=high	lt=light	M=medium	gy=gray	pk=pink	y=yellow
o=overfired	v=very light	L=large	lt=light	r=red	

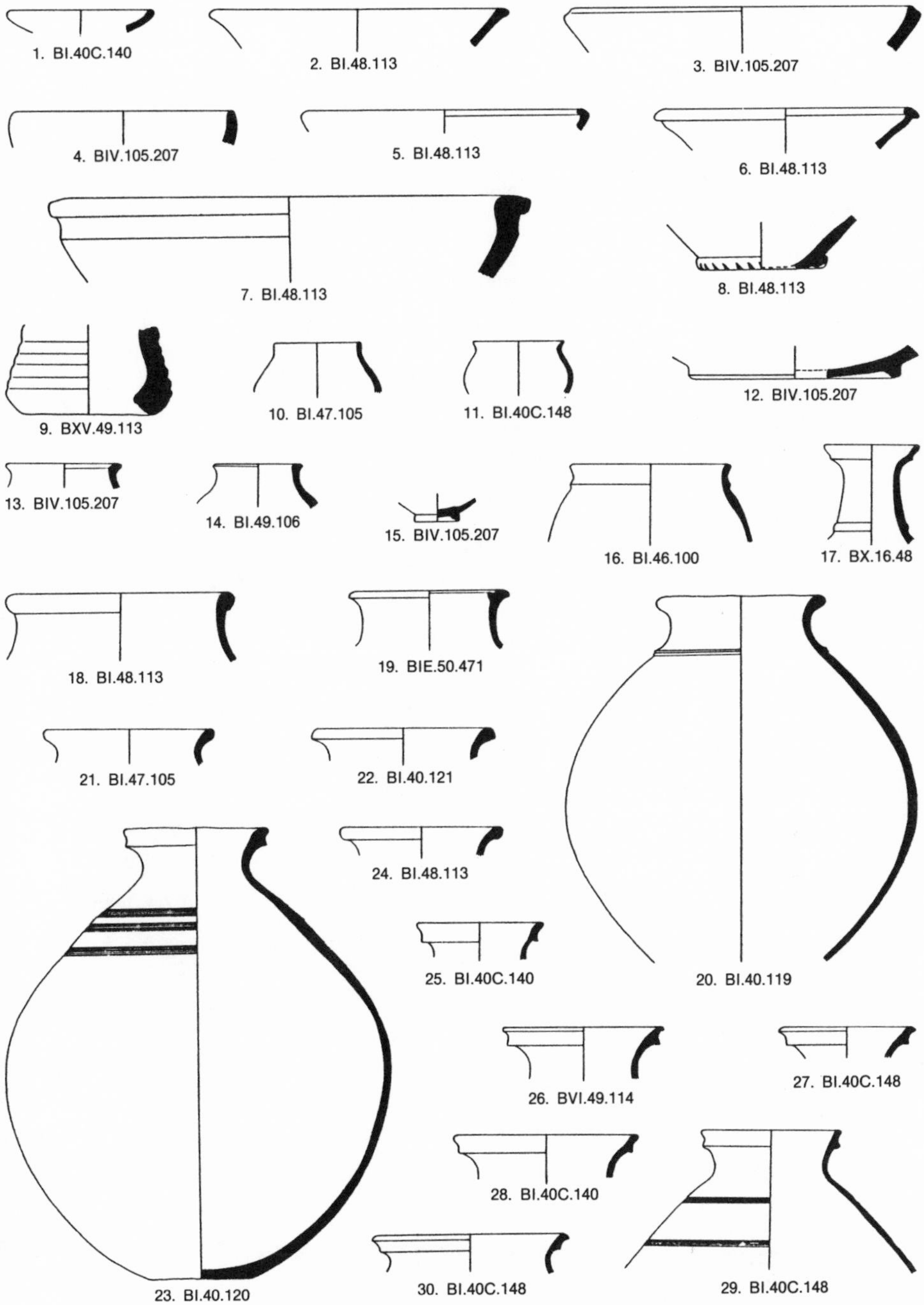

Figure 3. Middle Bronze IIB bowls, cups, and narrow-necked jars.

Figure 4

Figure	Area Locus.Basket	Size Ht/Dia	Clay Firing	Inclusions			Ware Color	Surface Color In	Surface Color Out
4:1[a]	BI	374/135	m	sand	m	F MF	7.5YR6/4	7.5YR7/4	5Y8/3
	40B.142			straw	lt	F	lt b	pk	p y
4:2[a]	BIV	126/160	m	sand	h	F	7.5YR7/6	7.5YR7/6	5Y8/3
	105.207			straw	lt	F	r y	r y	p y
4:3	BI	91/85	m	sand	lt	F MF	5YR6/6	2.5YR5/8	5YR6/6
	50.435			straw	lt	F	r y	r	r y
4:4	BIV	90/142	m	sand	m	F MF	5YR6/6	7.5YR7/4	10YR6/4
	105.210			straw	m	F	r y	pk	lt y b
4:5[a]	BIE	142/180	m	sand	h	F MF	7.5YR7/4	7.5YR8/4	5Y8/3
	50.465			straw	m	F	pk	pk	p y
4:6	BI	32/203	m	sand	m	F MF	5Y8/3	2.5Y8/4	5Y8/3
	50.437			straw	lt	F	p y	p y	p y
4:7	BIV	46/260	m	quartz	m	M L	7.5YR6/4	10YR7/3	10YR7/4
	105.210			straw	lt	F	lt b	v p b	v p b
4:8	BI	35/260	m	sand	h	F MF	2.5Y7/2	5Y8/2	5Y7/2
	40C.140			straw	h	F M	lt gy	w	lt gy
				quartz	v	L			
4:9	BIV	56/310	m	sand	h	F	5YR7/6	7.5YR7/6	5Y8/3
	105.180			straw	h	F M	r y	r y	p y
				quartz	m	M L			
4:10	BI	50/223	m	sand	h	F MF	7.5YR6/4	7.5YR7/4	5Y8/2
	50.433			straw	m	F	lt b	pk	w
				quartz	lt	m			
				quartz	v	L			
4:11	BI	30/266	m	sand	lt	F	5YR6/6	10YR7/3	10YR8/3
	48.113			straw	lt	F	r y	v p b	v p b
4:12[a]	BI	50/236	m	sand	lt	F M	10YR5/2	2.5Y6/2	2.5Y7/2
	48.113			straw	lt	F	gy b	lt b gy	lt gy
4:13	BIV	47/184	m	sand	h	F MF	7.5YR7/4	10YR7/3	2.5Y8/2
	105.207			straw	m	F M	pk	v p b	w
4:14[a]	BIE	78/211	m	sand	m	F MF	10YR7/4	2.5Y8/2	2.5Y8/2
	50.469			straw	m	F M	v p b	w	w
				quartz	v	L			
4:15	BIV	40/221	m	sand	m	F	7.5YR7/6	7.5YR7/4	10YR8/3
	105.207			straw	lt	F	r y	r y	v p b

Surface Treatment: [a]comb-incised decoration.

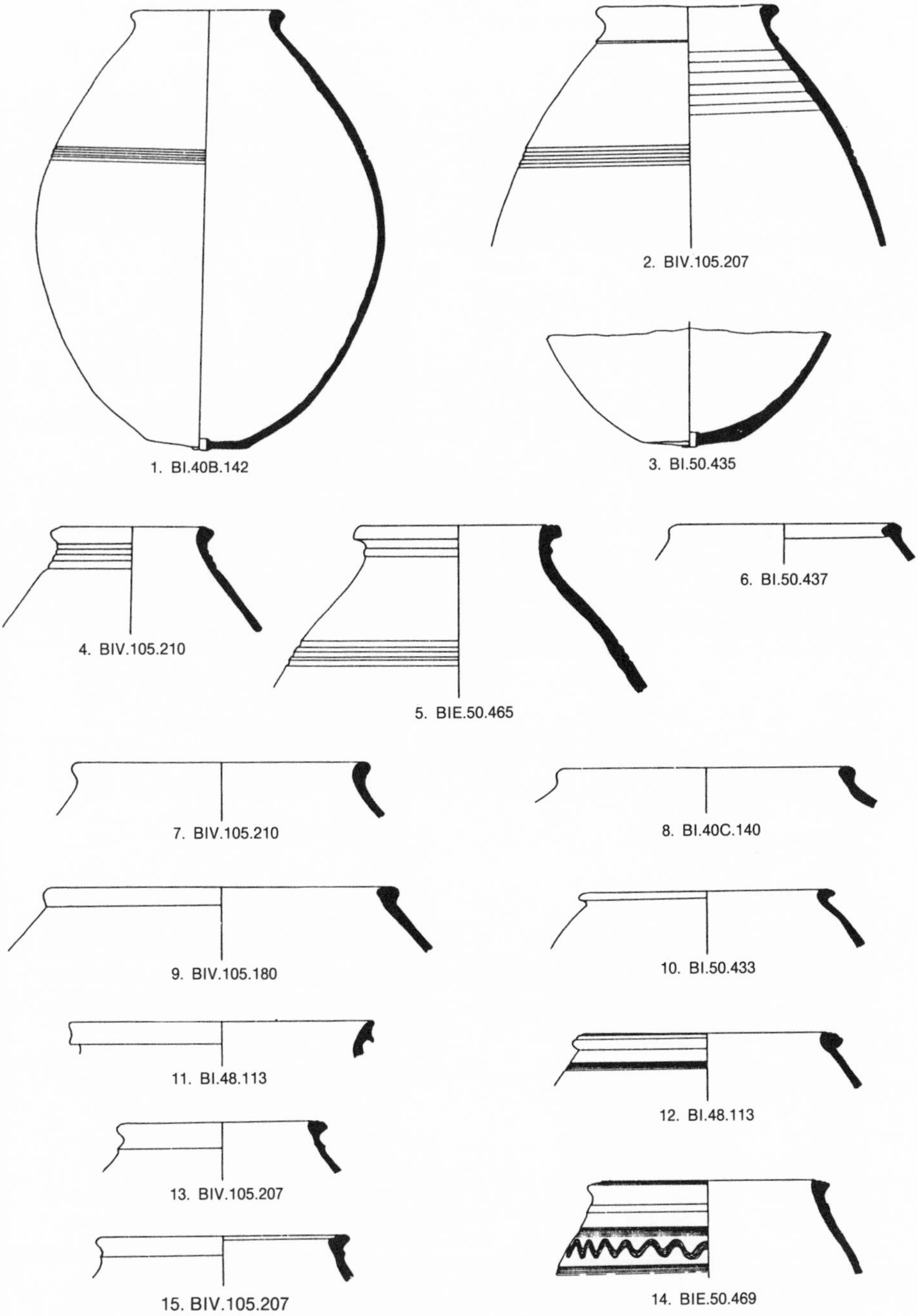

Figure 4. Middle Bronze IIB jars and cooking pots.

Figure 5

Figure	Area Locus.Basket	Size Ht/Dia	Clay Firing	Inclusions			Ware Color	Surface Color In	Surface Color Out
5:1[a]	BIV	127/230	m	sand	h	F M	10YR6/2	2.5Y7/2	2.5Y7/2
	105.187			straw	lt	F M	lt b gy	lt gy	lt gy
5:2	BIV	45/301	m	sand	h	F	7.5YR7/6	10YR8/4	10YR8/3
	105.180			straw	lt	F M	r y	v p b	v p b
5:3[b]	BI	273/250	o	sand	m	F MF	2.5Y7/4	2.5Y7/2	5Y7/3
	40.120			straw	lt	F	p y	lt gy	p y
				chalk	v	L			
5:4[a]	BIV	241/178	m	sand	m	F	7.5YR6/4	7.5YR7/4	10YR7/4
	105.216			straw	lt	F	lt b	pk	v p b
5:5	BIV	80/145	m	sand	h	F MF	5Y7/2	5Y7/3	5Y8/2
	105.216			straw	m	F M	lt gy	p y	w
				sand	v	L			
5:6[a]	BIV	145/293	m	sand	h	F M	2.5Y7/2	5Y7/2	5Y7/3
	105.180			straw	m	F M	lt gy	w	p y
5:7	BIE	30/178	m	sand	m	F MF	10YR7/3	10YR7/2	2.5Y8/2
	50.468			straw	lt	F	v p b	lt gy	w
5:8	BI	140/278	m	sand	h	F M	10YR8/3	2.5Y7/4	2.5Y8/4
	33B.153			straw	m	F M	lt b gy	p y	p y
				sand	v	L			
5:9[c]	BI	56/372	m	sand	h	F M	7.5YR7/4	5Y8/3	5Y8/3
	1+Fall.400			straw	m	F	pk	p y	p y
5:10	BI	71/465	m	sand	h	F	5YR6/6	5Y7/6	2.5Y8/2
	33B.153			straw	m	F M	r y	y	w
5:11[c]	BIE	85/528	m	sand	h	F MF	10YR7/1	5Y7/3	5Y7/3
	50.468			straw	m	F	lt gy	p y	p y

Surface Treatment: [a]comb-incised decoration; [b]comb-incised decoration impressed string decoration; [c]nicked-rib decoration.

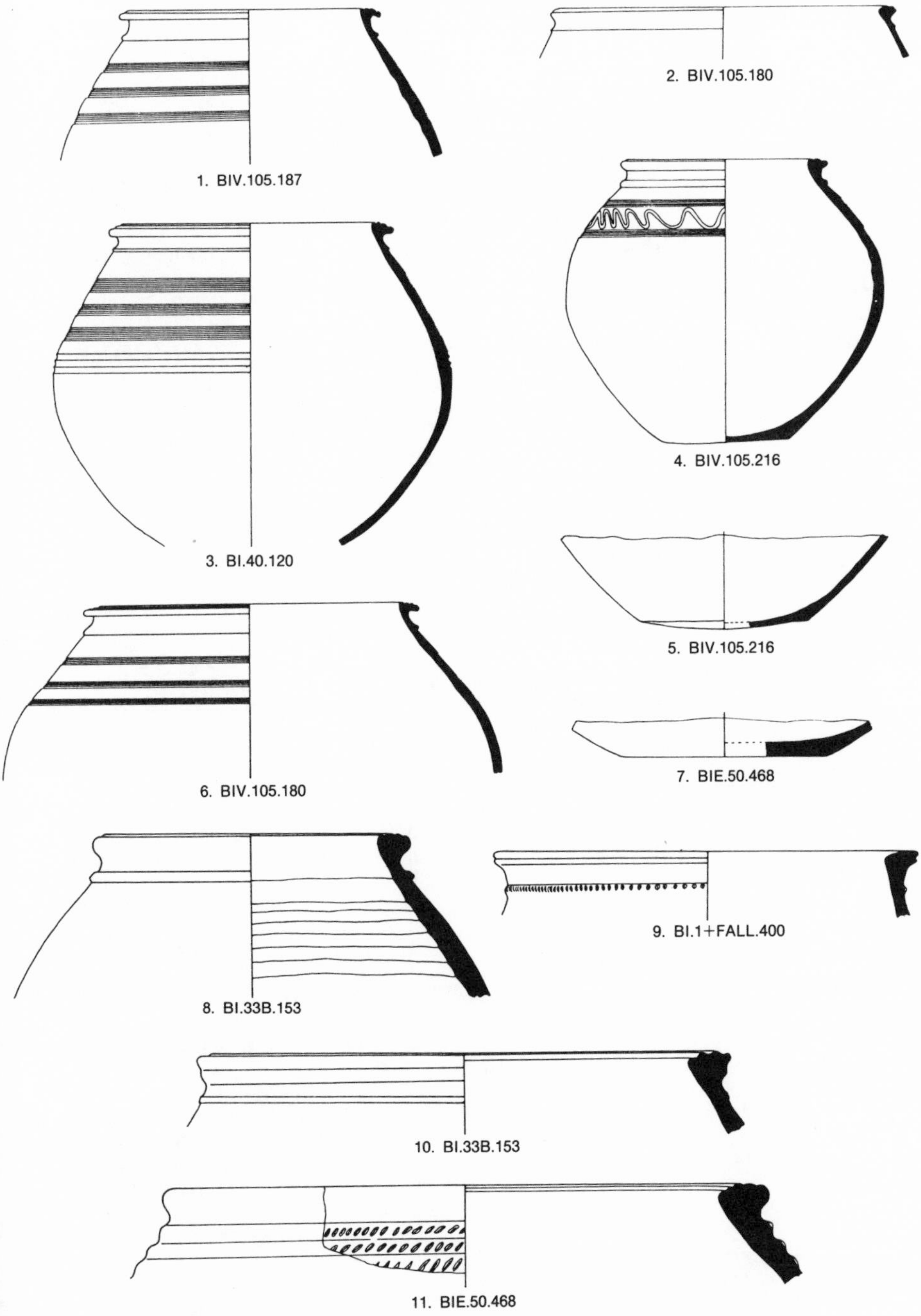

Figure 5. Middle Bronze IIB medium-sized jars, bases, and large storage jars.

Figure 6

Figure	Area Locus.Basket	Size Ht/Dia	Clay Firing	Inclusions			Ware Color	Surface Color In	Surface Color Out
6:1[a]	BIV	205/370	m	sand	lt	F	5YR6/3	7.5YR7/4	10YR7/3
	105.216			straw	lt	F M	lt r b	pk	v p b
6:2[b]	BI	141/530	m	sand	h	F MF	7.5YR3/2	10YR7/3	7.5YR7/4
	33B.153			straw	h	F	d b	v p b	pk
				sand	v	L			
6:3	BIE	68/518	m	sand	m	F MF	10YR6/1	10YR6/2	5Y7/2
	50.465			straw	lt	F M	gy	lt b gy	lt gy
6:4[b]	BI	300/540	m	sand	m	F MF	2.5YR7/4	5Y8/3	2.5Y8/2
	50.435			straw	lt	F	p y	p y	w
6:5	BI	91/520	m	sand	h	F MF	2.5Y6/2	2.5Y7/4	5Y7/3
	33B.153			straw	m	F	lt b gy	p y	p y

Surface Treatment: [a]incised decoration, nicked-rib decoration; [b]nicked-rib decoration.

Figure 3 (cont. from p. 88)

Figure	Area Locus.Basket	Size Ht/Dia	Clay Firing	Inclusions			Ware Color	Surface Color In	Surface Color Out
3:19	BIE	102/138	m	sand	lt	F MF	10YR6/4	7.5YR7/4	5Y8/3
	50.471			straw	lt	F M	lt y b	pk	p y
3:20	BI	310/148	m	sand	h	F MF	7.5YR7/4	10YR7/3	2.5Y7/2
	40.119			straw	lt	F	pk	v p b	lt gy
3:21	BI	30/148	m	sand	lt	MF	10YR7/2	2.5Y7/2	2.5Y7/2
	47.105			straw	lt	F	lt gy	lt gy	lt gy
3:22	BI	26/160	m	sand	lt	MF M	7.5YR7/6	10YR8/3	2.5Y8/4
	40.121			straw	lt	F	r y	v p b	p y
3:23[c]	BI	383/127	m	sand	m	F M	10YR7/3	10YR7/3	2.5Y7/2
	40.120			straw	m	F M	v p b	v p b	lt gy
3:24	BI	24/140	m	sand	h	F MF	7.5YR6/4	2.5Y8/2	2.5Y8/2
	48.113			straw	lt	F	lt b	w	w
3:25	BI	32/110	mh	sand	h	F MF	10YR7/3	5Y8/3	5Y8/3
	40C.140						v p b	p y	p y
3:26	BIV	44/141	m	sand	m	F	2.5Y7/4	5Y8/3	5Y8/3
	49.114			straw	lt	F	r y	v p b	pk
3:28	BI	37/160	m	sand	h	F MF	5Y6/2	2.5Y7/2	2.5Y7/2
	40C.140			straw	m	F	lt ol gy	lt gy	lt gy
				sand	v	L			
3:29[c]	BI	122/122	m	sand	m	F MF	10YR8/3	5Y8/3	5Y7/2
	40C.148			straw	m	F	v p b	p y	lt gy
3:30	BI	70/172	m	sand	lt	MF	7.5YR7/4	5Y8/3	5Y8/3
	40C.148			straw	lt	F	pk	p y	p y

Surface Treatment: [c]comb-incised decoration

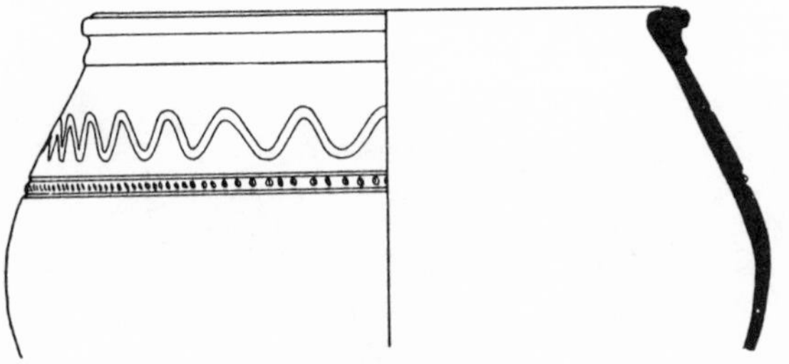

1. BIV.105.216

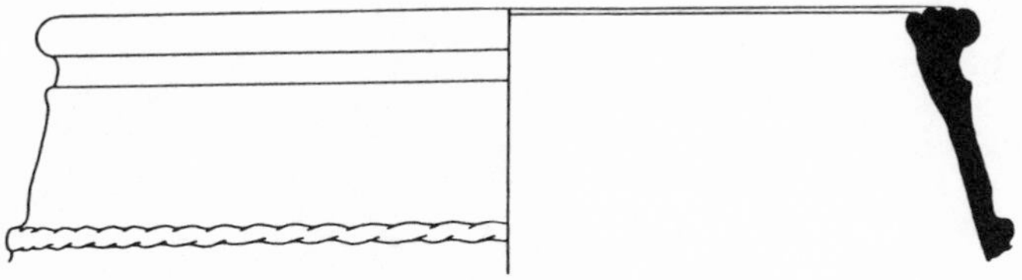

2. BI.33B.153

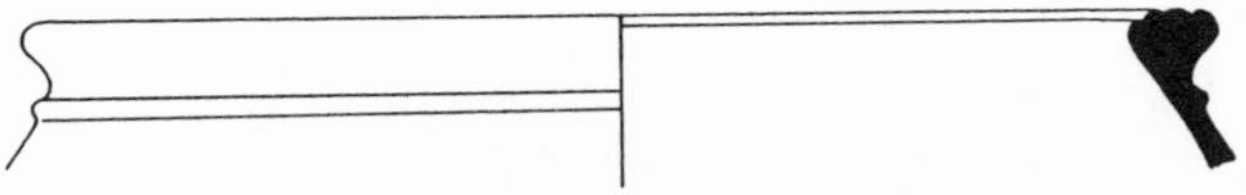

3. BIE.50.465

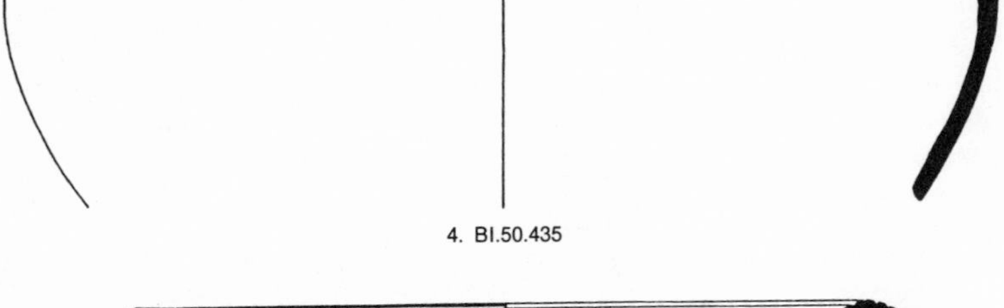

4. BI.50.435

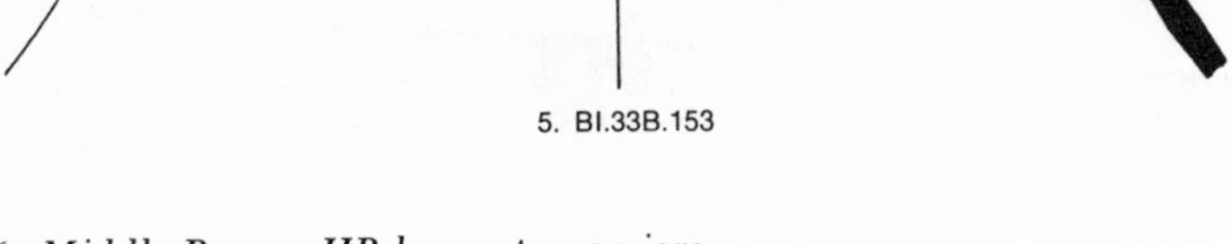

5. BI.33B.153

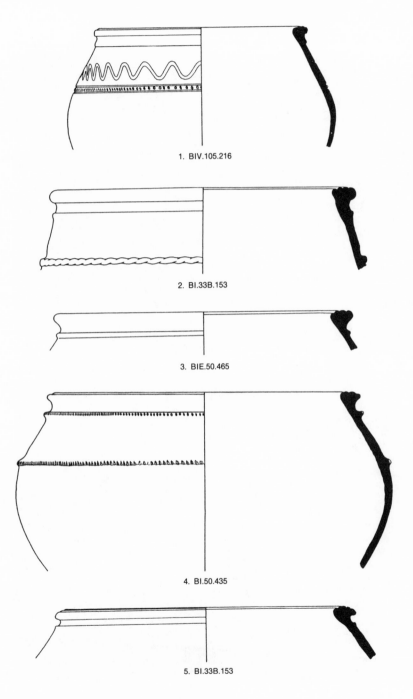

Figure 6. Middle Bronze IIB large storage jars.

Figure 7. Globular, narrow-necked jar from BVI.95.171.

Figure 8. Globular jar and elongated, neckless jar sherds.

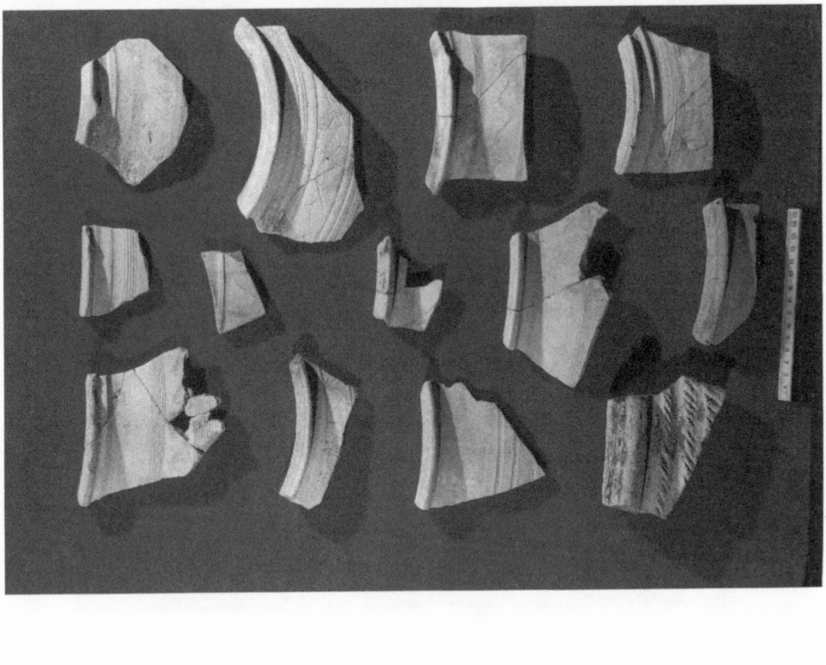

Figure 9. Neckless jar rims and one storage jar rim.

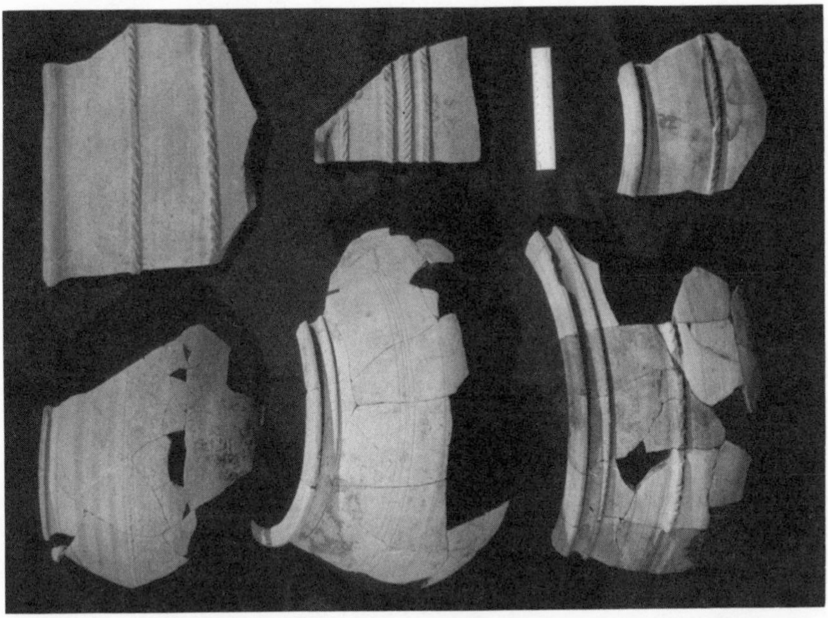

Figure 10. Krater and storage jar sherds.

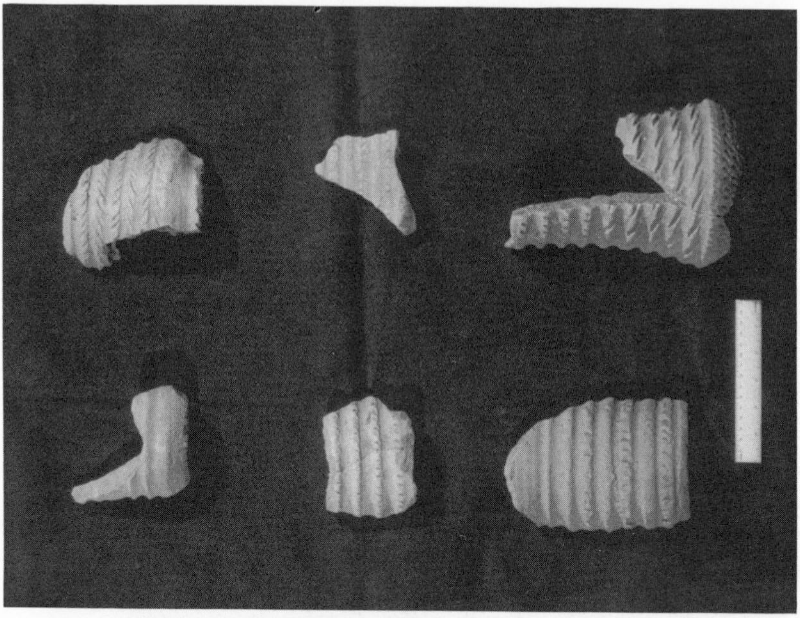

Figure 12. Tall vases with incised decoration.

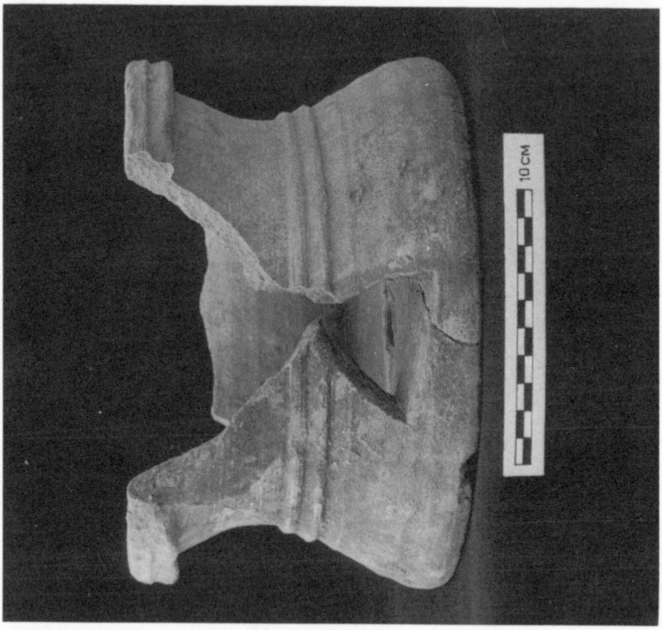

Figure 11. Heavy fenestrated jar stand.

Figure 14. Selection of Middle Bronze Age painted sherds.

Figure 13. Selection of incised body sherds and rims with incised decoration.

Figure 15

Figure	Area Locus.Basket	Size Ht/Dia	Clay Firing	Inclusions			Ware Color	Surface Color In	Surface Color Out
15:1	BI	35/155	h	sand	m	F	7.5YR7/4	5Y8/3	5Y8/3
	51.158			straw	lt	F	pk	p y	p y
15:2	BI-IV	20/170	m	sand	m	F M	5YR7/6	5YR7/6	10YR8/4
	128C.544			straw	lt	F	r y	r y	v p b
15:3	BI	20/210	m	sand	m	F M	10YR6/2	10YR6/2	10YR6/3
	53.112			straw	lt	F	lt b gy	lt b gy	p b
15:4[a]	BI	26/120	m	sand	m	F	5YR6/6	2.5Y8/2	2.5Y8/2
	445.581						r y	w	w
15:5	BI-IV	23/162	m	sand	h	F	7.5YR7/4	2.5Y8/2	2.5Y8/2
	128C.544			straw	lt	F	pk	w	w
15:6	BI	35/210	m	sand	m	F	5YR7/6	5YR7/6	7.5YR8/4
	51.110						r y	r y	pk
15:7	BI	25/200	h	sand	m	F M	7.5YR7/4	2.5Y8/2	5YR7/6
	52A.132			straw	lt	F	pk	w	r y
15:8	BI	30/90	m	sand	h	MF	10YR7/3	10YR7/3	2.5Y7/2
	55.131			straw	lt	F	v p b	v p b	lt gy
15:9	BI-II	97/95	m	-	-	-	-	-	5Y7/3
	406D.441								p y
15:10	BI	10/100	m	sand	m	MF	7.5YR7/4	2.5Y8/2	2.5Y8/2
	51A.162			straw	lt	F	pk	w	w
15:11	BIV	60/130	m	sand	m	F	5YR6/6	5YR6/6	10YR8/3
	422.494			straw	lt	F	r y	r y	v p b
15:12	BI	30/120	h	sand	lt	F	7.5YR7/6	10YR8/3	2.5Y8/2
	51.139						r y	v p b	w
15:13[b]	BI	55/150	m	sand	h	MF	10YR7/4	10YR7/2	2.5Y7/2
	448D.754						v p b	lt gy	lt gy
15:14	BIV	20/35	h	sand	m	MF	10YR7/3	10YR8/3	10YR8/3
	155.252			limestone	v	M	v p b	v p b	v p b
15:15	BI	40/35	m	sand	m	MF	5YR7/6	5YR7/6	5YR7/6
	59.88						r y	r y	r y
15:16	BI	20/140	m	sand	lt	F	5YR7/6	10YR8/4	7.5YR7/8
	40E.157			straw	lt	F	r y	v p b	r y
15:17[b]	BIV	55/120	o	sand	h	MF	5Y7/3	5Y7/3	5Y7/3
	155.252			straw	lt	F	p y	p y	p y
15:18[b]	BI	177/158	h	sand	lt	F M	7.5YR7/2	5Y8/3	2.5Y8/2
	51.110			straw	lt	F	pk gy	p y	w
15:19	BI	25/130	m	sand	h	F M	10YR7/2	10YR7/2	10YR7/2
	59.88			straw	lt	F	lt gy	lt gy	lt gy
15:20	BI	35/160	m	sand	m	F	5YR7/6	10YR8/3	10YR8/3
	462C.633						r y	v p b	v p b
15:21	BI	13/132	m	quartz	m	L	7.5YR7/6	7.5YR7/6	5YR6/6
	51A.162			straw	m	M	r y	r y	r y
15:22	BIV	40/410	m	straw	h	F	7.5YR5/4	10YR5/2	10YR7/3
	424.501			sand	m	F	b	gy b	v p b
				quartz	m	M L			
15:23[c]	BI	35/330	m	sand	m	F M	10YR6/2	10YR7/3	2.5Y8/2
	55.131			straw	lt	F	lt b gy	v p b	w
15:24	BI	30/330	m	sand	h	F	2.5Y6/2	5Y7/2	5Y7/3
	446C.575						lt b gy	lt gy	p y
15:25	BI	60/420	h	sand	m	M	5YR5/3	2.5Y8/2	2.5Y7/2
	40E.160			straw	m	F	r b	lt gy	lt gy
				chalk	v	L			

[Caption continued on p. 106]

Surface Treatment: [a]nicked rim [b]comb-incised decoration [c]possible slip

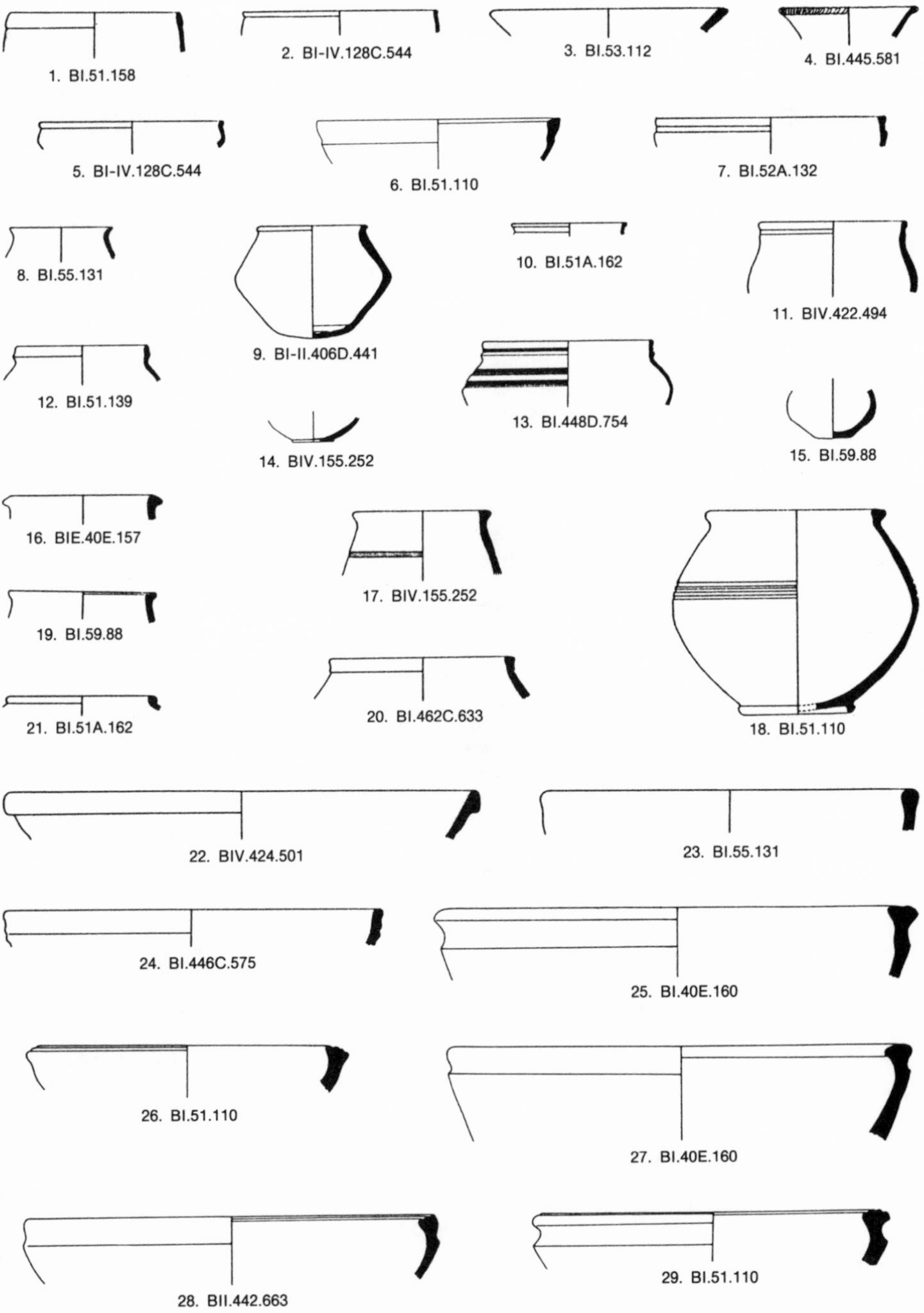

Figure 15. Middle Bronze IIA bowls and cups.

Figure 16

Figure	Area Locus.Basket	Size Ht/Dia	Clay Firing	Inclusions			Ware Color	Surface Color In	Surface Color Out
16:1	BI-II	120/420	m	sand	m	F M	5YR6/6	7.5YR6/4	2.5Y8/2
	406D.441			straw	lt	F	r y	lt b	w
16:2	BI	25/71	m	sand	m	F	7.5YR7/4	10YR7/3	10YR8/2
	51.110						pk	v p b	w
16:3	BI	26/90	m	sand	lt	M	5YR5/6	5YR6/6	10YR7/3
	40E.160			straw	lt	F	y r	r y	v p b
				sand	v	L			
16:4[a]	BIV	76/360	m	sand	m	F M	10YR7/4	7.5YR6/4	2.5Y8/2
	237.142			straw	lt	F	v p b	lt b	w
16:5[a]	BI	27/208	m	sand	m	F	7.5YR6/4	7.5YR6/4	2.5Y8/2
	53.112			straw	lt	F	lt b	lt b	w
16:6	BIV	110/520	m	sand	m	F M	5YR6/6	10YR7/3	10YR7/3
	112C.361			straw	lt	F	r y	v p b	v p b
16:7	BIE	41/190	m	sand	lt	F M	5YR6/6	5YR6/6	5YR6/6
	625.470			straw	lt	F	r y	r y	r y
16:8	BI-IV	43/160	mh	sand	m	F M	7.5YR7/4	10YR7/3	5Y8/3
	128C.544			straw	lt	F	pk	v p b	p y
16:9[b]	BI-II	240/110	m	sand	m	F MF	5YR6/6	5YR6/6	5YR6/6
	406D.441						r y	r y	r y
16:10	BI	57/110	m	sand	m	F M	10YR7/4	10YR7/4	5YR6/6
	53.112			straw	lt	F	v p b	v p b	r y
16:11[c]	BIV	150/118	m	sand	m	F	2.5YR6/6	10YR8/3	2.5Y8/2
	114.175			straw	lt	F	lt r	v p b	w
				limestone	v	L			
				quartz	v	L			
16:12	BI	30/100	m	sand	m	F M	10YR7/3	5Y6/3	5Y7/3
	446C.575			straw	lt	F	v p b	p ol	p y
16:13[d]	BI	18/130	m	sand	h	F	5YR7/8	5YR7/6	10YR8/3
	128C.550			straw	lt	F	r y	r y	v p b
				limestone	lt	M			
16:14	BI	19/120	m	sand	m	F M	7.5YR6/4	2.5Y8/2	2.5Y8/2
	59.88			straw	lt	F	lt b	w	w
				limestone	v	L			
16:15	BI	22/140	m	sand	m	F MF	10YR6/2	2.5Y7/2	2.5Y7/2
	51.110						lt b gy	lt gy	lt gy
16:16	BI	32/130	m	sand	m	F	7.5YR7/4	10YR8/3	10YR8/3
	52A.132			straw	lt	F	pk	v p b	v p b
16:17	BI	61/140	m	sand	lt	MF	10YR5/8	5YR7/6	10YR8/4
	54.117			straw	lt	F	y b	r y	v p b
16:18[e]	BI	92/177	m	sand	m	F MF	7.5YR7/4	5YR8/4	2.5Y8/2
	51.155			straw	m	F	pk	pk	w
16:19	BI	30/220	m	sand	m	MF M	7.5YR6/4	10YR8/3	2.5Y8/2
	55.131						lt b	v p b	w

Surface Treatment: [a]nicked rib decoration [b]burnished in (rim and neck) and out (completely) [c]slipped in and out, burnished in (rim and neck) and out (completely) [d]burnished in (rim only) [e]comb-incised decoration

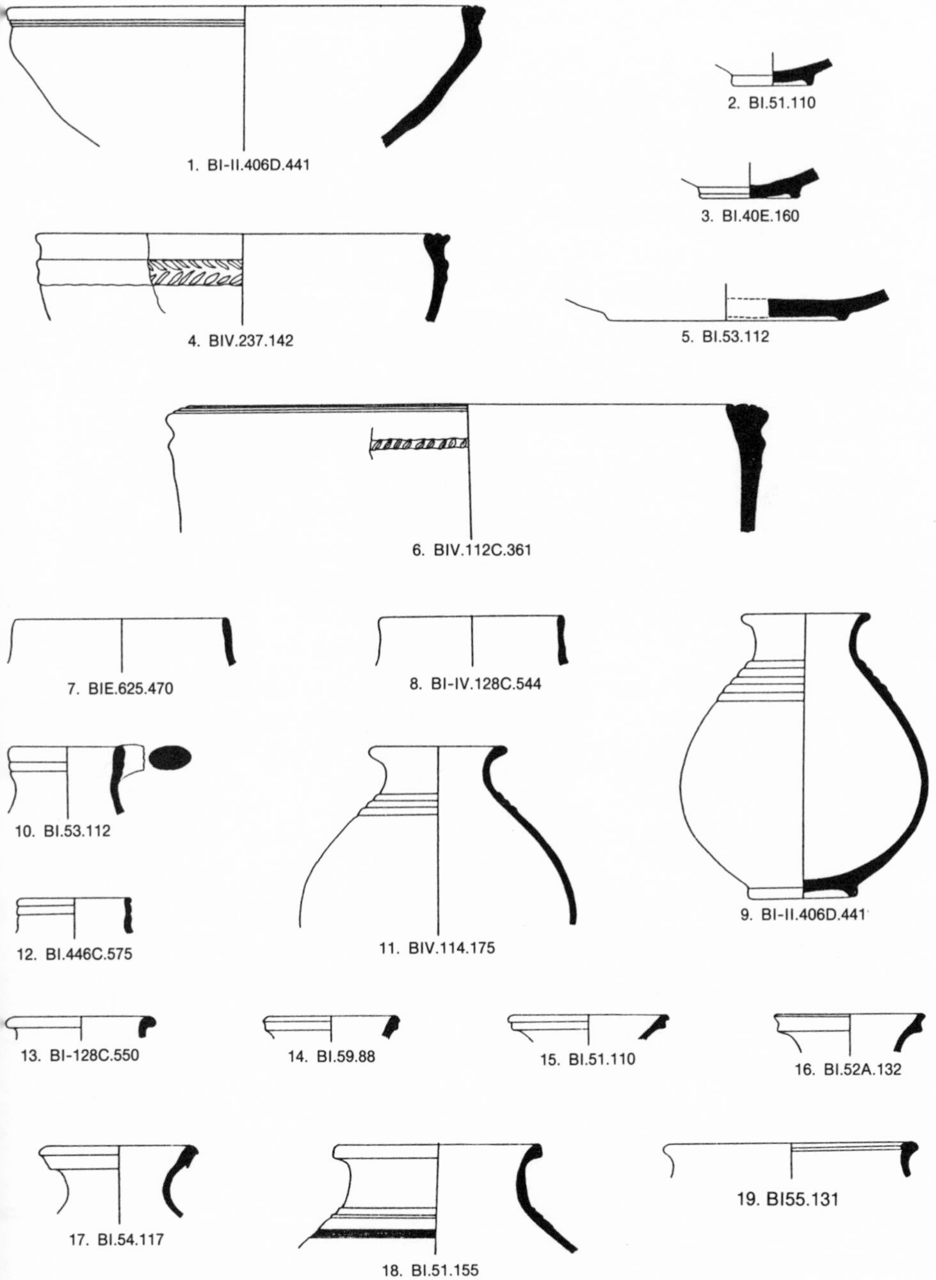

Figure 16. Middle Bronze IIA bowls, bases, vat, and narrow-necked jars.

Figure 17

Figure	Area Locus.Basket	Size Ht/Dia	Clay Firing	Inclusions			Ware Color	Surface Color In	Surface Color Out
17.1	BI	35/95	m	sand	m	F M	7.5YR6/4	7.5YR6/4	7.5YR7/4
	51.110			straw	lt	F	lt b	lt b	pk
17:2[a]	BIV	87/120	m	sand	m	F M	10YR7/3	10YR7/3	2.5Y7/4
	169.281						v p b	v p b	p y
17:3[b]	BIV	135/155	m	sand	h	F M	7.5YR7/4	2.5Y8/2	2.5Y8/2
	422.494			straw	m	M	pk	w	w
17:4	BI	35/220	m	sand	m	F M	2.5YR6/6	5YR7/6	5YR6/3
	40E.160			straw	lt	F	lt r	r y	lt r b
				quartz	lt	L			
17:5	BII	105/218	m	sand	m	MF M	5YR7/6	5YR7/6	10YR8/3
	442.663			straw	lt	F	r y	r y	v p b
				quartz	lt	L			
17:6	BI	60/210	m	sand	m	MF	5YR6/6	7.5YR7/4	10YR7/3
	51.158			straw	lt	F	r y	pk	v p b
				quartz	lt	L			
17:7	BI	50/130	m	sand	m	F MF	7.5YR6/4	7.5YR6/4	10YR5/3
	40E.160			straw	m	F M	lt b	lt b	b
				quartz	m	M L			
17:8	BI	80/245	m	sand	h	MF	10YR7/4	7.5YR7/4	2.5Y8/2
	442.690			straw	m	F	v p b	pk	w
17:9[c]	BIV	145/230	m	quartz	h	M L	7.5YR7/4	10YR7/3	5Y8/3
	424.501			straw	lt	F	pk	v p b	p y
17:10	BI	45/300	m	quartz	m	M	2.5YR5/6	7.5YR5/4	7.5YR5/4
	51.158			sand	v	L	r	b	b
17:11	BI	27/290	m	sand	m	F	10YR5/3	10YR7/4	10YR7/3
	128C.550			quartz	m	F M	b	v p b	v p b
				straw	h	F			
17:12	BI	115/240	mh	sand	lt	F	7.5YR7/4	5YR6/6	5YR3/1
	57.140			straw	lt	F	pk	r y	v d gy
				quartz	v	L			
17:13	BI	40/260	m	quartz	lt	M L	2.5YR4/6	7.5YR5/4	7.5YR5/4
	59.88			sand	lt	F	r	b	b
17:14	BI-II	77/217	m	sand	m	F	7.5YR7/6	7.5YR7/6	2.5Y8/2
	406D.442			straw	lt	F	r y	r y	w
				sand	v	L			
17:15	BI	100/160	m	sand	lt	MF	7.5YR7/4	10YR7/3	2.5Y7/2
	132A.677			straw	lt	F	pk	v p b	lt gy
17:16	BI	50/198	m	sand	h	F M	10YR6/3	5Y8/3	5Y7/3
	445.581			straw	lt	F	p b	p y	p y
17:17	BI-IV	50/200	mh	sand	m	F	7.5YR7/4	10YR7/3	5Y8/3
	128C.544						pk	v p b	p y
17:18	BVII	20/210	m	sand	m	F M	2.5YR6/6	5YR6/6	2.5Y8/2
	161.309			straw	lt	F	lt r	r y	w

Surface Treatment: [a]nicked rib decoration [b]nicked ring base, nicked rib decoration; [c]comb-incised decoration.

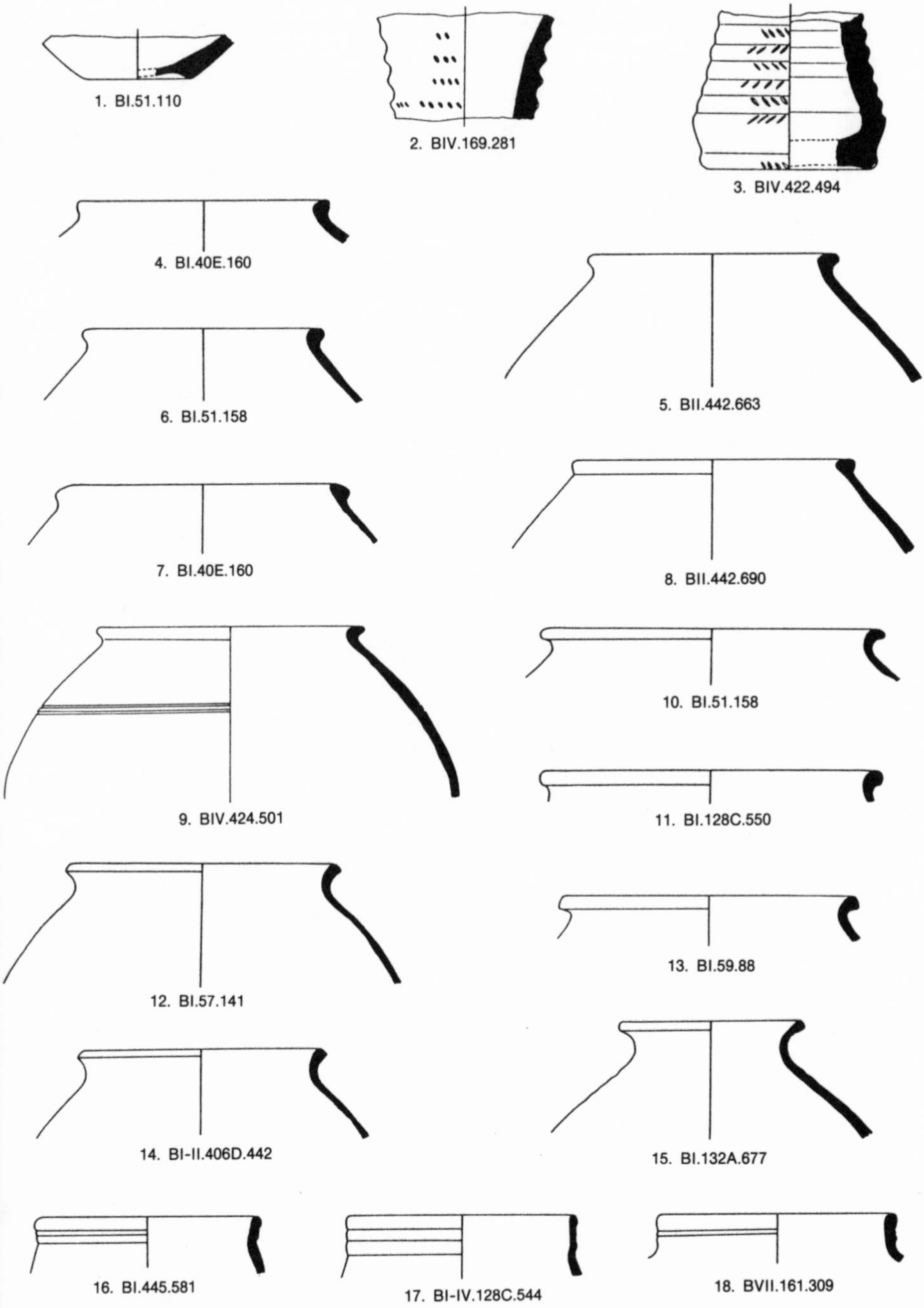

Figure 17. Middle Bronze IIA base, jars, and cooking pots.

Figure 18

Figure	Area Locus.Basket	Size Ht/Dia	Clay Firing	Inclusions			Ware Color	Surface Color In	Surface Color Out
18:1	BI	37/218	m	sand	m	F MF	7.5YR7/4	5Y8/2	5Y8/2
	128C.550			straw	m	F	pk	w	w
18:2	BI	36/260	m	sand	m	F M	10YR7/3	2.5Y8/2	5Y8/3
	128C.550						v p b	w	p y
18:3	BI	44/370	m	sand	m	F MF	10YR7/2	2.5Y8/2	2.5Y8/2
	448C.752			straw	lt	F	lt gy	w	w
18:4	BI	62/217	m	sand	m	F MF	5YR6/6	7.5YR6/4	7.5YR7/4
	456.518			straw	lt	F	ry	lt b	pk
				chalk	v	L			
18:5	BI	86/280	mh	sand	lt	MF	7.5YR6/4	7.5YR7/4	5Y8/3
	439.575			straw	lt	F	lt b	pk	p y
18:6	BI-II	62/280	m	sand	h	F M	5YR6/6	5YR7/6	2.5Y8/2
	406D.442			straw	lt	F M	r y	r y	w
18:7[a]	BI	48/230	m	sand	m	F	10YR7/2	10YR7/2	10YR7/3
	54.17			straw	m	F	lt gy	lt gy	v p b
18:8[a]	BIV	92/285	m	sand	h	F	2.5YR6/6	7.5YR7/4	10YR7/4
	141.235						lt r	pk	v p b
18:9	BI	22/260	m	sand	lt	F	7.5YR7/6	10YR7/4	2.5Y8/4
	51.110			straw	lt	F	r y	v p b	p y
				sand	v	L			
18:10	BI	42/250	m	sand	h	MF	2.5Y7/4	2.5Y8/2	5Y8/3
	40E.157			straw	m	F	p y	w	p y
18:11	BI	65/287	m	straw	m	F M	5YR6/6	7.5YR7/6	10YR8/4
	40E.160			sand	lt	F M	r y	r y	v p b
				chalk	v	L			
18:12	BI	52/250	m	sand	h	F MF	10YR7/3	2.5Y7/4	2.5Y7/4
	472.674			straw	m	F	v p b	p y	p y
				sand	v	L			
18:13[a]	BI	105/229	m	sand	m	F	7.5YR7/4	10YR7/3	5Y7/3
	456.518			straw	lt	F	pk	v p b	p y
				limestone	v	L			
18:14	BI	62/334	m	sand	m	F	5YR7/6	10YR8/3	10YR7/4
	472.672			straw	lt	F	r y	v p b	v p b
18:15	BII-IV	55/400	m	sand	h	F MF	7.5YR6/4	7.5YR7/4	10YR8/3
	98.486			straw	lt	F	lt b	pk	v p b
18:16	BI	69/400	m	sand	m	MF	5Y6/2	5Y7/2	5Y7/2
	54.117			straw	lt	F	lt ol gy	lt gy	lt gy

Surface Treatment: [a]comb-incised decoration.

Figure 15 (cont. from p. 100)

Figure	Area Locus.Basket	Size Ht/Dia	Clay Firing	Inclusions			Ware Color	Surface Color In	Surface Color Out
15:26	BI	40/280	m	sand	m	MF	7.5YR6/4	10YR8/2	2.5Y8/2
	51.110			straw	m	F	lt b	w	w
15:27	BI	80/400	m	sand	m	MF	5YR6/6	5YR6/6	5YR7/6
	40E.160			straw	lt	F	r y	r y	r y
15:28	BII	55/360	mh	sand	m	F	2.5YR6/8	2.5Y8/2	2.5Y8/2
	442.663			straw	lt	F	lt r	w	w
15:29	BI	45/310	m	sand	m	M	7.5YR7/4	5Y8/3	2.5Y8/2
	51.110			straw	m	M	pk	p y	w

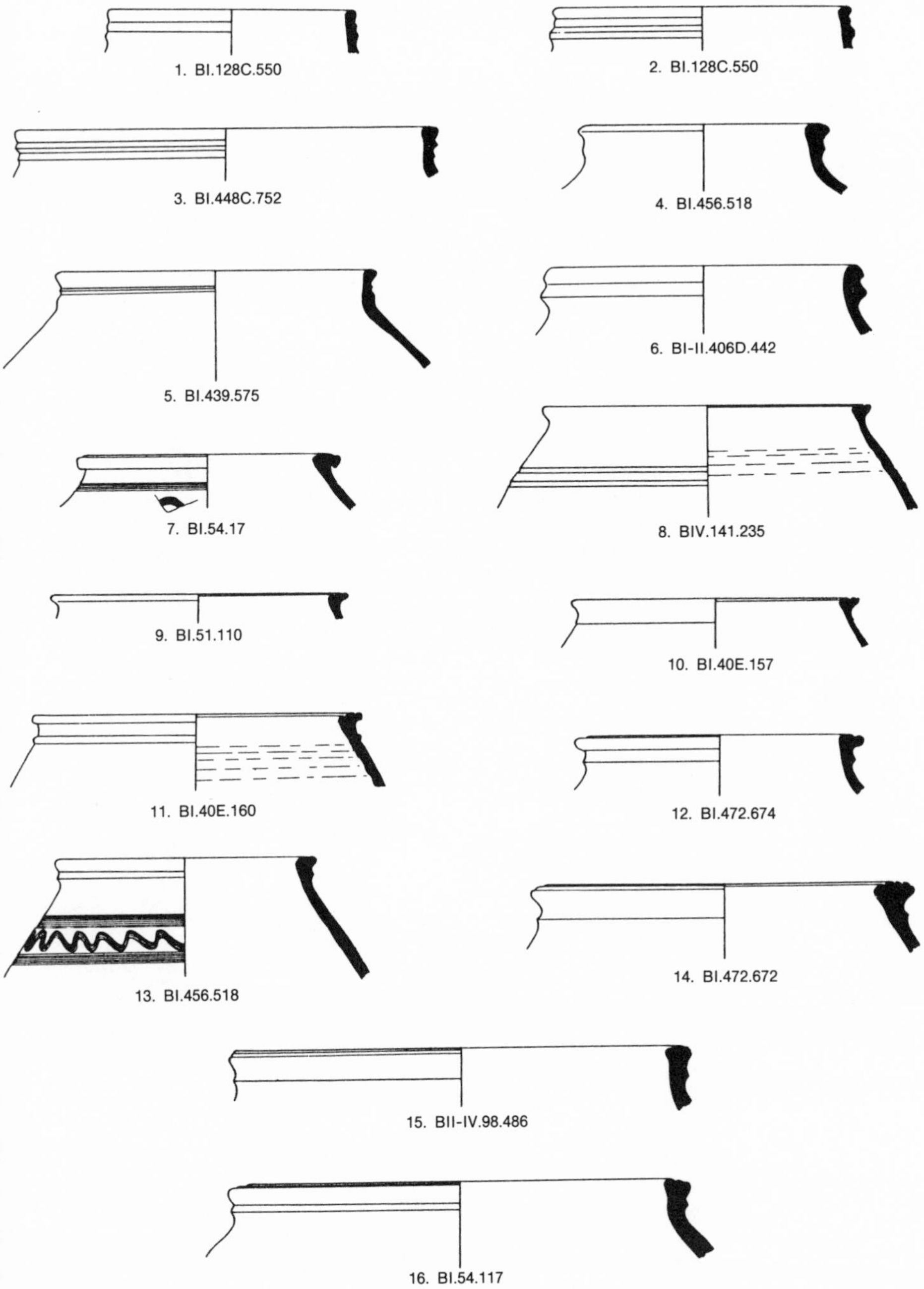

Figure 18. Middle Bronze IIA jars and kraters.

Figure 19

Figure	Area Locus.Basket	Size Ht/Dia	Clay Firing	Inclusions			Ware Color	Surface Color In	Surface Color Out
19:1	BIV	38/412	m	sand	m	F MF	5YR5/6	7.5YR7/6	10YR7/3
	141.235						y r	r y	v p b
19:2	BIV	35/510	m	straw	m	F	2.5YR6/8	5YR7/6	7.5YR7/4
	141.233			sand	lt	F	lt r	r y	pk
19:3	BI	67/519	m	sand	h	F	5Y6/2	5Y8/2	5Y8/2
	1+Fall.400			straw	m	M	lt ol gy	w	w
19:4	BI	123/360	m	sand	m	F	10YR6/3	5YR5/6	7.5YR5/4
	51.158			straw	lt	F	p b	y r	b
19:5	BI	75/500	m	sand	h	F	5YR7/6	5YR7/6	5Y8/3
	52A.132			straw	lt	F	r y	r y	p y
19:6	BI	107/588	m	sand	m	F M	5YR6/6	5YR6/6	5YR7/6
	51.110			straw	lt	F	r y	r y	r y
				sand	v	L			
19:7	BII-IV	47/566	m	sand	h	F MF	10YR6/4	5YR7/6	5YR7/6
	98.486			straw	lt	F	lt y b	r y	r y
				sand	v	L			

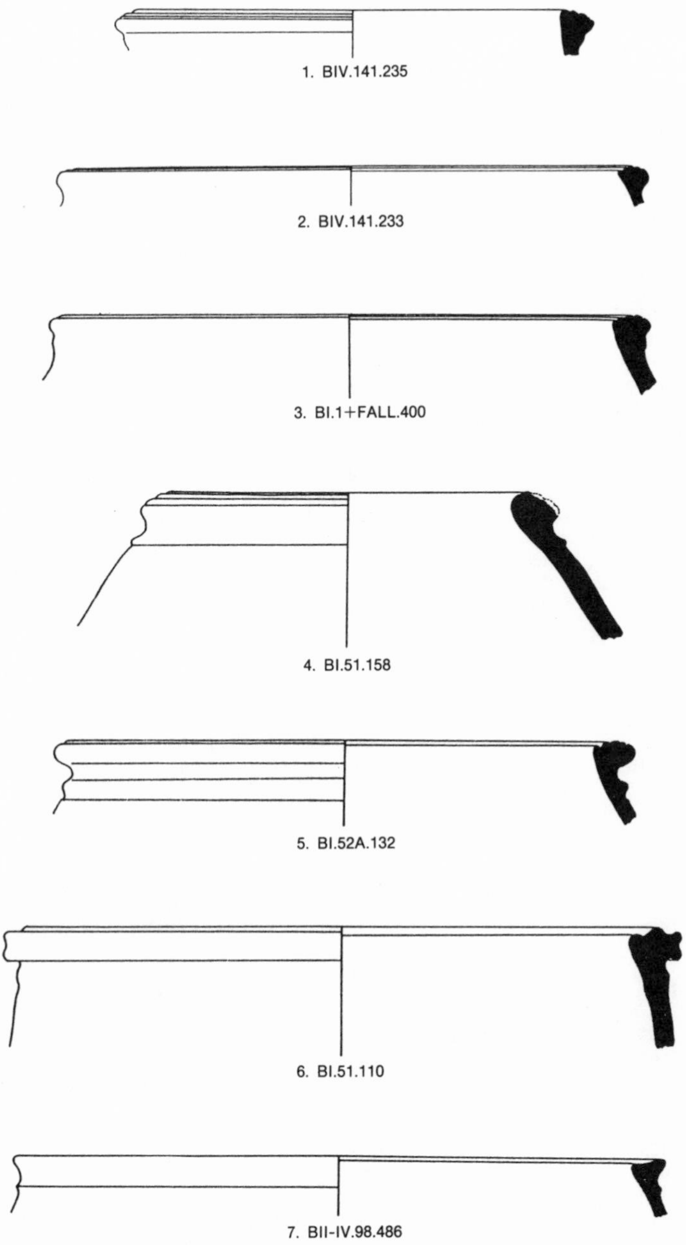

Figure 19. Middle Bronze IIA storage jars.

Figure 20

Figure	Area Locus.Basket	Size Ht/Dia	Clay Firing	Inclusions			Ware Color	Surface Color In	Surface Color Out
20:1	BIV	42/295	m	quartz	h	F M L	5YR6/6	7.5YR7/4	10YR7/4
	101B.53			straw	m	F	r y	pk	v p b
20:2	BIV	55/320	m	sand	m	F	5YR6/6	10YR8/3	5Y8/3
	101B.542			straw	m	F	r y	v p b	p y
20:3	BIV	29/237	m	sand	m	F MF	5YR7/6	10YR7/3	10YR8/3
	101B.542			straw	lt	F	r y	v p b	v p b
20:4[a]	BIV	45/78	m	sand	h	F MF	5YR6/8	10YR8/3	7.5YR7/4
	101B.531			straw	lt	f	r y	v p b	pk
20:5	BIV	36/127	o	sand	h	F	7.5YR7/4	10YR7/3	2.5Y7/4
	101B.542			straw	lt	F	pk	v p b	p y
				limestone	v	L			
20:6	BIV	40/131	m	sand	h	F	2.5YR6/8	5YR5/6	10YR8/3
	101B.531			straw	lt	F	lt r	y r	v p b
20:7	BIV	30/133	m	sand	h	F MF	7.5YR7/4	10YR8/3	5Y8/3
	101B.542			straw	lt	F	pk	v p b	p y
20:8	BIV	44/100	m	sand	m	F MF	7.5YR7/4	2.5Y7/4	5Y8/3
	101B.542			straw	lt	F	pk	p y	p y
				limestone	v	L			
20:9[b]	BIV	36/110	m	sand	m	F MF	5Y7/1	2.5Y7/2	5Y7/1
	101B.542			straw	lt	F	lt gy	lt gy	lt gy
20:10	BIV	25/140	m	sand	m	F M	5Y7/6	7.5YR7/4	2.5Y8/2
	101B.542			straw	lt	F M	y	pk	w
20:11	BIV	112/188	m	sand	lt	F MF	5YR6/6	2.5YR6/6	10YR7/3
	101B.542			straw	lt	F	r y	lt r	v p b
20:12[c]	BIV	38/271	m	sand	m	F M L	10YR5/2	10YR5/2	10YR7/4
	101B.542			straw	m	F	gy b	gy b	v p b
20:13	BIV	40/240	m	quartz	h	F M L	7.5YR5/4	10YR4/1	10YR7/2
	101B.542			straw	m	F	b	d gy	lt gy
20:14	BIV	28/200	m	quartz	h	F M L	10YR5/2	10YR5/1	10YR7/3
	101B.531			straw	m	F	gy b	gy	v p b
20:15	BIV	50/198	mh	sand	m	F MF	5YR7/6	7.5YR7/6	2.5Y8/2
	101B.542			straw	m	F M	r y	r y	w
20:16	BIV	31/85	m	sand	m	F M	5YR6/6	5YR7/6	10YR8/3
	101B.542			straw	lt	F	r y	r y	v p b
20:17	BIV	35/45	m	sand	m	F MF	5YR6/6	5YR7/6	10YR7/3
	101B.531			straw	lt	F	r y	r y	v p b
20:18	BIV	70/-	m	sand	m	F M	5YR7/6	7.5YR7/4	10YR8/3
	101B.531			straw	m	F M	r y	pk	v p b
				limestone	v	L			
20:19[d]	BIV	117/520	m	straw	h	F M	7.5YR7/4	10YR7/3	5Y8/3
	101B.531			sand	m	F M L	pk	v p b	p y
20:20	BIV	100/486	m	sand	h	F	5YR7/6	10YR8/3	10YR8/3
	103.505			straw	lt	F	r y	v p b	v p b
20:21	BIV	63/378	m	sand	h	F	5YR7/6	10YR8/3	5Y8/3
	103.483			straw	lt	F	r y	v p b	p y
20:22[e]	BIV	81/167	m	sand	h	F	5Y7/3	5Y8/3	5Y8/3
	103.505			straw	lt	F	p y	p y	p y
20:23	BIV	48/387	m	sand	m	F M	2.5Y7/4	2.5Y8/2	2.5Y8/2
	103.505			straw	lt	F M	p y	w	w
20:24	BIV	53/306	m	sand	m	F	10YR5/1	10YR6/2	10YR5/1
	103.505						gy	lt b gy	gy
20:25	BIV	139/458	m	sand	h	F MF	5YR6/4	7.5YR7/4	10YR8/3
	103.505			straw	m	F M L	lt r b	pk	v p b
20:26	BIV	78/118	m	sand	m	F M	5YR7/6	10YR7/3	10YR7/3
	103.483			straw	lt	F	r y	v p b	v p b

Surface Treatment: [a]possible slip, in [b]burnished out (not rim) [c]burnished in and out [d]incised mark, possible slip, out [e]comb-incised decoration

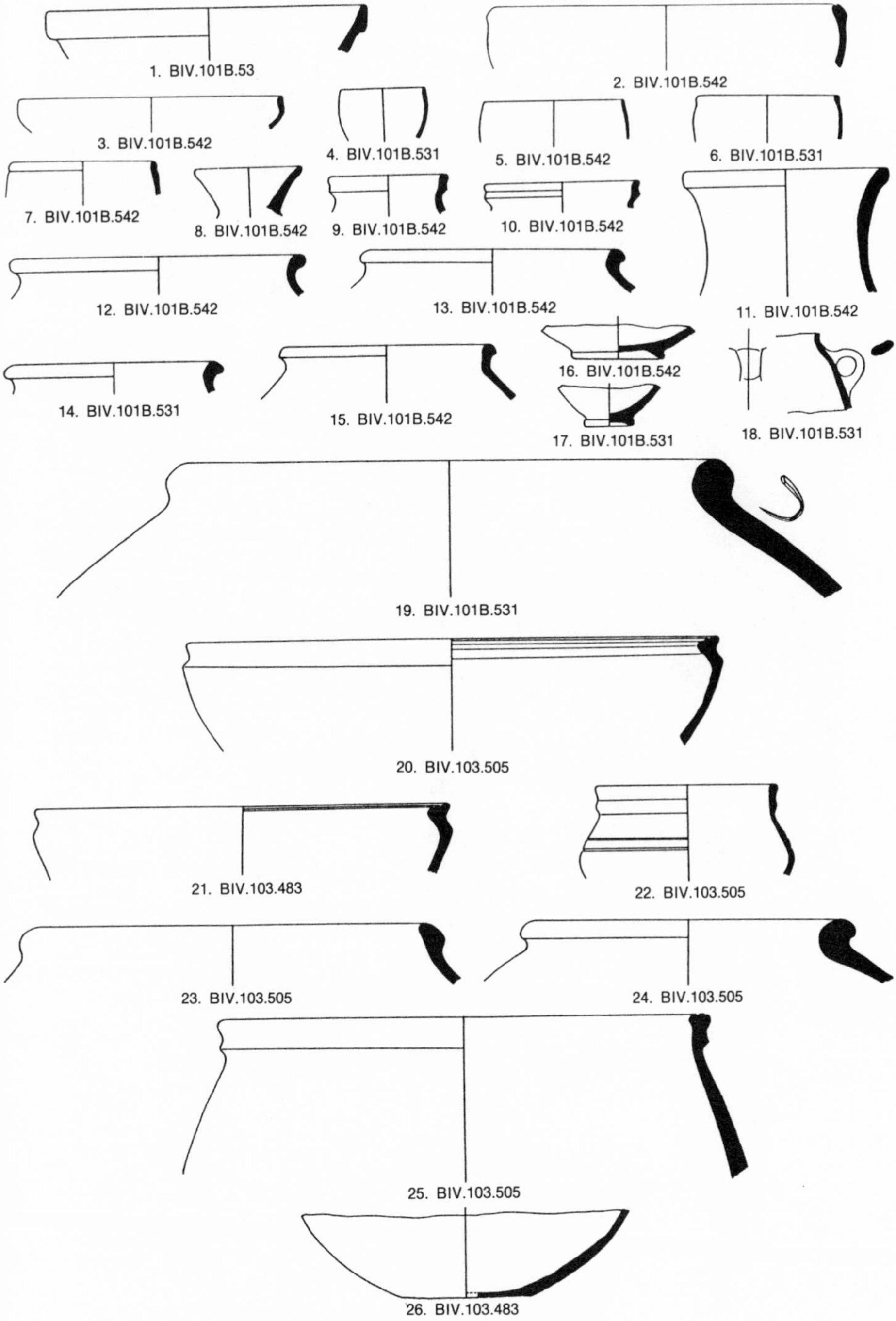

Figure 20. Selection of Middle Bronze I forms.

Figure 21. Middle Bronze IIB plaque with representation of "beer drinking" ceremony.

The *Mubassirū* Messengers at Mari

Robert W. Fisher

Wilfrid Laurier University

The Mari texts are well-known for the correspondence which they contain, and, over the fifty years since their discovery, these letters have been the object of much attention. Considerably less study, however, has been directed toward the means by which these letters reached their destinations: the messengers—the postmen of ancient Mari, if you will.

A survey of the materials reveals a variety of such functionaries. By far the most frequently mentioned is the *mār šiprim,* the regular messenger.[1] In addition one finds: the *wābil/bābil tuppim,* the letter carrier;[2] the *awīlum qallum* or *mārum qallum,* the fast courier;[3] the *lāsimum,* the express messenger;[4] the *rākibum,* the mounted messenger;[5] and a collective reference to *awīlū să tuppātim . . . ublūnim,* "the men who brought the tablets."[6] A discussion of all the messengers at Mari lies beyond the limits of this investigation, and therefore it will confine itself to the function of certain messengers called *mubassirū.*[7] The reason for this particular selection is the fact that the precise nature of these *mubassirū* is not immediately clear—certainly less so than the other kinds of messengers encountered, and it is hoped that the present effort will contribute to our understanding of them.

Mubassirū is the plural participle of the D-stem verb *bussurum,* "to bring news" (quite often, "to bring good news"),[8] and is found in the following texts from Mari: ARM 5 17, a letter from Išḫi-Addu, king of

Author's note: The author wishes to acknowledge the support of the Social Sciences and Humanities Research Council of Canada in the preparation of this article.

[1]ARM *passim;* see CAD M/1 261–62 and AHw 616, 1245–46.

[2]ARM 1 40: 26; 4 3: 6; 5 38: 5; 10 32: 9′; 85: 17; 176: 18; see AHw 1450.

[3]ARM 1 39: 17′; 45: 13; 84: 18; 93: 11, 14; 97: 16; 105: 9; 2 10: 4′; 45: 6; 72: 6; 4 31: 13; see CAD Q 62 and AHw 894.

[4]ARM 1 120: 9; 6 21: 11; 24: 5; 62: 7; 7 185: ii:3′; 9 131: 5′; 13 131: 5′; see CAD L 107 and AHw 539.

[5]ARM 2 55: 5, 7; 99: 40, 47; see AHw 947–48.

[6]ARM 7 21.

[7]See CAD M/2 158–59 and AHw 665.

[8]See CAD B 347–48 and AHw 142.

Qatna, to Yasmaḫ-Addu, governor at Mari; ARM 7 75, a "delivery receipt"; and ARM 7 156, a "note of payment."[9] In addition, the verb is encountered in the indicative in ARM 5 16, another letter from Išḫi-Addu to Yasmaḫ-Addu, which will also be considered.

ARM 5 17

During the period known as the Assyrian interregnum at Mari, the kingdom of Qatna in upper Syria enjoyed very good relations with Mari and Aššur. Šamši-Adad, king of Assyria, had even succeeded in obtaining the daughter of the king of Qatna as a wife for his son Yasmaḫ-Addu.[10] We learn from the archives that Mari and Qatna pastured their flocks together,[11] made war together,[12] and exchanged contingents of troops for various purposes.[13] ARM 5 17 belongs to this context.

1. *a-na Ia-ás-ma-aḫ-*^{d}IM *qí-bí-ma*
um-ma Iš-ḫi-^{d}IM *a-ḫu-ka-ma*
^{I}*Su-mu-e-pu-uḫ nu-zé-e*
ù ^{LÚ}*mu-ba-si-ri a-na Ma-mu-ka-ti-ša-ša*
5. [*iš-ta-n*]*a-ap -pa-ar tu*[*p*]*-p*[*a-*]
. . . .
Rev. . . . .
1′. [x x x *i*]*t-ti-ka e-er-r*[*i-iš* (?)]
[*a*]*-wa-tam an-ni-tam ša Su-mu-e-pu-u*[*ḫ*]
[*šum*]*-ma s*[*à-a*]*n-qa šum-ma la sà-an-qa*
[*an-ni-ta*]*m la an-ni-tam a*[*r*]*-ḫi-iš*
5′. [*šu-u*]*p-ra-am-ma li-ib-bi lu i-de*
Tr. *ù uz-ni-ia šu-up-te*

Say to Yasmaḫ-Addu: Your brother Išḫi-Addu sends the following message. (3) Sumu-epuḫ sends Nuzians and *mubassirū* to Mamukatišaša at regular intervals. The tablet . . . (Rev.) . . . he demands of you. (?) If this matter concerning Sumu-epuḫ is accurate, or if it is not accurate, (4′) (if it is) this or that, write to me immediately so that my heart may know, and open my ears.

The relatively fragmentary nature of this tablet demands a certain amount of caution in dealing with it, but it is clear that it contains a

[9]See n 15, below, for "delivery receipts" and "notes of payment."
[10]ARM 1 77; see ARMT 5 p. i.
[11]ARM 5 15.
[12]ARM 5 16.
[13]ARM 5 18; 19.

request from Išḫi-Addu to Yasmaḫ-Addu for more information concerning the "subversive activities" of a certain Sumu-epuḫ, an unfriendly neighboring chieftain to the north. The *mubassirū* of this text were apparently couriers who carried tablets back and forth between Sumu-epuḫ and Mamukatišaša. Not much more can be safely derived from this occurrence of *mubassirū,* but ARM 5 16, another letter from Išḫi-Addu to Yasmaḫ-Addu, sheds additional light. Here the indicative form of the verb *bussurum* is used.

ARM 5 16

[a-na Ia-á]s-ma-aḫ-^{d}IM *qí-bí-ma*
[um]-ma Iš-ḫi-^{d}IM
[a]-ḫu-ka-a-ma
aš-šum ṭe$_4$*-em* ^{I}*Iš-me-*^{d}*Da-gan*
tu-ba-si-ra-an-ni-ma
ma-di-iš-ma aḫ-du
ša-ni-tam aš-šum ṭe$_4$*-e-em*
e-li-ka an-ni-iš
a-aḫ-ka la na-di
sí-ma-nu-um ša e-li-ka
ṣa-ba-ka ša-al-la-tam
šu-ki-il-ma
Tr. *ù li-ik-ru-bu-ni-kum*
Rev. 3 *a-la-nu an-nu-tum*
ú-ul da-an-nu
UD 1 KAM *ni-ṣa-ab-ba-sú-nu-ti*
ar-ḫi-iš
e-li-im-ma
ù a-la-ni an-nu-tim
i ni-iṣ-ba-at-ma
ù ṣa-bu-ka ša-l[a]-tam
li-ku-ul
šum-ma a-ḫi at-ta
ar-ḫi-iš
[e]-li-im

Say to Yasmaḫ-Addu: Your brother Išḫi-Addu sends the following message. With reference to the report concerning Išme-Dagan, (5) you have brought me good news, and I have rejoiced greatly. (7) Another thing: with reference to the report of your coming here, do not be negligent. (10) (It is) the right time for you to come up. Cause your troops to take booty so that they will bless you.

(Rev.) These three cities (are) not fortified. (16) In one day we shall take them. come up to me without delay and let us take these cities, (21) and let your troops take booty. (23) If you are my brother, come up to me without delay.

Tu-ba-si-ra-an-ni-ma in line 5 of this letter is the second person masculine singular of the D-stem preterite of *bussurum*. I have translated, "you have brought me good news," a rendering which agrees with Dossin's translation in ARMT 5 and with the meaning of the verb given by Finet in his lexicon of volumes 1–5 of ARM.[14] It is unfortunate that the nature of the good news concerning Išme-Dagan which Yasmaḫ-Addu had sent Išḫi-Addu is not known, for this might have clarified the situation somewhat. In view of the fact of Išme-Dagan's numerous and successful military undertakings, it is quite possible that this message was news of one of his many victories in the field. This supposition is supported by the fact that the letter as a whole is concerned with military affairs. It seems unlikely that Išḫi-Addu would comment on some comparatively irrelevant good fortune of Išme-Dagan, and then turn immediately to a discussion of a proposed military expedition, although this is certainly not impossible. It seems much more likely that Išḫi-Addu would use an acknowledgment of the news of one of Išme-Dagan's military successes as an appropriate introduction to a letter whose main purpose was to urge Yasmaḫ-Addu to join quickly what Išḫi-Addu envisioned as a military success of their own. That this news was good is evident, apart from other considerations, from the simple statement that Išḫi-Addu "rejoiced greatly" over it. Thus, ARM 5 16 gives an indication of the possible activities of the *mubassirū*: some idea of the kind of message that they may have carried, i.e., the good news of a military victory.

The two other occurrences of *mubassirū* in the Mari archives are in very brief administrative texts: ARM 7 75, what Bottéro calls a "delivery receipt"; and ARM 7 156, a "statement of account," or perhaps better, a "note of payment."[15]

ARM 7 75

1. 11 SÌLA 5 GÍN Ì.SAG
a-na pa-ša-aš
mu̯-ba-si-ri
ša iš-tu IGI

[14]See also CAD B 347–48 and AHw 142, although the present writer takes a slightly different position with regard to the exact translation.

[15]See ARMT 7 pp. 176, 179, and 218–19 for these typologies. The fact that these two tablets come from different periods in Mari's history (ARM 7 75 from the Assyrian interregnum and ARM 7 156 from the time of Zimri-Lim) appears to have no significance. The

Rev. ^{I}*Iš-me-*^{d}*Da-gan*
il-li-ku-nim
ITI *ki-nu-nim*
UD 20.KAM
li-mu EGIR *Ṭà-ab-ṣíl-li-*
Tr. ^{d}*A-šur*

11 SÌLA, 5 GÍN (ca. 11.5 liters) of "prime" oil (oil of superior quality) for the anointing (3) of the *mubassirū* who have come from Išme-Dagan. (7) Month of Kinunim, 20th day, *līmu* following that of Ṭab-ṣilli-Assur.

ARM 7 156

1 ḪÚB?.TI?.LÁ? KÙ.[GI 6? GÍN K]I.L[Á.B]I
1 ^{GIŠ}TUKUL KÙ.BABBAR *Ḫa-am-mi-ta-ki-im*
1 ḪÚB?.TI?.LA? KÙ.GI 6 GÍN KI.LÁ.BI
1 ^{GIŠ}TUKUL K[Ù.B]ABBAR ^{d}*Na-bu-um-ma-lik*
1 ḪÚB?.TI?.LÁ? KÙ.GI 6 GÍN KI.LÁ.BI
1 Ḫ[AR.Š]U? ^{d}UTU-*mu-ba-li-iṭ*
Tr. 3 LÚ ERÍN^{MEŠ}
Rev. *mu-ba-si-ru*
ITI *la-ḫi-im*
UD 9.KAM
Tr. MU *Zi-im-ri-li-im* BÀD^{KI}-*Ia-aḫ-du-*[*li-im*] *i-pu-šu*

One ḪÚB.TI.LÁ[16] of gold weighing 6 shekels, (and) one silver mace: Ḫammi-takim. (3) One ḪÚB.TI.LÁ of gold weighing 6 shekels, and one silver mace: Nabum-Malik. (5) One ḪÚB.TI.LÁ of gold weighing 6 shekels, (and) one br[ace]l[et]: Šamši-muballiṭ. (Tr.) Three soldiers, (Rev.) *mubassirū*. (9) Month of Laḫḫum, 9th day. (11) The year when Zimri-Lim built Dūr-Yaḫdun-Lim.

While at first glance the documents do not appear to reveal much about the *mubassirū*, closer scrutiny reveals two interesting facts.[17] In ARM 7 75, the *mubassirū* received over 11 liters of oil of superior quality

bureaucracy continued to function relatively unchanged; messengers, including *mubassirū*, continued to carry their messages regardless of who wore the crown. Bottéro notes, in this regard, that we cannot readily distinguish between the orthography of the two periods (ARMT 7 pp. 204–5).

[16]See ARMT 7 p. 185 for ḪÚB.TI.LÁ.

[17]It seems worthwhile at this point to remind the reader that these oft-scorned administrative and economic documents are only properly studied in bulk. Seldom can the yield of these tablets be revealed, or even intimated, when studied singly.

for their anointing. In similar texts, greater quantities of this oil were distributed only to what seem to have been large numbers of people—usually soldiers or officials, often gathered together for a banquet.[18] yet other groups of messengers received less than one-tenth as much as the *mubassirū*. For example, the "men who brought the tablets from Išme-Dagan," the same place of origin as the *mubassirū*, received only one liter for anointing.[19] Likewise, the "men who arrived from Ekallātum," Išme-Dagan's capital, received only one liter.[20] It is unfortunate that the exact number of men in these groups is not mentioned, so that an accurate comparison of the amount received by each man could be made. It is interesting, however, that two groups of men received only one liter of oil, while the *mubassirū* coming from the same place received over eleven liters. Either this group of *mubassirū* was many times larger than the others, or there was something special about them. Perhaps the *mubassirū* were of considerably higher rank or station, or perhaps, as seems reasonable, they brought particularly good news.

ARM 7 156 seems to militate against the possibility of the *mubassirū* being a large group, and to favour their being either of high rank, or the bringers of good news (or both). The size of this group of *mubassirū* is clearly stated, and it is small—only three. Moreover, here again the materials given them seem to be rather extravagant. They each received a ḪÚB.TI.LÁ (perhaps a pendant of some kind[21]) made of gold and weighing six shekels (about 50 grams) apiece, plus either a silver mace, or a bracelet. The only other ḪÚB.TI.LÁ*s* of gold at Mari belonged to goddesses, and most of these were smaller, weighing eight to ten grams.[22] Only two larger ones are mentioned, "great" ḪÚB.TI.LÁ*s* of 80 to 120 grams, and these are clearly designated as part of the goddesses' treasuries.[23]

An interesting comparison can be made with ARM 7 117 in which are listed gifts given to men returning from various important missions. The largest sum was 18.3 shekels of silver (equal to about 6 shekels of gold) given to Aqba-Aḫum for two trips to the important court of Qarni-Lim. That is about 3 shekels of gold per trip. Ten shekels of silver (equal to about 3.5 shekels of gold) were given to Ḫabdu-Mālik for a mission to Ḫammurapi, king of Kurdā. Another 9.5 shekels (equal to about 3 shekels of gold) were given to a second Išḫi-Addu for a mission Šarriya, king of Razama. The list continues at length to record even smaller amounts. These were all men of high station who had performed significant services, yet the *mubassirū* of ARM 7 156 received at least

[18]See ARM 7 49; 40; and 47.
[19]ARM 7 21.
[20]ARM 7 42.
[21]See n 16, above.
[22]ARM 7 4: 1, 11, 4′; see also ARMT 7 p. 185.
[23]ARM 7 4: 9, 7′; see also ARMT 7 p. 185.

twice as much compensation. What was the reason for this preferential treatment? Again, perhaps these were men of especially high station, or else they brought especially good news.

The latter possibility would agree with the use of *tu-ba-si-ra-an-ni-ma* in ARM 5 16, and also with the fact that the three men named as *mubassirū* in ARM 7 156 do not appear elsewhere in the Mari texts, as far as can be ascertained to date. One would expect that, if they were high ranking officials, at least one of them would be mentioned in at least one other text in a body of material as large as that of Mari, although the last two names appear to be Akkadian and these men may have been emissaries from another locality. It is also strange that this participle, *mubassirū*, occurs only three times in the vast corpus of Mari texts, despite many references to messengers and the bringing of news. Was it reserved only for very special occasions when the messenger brought good news of some particular kind, perhaps?

The second interesting observation to be made concerning the *mubassirū* of the two administrative texts presented above is the fact that in ARM 7 156, they are called ^{LÚ}ERÍN^{MEŠ} *mubassirū*, "soldiers (performing the function of) heralds," according to Bottéro.[24] This juxtaposition of ERÍN (*ṣābu*) and *mubassirū* reinforces the military connotations of the latter considerably.[25] It also strengthens the possibility that, if these messengers were in fact bringers of good news, as suggested above, the content of that news was military victory. This usage is richly attested in later texts, especially in materials from the time of Aššurbanipal, where the D-stem verb *bussurum* is the relatively fixed and technical term signifying the bringing of good news of victory from the battlefield.[26] As far as the Mari texts are concerned, though, this interpretation, while highly probable, must remain a conjecture.

Thus the participial occurrences of the D-stem verb *bussurum* in the Mari texts suggest the following conclusion: the *mubassirū* were very likely military couriers who were the bringers of the good news of military victory.

In view of this probability, it is interesting to compare these Mari occurrences of *mubassirū* with the use of the Hebrew *pi*^{c}*el* participle *m*^{e}*baśśēr* in Second Isaiah, namely Isa 40:9, 41:27, and 52:7. There the word refers to the prophet himself as he brings to exiled Israel the ultimate good news of Yahweh's great eschatological victory over his

[24]ARMT 7 p. 244.

[25]The same military usage of *mubassirū* is also found in a very fragmentary middle Assyrian letter from Aššur, KAV 202, which is too broken, unfortunately, to provide a satisfactory context. Enough of the text is legible, however, to indicate that someone is communicating with his superior concerning military matters. Mention is made of charioteers, horses, and *mubassirū* who arrive(?) on a certain day.

[26]See Fisher (1966) 93–108, 153.

enemies and the imminent salvation and redemption of his people.[27] Even allowing for the differences in time and space, not to mention the cultural milieu, the suggested meaning of *mubassirū* would seem to elevate and define, a bit more than it has been in the past, the misty figure of the unknown prophet of the Exile.

Finally, a word should be said about the method by which this conclusion was reached. The preceding investigation illustrates clearly the crucial importance of the maximum utilization of the minute details of the economic and administrative documents which are so numerous in cuneiform literature. More numerous than any other single type of extant cuneiform material, they are nevertheless often set aside as dull, uninteresting, even unproductive and unimportant, compared with more exciting genres such as myths, letters, narratives of various sorts, and the like, which are pursued with great vigour. There are important exceptions to this charge, of course, but it holds true in general. Neglect of the economic and administrative texts can only impede the progress of Assyriology. The modest findings of this study are based to a significant degree upon a careful scrutiny of two humble "delivery receipts," part of the vast and often ignored corpus of texts contemptuously dismissed as "laundry lists." A great deal more remains to be discovered, and one wonders what riches of knowledge concerning Mesopotamian life, history and culture beyond the purely economic and administrative realms—in themselves of no small importance—remain to be gleaned from these lowly tablets. This is a question which cuneiform scholarship cannot afford to disregard.[28]

[27] See Fisher (1974).

[28] Others have voiced these sentiments in the past; see, for example, Gelb (1967) 1–8. The present writer only wishes to add his testimony to theirs.

Mari and the Kish Civilization

I. J. Gelb†

The Oriental Institute, The University of Chicago

1. *Introductory Remarks*

Ultimately, the present paper is the outgrowth of my interest in Old Akkadian. Involved as I was in the study and publication of Old Akkadian texts in the years just before and after the Second World War, originally my interests in the texts were primarily linguistic, specifically language and writing. However, on a broader basis, almost from the beginning, I saw: (a) that the northern part of Babylonia was occupied by the Akkadians, with their own writing system and language which were different from those used by the Sumerians in the southern part of Babylonia; (b) that the theories of the so-called "temple economy," claimed by Deimel and others, and the "state economy," posited by Landsberger, Koschaker, and others, were untenable.

As a result, I read two papers in 1960: (a) in Geneva, in ethnolinguistic history, on the horizontal classification of two peoples, the Akkadians and Sumerians; (b) in Moscow, in socio-economic history, on the vertical stratification of the upper and lower classes, the mighty and the poor, the "haves" and the "have-nots."

At that time (around 1960), the picture of most ancient Babylonia, and the Near East in general, was simple and consistent. Since the Sumerian sources are the oldest, the Sumerian civilization was the oldest and everything anywhere else was borrowed from Sumer. The consequence of this was that the Sumerians, surrounded on all sides by nomadic Semites, culturally dominated Babylonia, as well as a vast area extending from the Persian Gulf in the east to the Mediterranean Sea in

Author's note: Broad aspects of this paper were presented in a series of lectures that I gave in the spring of 1982 at the universities of Freiburg, Munster, Heidelberg, and Berlin in Germany and at UCLA, Harvard, and Brandeis in the United States.

Although anachronistic, the convenient term "Babylonia" is used in this paper for the area extending from the Tigris-Euphrates neck southward to the Persian Gulf, "Mesopotamia" for the vast area lying between the two rivers north of the Tigris-Euphrates neck, and "Assyria" for the area lying east of Mesopotamia between the Tigris and the mountains.

Abbreviations for frequently cited texts: adm. = ARMT 19; legal = Durand 1982c; liver = Rutten 1938.

the west. This is the gist of Kramer's *From the Tablets of Sumer: 25 Firsts in Man's Recorded History* (see Kramer 1956).

This "Pan-Sumerianism" is presently being attacked on all sides; first, by the archeological discoveries dated to proto-historical times and extending from Habuba Kabira and other sites in Syria, in the west, to Tepe Yahya in Iran and other sites around the Persian Gulf, in the east; and by the great epigraphic revelations dated to the middle of the third millennium B.C., and extending from Ebla in Syria, in the west, to Kish and other sites in Babylonia, in the east.

Our knowledge of the epigraphic sources of Ebla begins with the publication of Pettinato (1975) on the 42 texts and fragments that were excavated in 1974 at the modern site of Tell Mardikh, situated about 55 km. south of Aleppo in Syria. Towards the end of 1975, the great palace archive of about 15,000 tablets and fragments was discovered, and a few more texts were found during the campaigns of subsequent years. In the years 1975 to 1976, several articles by Matthiae and Pettinato appeared in print, and then in November, 1976, Matthiae and Pettinato came to Chicago to give a series of lectures and to discuss informally many questions related to Ebla with the staff of the Oriental Institute.

Early in 1977, I went to California to give a series of talks on Ebla, which I put together in a preliminary article entitled "Thoughts about Ibla" (Gelb 1977). Since then the written materials on Ebla have increased immensely.

In 1981 I wrote a second article on Ebla, entitled "Ebla and the Kish Civilization" (published in 1981). This article is a revised and much enlarged version of my first article published four years earlier.

In my first article (Gelb 1977) I wrote *Ibla* (not *Ebla*), justifying my spelling on p. 5. I changed the spelling to *Ebla* in the second article, not out of persuasion, but in deference to the precept *nec Hercules contra plures.*

Despite the objections of Matthiae and others, the Ebla archive is to be dated to the Pre-Sargonic period, with the proviso that "Pre-Sargonic" extends in time to include the early years of Sargon, when he was still battling for the domination of what later in his life became the Akkadē Empire. The occurrence of Jiblul-ᵓIl, king of Mari, both at Mari and Ebla makes the Mari texts synchronous with the Ebla archive (see Gelb 1977: 5–8, Gelb 1981: 57–59, and below, § 5).

In line with the main topic of the Chicago Conference, the present paper stresses the role of Mari within the frame of the Kish Civilization. Let me add here that while the place of Kish and Ebla within the frame of the Kish Civilization has been clear to me from the outset, I never realized until I began writing this paper what an important role Mari played in this picture.

2. *Concept of the Kish Civilization*

The concept of what I had dubbed "The Kish Tradition" in 1960 grew out of the investigation of three kinds of sources.

(a) The royal inscriptions of Sargon and Rimush, in which we must recognize the existence of two writing systems that were used by the Akkadians in the early Sargonic period: an earlier, northern variety which was localized around Kish; and a later, southern variety, which the Akkadians borrowed from the Sumerians at Nippur.

(b) The ancient kudurrus, votive inscriptions, and administrative texts of the Fara, Pre-Sargonic, and Sargonic periods, according to which the north (later Akkad) was mainly Semitic in language, population, and culture, while the south (Sumer) was mainly Sumerian.

(c) The Sumerian King List, and the references and allusions to the kings of Kish, and to Kishites, in the Sumerian royal inscriptions dating as far back as one to two hundred years before the rise of the Sargonic dynasty, which force us to reckon with the existence of a Semitic power in the north, rivaling that of the Sumerians in the south.

I popularized the term "Kish Tradition" (Gelb 1977: 13f.) with cross-references to my earlier discussions of the topic (Gelb 1961: 20–22; enlarged from Gelb 1952: 29; and especially in Gelb 1960: 266f.). As pointed out in Gelb (1977: 14), Edzard (1960: 248f.) stressed the importance of the city and state of Kish and of the title "King of Kish" in Early Dynastic times.

To avoid all misunderstanding, let me make it clear that the Kish Tradition, as originally conceived, was concerned not with the Sargonic period, but with the Early Dynastic era preceding the Sargonic period, and not with the Akkadians, but with a closely related people living in the area of Kish.

The great discoveries at Ebla in 1974 and subsequent years have enabled us to view the Kish Tradition in a much clearer light and to extend its horizons considerably both in space—from Kish to Abu Salabikh and other sites in Babylonia, and then, via Mari and Terqa on the Euphrates, to Ebla and possibly other sites in north Syria—and in time—from the Early Dynastic to post-Ur III times.

At the time that I introduced the concept of the "Kish Tradition," the word "tradition" seemed appropriate to describe a hypothetical power around Kish, which could be reconstructed mainly from later sources. An in-depth study of the ancient kudurrus in the Kish area and beyond, of the votive and administrative texts from Mari, and—above all—the recent discoveries at Ebla and Abu Salabikh allow us to view what I once had called "Kish Tradition" not just through the eyes of later scribes, but through the contemporary testimony of Early Dynastic times. For that purpose, the term "Kish Tradition" is no longer appropriate. It appears therefore that a new term, "Kish Civilization," should be introduced to describe the complex of cultural features which arose around Kish and extended up to Ebla in Syria.

Among the features characterizing the Kish Civilization we may list the following:

(1) Identical writing system everywhere.

(2) Scribal contacts between Ebla and Kish, and between Ebla and Mari.

(3) The language of Ebla and Mari and its relation to "Kishite," the language of the Kish area.

(4) Decimal system at Abu Salabikh, Ebla, and Mari.

(5) Systems of measures of Ebla in relation to those of the Kish area.

(6) Semitic month names everywhere.

(7) Identical systems of year dates at Abu Salabikh and Mari.

(8) Semitic personal, divine, and geographical names everywhere.

No unifying features may be detected in the spheres of law, art, and material culture (see also § 5 below), but we are able to view the concept of the Kish Civilization in the light of three aspects: the ethnolinguistic, political, and cultural.

There is no reason to speak about a unified ethnolinguistic situation embracing all the lands of the Kish Civilization. Such an assumption seems *a priori* implausible if we take into consideration the long distance between Kish and Ebla and the lack of a "chancery language," controlled by a central political agency. In contrast to the west, where it may be safely assumed that the languages of Ebla and Mari were either identical or closely related, the situation in the east is controversial. In the past, it has been generally assumed that the Early Dynastic language of the Kish area represented the older stage of the Sargonic Old Akkadian, and the possibility that the language of Kish and Abu Salabikh may have been identical with that of Ebla and Mari could not even be considered. In restudying the situation recently, I pointed to several features of the Kish area which cannot be duplicated in the Sargonic dialect and suggested the existence of a local linguistic entity around Kish which was different and separate from the Old Akkadian of the Sargonic period and the language of Ebla-Mari. In dubbing this early language of Babylonia "Kishite," I also suggested that the ancestral home of the Akkadians, who under Sargon founded a new dynasty in Babylonia, was not Akkadē in Babylonia, but an area north of Babylonia proper, which was bounded by the Tigris, the Lower Zab, the mountains, and the Diyala River (see Gelb 1981: §§ 9.3 and 9.4).

Similarly, there is no way to see a unified political control over all the lands of the Kish Civilization. Kings of Kish ruled over Kish and Babylonia, kings of Ebla ruled over Ebla and northern Syria, and Mari rulers dominated Mari and its area.

Among the cultural features that characterize all or some of the lands of the Kish Civilization, we find a unified system of writing, scribal contacts within the whole area, the use of the decimal system, and the systems of measures, year dates, month names, and religion. In this list, we may recognize certain features, such as the writing system, the decimal system, and the systems of year dates and month names, each of which was capable of developing a unified system throughout the whole area of the Kish Civilization, and others such as religion and systems of measures, each of which is apt to be widely diversified and, therefore, not likely to develop a unified system throughout the whole area.

With all the existing and potential variations, it is still necessary to recognize a cultural entity that is encompassed under the term "Kish Civilization," but only in the broad sense of a Semitic cultural area, as contrasted, in our case, with the Sumerian cultural area.

In the original embracement of "*Ex Ebla Lux*," claims were made that Eblaic was the oldest known Semitic language and that the mighty "Eblaic empire" extended as far as Akkadē politically and Abu Salabikh culturally. Such claims were once possible only by paying scant attention to the known facts about the Semites in Babylonia in the Fara and Pre-Sargonic periods, the ancient kudurrus and votive inscriptions written in a Semitic language, the political power of the kings of Kish, and the reconstruction of a Semitic cultural entity around Kish in northern Babylonia, which rivaled the Sumerian cultural entity in southern Babylonia.

Meśalim and the kings of Kish and the Kishite civilization lived and flourished long before Ebla, and it is no longer possible to claim the temporal priority of the Eblaic civilization in the Semitic world of the third millennium B.C. This is also acknowledged by Biggs (1980: 84), who writes of cultural transmissions emanating from Kish to Abu Salabikh and Ebla.

3. *Mari in the Third Millennium B.C.*

The sources are ordered in the following discussion by periods: (1) Pre-Sargonic, including everything before Sargon of Akkadē, partly overlapping the following; (2) Sargonic; (3) Ur III, partly overlapping the following; (4) Post-Ur III times. The sources may be distinguished as those originating in Babylonia and those excavated at Ebla and Mari.

3.1. *Pre-Sargonic Period*

3.1.1. *Introductory Remarks*

Our knowledge about Mari in the Pre-Sargonic period comes from the scattered sources originating in Babylonia, such as the Sumerian King List (below, SKL; § 3.1.2), from the ʾEnna-Dagan Letter (E.-D.) and references to Mari found in the Ebla texts (below § 3.1.2), and from the votive inscriptions (below, § 3.1.3) and administrative texts (below, § 3.1.4) excavated at Mari (see already Gelb 1977: 11).

3.1.2. *Sumerian and Eblaic Sources*

Fourteen kings of Mari occur in the listing of personal names connected with Mari in the Pre-Sargonic period. Of these, one king, ʾIlum-Pu, is attested only in SKL; four kings are named in the E.-D. Letter, of whom Śaʾʾumu ocurs also in SKL, Jiblul-ʾIl also in the administrative texts and dates of Ebla, and Jiśṭup-Śarr occurs only in the E.-D. Letter; five kings, namely, *Ḫi-da-ar, I-gi,* Jikûn-Śarr, NI-*zi,* and *Šu-ra* are attested only in the administrative texts of Ebla; and four kings, namely, Jikûn-Mari, Jikûn-Śamša, Jikûn-Šamakan, and *Iš*$_{x}$(LAM)-*gi*$_{4}$-*Ma-rí* are known only as votants in their votive inscriptions of Mari.

The titles borne by the kings and queens of Mari are LUGAL, EN, and NIN. See full discussion below, § 3.1.8.

The number of fourteen kings of Mari compares with the number of nine kings given by Archi (1981a: 161) and Michałowski in this volume, both of whom discuss kings of Mari who are attested at Ebla and omit kings who are named only in SKL (ʾIlum-Pu) and in the votive inscriptions of Mari (Jikûn-Mari, Jikûn-Śamša, Jikûn-Šamakan, and *Iš*$_{x}$-(LAM)-*gi*$_{4}$-*Ma-rí* are known only as votants in their votive inscriptions of Mari.

The following may be said about the sequence of the fourteen kings of Mari. ʾIlum-Pu, the first king of Mari according to the SKL, was followed by Śaʾʾumu; four kings, namely, Śaʾʾumu, Jiśṭup-Śarr, Jiblul-ʾIl, and ʾEnna-Dagan, are successively named in the E.-D. Letter; and seven kings, namely, Jiblul-ʾIl, ʾEnna-Dagan, Jikûn-Śarr, *Ḫi-da-ar, I-gi,* NI-*zi,* and *Šu-ra,* occur in the administrative texts of Ebla, and their approximate sequence may be established by the dates and correlation with the five kings of Ebla. Since I do not control the unpublished material of Ebla, all I can do at present is to refer to Archi (1981a: 161), who attempted to date successively the nine kings of Mari that were known to him. The chronological relation of the four kings of Mari, Jikûn-Mari, Jikûn-Śamša, Jikûn-Šamakan, and *Iš*$_{x}$(LAM)-*gi*$_{4}$-*Ma-rí,* who are attested solely in the votive inscriptions of Mari, to the kings of Ebla is completely unknown.

The Sumerian King List registers six kings who supposedly ruled in Babylonia for one hundred and thirty-six years between the rulers Lugal-ane-mundu of Adab and Ku-Bau of Kish (see Jacobsen 1939: 103f.).

Of the six names of the kings of Mari, only the first one is fully preserved and reads clearly AN.BU, not *An-sud*$_{4}$ (BU*gunu*) as in SKL 103 n 189. AN.BU was interpreted as an Akkadian name DINGIR-*Pu* /ʾIlum-Pu/

in MAD 3 210f., with the second element corresponding to the deified *Pum* 'mouth', 'word', 'logos', on the basis of such parallels as DINGIR-*Pu* (UE 2 322, 378, pl. 183c. UET 1 12), DINGIR-*Pum* /ʾIlum-Pum/ 'God is Pum', or 'Logos is god' (ITT 1/1 no. 923 rev. 1 and 7, Ur III), LUGAL-*Pum* /Šarrum-Pum/ 'Logos is king' (OIP 47 41), *I-sar-Pum* /Jiśar-Pum/ 'Logos is just' (see below, § 3.1.6), and others. Biggs (1967: 63f.) read BU as su_x and interpreted AN.BU as *Ìl*-su_x(BU) on the basis of such parallels as *Il*-su_x(BU)- or *Il-su-* and Su_x(BU)-*ma-* or *Su-ma* in the Abu Salabikh names (OIP 99 35, 71, and 112) and elsewhere, as in *Ìl*-su_x(BU), *Ìl-su* (MAD 3 31 = RTC 133) or *Il-su* (OIP 14 58 i; BIN 8 41, both Pre-Sargonic). No matter how interpreted, the name is clearly Akkadian or generally Semitic. While the name written AN.BU occurs on the seal impressions of Ur (UET 1 12; UE 2 322, 378, and pl. 183c), it is not followed by the LUGAL sign, thus disproving the connection between the AN.BU of Ur and the name of the king of Mari, which was proposed in SKL 103 n 189. The reading of AN.BU king of Mari on the Mesanepada pearl discovered at Mari (Dossin in MAM 4 53–59) has been disproved by Sollberger (1969: 169f.).

Of the remaining five names of the kings of Mari in the king list, only the final sign(s) are preserved: *-zi*, -LUGAL, -LUGAL, *-bi-im?*, and -NI are visible. These signs are likely to appear in Akkadian (Semitic) names. I have just learned, courtesy of Professor Markham Geller of London, that he reads the second of the six names *Sa-ú-mu*, making him synchronous with *Sá-ù-mu* EN *Ma-rí*KI, the "Śaʾʾumu king of Mari" of the ʾEnna-Dagan Letter discussed just below.

The discovery of the so-called "Treasury of Mesanepada" at Mari, including the pearl, raises the interesting question as to what extent Mesanepada, who called himself LUGAL *Kiš*, 'king of Kish' (UE 2 312f.), was in political control not only of Kish, that is, of northern Babylonia, but also of the kingdom of Mari (see Gelb 1981: 53).

The overthrow of Kish, Upi, and Mari was recorded in an inscription of Eanatum, king of Lagash (Thureau-Dangin 1907: 22; Feldstein A–B vi 21f.), who also writes of having been given the kingship of Kish (ibid., vi 4).

There is much information in the Ebla archives on the political and economic relations between Ebla and Mari. The political relations are amply treated in the well-known letter that *En-na-Da-gan* EN *Ma-rí*KI, 'ʾEnna-Dagan, king of Mari', wrote to an unnamed ruler of Ebla. As clearly stated in the title of his article, "Bolletino militare della campagna di Ebla contro la città di Mari," Pettinato (1980b) interpreted the letter as a military report of the conquest of Mari which ʾEnna-Dagan, allegedly an Ebla general, wrote to his superior, the king of Ebla. Compare similarly Pettinato (1977b, 1979b, 1981a) and Kienast (1980). Edzard (1981c) and Archi (1981a) interpreted the letter in a different way, a view that I share completely. Accordingly, ʾEnna-Dagan, king of Mari, wrote a diplomatic letter to his equal, the king of Ebla, informing him of the military campaigns which he and three of his predecessors on the throne of Mari conducted in the area of Mari.

The four rulers of Mari are named in the ʾEnna-Dagan letter in the following order: *Sá-ù-mu* EN *Ma-rí*^{KI}, 'Śaʾʾumu king of Mari' (i 3–iv 12); *Iš-dub-Sar* LUGAL *Ma-rí*^{KI}, 'Jišṭup-Śarr, King of Mari' (iv 13–v 13); *Ib-lul-Il* EN *Ma-rí*^{KI} *ú A-bar*-SILÀ^{KI}, 'Jiblul-ʾIl, king of Mari and ʾAparśal?' (vi 5–9), alternating with *Ib-lul-Il* EN *Ma-rí*^{KI} (vii 2–3) and *Ib-lul-Il* LUGAL *Ma-rí*^{KI} (viii 9–11; ix 8–10; rev. i 9–11; ii 13–iii 1; iv 12–14); and *En-na-Dagan* EN *Ma-rí*^{KI}, 'ʾEnna-Dagan, king of Mari' (rev. iii 2–iv 7?). Of these four names, Śaʾʾumu reappears as the king of Mari in the Sumerian King List (above, § 3.1.2), and Jiblul-ʾIl as the king of Mari in his votive inscriptions (below, § 3.1.5).

Archi (1981a: 154) briefly discussed an Ebla text, TM.75.G.2268, which he calls a political treaty (DUB *ù-šu-rí*, "documento dell'editto', da *WŠR?") between Mari and Ebla. Other treaties and political relations between Ebla and Mari are briefly described in MEE 1: nos. 1706, 1728, and 2000. Ebla administrative texts and year dates referring to *Ib-lul-Il* and *Šu-ra*, kings of Mari, are discussed in MEE 1: xxxiif. and Archi (1981a) 161f.

3.1.3. *Votive Inscriptions of Mari*

Votive inscriptions of the kings of Mari and other individuals were published mainly by Parrot (1967). Scattered sources are found in Thureau-Dangin (1934) 140–43, CT 5 2, Parrot (1965b) pl. XIII nos. 1 and 4 (photos), MAM 1 122 and pl. L, and Sollberger (1967) 104 (late copy). (See Gelb 1977: 11.) The circumstances of the discovery of the inscriptions in the temples of the so-called "Ištarat" and "Ninnizaza" deities (mainly MAM 3) were described by Börker-Klähm (1980).

New is the votive inscription of [1]*Al* (= form of MAḪ)-*ma* [2]DAM [3]*I-kùn*(KUM)-*Ma-rí*^{KI} [4]LUGAL *Ma-rí*^{KI}, 'ʿAlma, wife of Jikûn-Mari, king of Mari', a photograph of which is available to me courtesy of Vaughn Crawford and Robert D. Biggs. The Mari feminine name *Al-ma* is identical with the *Al-ma* of Ebla (MEE 2 43 viii 3, not in index; Archi 1981a: 155–60 i 6 and iv 4) and probably corresponds to Amorite *Ḫa-al-ma-tum* (Gelb 1980: 48, and elsewhere). For the interchange of the two feminine suffixes, *-a* and *-atum*, see below, § 3.1.8. The writing with ḪA in Amorite *Ḫa-al-ma-tum* suggests initial ʿ (Ġ) or, less likely, Ḥ. Accordingly, the most likely translation of *Al-ma* is 'girl', comparable with Arabic *ġulām* 'boy'. The votive deity, ^{d}*Nin-zi-Wa-ra-ne*^{KI}, is discussed below, § 3.1.6. The inscription has just been published by Fales (1984: 269f.).

3.1.4. *Administrative Texts of Mari*

A small group of Pre-Sargonic texts was registered in Gelb (1977) 11. Among their linguistic features we note the use of the lexical item *mi-at* /miʾat/, 'one hundred' (Parrot 1965b: 16 fig. 12), which recurs at Abu Salabikh and in a Sargonic text from Tell Brak in Upper Mesopotamia (see Gelb 1981: 62f.), and LUGAL, presumably for *malkum* 'king' and *ma-⸢lik⸣-[tum]* 'queen', which occur in Parrot (1965a) 15 no. 13, and are to be compared with EN *malkum* 'king' and *ma-lik-tum* 'queen' at Ebla, and LUGAL *šarrum* 'king' and NIN *bêlatum* 'queen' in Old Akkadian.

Additional administrative texts, which were excavated at Mari in 1980, are to be published by J. M. Durand and D. Charpin in a forthcoming issue of *Syria*. In a brief note devoted to the new readings of the post-Ur III text published by Dossin (1967c: 97–104), Durand (1980: 174) cited excerpts from two Pre-Sargonic administrative texts from Mari, reading ᵈINNIN-*Zar-bat* 'ʾInnin of Ṣarbat' (T 66 iv 2, photo in Parrot 1964: 8) and *iš Zar-bat*ᴷᴵ, 'to Ṣarbat' (T 70 ii 3). According to Charpin (1982: 3-4), there are a total of thirty-four administrative texts, "dites 'présargoniques'," equally divided between those excavated before and after 1980. They are said to be mainly concerned with rations to persons and gods.

A picture of economic relations between Ebla and Mari may be sketchily reconstructed on the basis of the descriptions of the Ebla administrative texts given by Pettinato (1979a = MEE 1) and the publication of the nine administrative texts in Archi (1981a) 131–66.

Judging from the frequency of occurrences in Pettinato (1979a), the economic relations of Ebla with the outside world were strongest with two cities lying on the Euphrates, namely Mari and Emar /Ḥimār/.

According to Pettinato (1979a), the object of the economic relations between Ebla and Mari were: Ì.GIŠ oil (nos. 3, 29), wooden objects (no. 813), and textiles (nos. 997, 1095, 1391). In one case, the word was about a KUG.DÍM *Ma-rí*ᴷᴵ, 'worker in precious metals of Mari' (no. 1046); in most cases, the description offered by Pettinato does not allow a determination of whether the texts concerned imports to Ebla or exports to Mari.

The nine administrative texts published by Archi (1981a) treat mainly varied amounts of silver and gold as well as daggers, precious stones, textiles, and different kinds of objects, described as NÍG.BA of the kings, elders, and high officials of Mari and other cities. The crux lies in our understanding of NÍG.BA LUGAL *Ma-rí*ᴷᴵ, 'gift of the king of Mari'. As in the ambiguous meaning of *amor dei* 'love of god', which may mean either the love of the god (for men), or the love (of men) for the god, the meaning of 'gift of the king of Mari' may be either the gift of the king of Mari (for Ebla) or the gift (of Ebla) for the king of Mari. While it is possible to establish from the context that some of the nine texts deal with gifts that were destined for Ebla and others that were destined for Mari, the matter is irrevelevant: we are clearly dealing with the exchange of gifts between equals and not with gifts offered by a subject to his sovereign.

The statements, "very important exchanges of goods [of Ebla] took place with Mari, the main export of which was wool that was manufactured at Ebla" (Archi 1980: 4), and "numerose citazioni di Mari nei testi di Ebla confermano . . . che Ebla esercitava un'egemonia economica su Mari" (Archi 1981a: 154) are beyond my control.

The nine administrative texts of Ebla which Archi published (1981a: 131–66; see above, § 3.1.4) are full of names, some connected with Mari and some not. Among the names connected with Mari in these texts and others cited by Archi are: *Ab-ba* (p. 154), *Ar-ri-a*-LUM (p. 160), *Bí-bí* (p. 156), GAL-*iš*-DÙG (p. 157), *I-ku-Il* (p. 159), *I-ti* (p. 154), *I-ti*-LUM (p. 151), *Il* (p. 157), *Ìr-ì-ba* (p. 154), *Iš-dub-Il* (p. 160), *Iš-má-ì-lum* (p. 160), *Iš-má-Il* (p. 157), PÙ.ŠA-*ra*-^{d}UTU (p. 154), *Sá-ba* (p. 154), Ù.BÍ.BÍ (p. 154), UR-*na* (p. 154). Most of these names reappear at Ebla.

3.1.5. *Votants and Kings*

The following is a list of the names of the votants and related persons who occur in the votive inscriptions and of the kings of Mari (marked by an asterisk). The abbreviations used are "E.-D. Letter" for the ᵓEnna-Dagan Letter (above § 3.1.2), SKL for Jacobsen (1939; above, § 3.1.2), "adm." for administrative, and "vot." for votive inscription.

AB+ÁŠ (MAM 3 309, vot.). The name AB+ÁŠ *Šîbum*, 'old man', 'elder', occurs frequently in ancient kudurrus.

Al-ma, wife of *I-kùn*(KUM)-*Ma-rí*^{KI} LUGAL *Ma-rí*^{KI}. Vot., see above, § 3.1.3.

AMAR-DINGIR (MAM 3 318, vot.).

Aw(WA)-*na-ni-*[*im*] (MAM 3 320, vot.). *Mar*ᵓ *ᵓAwnānim* is possibly a member of the *ᵓAwnān* tribe; see below, § 3.1.5.

Ar-ši-a-ḫa (Sollberger 1967: 104; vot.) and *Ar-si-a-ḫa* (MAM 3 320, vot.).

Be-bu-BÀD (MAM 3 329, vot.).

Dab$_{x}$(URUDU)-*rúm*(BÍ.RU) (MAM 3 315, 331, vot.).

*DINGIR-*Pu* LUGAL *Ma-rí*^{KI}. SKL, see above, § 3.1.2.

DUB-*la*, son of KUM.BÀD, brother of an unnamed king of Mari (MAM 3 319, vot.).

**En-na-Da-gan* EN *Ma-rí*^{KI} in E.-D. Letter, see above, § 3.1.2. Cf. also the following spellings and occurrences in administrative texts: *En-na-Da-gan* (Archi 1981a: 133), *En-na-*^{d}*Da-gan* (145), *En-na-*^{d}*Da-gan* LUGAL (143), *Gul-la* ŠEŠ *En-na-*^{d}*Da-gan* (142), and *En-na-Da-ga-an* (142f., *passim*); *Gul-la* is attested also (145).

EN.TI-*il* (Thureau-Dangin 1934: 143, vot.).

(LÚ) *Èš-pum* (Thureau-Dangin 1934: 142, vot.).

Gul-la, see *En-na-Da-gan*.

**Ḫi-da-ar* LUGAL *Ma-rí*KI (Archi 1981a: 162h, adm. unpubl.); *Ḫi-da-ar* without titles is named also in two administrative texts (ibid., 147 and 152).
I-bí-[....] (MAM 3 324, vot.).
**Ib-lul-Il* LUGAL *Ma-rí*KI (MAM 3 318, 323?, 327, 328, vot.; Pettinato 1977b: no. 2, p. 22, date; Archi 1981a: 132 twice, 161f.). For LUGAL *Ma-rí*KI alternating with EN *Ma-rí*KI, see E.-D. Letter, above, § 3.1.2.
**I-gi* LUGAL *Ma-rí*KI (Archi 1981a: 162g, adm., unpubl.).
**I-ku-Sar* EN *Ma-rí*KI (MEE 2 134f. = Archi [1981a] 162f., adm.).
**I-ku-*dŠ*a-ma-gan* LUGAL *Ma-rí*KI (MAM 3 309, 310, 329, vot.).
**I-kùn*(KUM)-*Ma-rí*KI LUGAL *Ma-rí*KI. Vot., see above, § 3.1.3.
Ì-li (MAM 3 330, vot.).
I-sar-Pum (MAM 3 315, vot.; sequence of signs in accordance with Jestin 1937: 750).
**Iš-dub-Sar* LUGAL *Ma-rí*KI. E.-D. Letter, see above, § 3.1.2.
Iš$_x$-*gi*$_4$ (reported as "Lamgi" in Parrot (1965b) 214, vot., but cf. LAM-*ki* in ARMT 19 311 and 312).
**Iš*$_x$(LAM)-*gi*$_4$-*Ma-rí* LUGAL *Ma-rí*KI (Thureau-Dangin 1934: 140, vot.).
*I-ti-*dÍD (Thureau-Dangin 1934: 142, vot.; MAM 3 322, vot.).
[*I*]-*ti-Il* (Sollberger 1967: 104, vot.).
KIN.URI (MAM 3 324, vot.; or URI.KIN as in Parrot (1965b) pl. 15 no. 13, Pre-Sargonic adm. Mari).
KUM.BÀD, brother of an unnamed king of Mari (MAM 3 325, vot.). See DUB-*la*.
Mi(*m*)-*ma-ḫir-su*(*d*) (MAM 3 323, vot.).
Munu$_x$(PAB)-*gá* NIN, 'queen', wife of [*Ib-lul*]?-*Il* LUGAL *Ma-rí*KI (MAM 3 318, vot.).
[*Na*]-*ni* (MAM 3 312, vot.).
**Ni-zi* LUGAL *Ma-rí*KI (Archi 1981a: 162d, citing p. 139 no. 5, and other occurrences of NI-*zi* on pp. 136, 137f. no. 3, and 139 no. 4).
Sá-lim (MAM 3 311, vot.).
**Sá-ù-mu* EN *Ma-rí*KI (E.-D. Letter, see above, § 3.1.2, and **Sa-ú-mu* (SKL, see above, § 3.1.2).
Su-wa-d[*a*] (MAM 3 329, vot.).
ŠUM.U (MAM 3 317 twice, vot.; the sign U is written in the form of an oblique wedge).
**Šu-ra* LUGAL *Ma-rí*KI (Pettinato 1977b: no. 2, p. 23; Archi 1981a: 162i, adm., date). Pettinato (1977b: no. 2, p. 23) and in (1981a) 146, adds what he considers a variant, *Šu-ra-Da-mu*, which Archi (1981a: 162i) does not register.
*Ur-*d*Nanše* (MAM 3 327, 328, vot.).
*Ur-*dUTU-*ša* (MAM 3 318, vot.).
X-ba-rúm(BÍ.RU) (MAM 3 312, vot.).
[...]-*lum* (MAM 1 122, vot.).
[...]-⌜*zi*⌝-[...] (Sollberger 1967: 104, vot.).

Two (or one?) unnamed kings of Mari occur in the inscriptions of DUB-*la* and KUM.BÀD (see just above), and the names of two kings of Mari are destroyed (MAM 3 314 and 316).

To judge from the names of individuals and deities that occur as part of those names in the known Pre-Sargonic texts pertaining to Mari, the general population of Mari was Semitic, not Sumerian, as were the deities they worshiped.

Two personal names begin with the element UR-, and give the appearance of being Sumerian. Of these, UR-^{d}NANŠE is composed of two Sumerian elements, and the name is, therefore, Sumerian. However, he was a singer/musician, and, as a wandering artist, he may very well have come to Mari from his homeland in southern Babylonia. The second name, UR-^{d}UTU-ŠA father of AMAR-DINGIR /Bûr-ʾilim/, is borne by a native of Mari; it is composed of the Sumerian element UR- and the non-Sumerian element ^{d}UTU-ŠA, and is, therefore, non-Sumerian. In the case of this Mari name, we are faced with the same problem as we are with many other names beginning with UR-, as, for instance, in the two names inserted among good Akkadian names of kings of the First Dynasty of Isin, and similarly at Kish (see MAD 2^2 12). For Akkadian names composed of *Bûr-*, written *Bur-* or AMAR-, see MAD 3 91f. A true Sumerian name, PAB.GÁ = MUNU$_x$-GÁ, meaning '(The child) of my. . . .', was borne by a wife of [*Ib-lul*]?-*Il*, who was the queen of Mari. The formation MUNU$_x$-GÁ, derived from MUNU+ZU+A(K), is paralleled by such names as NIN-GÁ, '(The child) of my lady'. MUNU$_x$-GÁ queen of Mari was obviously a foreigner in the midst of the Semitic rulers of Mari. For similar examples, see the case of the daughter of Narâm-Sin of Akkadē at Mari (below, § 3.2), and the daughter of Apil-kîn of Mari going to Ur to marry the son of Ur-Nammu, the first king of the Third Dynasty (below, § 3.3.2).

The name *ʾAwnānim*, in genitive, corresponds to the tribal name *ʾAwnān*, *ʾAmnān*, *ʾAmnānum* at Mari and in Babylonia in the Old Babylonia period, and provides important information on the tribal component of Mari civilization in the Pre-Sargonic period. For this Old Babylonian tribal name, see Kupper (1957) 49ff. and Index, 268. The existence of tribal elements at Mari in the Sargonic period is implied by the occurrence of the tribal term *gajjum* (see below, § 3.2).

A number of the names listed in § 3.1.5 above are at the present time not understandable. Among them are the names of four kings of Mari, *Ḫi-da-ar*, *I-gi*, NI-*zi*, and *Šu-ra*; *Gul-la*, brother of ʾEnna-Dagan; DUB-*la*, son of KUM.BÀD; *Su-wa-d*[*a*], son of BE-*bu*-BÀD; and ŠUM.U. They are all Semitic rather than non-Semitic.

The names exhibit standard formations, such as a noun, a noun plus construct state of a noun, and a noun plus a verb. The lexical *lemmata* *Jiblul-*, *Jiśqî-*, and *Jiśṭup-* recur at Ebla, the last two in Old Akkadian, and *Jiśṭup-* in Pre-Sargonic administrative texts (above, § 3.1.4), and Ur

III votive texts at Mari (below, § 3.3.2). See also § 3.1.4 for PNs in administrative texts.

3.1.6. *Deities*

The DNs appear in most cases independently as the names of the deities to whom the votive objectives were dedicated or in whose temple households the votants served, or as divine elements in the names of the votants and their relatives (above, § 3.1.3). As may be seen from the discussion below, the divine names are written syllabically, logographically, or as logograms plus phonetic indicators; and while most of them are Semitic, some (very few) are either Sumerian or not understandable. Added to the listing are DNs that occur in administrative texts, especially Parrot (1964) 8. The DNs are listed below alphabetically:

^{d}*A-bir*$_5$(NAM)-*tum* /ᶜAbirtum/ (Parrot 1964: 8 ii 6. adm.). Cf. PN *A-bir*$_5$*-tu*[*m*] (ARMT 19 430, cited below, § 3.1.8).

^{d}*Ama-ušum-gal* or ^{d}AMA.UŠUM.GAL (Parrot 1965b: 214, adm.; temple of A.).

ᵓ*Apiḫ-* in the name of a votant EN.TI-*il*, 'ᵓApiḫ is god'. ᵓ*Apiḫ*, later *Epiḫ*, is the deified name of the Hamrin range. Its initial and final consonants are uncertain. See also Gelb (1938) 67f.

^{d}*Aš-dar-ra-at* (MAM 3 329 and 330, votive deity). The first sign after the divine indicator is written with an oblique wedge whose allographs in the pre-Old Babylonian periods are a horizontal or vertical wedge. At the same time—that is, in the Pre-Sargonic period—the male god and his female counterpart are normally transliterated as ^{d}*Aš-tár* and ^{d}*Aš-tár-ra-at* by Pettinato, presupposing the existence of a sign written in its horizontal form. These two forms, a horizontal or oblique wedge, as well as a vertical wedge, occur as the signs AŠ and EŠ$_4$ from the Old Babylonian period on, just as the horizontal, oblique, and vertical allographs of a single sign correspond to the later sign EŠ written in the form of three "Winkelhakens." See MAD 2^2 47f. *ad* no. 1, and 100 *ad* no. 242. Phonologically, the forms ᶜAštar and ᶜAštarat show the preservation of *a* when preceded by ᶜ and followed by two consonants, as also in the name *Al-ma* /ᶜAlma/ (see above, § 3.1.3, and below, § 3.1.8. See also ^{d}*Innin* below.

Da-gan (Edzard 1967: 69), *-Da-gan* in the name of *En-na-Da-gan* king of Mari (above, § 3.1.3).

DINGIR.DINGIR (Parrot 1964: 8 ii 2). See also ^{d}*Pù-ra*-DINGIR.DINGIR, below, and MAD 3 34.

^{d}*En-líl* (CT 5 2; Thureau-Dangin 1934: 140). Both occurrences in the royal title EN$_5$.SI.GAL ^{d}*En-líl*, '(RN), viceroy of Enlil'.

EN.TI, see ᵓ*Apiḫ*.

^{d}ÍD, see *Nârum*.

-ʾ*Il* in PNs *Ib-lul-Il* and [*I*]-*ti-Il*.

^{d}IM (Parrot 1964: 8 ii 4).

^{d}*Innin-* in the compound names of votive deities ^{d}INNIN-GIŠ.TIR, 'ʾInnin of the forest' (MAM 3 319); ^{d}INNIN-NITA, 'The male ʾ*Innin*' (Thureau-Dangin 1934: 140, 142, 143); ^{d}INNIN-ZA.ZA (MAM 3 309, 311, 312, 314, 315 twice, 316, 318, 323, 326?, 327, 328, interpretation unknown); ^{d}INNIN-*Zar-bat*, 'ʾ*Innin* of Ṣarbat' (adm. text, see above, § 3.1.4), or, 'ʾInnin of *ṣarbat* (the Euphrates poplar)' (adm. text, see above, § 3.1.4).

^{d}LUGAL-*Ban-ga* 'King of Banga' (Parrot 1964: 8 iii 4).

^{d}LUGAL.KALAM.[MA], see *Śarru-mâtim* below.

-*Ma-rí*$^{<KI>}$ a deified geographical name in PNs *I-kùn*(KUM)-*Marí*^{KI} and *Iš*$_{x}$(LAM)-*gi*$_{4}$-*Ma-rí*.

-^{d}*Nanše* in the Sumerian name UR-^{d}NANŠE; see above, § 3.1.5.

^{d}*Nârum* and -^{d}*Nârum*, a deified river written ^{d}ÍD (Sollberger 1967: 106; MAM 3 329, temple household of ^{d}N.), and -^{d}ÍD in the PN *I-ti*-^{d}ÍD.

^{d}NIN-*da*?-*ra-at*? (MAM 3 320, votive deity). Interpretation unknown.

^{d}*Nin-zi-Wa-ra-ne*^{KI}, 'Ninzi of Warane', a compound deity in the votive inscription discussed above, § 3.1.3. ^{d}*Nin-zi* recurs in Deimel (1922) 1 v, ^{d}*Nin-zi-da* in Deimel (1914) no. 2571. GNs *Ù-ra-nè*^{KI}, *U*$_{9}$*-ra-na-a*^{KI}, and *Wa-ra-nu*^{KI} occur at Ebla (MEE 2 360f.), also *Wa-a-ra-an*^{KI} (MEE 1 nos. 4174–80). Cf. also *U-ra*-NI-*im*^{KI} (CT 50 70, Sargonic).

-*Pum* in PN *I-sar-Pum* /Jiśar-Pum/, '(god) Logos is just', and -*Pu* in PN DINGIR-*Pu* /ʾIlum-Pu/, 'Logos is god'; see above, § 3.1.2.

^{d}*Pù-ra*-DINGIR.DINGIR (Parrot 1964: 8 iii 6). See also DINGIR.DINGIR, above.

-^{d}*Ša-ma-gan* in PN *I-ku*-^{d}*Ša-ma-gan* /Jikûn-Šamakan/.

Śamša, or *Šamša*, the name of the sun god, appears in the form ^{d}UTU (CT 5 2; Sollberger 1967: 104, both votive deity), -^{d}UTU in the name of the votant *I-sar*-^{d}UTU, 'The sun god is just', and -^{d}UTU-*sa* in the name of a votant *Ur*-^{d}UTU-*ša* (see above, § 3.1.5). The first sibilant in the spelling of the second element -^{d}UTU-*ša* is unknown. The name corresponds, therefore, to either *Śamša*, or *Šamša*. Either form is in disagreement with Old Akkadian *śamś*, as in the names *Sa-am-si* /Śamśī/, 'My sun' (Gelb 1955: 18 and 19), and (*Be-lí-*)^{d}UTU-*si* /-Śamśī/ (MAD 1 109, both from Tell Asmar in the Diyala River region); (PÙ.ŠA-)^{d}*Sa-mu-uš* (MAD 1 215 and 241, both from Khafaje in the Diyala) is /-Śamuš/ or /-Śamuś/; the name read as (*Pù-*)*Ša-mu-sa*? /-Šamuśa/ or (PÙ.ŠA-)*Mu-sa*? in MAD 5 51 and p. 114, from Kish) may possibly be interpreted (PÙ.ŠA-)<*Sa*>-*mu-sa*? /-Śamuśa/, or (PÙ.ŠA-)<*Ša*>-*mu-sa*? /-Šamuśa/. It is interesting to note that all of these spellings are found at Tell Asmar and Khafaje in the Diyala region and Kish in northern Babylonia, both of which lie within the span of the Kish Civilization, which is deeply interwoven with features flourishing at Ebla-Mari. See Gelb 1981: §§ 9.2 and 9.3, and below, § 5. It is, therefore, natural to assume that the exact form of the name of the sun god recorded as ^{d}UTU-*ša* at Mari is reflected in some of the occurrences from the Diyala region and Babylonia cited above. For post-Ur III Mari there is a PN *Ša-maš-ì-lí* (ARMT 19 294).

-*Śarr* in the name of kings of Mari *Iš-dub-Sar* (above, § 3.1.2). and *I-ku-Sar.*

^{d}*Śarru-mâtim* or ^{d}*Śarr-mâtim,* 'King of the land', is written logographically ^{d}LUGAL.KALAM.[MA] (MAM 3 311, temple household of Ś.). ^{d}LUGAL-*ma-tim* is also known from the Mari votive inscriptions of the Ur III period (below, § 3.1.2) and ^{d}LUGAL-*ma-tim*$_{x}$ occurs in a post-Ur III administrative text (M. Lambert 1970: 247 no. 3).

^{d}UTU, see *Śamša.*

Some of the divine names listed above, such as ^{d}*Ama-ušum-gal,* ^{d}INNIN-GIŠ.TIR, ^{d}INNIN-NITA, ^{d}INNIN-ZA.ZA, ^{d}INNIN-*Zar-bat,* ^{d}LUGAL-KALAM. [MA] /Śarru-mâtim/, and ^{d}*Nin-zi-Wa-ra-nè*^{KI}, belong to a class that I have named "compound divine names" of type 3, DN + Description. The Pre-Sargonic divine names of Mari were studied by Edzard (1967). It is interesting to note that of the two chief gods of Mari in later periods, Dagan occurs only twice in the listing provided above, and Lîm not at all.

3.1.7. *Calendars*

The old "Semitic" calendar of Ebla in the Pre-Sargonic period was reconstructed by Pettinato (1977c). Additional variant spellings were registered in *MEE* 1 xxxivff. and 281f. As pointed out (Gelb 1977: 8 and 12), some of these month names reappear at Mari and at Abu Salabikh in Babylonia. Many of them are attested in the Sargonic period in scattered Babylonian and Assyrian sites. Cf. MAD 1 233f.

In Gelb (1981) 62, I was loath to draw any conclusions about the months of the Semitic calendar at Ebla, Mari, and Abu Salabikh, since "certain month names (and not others) of the Eblaic calendar may appear in different calendar systems of the same period." The newly discovered administrative texts of Mari have changed the picture completely. They allowed Charpin (1982) to reconstruct the names and the sequence of the Semitic calendar of Mari, which corresponds exactly to that of Ebla.

In the following discussion, the month names of Ebla are cited from Pettinato, those of Mari from Charpin, and those of Babylonia-Assyrian from Gelb.

Notes on Ebla-Mari MNs and Parallels (see Fig. 1)

I. *I-si*: This MN also occurs at Pre-Sargonic Abu Salabikh (OIP 99 508 iv). Possibilities are *ᵓIśiᵓum, ᵓIśśiᵓum, Jiśiᵓum,* or *Jiśśiᵓum,* with no apparent meaning. The interpretation of ITI *I-si* as "wohl Genetiv eines Names **iś(ś)um*" in Edzard (1967) 54 is contrary to the assumption expressed below, that MNs with the suffix -Ø are in the indeterminate state.

II. *Iq-za, I-iq-za, Iq-zum*: Interpretation: *Jiqṣum* 'heat'? The spelling *I-iq-za* suggests that the MN begins with *ji*, as in the Old Akkadian spelling *i-ik-mi* /jikmî/ 'he has bound', 'he has taken captive' (MAD 2^2 28). The spelling of *Jiqṣum* with *qṣ* conforms with the phonology of Ebla-Mari, and not with that of later Akkadian, which dissimilates *qṣ* to *kṣ*. See below, § 3.1.8. The reconstructed MN *Jiqṣum*, a noun of the *qitl* formation, may be derived from a root that occurs as JKṢ in Akkadian, and JQṢ in Hebrew, with the meaning 'to be awake'. Such a meaning is hardly appropriate for a month name. Not registered either in CAD or AHw, the MN *ik-zum* (the only spelling known at the time) was interpreted as *ikṣûm* 'cold' in MAD 3 26, by comparison with a sentence that was read and translated as *likṣî lu ba-ḫir* 'er möge erkalten, abkühlen', in Küchler (1904) 26f. line 45 = Langdon (1935) 16, and as *tukaṣṣa lu ba-ḫir* 'let it cool, but it should be still hot' in CAD B 29a. Thus the contrast between *kaṣûm* 'to be cold' and *baḫum* 'hot' and, similarly, between *kaṣûm* 'cold' and *emmum* 'hot' (and corresponding verbs), adds weight not only to the interpretation of the MN *Jiqṣum* 'cold', but also to that of the MN *Baḫīrum* 'heat' (see below). Related to the verb *kaṣûm* 'to be cold' may be the Old Akkadian noun *kiṣʾum* (or *qiṣjum*) 'morning', which may be so called after the cool of the morning (MAD 3 153). Unrelated is the *hapax* noun *i*G-*zum* in the entry *i*G-*zum šu* GUR_7 *na-ar-ki-im*, '. . . of the old grain storage' (MAD 1 270, perforated tag), parallel to x ŠE GUR *šu* GUR_7 BÍL 'x *gur* of barley of the new grain storage'. The lemma *i*G-*zum* is entered without a translation in MAD 3 26, CAD I 664, and AHw 370a. The connection between the root JQṢ of the MN *Jiqṣum*, the root QṢJ of the verb *kaṣûm* 'to be cold', and adjective *kaṣûm* 'cold' is justified by the assumption that the roots of JQṢ and QṢJ are based on the biconsonantal root QṢ which could be augmented by the weak consonants J or W in the initial, final, or medial positions, as in the allomorphs JQṢ and QṢJ, as well as QJṢ, which is attested in the Hebrew verb that occurs as JQṢ 'to awaken' in the *qal* stem, but as QJṢ (QWṢ) in other stems. The root QJṢ occurs in the noun, also a month name that means 'heat', 'summer' in Hebrew, the Gezer Calendar, and ancient South Arabic.

The choice of the meaning of the MN *Jiqṣum* lies between 'cold' and 'heat'. The adduced parallel with the noun based on QJṢ, which in other Semitic languages means 'heat', 'summer', or in which it denotes a month name, favors the meaning 'heat' for *Jiqṣum*. On the other hand, the existence of the Akkadian opposites *kaṣûm* (QṢJ) 'cold' and *baḫīrum* 'heat' (cited just above) leads to the conclusion that if the MN *Baḫīr* means 'heat', as argued below, then the MN *Jiqṣum* must denote its opposite, namely 'cold'.

Fig. 1. Earlier Calendar of Ebla-Mari and Parallels.

	Ebla, Pre-Sargonic	*Mari, Pre-Sargonic*	*Babylonia and Assyria, Sargonic*
I.	*I-si* (also Abu Salabikh)	*I-si*	-----
II.	*Iq-za*	*Iq-za, I-iq-za*	*Iq-zum*
III.	*Za-ʾà-tum* (also Abu Salabikh), *Za-ʾà-na, Za-ʾà-na-at*	*Za-ʾà-tum*	*Za-ʾà-tum*
IV.	*Gi-ì* (or *Gi-lí*)	*Gi-ì* (or *Gi-lí*)	*Gi-um*
V.	*Ḫa-li-du, Ḫa-li, Ḫa-li-ì*	*Ḫa-li-du, Ḫa-li*	*Ḫa-lí-it, Ḫa-lí-da* (MCS 9/1 233, collated, Umma), *Ḫa-lí-ì*
VI.	*I-rí-sá, Rí-sá*	*I-rí-sá*	*I-rí-sa-at*
VII.	*Ga-sum*	*Ga-sum*	-----
VIII.	Ì.NUN, Ì.NUN.NA, Ì.NUN.NA-*at*	Ì.NUN, Ì.NUN.NA	-----
IX.	*Za-nar* (or *Za-lul*)	*Za-nar* (or *Za-lul*)	*Za-nar* (or *Za-lul*)
X.	*I-ba*$_4$*-sa*	*I-ba*$_4$*-sa*	*I-ba-ša-áš*
XI.	MA+GÁN*tenû*.SAG	MA+GÁN*tenû*.SAG, MA+GÁN.SAG	-----
XII.	MA+GÁN*tenû*.SIG$_7$	MA+GÁN*tẹnû*.SIG$_7$	-----
XIII.	*Iq-za* MIN		
			a) *Ba-ḫi-ir* IGI, *Ba-ḫi-ir* IGI.ME, *Ba-ḫi-ir ma-*<*aḫ-rí*>? (also Mari, Sargonic)
			b) *Ba-ḫi-ir* EGIR
			c) *Ga-da-ad*
			d) *Ḫa-lu(l)-ut*
			e) *Ša-ni-í*
			f) *Ti-ru*

The words with opposite meanings, such as 'cold' and 'heat', belong to the class of *ʾaḍdād* words that have been amply discussed by Littmann (1910: 67–108). Unfortunately, the opposites 'cold' and 'heat' are nowhere discussed in that chapter.

Irrespective of whether the MN *Jiqṣum* is interpreted as the month of the greatest cold or the greatest heat, its placement as the tenth month of the Semitic Calendar by Pettinato, or the second month by Charpin, cannot possibly be right.

Besides the MN *ig-za,* Pettinato (1977c) 273, 278–81, knows of three occurrences of the MN *ig-za-mìn* at Ebla. They are not mentioned in Charpin's article (see also below).

III. *Za-ʾà-tum, Za-ʾà-na, Za-ʾà-na-at*: The first form also occurs at Abu Salabikh (OIP 99 513). Interpretation: *Ṣaʾattum* 'sheep and goats' (German *Kleinvieh*). My reading and interpretation of the MN occurring at Išnun and Lagaš as *Ṣaliltum* (MAD 3 243) was corrected by Pettinato (1977c: 275) to *Ṣaʾattum* on the basis of other spellings occurring at Ebla and Mari. The word is related to Hebrew *ṣōʾn* from **ṣaʾn* meaning 'sheep and goats'. Obviously the month was named after the period during which sheep and goats yeaned, that is, bore their lambs and kids. This normally takes place in the spring in the Near East.

IV. *Gi-í, (I)gi-ì, Gi-um*: The hapax spelling IGI-*lí* is cited in MEE 1 xxxv and 282. Pettinato and Charpin read *Gi*-NI as *Gi-lí*. If it turns out that there is no spelling *Gi-li* to support this reading, then I suggest that the spelling *Gi-um* in Old Akkadian favors the interpretation of *GI*-NI as *Gi-ì* at Ebla and Mari. Possibilities are *Giʾum, Kiʾum,* and *Qiʾum*. No interpretation.

V. *Ḫa-li-du, Ḫa-lí-da, Ḫa-lí-it, Ḫa-li, Ḫa-lí, Ḫa-li-ì*: Dahood (*apud* Pettinato 1977c: 272 and n 8) suggests comparison with the Ugaritic month name *ḤLT* (Gordon 1965: 232 and 397; Aistleitner 1967: 103 and 136), which leads, presumably, to *Ḥalîtum,* etc., at Ebla-Mari and Babylonia-Assyria. There are too many possibilities and no plausible interpretations.

VI. *I-rí-sá, Rí-sá, I-rí-sa-at*: The unexplainable apocopation of the initial *I-* in *Rí-sá* is attested several times at Ebla. The most plausible interpretation of the MN *Ḥiriśatum* as the month of cultivation and seeding (MAD 3 66f.) stumbles on the problem of the sibilants (see below). The spellings of the MN with SÁ and SA, and of the underlying verb *e-ra-si-iš* (HSS 10 5:25) with SI, suggest the root ʿRŚ or ḤRŚ, contrariwise to the root ḪRŠ in Ugaritic, ḤRT in Aramaic, ḤRṮ in Arabic, which should be spelled with ŠA and ŠI at Ebla-Mari, as in Old Akkadian. Apparently, there is a confusion between two roots, one ḤRŠ, ḤRT, ḤRṮ 'to cultivate', 'to seed', and the other ʿRŚ that is known from Arabic *ġarasa* 'to plant (trees, herbs, etc.)'.

VII. *Ga-sum*: The possibilities are *G/K/Qaśśum, G/K/Qaššum,* or *G/K/Qaḏḏum* (= *G/K/Qažžum*). Since the initial sibilant of -SUM is *ḏ* (= *ž*) at Ebla, the most plausible connections are with Akkadian *gazāzum* 'to shear (sheep)', *gazzum* 'shorn', and also *kazāzum, kasāsum, kaṣāṣum,* etc. The shearing of sheep took place in the third month of the Adab Calendar in the Sargonic period (Gelb *apud* Hunger, *RLA* 5 299), and in an unknown month registered in an Ur III tablet (MVN 3 246).

VIII. Ì.NUN, Ì.NUN.NA, Ì.NUN.NA-*at*: The logographic spellings Ì.NUN and Ì.NUN.NA, plus the phonetic indicator *-at* in the third example, lead to the reading *Ḫimʾat* 'butter', 'ghee', later *ḫimêtum* in Akkadian. The interpretation of the month name as butter (or ghee) makes sense only if it is assumed that the month was so named because the best kind of butter (or ghee) was produced only during that month of the year. This suggestion is partly confirmed by the existence of Ì.NUN.NUN 'noble butter', that is, the best kind of butter, as a basis of Ì.NUN, the non-canonical names of the month IV in the new Calendar of Ebla (see below). For similar adjectives, cf. *ì-dùg-nun* (Thureau-Dangin 1907: 112 xxii 5, from Civil), *ì-dùg-nun-na* (Scheil 1921: 53 ii 13, from Civil) or *ì-nun-dùg* (MSL 11 121:9, from Civil; Gelb 1955: 34:5), *ì-nun-dùg-ga* (Scheil 1921: 53 ii 11, from Civil; RTC 215). Unfortunately, despite a diligent search, I am not able to produce any evidence from modern times that a certain month of the year was better suited than any other to clarify, or to heat, butter in the form of ghee.

IX. *Za-nar*: There is no more reason to read the MN *Za*-LUL as *Za-lul* or *Ṣa-lul*, as Gelb, Pettinato, and Charpin did, than as *Za-nar*. Judging from the collections of month names gathered by Langdon (1935: 1-47), the root ṢLL is not productive in the menology of the Semitic peoples. On the other hand, the reading of the MN as *Za-nar* finds support in several parallels: PNs *Za-na-r*[*-i*] (IM 61406, Sargonic, unpublished) and *Za-na-ru-um* (Birot 1969: 60, OB); DN ^{d}*Za-na-ru*, and lexical ^{GIŠ}ZA-NA-RU in Sumerian, and *zannarum* in Akkadian, denoting a musical instrument (Sjøberg 1965: 64f.; Castellino 1972: 48:166; W. G. Lambert 1982: 213).

X. *I-ba*$_{4}$*-sa*, *I-ba-ša-áš*: A collation of *I-ba-ša-áš* in OIP 14 leaves little room for any other reading of this Adab MN. Its derivation from *pašāšum* 'to anoint' in MAD 3 219, and its relation to *I-ba*$_{4}$*-sa* of Ebla-Mari, are unexplainable. The spelling *I-ba*$_{4}$*-sa* occurs several times and cannot easily be corrected to *I-ba*$_{4}$*-sa-áš*, which, in addition, suffers from the difficulty of adjusting the divergent sibilants in the spellings ŠA and SA.

XI. MA+GÁN*tenû*-SAG, MA+GÁN.SAG: The reading is Pettinato's and Charpin's. Besides these forms, Pettinato (1977c: 275) also has a single occurrence of the MN MA+*ganatenu*-sag-mìn, the last sign of which is transliterated as ⸢mìn⸣ on p. 277. This MN is not recognized by Charpin.

XII. MA+GÁN*tenû*.SIG$_{7}$: Edzard (1967: 54) reads MA×GÁN-*tenû*+IGI-*gunû*×KASKAL; Pettinato (1977c: 274) reads MA×*ganatenû*-gudu$_{4}$ (with gudu$_{4}$ composed of KISIM$_{5}$×IR+ME) at Ebla, and MA×*ganatenû*-KISIM$_{5}$×IR at Mari (p. 283). Charpin (1982: 5 n 13) terms his reading MA×GÁN*tenû*-sig$_{7}$ an "approximation" and "transcription simplifiée" from MA+GÁN-*tenû*+SIG$_{7}$(×KÚR). Since both MA+GÁN*tenû*.SAG and MA+GÁN*tenû*+SIG$_{7}$ occur in the Mari text T 67 (= Charpin 1982: 5), they must be taken as two independent month names, not variants. Used as a noun, the Sumerian SAG corresponds to *raʾšum* 'head', 'front', and is contrasted by the syllabically written *warkum* 'back' in Old Akkadian (MAD 3 64 and 232). Used as an adjective, SAG **raʾšijum*, **raʾštijum* 'earlier' of month name XI is contrasted by the Sumerian root that was symbolized as "SIG$_{7}$" by Charpin in the month name XII. Whatever its reading and the Semitic correspondence, "SIG$_{7}$," as the opposite of SAG, must have the meaning of

EGIR *warkijum* 'later' which occurs in the pair of months *Ba-ḫi-ir* IGI+ /Baḫīr maḫrî/ 'Earlier Baḫīr' and *Ba-ḫi-ir* EGIR /Baḫīr warkî/ 'Later Baḫīr', discussed below. The stumbling points to a successful interpretation are the first sign in MNs XI and XII, which is found nowhere else and was read as MA+GÁN*tenû* by Edzard, Pettinato, and Charpin, and the second sign in MN XII, which was described in different ways by Edzard and Pettinato and was symbolized by Charpin as "SIG_7." This sign has several meanings, none of which approximate EGIR. See also below for a possible identification of the Ebla-Mari month names XI-XII with *Baḫīr maḫrî* and *Baḫīr warkî*.

Since the ten month names of Ebla-Mari are written syllabically, as are all the month names that are attested in Babylonia-Assyria (see below), and all of them are Semitic, I have no doubts that the Ebla-Mari month names XI-XII are not Sumerian, but Semitic names that are written logographically.

As may be seen from the above discussion, all twelve months of the old Semitic Calendar are attested at both Ebla and Mari in the Pre-Sargonic period. Its further areal and temporal distribution is indicated below:

1) Two Pre-Sargonic Ebla-Mari MNs recur at Pre-Sargonic Abu-Salabikh:
   - I. *I-si* (OIP 99 508 iv)
   - III. *Za-ʾà-tum* (OIP 99 513 rev.)

2) Seven Pre-Sargonic Ebla-Mari MNs recur in Sargonic Babylonia-Assyria:
   - II. *Iq-zum* (HSS 10 96, Gasur; ITT 1 1291, Lagaš)
   - III. *Za-ʾà-tum* (MAD 1 296, 330, Išnun; RTC 106, Lagaš)
   - IV. *Gi-um* (MAD 1 102, 292, 299, Išnun)
   - V. *Ḫa-lí-it* (HSS 10 41, 82, 125, Gasur; MAD 4 10, of unknown origin); *Ḫa-lí-da* (MCS 9/1 233, collated, Umma); *Ḫa-lí-i* (RTC 117, Lagaš)
   - VI. *I-rí-sa-at* (MAD 1 273, 306, Išnun)
   - IX. *Za-nar* (HSS 10 63, 144, 170, Gasur)
   - X. *I-ba-ša-áš* (OIP 14 165, Adab)

3) Six Pre-Sargonic Ebla-Mari MNs are not attested in Sargonic Babylonia-Assyria.
   - I. *I-si*
   - IIb. *Iq-za* MIN
   - VII. *Ga-sum*
   - VIII. Ì.NUN+
   - XI. MA+GÁN*tenû*.SAG+
   - XII. MA+GÁN*tenû*.SIG_7?

4) Six Sargonic Babylonian-Assyrian MNs are not attested at Pre-Sargonic Ebla-Mari. Since their position within the Semitic Calendar is unknown, they are listed below in alphabetical order:

a) *Ba-ḫi-ir* IGI (OIP 14 92, Adab); *Ba-ḫi-ir* IGI.ME (PBS 9 119, AS 17 12, both Nippur); *Ba-ḫi-ir ma-<aḫ-rí>*? (MAD 1 154, Išnun).

b) *Ba-ḫi-ir* EGIR (MAD 1 184, Išnun; ITT 1 1079, Lagaš).

The spelling *Ba-ḫi-ir* was derived from the noun *baḫīrum* 'heat?' in MAD 3 94f.; CAD B 28 connects the MN with the Akkadian adjective *baḫrum* 'hot'. The interpretation of *Ba-ḫi-ir* as a noun, rather than an adjective, is preferred because all other month names are nouns. AHw 96a leaves the month name unexplained but connects it possibly with *baḫrum* 'well-done', 'well-cooked'. The interpretation of *Ba-ḫi-ir* as 'heat' is supported by the Arabic *baḫara* 'to steam'. Both spellings of the adjective qualifying *Ba-ḫi-ir*, IGI and IGI.ME, occur as prepositions with the correspondence *maḫar* 'before', 'in front' in Old Akkadian (MAD 3 173f.). The spelling IGI.ME (for IGI) is known from a bilingual inscription of Rîmuš (MAD 3 173), from the Pre-Sargonic votive inscriptions of Mari (MAM 3 319, 325, 326), and from Ebla (MEE 4 357: 0128). The adjectival meaning *maḫrijum* 'first', 'earlier' for IGI and IGI.ME is not attested in Old Akkadian, but is necessitated by the opposition of IGI and IGI.ME to EGIR *warkijum* 'later' in the MN *Ba-ḫi-ir* EGIR. The reconstruction of *Ba-ḫi-ir* MA to *Ba-ḫi-ir ma-<aḫ-rí>*?, which is in indeterminate state (see below), is based on the same reasoning. The spelling *Ba-ḫi-ir* MA occurs in a Sargonic text of Mari, recently published by Durand (1984b: 264) and cannot be taken, therefore, as a scribal error. Durand read *Ba-ḫi-ir-ma* and noted that "la date est soulignée par l'enclitique *-ma*." Similar use of *-ma* is known, for instance, from royal titulary, as in RN_1 LUGAL *Aššur* DUMU RN_2 LUGAL *Aššur-ma* 'RN_1, king of Aššur, son of RN_2, *also* king of Aššur' (KAH 2 80; KAV 1 ii). With month names it does not make much sense.

The outward similarity between the two pairs of months, *Ba-ḫi-ir* IGI and *Ba-ḫi-ir* EGIR, used in Babylonia-Assyria in the Sargonic period, and MA+GÁN*tenû*.SAG and MA.GÁN*tenû*."SIG_7", used at Ebla-Mari in the Pre-Sargonic period (above) is great enough to suggest that they might be identified, as was actually done by Pettinato (1977c: 264). This identification clashes with some obstacles. The first is the reading and identification of the initial sign, MA+GÁN*tenû*, occurring in months XI and XII, and of the second sign, "SIG_7", occurring in month XII of the Pre-Sargonic Calendar; the second is the placement of MNs XI and XII in the cold months, at the end of the Semitic Calendar, contrasting with the meaning of the two *Baḫīr* months as 'heat' and their placement in the summer. Still, it is possible that renewed collations of the Ebla-Mari texts and a corrected placement of MNs XI and XII within the Semitic Calendar may yet overcome the apparent difficulties and bring the two pairs of months together.

c) *Ga-da-ad* (HSS 10 166, 184, Gasur): No parallels, no interpretation.

d) *Ḫa-lu(l)-ut* (MAD 1 153, 163, 293, 331, Išnun): No parallels, no interpretation.

e) *Ša-ni-i* (OIP 14 117, Adab; Scheil 1925: 159, Lagaš): A month named *Šanî* 'Second' apparently refers to an intercalary month, as denoted at Mari by ITI *Taš-ni-tim*$_x$ in the post-Ur III period (ARMT 19 32+), and ITI *E-bu-ur Taš-ni-tim,* ITI *E-bu-ri* MIN, ITI *Ta-aš-ni-it Ḫi-b*[*ir*$_5$*-ti*]*m,* and ITI *Ḫi-bi-ir-tim* MIN in the Old Babylonian period (ARMT 19, p. 11). See also below.

f) *Ti-ru* (MAD 1 287, Išnun; MAD 4 44, Kiš): For the Old Babylonian MNs written *Ti-ri-im* or *Ti-ri,* see AHw 136 under *Tīrum,* MAD 3 299, and Edzard 1970: no. 117. A related dating of the type UD *Ti-ru-um*-ŠÈ, parallel to UD *E-lu-um*-ŠÈ, occurs in TA 1931.326, an unpublished Tell Asmar tablet of the Ur III–post-Ur III period. Derived occurrences in PNs and DNs were noted in MAD 3 299; several Old Babylonian occurrences of the PN dEN.ZU-*ti-ri* were collected in ARMT 15 155. The underlying lexeme *ti-ru* occurs in the Sargonic texts MDP 14 24 end, 25 end, registered in MAD 3 299, MDP 14 6 rev. ii; and *in te-ir,* UDU *te-ir,* and SILÀ *te-ir* at post-Ur III Mari (ARMT 19 166, and below). See also AHw 1351a under *tēru(m).*

5) One Sargonic Babylonian-Assyrian MN is attested at Sargonic Mari:

a) *Ba-ḫi-ir ma-*<*aḫ-rì*>? (Durand 1984b: 264). See above under 4a.

Several of the proposed interpretations, some quite tentative, may help to establish the sequence of the Semitic calendar at Ebla-Mari. Among them, note especially the following.

Iq-za /Jiqṣa/ 'Cold?', the coldest month of the year, which is January/February. It is classified as month X of the Semitic calendar by Pettinato and month II by Charpin.

*Za-*ʾ*àtum* /Ṣaʾattum/ 'Sheep and goats' (*'Kleinvieh'*), the month of yeaning, which greatly varies from country to country. Cf. Kraus 1966: 51f. It is denoted as month III or month XI, respectively, by Pettinato and Charpin.

Ga-sum /Gazzum/? 'Shearing', the month of shearing sheep, which is normally around February/March in ancient Babylonia, April/May in Syria and Palestine. See Kraus 1966: 46f.; Waetzoldt 1972: 10f. It is classified as month III or VII, respectively, by Pettinato and Charpin.

I-rí-sá /ᶜIrīša/ 'Cultivation', the month of cultivating (including sowing) the fields, which is October/November in ancient Babylonia. It is classified as month II or VI, respectively, by Pettinato and Charpin.

Ba-ḫi-ir IGI+ /Baḫīr maḫrî/ 'Earlier Heat' and *Ba-ḫi-ir* EGIR /Baḫīr warkî/ 'Later Heat' of the Babylonian-Assyrian calendar (above), the two months of greatest heat, which are July and August. These two months may correspond to the MA+GÁN*tenû*.SAG and MA+GÁN*tenû*."SIG_7" of the Ebla-Mari calendar that were classified as months VII and VIII by Pettinato, or months XI and XII by Charpin.

As may be seen from the foregoing, there are serious differences between Pettinato and Charpin in their placement of the individual months within the Semitic Calendar (and between their placements that are solely based on the sequence in which the month names are listed in the texts) and my interpretations that are based solely on meaning. It seems inappropriate to discuss in detail all of these divergencies until the following points are fully established: the exact meaning of the individual month names, the sequence of the ancient calendar, the beginning of the ancient calendar (Spring or Fall), and the place of the individual months within the sequence of the ancient and modern calendars.

All twelve month names occur in the texts written in the language of Ebla-Mari or Akkadian, and all are Semitic, not Sumerian. This applies, obviously, to the nine months of the Ebla-Mari Calendar and the Babylonian-Assyrian month names, all of which are written syllabically. Since the Sumerian influence at Ebla-Mari is restricted to didactic and literary literature, there is no reason, in my judgment, to interpret the three Ebla-Mari MNs that are not written syllabically as Sumerian, rather than Semitic. This applies in the first place to Ì.NUN, Ì.NUN.NA, which, as shown by the spelling Ì.NUN.NA-*at*, are logograms to be read in Semitic; and this is also true of the logograms MA+GÁN*tenû*.SAG and MA+GÁN*tenû*. SIG_7 of the Ebla-Mari Calendar, which may even correspond to the two *Baḫīr* months of the Semitic Calendar of Babylonia-Assyria and Mari in the Sargonic period.

The month names appear either in the normal state with the suffix *-um*, with or without mimation, as in *Iq-zum* and *Ti-ru*, or in the indeterminate state with the suffix -Ø, as in *Za-nar* and *Ba-ḫi-ir*, or the suffix *-a*, as in *Iq-za* and *Ḫa-lí-da*. For examples and discussion, see below (§ 3.1.8). The occurrence of the names in the normal or indeterminate states clearly indicates that ITI in the structure ITI MN is a graphic auxiliary ("determinative" or "semantic indicator"), and it does not form part of the construct with the MN in genitive, as in Post-Ur III and Old Babylonian Mari, or in Old Assyrian, for example.

In part repeating the information gathered above, we shall investigate the distribution of the Semitic Calendar in terms of time and space in the following pages. In the Pre-Sargonic period, the Semitic Calendar is attested at Ebla-Mari in the west and at Abu Salabikh in Babylonia in the east. In the Sargonic period, it occurs primarily in Babylonia-Assyria, and once at Mari. Most of the Babylonian-Assyrian attestations come from Išnun (14) in the Diyala River district, and Gasur (9) in Assyria, the two outposts of what I have dubbed "the Kish Civilization." Strangely, only one occurrence is attested at Kish itelf, in the heartland of the Kish Civilization. The few attestations at Lagaš, Adab, Nippur, and Umma in the Sumerian area of Babylonia may be explained as due to their exposure to the Akkadian (Semitic) influence emanating from the north, around Kish. All of the month names of the Semitic Calendar disappear after the Sargonic period, except MN Ì.NUN+, which appears in the new calendar of Ebla, MN *Ti-ru*, which is also known in the Old Babylonian period, and MN *Ḫa-li-du*+ (all referred to above), which may correspond to the MN ḤLT at Ugarit.

There are twelve regular months at Pre-Sargonic Ebla, including a pair of months, XI and XII, which bear the same name, MA+GÁN*tenû*, and different qualifications, SAG and "SIG$_7$." In addition, an intercalary month *Iq-za* MIN is used at Ebla, but apparently not at Mari. Another intercalary month, read MA+*ganatenû-sag-mìn* and MA+*ganatenû-sag-*⌈*min*⌉ by Pettinato (1977c: 275 and 277), is too doubtful for serious consideration. Thirteen months are attested at Pre-Sargonic Mari, as well as in Sargonic Babylonia-Assyria, including an intercalary month *Ša-ni-i*. Of these, seven months are attested at Ebla-Mari in the Pre-Sargonic period, while six months, including a pair of months, 5a and 5b, which bear the same name, *Ba-ḫi-ir*, plus different qualifications, IGI+ and EGIR, are not. Even admitting that Pre-Sargonic month names XI and XII correspond to Sargonic month names 5a and 5b, as argued above, the divergences are great enough to force the conclusion that the Pre-Sargonic calendar of Ebla-Mari was not operative in the Sargonic calendars of Babylonia-Assyria and Mari. We may, therefore, conclude that there was a single Pre-Sargonic calendar at Ebla-Mari, which is partly attested at Abu Salabikh in Babylonia, and whose origin lies in the heartland of the Kish Civilization. Our knowledge of the Sargonic month names was culled over the years from many sites in Babylonia-Assyria and from Mari, and many more are expected to come to light in the future. Apparently, there were several city calendars in the Sargonic period which drew their month names partly from the common patrimony of the Pre-Sargonic period and partly from the various local traditions. For parallels, compare, for instance, the history of the city calendars of the Ur III and early Old Babylonian periods.

Besides the Semitic calendar (discussed above), which Pettinato (1977c) called "calendario vecchio" or "calendario semitico," there is a slightly later calendar, which Pettinato called "calendario nuovo" (1974–77). An alphabetical listing of the month names plus their "variants" was provided by Pettinato in MEE 1 xxxvif. and 281f. In comparison with the older calendar, the areal and temporal coverage of the new calendar is very limited, as it was used only at Ebla and only at the time of the last king of Mari, Jibbiʾ-Zikir. Thus, the new calendar partly overlaps the old calendar. See Pettinato 1977c: 257, 278–79; 1974–77: 1; and Charpin 1982: 3.

A listing of the twelve months of the new calendar plus ten "variants," for a total of twenty-two entries, is given by Pettinato (1974–77: 35); an abbreviated listing, without "variants," is also provided by Charpin (1982: 2). For unclear reasons, both scholars treat the intercalary month ŠE.GUR.KUD MIN together with ŠE.GUR$_{10}$.KUD.

The MNs in fig. 2 are listed under three headings, "Main," "Variants," and "Non-Canonical." When the MN has different forms or spellings, one of them was placed under Main and the others under Variants. The variants are either abbreviated forms of the main entry, as in MNs II, IV, XIII, or are graphic (XII), phonetic (V, VI), or morphemic (IX) variants of the main entry. Forms that cannot be interpreted as variants along these lines are placed under Non-Canonical. They include MNs apparently taken over from a different tradition or calendar. The most interesting of the non-canonical names are Ì.NUN, Ì.NUN.NUN, and A.NUN.NUN (listed under IV). Of these, Ì.NUN means 'butter', 'ghee', Ì.NUN.NUN 'noble butter', that is, the best kind of butter, and A.NUN.NUN may possibly be a phonetic variant of Ì.NUN.NUN. The MN Ì.NUN + is the only one that was inherited from the Semitic Calendar. For an interpretation of this MN, see above. The non-canonical MN IZI.GAR is connected with the Sumerian compound word IZI-GAR, with all its meanings associated with 'fire', and the Ur III MN IZI-IZI-GAR. Any relation between the Eblaic MNs IZI.GAR and *Ḫurmu+* is unprovable.

Since the new calendar is limited in its use to Ebla, the following brief remarks affect directly the writing and language of Ebla, and only indirectly those of Mari.

Notes on the Later Calendar of Ebla (see Fig. 2)

Ad I. BE.LI: Written with the sign LI, this MN cannot be interpreted as /Beʿlī/.

Ad II, IV, and XIII: These MNs are written either INNIN.ŠUKU+DN, in which INNIN.ŠUKU stands for the normal ŠUKU.INNIN or ŠUKU.^{d}INNIN, Akkadian *nindabûm* 'food offering' or simply DN.

Ad II. ^{d}*Aš-da-bi*$_{5}$: This DN, after whom the month was named, was called "grand dieu hourrite, identique à NINURTA ou à ZABABA" by Laroche (1946/47: 46). See also note to IX.

Ad IV. ^{d}*À-da*: This spelling of the weather god is known at Ebla. See, e.g., Pettinato (1979c: 125).

Fig. 2. The Later Calendar of Ebla.

	Main	*Variants*	*Non-Canonical*
I.	BE.LI		
II.	ŠUKU.INNIN-^{d}*Aš-da-*bi_5	a) ^{d}*Aš-da-*bi_5	
III.	NI.DU		
IV.	ŠUKU.INNIN-^{d}*Ã-da*	^{d}*Ã-da*	a) Ì.NUN b) Ì.NUN.NUN c) A.NUN.NUN
V.	*Ĩ-la-mu*	a) *Ir-me* b) *Ir-mi*	
VI.	*Ḫu-lu-mu*	a) *Ḫu-la-mu* b) *Ḫur-mu* c) *Ḫu-*ru_x(EN)*-lu*	a) IZI.GAR
VII.	È		
VIII.	ŠUKU		
IX.	^{d}*A-dam-ma-um*	a) ^{d}*A-da-ma-um* b) ^{d}*A-dam-ma*	
X.	ŠE.GUR_{10}.KUD		
XI.	ŠE.GUR_{10}.KUD MIN		
XII.	^{d}AMA.RA		
XIII.	ŠUKU.INNIN-^{d}*Ga-mi-iš*	a) ŠUKU.INNIN-^{d}*Ga-me-iš* b) ^{d}*Ga-mi-iš*	

Ad V and VI: The spellings of V—*Ĩ-la-mu, Ir-me, Ir-mi*—and of VI—*Ḫu-lu-mu, Ḫu-la-mu, Ḫur-mu*—show the *r/l* alternation and vocalic alternation and elision, all known at Ebla.

Ad V and XIII. The alternation of the signs ME/MI in V—*Ir-me, Ir-mi*—and in VII—^{d}*Ga-me-iš*, ^{d}*Ga-mi-iš*—is known at Ebla.

Ad VI. The variant *Ḫu-*ru_x(EN)*-lu* in relation to *Ḫu-lu-mu, Ḫu-la-mu,* and *Ḫur-mu* shows a rather far-fetched *l/m* alternation.

Ad IX. ^{d}*A-dam-ma-um*, ^{d}*A-da-ma-um*, ^{d}*A-dam-ma*: Discussed by Pettinato (1974/77: 28 and n 43), the DN Adamma, after whom the MN was named, was taken as a Hurrian goddess of the circle of Kubaba by Laroche (1946/47: 46). See also note to II. Linguistically noteworthy is the omission of the suffix *-um*, which is well known in the language of Ebla-Mari (see above).

Ad XII. ^{d}AMA.RA: For ^{d}AMA.RA = ^{d}$BARA_{10}$*-ra* = *Iš-ḫa-ra,* see Pettinato (1979b: 281).

Ad XIII. ^{d}*Ga-me/iš*: See above *ad* V, Pettinato (1979c: 126), and (1976: 11-15).

Of the thirteen month names and their variants plus two non-canonical names, four are unintelligible (I, III, V, VI), six are written in "Sumerian" (VII, VIII, X, XI, plus non-canonical IV, VI), and five are either composed of "Sumerian" ŠUKU.INNIN+DN, or correspond to a DN (II, IV, IX, XII, XIII). As indicated by the capitalization, "Sumerian" elements are logograms to be read in the Semitic language of Ebla, not in Sumerian. For a similar situation in the earlier calendar, see above. Even though none of the names is written clearly in Eblaic, their phonetic and morphemic features (*r/l*, omission of *-um*, vowel alternation and elision) leave little doubt that the later calendar is written in that language.

There are very few connections between the later calendar of Ebla and other calendars. The MNs X ŠE.GUR$_{10}$.KUD and XI ŠE.GUR$_{10}$.KUD MIN recur in the Ur III calendars, and the non-canonical MN IV Ì.NUN+ is identical with the MN VIII of the Semitic Calendar at Ebla and Mari (above).

With at least fifteen month names plus their variants presently attested, the short-lived new calendar, like the older, Semitic Calendar of the Sargonic period (above), must have drawn its inventory of month names from more than one source.

The year dates are marked in two ways at Ebla-Mari: by 1) the number of the reign of an unnamed king, such as 1 MU, 2 MU, etc., or 2) an event in his reign, such as MU LUGAL *Ma-rí*^{KI} UG$_5$ 'the year in which the king of Mari died'. The former form of dating is attested at Ebla and Mari, the latter only at Ebla. Both kinds of dating are known from Babylonia long before the Sargonic period.

3.1.8. *Writing and Language*

This study of the writing and language of Pre-Sargonic Mari is based almost exclusively on personal, divine, and month names, rarely on living examples culled from the language of the inscriptions. Occurrences found in names are given in the listings provided above (§ 3.1.5, PNs; § 3.1.6, DNs, § 3.1.7, MNs). All other occurrences are cited directly. Outside of the names of the native rulers of Mari, other information concerning the writing and language of Mari contained in the ʾEnna-Dagan Letter was not utilized here in order not to prejudice the matter of the identity or diversity of the languages of Mari and Ebla. Theoretically, ʾEnna-Dagan could have written the letter either in his own language or in the language of the king of Ebla. In the long run, it matters little since, in my judgment, the language of Mari and Ebla is identical.

In the field of writing, the logograms AB+ÁŠ *šîbum* 'old man', 'elder', here a PN, DÙL *ṣalmum* 'statue' (*passim*), IGI.ME *maḫar* 'before' (MAM 3 319, 325, 326), Ì.GUB *jizziz* 'stands' (ibid.). and SAG.ḪÚB.DU *jiśruk* 'he offered ex-voto' (*passim*), recur in Old Akkadian (MAD 3 under the respective entries) and their use indicates one of the features of the Kish Tradition. The structure DUMU.NITA PN 'son of PN' (MAM 3 329, 322, 332), is regular at Ebla and interchanges with the structure DUMU PN (MAM 3 318, 319, 320; Sollberger 1967: 104, twice).

The use of the logograms for "king" and "queen" at Mari requires fuller discussion. As may be seen from the listing of the kings of Mari (above, § 3.1.5), the title they bear in their own votive inscriptions is normally LUGAL. Only the ʾEnna-Dagan Letter, written by a king of Mari to a king of Ebla, applies the title EN to ˀEnna-Dagan and Śaˀˀumu, the title LUGAL to Jiśṭup-Śarr, and both EN and LUGAL to Jiblul-ˀIl. The word for '(deified) king' occurs in Jikûn-Śarr and Jiśṭup-Śarr. The female counterpart of the male LUGAL or EN is NIN 'queen' in the votive inscription published in MAM 3 318, which names *[Ib-lul]?-Il* LUGAL *Ma-rí*^{KI}, and PAB.GÁ (= Sumerian MUNU$_x$-GÁ) NIN. A Mari administrative text (Parrot 1965a: 15 no. 12) has both LUGAL and *ma-⌜lik⌝-[tum]* (above, § 3.1.3). The Ebla sources normally apply the title LUGAL to the kings of Mari, including ˀEnna-Dagan who calls himself EN in his own letter, but the title EN *Ma-rí*^{KI} is applied to Jikûn-Śarr and an unknown person (Archi 1981a: 147) in administrative texts. Thus the known royal titles at Mari are LUGAL = EN for 'king' and NIN *maliktum* for 'queen'. The corresponding titles are Ebla are EN *malkum* for 'king' and NIN *maliktum* for 'queen'. In Old Akkadian, the title for the 'king' is LUGAL *śarrum*, while EN is reserved for foreign rulers; the female counterpart of LUGAL is NIN, as, for instance, in *na-ˀà-áš* LUGAL *ù na-ˀà-áš* NIN 'for the life of the king and the life of the queen' (Scheil 1921: 25), while *śarratum* is applied to divine rulers. For Old Akkadian references, see MAD 3 86–90 and 286–89. In conclusion, I suggest that the royal titles are LUGAL or EN *malkum* 'king' and NIN *maliktum* 'queen' at Mari, EN *malkum* and NIN *maliktum* at Ebla, and LUGAL *śarrum* and NIN *bêlatum* in Old Akkadian. Not directly pertinent to the royal titulary is the noun DAM in *Al-ma* DAM *I-kùn*(KUM)*-Ma-rí*^{KI} 'ˁAlma, wife of Jikûn-Mari' (above, § 3.1.3). While DAM means 'wife' and ˁAlma is but one of the royal wives of Jikûn-Mari, the title NIN means 'queen' and PAB.GÁ is not only the wife of Jiblul-ˀIl, but also the crowned queen of Mari.

The use of the following syllabic signs is characteristic of Pre-Sargonic Mari. The sign ˀa_x(Ì) in *ˀa_x-na* /ˀana/ 'for (DN)' (MAM 3 317), besides *a-na* (Thureau-Dangin 1934: 142; MAM 3 315), is used regularly at Ebla in the Pre-Sargonic period and at Mari in the Ur III (below, § 3.3.5) and post-Ur III (below, § 3.4.6.7) periods. Occasionally it also occurs in Old Akkadian. For the reading *ˀa_x-na*, not *ì-na*, see Krebernik (1982: 221) and a forthcoming article of L. Milano. For other syllabic signs note *ˀà* in MN *Za-ˀà-tum* /Ṣaˀattum/; *dab$_x$*(URUDU) in PN *Dab$_x$-rúm* (BÍ.RU); *aw*(WA) in *Aw-na-ni-[im]* /ˀAwnānim/; *ba$_4$* in MN *I-ba$_4$-sa*; *gi$_4$* and *iš$_x$*(LAM) in *Iš$_x$-gi$_4$* and *Iš$_x$-gi$_4$-Ma-rí* /Jiśqî-/; *kùn*(KUM) in *I-kùn-Ma-rí*^{KI} /Jikûn-/; *rúm*(BÍ.RU) in *Dab$_x$*(URUDU)*-rúm* and *X-ba-rúm*; *su*(*d*) mainly in the writing of the third person masculine pronominal suffix *-śu*, as in DÙL-*su*(*d*) 'his statue' (*passim*); *ù* for *ˀu* in PN *Śa-ù-mu* /Śaˀˀumu/.

The spelling *I-iq-* in MN *I-iq-za*, besides *Iq-za*, suggests the pronunciation *Jiq-*, as in Old Akkadian *i-ik-mi* /jikmî/ 'he has bound', 'he has taken captive' (MAD 2² 28).

The spellings (*En-na*)*-Da-gan* besides (*En-na*)-^{d}*Da-gan*, (*Iš$_x$*(LAM)*-gi$_4$*)*-Ma-rí* besides (*I-kùn*)*-Ma-rí*^{KI}, and of (^{d}INNIN)*-Zar-bat* besides *Zar-bat*^{KI} (both above, § 3.1.4), with and without the semantic indicators ^{d} and

KI, are optional in the period. The occasional omission of the prepositions ᵓ*ana* in the structure 'for DN', as in MAM 3 309, 328, 330, 336; CT 5 2; Thureau-Dangin (1934: 140, 143); and Sollberger (1967: 104), abnormal in Babylonia, belongs to the class of "Unique Characteristics of the Ebla Writing" (Gelb 1981: § 2.3).

In the field of phonology, we note that the vowel *a* is preserved when preceded by ᶜ and followed by two consonants in *Al-ma* /ᶜAlma/ and DN ᵈ*Aš-dar-ra-at* /ᶜAštarat/, but not at Ebla where it becomes *e,* as in ᶜ*ebdum* 'slave'. The vowel *a* preceded by ᶜ in an open syllable is also preserved, as in ᵈ*A-bir*$_5$(NAM)-*tum* /ᶜAbirtum/, possibly comparable with Old Akkadian ᶜ*abartum* 'crossing' (MAD 3 14). The vowel *a* followed by ᶜ becomes *e* at Mari, as in *be-lí-su*(*d*) /beᶜlišu/ (MAM 3 317). For the treatment of the vowel *a* in the vicinity of ᶜ in Old Akkadian and Eblaic, see MAD 2^2 124f. and Gelb 1981: 18–21. The writing of the sibilants yields unexpected results at Mari: The spelling with ŠA in DNs -ᵈUTU-*ša* and -ᵈ*Ša-ma-gan* indicates the phoneme /š/, Arabic *ṯ*, not /ś/, as expected, and the interchangeable spellings of PNs *Ar-si-* and *Ar-ši-* and MN spelled *I-ba*$_4$*-sa* at Mari and Ebla and *I-ba-ša-áš* in Babylonia, indicates the possible existence of the phoneme /ž/, which I intend to discuss in the near future. The sign SÁ in the month name *I-rí-sá* stands for *ś,* contrary to the etymology, which requires spelling with ŠA, as in Ugaritic, Aramaic, and Arabic ḤRṮ and the like. The initial syllable *ja-* becomes *ji-* in the name *I-sar-* /Jiśar-/ 'he is just'. The phoneme *n* assimilates to the following ᶜ, as in [*I*]-*ti-Il* /Jiddin-ᵓIl/ (as in the Akkadian examples discussed in OIP 27 30f.), and to *š* or *ś,* and *t,* as in *I-ku-*ᵈ*Ša-ma-gan* /Jikûn-Šamakan/ and *I-ku-*ᵈUTU /Jikûn-Śamaś/, MN *Za-*ᵓ*à-tum* /Ṣaᵓattum/ from **Ṣa*ᵓ*antum.* In accordance with the Semitic languages, *qṣ* is preserved in Jiqṣum and does not become *kṣ* as in Akkadian.

In the field of grammar, we know of pronominal suffixes -*ī* in PNs *Ì-li* /ᵓIlī/ 'My god' and ⸢*Na*⸣-*ni* /Nannī/ 'My . . .', and -*śu* in PN *Mi*(*m*)-*ma-ḫir-su*(*d*) /Mi-māḫirśu/ 'Who is his opponent?', and in the language of the texts, as in DÙL-*su*(*d*) /ṣalamśu/ 'his statue' (*passim*). The interrogative personal pronoun *mi* 'who?' in the PN /Mi-māḫirśu/ just cited, and *Mi-ga-Il* /Mi-ka-ᵓIl/ 'Who is like ᵓIl?' at Ebla corresponds to *mi* 'who?' of Hebrew and Ugaritic, but is different from *man* of post-Ur III Mari (below, § 3.4.6.5) and Old Akkadian (later *mannum*).

The noun exhibits a few cases of regular declension, such as nom. masc. in PNs *Dab*$_x$(URUDU)-*rúm*(BÍ.RU), *Èš-pum, X-ba-rúm*(BÍ.RU), DN -*Pum,* MNs *Ga-sum,* Iq-zum, gen. in *Aw-na-ni-*[*im*] /ᵓAwnānim/, and *be-lí-su*(*d*) /beᶜlišu/ (MAM 3 317), fem. in DN ᵈ*A-bir*$_5$(NAM)-*tum* /ᵓAbirtum/, and MN *Za-*ᵓ*à-tum* /Ṣaᵓattum/. In comparison, we note the following: the lack of mimation in PNs *Sá-ù-mu* /Śaᵓᵓumu/ and *Ar-si-a-ḫa* or *Ar-ši-a-ḫa* /ᵓArśî-ᵓaḫa/, DN -*Pu* /-Pu/, and MN *Ḫa-lí-du;* the lack of -*um* in masc. PNs *Ḫi-da-ar* and *Sá-lim,* DNs -*Da-gan, -Il, -Šar,* and ᵈ*Ša-ma-gan,* and MNs *Gi-ì, I-si* (not understandable), *Za-nar,* and MN (from DN) ^{d}*A-dam-ma*, in fem. DNs ^{d}*Aš-dar-ra-at* and ^{d}NIN-*da*?-ra-at? (not understandable), GN *Zar-bat*$^{(KI)}$ /Ṣarbat/, and MNs *Ḫa-lí-it*, Ì.NUN.NA-*at*, *I-rí-sa-at*, and *Za-ʾà-na-at*; the lack of *-tum* in the fem. PN *Al-ma* and MNs *Ḫa-li*, etc., *I-rí-sá*, Ì.NUN.NA, and *Za-ʾà-na* (Ebla). The suffix *-a* occurs in PNs DUB-*la*, *Gul-la*, *Su-wa-d*[*a*], and *Šu-ra*, DN ^{d}UTU-*śa* /Śamša/ or /Šamša/, and MNs *Iq-za* or *I-iq-za* and *I-ba*$_4$-*sa* (not understandable). The element *En-na-* in PN *En-na-Da-gan* has several parallels in the forms *En-na*-DN, *En-nam*-DN, *En-ni*-DN, *En-nu-um*-DN, and their allographs in the Pre-Sargonic, Sargonic, and Ur III periods in Babylonia (MAD 3 51ff.), at Ebla in the Pre-Sargonic period (M. Lambert 1975: 50; Pettinato 1976: 48 and 50; and Gelb 1977: 18), and in *En-na-ì-lí* in post-Ur III Mari (ARMT 19 377, 385+). In one case each, *-en-núm* and *-en-nam* occur as the second element in *Ì-lí-en-núm* and *Ma-da-en-nam* (MAD 3 53). In MAD 2^2 124, MAD 3 51f., Gelb 1977: 18, and Gelb 1981: 19, I derived it from the root ḤNN, with or without question marks, and translated it variously as '(my) grace', 'request', 'please'. The interchange of the masculine MN Ì.NUN and the feminine MN Ì.NUN.NA, Ì.NUN.NA-*at* is discussed above (§ 3.1.7). All these ossified features occur in the names of various types, not in the living language of the texts. For extensive parallels at Ebla, cf. Gelb 1981: 32f. and MAD 2^2 159ff. in Old Akkadian.

A most noteworthy feature of the verbal system at Pre-Sargonic Mari is that as many as eleven names in the votive inscriptions (above, § 3.1.3) and at least five names in the administrative texts (above, § 3.1.4) begin with *I-*, indicating that the prefix of the third person masculine singular was *ji-*, and not *ja-*, as in Arabic, for example. See Gelb 1977: 21 and 1981: 33f. The name *Sá-ù-mu*, known from a letter of ʾEnna-Dagan of Mari that was found at Ebla, stands for *Śaʾʾumu* 'bought' (from a deity?), a passive participle of the D stem. It may testify to the existence of the *parrusum* participle in the living language of Mari, as in *qaṭṭurum* at Ebla (Gelb 1981: 39 and 42), and *passim* in the Old Assyrian dialect, and contrary to the *purrusum* participle in Old Akkadian and the Babylonian dialect.

The prepositions *a-na* 'to', 'for' (MAM 3 315; Thureau-Dangin 1934: 40)=ʾa_x(NI)-*na* (MAM 3 317), *in* 'in' (MAM 3 316), and *iš* 'to' (see above, § 3.1.4), recur at Ebla; *a-na*, *in*, and very rarely *iš* in Old Akkadian.

3.1.9. *Conclusions*

1. As evidenced by the preserved names of the Pre-Sargonic kings of Mari in the Sumerian King List, the ruling dynasty was of Semitic origin as was probably the earliest population.

2. According to the votive inscriptions and administrative texts, the rulers of Mari, the general population, and the deities they worshiped were Semitic.

3. As evidenced by the votive inscriptions and administrative texts, the writing, language, and calendar of Mari are practically identical with those at Ebla.

4. The features of the writing system and most of the linguistic features used at Mari-Ebla are part of the "Kish Tradition" that arose around Kish in Babylonia and spread westward toward Mari and Ebla. See below, §§ 4 and 5.

3.2. *Sargonic Period*

Mari is less well known in the Sargonic than in the Pre-Sargonic period, and what we know about it comes mainly from the Akkadian sources in Babylonia. Sargon reports the conquest of Mari and Elam (Hirsch 1952/53: 36 iv 20–22; 43 ix 8–10), as well as of Mari, Jarmuti, and Ebla (Hirsch 1952/53: 38 v 22–24 = vi 27–29; 49 xiv 24–26). The conquest of Mari, presumably by Sargon, is also the topic of a date formula, reading MU *Ma-rí*[KI] ḪUL.A 'the year in which Mari was destroyed' (PBS 13 27 and TMH 5 80).

According to a late pseudo-historical text, ten kings revolted against Narâm-Sin, among them Migir-Dagan, king of Mari (written *Má-rí*[KI]). See Boissier (1919: 163: 38); reedited by Grayson and Sollberger (1976: 112: 32).

The presence of a votive bowl of ME-*Ul*$_x$-*maš*, daughter of Narâm-Sin, at Mari (Parrot 1955: 185ff. and pl. XVI/1) suggests that she may have gone to Mari in order to marry a local ruler or his son. For similar examples, see the case of the Sumerian queen at Mari (above, § 3.1.5) and of the daughter of a king of Mari who went to Ur to marry the son of Ur-Nammu, the first king of the Ur III Dynasty (below, § 3.3.2).

Mari occurs very rarely in the administrative texts of Babylonia. The most interesting of these is a small group of texts from the archive of Qurādum, which deal with silver and silver objects (CT 50 72, 74), inventory (CT 50 73; Metr. Mus. 86.11.134, unpubl.), a message (CT 50 71), and a sale contract (Sollberger 1956: 13f. and 26). At least one of these texts, which presumably stem from Sippar (see CT 50, p. 8), refers to the price paid for a large quantity of about five hundred quarts of lard acquired at *Ma-rí*[KI] (CT 50 72).

Nothing is known about the few administrative texts that were excavated by the French at Mari, including one text that has important references to *gajjum*, a tribal term that heretofore has been known only from the classical Old Babylonian texts of Mari (see Gelb 1981: 59). Just recently, Durant (1984b: 265) has published a small Sargonic text coming from the French excavations at Mari.

3.3. *Ur III Period*

3.3.1. *Introductory Remarks*

Mari in the Ur III period is known to us almost exclusively from a number of votive inscriptions and seal impressions of the GÌR.NITA 'governor-generals' of Mari and from the Sumerian administrative texts originating in Babylonia. For a justification of the spelling 'governor-generals', rather than 'governors-general', see below, § 3.3.4.

3.3.2. *Votive and Seal Inscriptions of Governor-generals of Mari*

The votive inscriptions of the governor-generals of Mari have appeared in scattered publications. Their seal impressions were described by Marie-Thérèse Barrelet and André Parrot in MAM 2/3 146f., 156–60, and their inscriptions were transliterated and translated by R. Dossin, MAM 2/3 250f., and collated and revised by J.-M. Durand (1981a: 180f.). The Ur III administrative texts bearing on the Mari synchronisms have never been collected before.

The votive inscriptions of the governor-generals of Mari were briefly treated by Kupper (1969: 123–25, and 1971: 113–18). In his first article, Kupper assumed that the only *šakkanakkum* of Mari certainly datable to the Ur III period was Apil-kîn, who lived at the time of Ur-Nammu, and was generally inclined to place the early *šakkanakkū* of Mari in the Ur III period. In the second article, he revised his dating. On the basis of the archeological evidence and seal impressions (recently discussed in Durand 1981a: 180f.), he assumed that most of the *šakkanakkū*s of Mari are to be dated to the Old Babylonian period, and concluded on p. 118 that "nos quatorze noms [des *šakkanakkū*] . . . ont regné sur Mari pendant les deux siècles et demi environ qui séparent la fondation de la IIIe dynastie d'Ur de l'arrivée des ancêtres de Zimri-Lim dans la capitale du Moyen Euphrate." In comment to the above, the following may be said. As may be seen from the survey given below (§ 3.3), as many as ten *šakkanakkū* are to be placed in the Ur III period, mainly on the basis of the synchronisms between Mari and Ur III Babylonia (see fig. 3, below), while ten *šakkanakkū* are at present undatable and may be placed either in Ur III or post-Ur III times. The question is: what is the temporal extension of the period of the *šakkanakkū*, a term which was used, among others, by Barrelet and Parrot (in MAM 2/3 157), Durand (1981a: 180), and Limet (ARM 19 p. 11, and the title of his TCM 3 [= ARM 19])? Does it cover the administrative texts of Limet and the majority of the seal impressions of Parrot and others, which are dated to the obscure period between the end of Ur III and the beginning of classical Babylonian around the time of Hammurapi? Or, does it also include the votive inscriptions of the governor-generals of Mari which are dated to the Ur III period? I have always understood that the period of the *šakkanakkū* covers only the post-Ur III period at Mari, in the same sense that the term *Zwischenzeit* is used by Edzard and others to cover post-Ur III times in Babylonia. There is need for agreement among scholars working in the Mari field on this point. The term "Period of the *šakkanakkū*" should not be applied to the Ur III period, a term that is well established in Assyriology. What is needed is a convenient term for the dark age extending from the first years of Ibbî-Sin, when he lost control of most of Babylonia and of all the outlying territories, to the rise of the Lîm Dynasty. During that period Mari was independent of Babylonian suzerainty and used its own writing system and language (see also below, § 3.4.1).

The following governor-generals are datable to the Ur III period:

1) *Apil-kîn*

The oldest inscription pertaining to a governor-general of Mari who is also called 'king of Mari' comes from Nippur. Published by M. Civil (1962: 213) and dated to the time of Ur-Nammu, the first king of the Third Dynasty of Ur, it names the votant $^{3)}$*Da-ra-am*-ŠEŠ.AB^{KI}-*am* $^{4)}$DUMU-SAL *A-pil-ki-in* $^{5)}$LUGAL *Ma-rí*^{KI}-*ka* $^{6)}$É-GI$_4$-A $^{7)}$*Ur*-^{d}*Nammu* LUGAL ŠEŠ.⌜AB^{KI}-*ma*⌝ 'Tarâm-Uram, the daughter of Apil-kîn, king of Mari, the daughter-in-law of Ur-Nammu, king of Ur'.

Apil-kîn, father of the Tarâm-Uram of the above inscription, is identical with $^{1)}$*A-pil*$_x$(GIŠ.BÍL)-GI $^{2)}$*da-núm* $^{3)}$GÌR.NITA $^{4)}$*Ma-rí*^{KI} 'Apil-kîn, the mighty, the governor-general of Mari' of the votive inscription from Mari, which was published by Dossin (1940: 159).

Several noteworthy observations may be made about these two inscriptions. While the inscription of Apil-kîn is written in Akkadian, as expected in this period at Mari, the inscription of his daughter, Tarâm-Uram, is written in Sumerian. The reason for the latter is obviously that the inscription was not written at Mari, but in Babylonia, where she must have gone to marry the son of Ur-Nammu. The name that Turâm-Uram bore is also illustrative of the ethno-linguistic situation. This is, obviously, not her native Mari name, but an Akkadian name, meaning 'She loves Ur', a name she had acquired in Babylonia. See Civil (1962: 213 n 4) with reference to the general question of metonymy among the Hittites, Sumerians, Assyrians, Hebrews, and Egyptians, described by Gelb (1953: 146–54, especially 151–52).

The second noteworthy feature of the two inscriptions concerns the titles borne by Apil-kîn: 'king of Mari' in the first inscription, and 'the mighty, the governor-general of Mari' in the second. The title *da-núm* 'mighty' is regularly applied to rulers and has the same weight as the title 'king'. See Hallo (1957: 65–76) and below, § 3.3.4.

Following Apil-kîn, we are inclined to place a series of three kings, or governor-generals, of Mari:

2) [*PN*] *king, father of Puzur-*ᶜ*Eštar I*

3) *Puzur-*ᶜ*Eštar I, king, son of the king*

4) [*PN*] *king, son of Puzur-*ᶜ*Eštar I*

Puzur-ᶜEštar and his unnamed son occur in a late copy of a votive inscription (Sollberger 1967: 104). It reads: *ḫi-bi* ('destroyed [in the original]') LUGAL <*Ma*>-*ri*^{KI} DUMU KA.ŠA-*Eš*$_4$-*dar* LUGAL '[PN], king of Mari, son of Puzur-ᶜEštar, the king'.

Fig. 3. Synchronisms between governor-generals of Mari and Ur III kings.

Ur III	*Mari*
Ur-Nammu (18 years)	Apil-kîn
Šulgi (48 years)	
	[PN]
44th year	Puzur-^{c}Eštar I
Bûr-Sin (9 years)	[PN]
1st year	Jiśma^{c}-Dagan
3rd year	Tûra-Dagan
Šu-Sin (9 years)	Jiśṭup-^{ᵓ}ilum
	(Da?/Iš? . . .?)
Ibbî-Sin (25 years)	
2nd year	Puzur ^{c}Eštar II
24th year	Jiśbî-Era

The Puzur-ᶜEštar of this inscription cannot be equated with Puzur-ᶜEštar, son of Tûra-Dagan, because the latter is dated to the Bûr-Sin–Ibbî-Sin period (see below) and the former's place early in the Ur III period is suggested by his use of the title LUGAL 'king', also borne by his predecessor, Apil-kîn. Accordingly, he is to be identified with PÚ.ŠA-*Eš$_5$-dar* DUMU LUGAL 'P., son of the king' in the Ur III administrative text dealing with the issue of beer and bread (MVN 2 238), without year date, but taken as referring to a son of Šulgi by Sollberger (1954–56: 21 and n 48; the text also concerns Tuttuli, close to Mari), and with PÙ.ŠA-*Eš$_4$-dar* GÌR.NITA (Holma and Salonen 1940: no. 22) in a text recording the delivery of animals, dated to Šulgi 44. This Puzur-ᶜEštar is denoted here as Puzur-ᶜEštar I to distinguish him from the later Puzur-ᶜEštar II (below).

The votive inscription published by Sollberger (1967: 104) is noteworthy for its writing *ʾa$_x$*(NI)*-na maḫ-ri* DN 'in front of DN' for *a-na maḫ-rí* DN in older Akkadian and *a-na ma-ḫar* DN in standard Akkadian (see above, § 3.1.8). Another remarkable feature of this inscription is the final line, after the curse formula, reading *a-ti* SI.DAR.KI-*šu*, exactly as in the inscription of Tûra-Dagan and his son, Puzur-ᶜEštar, discussed below, § 3.3.2. The expected meaning of the phrase is something like 'forever'. Accordingly, we would read it *a-ti si-dar* KI-*šu* /adî šiṭ(a)r erṣetišu/ and translate it 'as long as "the writing of the earth" (lasts)'. 'The writing of the earth' may be compared with *šiṭ(i)r šamê* or *šiṭirti šamâmî* 'Himmelschrift = Sterne' in Akkadian (AHw 1253). The preposition *adî* 'until', 'as long as' is frequently construed with a noun plus a pronominal suffix, such as 'his', 'her', 'their'. With the writing *si-dar*, instead of *si-ṭir*, for the construct state of *šiṭrum*, compare *ki-ra-ab*, instead of *ki-ri-ib*, for the construct state of *qirbum*, known from the liver omina (see below, § 3.4.5).

Next in time is a series of five governor-generals who are all probably related by descendance.

5) *Jišmaᶜ-Dagan father of Jišṭup-ʾilum and Tûra-Dagan? (below)*

The exact dating of *Iš-má-ᵈDa-gan* governor-general of Mari is based on the occurrence of *Iš-me-ᵈDa-gan* LÚ *Ma-rí*ᴷᴵ 'Išmê-Dagan of Mari' in an Ur III administrative text, PDTI 594, a delivery of animals, dated Bûr-Sin 1; the text also concerns Tuttuli, close to Mari. For the discussion of LÚ *Ma-rí*ᴷᴵ 'he of Mari', see below, § 3.3.3. The identity of the *Iš-má/me-ᵈDa-gan* of Mari and the *Iš-má-ᵈDa-gan* (without titles) who is named in one of the liver omina of Mari (Rutten 1938: 44 no. 11b; see below, § 3.4.5) cannot be maintained because the latter is mentioned in connection with the conquest of Kish in Babylonia, and is thus one of the rulers cited in the liver omina of Mari who were concerned with events taking place in Babylonia, and not at Mari. Consequently, despite the spelling with *má*, *Iš-má-ᵈDa-gan* of the liver omina should be identified with *Išmê-Dagan*, king of Isin in the early Old Babylonian period.

Note the form *jiśma*^{c} in the native language of Mari. It coincides with the older Akkadian *jiśma*^{c}, but differs from the form *išmê* in the Akkadian of the Ur III period and later.

6) *Jišṭup-*$^{\supset}$*ilum son of Jiśma*^{c}*-Dagan*

a) *Iš-má-*^{d}*Da-gan* GÌR.NITA *Ma-rí*^{KI} *Iš-dub-*DINGIR GÌR.NITA *Ma-rí*^{KI} DUMU-*su* 'Jiśma^{c}-Dagan, governor-general of Mari, Jišṭup-$^{\supset}$ilum, governor-general of Mari, his son' or "Jišṭup-$^{\supset}$ilum, governor-general of Mari, son of Jiśma^{c}-Dagan, governor-general of Mari" (Dossin 1940: 163, votive inscription). Note the use of older *-su* in DUMU-*su* instead of *-šu* as in other votive inscriptions.

b) *Iš-dub-*DINGIR GÌR.NITA *Ma-rí*^{KI} DUMU *Iš-má-*^{d}*Da-gan* GÌR.NITA *Ma-rí*^{KI} 'Jišṭup-$^{\supset}$ilum, governor-general of Mari, son of Jiśma^{c}-Dagan, governor-general of Mari' (Dossin 1940: 162, votive).

c) *Iš-dub-*DINGIR GÌR.NITA *Ma-rí*^{KI} 'Jišṭup-$^{\supset}$ilum, governor-general of Mari' (Parrot 1936a: pl. VII, opp. p. 24 = MAM 2/3 3f., and pls. I–III, votive).

Inscriptions *a* and *b* record the building of the temple of ^{d}LUGAL-*ma-tim* /Šarr-mâtim/, who is also known from a Pre-Sargonic inscription of Mari (above, § 3.1.6).

7) *Tûra-Dagan son? of Jiśma*^{c}*-Dagan, father of Puzur-*^{c}*Eštar II and Da?-/Iš?-*[...] *(below)*

The dating of Tûra-Dagan, governor-general of Mari, close to Jiśma^{c}-Dagan (Bûr-Sin 1) is suggested by the occurrence of *Du-a-ra-am-*^{d}*Da-gan* LÚ *Ma-rí*^{KI} in an Ur III administrative text, SET 59, that was transliterated by Jones and Snyder (1961), a delivery of animals, dated to Bûr-Sin 3. Certain readings in this transliteration are in need of collation: *Du-a-ra-am-* for *Du-ra-am-* and *Ma-ri*^{KI} for *Ma-rí*^{KI}. Note Mari *tûra-* for Akkadian *tûram-*, discussed below, § 3.3.5. A certain Tûram-Dagan, without the GÌR.NITA title, is named in the year Bûr-Sin 5 (Legrain, TRU 47, 227, and 230) and Bûr-Sin 6 (TRU 52). An unpublished administrative text, Dr. Serota no. 13, dated to Bûr-Sin 7, refers to LÚ *Ma-rí*^{KI} in connection with LÚ *Ur-šu*^{KI} and LÚ *Tu-tu-ul*^{KI}.

Tûra-Dagan is possibly mentioned in a letter to Zimrī-Lîm from his wife $^{\supset}$Addu-nûrī, who reports to him of having heard a hostile voice in a dream shouting *tu-ra* ^{d}*Da-gan tu-ra* ^{d}*Da-gan* or *Tu-ra-*^{d}*Da-gan Tu-ra-*^{d}*Da-gan* (ARMT 10 50: 19f.). This was taken as two words meaning 'reviens Dagan, reviens Dagan' in the translation on p. 57, and as a name 'Tūra-Dagan' on pp. 6 and 22. Kupper (1971: 118 n 3) pointed out that the obligatory form of the allative in the classical Old Babylonian period at Mari was *-am*, not *-a*, and, consequently, the two words should be interpreted as a name Tûra-Dagan and identified with Tûra-Dagan of Mari. However, the identification of the Tûra-Dagan of the dream with Tûra-Dagan of Mari is not completely assured since the name is used in the Old Babylonian period for various persons (see ARMT 16/1 205, and

ARMT 21 9: 2). See the discussion by Jack M. Sasson (1983: 286–89, and 1984: 112), who weighs both interpretations.

8) *Puzur-ᶜEštar II son of Tûra-Dagan*

a) *Tu-ra-*^{d}*Da-gan* GÌR.NITA *Ma-rí*$^{[\mathrm{KI}]}$ PÙ.ŠA-*Eš*$_4$*-dar* GÌR.NITA DUMU-*šu* 'Tûra-Dagan, governor-general of Mari, Puzur-ᶜEštar, governor-general, his son' (Nassouhi 1926: 112, votive), also PÙ.ŠA-*Eš*$_4$*-dar* GÌR.NITA *Ma-rí*$^{[\mathrm{KI}]}$ MI-*lá-*⌜*A-ga*⌝ NU.[ÈŠ] ŠE[Š-*šu*] 'P., governor-general of Mari, Ṣill-ᵓAkka . . . , his brother' (ibid.). Ṣill-ᵓAkka is identified as a NU.[ÈŠ], a kind of temple functionary, not a governor-general. As pointed out by Limet (ARMT 19 p. 8), the reading of MI-*lá-*⌜*A-ga*⌝ of Nassouhi (1926: 112) is to be reconstructed on the basis of the name fully spelled MI-*lá-A-ga* in ARMT 19 319. The conjunction 'and' in this inscription is written with the sign Ú, contrary to the other votive inscriptions which write Ù exclusively and to Akkadian generally. An archaic value AL = el$_x$ occurs twice in the DN *be-*AL *puḫrim* (UKKIN).

For the final line of the inscription, reading *a-ti si-dar* KI-*šu*, see the discussion of Puzur-ᶜEštar I, above.

b) PÙ.ŠA-[*Eš*$_4$*-dar*] GÌR.[NITA] [*M*]*a-rí*$^{[\mathrm{KI}]}$ 'Puzur-ᶜEštar, governor-general of Mari' (MAM 2/3 158, ME 68, seal impression). The reading by Dossin (1959: 252) was collated by Durand (1981a: 180).

Puzur-ᶜEštar governor-general of Mari apparently occurs as Puzur-Eštar governor-general in Ur III administrative texts also, such as TRU 342 (a delivery of animals, dated to Ibbî-Sin 2), and, possibly, HLC 3 pl. 103 no. 162 rev. (a delivery of flour, without year date). We designate him as Puzur-ᶜEštar II to distinguish him from the earlier Puzur-ᶜEštar I (above).

9) *Da?/Iš? . . . son of Tûra-Dagan*

Tu-ra-^{d}*Da-ga*[*n*] GÌR.[NITA] [*Ma-rí*^{KI}] *Da?/Iš?-*[...] DUMU-*šu* 'Tûra-Dagan, governor-general of Mari, Da?Iš? . . . , his son' (MAM 2/3 157 and pl. XLV, ME 56, seal impression). Dossin's transliteration (1959: 251) is to be corrected in accordance with Durand (1981a: 180), who states that there is no evidence that *Da?/Iš?-*[. . .] bore the title of governor-general.

10) The last ruler of Mari who may be dated with certainty to the Ur III period is ^{d}*Iš-bi-Ìr-ra* LÚ *Ma-rí*^{KI} 'Jišbî-ᵓEra of Mari', who, together with the Elamites and Subarians, brought an end to the rule of Ibbî-Sin in Babylonia, and established himself on the throne of Isin.

Ten other governor-generals of Mari cannot be dated through synchronisms with the Ur III period.

11) *Jiddin-ᵓilum father of Jiddin-Dagan (below)*

*I-ti-*DINGIR GÌR.NITA *Ma-rí*^{KI} 'Jiddin-ᵓilum, governor-general of Mari' (Thureau-Dangin 1937: 173f.; MAM 2/3 17f., and pls. IX–XI, votive). The inscription uses both archaic *-su* and later *-šu* 'his'.

12) *Jiddin-Dagan son of Jiddin-ᵓilum*

I-ti-DINGIR GÌR.NITA *Ma-rí*^{KI} *I-ti-*^{d}*Da-gan* <DUMU-*su*> 'Jiddin-ᵓilum, governor-general of Mari, Jiddin-Dagan, <his son>' (MAM 2/3 146f., and pl. XXXIX, seal impression). Durand (1981a: p. 180 n 4) knows of an unpublished seal of "un fils d'Iddin-Ilum."

13) *ᵓIlum-Jiśar*

DINGIR-*I-sar* GÌR.NITA *Ma-rí*^{KI} 'ᵓIlum-Jiśar, governor-general of Mari' (Thureau-Dangin 1936: 178, votive). The inscription is remarkable for its free syntax, PN *ù-šu-rí-id* ^{d}*Ḫu-bu-ur a-na* KÂ *Me-ir*^{KI} 'PN installed DN Ḫubur in the gate of Mer (= Mari)', which is not in agreement with Akkadian. In the spelling DINGIR-*I-sar*, meaning 'Verily, god is Jiśar' or 'Jiśar is verily god', Jiśar is a DN, as in ^{d}*I-sar* (Dossin 1967c: 100:28), and Hebrew *Jašar*; *jiśar* is a predicate noun meaning 'he is just' in PN *I-sar-Pum* '(god) Logos is just' (above, § 3.1.5). The logogram DINGIR in DINGIR-*I-sar* probably corresponds to *ᵓilum*, rather than *ᵓil*, and similarly in DINGIR-*Pu* (above, § 3.1.2; cf. also *ᵓÀ-num-*^{d}*Da-gan* (below).

14) *Niwar-Mer*

Ni-wa-ar-Me-ir GÌR.NITA *Ma-rí*^{KI} 'Niwar-Mer governor-general of Mari' (Dossin 1940: 153, votive)

15) *Jitûr-*[*Mer*]*?, see Tir-Dagan? (below)*

16) *Tir-Dagan?, son of Jitûr-*[*Mer*]*?*

Ti-ir-^{d}*Da?-*[*gan*]? GÌR.NITA *Ma-rí*^{KI} DUMU *I-dur-*^{d}[*Me-ir*]? GÌR.[NITA] 'Tir-Dagan?, governor-general of Mari, son of Jitûr-[Mer]? governor-general' (MAM 2/3 157f., and pl. XLV, ME 64, seal impression). The transliteration of Dossin (1959: 251f.) was revised by Durand (1981a: 180), who cites several parallels from unpublished Mari texts, such as *Ti-ir-An-nu*, *Ti-ir-Eš*$_{4}$*-dar*, and *Ti-ir-*^{d}*Nu-nu*. The last name also occurs in the post-Ur III legal text discussed below (§ 3.4.2).

17) *ᵓĀmir-Nunu*

[*A*]*-me-ir-*^{d}*Nu-nu* GÌR.NITA *Ma-rí*^{KI} [. . .] 'ᵓĀmir-Nunu, governor-general of Mari . . .' (MAM 2/3 157, and pl. XLV, ME 57, seal impression). The transliteration of Dossin (1959: 251) was revised by Durand (1981a: 180), who cites several parallels from unpublished Mari texts, such as *A-me-ir-An-nu*, *A-me-ir-ᵓÀ-a*, *A-me-ir-Gag-ga*, *A-me-ir-Ma-ma*, and *A-me-ir-*^{d}*Nu-nu*.

18) *Jîṣiᵓ-Dagan father of ᵓEnnin-Dagan (below)*

I-zi-^{d}*Da-gan* GÌR.NITA *Ma-rí* 'Jîṣiᵓ-Dagan, governor-general of Mari' (Andrae 1922: 102, and pl. 59, seal impression found at Assur).

19) [*ᵓEn*]*nin-Dagan son of* [*Jîṣ*]*iᵓ-Dagan*

[*En*]*-nin-*^{d}[*D*]*a-gan* [G]ÌR.NITA [*Ma-rí*]^{KI} [DUMU *I-z*]*i-*^{d}*Da-gan* GÌR.NITA, '[ᵓEn]nin-Dagan, governor-general of Mari, son of [Jîṣ]iᵓ-Dagan, governor-general' (MAM 2/3 156f., and pl. XLV, ME 14, seal impression).

The transliteration of Dossin (1959: 251) was corrected by Durand (1981a: 180), who cites parallels from unpublished Mari texts, such as *En-nin-x-*[. . .] and *En-nin*$_9$*-Ma-ma*. The closest parallel to the element *en-nin-* at Mari appears in the Amorite names *En-ne-nu-um* and *En-ni-nu-um*, which were interpreted as *Ḫinninum* from ḪNN 'to be gracious/merciful' in Gelb (1980: 20, 83, etc.). The relationship of the elements *ʾEnnin-* and *ʾAnnum-* (just below) cannot be established.

20) *ʾAnnum-Dagan*

a) *ʾÀ-num-*^{d}*Da-gan* LUGAL *Me-ir*$^{K[I]}$ 'ʾAnnum-Dagan, king of Mer (= Mari)' (Parrot 1938: 16, and fig. 10; MAM 2/1 12, and pl. XII/2; MAM 2/3 81, and pl. XXXII, ARM HC M.1572, votive inscription on a door socket; MAM 4 58f., and fig. 42, copy). The statement 'roi de Mari, non "der Mer"' in Durand (1981a: 181 n 10) is not clear to me. The relationship between the elements *ʾAnnum-* and *ʾEnnin-* (just above) and between *ʾAnnum-* and *-ʾAnnu*, written (*A-me-ir*)-*An-nu*, cited above (§ 3.3.2) under *ʾĀmir-Nunu*, cannot be established.

b) Two impressions of a seal published in MAM 2/3 160, ME 197 and ME 213. The transliteration of Dossin (1959: 252), revised by Durand (1981a: 81), reads: $^{1)}$*ʾÀ-num-*[^{d}*Da-gan*] $^{2)}$DUMU GÌR. NITA 'ʾÀnnum-[Dagan], son of the governor-general'.

c) Two impressions of a seal published in MAM 2/3 159, and pl. XLV, ME 189 and ME 194. The transliteration of Dossin (1959: 252), revised by Durand (1981a: 81), reads: $^{1)}$[DU]MU GÌR.[NITA] $^{2)}$*ʾÀ-num-*^{d}[Da-gan], apparently the reverse of *b*.

In résumé of the discussion given above, we find that ten governor-generals of Mari may be dated to the Ur III period by identification with individuals who are called either 'governor-generals' or are designated as being LÚ *Ma-rí*^{KI} 'of Mari' in the administrative texts of the Ur III period. Their chronological distribution is shown here in figure 3.

To some readers, the seven synchronisms established between the governor-generals of Mari and the individuals occurring in the Ur III administrative texts (§ 3.3.2) may appear inconclusive since the latter bear only the title of governor-general (not necessarily of Mari) or are described simply as being LÚ *Ma-rí*^{KI} 'of Mari'. "The proof of the pudding is in the eating!" The best evidence in favor of the synchronisms is the fact that the year dates found in the administrative texts fit rather well the sequence of the governor-generals of Mari, which was established on the basis of their descendance given in their votive inscriptions or seals.

In addition there are ten governor-generals of Mari who cannot be dated exactly through synchronisms with the Ur III period. They may belong either to the Ur III period or to post-Ur III times following the downfall of the Third Dynasty of Ur. The latter are briefly discussed below, § 3.4.2.

Listed in the following are the names of the governor-generals of Mari of the Ur III period and of those who may be dated either to the Ur III period or the post-Ur III period (above, § 3.3.2). Included are a few names of persons who bear the title LUGAL 'king' of Mari or are designated as LÚ *Ma-rí*^KI^ 'of Mari'.

[*A*]-*me-ir*-^d^*Nu-nu* GÌR.NITA
A-pil-ki-in lugal, GÌR.NITA
ᵓ*À-num*-^d^*Da-gan* LUGAL
Da?/*Iš*?-[. . .] (GÌR.NITA?)
DINGIR-*I-sar* GÌR.NITA
[*En*]-*nin*-^d^[*D*]*a-gan* GÌR.NITA
I-dur-^d^[*Me-ir*]? GÌR.NITA
I-ti-^d^*Da-gan* GÌR.NITA
I-ti-DINGIR GÌR.NITA
I-zi-^d^*Da-gan* GÌR.NITA
Iš-bi-Ìr-ra (LÚ *Ma-rí*^KI^ 'of Mari' at the time of Ibbî-Sin; the future king of Isin)
Iš-dub-DINGIR GÌR.NITA
Iš-má-^d^*Da-gan* GÌR.NITA (and *Iš-me*-^d^*Da-gan* LÚ *Ma-rí*^KI^)
MI-*lá*-⌜*A-ga*⌝ (= Ṣill-ᵓAkka, not a GÌR.NITA, brother of PÙ.ŠA-*Eš*$_4$-*dar*)
Ni-wa-ar-Me-ir GÌR.NITA
PÙ.ŠA-*Eš*$_4$-*dar* I LUGAL
PÙ.ŠA-*Eš*$_4$-*dar* II GÌR.NITA
Ti-ir-^d^*D*[*a*?-*gan*?] GÌR.NITA
Tu-ra-^d^*Da-gan* GÌR.NITA (and *Du*≪-*a*≫-*ra-am*-^d^*Da-gan* LÚ *Ma-rí*^KI^)

3.3.3. *Sumerian Administrative Texts of Babylonia*

Outside of a few scattered references to commodities linked with Mari in the administrative texts of the Ur III period, the only solid body of material consists of the names of individuals who are said to be LÚ *Ma-rí*^KI^ 'of Mari'. In Gelb (1938: 80f.), I listed the sources that were known to me at the time. They were collected again in Edzard and Farber (1974: 128f.). Brought up to date, this is the listing:

A-bu-DÙG
A-da-tum LÚ *Ma-r*[*í*?^KI^] (ARM HC A.3188, unpubl.)
AG-*ba-ni* (cf. *I-din*-AG)
A-mi-ir-^d^*Šul-gi* (cf. below)
A-mur-^d^*Šul-gi* (cf. above)
E?-*la-ag-ì-lí* (transliterated as [*Kur*]-⌜*bi*⌝-*la-ag* ⌜NI⌝.NI in PDTI 161)
É.MES (see discussion below)
Ga-ba-LUM
I-din-AG (cf. AG-ba-ni)
Ì-lí-^d^*Da-gan* (Goetze 1953b: 104a:10)

Ì-lí-dan (Dawson no. 9, unpubl.)
Ì-lí-iš-ti-gal
Ì-lum-a-ḫi (DINGIR-*a-ḫi* of ARM HC A.5439 cannot be found)
Iš-bi-Ìr-ra (see above)
Iš-me-^{d}*Da-gan* (see above)
La-gi-pu-um
PÙ.ŠA-*Ma-ma*
Šu-^{d}*Da-gan*
Šu-^{d}*Iš-ḫa-ra*
^{d}*Šul-gi-pa-lí-il*
Du≪-a≫-ra-am-^{d}*Da-gan* (see above)

Included in the listing is what occurs as É.DUB LÚ *Ma-rí*^{KI} in seven administrative texts: Weidner (1921/23: 474); BIN 3 221; MVN 3 384; TLB 3 25; Oppenheim (1948: R 11); Sollberger (1960: 121); AnOr 9 99. Generally, the two signs were read as É.MES and interpreted as a personal name, as for instance, Edzard and Farber (1974: 129). Sollberger (1960: 121) proposed to read the two signs as a name *líl-la,* a proposal extended to the reading of AnOr 9 99 by Cagni (1983: 90), who collated the text. Oppenheim (1948: R 11) read them as É-KIŠIB$_2$ LÚ *Ma-rí*^{KI}, and translated them as 'store-house of the *Ma-rí*^{KI}-men'.

All individuals who are said to be LÚ *Ma-rí*^{KI} 'of Mari' in the Sumerian administrative texts of the Ur III period appear to bear Akkadian names, or Mari names that are written in Akkadian garb. See especially above (§ 3.3.2), where the Mari name *Iš-má-*^{d}*Da-gan* /Jiśma^{c}-Dagan/ appears as *Iš-me-*^{d}*Da-gan* /Išmê-Dagan/ in Ur III administrative texts.

3.3.4. *Discussion of GÌR.NITA, LUGAL, and LÚ*

Three designations occur with the governor-generals of Mari: GÌR. NITA, LUGAL, and LÚ. GÌR.NITA is by far the most common title of the governor-generals of Mari. The logogram GÌR.NITA is read as ŠAGAN in Sumerian and *šakkanakkum* in Akkadian. Originally, ŠAGAN meant 'equid', and *šakkanakkum,* a loanword from Sumerian ŠAGAN.AK 'of the equid', denoted an attendant in charge of equids. From that original meaning, the word acquired the current meaning of 'general', as in GÌR.NITA LÚ.GIŠ.TI 'general of the archers' and GÌR.NITA LÚ.GIŠ.GÍD.DA 'general of the lancers' of the Man-ištušu Obelisk (MDP 2 A xii 5f. and 14f.). It is such generals who were appointed by the Babylonian kings to serve as governor-generals in charge of the outlying and unruly provinces, such as Mari, Assur, and Elam. This is the reason why I spell the plural of the English word as 'governor-generals', rather than 'governors-general'.

A good parallel to the semantic evolution from 'the man in charge of equids' to 'general' is provided by the English word 'marshal', a borrowing from the French *maréchal,* which, like German *Marshall,* goes back to

Old High German *marah-scalc*, meaning 'man in charge of horses', later 'marshal'. For a similar development, compare the Polish (and Russian) word *koniuszy*, originally, 'man in charge of horses' (*koń* 'horse'), later 'marshal'.

Mari was conquered by Sargon of Akkadē (see above, § 3.2), and since then Mari was, presumably, under the control of military governors. In contrast to Assur and Elam, Mari was never fully integrated within the frame of Babylonian authority, since ENSIS, the civilian governors of the province, are unknown there.

We meet with the title LUGAL 'king' at Mari in the Ur III period five times: Apil-kîn is LUGAL in one inscription and GÌR.NITA in another (above, § 3.3.2, time of Ur-Nammu); [PN] LUGAL is the father of Puzur-ᶜEštar LUGAL or GÌR.NITA, and the grandfather of [PN] LUGAL (above, § 3.3.2, time of Šulgi); and ᵓAnnum-Dagan calls himself LUGAL (above, § 3.3.2, time unknown). This double titulary, 'king' and 'governor-general', of rulers of Mari had its origin in the political evolution of the times. Originally, the governor-generals of Mari were dependents of Babylonia. With the weakening of political authority in Babylonia, some of these governor-generals declared themselves independent, partly retaining the old title of governor-general, partly acquiring royal titulary. The double status of Mari, dependent and independent, is reflected in other sources. The continued dependence of the governor-generals of Mari is witnessed by Ur III administrative texts which show that the governor-generals of Mari fully participated in the economic and religious life of Babylonia. At the same time, their independence is manifested in their votive inscriptions which, contrary to tradition, never refer to their Babylonian overlords. For similar developments, compare the history of Eshnuna and Elam during periods of Babylonian political disorganization.

Above, we have encountered the designation PN LÚ *Ma-rí*^{KI} three times: *Iš-me-*^{d}*Da-gan* LÚ *Ma-rí*^{KI} 'J. of Mari' occurs in an Ur III administrative text, while *Iš-má-*^{d}*Da-gan* is a GÌR.NITA in his own inscription (above, § 3.3.2, time of Bûr-Sin); *Tûra*(*m*)*-Dagan* is called LÚ *Ma-rí*^{KI} in an administrative text, but GÌR.NITA in his inscription (above, § 3.3.2, time of Bûr-Sin); and Jiśbî-ᵓEra is known as LÚ *Ma-rí*^{KI} in the Ibbî-Sin Correspondence (above, § 3.3.2).

The interchangeable use of PN LÚ GN with PN GÌR.NITA GN does not indicate, of course, that LÚ *equals* GÌR.NITA. Limiting the meaning of PN LÚ GN to the governor-generals can hardly be applied to the twenty or so names which are said to be LÚ *Ma-rí*^{KI} (above, § 3.3.3), let alone to the dozens of names of individuals who are known by the LÚ GN designation in hundreds of administrative texts of the Ur III period. We may conclude, therefore, that many individuals designated as PN GÌR.NITA *Ma-rí*^{KI} may also be called PN LÚ *Ma-rí*^{KI}, but not that all occurrences of PN LÚ *Ma-rí*^{KI} must be interpreted in the sense of PN GÌR.NITA GN.

The normal meaning of Sumerian LÚ and Akkadian *awīlum* is 'man' (as in Latin *homo*, German *Mensch*, not *vir* or *Mann*), but the Sumerian structure PN LÚ GN cannot be translated as 'PN, man of GN' (as generally done in Assyriology), because the corresponding Akkadian structure is not PN *awīl* GN, but either PN *ša* GN 'PN of GN' or a gentilic formation, such as *Marijum* 'Marite', 'Marian'.

3.3.5. *Writing and Language*

The votive inscriptions of Mari of the Ur III period are written in the cuneiform system and the Akkadian dialect of the period. At the same time, they exhibit certain features that reflect the imprint of the local writing system and of the non-Akkadian but Semitic language used in the area of Mari.

In the field of writing we note: the standard preposition 'to', 'for' is written *ʾa*$_x$(NI)-*na* in *ʾa*$_x$(NI)-*na maḫ-ri* DN 'in front of DN' (above, § 3.3.2), as in Pre-Sargonic Ebla, a single votive inscription from Mari, and *passim* in the post-Ur III Mari texts, and not *a-na* as in other Ur III votive inscriptions, and, generally, in Akkadian. The pronominal suffix is written *-su* (above, § 3.3.2), and both *-su* and *-šu* (above, § 3.3.2), against *-šu* in other votive inscriptions. The conjunction 'and' is written uniquely *ú* (§ 3.3.2), as in the liver omina from Mari and in Old Assyrian, but not in other Ur III votive inscriptions and not in standard Akkadian.

The following observations may be made on the language: The vocalic phoneme *a* is preserved in the vicinity of the consonantal phoneme ᶜ in *Iš-má-* /Jišmaᶜ/, as in Pre-Sargonic Mari, Ebla, and Babylonia, contrariwise to *Iš-me* /Jišmê/ in the Babylonia of the Ur III period and later (above, § 3.3.2). The prefix *ji-* of *Jišma*ᶜ-, *Jišṭup-*, etc. (above, § 3.3.2) is in agreement with Pre-Sargonic Mari, Ebla, Akkadian (generally), and Amorite (generally), but in disagreement with Arabic *ja-*. The dative-allative morpheme *-a* 'to me' in the name *Tûr+a+Dagan* 'Return to me, Dagan!' occurs as *-am* in *Tûr+am-Dagan* in Ur III Akkadian (above, § 3.3.2). Tentatively suggested in Gelb (1977: 22 and Gelb 1981: 41), the existence of the Mari morpheme *-a* contrasted with Akkadian *-am* is confirmed by the forms *ûṣiʾa* and *ûṣiʾam* in Mari liver omina (below, § 3.4.5); the morpheme *-a* is also attested in Amorite, as in *Šûb+a+ʾIl* 'Return to me, ʾIl!' (see Gelb 1980: 195, etc.). Free syntactical order exemplified in PN *ù-šu-rí-id* DN *a-na* KÁ *Me-ir*^{KI} 'PN installed DN in the gate of Mer' (above, § 3.3.2) is characteristic of Pre-Sargonic Ebla, but not of Akkadian.

One noteworthy feature of Mari in the Ur III period is that it is completely devoid of Sumerian influence. All votive inscriptions are written in Akkadian. The single votive inscription of Tarâm-Uram, daughter of Apil-kîn, which was written in Sumerian may have been composed not at Mari, but in Babylonia where she must have gone to marry the son of Ur-Nammu. All names of the votants are either Akkadian or in the native language of Mari (above, § 3.3.2), and the same is true of the individuals called LÚ *Ma-rí*^{KI} 'of Mari' in the Ur III administrative texts (above, § 3.3.3) and of the Post-Ur III period personal names (§ 3.4.3).

As in Post-Ur III Mari, the most frequent divine name forming part of the names of the Ur III governor-generals of Mari and of the LÚ *Ma-rí*^{KI} individuals was Dagan, the patron god of Mari. There are no Sumerian gods among them.

3.3.6. *Conclusions*

1. Mari was ruled in the Ur III period by governor-generals, who, theoretically appointed by the Babylonian kings, were *de facto* semi-independent.

2. The votive inscriptions of the governor-generals of Mari were written in a writing system that was borrowed directly from Babylonia; their language was Akkadian, the second (after Sumerian) official language of the kingdom.

3. Certain linguistic features of these inscriptions reflect the imprint of the local, non-Akkadian but Semitic, language.

4. The governor-generals of Mari bore names that were partly Akkadian, partly native, as were the deities they worshiped.

3.4. *Post-Ur III Period*

3.4.1. *Introductory Remarks*

In accordance with the discussion above (§ 3.3.2), the post-Ur III period extends at Mari from the first years of Ibbî-Sin, when he lost control of most of Babylonia and of all adjacent territories, including Mari, to the rise of the Lîm Dynasty. During this long span of about 270 years, Mari became fully independent of Babylonian suzerainty and used its own writing system and language.

Under this broad classification we include a few votive inscriptions of the governor-generals of Mari, the administrative texts, a legal text, and the liver omina, all excavated at Mari.

3.4.2. *Inscriptions of Governor-Generals of Mari*

It has been suggested above that some of the ten governor-generals of Mari who cannot be assigned to the Ur III period definitely, especially those recorded not on the votive inscriptions but on seal impressions, may belong to the post-Ur III era. Supporting this suggestion are the parallels between the elements *A-me-ir-*, *En-nin-*, and *Ti-ir-* occurring in the names of the later governor-generals (above, § 3.3.2) with those in the post-Ur III administrative texts published in ARMT 19. As in the previous periods (above, § 3.3.5), Dagan is the most common divine element in the names of the governor-generals. God Nunu, in the name of the governor-general *[A]-me-ir-*^{d}*Nu-nu*, recurs in *Ti-ir-*^{d}*Nu-nu* in the legal text (below, § 3.4.4) and in the administrative text ARMT 19 373.

3.4.3. *Administrative Texts*

Fifty-eight administrative texts were published by Jestin (1952). These texts created a sensation in our field. Due to their extraordinary interest, I discussed them, as well as the liver omina of Mari published by Rutten in 1933 (see below, § 3.4.5) in an article (Gelb 1956). In that article, I proposed to change the date of the administrative texts from the Ur III period (assumed by Jestin and others) to the post-Ur III period and concluded that the writing and language of the administrative texts are completely different from those of the classical Old Babylonian period at Mari.

A greater number of administrative texts was published in ARM 19 = TCM 3 (copies), and ARMT 19 (transliterations and translations). Many new texts are provided, in addition to those previously published by Jestin.

A handful of administrative texts of the same type as those at Mari have recently been discovered at Tell Ashara, ancient Tirqa, some 60 kilometers up the Euphrates from Mari, and published by Buccellati (1977).

The exact dating of the administrative texts within the span of about 270 years of the post-Ur III period is not easy, since they contain no synchronisms that would enable us to link the administrative texts with dates firmly established in Babylonia. Indirectly, it may be suggested that the administrative texts of the post-Ur III period give the appearance of being epigraphically much closer to the Old Babylonian of the Lîm Dynasty than to the Ur III period.

On the surface, the occurrence of the name *A-mu-ra-bi-*⌜*ì-lí*⌝ in ARMT 19 308 is disconcerting for the pre-Old Babylonian date of the administrative texts. The last two signs were transliterated as *-ì-*[*lí*] on p. 108 and *-ì?-lí?* on p. 159. The name can mean only '(king) ᶜAmmu-rāpiᵓ is my god' and has the same structure as many names of individuals which are composed of the names of the Old Babylonian rulers, such as Śumu-ᵓabum, Śamśu-ᵓiluna, ᵓAbī-ješuᵓ or ᵓAbī-Ješuᶜ, and ᶜAmmī-ditana. There is no way to connect the ᶜAmmu-rāpiᵓ of ARMT 19 with the great Ḫammurapi of Babylon and to lower the date of the Mari administrative texts beyond the Lîm Dynasty to the age of Ḫammurapi. Clearly, the ᶜAmmu-rāpiᵓ of ARMT 19 is a king of local renown, as yet unknown to us, who lived many years before Ḫammurapi of Babylon. For a similar judgment, cf. Durand (1984a: 132 n 23).

Limet wrote a philological treatment of the administrative texts in his article published in *Syria* (Limet 1975) and in the introduction to ARMT 19 1-37. Their writing and language have been constructively evaluated by Westenholz (1978: 160-69).

The graphic and linguistic features of the post-Ur III administrative texts (of Jestin) and the liver omina (below, § 3.4.5) of Mari were collected and discussed in Gelb 1956: 1-10; the linguistic features relating post-Ur III Mari to Pre-Sargonic Mari and Ebla in Gelb (1977: 3f.). The large body of material made available through the publication of the administrative texts in ARMT 19 made possible a broader evaluation of the linguistic features in Gelb (1981: 59 and 63f.). Facts relating to writing and language are collected below in § 3.4.6.

As already suggested in Gelb (1956: 3, 4, and 7), I concluded in Gelb (1981: 59) that the Mari texts of this period "are written in a new and unique type of writing that shows certain features recurring only in the Old Assyrian writing system."

The sign inventory of the post-Ur III administrative texts was evaluated by Limet, ARMT 19 5-7, and 152-58, and that of the liver omina by Snell (1974). In accordance with the conclusions reached below (§ 3.4.6.2), four types of syllabic signs are employed in the post-Ur III administrative texts, including one type that is attested in Old Assyrian and nowhere else.

The administrative texts of Mari team with lexical items that are either rare or unique. X *li-im* 'x thousands' (462); x *me-at* 'x hundreds' (389, 462), comparable with x *mi-at* at Pre-Sargonic Ebla and Abu Salabikh and in a Sargonic text from Tell Brak in Upper Mesopotamia (see above, § 3.1.3); *ma-az-um* (210), *tim-za-u* (38-45), *im-za-ʾà* (46-50) from *mazāʾum* 'to mix' or *masājum* 'to wash' (cloth or metal); *ra-ʾà-at, ra-ʾà-te* (460), comparable with *ra-ʾà-tum* at Pre-Sargonic Ebla and with *rittum* 'hand', 'span' in Akkadian and other relatives of RḤT in Ugaritic, Hebrew, etc. (see below, § 3.4.6.2); *ru-si* (38-50, regularly with MZʾ or MSJ), comparable with *ru-si-in,* a metallurgical term at Pre-Sargonic Ebla (see Gelb 1981: 64); *sá-ni-en* 'sandals' (300, dual genitive-accusative), comparable with *sa-na* in a Pre-Sargonic lexical text from Ebla (MEE 4 335: 1323′, cited courtesy of Steinkeller), and with Akkadian *šēnum.* Mystifying is the relation of the lexeme *te-ir* in the administrative texts, such as GURUŠ *in te-ir* (35, 36+), x UDU *te-ir* (193, 194+), x SILÀ *te-ir* (238, 258+), to *Ti-ir* that occurs at Pre-Sargonic Ebla (MEE 1 676, 929, marked "NPrf," and MEE 1 1124, 1649, marked "Prf.," collected on p. 274 under professions), and to the element *Ti-ir-* that forms part of the names of post-Ur III Mari, such as *Ti-ir*-EŠ$_4$.DAR etc. (see above, § 3.4.2 and below, § 3.4.4). Other interesting lexemes in administrative texts may be gleaned from § 3.4.6.

In the case of the administrative texts of post-Ur III Mari, we are in the rather fortunate position of being able to compare two large bodies of material, the texts proper, and the personal names contained in them. A study of the list of personal names gathered in ARMT 19 159–62 shows conclusively that the population of Mari in post-Ur III times consisted primarily of individuals who spoke the language in which their texts were composed. A scattering of Akkadians and Amorites forms an insignificant admixture in the population.

Fruitful results about the ethno-linguistic affiliation of native and foreign deities that were worshiped at Mari in the post-Ur III era may come from a comparative study of three kinds of sources: the names of deities scattered in the texts, the names of deities forming parts of personal names, and the names of deities gathered in the so-called god-lists. The last two kinds of sources were studied by Limet (1976c). The god-lists in the administrative texts of Mari, some of which may go back to post-Ur III times, some to the classical Old Babylonian period, were studied by Dossin (1950b and 1967c), Durand (1980: 174–75); and Talon (1980). The divine names occurring in the administrative texts were studied by Edzard (1967: 57–60 and 70) and Limet (1976c).

The calendar of twelve months used in the administrative texts in the post-Ur III period is completely different from the "Semitic Calendar" used at Mari and Ebla in the Pre-Sargonic period (see above, § 3.1.7), but it is almost identical with the calendar known at Mari in classical Old Babylonian times. See ARMT 19 10–14, and Gallery (1981: 346f.).

3.4.4. *A Legal Text*

In addition to the administrative texts previously published by Jestin and Limet (see above, § 3.4.3), about one hundred texts are known to come from the excavations of Mari. A legal text found among them has recently been published by Durand (1982c).

Generally sound in its philological treatment, Durand's article, including its title, contains a number of terms that hardly apply to the document he published, such as his terms "Sumérien," "Akkadien," "Amorite" (for a document written not in Sumerian, but in its own system of writing, and in a language that is not Akkadian spoken in the land of the Amorites, but is identical with the local language of Mari and Ebla), and "archaïque" (for a period that is at least four hundred years younger than the "archaic" period of the Pre-Sargonic texts of Mari). Durand's statement on pp. 79–81 about the relation of the new text to those published by Jestin (1952) and Limet in ARMT 19 is not clear since it is hard to know whether he is writing about the form of the tablets or the writing and language of the texts. Clear is what he says on p. 83: "La graphie de notre texte . . . rappelle les documents publiées dans *BIN* IX par Crawford." The statement is remarkable in what Durand chose to compare (BIN 9 texts written in Sumerian in far-away Isin), and what he did not (the relation to the Old Assyrian systems of writing, for example).

Durand's text is a unique contract concerning the sale of 1½ *iku* 'acres' of field by Jiddin-Mama, the cupbearer, to ᵓIlī-Jiddinam, the captain-overseer, for 12 shekels of silver plus an additional payment of 1 SILÀ 'quart' of oil. The witnessed contract concludes in the following way: 14-19) 7 PNs 20) ÉŠ. GÍD *šu zi-ga-tim*$_x$(TÍ) 21) *tim-ḫa-zu* 22) NINDA *ti-ku-lu* 23) KAŠ *ti-iš-da-u* 24) *ú* Ì *ti-il-tap-tu* 25) *in* É PN 26) *a-lu-zi-nim* '7 PNs, surveyors, who have driven the clay-nails (into the wall of the house), eaten bread, drunk beer, and anointed themselves with oil in the house of PN, the bear ward'.

This concluding statement of the Durand contract corresponds to two parts in the Mari contracts of the Lîm Dynasty and in the ancient kudurrus and related sale contracts of Babylonia in the third millennium B.C.

As noted by Durand (1982c: 85f.), the rite of driving the nail recurs at Mari in ARM 8 12, and p. 194. The ceremonial feast celebrating the conclusion of the contractual agreement, which consists of eating bread, drinking beer, and anointing oneself with oil, also recurs in later Mari, in ARM 8 13, as noted by Durand (1982c: 86ff.). In Sumerian, the rite of sanctioning the sale of a landed property is expressed by two actions, kag . . . dú 'driving of the nail' and ì . . . ag 'spreading of the oil' (see §§ 8.12.5.1 and 8.12.5.2 in the forthcoming publication of the ancient kudurrus); furthermore, the feast is limited in Babylonia to eating bread, or eating bread and drinking beer (§ 8.12.5.8). However, the custom of anointing oneself with oil is attested in later periods in an Old Babylonian contract from Khafaje (Jacobsen 1955: 107 no. 59).

The main difference between Durand's and our interpretation is the following: While Durand breaks up the final statement into three parts, "7 PN's (sont) les arpenteurs qui ont frappé les piquets," "on a mangé le pain . . . ," and "l'acte s'est passé dans la demure d'Irra-dalîlî, le baladin," they are linked together in our translation. The main questions are: who participates in the feast, and where did it take place? In Babylonia, the participants of the feast vary greatly from text to text. They may include the primary witnesses (= secondary sellers), mainly culled from among the relatives of the main seller, as well as scribes and surveyors, and even the citizens of the adjoining settlements. Whatever the composition of the participants, the feast took place regularly in the house of the buyer of the property. Only in one case did the feast take place on the threshing floor of the property of the steward of the household of a man who is known to be the son of Sargon, and, therefore, a brother of Man-ištušu, the buyer of the property (cf. MDP 2 1, the Man-ištušu Obelisk C xiii 2, and xix 26). In Durand's text, the feast took place not in the house of the buyer or his relative, but in the house of an *aluzinnum,* translated '*baladin*' by Durand, and 'bear ward' by me (Gelb 1975: 61ff.). In light of the very strict limitations of social mobility, I leave unanswered the question whether a man of such a lowly status as a bear ward could have been a relative of the buyer, who was a middle-class official of the rank of captain-overseer.

The writing and language of the Durand text are in agreement with those of the administrative texts. In the field of writing, the sign inventory and its use are identical. The same is true of the language, but for some important morphological and lexical additions that are likely to be found in a legal contract, and not in administrative texts. See below, § 3.4.6.2.

In the lexicon of the legal text, we note the use of the verb *lapātum* 'to anoint oneself' (line 24), instead of *pašāšum*; of the elements *Ìr-maš-*, *Iš-làl-*, and *Ti-ir-* in personal names, of whom *Ìr-maš-* is attested in adm. 373 and *Ti-ir-* in the name of a governor-general (above, § 3.4.2); and of the DNs *-Da-gan*, dKUR, -d*Ma-ma*, and -d*Nu-nu*, all of which recur in ARMT 19.

3.4.5. *Liver Omina*

Thirty-two clay models of liver omina were published by M. Rutten (1938). Durand (1983: 218) offered a collation and new interpretation of Rutten (1938: 50 no. 31).

Although several Babylonian kings of different date are named in the liver omina, such as Sargon, Rîmuš, and Narâm-Sin of Akkadē, Šulgi and Ibbî-Sin of Ur III, and Išbî-Era and Išmê-Dagan of Isin, their final composition cannot be earlier than ca. 2022–1935 B.C., the time of the two rulers of Isin, or very close to the date of the Mari administrative texts, suggested above (§ 3.4.3). The tradition about the Sargonic kings Sargon and Narâm-Sin continued at Mari into the period of the Lîm Dynasty, when offerings were made to their divine statues (see Birot 1980: 139 i 5–7, and pp. 16–17 and 142).

The question of the writing and language of the Mari liver omina has to be tackled very delicately since they show a much greater diversity than the administrative texts. The explanation lies simply in the fact that while the administrative texts are all more or less synchronous, the liver omina are not. While the final edition of the omina was accomplished in the post-Ur III period, that is, at the time of the administrative texts, the large number of differentiations in writing and language that the omina contain indicates that not all of them were composed in the language of the compiler in the post-Ur III period, but were copied from the original which were written in different languages, Akkadian or local Mari, as well as in the dialects of different periods, between the time of Sargon of Akkadē and Išmê-Dagan of Isin.

In the field of writing, we note, generally, the occurrence of the four types of signs which were found in the administrative texts (see below, § 3.4.6.2), but there are also important divergencies. The noun *ʾawatum* 'word' is generally written with the initial sign ʾÀ (nos. 30a, 31a, and 33a,

33b), once with A (no. 19), and the verb *il-ga-ʾà* 'he has taken' (no. 3) interchanges with *il-ga-a* (no. 9). The word for 'omen' is generally written with A in *a-mu-ut* (nos. 1, 2, 3, etc.), and twice with UD (= u_4) in UD-*mu-ut* (nos. 4a and 16). The noun *beᶜlum* 'lord' is written with AL in *be*-AL (no. 34a), but the verb *beᶜālum* 'to dominate' appears with IL in *i-be-il* (no. 35). The sign MI usually occurs (nos. 7, 10, and 27b), but once ME is used (no. 24a). The verb *śakānum* 'to put', 'to place' is written either with SÁ (nos. 7, 21a, 23, and 29) or ŠA (nos. 10, 12, and 19); note also *i-sá-ni* (no. 11a), but *i-ša-pil* (no. 35b) and *ša-aḫ-lu-uq-tim*$_x$(TÍ) (nos. 4 and 28). The intervocalic phoneme ʾ is expressed by means of the sign ḪA in *da-ri*-ḪA-*tim*$_x$(TÍ) /dariʾātim/ 'eternity' (no. 17), as in Old Babylonian. A late, and most unusual Akkadian syllabic value, A = ME$_5$ is attexted in *a-na ti-li ú gìr-me*$_5$ /karmē/ (no. 8).

In the field of language, the variations are more numerous and more serious. Uncontracted *ru-ba-um* /rubāʾum/ 'prince' (no. 35), and, similarly, *ru-ba-i-im* in genitive (no. 31a), becomes contracted *ru-bu-um* (no. 24b). For a similar example, note uncontracted *wa-zi-ʾa*$_x$(NI) in masculine (no. 18b and probably 24a), but contracted *wa-za-at* in feminine (nos. 31d and 32b). Strangely, a similar case with *waṣāʾum* 'to go out' is provided at Pre-Sargonic Ebla in *wa-za-ù-um, wa-za-um,* and *wa-zu-um* (MEE 4 257: 507, cited in Gelb 1981: 41, and Krebernik 1983: 18 and n 65). The determinative-relative pronoun is attested in singular nominative as *šu* (no. 3e) as well as *sá* (no. 1b), genitive as *si* (no. 6), and plural nominative as *šu-ut* (no. 13a). The construct state of the *qitl* formation occurs in *mi-lik* 'counsel' (no. 30b), as well as, as in Old Assyrian, in *ki-ra-ab* 'midst' (no. 31d); cf. possibly also *si-dar,* not *si-ṭir,* construct state of *šiṭrum* 'writings', discussed above, § 3.3.2. The adjective *ṣaḫum* (Akkadian *ṣiḫum*) 'small' appears in plural not only as *za-aḫ-ru-tim*$_x$(TÍ) (no. 28), but also *za-ḫa-ru-tim*$_x$(TÍ) (no. 18a). The feminine noun *ʾawatum* 'word' goes with the verb *ú-zi-ʾa*$_x$(NI) 'has gone out' (no. 30a) or *ú-zi-a-am* (no. 19), which have the prefix *u-* (or *ju-*) of the third person feminine singular that occurs in standard Old Babylonian, in contrast to *tu-* (or *ta-, ti-*) found in all Semitic languages, including Ebla, Mari, and Old Akkadian (and partially Old Assyrian). Above and below, the sign NI is transliterated as *ʾa*$_x$(NI), and not *ià,* in accordance with the evidence discussed above, § 3.1.8. The alternation of *ú-zi-ʾa*$_x$(NI) (no. 30a) and *ú-zi-a-am* (no. 19), just listed, shows that the standard Old Babylonian allative suffix *-am* has the form *-a* at Mari. The affixes of the third person masculine plural are *i . . . ū* (or *ji . . . ū*) in *iš-ta-ba-ru* 'they sent' (no. 10), *i-za-aḫ-ru* 'they turned' (no. 10), *i-ba-al-šu* /jippalšū/ (no. 11b), as regularly in Akkadian, and not *ti . . . ū,* as in *timḫaṣū* 'they have driven', *tîkulū, tištajū,* and *tiltaptū,* in a legal text and *timzaʾū* and *tîkulū* in administrative texts of Mari in the Post-Ur III period (see below, § 3.4.6.6). There are great variations in the form of the subjunctive. The standard suffix *-u* (-ū in plural) appears in nos. 7 and 17, singular, and nos. 10 (twice), 11b, plural;

but there is also the suffix *-a* in *il-ga-ʾā* (no. 3) and *il-ga-a* (no. 9) 'he has taken' and in *in*-TI-*ʾa*$_x$(NI) with uncertain meaning (no. 5), the suffix *-i* in *i-ba-al-ki-ti-šu* 'he has rebelled' (no. 6) and possibly *i-lá-ki-i* 'it will be taken' (no. 11b), and the suffix *-una* in *i-za-aḫ-ru-na* (no. 10) and *ú-ti-ru-na* (no. 22). All of these morphemes are discussed further, below, § 3.4.6.6. The suffix of the dative-allative is *-am* in *ú-zi-a-am* 'he has gone out' (no. 19), but *-a* in *ú-zi-ʾa*$_x$(NI) (no. 31a), both preterites (cited above, § 3.4.5) and in *wa-zi-ʾa*$_x$(NI) (nos. 18b and probably 24a where the interpretation as *ú wa-zi-ʾa*$_x$[NI] may be preferred to *ú-wa-zi-ʾa*$_x$[NI]), masculine participle to the feminine *wa-za-at* (nos. 31d and 32b). These examples from the Mari liver omina add force to the suggestion offered above, § 3.3.5, that the standard Akkadian suffix *-am* corresponds to *-a* in the native language of Mari. See also below, § 3.4.6.5.

The preposition *i-na* 'in' (nos. 13a and 27b) occurs in Akkadian, while the older form *ʾin* 'in' (nos. 11b, 12a, 24a, etc.) is found in Old Akkadian, Eblaic, and the administrative texts of Mari; the preposition written *ʾa*$_x$(NI)*-na* 'to', known from Eblaic and votive inscriptions from Mari of the Pre-Sargonic and Ur III periods, does not appear in the liver omina of Mari; the preposition written *a-na* 'to', 'for' (nos. 8, 10, 11b, 19, 22, 23, 24b, 29, and 30a) occurs in standard Akkadian, Eblaic, and votive and administrative texts of Mari, while the synonymous preposition *iš* 'to', 'for' (nos. 31b, 31d, and 32a), is known from Eblaic, occasionally Old Akkadian, and votive and administrative texts of Mari.

These are serious discrepancies. They force us to conclude that the liver omina were not necessarily composed in the language of the compiler in the post-Ur III period, but were copied from originals that were written in the languages or dialects of the different periods. The possibilities are: 1) Old Akkadian and its dialects, 2) Old Akkadian plus some features borrowed from the local language of Mari, 3) the local language of Mari and its dialects, and 4) the local language of Mari plus some features borrowed from Old Akkadian.

To provide some order in this jumble of possibilities in the liver omina, we have followed a simplified procedure. We have decided to assign to the local Mari language all those features that agree with the Mari features that may be reconstructed from the administrative texts and votive inscriptions of Mari in the Pre-Sargonic and Ur III periods. They are listed in fig. 4, which provides a comprehensive view of the language of Mari in all its periods of attestation.

3.4.6. *Writing and Language*

3.4.6.1. *Introductory Remarks*

In the following evaluation of the writing and language of Mari in post-Ur III times, the material based on personal names that occurs in the administrative texts (ARMT 19 159–62) must be used with caution because of the difficulties in disentangling the local Mari names from those of Akkadian or Amorite origin. A similar note of caution must be sounded in the case of the liver omina which were composed in post-Ur III times from originals that were written in different languages or dialects of different periods (see immediately above).

This section contains a full discussion of the linguistic features of post-Ur III Mari, plus brief discussions and/or cross-references to similar or different features fully treated in previous sections. This part may, therefore, be considered as containing a discussion of the language of Mari not only in post-Ur III times, but throughout the third millennium B.C. General implications in its relationship to and identification with the language of Ebla are taken up in § 4.

The sources are cited in the following way: "adm. + no." for administrative texts published in ARMT 19 = TCM 3, "legal + line" for the legal text published by Durand (1982c; above, § 3.4.4), "liver + no." for liver omina published by Rutten (1938; above, § 3.4.5); and "vot." for the few votive inscriptions discussed above (§ 3.3.2).

3.4.6.2. *Writing*

The sign inventory of the administrative texts of Mari is unique in that it is different from those in both the preceding Pre-Sargonic, Sargonic, and Ur III periods, and the following classical Old Babylonian.

We may distinguish four types of signs:

1) Standard syllabic values that do not indicate the distinction between voiced, voiceless, and emphatic phonemes, such as GA with the values of *ga, kà,* and *qá.* Inherited from Old Akkadian, they are used not only at post-Ur III Mari, but also in Old Assyrian.

2) Standard syllabic values, such as EN (IN only in the writing of the preposition *in*), LÁ, ME, DÍ (= *dí, tí,* and, in final position, tim_x), DU (tum_x in final position), and Ú in the writing of the copula written elsewhere Ù 'and'. As standard values, they are used only at post-Ur III Mari and, except for tim_x and tum_x, in Old Assyrian.

3) Archaic syllabic values, such as ᵓÀ (= É), BÍ, ÍL, LÍ, MÁ, RÍ, SÁ, and ŠÈ. Inherited from Old Akkadian, the distinction between the signs with "simple" values, such as LI in *u-li-id* /jûlid/ 'he bore children' or MA in *i-ma-ḫa-ru* /jimaḫḫarū/ 'they will receive', and the signs with corresponding "long" values, such as LÍ in *ì-lí* /ᵓilī/ 'my god' or MÁ in *iš-má* /jiśmaᶜ/ 'he has heard' (see MAD 2² 26f.), is rather consistently observed at Mari, as in the personal names (*Ìr-ra-*)*da-li-lí, passim* in *-ì-lí, -be-lí, -lá-lí, iš-má-,* and *-ni-rí,* and in the month name *Li-lí-a-*tim_x(TÍ).

The Old Akkadian distinction between the signs U, with the value *ju,* and Ù (rarely Ú), with the value ᵓ*u* (MAD 2² 26, 28, and 164f.) is generally observed at Mari: *a-li-u-um* /ᶜalijum/ (legal, line 1), *ti-iš-da-u* /tiśtajū/

(legal, line 23), possibly *i-da-u-um* /ʾitajum/? (legal, lines 2, 4), *Kar-ga-[m]e-si-u-um* /Karkamiśijum/ (adm. 397), possibly *tim-za-u* /timsajū/? (adm. 38–45) and *a-ni-u-um* /ʾannijum/ (livers 7, 10, etc.).

4) Standard syllabic values, such as IL, TE, TU, U, and those listed above under *3* that are known at Post-Ur III Mari, but are unknown (or are very rare) in Old Assyrian.

Especially important is point *2*, listing the syllabic values that are part of the standard syllabary at post-Ur III Mari, as well as in Old Assyrian, but nowhere else. Their background is a mystery at Mari, as is the origin of the Old Assyrian system of writing generally.

In contrast to the unique character of the writing system of the Mari administrative texts of the post-Ur III period, their language shows clear connections with that of Pre-Sargonic Mari and Ebla. The diverse origin of the writing and language at Mari is not surprising, as similar developments are widely attested. For instance, the royal inscriptions of the New Assyrian kings are written in the inherited Assyrian system of writing, but in the borrowed Babylonian dialect; written English is an inherited Germanic language that uses the borrowed Latin alphabet.

The writing system of the legal texts conforms with the features of the administrative texts. By contrast, liver omina, which originated at different times between the Sargonic and Old Babylonian periods, have certain characteristics reflecting all these periods (see above, § 3.4.4). While generally conforming to the writing system of the administrative texts, two new syllabic values are attested: UD with the value u_4, and AL with the value el_x. The word for 'omen' is generally written with A, in *a-mu-ut*, and twice with UD, in UD-*mu-ut*. The sign UD with the syllabic value u_4 recurs in Old Babylonian lexical texts, and the two spellings imply the existence of *ʾamûtum* and its allomorph *ʾumûtum* that is not attested anywhere. The noun *beʿlum* 'lord' is written with AL in *be*-AL, but the verb *baʾālum* (or *beʾālum*) 'to dominate' appears with IL in *i-be-il*; sign AL with the value al_x occurs in Old Akkadian *be*-AL and *i-be*-AL (MAD 3 86), and in *be*-AL in the votive inscription of a governor-general of Mari in the Ur III period (above, § 3.3.2).

A common feature of the writing of all sources of the post-Ur III period, as of all preceding periods, is that double (long) consonants and long (double) vowels are regularly written singly. The exceptions are very few, as in *ga-bi-an-nu* (adm. 330) and *ga-bi-a-nu* (adm. 315); *Bi-rí-iz-zi-rí-im* of ARM 19 248, twice, is read *pí-rí-is ṣe-rí-im* by Durand (1980: 174); *sá na-aḫ-li-i* (adm. 427) may be compared with KÁ *na-aḫ-lim* (442), and *sá na-ab-rí?-i* (381) with *in na-ab-rí-im* (324); also, *gur-na-a-tum* (365 twice), *te-rí-i* (427), possibly plurals, and ${}^{\text{GIŠ}}$*man-za-a-tum* (1460 = M. Lambert 1970: 254), plural, is to be corrected to ${}^{\text{GIŠ}}$*man-za-za?!-tum*.

Phonemes known as "weak consonants" in Akkadian are represented in the writing in the following way:

ᵓ (= ᵓ$_1$) *wa-zi-ᵓà* /waṣiᵓa/ (liver nos. 18b and 24a?) *ú-zi-ᵓà* (liver 31a).
A-me-ir- /ᵓĀmir/ (vot. above, § 3.3.2, and sev. adm.).
lu-ku-ᵓà-a-um /luquḫḫāᵓum/ (adm. 396).

h (= ᵓ$_2$) *ᵓà-wa-tum* /hawatum/ (livers 30a, 31d) *ᵓà-wa-at* (livers 32a, 32b).
ra-ᵓà-at /raḥat/ and *ra-ᵓà-te* (adm. 460).

ḥ (= ᵓ$_3$) *il-ga-ᵓà* /jilqaḥa/ (liver 3), *il-ga-a* (liver 5), and *lu-ku-ᵓà-a-um* /luquḫḫāᵓum/ (adm. 396).
I-šu-ub-Ja wr. ia$_8$)*-ᵓà-ad* /Jaḥad/ (Durand 1980: 175 adm., comparable with *Ia-su-ub-Ia-ḫa-ad* and other OB Mari names with the DN *Jaḥad* in Gelb 1980: 102). See also ᶜ.

ᶜ (= ᵓ$_{4\text{-}5}$) The initial consonant is ᶜ or *ḥ* in the following names:
PN *A-bir$_5$-tu*[*m*] (adm. 430).
DN ᵈNIN+*E-bir$_5$-tum* (Durand 1980: 175 adm.). Cf. ᵈ*A-bir$_5$-tum* (Parrot 1964: 8 ii, Pre-Sargonic, cited above, § 3.1.6).
MN *E-bir$_5$-tim$_x$* (adm.). Cf. ITI *Ḫi-bir$_5$-tim* at OB Mari.
DN ᵈNIN+*E-sá-me-tum* (Durand 1980: 174 adm.). Cf. OB DN *Ḫi-ša-mi-tim* (Dossin 1950b: 43:22) and GN *Ḫi-ša-am-ta*ᴷᴵ (ARMT 14 126).
ᶜà-ba-áš /ᶜapāś/ or /ḥapāś/ (adm. 96).
a-li-u-um /ᶜalijum/ (legal, line 1).
Iš-má- /Jiśmaᶜ/ (legal, lines 3 and 18; vot. § 3.3.2).
ú-ša-ti-ú /juśâdiᶜū/ (liver 14).
maš-a-na-an /maśᶜānân/ and sim. (adm. 279+).
sá-ni-en /śaᶜnên/ (adm. 300).
na-ra-ab /naᶜrāb/ ? (adm. 363 and 365?).

w (= ᵓ$_6$) *wa-at-rí-iš* /watriš/ (legal, line 9)
ᵓà-wa-tum /hawatum/ (livers 30a, 31d) and *ᵓà-wa-at* (livers 32a, 32b).
sá-bu-wa-an /śappuwân/ (adm. 295+), and *sá-bu-a-an* (adm. 279).
šu-tu-wa-tim$_x$ (adm. 314).
a-mu-wa-tum (adm. 381), plural of *a-mu-tum* (liver 18a).
ᵓà-ba-al /(w)abāl/ (adm. 378).
a-ak-lu-tum /(w)aklûtum/ (adm. 351+).

j (= ᵓ$_7$) *ti-iš-da-u* /tiśtajū/ (legal, line 23).
a-li-i-um /ᶜalijum/ (legal, line 1).
i-da-u-um /ᶜitajum/ ? (legal, lines 2 and 4).
Kar-ga-[*m*]*e-si-u-um* /Karkamiśijum/ (adm. 299).
tim-za-u /timsajū/? (adm. 38+).

ru-ba-um /rubājum/ (liver 35), and *ru-ba-i-im* (liver 31a).
a-ni-u-um /ʾannijum/ (livers 7, 10, 19, 22, 29).
ḫa-ra-iš /ḫarājiš/ (liver 14).
*da-rí-*ḪA*-tim*ₓ /dârijātim/ (liver 17), probably OB /dâriʾātim/.
da-li-ja(WI)*-tim*ₓ /dalijātim/ (adm. 393).
Ja(WA)*-bi-sa-tum* (adm. 462).
ja(WA)*-si-bi-im* (liver 27b).
I-šu-ub-Ja(wr. ia_8)*-ʾà-ad* /Jaḥad/ (Durand 1980: 175 adm.).

Individual consonants are not regularly distinguished by discrete signs. They are either marked by certain signs, as in *ʾà-wa-tum* /hawatum/, *wa-zi-ʾà* /waṣiʾa/, *Iš-má-* /Jiśmaʾ/, or they are unmarked, as in *A-me-ir-* /ʾĀmir/, *a-li-u-um* /ʿalijum/.

3.4.6.3. *Phonology*

The following phonemes may be posited for the language of post-Ur III Mari.

Vowels, *a, e, i, o,* and *u*. The existence of *o* may be posited by the principle of symmetry, but cannot be proved.

Consonants: ʾ, ʿ, *b, d, g, h, ḥ, ḫ, j, k, l, m, n, p, q, r, s, ś, š* (= *ṯ*), *ṣ, t, ṭ, w, z,* and *ž* (= *ḏ*).

The Akkadian "weak consonants" are illustrated above, § 3.4.6.2. They are all strong in the language of Mari, except that *j* and *w* may also form part of the diphthongs *aj, aw,* and the like, or serve as glides. See below.

Vowel *a* is preserved (not *e*) in the vicinity of *ḥ* and ʿ. See *jilqaḥ, jiśmaʿ, ʿapāś, ʿalijum, ʿAbirtum, maśʿānān, śáʿnên,* above.

We surmise that the Akkadian consonantal incompatibility does not affect the language of Mari, as in *ga-za-rí-en* /qaṣṣārên/ (adm. 248), against Akkadian /kaṣṣārên/. Cf. also the MN *Iq-zum* /Jiqṣum/ at Pre-Sargonic Ebla–Mari (above, § 3.1.7).

The distinction between the morphemes ś and š, neatly observed at Ebla and Mari in the Pre-Sargonic and Sargonic periods, is no longer valid at post-Ur III Mari. Cf. *li-sá-nu* /liśānu/ (adm. 304), *sá-sá-lum* /śaśallum/ (adm. 103) and sim., *da-sá-an* /daśśan/ (adm. 160+) and *da-si* /daśśi/ (adm. 107+), *Su-mu-*EŠ₄.DAR /Śumu/ (adm. 462) and *Šu-mu-*EŠ₄.DAR (adm. 283), *da-šu-ba-tim*ₓ /daśśubātim/ (adm. 393), *A-šu-ru-um* /ʾAśurum/ or /ʾAšurum/ (adm. 370+). In the case of *Ša-maš-ì-lí* (adm. 294), the sun-god may be /Šamaš/ or /Śamaš/, see above, § 3.1.6. For divergent spellings of the sibilants in Pre-Sargonic, see above, § 3.1.8, and in liver omina, above, § 3.4.5. The determinative-relative pronoun is written regularly with the ŠU, ŠI, ŠA signs, standing for the phoneme *ś* at Pre-Sargonic Ebla and in Sargonic Babylonia. At post-Ur III Mari, it is written indiscriminantly *šu, šu-ut, ša-at* as well as *sá, si.* See below, § 3.4.6.5. The old pronominal suffix *śu* is written *-šu* in the few cases listed below, § 3.4.6.5.

Five examples of the *maprās* formation, cited below, § 3.4.6.4, such as *na-aṭ-ba-ḫu* /naṭbāḫū/, show the phonetic change *m* > *n* > in proximity of a labial, which is preserved in Akkadian, but not in other Semitic languages, including Ebla-Mari.

Phoneme *n* is assimilated to the following *t* in the MN *Za-ʾà-tum* /Ṣaʾattum/ from **Ṣaʾantum* in Pre-Sargonic (above, § 3.1.7), but not assimilated in *šu-un-ti-šu,* 'in his dream' (liver 26).

The abnormal spellings of *ʾà-ba-al* /wabāl/ (adm. 378) and *a-ak-lu-tum* /waklûtum/ (adm. 351), raise the possibility that the initial phoneme *w* was in the process of being elided, as in later Akkadian.

The initial phoneme *j* is apparently preserved in the PN *Ja*(WA)*-bi-sa-tum* (adm. 462) and *ja*(WA)*-si-bi-im* (liver 27b).

Glide *w* is found in *a-mu-wa-tum* /$ʾ_x$amuwātum/ or /$ʾ_x$amu^{w}ātum/ (adm. 381), plural of *a-mu-tum* /$ʾ_x$amûtum/ (liver 18a), *sá-bu-wa-an* (adm. 295+) compared with *sá-bu-a-an* (adm. 279), and *šu-tu-wa-tim*$_x$ (adm. 314). Glide *j* occurs in *da-lí-ja*(WA)*-tim*$_x$ (adm. 393, where Limet read *da-li-wa-tim*$_x$ and compared it with the OB *da-lu-wa-tim* of ARM 6 31). The reading *da-lí-ja-tim*$_x$ is justified by the incompatibility of *i*+*w* in the reading *da-lí-wa-tim*$_x$. Apparently DLJ of post-Ur III Mari corresponds to DLW of OB Mari. Glide *j* is attested also in the personal names ^{d}*Nu-nu-li-tí-ja* (adm. 408), compared with ^{d}*Nu-nu-li-tí-a* (adm. 321), and in the month name *Li-lí-a-tim*$_x$ in post-Ur III Mari compared with *Li-li-ja/a-tim* in OB (ARMT 19 11).

The development of the diphthong *aj* > *ê* > *î* stopped at *ê* in the language of Mari, as shown by the oblique case of the dual, *maš-a-ni-en* /maśᶜānên/ (adm. 37+), *ga-za-rí-en* /qaṣṣarên/ (adm. 48), etc., especially *ku-ba-e-en* (adm. 103). We assume that the diphthong *aw* developed to *ô* by analogy to *âj* > *ê.* This development is paralleled by Old Assyrian, where we have *ênên* 'two wells' from **ᶜajnajn* and, presumably, *ômum* 'day' from **jawmum,* contrasting with Babylonian *ênîn* and *ûmum.* A different development is known at Ebla in the Pre-Sargonic period, where *aj* either stayed *aj* or it developed to *â,* just as *aw* either stayed *aw* or developed to *â.* See Gelb 1981: 23ff.

Variations between full and contracted forms are illustrated in the liver omina, which express both local Mari, as well as Akkadian, linguistic elements. See above, § 3.4.5. Such are *ru-ba-am* /rubāʾam/ (35), *ru-ba-i-im* (31a), and *ru-bu-um; a-ni-u-um* (7, 10, 12), *a-ni-um* (19, 29), *a-nu-um* (23) and *a-nu-tùm* (12c); *wa-zé-ʾà* /waṣiʾa/ (18b), *ú-zi-ʾà* (31a), and *wa-za-at* (31d, 32b). The case of *wa-za-ù-um, wa-za-um,* and *wa-zu-um* at Pre-Sargonic Ebla, cited there, gives a warning that contracted forms are not necessarily limited to late Akkadian.

Vowel apocopation in *ṣaḫarum* > *ṣaḫrum* 'small' is shown in *za-ḫa-ru-tim*$_x$ (liver no. 18a) compared with *za-aḫ-ru-tim*$_x$ (liver no. 28), and the forms *ṣaḫarum, ṣaḫrum* alternate with the form *ṣaḫirum* (or *ṣaḫrum*) in the PN *Za-ḫir-tum* (adm. 212+, taken as an appellative noun in ARMT 19 166).

3.4.6.4. *Noun*

The following nominal formations are worth noticing.

PIRS: *ki-ra-ab* /qirab/ in construct state (liver no. 31a), but *mi-li-ik* /milik/ (liver no. 30b). Comparable with the former is possibly *si-dar* /šiṭar/ in place of Akkadian *šiṭir,* in a votive inscription of the Ur III period, discussed above, § 3.3.2, and several occurrences in Old Assyrian of *piras* which contrast with the *piris* of Old Akkadian and later Babylonian.

PURĀS: *ú-ra-zum* /ʾurāṣum/ and others (adm. 114), an original *purajs* diminutive formation which is realized as *purās.*

PARRĀS: *ga-za-rí-en* /qaṣṣārên/ (adm. 248).

PARRŪS: *da-šu-ba-tim*$_x$ /daššubātim/ 'sweets' (adm. 393), comparable with Assyrian *daššupum,* Babylonian *duššupum* 'very sweet'.

MAPRĀS: *ma-ga-lu* (adm. 389).
ma-ga-rí /magarrī' (adm. 459).
^{GIŠ}*man-za-za*$^!$(or A)-*tum* /manzāzātum/ (adm. 460).
maš-a-na-am /maśᶜānān/ and others (adm. 279+).
^{GIŠ}*maš-ga-ga-tum* /maśkākātum/ (adm. 460).
ma-za-ra-tim$_x$ /maṣṣārātim/ and others (adm. 365).
^{GIŠ}*na-ba-lu* (adm. 460), root unknown.
na-ba-tim$_x$ (adm. 413), root unknown.
na-ra-ab /naᶜrāb/ ? (adm. 363 and 365?).
na-áš?-da-ap-tum /našṭaptum/ ? (liver no. 22) according to von Soden 1953: 260 n 1.
^{GIŠ}*na-aṭ-ba-ḫu* /naṭbāḫū/ (adm. 460).
For the phonetic change *m* > *n* in the four previous cases, see above, § 3.4.6.3.

MAPRĪS: ^{NA4}*mar-si-da-tum* /marśīdātum/ (adm. 460).

PURUSSĀʾum: *lu-ku-a-um* /luquḫḫāʾum/ (adm. 396).
mu-ku-tum /muquttûm/? (adm. 326+). Very doubtful since it involves a contraction from *muquttāʾum*; see Gelb 1956: 9.
šu-ku-na-ì /śukunnāʾi/ (Durand 1980: 176 adm.).
zu-ḫu-ra-im /ṣuḫurrāʾim/ (liver 6).

ŠAPRUS: *ša-aḫ-lu-uq-ì* (livers 4, 28).

TAPRĀS: *tap-ḫa-ru-um* /tapḫārum/ (adm. 252).

TAPRĪS: *da-aḫ-bi-sá-tim*$_x$ /taḫbīśātim/ or /taḫpīśātim/ (adm. 306). Cf. 1 GI *da-ḫa-ba-áš-tum* (TCL 5 6036 x, Ur III) and later Akkadian *taḫabšum*, both cited in MAD 3 125.
MN *Taš-ni-tim*$_x$ /Tašnîtim/ (adm. 32+).

-ānum: *ga-bi-an-nu* (adm. 330) and *ga-bi-a-nu* (adm. 315).
MN *Ma-al-ga-ni-en* /Malkānên/ (adm. 33+) and MN *Ma-al-ga-ni* (adm. 17+).
za-mu-ga-ne /samūkānī/ with *jaśibum*, a kind of siege engine (liver 27b), comparable with *sāmūkānum* and *jašibum* in an Old Babylonian Diyala Region letter to be published by Robert M. Whiting. Cf. also *-ān* in PN *Sá-tu-ba-an* /Śatupān/ (adm. 279).

-ijum: *Kar-ga-[m]e-si-u-um* /Karkamiśijum/ (adm. 397).
Šu-ba-ri-ú /Šubarijū/ (liver 10 twice).
dNIN *E-sá-me-tum* /ʾEśamîtum/ (Durand 1980: 174, adm.). Cf. OB DN d*Ḫi-ša-mi-tim* (Dossin 1950b: 43:22) and OB GN *Ḫi-ša-am-ta*KI (ARMT 15 126).
dNIN *Ti-rí-tum* /Dîrîtum/ (Durand 1980: 174 adm.). Cf. OB DN d*Di-ri-tim* (Dossin 1950b: 43:10).

-illum: *a-za-me-lum* /ʾazamillum/ (adm. 96).
bar-zi-lum /parzillum/ (adm. 337). Doubtful.

-innum: *a-lu-zi-nu* /ʾaluzinnu/ (adm. 364).

-ûtum: *a-mu-ut* /ʾa$_x$mût/ (liver 1+), *u(d)-mu-ut* (livers 4, 17), *a-mu-tum* (liver 18a), and *a-mu-wa-tum* (adm. 381, plural).
a-a-bu-dam /ʾajjābûtam/ (liver 30a) and *a-a-bu-tim*$_x$ (liver 31b).

The following declension includes all declinable speech elements: nouns (proper or substantive), adjectives, participles, infinitives, and numerals, except the pronouns which are discussed below, § 3.4.6.5.

Masc. Sg. N. *-um*: *a-li-u-um* (legal, lines 2, 4), *a-lu-zi-nu* (adm. 364), *bar-šum* (adm. 223+), *bi-li-lum* (260+), *bi-*

tum (152+), *bi-tu-ru-um* (258), *Da-i-ru-um* (194), *da-šum* (166+), *ḫa-u* (313), *ku-ku-šu* (339), *lu-ku-a-um* (396), *mar-zum* (18+), TÚG . . . *ma-az-um* (310), *mu-ku-tum* (326+), *na-ru-kum* (307), *na-zi-zum* (332), *Sá-da-šum* (266), *sá-ap-lum* (legal, line 4), *sá-sá-lum* (303), *Sál-la-šum* (267), *tap-ḫa-ru-um* (252), Ì *za-kum* (316+), *zu-gu* (316+).

G. *-im*: *a-ḫu-rí-im* (adm. 391), *ba-lá-lim* (347), *bi-tim* (342), *da-šim* (324) and *da-si* (207+), Ì *gur-nim* (327), *ḫu?-da-lim* (427), *ja*(WA)*-si-bi-im* (liver 27b), *ki-si* (adm. 110), *ki-šèr-šim*? (258), *ku-bu-li* (106+), *ku-ru-nim* (Durand 1980: 185 adm.), MN *Lá-ḫi-im*, *na-ab-rí*!*-i*[*m*] (324*) and *na-ab-rí?-i* (424), *na-aḫ-lim* (442) and *na-aḫ-li-i* (427), *ru-si* (38+), *sá-ba-rí* (84), *si-ki* (288), *śu-gur-rí* (334), *šu-ku-na-ì* (Durand 1980: 176 adm.), *te-rí-i* (427), *ú-ba-si* (382), *za-aḫ-ti* (407+, *zi-rí-im* /ṣêrim/ (248).

A. *-am*: *ì-ga-mu u ba-al-ga-am* (liver 14), *maš-a-na-am* . . . *gur-nam* (adm. 296), *Ú-ra-am* (liver 8), *za-ba-am* (liver 24a).

Pl. N. *-ū*: x *a-bi-nu-šu* (adm. 460), x UDU *ba-ag-ru* (303), *bi-il-šu* (liver 11b), x GIŠ*bi-it-nu* (adm. 460), x *ḫi!-ru* (277+), x GIŠ*ki-da-nu* (460), 2? *ki-ru* (182), x *li-sá-nu* (304), x *lu-ru* (460 twice), x *ma-ga-lu* (389+), x *maš-a-nu* (293), x *maš-a-nu tab-ú-tum* (280+), x GIŠ*na-ba-lu* (460 twice), x GIŠ*na-aṭ-ba-ḫu* (460), x *ra-bi-ku* (277+), *Šu-ba-ri-ú* (liver 10 twice), x *tir-ku* (adm. 280+), x GIŠ*zi-tu* (460).

-ûtum: with adjectives or substantivized adjectives: *a-ak-lu-tum* (adm. 351+), x TÚG . . . *ma-az-ú*]*-tum* (309), x *maš-a-nu tab-ú-tum*, just above.

G.-A. *-ī*: *a-li* (livers 18a, 28), x *ma-ga-rí* (adm. 459), x *maš-a-ni* (291), x TÚG*na-zi-zi* (311), x KÚŠ *ra-ʾà-te* (460), *a-na ti-li ú gàr-me*$_5$ (liver 8), x KUŠ *ú-ra-zi* (adm. 133+), *za-mu-ga-ne* /samūkānī/ (liver 27b).

-ûtim: with adjectives or substantivized adjectives: *iš-ra-at-ú-tim*$_x$ (adm. 395, or abstract), *za-ḫa-ru-tim*$_x$ /ṣaḫarûtim/ (liver 18a), and *za-aḫ-ru-tim*$_x$ (liver 28).

Du. N. *-ān*: 2 *bi-da-an* (adm. 164), 2 *ḫar-ʾà-an* (301), 2 *da-sá-an* (184), 2 *maš-a-na-an* (284+), 2 *maš-a-na-an tab-a-an* (279+), 1 *maš-a-na-an* (280+), 1 *maš-a-na-an tab-a-an* (282+), 1 *maš-a-na-an ra-bu-a-an* (292), 1 *maš-a-na-an sá-bu-a-an ra-bu-a-an* (279+); 1 *maš-a-na-an* . . . TUR-*ki-na-an* (295), 1 *maš-a-na-an* . . . *gur-nam* (296), 2 *sá-sá-lá-an* (302), 2 *tir-ga-an* (286), 2 *za-aḫ-da-an* (463), 2 *zu-ba-ʾà-an* (258).

G.-A. *-în*: *ma-al-ku-i-in* (liver 23, unusual).

G.-A. *-ên*: *a-lu-zi-ni-en* (adm. 304), 2 *ga-za-rí-en* (248), *ki-ba-en* (61), *ku-ba-a-en* (103), *li-li-en* and *li-li* (both in ARMT 19 163), MN *ma-al-ga-ni-en* (33+) and MN *Ma-al-ga-ni* (17+), 2 *maš-a-ni-en* (290), 1 *maš-a-ni-en* (37), and *maš-a-ni-en* (287), *ma-za-en* (59), *sá-ni-en* (300), *šè-ir-te-en* (331+).

Fem. Sg. N. *-(a)tum*: *A-bir*$_5$*-tu[m]* (adm. 247), *a-mu-tum* (liver 18a), *ʾà-wa-tum* (livers 30a, 31d), *Da-lu-uḫ-tum* (adm. 384), *ga-za-tum* (258), ^{d}*Ga-ma-šu-ra-tum* (Durand 1980: 174 adm.), *Taš-ni-tum* (247), WA-*bi-sa-tum* (462), *Za-ḫir-tum* (212+).

G. *-tim*: MN *E-bir*$_5$*-tim*$_x$ (adm. 1+), *ḫir-tim*$_x$ (258), MN *Taš-ni-tim*$_x$ (32+), *a-a-bu-tim*$_x$ /ʾajjābûtim/ (liver 31b).

A.: *-tam*: *a-a-bu-dam* /ʾajjābûtam/ (liver 30a).

Pl. N.: *-ātum*: *a-mu-wa-tum* (adm. 381), x *ḫu-ba-tum* (Durand 1980: 175 adm.), *ir-ma-tum* (adm. 339), x *ki-a-tum* (389), x ${}^{\text{GIŠ}}$*ki-is-gàr-ra-tum* (460), x ${}^{\text{GIŠ}}$*man-za-za?!-tum* (460), x ${}^{\text{NA}_4}$*mar-si-da-tum* (460), x *ma-lá-tum* (Durand 1980: 175 adm.), x ${}^{\text{GIŠ}}$*maš-ga-ga-tum* (460), x *sá-sá-lá-tum* (302).

G.-A. *-ātim*: *a-na-tim*$_x$ (365 adm. twice), *da-aḫ-bi-sátim*$_x$ (306), *da-lu?!-wa-tim*$_x$ (393), *da-šu-ba-tim*$_x$ (393), *gìr-tap-ba-tim*$_x$ (104), *gur-bi-za-tim*$_x$ (463), MN *Li-lí-a-tim*$_x$ (20), *ma-za-ra-tim*$_x$ (365), *ma-ba-tim*$_x$ (413), *na-ru-ga-tim*$_x$ (324), *sá-ak-sá-tim*$_x$ (324), *šu-tu-wa-tim*$_x$ (314), *zi-me-da-tim*$_x$ (248).

Du. N. *-ān*: - - -

G.-A. *-ên*: *šè-ir-te-en* (adm. ARMT 19 163).

Construct State:	
Masc. Sg. -Ø:	*ʾà-ba-al* (adm. 378), *ʾà-ba-áš* (96), *ga-sur* (61+), *ki-kir* (61+).
Fem. Sg. -Ø:	*a-mu-ut* (liver 1+), *ʾà-wa-at* (livers 32a, 32b), *ma-za-ra-at* (adm. 381), *uk-lá-at* (Durand 1980: 176 adm.).
Fem. Sg. *-ti*:	*ša-aḫ-lu-uq-tí* (livers 4, 28).
Predicate State:	
Masc. Sg. -Ø:	in PNs, as in *E-a-ma-lik* (adm. 376), etc., *ma-zi-i* /maṣî/ (liver 31a).
Du. *-ā*:	*mar-za* (adm. 55, 57).
Fem. Sg. *-at*:	*mar-za-at* (adm. 14+).
Du. *-ā*:	*mar-za* (adm. 19, 20+).
Fem. Sg. *-a*:	only in PNs EŠ$_4$.DAR-*a-li-a* (adm. 384+), EŠ$_4$.DAR-*dam-ga* (303+). *Lá-da-ba*-DINGIR /La-ṭâba-ʾIl/ (461), *Ma-ma-a-li-a* (37+).
Absolute State:	x SILÀ *kir-ba-at* (adm. 212+), *a-na na-ap-da?-an* (389), *šu na-ra-ab* (363), x KÚŠ *ra-ʾà-at* (460), *in te-ir*, and similar (35+), ^{d}NIN-*mu-ra-ra-at* /murārāt/ (Lady of certain plants) (Durand 1980: 174 adm.). Cf. also the structure of numerals in absolute state, plus things connoted in apposition: 1 *me-at ma-ga-lu* (389), 7 *me-at* 10 ÙZ (462 sev.), 1 *li-im* 3 *me-at* 80 ÙZ (462), 1 *rí-ba-at* 3 *li-me* 4 *me-at* UD[U.UD]U (Durand 1984c: 278 adm.).

In the listing provided just above, we find several noteworthy features: singular *śaśallum* 'rump' occurs as *śaśallān* in dual and *śaśallātum* in plural; singular *naruqqum* 'basket' has *naruqqātim* in plural; *kirtappātim* is a plural of unattested *kirtappum* 'footstool', which is known in various other forms in Akkadian; and *gurbisātim* is a plural of *gurpisum*, which occurs in an unpublished Mari text, according to Limet (1975: 44), and in several differing forms also in later Akkadian, where it denotes a protective device, probably a helmet.

The suffixes *-ûtum*, *-ûtim* stand for the masculine plural of adjectives or substantivized adjectives, as in *ṣaḫarum*, *ṣaḫrum* 'small', plural *ṣaḫarûtum*, *ṣaḫrûtum*, and correspond to the suffixes that are used to denote abstract formations, as in *ʾajjābûtum* 'hostility' (above), but contrast with the suffixes *-ū*, *-ī* of the substantives. No such contrast takes place in the suffixes of the feminine plural and of the dual (only masculine attested) of the adjectives (or substantivized adjectives) and substantives.

As may be seen from the examples provided above, the dual forms are preceded by number 2, as in 2 *maš-a-na-an*, 2 *maš-a-ni-en*, or 2 *ma-za-rí-en*, number 1, as in 1 *maš-a-na-an* or 1 *maš-a-ni-en*, or number Ø, as in *maš-a-ni-en* or *a-lu-zi-ni-en*. The number of 2 *ki-ru* (adm. 182) should probably be corrected to 3 (or more) *ki-ru*.

The form *mar-za* /marṣā/ is the predicate of two male subjects (adm. 55, 57) as well as two female subjects (adm. 19, 20), contrary to Old Akkadian where the corresponding forms are *marṣā* in masculine (MAD 1 178), and *śalimtā* in feminine (MAD 1 185).

Mimation is strictly observed in the legal text. The use or the absence of mimation in the liver omina may be explained by the difference in their temporal composition. Strict preservation of the mimation in *-tum*, *-tim*, *-ātum*, *-ātim* of the feminine singular and plural and of the nunation *-ān*, *-ên* of the dual in administrative texts raises the suspicion that many of the masculine forms ending in *-u* and *-i* are plurals, rather than defectively written singulars, as here taken.

One of the surprising features of the listing is the almost total absence of the accusative case.

The most bewildering forms occur in words designating the time of the day and month. The time of the day is denoted *in šè-ir-te-en* 'in the morning'' and *in li-li-en* 'in the evening' at post-Ur III Mari. The former is identical with Akkadian *šêrtum* (also *šêrum*), plural *šêrētum*, Hebrew *šaḫar* 'dawn', etc., the latter with Akkadian *lîlum*, plural *lîlijātum*, *lîlâtum*, Hebrew *lajil*, *lajla* 'night', etc. The lack of nunation may be noted in the forms *li-li*, ITI *Ma-al-ga-ni*, besides ITI *Ma-al-ga-ni-en*, and a plural form *Lîlijātum* occurs as a month name. The reason for the dual in *šêrtān*, *lîlān*, and MN *Malkānān*, and the relation of these duals to the plural in MN *Lîlijātum* and to the singular in MN *Malkānum* (also at OB Mari) remains baffling.

As may be seen from examples of the absolute state (just above), the cardinal numerals *me-at* 'hundred', *li-im* 'thousand', and *rí-ba-at* 'ten thousand' regularly occur in the absolute case in the post-Ur III period. The spelling *mi-at* is attested in the Pre-Sargonic period (above, § 3.1.4), and a variant *li-me* for *li-im* in Durand (1984c: 278).

The post-Ur III form *rí-ba-at*, which is a feminine *ribbat*, from *ribbatum*, corresponds to *ri-ib-ba-at* at Old Babylonian Alalakh (AT 55:27 and 56:36, 40), and similarly in Ugaritic, Hebrew, and Aramaic, and contrasts with the Ebla form *rí-bab* (e.g., MEE 3 134 and 156), which is a masculine *ribb*, from *ribbum*. The difference between the masculine *ribb* at Pre-Sargonic Ebla and the feminine *ribbat* at post-Ur III Mari may be listed under the very few dialectal variations which may have been occasioned by the difference in time and area. Noteworthy is the fact that *ribbum, ribbatum* is at home in the West Semitic area (Mari, Ebla, Alalakh, Hebrew, and Aramaic), but not in East Semitic Akkadian.

Besides the masculine *-um* and feminine *-(a)tum* in normal state, forms in indeterminate state occur in the PNs, DNs, GNs, and MNs of the Pre-Sargonic period (§ 3.1.8). Note -Ø in *Sá-lim* /Śalim/ and ᵈ*Aš-dar-ra-at* /ᶜAštarat/; ITI Ì.NUN.NA-*at* /Ḫimᵓat/; the masculine suffix *-a*, as in ITI *Iq-za* /Jiqṣa/, besides ITI *Iq-zum*, with the normal *-um* suffix, at Išnun, Gasur, and Lagash. Similar cases are attested in the post-Ur III period: -Ø in *Sá-tu-ba-an* /Śaṭupān/ (adm. 279), PN *Lá-as-ga-an* (adm. 333+), DN /Jaḥad/ in *I-šu-ub-Ja* (or *Ia*$_8$)-ᵓ*à-ad* (Durand 1980: 175 adm., comparable with *Ia-šu-ub-Ia-ḫa-ad* and other OB Mari names listed in Gelb 1980: 102), DNs ᵈ*I-sar* and ᵈ*Me-sar* (Dossin 1967c: 100:28f., adm.), GN /Ṣarbat/ in ᵈEŠ.DAR-*Za-ar-ba-at* (Durand 1980: 174 adm.; cf. also § 3.1.8, Pre-Sargonic); the suffix *-a* in ᵈ*Ga-as-ba* /Kaspa/ (Dossin 1967c: 100:32 adm.), and /Kakka/ in PN PÙ.ŠA-*Kag-ga* (adm. 316+).

3.4.6.5. *Pronoun*

Independent personal forms are not attested anywhere.

Pronominal Suffixes

The declension of the pronominal suffix is illustrated in the following examples:

Noun + pron. suffix in Gen.

Sg. 1st	*-i*:	ᵈ*Da-gan-a-bi* (adm. 376), ᵈIM-*ì-lí* (adm. 285), etc.
3rd	*-šu*:	ŠEŠ-*šu* (legal, line 3), *Ma-na-áš-tu-šu*(liver 2), etc.
Du. 3rd	*-šuni*:	*iš la-*ᵓ*à-me-šu-ni* 'for their consumption' (adm. 248, according to Westenholz 1978: 164, 165, 167), *ra-*ᵓ*à-te-šu-ni* 'their handles' (adm. 460 rev.), GUD-*šu* (or *si*)*-ni* 'their oxen' (adm. 379, according to Whiting 1977: 210f., Westenholz 1978: 164, 165, 167).

Verb + pron. suffix in Acc.

Sg. 1st	*-i*:	*Ku-um-li-*ᵈIM (adm. 200+), *Rí-im-si-*ᵈ*Da-gan* (adm. 205+).
	-ija:	ᵈ*Nu-nu-li-tí-a* (adm. 321) or ᵈ*Nu-nu-li-tí-ja*(WA) (adm. 408).
	-anni:	*Iš-ma-ni-*ᵈ*Nu-nu*? (adm. 461), *Ì-lí-iš-ma-*[*ni*] (adm. 308).
3rd	*-šu*:	*iš-am-šu* (legal, line 13), *Ì-lí-i-ti-šu* (adm. 199), *ú-ša-ti-ú-šu* (liver 14), *i-ba-al-ki-ti-šu* (liver 6).
	-aššu	(from *+am+šu*): *Ì-lí-i-ti-na-šu* (adm. 314), DINGIR-*i-ti-na-šu* (adm. 389).

Verb + pron. suffix in Dat.

1st	*-a*:	*ú-zi-*ʾ*à* (liver 31a), *Rí-za-*^{d}*À-a-a*: 'Come to help me, Ḫajja!' (adm. 369+), *Rí-im-sá-ì-lí* '. . . to me, my god!' (adm. 18+).
	-aja:	DINGIR-*aš-ra-a* (adm. 289), ^{d}*Da-gan-nu-uṣ-ra-a* (341, 449), ^{d}IM-*tu-ra-a* (322, 325).
	-am:	*ú-zi-a-am* (liver 19).
3rd	*-śum*:	*i-ti-šum* (legal, lines 8, 11; adm. 308).

Two morphemes require further attention: the dual *-śuni* with the noun, and the singular accusative *-i, -ija, -anni*, and the dative *-a, -aja, -am* with the verb.

The discovery of the morpheme *-šuni* of the dual belongs to Whiting (1972), as supplemented (Whiting 1977). To be added to the material is KUG.BABBAR-*šu-ni* in EA 246 rev. 5–7, from Megiddo. The word *la-*ʾ*à-me-šu-ni* may be either an infinitive *la*ʾ*āmum*, for which see MAD 3 159 under LḤM, later *lêmum*, etc., or a noun *la*ʾ*amum, la*ʾ*mum*, for which see MAD 3 161 under LḪM (= LḤM). The word *ra-*ʾ*à-te-šu-ni* occurs as *ra-*ʾ*à-at* in indeterminate case in the same text, and as *ra-*ʾ*à-tum* at Pre-Sargonic Ebla (MEE 1 4973). The word occurs as *rittum* 'hand', 'hand-span' in Akkadian and has relations in the form RḤT with the meaning 'hand', 'palm', a measure of length, etc. in Ugaritic, Hebrew, and other Semitic languages.

The most noteworthy variations are shown in the suffixes of the first person singular: *-i, -ija, -anni* in accusative, and *-a, -aja, -am* in dative.

The following comparative material may be adduced. "M" refers to the Mari names of the OB period collected in ARMT 16/1 and Gelb (1980).

To *-i* in *Ku-um-li-*^{d}IM (adm. 200+): *Ku-um-li-A-du* (Wiseman 1953: Index), ^{d}*Iš-ḫa-ra-gu-um-li* (M, fem.). Cf. also under *-ija*, below, and the discussion under the imperative below, § 3.4.6.6.

To *-i* in *Rí-im-si-*^{d}*Da-gan* (adm. 205+): *Ri-im-ši-ì-lí* and *Ri-im-ši-*DINGIR (M+). Cf. also under *-a* below, the discussion under the imperative below, § 3.4.6.6, and *Tu-ri-*^{d}*Da-gan* (TCL 1 237+, Hana), *Šu-bi-*^{d}IM /Šûbi-Haddu/ (M).

To *-ija* in ^{d}*Nu-nu-li-tí-a* (adm. 321) and ^{d}*Nu-nu-li-tí-ja* (408): cf. with the verb EŠ$_{4}$DAR-*tu-ri-ia* (M. fem.), *Ì-lí-gu-um-li-ia* (M), *Ì-lí-tu-ri-ia* (M+), *Ka-ka-tu-ri-ia* (M) and with the noun *A-du-ni-a-bi-ia* (Dossin 1930: 87, Mari), *Bi-in-ì-lí-ia* (M), *Ia-ku-un-bi-ia* (M) and *Ku-um-li-*^{d}IM under *-i*, above.

To *-anni* in the Akkadian type Sin-gimlanni, etc.: the suffix corresponds to the Mari suffixes *-i* and *-ija* in *Ku-um-li-*^{d}IM /Gumli-Haddu/ (adm. 200+), and *Ì-lí-gu-um-li-ia* (M).

To *-a* in *Rí-im-sá-ì-lí* (adm. 18+); cf. *Rí-im-si-*^{d}*Da-gan* under *-i* above.

To *-a* in *Rí-im-sá-ì-lí* (adm. 18+) and *Rí-za-dDa-gan* /Rîṣa-Dagan/ (369+): cf. *Tu-ra-dDa-gan* (M+), *Tu-ra-dDa-gan* (Ur III Mari = *Tu-ra-am-dDa-gan* [Akk. Ur III Mari], for which see above, § 3.3.2), *Tu-ra-ì-lí* MAR.TU (MVN 2 205 v, Ur III), *Ì-lí-tu-ra* (M+), *Šu-ba-d*DINGIR /Šûba-ʾIl/ (Gelb 1980: 362), *ú-zi-ʾà* (liver 31a) = *ú-zi-a-am* (liver 19).

To *-aja* in DINGIR-*aš-ra-a* (adm. 289): cf. *Ì-lí-aš-ra-ia* (M+).

To *-aja* in *dDa-gan-nu-uṣ-ra-a* (adm. 391, 449): cf. *dDa-gan-nu?-uṣ?-ra-ia* (ARM 8 1:40).

To *-aja* in dIM-*tu-ra-a* (adm. 322, 325): cf. *Ì-lí-tu-ra-ia* (M+); *Ša-la-aš-tu-ra-ia* (*Iraq* 7 p. 41, Chagar Bazar, fem.).

To *-am* in the Akkadian *Tu-ra-am-dDa-gan* (Ur III), and *ú-zi-a-am* (liver 19): cf. *-a* in the Mari name *Tu-ra-dDa-gan* (Ur III) and *ú-zi-ʾà* (liver 31a).

We may draw the following conclusions:

1. The suffix *-i* corresponds to the suffix *-ija*: *gumli-* and *-gumlija*, *Tûri-* and *-tûrija*.

2. The suffixes *-i* and *-ija* correspond to the Akkadian *-anni*: *Gumli-*, *-gumlija*, and Akkadian *-gimlanni*.

3. The suffix *-a* corresponds to the suffix *-aja*: *Tûra-*, *-tûra*, and *-tûraja*.

4. The suffixes *-a* and *-aja* correspond to the Akkadian *-am*: *Tûra-*, *-tûra*, *-tûraja*, and Akkadian *Tûram-*, also *ûṣiʾa* and Akkadian *ûṣiʾam*.

5. The suffixes *-am* and *-anni* are Akkadian only.

6. The suffix *-i* is used at Mari in post-Ur III and OB Amorite, and in later dialectal Akkadian.

7. The suffix *-a* is used at Mari in Ur III and post-Ur III periods and in OB Amorite.

8. The suffixes *-ija* and *-aja* are attested at Mari in post-Ur III and OB periods.

9. The suffixes *-ija* and *-aja*, which mainly occur at the end of words (names), are phonetic extensions of *-i* and *-a*, respectively. For similar cases, cf. *ʾana ʾabī* 'to my father' in Old Akkadian (MAD 2^2 128f.) and *ana abija* in later Akkadian.

10. The function of the accusative suffix *-i* (also *-ija* and Akkadian *-anni*) parallels that of the dative suffix *-a* (also *-aja* and Akkadian *-am*): *Rimši-*, *Tûri-*, *Tûra-*, and *Tûram-* in post-Ur III, *Šûbi-* and *Šûba-* at OB Mari.

11. The parallel use of the accusative suffix *-i* (also *-ja*) and the dative suffix *-a* (also *-aja*) recurs in certain verbs in later Mari, and the same is true of the accusative suffix *-anni* and the dative suffix *-am* in later Akkadian. Note, for instance, the dative *rîṣam*, *Sin-rîṣam*, *Ili-irîṣa* and accusative *irîṣam* cited in AHw 970.

The dative pronominal suffixes frequently function in the role of the dative-allative, as in *tûra*, *tûram*, 'turn to me!', 'return (here)'.

Determinative-relative Pronoun

A complete survey of the administrative texts, a legal text, and the liver omina yields the following declension of the determinative-relative pronoun:

Masc.	Sg. N.	*šu* (adm. *passim*; legal, lines 15, 19; liver 3b)
		sá (adm. 303; liver *passim*)
	G.	*si* (adm. 254, 442; liver 6)
		sá (adm. *passim*)
	A.	*šu* (legal, line 6)
	Pl. N.	*šu* (adm. *passim*; legal, line 20)
		sá (adm. 60, 201, 202, 230)
		šu-ut (liver 13a)
	G.-A.	*šu* (adm. 34, 291)
	Du. N.	*šu* (adm. *passim*)
		sá (adm. 284, 288, 463)
	G.-A.	*sá* (adm. 37, 287, 300)
Fem.	Sg. N.	*sá* (adm. *passim*)
	G.	---
	A.	---
	Pl. N.	*šu* (adm. 96)
		sá (adm. *passim*)
		ša-at NIM^{KI} (adm. 303, probably wrong)
	G.-A.	*sá* (adm. 314, 381)
	Du. N.	*sá* (adm. *passim*)
	G.-A.	---

The examples just cited show a complete breakdown in phonology and morphology from the original forms Masc. Sg. N. *šu,* G. *ši,* A. *ša,* Fem. Sg. N. *šat,* G. *šati,* A. *šat,* etc., attested at Sargonic Ebla and Mari and Pre-Sargonic Babylonia, including the Diyala River district.

Other Pronouns

The interrogative pronoun *man* 'who?' in the name *Ma-na-áš-tu-šu* /Man-ᵓaśtuśu/ (liver 2) corresponds to *man* in *Ma-ni-iš-tu-su* /Man-ᵓiśtuśu/ of the Sargonic period, but disagrees with *mi* 'who?' of Ebla-Mari in the Pre-Sargonic period (above, § 3.1.8).

The demonstrative and indefinite pronouns used as adjectives occur only in liver omina: *ᵓannijum* 'this' (9+) and other forms (see above, § 3.4.6.3) and *ᵓajjûmme* 'any' in *a-na a-li-im a-i-me* (19), for Akkadian *ᵓajjîma.*

3.4.6.6. *Verb*

Verbal conjugation is represented in the following occurrences:

Sg. 1	*ᵓa-*:	*a-ga-al-ma* (liver 29), *a-mur* (36), *am-ḫur* (adm. 326+), *A-na-aḫ-ì-lí* (326+).
2 m.	*ta-*:	---
2 f.	*ta . . . i*:	---
3 m.	*ji-*:	*Passim* spelled with *I-*, once *i-is-ḫu-ur* /jisḫur/ (liver 16).
	ju-:	*ú-ra-ad* (liver 27b) and probably *ú-<ta->ra-ad* (24b), *ú-ta-ma* (24a), *ú-ti-ru-na* (22) subjunctive, *ú-ša-me?-id?* (12c).
3 f.	*ta-*:	*dam-ḫur* (adm. 324+), EŠ$_4$.DAR-*tal-e* (393), EŠ$_4$.DAR-*ti-da* (397), ^{d}*Nu-nu-da-mur* (384), ^{d}*Nu-nu-da-ti* (418), *Tab-ni-Ma-ma* (218), ^{d}*Dar-am-Me-ir* (Durand 1980: 174 adm.; why fem.?), ^{d}NIN+*Taš-ki-Ma-ma* (ibid.; 'Lady of PN', a personal god of the type 4).
	ti-:	EŠ$_4$.DAR-*ti-da* (adm. 397).
	ju-:	(instead of *tu-*): *ú-zi-ᵓà* (liver 31a+).
Pl. 1	*ni-*:	*ni-dí* (adm. 165).
2 m.	*ta . . . ū*:	---
2 f.	*ta . . . ā*:	---
3 m.	*ji . . . ū*:	*i-ba-al-šu* (liver 1b), *iš-da-ba-ru-ma* (10), *i-za-aḫ-ru-ma* (10).
	ju . . . ū:	*ú-ša-ti-ú-šu* (14).
	ti . . . ū:	*tim-ḫa-zu* (legal, line 21), *ti-ku-lu* (legal, line 22 and adm. 382), *ti-iš-da-u* (legal, line 23), *ti-il-tap-tu* (legal, line 24), *tim-za-u* (adm. 38–45).
3 f.	*ji/ti . . . ā*:	---
Du. 2	*ta . . . ā*:	---
3	*ji . . . ā*:	*im-za-ᵓà* (adm. 46–50, including no. 46 where 1 GURUŠ may have to be corrected to 2 GURUŠ.

Notes on Conjugation

The prefixes of the 3m. Sg., Pl., and Du. are *ji-* in the verbs primae *j* in B, N, and derived T and TN stems, and *ju-* in the verbs primae *w* of B and N stems and in D, Š, and derived stems. The assumption that the normal prefix of the third person was *ji-* (not *i-*) in post-Ur III times, as it was from the Pre-Sargonic to Ur III periods, is based on the spelling *i-is-ḫu-ur* /jisḫur/ in the liver omen 16. For similar cases in Old Akkadian, cf. *i-ik-mi*, *I-iš-e-* cited in MAD 2^2 28. The existence of the prefix *ju-* (not *u-*) is assumed on analogy with *ji-* (not *i-*). This may be proved easily for Old Akkadian where the prefix of the third person is regularly spelled with the sign U, as in *u-sá-rí-ib* /juśaᶜrib/ 'he caused to enter', contrasting with the spellings of the first person with the sign Ù (or Ú), as in *ù-dam-me* /ᵓutammiᵓ/ 'I conjure' (MAD 2^2 26, 28, and 164f.). The situation at post-Ur III Mari is controversial. While the evidence in favor of the sign U to be read as *ju* exists in the spellings *ti-iš-da-u*

/tiśtajū/ 'they have drunk' (legal, line 23), and others discussed above, § 3.4.6.2, the prefix is written exclusively with the sign Ú (not U).

The levelizing of the three original prefixes *ja-*, *ji-*, *ju-* to *ji-* in the B stem is similar, in that respect, to what happened to Arabic, for example, where the three prefixes leveled off to *ja-*. The Barth-Ungnad Law, operative in Ugaritic, Hebrew, and partially in Amorite, does not apply to Akkadian and the language of Ebla-Mari.

The contrast between masc. *ji-* (or *ju-*) and fem. *ta-* (or *tu-*, *ti-*), also known at Ebla in the Pre-Sargonic period (Gelb 1981: 35) and in post-Ur III times (Gelb, "The Inscription of Jibbiṭ-Lîm, King of Ebla," lines 7 and 14, soon to appear), in Old Akkadian, the Assyrian dialect, and all other Semitic languages, is disregarded in the Akkadian dialect from the classical OB period until the beginning of the NB Empire, when the prefix *i-* is used for both the masc. and fem. The occurrence of the masculine prefix in *ú-zi-ʾà* 'has gone out' (liver 31a), or *ú-zi-a-am* (19) with the subject *ʾawatum* /hawatum/ 'word' is due to the Akkadian influence (see above, § 3.4.5).

New and by far the most important for the question of the linguistic position of post-Ur III Mari are the verbal forms *timḫaṣū*, *tîkulū*, *tiśtajū*, and *tiltaptū* in the legal text, and *tîkulû* and *tim-za-u* in administrative texts for the third person masculine plural. The new information derived from these forms is: 1) The prefix *ti-* for the third person feminine, etc., against Akkadian *ta-*; 2) the affixes *ti . . . ū* for the third person masculine plural, against Akkadian *ji . . . ū*; and 3) the pattern *jiśtâ* (*jiśtaj*), against Akkadian *jiśtê*, *jiśtî*.

The prefix *ta-* in different persons, genders, and numbers of the Akkadian conjugation appears as *ti-* in the affixes *ti . . . ū* at Mari. However, *ti-*, besides *ta-*, appears in Pre-Sargonic names of Ebla, as in *tiqîś* (and *taqîś*) or *tiśtê* (and *taśtâ*, *taśtî*) for 3f. sg., where the change from the masculine to the feminine gender was occasioned by the feminine gender of the bearer of the name. See Gelb (1981: 33 and 35), citing Edzard. Other cases at Pre-Sargonic Mari are *ji . . . ū* for 3m. pl., and *ta . . . ā* for 3f. pl. or Du. Three additional verbal forms beginning with *ti-* occur in the "incantations" that have been recently published by Edzard (1984). The clearest of them is the sentence ^{d}UTU *ti-a-ba-an* /tilabban/ SIG$_4$.GAR 'the sun god will make bricks' (3 i); note the feminine gender of ^{d}UTU and above, § 3.1.6, the elision of *l/r*, frequent in the incantations and elsewhere at Ebla, the pattern *jilabban*, instead of *jilabbin* in Akkadian (see below), and the free sentence syntax (see below, § 3.4.6.8). The other two forms, AN.AN *ti-da-ḫu-ru*$_{12}$ (6 xii) and AN.AN *ti-na-ḫu-úš* (6 xiii), are not clear. About one thousand years later the prefix *ti-* reappears in Syria-Palestine. Note, for instance, Böhl (1909: 52f.); Ebeling (1910: 46); Moran (1951: 34); and Huehnergard (1983: 40), for Amarna letters, esp. Byblos;

Gordon (1965: 75), and Huehnergard (1983: 40), for Ugaritic; and G. Wilhelm in Hachmann (1982: 123), for the Emar area.

The occurrence of *ti . . . ū* for 3m. pl. at Mari, of *ti-* for 3f. sg. at Ebla, and similarly in the examples from Syria–Palestine cited just above suggests that other cases of the prefix *ta-* given in the conjugation above, which are hitherto unattested, may turn out to be *ti-*, not *ta-*.

Robert M. Whiting reminds me that I have marked as worthy of attention certain cases of the prefixes *ti . . . ū* or *ti-*, such as *ti-ga-bi-ú* or *ti-ḫa-da-ar*, in the Old Babylonian Larsa letter, Walters (1970: no. 43), and elsewhere, as noted by Stol (1971: 366), but have failed to include them in the discussion given above. We may note that the use of these forms in south Babylonia in the Old Babylonian periods cannot be fully ascertained as long as the homeland of their users is unknown.

The important isogloss *ti-* for *ta-* in the conjunction links the language of Ebla–Mari with the language spoken mainly in Syria–Palestine.

Among the four verbs with the affixes *ti . . . ū* in the post-Ur III legal text, there is one, *ti-iš-da-u*, that is a verb *ultimae infirmae* with the pattern *jištâ*. This pattern known as *jištê, jištî* in Akkadian, recurs at Pre-Sargonic Ebla with either *-â* or *-ê*/*-î*, as in *jibnâ* 'he has created', Akkadian jibnî, Amorite *-jabnî*; *jilʾâ, jilʾê* 'he has prevailed', Akkadian *jilʾê*, Amorite *jalʾê*, but also *jilʾâ*; *jirʿâ*; *jirʿâ, jirʿê* 'he has pastured', Akkadian *jirʿê*, Amorite *jarʿê*; *jiśrâ*, Akkadian *jiśrî*, Hebrew *jiśrô* (in the name *Jiśrô-ʾEl*). For evidence, see Gelb 1981: 33ff. For a discussion of the problem and relation to Arabic, see Gelb 1981: 37ff.

The form *tištâ*, attested in *ti-iš-da-u* /tištajū/ 'they have drunk' is not just another example of the linguistic connections between post-Ur III Mari and Pre-Sargonic Ebla (and therefore Pre-Sargonic Mari); it furnishes new, living, textual documentation for a form for which hitherto only personal names were attested.

Vocalic Pattern

Imperative *gumul* (*guml*) 'spare!', 'save!', discussed above, posits the existence of the fientive forms *igmul, igammal*, which occur in Babylonia in the Sargonic and Ur III periods and possibly at Old Babylonian Mari in *ta-ta-ag-ma-lu-šum* /itagmal/ (ARM 1 19:18 and ARMT 15 201). The forms *igmul, igammal, guml, itagmal*, attested at Mari, differ from *igmil, igammil, giml, igdamil* in later Akkadian. Cf. also the divergent vocalic patterns of *igriś* at Pre-Sargonic and Post-Ur III Ebla and *igruś* in Old Akkadian (Gelb, "The Inscription of Jibbiṭ-Lîm, King of Ebla," soon to appear); *ibbiṭ* at post-Ur III Mari and in Babylon in the Ur III and OB periods and *ibbuṭ, inabbut* in later Akkadian (ibid.); *jidlal* in three post-Ur III personal names (ARMT 19 160) and *idlul* in the Sargonic and Ur

III periods (MAD 3 109); *išlal* in the name *Iš-làl-*[d]*Da-gan* (legal, line 17), and *išlul* in Old Akkadian (MAD 3 271); *jilabban* at Pre-Sargonic Ebla (see above) and *ilabbin* in Akkadian.

A different type of vowel variation is exemplified in the verbs *ultimae infirmae,* as in *jištâ,* written *ti-iš-da-u* in the legal text, line 23, and parallels, as contrasted with Akkadian *jištê, jišti.*

Tense

The two main tenses attested at Mari are preterit (*passim*) and present-future, attested only in the post-Ur III liver omina, which may possibly reflect the Akkadian, rather than Mari usage. Besides the few examples of the present-future at Pre-Sargonic Ebla that are illustrated in Gelb (1981: 40), a few more, such as *ʾaṣammid, jilabban, jinaʾʾaś, jipaḫḫir,* are used in the "incantations" that were recently published by Edzard (1984: see Glossary). Several examples of the third person stative were cited above, § 3.4.6.4, and the first person occurs in *sá-al-ma-ku* 'I am well' (liver 29). The West Semitic *qatala*-type perfect at Ebla discussed and illustrated in Gelb (1981: 36f.), as in *ba-na* 'he created', *la-a* 'he prevailed', is not attested at Mari. The two examples of the BT stem do not function in the sense of the Akkadian perfect tense, but as the reflexive-reciprocal mood. See below, under stems.

Imperative

All occurrences of an imperative are attested under names: *A-sur-*[d]*Da-gan* /ʾAśur-Dagan/ (376), comparable with *A-sur-*DINGIR (MAD 3 76); *Ku-um-li-*[d]IM /Gumli-Haddu/ 'Spare me, Haddu!' (200+), comparable with *Ku-um-li-A-du* in Wiseman (1955: Lexicon), *Gu-mu-ul-*[d]EN.ZU, *Ì-lí-gu-um-li-ia,* and [d]*Iš-ḫa-ra-gu-um-li* in Gelb (1980: 299), Mari, and *Sin-gimlanni,* etc., in Akkadian; *Ku-un-*[d]*Da-gan* (248); *Ri-im-si-*[d]*Da-gan* (205+), comparable with *Rí-im-sá-ì-lí* (18+), *Ri-im-si-ì-lí* (ARM 9 5, etc.), *Rí-za-ʾà-a* (369+). For the pronominal suffixes *-a* and *-i,* see above, § 3.4.6.5.

Subjunctive

As noted above (§ 3.4.6.5), there are great variations in the form of the subjunctive in liver omina: *-u* in *i-nu-mi . . . i-ba-al-ki-du-šu* (7, sg.), *i-nu-mi . . . iš-da-ba-ru-ma* (10, pl.), *sá . . . i-ba-al-šu* /ippalsū/ (11b, pl.), *sá . . . i-ku-lu-ma* (17, sg.); *-una* in *i-nu-mi . . . i-za-aḫ-ru-na* (10, pl.), *i-nu-mi . . . u-ti-ru-na* (22, sg.); *-i* in *si . . . i-ba-al-ki-ti-šu* (6, sg.), possibly *sá . . . i-lá-ki-i* (11b, sg.); *-a* in *sá . . . il-ga-ʾà* (3, sg.), *sá . . . il-ga-a* (9, sg.), *sá . . . in-*TI*-ʾ*a_x(NI), (5, sg.); -Ø in *sá . . . iš-ku-un* (8), *sá . . . i-is-ḫu-ur* (16). Of these four subjunctive suffixes, only *-u* is common in Akkadian. The suffix *-una* (and *-na* after *-am-*) also occurs in dialectal Old Babylonian (MAD 2^2 170; Robert M. Whiting, *Old Babylonian Letters from Tell Asmar* [AS 22; Chicago, 1987], commentary to letter no. 6), and possibly in Old Babylonian Mari, as in *iškunanna* and *imḫuranna* (Finet 1956: 33 and 263). For the occasional use of the subjunctive in *-i* in late Old Babylonian, see Gelb (1969: 106). The suffix *-a*, first discovered in the Sargonic texts of the Diyala Region (MAD 2[2] 170, *passim*), reappears in *ta-ú-bi-a* /tawpiᶜa/ in the post-Ur III inscription of Jibbiṭ-Lîm king of Ebla (Pettinato 1981a 24:7; W. G. Lambert 1981: 95f.). For the interpretation of the morphemes of the subjunctive, see the discussion in Gelb (1969: 98–107). As noted by Westenholz (1978: 165f.), two occurrences occur without subjunctive markers: *sá . . . iš-ku-un* (8), *sá . . . i-is-ḫu-ur* (16); others, registered by Westenholz, have the *-a* suffix. For similar cases, cf. *inûma . . . baliṭ, kīma . . . wašib* at Old Babylonian Mari (Finet 1956: 261) or *ša . . . tetêpaś, kī išme* at Middle Babylonian Ugarit (MRS 9 140ff.; Westenholz 1978: 165f.).

Participles

Active participles are attested in several names in the administrative texts, as in *A-me-ir-Ma-ma* (384), *A-me-ir-ᵈNu-nu* (31), *ᵈDa-gan-ba-ni* (173+), *Il-e-da-bi-bu* (338), and in liver omina, as in *a-ki-íl* (31c), *da-gi-íl-šu* (9), *za-i-il-šu* (15a). Many passive or stative participles, or substantivized adjectives, were listed above (§ 3.4.6.4): among them, *ᶜalijum* 'upper' (*a-li-u-um, -a-li-a*), *damqum* 'good' (*-dam-ga*), *marṣum* 'sick' (*mar-zum, mar-za-at, mar-za*), *ma-az-um*, also *ma-az-[ú]-tum, ra-bu-a-an, śaplum* 'lower' (*sá-ap-lum*), *ṣaḫarum* 'small' (*za-ḫa-ru-tim*$_x$), also *ṣaḫrum* (*za-aḫ-ru-tim*$_x$), *tab-ú-tum* and *tab-a-an, waklum* 'reliable' (*a-ak-lu-tum*). Other substantivized participles or adjectives are found among names: *Da-i-ru-um* (194), WA-*bi-sa-tum* (462), *Za-ḫir-tum* /ṣaḫirtum/ (212+), *Za-ki-ru-um* (205), *A-šu-ru-um* (370+), *Da-lu-ul-tum*? (384), *Sá-tu-ba-an* /Śaṭupān/ (279 and ARMT 19 161 n 21′). A case of a substantivized adjective occurs in *iš da-šu-ba-tim*$_x$ /daśśubātim/ 'for sweets' (393), showing a D Stem *daššubum* that corresponds to the Akkadian *duššupum*. The predicate of the passive participle, functioning as the stative/permansive, is attested in *sá-al-ma-ku* /śalmāku/ 'I am in good health' (liver no. 29) and the names *Sá-lim-ke-lí* (adm. 111+), etc.

Infinitives

The infinitive of the B stem is attested in *ᵓà-ba-áš* /ᶜapāś/ (adm. 96), *ᵓà-ba-al* /wabāl/ (378), and *na-ga-ar* /nakār/ (liver 18a) in construct state, and in *iš la-ᵓà-me-šu-ni* 'for their consumption' (adm. 248), where the main word may be either an infinitive *laᵓāmum* or a substantive *laᵓamum, laᵓmum*. See above, § 3.4.6.4. There is also *ḫa-ra-iš* /ḫarājiš/ 'to dig' (liver no. 14) and a late form of an infinitive is found possibly in *te-bi-am* (19). A single case of the construct state of the infinitive of stem II occurs in *iš ga-sur* /kaśśur/ 'for the repair' (adm. 64+). A construct state of a feminine Š stem in *ša-aḫ-lu-uq-tí* 'destruction' (livers 4, 28) corresponds to the

Akkadian *šaḫluqtum*, and an Š quadriconsonantal is illustrated in *sá-ḫu-ru-ri-im* 'stupor' (liver 16), which occurs as *šuḫurrurum, šaḫurrurum* in Akkadian.

Stem

The following stems are attested:

B: (*passim*).

BT: *ti-il-tap-tu* '(PNs) anointed themselves (with oil)' (legal, line 24), *i-ta-ú* /jîtawwû/ 'enemy conspires (an attack)' (liver 19), *i-da-ú* 'conspires (hostility)' (30a), *i-da-ú*? 'conspires (hostility)' (31b). To judge from the adduced parallels, the last reading is more plausible than the *i-da-ba* = *i-tá-be*$_4$ of Durand (1983c: 218).

BTN: *iš-ta-ba-ru-ma* 'they sent continuously' (liver 10).

D: *ú-ti-ru-na* (liver 22, subjunctive).
iš ga-sur /kaśśur/ 'in order to repair (objects)' (adm. 64, 114, 324, infinitive, construct state).
iš da-šu-ba-tim$_x$ /daśśubātim/ 'in order (to make) sweets' (adm. 393, verbal noun with the force of an elative).

Š: *ú-ša-ti-ú-šu* /juśâdiᶜūśu/ (liver 14), *ú-ša-me-id*? (120).
ša-aḫ-lu-uq-tí /śaḫluqti/ 'destruction' (livers 4, 28, verbal noun, construct state).

N: *i-lá-ki-i* /jillaqî/ (liver 11b).
i-ba-al-šu /jippalśû/ (liver 11b).
i-za-ḫé-ir /jissaḫir/ (liver 12b) and *i-za-aḫ-ru-na* (liver 10, subjunctive).
i-sá-kín /jiśśakin/ (livers 7, 22) and *i-ša-ki-in* (liver 10).

Quadriconsonantal of the N Type: *i-ba-al-ki-ti-šu* (liver 6, subjunctive), and *i-ba-al-ki-du-šu* (liver 7, subjunctive).

Quadriconsonantal of the Š type: *sá-ḫu-ru-ri-im* /śaḫurrurim/ 'stupor' (liver 16).

Notes on Stem

Ad BT: The reflexive-reciprocal meaning *litputum* 'to anoint each other', *ᵓatwuᵓum* 'to talk with each other', 'to conspire' is similar to that of Akkadian *mitḫuṣum* 'to fight with each other', 'to wrestle', or *šitᵓulum* 'to ask each other', 'to consult'.

Ad D: While *ú-ti-ru-na* is simply a causative of an intransitive verb, *kaśśurum* and *daśśupum* express the plurality of objects. Cf. also *Śaᵓᵓumu* 'bought' at Pre-Sargonic Mari (see above, § 3.1.9), *qaṭṭurum* 'to burn incense' at Ebla (Gelb 1981: 39), also *ᵓabbuḫum* and *dannumum* in Edzard (1984: 3 iv–v). For the *parrus* formation, see also just below.

Ad Š: The *śa* prefix of the verbal noun *śaḫluqtum* and of the quadriconsonantal *śaḫarrurum* recurs in the infinitive *śaᵓḫu-*

ḏum 'to cause to be taken' at Pre-Sargonic Ebla (Gelb 1981: 40). Together with the *parrus* formation (assumed just above), they recur in the Assyrian dialect, contrasting with the *šuprus*, *purrus* formations of Old Akkadian and later Babylonian.

3.4.6.7. *Indeclinables*

a-na 'to', 'for' (adm. 389, unique; livers 8, 10, etc.). Note also the use of *a-na* at Pre-Sargonic Mari–Ebla (above, § 3.1.8), Ur III Mari (above, § 3.3.5), and in Old Akkadian. The spelling *ˀa*$_x$(NI)*-na* is known at Pre-Sargonic Mari–Ebla (above, § 3.1.8) and Ur III Mari (above, § 3.3.5).

a-ša-ar '(in place) where' (liver 10). Akkadian.

áš-tu 'from', 'with' in the royal name *Ma-na-áš-tu-šu* /Man-ˀaś-tuśu/ 'Who is with him?' (liver 20). The preposition *áš-du* /ˀaśtu/ is known at Pre-Sargonic Ebla and in the form *iš-tu* in Old Akkadian.

bi-il-ti 'without' in the name *Bi-il-ti-*[d]*Da-gan* '(Who is) without Dagan?' (adm. 375, 391). The preposition occurs in the form *balti, balte* in such Amorite names as *Manna-balti-ˀEl* "Who is without El?' and the like (Gelb 1980: 116) and in Hebrew.

in 'in' (adm. 23, 266+; legal, lines 1, 25; livers 11b, 12a+), see above, § 3.4.5. Note also the use of *in* at Pre-Sargonic Mari–Ebla (above, § 3.1.8) and in Old Akkadian. The later form *i-na* is used, beside *in*, in livers 13c, 27b (above, § 3.4.5).

i-nu-mi 'when', with the verb in the subjunctive (livers 7, 10, 22). Akkadian.

iš 'to', 'for' (adm. 32 and *passim*; legal, line 7; livers 31b, 31d, 32a). Note also the use of *iš* at Pre-Sargonic Mari–Ebla (above, §§ 3.1.4 and 3.1.8) and, occasionally, in dialectal Akkadian.

-iš postpositional-adverbial suffix in *wa-at-rí-iš* 'additionally' (legal, line 9), *ḫa-ra-iš* 'in order to dig' (liver 14). Note also *da-rí-iš* 'forever' (Krebernik 1984: 194 and 319), *ga-ti-iš* /qâtiš/ (MEE 4 512a, and Krebernik 1984: 319), *ar-ḫi-iš ar-ḫi-iš* 'very quickly' (the so-called "Assyrian Treaty," Sollberger 1980: 142), and in several occurrences, such as *a-bar-rí-iš* 'on the other side', *da-ma-rí-iš*, etc., excerpted by Edzard (1984: 49–60) from an "incantation" recorded at Ebla and Abu Salabikh. A suffix *-iš* with an unknown function occurs in several names from Ebla (*A-ga-iš*, *A-ra-ḫé-iš*, etc., in MEE 2 335–53) and from the Diyala Region (*Sa-a-mi-iš* /Śaˀāmiš?/, *Sa-a-*NI*-iš* /Śaˀāliš/, etc., in Gelb 1955: 234). See also Gelb (1981: 69). The postpositional-adverbial *-iš* is also known in Old Akkadian and predominantly in its adverbial function also in later Akkadian, Aramaic and other Semitic languages.

ki-am 'thus' (livers 7, 10). Only Akkadian.

ki-ma 'like', 'as' in the name *Ki-ma*-DINGIR (adm. 394). Only Akkadian. Forms *ka, ki* are known from Eblaic, Amorite, and other Semitic languages.

lá 'truly', 'verily', a particle used with asseverative force in the name *Lá-da-ba*-DINGIR /La-ṭâba-ᵓIl/ 'Truly, god is good' (adm. 461). Asseverative *la* is known in Amorite.

lá 'not', see *ú-lá* below.

ma 'truly', 'verily' used with asseverative force in an Amorite name *Bi-nu-ma*-ᵈIM /Binu-ma-Haddu/ 'He is truly a son of Haddu' (adm. 298). The particle recurs in Eblaic, Akkadian, and other Semitic languages.

ma-lá 'as much as' (liver 31a). Only Akkadian.

šum-ma 'if' with verb in subjunctive *-u* (livers 19, 30a, 31b) or without (livers 11a, 12b, 21, 24a, similarly 18b, 31d, 32a, 32b). In the form *su-ma* known in Eblaic (Sollberger 1980: 142) and in the forms *su-ma, šum-ma* in Sargonic (MAD 3 255).

ú 'and' (adm. 92, 280, 286; legal, lines 3, 9, 24; livers 2, 8, 9, 14). Cf. also *ú* at Ur III Mari (above, § 3.3.5). Ebla has *ù* and *wa* (= *wu*?), Old Akkadian has *ù*, and *ú* is used in a Lullubum inscription (MAD 3 1).

ú-lá '(and) not' (liver 31a). Akkadian.

The following prepositions, known at Ebla, are as yet not attested at Mari: *a-dè* 'up to', 'until' in Eblaic and *a-ti* in Old Akkadian; al *'upon'* in Eblaic and Old Akkadian; *áš-ti, áš-da* 'with' at Ebla, and *iš-dè, iš-ti* in Old Akkadian, also *áš-da*, áš-dè, *áš-ti* in ancient kudurrus; *iš*$_{11}$*-ki* 'up to' in Eblaic; and *si-in* 'to', 'for' in Eblaic.

3.4.6.8. *Syntax*

In the sentence PNs *šu zi-ga-tim*$_x$ *tim-ḫa-zu* . . . *in* É PN 'PNs who have driven the clay nails . . . into the house of PN' (legal, lines 14–26), we have a good example of the free syntactical order, which is also attested at Ur III Mari (above, § 3.3.5) and at Pre-Sargonic and post-Ur III Ebla (see Gelb 1981: 42f.). Several examples of free sentence syntax at Ebla are also found in the "incantations" recently published by Edzard (1984).

3.4.6.9. *Lexicon and Onomastics*

A thorough discussion of the lexicon and the names contained in the texts of Mari is impossible. Lexical and onomastic data were included only to the extent that they affect the grammar, and not the semantics, of the language. Brief discussions are found above under:

Lexicon: § 3.1.4, PSarg. adm. (*miᵓatum* 'one hundred', *malkum* 'king', *maliktum* 'queen'); § 3.1.5, Sarg. adm. (*gajjum*, a tribal term);

§ 3.4.3 post-Ur III adm. (*liʾmum* 'one thousand', *miʾatum* 'one hundred', *mazāʾum* 'to mix' or *masājum* 'to wash', *raḥatum* 'hand', 'hand span', *ru-si*, *śaʾnum* 'sandal'); § 3.4.4, legal (*lapātum* 'to anoint').

PNs: § 3.1.5, PSarg. vot., § 3.1.4, adm.; § 3.3.2, Ur III vot.; § 3.3.3, § 3.4.2, § 3.4.4, post-Ur III vot. and seals, and adm. (*A-me-ir-*, *En-nin-*, *Ti-ir-*), legal (*Iš-làl-*, *Iš-má-*, *Ti-ir-*).

DNs: § 3.1.6, PSarg. vot. +; § 3.3.5, Ur III vot. and Sum. adm. (Dagan); § 3.4.2, post-Ur III vot. and seals (Dagan, Nunu), § 3.4.2, adm., § 3.4.4, legal (Dagan, Mama, Nunu, ᵈKUR).

GNs: § 3.1.4, PSarg. adm.

MNs: § 3.1.7, PSarg. adm.; § 3.4.3, post-Ur III adm.

Further information may be gathered from the listings of PNs: § 3.1.5, PSarg., § 3.3.2, Ur III vot., § 3.3.3, Ur III Sum. adm.; DNs: § 3.1.6, PSarg. vot. +; MNs: § 3.1.7, PSarg. adm.; post-Ur III livers, § 3.4.5, post-Ur III adm. +; and from the discussions of the writing and language given in each section, mainly at the end: § 3.1.8, PSarg.; § 3.3.5, Ur III; § 3.4.6.

Conclusions

The main sources pertaining to Mari of post-Ur III times are administrative texts, a legal text, and liver omina.

While the administrative and legal texts are practically synchronous, and are, therefore, fully utilizable in the reconstruction of the writing and language of Mari in post-Ur III times, the liver omina are not. They were copied from the originals of different periods and may, therefore, be utilized only when they agree with the conclusions that have been reached on the basis of the administrative and legal texts.

The administrative and legal texts, and partly liver omina, were written in a new system of writing that contains certain features relating it to the Old Assyrian system.

The administrative and legal texts, and partly liver omina, were written in a Semitic language which, with insignificant temporal and local variations, is identical with that of Mari and Ebla of the Pre-Sargonic period.

Keeping in mind that some of the governor-generals of Mari discussed above (§ 3.3.2) may and probably do belong to the post-Ur III period, the rulers of Mari in that period were native Marians. To judge from the other personal names, the population of Mari in post-Ur III times was native Marian as well, with an insignificant admixture of foreign elements, such as Amorites and Akkadians, but not Sumerians or Hurrians.

4. *Writing and Language of Mari in the Third Millennium* B.C.

Less than ten years ago, it was easy to explain the ethno-linguistic situation of Mari in the third millennium B.C. The votive inscriptions of

Mari of the Pre-Sargonic period appeared to be not much different from those found in the Diyala River District, for example. Mari was conquered by Sargon of Akkadē, and all throughout the Sargonic and Ur III periods Mari was a province of the Akkadian and Sumerian empires. Nothing stood in the way of considering Mari to be a linguistic outpost of Akkadian. Then came Ebla and the revelation of a new linguistic entity centered around Ebla and its identification with the native language of Mari.

The presently available documentation about the writing and language of Mari is abundant only in the Pre-Sargonic period, at one end, and post-Ur III times, at the other. In both periods, Mari possessed its own system of writing and its own language, both different from Akkadian. In between, in the Sargonic and Ur III periods, original sources written in the writing system and language of Mari are completely lacking, and our knowledge of them is derived solely from secondary sources, such as the administrative texts of Babylonia, which were written in Akkadian (Sargonic) or Sumerian (Ur III), and the votive inscriptions of the governor-generals of Mari in the Ur III period, which were written in Akkadian.

This great disparity in our knowledge of the writing and language of Mari requires comment. The full use of its own system of writing and its own language at Mari in the Pre-Sargonic period and post-Ur III era is easily explainable if we assume that Mari was independent of Babylonian suzerainty at the time. After the conquest of Mari by Sargon, Mari was ruled by governor-generals who were appointed to their office by the Babylonian kings, but became independent during the periods of weakness of the central authority. Traditionally, the governor-generals of Mari employed Akkadian in their inscriptions, the second, after Sumerian, official language of the Ur III period.

The native language of Mari was not dead during the Sargonic and Ur III periods. While textually not attested, its existence, at least in the Ur III period, is provable by the occurrence of the numerous features of the votive inscriptions of the governor-generals of Mari, which reflect the native language of Mari.

The direct and indirect evidence that proves the continued existence of the native language of Mari from the Pre-Sargonic period to post-Ur III times is much stronger in the case of Mari than of Ebla, where the texts written in the native language of Ebla are attested solely in the Pre-Sargonic period. Were it not for certain linguistic features recoverable in the Akkadian-written inscription of Jibbiṭ-Lîm, who ruled Ebla in post-Ur III times, we would have had no reason even to suspect that the language of Ebla, like that of Mari, continued in existence well into post-Ur III times. See Gelb (1981: 60) and the forthcoming article, "The Inscription of Jibbiṭ-Lîm, King of Ebla."

As frequently noted in this study, the native language of Mari is identical, but for insignificant local and temporal variations, with that of Ebla.

A discussion of the writing and language of Mari is usually given at the end of each section, from the Pre-Sargonic to the Post-Ur III periods. The discussion of the post-Ur III features contains, in addition, a bird's eye view of the features of the previous periods and may, therefore, be considered to give a total evaluation of the writing and grammar of Mari in the third millennium B.C. I have discussed in greater detail the Pre-Sargonic section, because of its relative importance. During this period, Ebla and Mari, though exposed to the cultural imprint of the Kish Civilization (for which see the next section), were relatively free of foreign linguistic interference, and it was in this period more than in any other that the linguistic identity of Ebla and Mari can be proved or disproved. During the subsequent Sargonic and Ur III periods, the language of Mari fell under Akkadian influence, and its lingering effect is strongly felt in the post-Ur III sources, especially in the liver omina that were written partly in Akkadian and partly in the language of Mari.

The close relations between the writing and language of Ebla–Mari and Old Assyrian have been noted in all sections, from the Pre-Sargonic to the post-Ur III periods. This important question must be left for the future to solve.

In contrast to the exaggerations of the "History-Begins-at-Sumer" school, one thing is clear: the impact of Sumer on Ebla–Mari was minimal. Writing, ultimately borrowed from Sumer, developed its own systems at Ebla–Mari, with many features borrowed from Kish and from Old Assyrian. Except for one brief Ur III inscription of a daughter of a king of Mari which was written in Sumerian when she went to marry a son of Ur-Nammu (above, § 3.3.2), all other texts of Mari are written in its own language or, rarely, in Akkadian. There are no Sumerian geographical names at Ebla and Mari. Except for some outsiders, such as singers-musicians in the Pre-Sargonic period (above, § 3.1.5), all personal names associated with Mari are non-Sumerian. All names of deities worshiped at Mari in the Pre-Sargonic period (§ 3.1.6) are in the language of Mari, and that includes the logograms, written in Sumerian, but most probably read in the language of Mari. In later periods, the divine names are all in the language of Mari–Ebla, except those found in the lists of deities (above, § 3.4.3), which include Sumerian names and derive from Babylonia. All month names used at Ebla–Mari in the Pre-Sargonic (§ 3.1.7, above) and post-Ur III periods (§ 3.4.3), written syllabically or logographically, are in the language of Ebla–Mari.

The language of Mari of the post-Ur III period is not simply related to that of Pre-Sargonic Mari and Ebla, but forms with them, with some small dialectal variations, a single linguistic unit.

Fig. 4. Linguistic Features of Mari in the Third Millennium B.C.

	Pre-Sargonic Mari	Pre-Sargonic Ebla	Ur III Mari	Post-Ur III Mari	Post-Ur III Ebla	Old Akkadian	Old Assyrian
Phonemes							
ś and *š*	+	+	+	+	( )	+	– (only *š*)
ᶜ *jiśma*ᶜ, but *bêlum*	+	+	+	+	( )	+	– (only *ê*)
aj > *â*	( )	*aj, â*	( )	*ê*	( )	*ê*	*ê*
aw >*â*	( )	*aw, â*	( )	*ô, û*	*aw*	*ô, û*	*ô, û*
Noun							
Indeterminate State Sg., Fem. *-a*	+	+	( )	+	( )	–	–
Dual, Nom. *-ā(n)* Gen.-Acc. *-aj(n)*	( )	+ +	( )	+ (*-ān*) – (*-ên*)	( )	+ (*-ān*) – (*-ên*)	+ (*-ān*) – (*-ên*)
Pronoun							
Det.-rel. *šu, ši, ša*	(+)	+	( )	+ (wr. *šu, si, sá* irreg.)	– (only *ša* attested)	+	– (only *ša*)
Interrogative *mi*, 'who?'	+	+	( )	( )	( )	– (only *man, mannum*)	– (only *mannum*)

Verb							
Conjugation 3rd masc. pl. *ti . . . ū*	( )	+	( )	+	( )	– (only *ji . . . ū*)	– (only *ji . . . ū*)
Pret. verbs ult. *j* (*w*) *jibnâ, jibnî*	–	+	( )	+	( )	– (only *jibnî*)	– (only *jibnî*)
Perfect qatal	( )	+	( )	–	( )	–	+ (rare)
Passive Participle *parrusum*	+	+	( )	+	( )	– (only *purussum*)	+
Subjunctive -*a*	( )	( )	+ (Ur III Ebla)	+ (also -*i* and -*u*)	+	+ (Diyala only)	–
Subjunctive -(*u*)*na*	–	–	( )	+	( )	– (only -*u*(*ni*))	– (only -*u*(*ni*))
Dative-allative -*a*	( )	+	+	+ (also -*am*)	( )	– (only -*am*)	– (only -*am*)
Indeclinables							
ʾ*in*, 'in'	+	+	+	+ (also *ina*)	– (only *ina*)	+	+ (*in*) – (*i-na*)
ʾa_x(NI)-*na* 'to', 'for'	+ (also *a-na*)	+ (also *a-na*)	+	+ (also *a-na*)	– (only *a-na*)	– (only *a-na*)	– (*an*) – (*a-na*)
ʾ*iš* 'to', 'for'	+	+	( )	+	( )	–	–
ʾ*aśtu* 'from'	( )	+	( )	+	( )	– (only ʾ*iśtu*)	– (only ʾ*ištu*)
Syntax							
Free word order	+	+	+	+	+	–	–

As I wrote in the conclusion of my forthcoming article on the inscription of Jibbiṭ-Lîm king of Mari, the fact that not all features may be duplicated at both Ebla and Mari, and that features occurring in later periods are not necessarily reflected in earlier times at Ebla and Mari, may be explained by the disparities in the nature and quantity of sources from the two sites, and partly by the areal and temporal differentiations.

Among the dialectal divergencies between Ebla and Mari are the following. 1) The phonetic exchange of the *r* and *l* phonemes of Ebla is not at home at Mari. 2) The diphthong *aj* either stays *aj* or becomes *â* at Pre-Sargonic Ebla, but becomes *ê* at post-Ur III Mari. 3) The present-future tense, frequent at Pre-Sargonic Ebla, is not attested at Mari except in the post-Ur III liver omina, where it may reflect the Akkadian, and not the Mari, usage. 4) The West Semitic *qatala*-type perfect, as in *ba-na* 'he created', *la-a* 'he prevailed', is attested only at Pre-Sargonic Ebla. 5) Several prepositions, such as *áš-ti* 'with', *si-in* 'to', 'for' occur frequently at Pre-Sargonic Ebla but not at Mari.

The difference between post-Ur III Mari and the Mari of the classical Old Babylonian period is enormous. The population of the latter consisted mainly of Amorites who were governed by kings of the Lîm Dynasty and adopted a new system of writing and a new language, borrowed directly from the Old Babylonian. In contrast to the strong imprint made by the local language of Mari on the Akkadian of the governor-generals of Mari, the features of the Amorite language that may be recognized in the Akkadian of the Lîm Dynasty are insignificant; the best known of these is the *-ijam* > *-iʾam* > *-iʾem* > *-eʾem* and -uwam > *-uʾam* > *-uʾem* > *-eʾem* change, as in *rabijam* > *rabiʾam* > *rabiʾem* > *rabeʾem* 'great' (acc.) and *asuwam* > *asuʾam* > *asuʾem* > *aseʾem* 'physician' (acc.).

The linguistic features linking Mari and Ebla, in comparison with Old Akkadian and Old Assyrian, are illustrated in fig. 4.

5. *The Role of Mari within the Frame of the Kish Civilization*

As noted above (§ 2), the eight Semitic features of the Kish Civilization, which had been first detected in the ancient kudurrus and the royal and votive inscriptions from the area of Kish in Babylonia, recur in the "literary" and administrative texts from Abu Salabikh and Ebla and the votive and administrative texts from Mari. Thanks to the discoveries of Ebla, the documentation concerning these features has increased tremendously, and new common features are being detected continuously. Many more are expected to come to light when the program of the publication of the Ebla and Mari sources is fully realized.

Some of these features encompass the whole area of the Kish Civilization, some large parts of it, and very few have been attested, up to now, in a single locality.

Clearly unified are the features linking Kish with Abu Salabikh and those linking Ebla with Mari. This is to be expected, if for no other reason, because of their geographical proximity.

The features linking Mari with Ebla include, above all, a common writing system, a common language, and a common calendar.

The early texts of Mari are dated to the same Pre-Sargonic period as the Ebla archive through the synchronism provided by the occurrence of Jiblul-ᵓIl, king of Mari, both at Mari and Ebla. See above, § 1.

We have been able to detect the unifying features of Mari and Ebla in the sphere of writing, language, and calendar, despite the great disparity of the available sources: at Mari, mainly votive inscriptions, a few administrative texts, and no "literary" texts; at Ebla, mainly administrative texts, a few "literary" texts, and no votive inscriptions.

There is no longer any doubt in my mind that, with a few local peculiarities, the same writing system and the same Semitic language prevailed at Mari and Ebla. Just recently, Charpin has shown that the "Semitic" Calendar" of twelve months was used not only at Ebla, but also at Mari (see above, § 3.1.7).

The many linguistic connections between Mari and Ebla led me to conclude in 1977 (Gelb 1977: 12): "*The so-called 'Iblaic' language was spoken not only at Ibla, but also around Mari.*" In respect to the direction of the cultural influence, from Ebla to Mari, or from Mari to Ebla, this what I said in the same article (p. 15): "*There is no good reason to think that the cultural radiation went from Ibla to Mari, rather than from Mari to Ibla.*"

On the basis of an unfortunate interpretation of the so-called "ᵓEnna-Dagan Letter," Pettinato (1980b) took it for granted that Mari was subjugated by Ebla (see above, § 3.1.2). Contrariwise, it is my firm belief not only that Mari was not subjugated by Ebla, but that the over-importance of Mari versus Ebla is paramount. Ebla flourished during a brief period just before Sargon of Akkadē, while Mari was widely known throughout the whole third millennium B.C., as well as later.

The importance of Mari within the frame of the Kish Civilization is evidenced by the existence of the Mari Dynasty which, according to the Sumerian King List, held hegemony over Babylonia and beyond just before the time of the second and third dynasties of Kish (see Jacobsen 1939: 103, and above, § 3.1.2). Junior scribes went from Ebla to Mari to learn their craft, just as a professor of mathematics went from Kish to Ebla to each the locals the intricacies of Babylonian metrology and accounting.

Dies diem docet. Before 1960, the historical picture of the ancient Near East seemed to be clear: the Sumerian civilization was the oldest, and everything everywhere was borrowed from the Sumerians. After 1960, the concept of the Kish civilization centered around the Semitic northern

Babylonia, and contrasting with Sumerian civilization in the south, was put on the map. From 1975 on, this concept was considerably extended with the great epigraphic discoveries at Ebla that have shown that the Semitic features derived from Kish in the east were flourishing at Ebla in the west. The question is: what was the role of Mari within the concept of the Kish civilization? The answer is not too difficult. *On the basis of what we now know about Mari, it appears that Mari played the role of the catalyst and transmitter of the Kish civilization from its homeland in northern Babylonia to Ebla in northern Syria.*

The discovery of a batch of Pre-Sargonic tablets in 1980 at Mari which were said to be "de l'âge eblaïte" made me jokingly remark to my friends and colleagues that had the new Mari discoveries been made about ten years earlier, the new language of Mari, and what goes with it, might have been called "Mariote" and then applied to Ebla.

My joking remark spread far-away. I was told by the organizer of this Symposium that he had heard the same remark on his recent trip to Jerusalem.

The *Nīšum* "Oath" in Mari

Paul Hoskisson

Brigham Young University

Though the *nīsum* "oath" is attested from the Old Akkadian period onward, the exact nature of it does not appear in cuneiform literature.[1] This communication, drawing upon the evidence made available through the Tell Hariri excavations, will discuss the oath as it was used in Mari.

There can be no doubt that the oath was spoken. The most common verb by far associated with *nīšum* is *zakārum*, "to declare."[2] It occurs in the G-stem *passim*, in the Š-stem (ARM 14 64: 8, *nīš* DINGER^{lim} *dannam ušazkiršunūtimma*), and probably also in the N-stem (ARM 4 78: 80ff, [*nī*]*š* DINGER^{MEŠ} *izzakram*). It also occurs twice in the G-stem stative. ARM 10 32: 11, *anāku nīš* DINGER^{lim} *zakrākuma*; and ARM HC BENJ. = Dossin (1939a) 990b: 18′–19′, *kīma atta ana zimri-lim nīš ilim zakrat/u anākuma qatamma ana mār-jamīna nīš ilim zakrāku.*

In addition to *zakārum*, the following verbs are used in conjunction with *nīšum*. *Tamûm*, "to swear," is used three times: ARM HC FOND. = Dossin (1940) 155a, *nīš* ^{d}*itūr-mer u šarrim* ^{d}*iasmaḫ*-^{d}*addu itmû*; ARM 3 19: 15–17, *nīš* ^{d}*dagan* ^{d}*itūr-mer u bēlīa utammīšunūt*[*imm*]*a*; and ARM 8 17: 5′–7′ in a broken context. *Ḫasāsum*, "to recall, to remember (in the sense of to keep, or to observe)," also appears three times, once in tandem with *zakārum*: ARM 14 89: 9′–12′, [*umma a*]*nāk*[*u*]*ma šumma nīš* DINGER^{lim} *azakkarakkunūšim* [*ṣe*]*ḫram u* ^{MÍ}*ṣeḫirtam ša ālānikunu ana dūr*^{KI}-*iaḫdu-l*[*im*] *kimsānimma nīš* DINGER^{lim} *luḫsusakkunūši*[*m*], "thus I, 'If I am to declare the oath of god for you, gather hither the children of your cities to Dūr-Yaḫdun-Lim so that I may evoke the oath of god for you;'" the same text, obv.: 9; and ARM 14 106: 14′–15′.[3] *Qabûm* (ARM HC AREP. = Dossin [1938a] 108: 20) and

[1]*Nīšum* literally means "life," from the verb *nêšum*. That it means "oath" can be induced from passages such as the Tukulti-Ninurta Epic vi: 25, where *nīšu* is parallel to *māmītu*. For the references to the various periods, including the latter passage, see CAD N/2 290–94.

[2]Of the thirty passages (not texts) where a verb is used in a way that could be construed as indicating the verbal action involved with the utterance of the oath, twenty use the verb *zakārum*.

[3]The translation of *ḫasāsum* here presents some problems. It could mean "to keep in remembrance, to observe." Cf. Weinfield (1973) 193 and n 57. Birot, ARMT 14, p. 262, says

dabābum (ARM 2 55: 37) are used once each. *Šakānum,* which will be discussed below, occurs twice: ARM HC IAMḪ. = Dossin (1939b) 51a: 7–10; and ARM 2 13: 31.

This spoken element of the oath could have reference to god and/or kings as the object, literally, "by the life of" god and/or king. In most cases, the personage to whom the oath was given remains unnamed, being designated simply as DINGER$^{(lim)}$, DINGER^{MEŠ}, *bēlum,* or LUGAL. In those cases where the gods were mentioned by name, Dagan (ARM 3 19: 15–17), the most prestigious god of Old Babylonian Mari, and Itūr-Mer (ARM 3 19: 15–17 and ARM HC FOND. = Dossin [1940] 155a), who was the titular king of Mari (ARM 10 63: 15–19), appear. The only known mortal by whom the oath was sworn was Yasmaḫ-Addu (ARM HC FOND. = Dossin [1940] 155a), the king of Mari, vassal of his father, Šamši-Adad.

In addition to the verbal element, there was also a "ritual gesture,"[4] presumably of the hand or hands, associated with the oath. The phrase used in the Mari tablets for this action element of the oath is *napištam lapātum,* or, in the noun chain, *lipit napištim.* While the exact denotation of these phrases remains elusive, they no doubt refer to touching or seizing the throat (AHw 535a), and connote the seriousness of the commitment undertaken by reciting the oath. Falkenstein saw "der Gestus des Halsabschneidens" behind these words for violation of the oath.[5]

Several Mari texts make it clear that the *lipit napištim* was an aspect of the oath ceremony. The best example is ARMT 13 147: 1–9, *ana bēlīa qibima umma iawi-ilā waradkama aššum ilāni tarādim bēlī išpuram ummāmi ilānīka ṭurdamma napištī lulput inanna anūmma ilāni aṭṭardam bēlī nīš ilāni lizkur,* "to my lord speak, thus Yawi-ilā, your servant. My lord wrote to me to send the gods, 'Send your gods that I may touch my throat.' Now then, I have sent the gods. Let my lord declare the oath of the gods." The king had requested that the (statues? of the) gods be sent so that he could touch his throat. When the gods had been sent to the king, it is precisely the oath that is demanded of him. In other words, the *lipit napištim* is used as a synonym for the *nīš ilāni.*

The author of ARM 2 77: 2′–8′ also employs *lipit napištim* parallel to *nīš ilāni*: *assurri kīma ḫammurapi nīš ilāni izkuru bēlī ilammadma*

---

that it could also retain its usual sense of "to remember," but goes on to cite Weinfield. I suggest that it may mean "evoke" in the Mari texts. This proposal is based on the fact that the oath could be repeated if necessary. For instance, it is stated in ARM 2 51: 10–11 that the oath was declared anew, *nīš* DINGIR *ūdiš azkurma.* And in ARM 14 89: 9′–12′ it would seem that the Amnaneans were now demanding of Yaqqim-Addu that he make good on an oath he had previously given, otherwise how could they demand of him that he "remember-evoke" the oath (1. 9)?

[4]See Oppenheim (1952) 132.

[5]Falkenstein (1954) 114.

wardū ša ḫammurapi ša maḫar bēlīa wašbū ana bēlīa awātam iṣabbatū umma šunuma bēlni napištašu [i]l[t]apat ana ilāni ša bēlini a[šrānu]m wašbū napištaka luput. "Surely my lord shall learn that Ḫammurapi has declared the oath of the gods, and the servants of Ḫammurapi, who live in Mari, shall take up the matter for my lord and say, 'Our lord [has already m]ade his *lipit napištim.* Make thou thy *lipit napištim* to the gods of our lord who dwell [ther]e.'" Here the phrase *lipit napištim* in the statement of the servants of Ḫammurapi replaces the *nīš ilāni* mentioned by the author in l. 3′. The synonymous nature of the two terms would also explain why in ARM 1 37: 19–26 a tablet of *nīš ilāni* can supply information about the *lipit napištim.*[6]

The wording of two other texts suggests that at least on some occasions the *asakkum*-"taboo" was connected with an oath ceremony.[7] Normally, this word is combined with the verb *akālum* to mean roughly "to infringe upon the taboo" of a god, king, or person of superior rank (e.g., ARM 2 13: 17–36; 8 1: 28–29; 8 85: 3′–5′; and 14 67: 8′). However, in ARM 8 16: 6′–8′ *akālum* is replaced by IN.PÁD.BA.DÈ.MEŠ, "they swore" (the taboo of Yaḫdun-Lim and Zimri-Lim). At first glance, it would seem as J. Aro stated in his review of ARM 8, that the oath ceremony, and the "infringement of a taboo" of a god or king have been contaminated,[8] or, as Falkenstein observed, "Hier ist offensichtlich die *asakku*-Formel und die Eidformel vermengt," (Here the *asakku* and the oath formulae have obviously been conflated).[9] More likely, as will be shown presently, the "infringement of a taboo" was either a type of, or a part, of an oath ceremony, and the "contamination" or "conflation" observed here is simply the use of roughly equivalent terms, at least in the mind of the Old Babylonian Mari scribe.

In another variant of the *asakkam akālum* formula, ARM 2 55: 35–37 replaces the usual *akālum* with *šakānum*, *[šumm]a* ^{GIŠ}APIN *ekallim ippuṣ* [. . .] *asak* LUGAL *ana pī* ^{LÚ}APIN *išku[n]*. Leaving aside the difficulties involved in understanding the import of these phrases,[10]

[6]Notice also the parallelism in the roughly contemporary Uruk letter, W 199000, 147 iv: 17–18 (= Falkenstein (1963) 59]: *ēma salīmim u damqātim nīš ilim innerrišu adi napištim lapatim* (reading with CAD L 84b) *libbum lā iqqippu.* "The *nīš ilāni* is called for wherever peace and goodwill are sought; until the performance of the *lipit napištim*, the heart is not trusting."

[7]On *asakkum*, see also Malamat (1966).

[8]Aro (1960) 261.

[9]Falkenstein (1960) 178a.

[10]Both dictionaries translate the phrase *asak . . . iškun* with caution. CAD A/2 327b has, "(if) he has made farmers infringe on a taboo of the king," for this passage. AHw 73b translates, "er überliess dem Bauern, was dem König vorbehalten ist (?)." An alternative translation would be, "[i]f the plow of the palace he has broken [?] (then) he has plac[ed] the taboo of the king in the mouth of the farmer [ ]." See also C.-F. Jean's translation in ARMT 2.

it is clear that the *asakkum* was placed in the mouth of the farmer.[11] Thus the phrase *asakkum akālum* connotes an infringement of a taboo, and also denotes a physical action: the placing of an object in the mouth, and possibly consuming it.

In turning now to ARM 2 13: 23–32, it becomes clear that there is a direct, though perhaps not one-to-one, correspondence between an oath ceremony and the infringement of a taboo. In this text, a commander of troops, Samādaḫum, tried to justify himself for not sending on to the king the booty that had been taken from the city Ṣibat. Apparently he was to receive his share, and the king's share, of the plunder (in this case slaves are mentioned) from the officers under him, but they did not deliver them. When pressed, the officers tried to send only six slaves which they had probably taken from the common soldiers. Samādaḫum then reminded the officers that it was an infringement of the taboo of Dagan, Itūr-Mer, Šamši-Adad, Yasmaḫ-Addu, and various officials to take away the spoil of the soldiers. To determine if any of the officers had taken the spoil of the soldiers, *ana pīya u* GAL.KUD[12] *nīš* LUGAL *aškunma šallat* ^{LU}AGA.UŠ *ul īṭer*. "In my mouth and (in the mouth of each) officer, I placed the oath of the king, and (the result was that) no one had seized the plunder of a soldier."

Both the juxtaposition of the taboo infringement next to the "placing of the oath of the king in the mouth," and the wording of the phrase "placing of the oath," indicate the direct relationship of the oath ceremony, and the infringement of a taboo. Samādaḫum "placed the oath of the king" in their mouths only after he had warned them about the *asak* DN/RN *akālum*, as if the latter were a necessary introduction to the former, an explanation thereof. And the wording *ana pīya . . . nīš* LUGAL *aškun* is simply a variation of the phrasing in ARM 2 55: 35–36, *asak* LUGAL *ana pī . . . iškun*, itself a variation of *asakkam akālum*. Thus, in ARM 2 13: 31, an otherwise intangible object, the "oath of the king," is placed in the mouth in the same manner as the *asakkum* would have been. On the other hand, in ARM 8 16: 6′–8′, the tangible *asakkum* is sworn in the same manner as the oath. By Ockham's razor, the problem is only in the mind of the modern reader; for the Old Babylonian scribe, the *asakkam akālum* and *nīš* DN/RN formulae, though not identical, could be used synonymously—the one being a subset of the other—just as *napištam lapātum* could be used for the *nīš* DN/RN.[13]

[11]What it was that was placed in the mouth is hinted at in ARM 8 11: 29–31, where, in the place of the usual *asakkam akālum* juxtaposed with the silver fine on a contract, the lines read, SAR^{MEŠ} ^{d}*šamši-*^{d}*adad u iasmaḫ-addu/u awin [r]abbi īkulū*. Even though CAD A/2 327a translates, "anyone who enters a claim has infringed on a taboo," the use of SAR, the Sumerogram for plant or herb, indicates that *asakkum* was not simply an object, but probably some kind of flora.

[12]For this professional designation, see Ellis (1974) 138.

[13]So far, the Mari texts indicate that the *napištam lapātum* and the *asakkum akālum* were mutually exclusive.

In vassal-suzerain relationships, the superior swore the oath for the inferior, and, if gods were mentioned, by the gods of the inferior. Thus, in ARMT 13 147: 1–9, Zimri-Lim was to have sworn by the (statues of the) gods that his underling, Yawi-ilā, had sent him. Similarly, in ARM 14 89: 4–10, and 9′–12′, Yaqqim-Addu reported to Zimri-Lim, LÚ.MEŠ*amnanayyu ša ina saḫrī*KI *wašbū illikūnimma kīam iqbūnim umma šunuma aššum* LÚMEŠ *aḫḫūni ša elēnum wašbū ittakrū ana napištini palhān*[*u*] [*nī*]*š* DINGER*lim* *ḫussannîšimma* [*libb*] *an*[*i*] *linūḫ*. "The Amnaneans that live in Saḫrū came to me and said, 'We are afraid for our lives because our brothers who live in the upper (country) have become belligerent. Evoke for us the oath of god that our heart may be calm.'" Note that it is Yaqqim-Addu who should repeat the oath of god for the Amnaneans. The same is evident again in lines 9′–12′, Yaqqim-Addu's answer.[14]

By extrapolation from the above two texts, the oath was sworn by the suzerain at his place of residence, or at some place under his jurisdiction, and not in the immediate territory of the inferior. In ARMT 13 147: 5–9, Yawi-ilā had sent his gods to Zimri-Lim so that Zimri-Lim could swear by them at his place of residence. Yaqqim-Addu proposed a site other than the seat of his governorship, but also undoubtedly removed from the cities of the Amnaneans.

There is only one text in which the relationship between the persons swearing the oath was probably parity, and not vassal-suzerain. In this missive, ARM 2 77, sent by Zimri-Lim's envoys at Ḫammurapi's court, it was reported that although Ḫammurapi had agreed to allow a matter to come to litigation, he had subsequently failed to perform his *lipit napištim*. The reverse, lines 2′–8′, containing the recommendations of the envoys for Zimri-Lim, was quoted above. In summary, Zimri-Lim's envoys reported back to him that Ḫammurapi did not perform the *lipit napištim,* or, as the second line states, the oath of the gods, and that Zimri-Lim would perhaps hear and/or be told by Ḫammurapi's envoys in Mari that Ḫammurapi had performed the "touching of the throat," and would demand of Zimri-Lim that he "touch his throat" for the gods of Ḫammurapi. The report continues with the recommendation that Zimri-Lim not perform the oath until the authors had returned to Mari, and have had an opportunity to explain the situation to their king. The fact that *both* Ḫammurapi and Zimri-Lim were to "touch the throat" underscores the parity relationship which is known to have existed historically during part of their respective reigns.[15] It is therefore of interest that Zimri-Lim was to touch his throat, that is, swear, by the

[14] *šumma nīš* DINGER*lim* *azakkarakunūšim* [*ṣe*]*ḫram u ṣeḫirtam* [*š*]*a ālānikunu ana dūr*KI*-iaḫdu-l*[*im*] [*k*]*imsānimma nīš* DINGER*lim* *luḫsusakkunūši*[*m*]. "If I am to declare the oath of god for you, gather hither the children of your cities to Dūr-Yaḫdun-Lim so that I may evoke the oath of the god for you."

[15] CAH 2/1^3 14.

god(s) of Ḫammurapi. By extrapolation, it may be assumed that Ḫammurapi, if he had performed the oath, would have sworn by the god(s) of Zimri-Lim. Indeed, this letter puts an excuse concerning the god Sin into the mouth of Ḫammurapi. Sin may have been the god, or part of the Mari contingent of deities, sent to Babylon for this purpose.[16]

The oath ceremony could be held in conjunction with or accompanying a celebration. In the economic texts of the Zimri-Lim period, six record the disbursement in each case of between two and 120 liters of *sasqû* (a certain type of fine flour); in three cases, various grain products; and in one case, in addition to the other items, also the legume *appānum.* No beverage or oil is ever mentioned—items commonly found in cultic and non-cultic ceremonies. In two instances, the disbursement of food stuffs for the oath of the gods is accompanied by rations for the king's meal, the *naptan šarrim.*[17]

Though there is no consistency to the dates on these economic tablets, and therefore no discernible fixed date, it must be noted that ARMT 12 21 is dated to the third of the month Lilliatum, and the disbursement is in conjunction with the king's meal. It is known that an Ištar festival took place annually in the first few days of the month Lilliatum,[18] and that the king made efforts to attend. It is possible that in the course of the Ištar festival, the king swore the oath of the gods. This might explain ARM HC AREP. = Dossin (1938a) 117: 22, in which Zimri-Lim had invited (subservient?) kings to come to the *nīqum*-"sacrifice" of Ištar.

The oaths, or perhaps more accurately, the purpose of the oaths, were at times, and certainly for all important affairs, recorded on clay tablets. ARM 1 37: 19–26 speaks of a *tuppi nīš ilāni,* "tablet of the oath of the gods" (which by the way, is juxtaposed with the "touching of the throat"), from which extracts were made concerning, probably, a treaty between Šamši-Adad and the king of Ešnunna. In ARM 2 77: 12, a *tuppi lipit napištim,* "tablet of touching the throat," appears in conjunction with a treaty.

The oath of the gods was used in both promisory and assertive senses. Simple promises were made more emphatic by the addition of the

[16]It is known that the temple of Sin in Ḫarrān was on occasion the scene of covenant making. See ARM HC BENJ. = Dossin (1939a) 986a: 10–15.

[17]The six texts recording disbursement of *sasqû* are ARM 9 168 vi: 20–21; 213 ii: 5; 218 iv: 47–48; 12 21: 6–7; 46: 5–6; 606: 1–3. In addition 12 21; 12 46; and 9 213 mention grain products, while the latter also contains the legume *appānu.* For disbursement of food-stuffs for the oath of the gods accompanying rations for the *naptan šarrim* see ARM 12 21: 1–16; and 46: 1–10. For a recent study of the *naptan šarrim* see R. R. Glaeseman, "The Practice of the King's Meal at Mari: A System of Food Distribution in the 2nd Millennium B.C.," Dissertation University of California, Los Angeles, 1978.

[18]Sasson (1979) 132–33.

oath. In ARM HC AREP. = Dossin (1938a) 108, we read, "I spoke to Qarni-Lim with an oath of the gods, saying, 'If you abandon Zimri-Lim, I will again become your adversary.'" Treaties were sealed, or received credibility, with the oath. An unnamed representative of Zimri-Lim wrote to him in ARM HC IAMḪ. = Dossin (1939b) 52a, "Amud-pī-El, the king of Qatanum, should come to Aleppo. A pleasant word between me and him, the oath of the god, and a binding contract we shall establish." When a question arose about the continued efficacy of a treaty, the oath could be invoked again. A tribe that had apparently entered into an agreement with Zimri-Lim's government came to his representative and said, "we are afraid for our lives because our brothers who live in the upper (country) have become belligerent. Evoke for us the oath of the gods that our heart may be calm" (ARM 14 89: 6–10, mentioned above).

The oath was used assertively to settle disputes. In ARM 1 30, a text concerning the fate of 200 sheep purchased with 2 *mana* of silver, and contested by a third party, king Šamši-Adad wrote to his son, Yasmaḫ-Addu, to have the third party's witnesses swear the oath of the gods, at which point the sheep would be turned over to the third party.[19]

The oath of the gods was respected and inviolate. Though this point has been taken for granted, ARM 2 77, mentioned twice above, verifies this point in an unusual way. Zimri-Lim and Ḫammurapi had their differences: the facts, unfortunately, are not given. Two envoys, one of them the high court official, Lāʾûm, had been sent from Mari to Babylon to discuss the matter with Ḫammurapi. After their arrival, and subsequent conversation, they dispatched a letter to Zimri-Lim, with their report and recommendation. In short, they took up the matter at hand, including what appears to be the finalizing of an agreement—an oath ceremony—with Ḫammurapi, who tried to avoid the crux of the matter by a shower of words. Not being satisfied with Ḫammurapi's evasiveness, they pursued the discussion carefully, and eventually thought that they had convinced Ḫammurapi to let the matter come to litigation. When the appointed day arrived for the litigation—including the oath ceremony—Ḫammurapi did not go through with it, offering instead a not quite intelligible excuse about honoring the god Sin. At this point, a break interrupts the text completely, and after the break, the text has already progressed to the envoys' recommendation for their king: even if Zimri-Lim has learned that Ḫammurapi has supposedly performed the oath ceremony, and even if the servants of Ḫammurapi stationed at the court of Mari have reported that Ḫammurapi has indeed performed the oath ceremony, Zimri-Lim should wait until his own envoys

[19]It is the silver, by the way, and not the sheep, which is in dispute.

return from Babylon, and personally give their report, before he performs his oath ceremony.

What Ḫammurapi hoped to gain specifically by this deception remains unsaid in this text, but the means seem clear. By not performing the oath ceremony himself, Ḫammurapi would be free of obligations, while Zimri-Lim, through performing it, would be unilaterally obligated.

Both the intrigue of Ḫammurapi, and the extraordinary report dispatched from Babylon itself (?) warning Zimri-Lim of the deceit, demonstrate the inviolability which the oath ceremony enjoyed. If Ḫammurapi had been so inclined, he could have reneged on the obligations incurred through performing the oath without going through the protracted machinations recorded in this letter. Instead he chose not to perform the oath ceremony, indicating his reverence for it. Likewise, neither did the envoys of Zimri-Lim need to risk sending a damning report from Babylon, nor could Ḫammurapi have hoped for success, if either had thought Zimri-Lim capable of repudiating his own oath after learning that the corresponding oath had not been sworn. It is no wonder, then, that Zimri-Lim wrote in ARM 10 177: 7–10, "now concerning Ḫammurapi, the man of Babylon, ask, 'will that man die, (or) will he speak honestly with us, (or) will he provoke us to belligerency . . . ?' "

In summary, "the oath of the gods," "the touching of the throat," and the *asakkum akālum*, while denoting different aspects of an oath ceremony, could by themselves connote an entire ceremony. The oath was used both promisorily and assertively, and could be sworn by the person superior in rank by the gods of the lesser party. In cases of parity, most likely each party swore by the gods of the other party. The ceremony could be held in conjunction with other celebrations, including the Ištar festival. Records were kept for at least the more important oaths. And finally, even the king of Babylon, who eventually defeated Mari militarily, showed a deference for the oath ceremony, despite his other devious political machinations.

The Divine Nature of the Mediterranean Sea in the Foundation Inscription of Yaḫdunlim

Abraham Malamat

The Hebrew University of Jerusalem

One of the central themes in comparative studies of Ugaritic poetry and biblical literature relates to the motifs concerning the myth of Yamm, god of the sea, and his rising against the gods of Ugarit, on the one hand, and the God of Israel, on the other. In the Ugaritic myths, this deity holds a lofty role in the pantheon, and bears the epithet *zbl ym*, *ṯpṭ nhr*, "Prince" Yamm, "Judge" Nahar (i.e., Ruler of the River).

Yamm was conceived as the cosmic force of the raging waters, but this personification undoubtedly originated in the nature and characteristics of the Mediterranean Sea, whose waters threaten the coast, and deluge it. Faint echoes of this concept, and a plethora of allusions to it, are found in the Bible, and, even more overtly, in Rabbinic literature, as has clearly been demonstrated by Cassuto.[1] We shall see below that this concept—of the Mediterranean Sea's mythical and divine nature—can be pushed back to a period several centuries earlier than the Ugaritic texts (14th–13th centuries B.C.).

The various references to Yamm (and the daemonic creatures associated with him) in the Ugaritic literature have been treated by Cassuto, and subsequently by O. Kaiser and S. Loewenstamm, among others. The extant material of the myth of Yamm—too fragmentary to provide a continuous narrative—can all be found in the works of the two latter scholars, as well as in the various collections of Ugaritic texts.[2] Briefly, in outline: the god Yamm, denoted the "friend" (*mdd*) of El (head of the Ugaritic pantheon), seeks majesty; El proclaims Yamm's majesty, and promotes the erection of his palace. This lofty aspiration is contested by Baal, Lord of the Earth and of fertility, who struggles with Yamm over

[1]Cassuto (1975) 80ff., and *s.v.* "Prince of the Sea," p. 285.

[2]Kaiser (1962); Loewenstamm (1980) 346–61; and cf. Haussig (1965) 85ff., *s.v.* *Jamm*. For the reconstruction of the myth of Baal and Yamm, see now Gibson (1978) 37–45 and 148, *s.v.* *ym*.

hegemony, and eventually strikes the victorious blow. Two further stories, poorly preserved, are the contest between Yamm and the goddess Anath, and his struggle with *ᵓAṯtr*.[3]

Of special relevance to our discussion is the inclusion of Yamm in two cultic lists from Ugarit recording sacrifices to the various gods,[4] demonstrating Yamm's integral position within the official pantheon of Ugarit. Furthermore, we may attach importance to Loewenstamm's assumption that the Ugaritic (no less than the biblical) material is derived from West Semitic traditions antedating them both.[5]

In their discussions of the Yamm myth, Cassuto, Loewenstamm and others (in contrast to Kaiser) ignore, or circumvent (out of lack of direct interest), a further source relating to the mythical nature of the Mediterranean Sea—i.e., Egyptian literature. In the Egyptian legends, too, the sea deity is denoted by the Canaanite appellation, "Yam." This loanword appears in Late Egyptian, from the 18th dynasty (15th century B.C.) onwards, as an alternative to the indigenous term *w3ḏ-wr* (lit., "Great Green"), not only in mythological usage, but even in ordinary contexts.[6]

The two main Egyptian legends involved, which we can only briefly review here, are found in full in Kaiser's study, and in various collections of Egyptian literature.[7] The one is known as "The Tale of Two Brothers" (Papyrus D'Orbiney), in which Yam snatches a lock of hair from the wife of the younger brother. The narrative takes place largely in the "Valley of the Cedar" (or the Pine), apparently in the Lebanon, or possibly in the Beqaᵓ.[8] Thus the story, we can reasonably assume, was influenced by Canaanite mythology. The second story (Astarte Papyrus) is from the early 19th dynasty (late 14th century B.C.).[9] In this very fragmentary text, Yam is enmeshed by the beauty of Astarte, and thus comes into conflict with the god Seth. Here, too, as has been noted, the Ugaritic myths are called to mind, or may even have served as its origin.[10]

[3]Loewenstamm (1980) 350, 354ff.

[4]KTU 1 39: 13; 46: 6; and cf. Kaiser (1962) 58.

[5]Loewenstamm (1980) 360.

[6]Cf. besides Kaiser (1962), Erman and Grapow (1926) 1 78; Helck and Otto (1980) 3 242f., *s.v.* Jam (Meer). Cf. also Faulkner (1962) 56, *s.v.* *w3ḏ-wr*, where one form should actually read *w3ḏ-wr ᵓim* (!), that is, "Great Green Yam."

[7]Kaiser (1962) 78ff., and the references therein. For the "Tale of the Two Brothers" see immediately below, and the recent translation in Lichtheim (1976) 2 203ff.

[8]Gardiner (1933) 128.

[9]Kaiser (1962) 81ff; and especially Stadelmann (1967) 125ff.

[10]Kaiser (1962) 38, and 90, even went so far as to postulate that the influence of the Canaanite myth of the god Yam entered Egypt, apparently from Ugarit, already during the Middle Kingdom—that is, during the first quarter of the second millennium B.C., though he cites no actual proof for this assumption.

It is in this light that we can now find implication of the Mediterranean Sea as a divine-mythological entity in an Akkadian text much earlier than the evidence cited hitherto. The text, the Foundation Inscription of Yaḫdunlim, King of Mari, was discovered in the temple of Shamash at Mari.[11] Yaḫdunlim—Zimri-Lim's father, who reigned around 1800 B.C. (middle chronology)—describes with fervor his campaign in the West, and his reaching the Mediterranean coast, an event which crowned the entire campaign. The relevant passage is as follows (i: 34–ii: 23):

> Since days of old, when god[12] built Mari, no king residing in Mari had reached the sea (*ti-a-am-ta-am*). To the Cedar Mountain, and the Boxwood (Mountain), the great mountains, they had not reached; they had not felled their trees. (But) Yaḫdunlim, the son of Yaggidlim, the mighty king, a wild ox among kings, marched to the shore of the sea (*ti-a-am-ta-am*) in irresistible strength. To the "Vast Sea" (*a-a-ab-ba*)[13] he offered his great royal sacrifices,[14] and his troops cleansed themselves with water in the "Vast Sea" (*a-a-ab-ba*). . . . He subjugated that land on the shore of the "Vast Sea" (*a-a-ab-ba*).

In an earlier treatment of this inscription, the author touched upon this passage, and on the illuminating distinction in Akkadian terminology here concerning the Mediterranean Sea. Twice we see the ordinary word for "sea"—*tiʾamtum, tâmtum*, properly used in a secular,

[11]ARM HC M.2802 = Dossin (1955) 1ff. For the passage discussed below, cf. pp. 13–14, and the notes on pp. 25–26, as well as Malamat (1965) 367ff., and A. L. Oppenheim's translation in Pritchard (1969) 556.

[12]The reading of the cuneiform sign is doubtful. In the version published by Dossin, the logogram AN appears, denoting divinity in both Sumerian and Akkadian, but in other versions of the inscription, the significant variant *i-lu-um* (in syllabic spelling) appears. The latter indicates that the word was read as *ʾilum,* whether representing the general Semitic term for divinity, or referring to a specific deity, Il/El, the well-known West Semitic god who was chief of the Ugaritic pantheon. Dossin (1955) 25 n 11 favors the latter interpretation, as do other scholars such as de Vaux (1969) 508. If we adopt this stance, we have here in Yaḫdunlim's inscription a clear "Canaanism," according to which the "founder" of the city of Mari was a decidedly West Semitic deity. On the other hand, Sollberger and Kupper (1971) regard the god here to be Dagan, supreme deity of the Middle Euphrates region.

[13]Our translation is in accord with the apposition of [*t*]*a-ma-ti* DAGAL-*ti* to A.AB.BA in a Gilgamesh fragment and other sources. Cf. Wiseman (1975) 160–61, l. 38.

[14]The text of ii: 10–11 is problematic, especially the relationship of the adjective *rabiam,* which we have translated here as "great," modifying the sacrifice(s)," as do Dossin and CAD A/1 221, *s.v. ajabba.* In Malamat (1965), we translated the phrase as "multitude of royal sacrifices," which would call for an Akkadian adverbial form like *rabiš.* In contrast, Oppenheim (n 11, above) translates the phrase as "and offered sacrifice to the Ocean as (befitting) his royal rank." That is, he connects the adjective *rabiam* with the noun "(royal) rank," rather than with "sacrifice."

empiric aspect; in contrast, the solemn term, *a-a-ab-ba* (spelled *a-ia-ba* in other versions of this text), having a mythological color to it, appears thrice—most likely the Akkadian phonetic equivalent of the Sumerogram A.AB.BA.[15] This term, often encountered in Sumerian-Akkadian literature, is also used several times in the El-Amarna letters to denote the Mediterranean Sea (especially in letters from the king of Byblos—and in a literary text which has escaped scholarly attention until recently).[16]

Moreover, A.AB.BA appears in an Akkadian list of the pantheon of Ugarit, in a position parallel to the name of the god Yamm in an equivalent list in Ugaritic.[17] In other words, the Canaanite word for "sea" was identified at Ugarit with the Sumerogram A.AB.BA. This is also demonstrated, *inter alia*, by the personal name *Abdi*-A.AB.BA, appearing in an Akkadian text from Ugarit. The name was most likely pronounced *Abdi-Yamm*, the second element appearing in names in Ugaritic, as well as in Mari and other sources.[18]

From terminology, we shall now proceed to the subject matter of our passage in the Yaḫdunlim inscription. The king of Mari (or rather, his scribes) praises his own "unprecedented" campaign to the Mediterranean Sea. The Akkadian term *illik* (lit. "he went") is used here in the meaning of "carried out a military campaign," and such usage is also found in the Bible for the parallel Hebrew *hlk* (cf., e.g., Num 32:21, 22; 2 Sam 5:6; 8:3; 12:29; 2 Kgs 8:3, 17; 28:11). The "Cedar Mountain and the Boxwood (Mountain)"—through which Yaḫdunlim passed, and where he felled trees—apparently refer to the Amanus range in northern Syria (an identification more acceptable than the Lebanon and Anti-Lebanon ranges).[19]

This extraordinary encounter with the Mediterranean Sea was accompanied by cultic ceremonies—the offering of sacrifices to the Sea by the king, and the washing of his troops in the water of the Sea, in what was surely a cultic ritual. This latter is presumably indicated also by the Akkadian verb employed, *ramāku*, meaning to cleanse the entire

[15]For this term, see CAD A/1 221, where the difficulty of its being a loanword from Sumerian is noted. Cf. also Albright and Moran (1950) 167, and Goetze (1955) 16 n 58. Dossin and Oppenheim (n 11, above) translate the word in this inscription as Ocean, in the mythical sense of the Homeric epics.

[16]As noted by P. Artzi in a lecture at the Eighth World Congress of Jewish Studies in Jerusalem in 1981, this very fragmentary literary text is EA 340. See Knudtzon (1915) 2 954. Though Knudtzon gives the reading A.AB.BA in a note, both he and Mercer (1939) 2 790 read *tâmtu* in line 6.

[17]See Nougayrol (1968) pp. 45 (l. 29) and 58. He reads the Sumerogram A.AB.BA as [d]*tâmtum*, but in his explanatory notes, postulates the reading *yâm*(*u*). Cf. Caquot, Sznycer, and Herder (1974) 110.

[18]Compare the Ugaritic personal names *Ymy*, *Ymn*, *Ym-il* and the like in Gröndahl (1967) 104, 144, and 316. For personal names at Mari with the element Yam. see Huffmon (1965) 210.

[19]For the location and identification of the kinds of trees, see Malamat (1965).

body in water, especially ritually.[20] Yaḫdunlim's description differs in essential details from the acts of the Neo-Assyrian kings in the first millennium B.C. upon arrival at the Mediterranean shore. Thus, for instance, Ashurnasirpal II and his son Shalmaneser III also offered sacrifices at the seashore, but the god worshipped was not the god of the sea, but rather "the gods" (in plural) in general; and they symbolically purified only their weapons by dipping them into the water, with no other ceremony involved.[21]

The conclusion deriving from Yaḫdunlim's inscription, then, is that already in the Mari period (and possibly earlier), the Mediterranean Sea was conceived as a divinity. This was undoubtedly based on early West Semitic-Canaanite concepts, which find clear expression centuries later in the Ugaritic texts, on the one hand, and in the Egyptian stories, on the other, and still later in the biblical and talmudic traditions. The Canaanite concept of the divine nature of the Mediterranean Sea could well have taken hold at Mari at the time of its close ties with the West in general, and with such centers as Ugarit in particular.[22] Moreover, it has been recently suggested, rather boldly but reasonably, that the Babylonian Creation epic, the *Enuma Eliš*, which describes the combat between the god Marduk and the primordial sea (in the person of Tiamat—*tehom* in Canaanite-Hebrew), is derived from the West, i.e., the Mediterranean coast—just as the Ugaritic Yamm myth. From that region, it is held, the myth spread to Babylonia (and not vice versa!), apparently by means of the Amorites during the Old Babylonian period.[23]

In other words, from our analysis of this passage of Yaḫdunlim's inscription—an Akkadian text displaying affinity with the conceptual world of the West Semites in its expressions, grammatical forms, and outlook[24]—an additional West Semiticism or Canaanism emerges: the divine nature of the Mediterranean Sea.[25]

[20]Though the verb *ramāku* does mean "wash," its ritualistic sense in certain contexts is indicated by the noun *rimku*. Cf. AHw 985: "Bad(ekult), Ganzwaschung."

[21]Cf. their inscriptions in Pritchard (1969) 276ff. An intriguing, late (6th century A.D.), but similar instance is noted by Procopius, *de bello pers.* II:xi:1. The Sassanian king Choseroes, after conquering Antioch from Justinian, went to the Mediterranean coast, and ". . . bathed himself alone in the seawater, and after sacrificing to the sun and other such divinities . . . , he went back." Text and translation in Dewing (1914) 350–51.

[22]See Malamat (1971) 32ff.

[23]See Jacobsen (1968).

[24]Cf. n 12, above, on the name Il/El, or, for another example, compare *ummatum* and Hebrew *ummah*. For this last, see Malamat (1979).

[25]This study was prepared within the framework of a grant from the Fund for Basic Research, administered by the Israel Academy of Sciences and Humanities.

The 1979–1982 Excavations at Mari: New Perspectives and Results

JEAN-CLAUDE MARGUERON

Director, Mission Archéologique de Mari
University of Strasbourg

Between 1933 and 1974, the late André Parrot led twenty-one expeditions to Mari.[1] As a result, our knowledge of Mesopotamia and Syria during the third and second millennia B.C. has been immensely broadened. While at first it was the religious institutions and their remains in the city upon which Parrot concentrated, subsequent discovery of the palace drew his attention in that direction. Initial construction of the palace probably began during the first half of the third millennium, and it lasted, subject to the vicissitudes of time, until the destruction of the city during the eighteenth century B.C. by Ḫammurapi of Babylon. This palace is a key building for the study of Mesopotamian monumental architecture, and thus it is to be regretted that certain phases of its life are still imperfectly known and remain a high priority on the agenda for future seasons of excavation. Yet, while it is proper to say that the full scope of his brilliant work at Mari still cannot be measured, André Parrot's contribution of materials for the fields of epigraphy, glyptic, painting, and sculpture form the bases for all major syntheses. They are his legacy, now entrusted to his archaeological and epigraphic successors.

A new interdisciplinary team composed of scholars from several branches of learning has been organized to continue the work at Mari. It is charged with the mission of increasing the accuracy of our knowledge of the city of Mari and its unique contributions to all of the fields of the study of the Oriental Bronze Age. Its proper place, and the precise part that it played as a link between Syria and Mesopotamia, as well as its role as a conveyor of oriental culture towards the Mediterranean areas, and *vice-versa*—questions of great concern to André Parrot—are also a major part of the new team's mandate.

[1]See Parrot (1974), his last major synthesis of the results of his many years at Mari, and among its materials.

Two important discoveries of the last decade have enriched our knowledge of ancient Syria, and are leading us to new approaches to many problems. The International Campaign for the Protection of the Antiquities of the Euphrates (Tabqa Dam Project) has drawn attention to the major importance of that loop of the river, especially as regards economic relations between Mesopotamia, Northern Syria, and the Mediterranean in the Bronze Age. In addition, excavation at Tell Mardikh-Ebla has resulted in the exceptional discovery of the archives and palace of the third millennium. The architecture of the building, the art objects found therein, as well as about 15,000 tablets and fragments give a new importance to North Syria and put the question of Syro-Mesopotamian relations in new terms.

It is obvious that the Kingdom of Mari was the intermediary between these two worlds, and that only the study of its history will help us understand the relations which existed between them. It will also enable us to state the share of each of the termini in that exchange, where culture and economy were inextricably linked. With this in mind, new targets were fixed in 1979 for the next ten archaeological campaigns at Mari. They may be grouped according to the main axes of our research.

I. THE NEW TARGETS

A. *The study of the capital of a kingdom on the Euphrates River*

Three aspects will draw special attention: (1) city planning at Mari during the 3rd and 2nd millennia: system of streets; localization of the city-gates; analysis of the city-wall and of the defensive works, and connections between the sacred area, the palace and the other parts of the city; (2) connections between the city and the river which caused its development; (3) study of the evolution of the city from its origins to its destruction.

B. *The study of the land which was the agricultural basis of the city*

We are trying to define the territorial unit which allowed the city to survive whenever it had to live on its own means. For that reason, we are systematically studying the entire territory which lies between the cliffs of Dura-Europos and those of Abou-Kemal, in order to discover: (1) the changes of the course of the river, and the exact course at the time of Mari; (2) the exact nature of the different kinds of earth in the valley, and those soils which may be considered as belonging to the time of Mari; (3) the different human activities in the neighborhood of the site, and especially those which belong to the 3rd and 2nd millenia B.C.; (4) the possibility of linking the territorial units to the North (at the level of Dura-Europos) and to the South (Abou-Kemal).

C. *The study of the axis of expansion of this kingdom*

Even if the road which led southwards to Babylonia played an important part at certain times, it was mainly the middle valley of the Euphrates, with its affluents (the Khabur and Balikh), which seems to have played the essential role in the life of the country. Here, archaeology and epigraphy are strictly complementary, the first aim being to localize sites which belong to the time of Mari, and the second aim being their identification in the documentary record.

D. *Research on connections between the kingdom of Mari and its neighbors*

In the present state of our documentation, this research must be directed towards: (1) Babylon, Sippar, and Eshnunna on the one hand; (2) Northern Syria (i.e., the kingdom of Ebla for the third millennium, and Aleppo for the second millennium) on the other hand.

E. *An inquiry into the geographical, economic and social, and historical (in the broad sense) conditions of ancient Mari*

Mari may be considered an exemplary phenomenon which must be thoroughly analyzed. Numerous studies, both general and specific, will permit us to chart the historical fortunes, good and bad, of an important Mesopotamian city of the Bronze Age.

II. INITIAL RESULTS OF OUR ACTIVITY ON THE SITE, 1979-82.

Three seasons of excavation have followed the elaboration of our program: 1979;[2] 1980;[3] and 1982.[4] In each season, we have been able to explore four areas of the site and its surroundings. What follows is a summary of the six areas excavated during these seasons.

A. *Excavations in the city-wall*

Several soundings have been made in the little "Hariri" tell, south of the main tell and connected to the earth dike surrounding the southern half of the site. The results, however, are not yet clear enough to permit a detailed evaluation of these structures. Excavation on the little "Hariri" tell reveals a hill of earth without any noticeable stratification, materials, or sherds. Consequently, it is still impossible to place a precise date on the construction of this impressive work. Nor has it been possible to determine the reason for its construction. It could be the

[2]See Margueron (1982).
[3]See Margueron (1983).
[4]A preliminary report on the 1982 season will appear in *MARI* 3, 1984.

lower part of a high terrace, but the question of its function and why it was built outside the tell remains.

With regard to the earthen dike, excavation has yet to make clear that it forms the city wall, as is usually the case. A wall made of mud-bricks without plastered faces has been found outside the ridge, but its thickness (barely two meters) is obviously insufficient for a city wall. This wall was supported on its inner face by a great mass of gravelled earth, probably in the shape of a *glacis*. We may presume that this structure was built during the Shakkanakku period. Whether it was a defensive wall, or a dike to protect against floods, remains for future excavation to determine.

B. *Area A (fig. 1)*

The principal objective of excavation in this area was to locate a complete stratigraphic sequence near the focal point of the main tell. A large building was discovered on the first level, lying on an artificial earth foundation more than 3.5 m. deep, surrounding an impressively built tomb (figs. 4, 8, 9, and 10). As a consequence, we discarded our original plan and concentrated our efforts on determining the plan of the building. A very important structure emerged, probably built at the height of the Shakkanakku era and destroyed at the end of the reign of Zimri-Lim, during the destruction of Ḫammurapi. This structure has only been partially excavated to date, but we have uncovered 23 rooms, with an approximate surface area of 1,000 square meters, including the west corner, 30 m. of the northwest wall, and 35 m. of the southwest wall. During its lifetime, the building became dilapidated one or two times, and there are signs of numerous repairs. Three levels of occupation were found in some of the rooms: the first, of very good quality plaster and paving stones in one spot; on top of this floor-tiles were later laid; the last layer was simple earth. The first layer was, obviously, the most impressive, the decorations of this period closely resembling those of a palace.

The primary characteristic feature of this area is the existence of two very large rooms (I and XVI, both partially excavated). During the first period, room XVI was furnished with a throne under a dais, if the traces and the holes near the middle of the northwest wall are correctly interpreted (fig. 7). Other interesting features of the building include a well-preserved chimney in the north corner of room XX (fig. 6)—which also had a Turkish toilet in the south corner—and a large bread-oven in room XIII (fig. 5).

There were not very many artifacts, apart from sealings, most of which date to the Shakkanakku period, but there were more than one hundred tablets, one dating back to the same period. The bulk of the tablets indicate, however, that this building was the house of Asqudum, the soothsayer well known from the palace archives of the time of Zimri-Lim.[5]

The last feature to be discussed, and an unusual one, was the tomb which lies under room I. This monument, found in a very good state of repair despite repeated attacks by looters (illustrated by a great number of pits, one of which reaches the top of the tomb), was planned with two rooms. The first (fig. 10) is square shaped, built in brick-work, with four buttresses (one in the middle of each inside face), and has a corbel vault 2.5 m. high. A triangular opening in the east wall (fig. 9) gives access to a second room of rectangular shape, built of stone, the walls being strengthened by three buttresses which help support the roof and keep the slabs in place. This room appears to be an anteroom—a kind of *dromos,* despite the lack of stairs. Substantial proof exists to show that the tomb was reopened for a short time after it was first sealed (perhaps at the time of its construction). Unfortunately, this monumental tomb was completely empty when we opened it, except for two or three broken ceramic pieces.

C. *Area B (figs. 2 and 11)*

Our aim for Area B was to study the stratigraphy of the northern edge of the tell in order to clarify the history of this area. The first observation of consequence from the results of our efforts is that the ancient boundaries of the city have proved to be farther north than has yet been uncovered. Even if it has proved impossible to be certain of the ancient boundaries, it is beyond question that the city of Mari extended farther north in the 3rd millennium than the tell does now. It is a reasonable possibility that the Euphrates was responsible for its destruction by erosion at an unknown date.

A second important result has been the clearance of part of a building which appears to be an auxiliary temple building. Of greater importance was the discovery on the floor of a group of 20 tablets of mid-third millennium date. The potential relationship between these texts and the roughly contemporary Ebla documents is of great importance indeed.

Our trench in Area B also reveals a stratigraphic sequence represented by a collection of graves from the ED III to the Ur III periods. Unfortunately, however, we are still unable to state when this part of the tell was first occupied.

Among other features of great interest is a fine toilet built of tiles, stone, and bitumen which is connected to a main sewer, running into a great pit. The quality of the building in which the tablets and toilet

[5]Cf. the remarks of D. Charpin in this volume, pp. 61–63, 67–68.

were found gives us an idea of the very high standard reached by the city of Mari in the third millennium.

Finally, we should mention a system of bitumen-coated basins connected to a sewage system which may have been used by a dye-works, and note that ceramics and other artifacts were found in great abundance in the numerous graves.

D. *The palace of the third millennium (fig. 3)*

The importance of this building, well established by the work of André Parrot, prompted us to resume excavations in this area. The place chosen was situated west of courtyard IV. Two rooms and one corridor were found and partially excavated. These contained a good quantity of ceramics found in place and established the fact that after a great fire a new coat of plaster was applied to the walls over the half-baked plaster. This means that this part of the building, at least, was reoccupied after the fire, evidence of which was found in other parts of the palace.

The second important discovery was the clearance of a large room (15 × 15.5 m.) divided by two rows of three-stepped pillars (figs. 12 and 13). Its front was decorated with niches and strengthened by buttresses. While the excavation of this room has not been completed, the results to date point to a new kind of architecture which may characterize the Agade period at Mari—something without parallel in any Mesopotamian site of the time. It appears also that the last phase of the Palace (phase P-1 and P-0) was built later than previously thought, and that the palace was in use during the Agade period.

Finally, archaeological evidence shows that the palace of the third millennium was a very large building, which extended farther west than the later palace and contained features of considerable interest and novelty.

E. *Area D*

This area was chosen at the end of the last season when it became clear that area A would not be able to give us the stratigraphic sequence of the center of the city. Set up at some 50 meters or so to the south, on a slight slope, this sounding proved to be of immediate interest because the first encountered level belonged to the Shakkanakku period and substantiates the link with area A. Thus, the excavations in this area look very promising.

F. *Research on the plain of Mari*

We have begun the survey on the outskirts of the city. While we had intended to study the valley beyond Abou Kemal and Salihiye, we are now concentrating our efforts on the search for activity around the city during the third and early second millennia, using soil analysis, study of different geological terraces, the variations of the river, and the lost meanders. Research on ancient channels and human occupation is under way, but it is too early at present to draw conclusions, as the information does not appear to be as rich as we had hoped.

III. CONCLUSIONS

The last three campaigns have allowed us to begin the study of the neighborhood and to gain new information about the organization of the city, its extent, and its history. We have found an important new series of tablets, some of which give new evidence about relations with Ebla. We have cleared out a new building which has a completely new kind of architecture. And finally, we have been able to make stratigraphical and historical observations which reintroduce the time of Agade into the history of the palace and increase the importance of Mari at the time of the Shakkanakku.

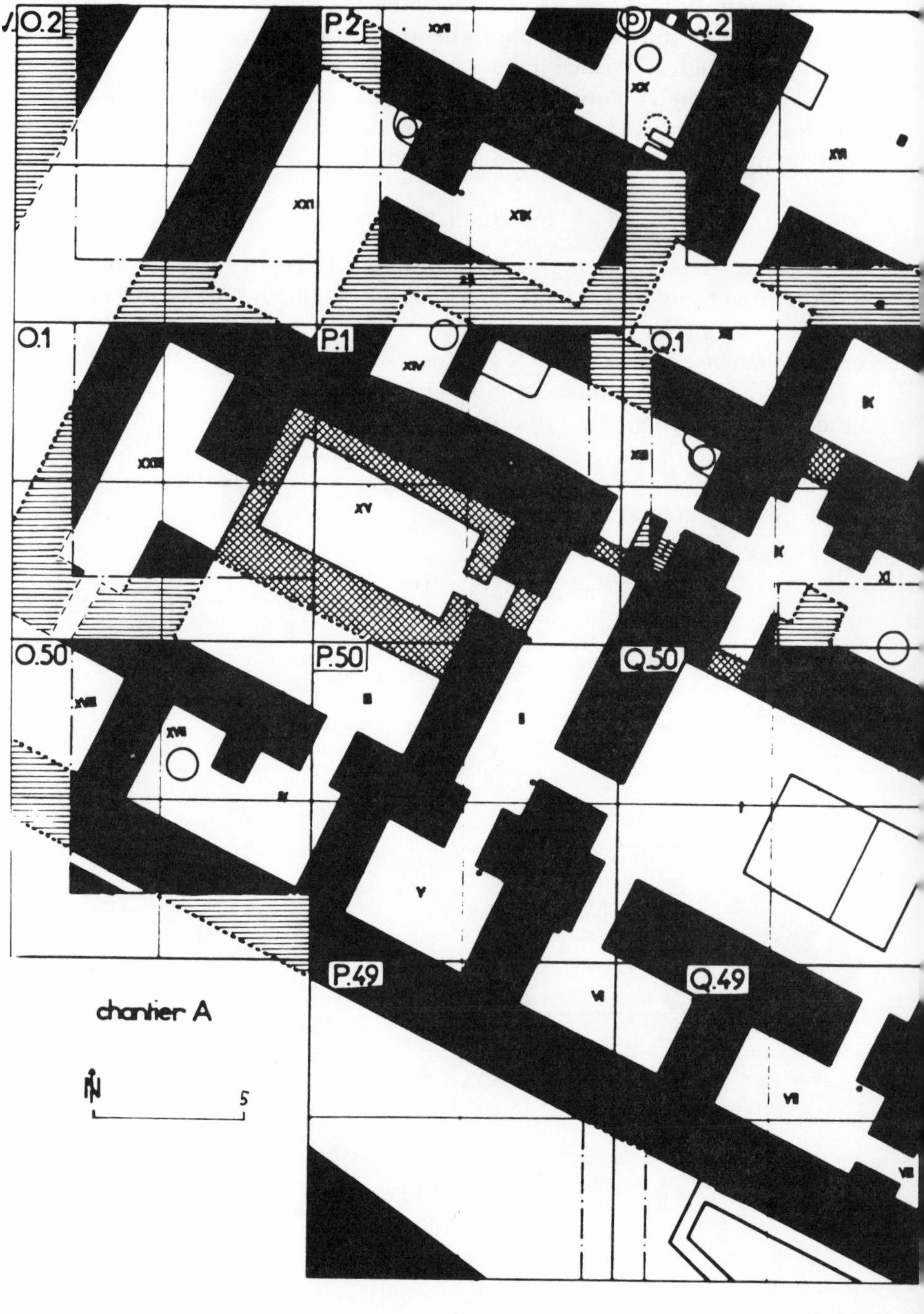

Fig. 1. Plan of Area A.

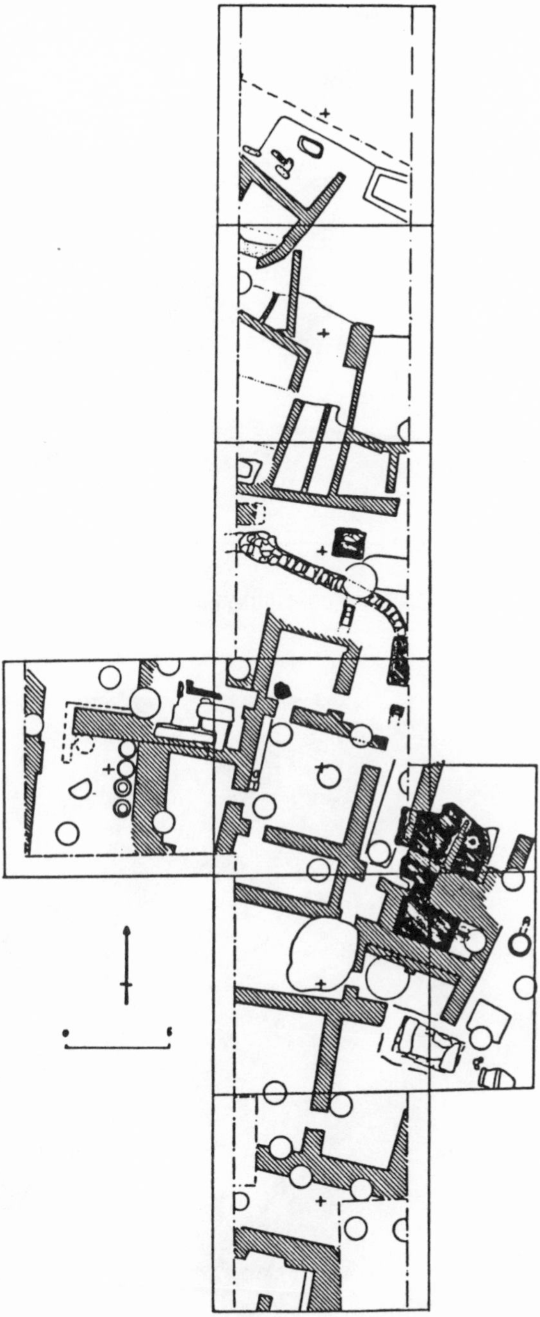

Fig. 2. Plan of Area B.

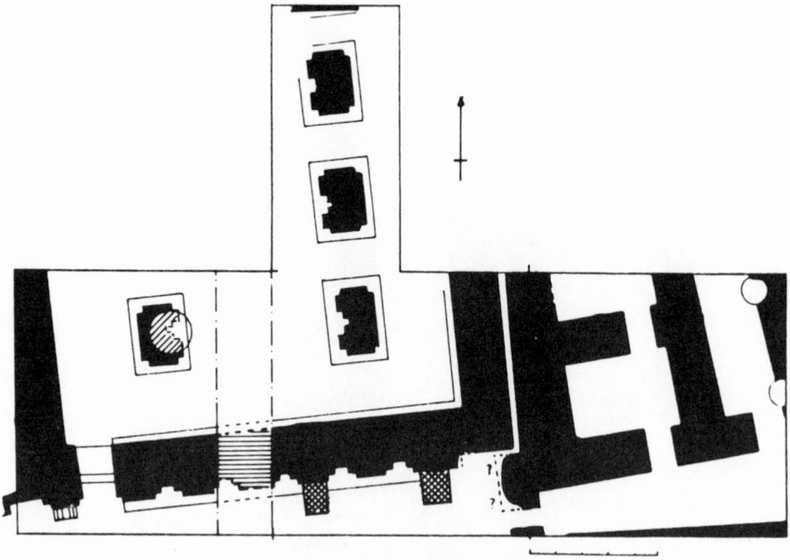

Fig. 3. New rooms in the palace of the third millennium.

Fig. 4. Walls of the large building of Area A.

Fig. 5. Bread oven in room XIII.

Fig. 6. The chimney in room XX.

Fig. 7. Holes of a dais against the northwest wall of room XVI.

Fig. 8. The top of the tomb under room I.

Fig. 9. Triangular opening between the anteroom and main room of the tomb.

Fig. 10. Walls of the main room of the tomb.

Fig. 11. View of Area B under excavation.

Fig. 12. Front wall of the room with pillars in the palace of the third millennium.

Fig. 13. The eastern row of pillars.

The Amorite Migrations

George E. Mendenhall
The University of Michigan

The fifty years that have elapsed since the discovery of the Mari archives, the importance of which is celebrated and delineated in this volume, have brought about a change in the entire context of scholarly work in both the ancient and biblical fields of academia to an extent that those who have not lived through it can only with difficulty understand or even imagine. The vivid picture of life in what must have been a fairly typical "Amorite" city-state and empire of the eighteenth century B.C. afforded us by these documents is, however, clouded considerably by the attempt on the part of modern scholars to force the new evidence into the inherited framework of old scholarly ideas deriving from the nineteenth century. Foremost among those ideas is the remarkable persistence of racial theories, so that the Amorites, Babylonians, Canaanites, Philistines, ancient Israelites, and other cultural entities are regarded as distinct and separate "racial" or ethnic entities. Not far behind is the persistent foisting of comparatively recent cultural developments involving animal husbandry upon the ancient societies, so that the Amorites automatically become "nomads" if they have more than two sheep, or if pasturage for their flocks demands that they stay away from home overnight.

It should not be surprising then that there has been considerable controversy over the topic of the so-called "Amorite Migrations." The problem involves not only the interpretation of archaeological strata, but also the interpretation of the entire Abraham cycle of narratives in the Bible. From the published literature on the subject, one would receive the impression that there exists a considerably over-hasty consensus that the Abraham cycle of narratives have nothing to do with pre-Israelite cultural history (Van Seters [1975]; Thompson [1974]). But contrast the treatment of Dever (1977), who approaches the problem from the vantage point of field archaeology. It is understandable that there should be a reaction against plausible correlations made nearly a half century ago between the biblical narratives and extra-biblical realities known from excavations and written documents that were then available, but a literary-critical escapism into a neo-docetic ideology represents no advance in our understanding either of the course of ancient history, or of the literary record of ancient peoples' understanding of and reaction to that history.

A basic and unfaced problem is that of the intrinsic incompatability of two conflicting purposes in biblical studies. The first is the understanding of the biblical text in its *own* context, which is fundamentally a historical problem—and one that requires a historical method, not a method derived from some contemporary fad or fashion in the literary manipulation of ancient or more recent literary works. One of the best indicators of the abysmal incompetence of much biblical scholarship today is the idea that literary-critical methods are historical methods.

The second purpose is illustrated by the frequent dismissal of historical research as "mere history," or as old-fashioned "historicism," and is characterized by a primary concern to utilize the prestige of the Bible for legitimizing and furnishing authority for modern social and ideological systems. It is not to be questioned that in contemporary culture there is an almost vehement rejection of "history," and much "history" deserves such rejection—after all, "1984" is past, together with its quaint custom of rewriting history every time some ambitious politician wants justification for his grandiose schemes and delusions of grandeur. It is certainly an unconscious recognition of the fact that the realities of the biblical history do not support those modern ideologies that exploit the Bible for modern purposes that explains the dogmatic retreat into various sorts of fundamentalism, political as well as religious. Uneasy coalitions of the two kinds of fundamentalism are only to be expected, as well as their sad historical consequences.

The Abraham narratives and the Amorite migrations are, then, a sort of paradigm problem for historical method. Unfortunately, the results are too shocking to traditional religious and academic establishments to be very popular, at least at first glance, for the acceptance of the historical basis of the Abraham narrative implies the fact that Abraham had originally nothing to do with biblical Israel, which didn't even exist until a couple of archaeological eras later. Perhaps most difficult for academics is the implication that people in ancient times also had some historical memory of very remote events and made use of those events as precedents for much later purposes. The means for arriving at a more adequate understanding of those narratives involves, as well as other more traditional methods, a new disciplinary approach that hardly existed several decades ago, namely, that of historical linguistics, over against the old nineteenth century "comparative philology."

There seems to be little or no doubt concerning the migration or infiltration of population elements into Mesopotamia from the West, though of course there is plenty of room for difference of opinion concerning the extent and the nature of such a population movement. At least one problem involved in the historical enigma is one of definition: what was an Amorite, and how did he contrast culturally and linguistically with other Semitic-speaking ethnic elements? Without attempting at present to answer this question, it seems to be a reasonable assumption, or even working hypothesis, that the term was not a designation of some homogeneous "ethnic" group, but one that from the ancient Mesopotamians' point of view designated any of a variety of groups who had little more than one feature in common: they weren't Sumerians or Akkadians either culturally or linguistically. We are faced with the "all foreigners look alike" syndrome, and this seems to be carried over into scholarly theories in some recent discussion of the subject. Add to that the scurrilous denigration of the *MARTU* in the famous Sumerian description of him, and the way is open for an enormous misconception of what is involved in the Amorite migration.

Thanks to the Syllabic Inscriptions from Byblos we now have a corpus of usable materials that gives us a perspective from which to look anew at the Amorite migration hypothesis. After thirty-seven years of off-and-on work on the corpus excavated by the French expedition to Byblos from 1929 to 1932, and published in 1945, a considerable amount of linguistic evidence is now available, and the monograph should be in press by the time this essay is published (Mendenhall [1985]). From internal evidence alone it is necessary to date them, against what seems to be the general consensus, to the late phases of the Early Bronze Age—precisely because they exhibit little or none of the features that we can now reasonably assume to be characteristic Amorite traits. Regardless of the dating problem, these inscriptions illustrate such a radical contrast to linguistic features of the entire Inland region of Semitic, that two observations become not only possible but necessary: (1) the contrast to what would be expected from our previous knowledge of Bronze Age West Semitic such as Ugaritic, the Amarna glosses, and Amorite itself, is so great that it constituted for years a most formidable obstacle to the process of decipherment, for the language stubbornly refused to be in reasonable conformity to the "laws" of comparative Northwest Semitic; and (2) the results necessitated a radical revision of ideas about Semitic linguistic history. In retrospect this seemed long overdue, particularly in view of the idea held by some that the Early Bronze population of the coastal region didn't even speak a version of Semitic.

A good part of the impasse over the Amorite migration to the West is to be attributed to the tendency of scholars to interpret the evidence they themselves accumulate, especially in field archaeology, and to work consciously or unconsciously with operating assumptions they absorbed from authoritative sources while they were still in graduate school; or, on the other hand, to integrate their data into theories generated by their contemporaries in the same specialized discipline. This tendency has already been deplored by several scholars who deal with the humanities and need not be further belabored here. What it amounts to, of course, is an increasing narrowness of specialization, which is counterproductive when it comes to the understanding especially of juncture periods in human culture, of which the Early Bronze to Middle Bronze transition period is crucially important and so complex that no consensus has been obtained.

The argument from language is definitive. When we had no usable linguistic evidence, it was not possible to reach firm conclusions concerning folk migrations, but since a new language is among the most difficult of cultural traits for individuals to acquire, language constitutes the most important index of cultural and "ethnic" relationships. We must, however, be aware of pitfalls even in this respect, for the Table of Nations in Genesis 10 clearly indicates, and quite correctly, that for historical purposes—and probably more emphatically in ancient times than in our own time—cultural relationships and derivations were far more significant than mere linguistic connections (Pulgram [1960]). However, when we are dealing with the problem of probable new population elements that could be correlated with the relatively sudden appearance of new artifactual traits of a culture that contrasts in significant ways to that which preceded, the carriers of that new complex of cultural traits may be identified through their language at least indirectly by its influence upon an earlier language, and through their personal and place names.

What I am suggesting here is that there is now a massive body of evidence that proves such an enormous linguistic change at Byblos itself that the change can be explained only on the hypothesis that there was an important and probably hegemonistic new population element, for language usually follows political power. The process is thus linguistically identical to what happened in Mesopotamia perhaps three centuries later. If the Mesopotamian cities were under the rule of kings who bore identifiable Amorite names in the nineteenth century B.C., it seems probable that a similar process had already taken place in the coastal regions of what is now Palestine and Lebanon in that destructive period between 2300 and 2100 B.C. The major difference in the West was the fact that urban and, therefore, politically centralized social organization probably did not exist after the destructions of the Early Bronze Age cities and cultures on any large scale until the Middle Bronze II period. The ruler of Byblos contemporary with the Ur III period, whose name is normalized probably correctly as *Entin,* from *Yantin,* illustrates a phonetic change that was not characteristic of the Coastal region, but abundantly illustrated from the inland dialects. The West knows the shift that occurs later from *ay* > *e,* but never independently from *ya* > *e* so far as our evidence now goes. There is absolutely nothing in the available evidence from the Byblos Syllabic texts that could conceivably explain such a name as *Entin.*

This is merely a lead illustration of the thesis that the Early Bronze Age language of Byblos is just as far removed from Ugaritic as the language of Chaucer is from that of the Anglo-Saxon Chronicle, but the discontinuity was not and could not be absolute. The difficulty of the decipherment of the Syllabic texts does not stem primarily from the strangeness of the writing system, for nearly all of the later alphabetic signs are already used, though often in a completely unexpected and at first glance unrecognizable form. The same observation may also be true of the Proto-Sinaitic inscriptions. The assumption that they are "Canaanite" seems to dominate all discussion and attempts at decipherment since Albright's early and unsuccessful attempt. The utilization of Ugaritic as the base for their decipherment is roughly analogous to an attempt to decipher Scandinavian Runes on the basis of Cicero's Latin.

Let us look at some of the contrasts that I believe can now be reasonably established between the Early Bronze coastal dialect and the Middle Bronze dialect that has long been called either "Canaanite" or "Northwest Semitic," depending on which scholar of a past generation conferred the degree on the modern scholar. Current speculation about the nature of the linguistic substratum exhibited in the Ebla texts has led to its designation as "Canaanite" also—which is about as logical as calling Old French Old English because modern English preserves a number of vocabulary items deriving from Old French. (I shall refrain from further references to psychological inertia.)

LINGUISTIC CONTRASTS

1. *Sibilant shift.* The causative /s/ is written with the *samek* sign, which is itself clearly a representation of the Egyptian *djed* pillar. It means evidently 'pillar', has the syllabic value /*sa*/ and contrasts to the *šafel* of Ugaritic and some Hebrew and Aramaic remnants. The *s*- causative survives in the inscriptions of Old South Arabic.

2. *The sibilant system.* The three sibilants, *sin, šin, ṯa* are fairly well attested in a system that has close similarity to pre-Islamic Arabic and later Arabic. At the Early Bronze to Middle Bronze transition, there was a massive sibilant shift that was not carried through systematically, as no such sound change is in the formative period of a language. As a result, some of the original /*s*/ sounds were preserved as /*s*/ as late as Biblical Hebrew (and these therefore coincided with Arabic). In other words, the /*s*/ shifted to /*š*/. Compare Hebrew *ns*ʾ to Ugaritic *nš*ʾ. In different dialects the shift took place in different vocabulary items: there was no "law," until it was concocted by grammarians and schoolteachers of professional scribes. (These we know already existed in Palestine in the Amarna Age.)

3. *The conjuctions.* Even though the Byblos Syllabic corpus is so meager, there is abundant evidence that the major conjunction is the syllable *pa*-. It introduces what seems to be a major change of subject, and certainly is identical to Arabic *fa*-. Inland dialect seems to have had ʾ*ap* = Hebr. ʾ*af*,

which is phonetically quite different, though the semantic function is analogous. There is no evidence at all for a prefixed conjunction *wa-*. Quite frequent is a suffixed *-ma* that usually cannot be translated. It is probably the origin of the Late Bronze and Hebrew enclitic *mem*. I have been playing with the idea that a suffixed *-ma* as a very weak conjunction may have led to the prefixed *wa-*, but against this is the fact that the *wa-* is already attested at the contemporary or earlier Eblaite.

4. *The causative.* Though the forms found so far are in part *st-* causatives (causative-reflexives), it is clear that this dialect has both *h-* and *s-* causatives. It is interesting that this becomes a systematic contrast attested in later Old South Arabic dialects from Yemen.

5. The *remarkable frequency of st- causative reflexive forms* corresponds also to the unusual frequency of this form in Old South Arabic.

6. One of the most unexpected aspects of this language is that fact that *Ugaritic cognates are relatively rare.* This has been one of the most powerful phenomena that compelled the conclusion that Ugaritic cannot be merely a descendant from the Early Bronze language of the coastal plain of Canaan. Though I have not yet made a statistical tabulation of relative frequency of cognates, it is classical and pre-Islamic Arabic that have almost always, together with Biblical Hebrew, furnished the cognate roots that yielded meaning in the context of the emerging decipherment.

7. There is, apart from the above mentioned enclitic *-ma, no trace of a mimation or nunation,* unless it be the sign that I read, for lack of a better idea, as a final *-m*. However, the function of this sign coincides in no discernible way with the mimation of Old Babylonian, or the nunation of classical Arabic, and unfortunately there is no certainty at all that the sign actually does represent a final */-m/*.

8. There is a *remarkable frequency of* a variety of forms that demand analysis as *verbal nouns.* Grammarians have identified some 40 different forms of the verbal noun of the Ist form in Arabic, and it is not yet clear just how many there are in the Byblos Syllabic corpus: certainly far more than the usual absolute and construct "infinitives," or the active and passive "participles" of traditional grammars of Iron Age West Semitic.

9. The *signs* of the Byblos syllabary *have remarkable formal and functional (i.e., phonetic) coincidence with those of Proto-Sinaitic.* The latter are in several cases more archaic typologically than the signs of Byblos Syllabic, in that they are much more "pictographic" than Byblos Syllabic. This strongly suggests caution in dating texts of early periods on the basis of an alleged evolution from "pictographic" to "linear" forms, or even at all on the basis of merely formal traits. Such formal evolutionary

schemes may be comforting to the modern academician, but they may easily have no necessary connection with ancient social and cultural reality.

10. Finally, *the priority of a clearly syllabic writing system* to a later alphabetic one is beyond question. The transition must have been made quite easy by the fact that already in the Byblos Syllabic writing system there are a number of contexts within which the vocalic element signalled by the sign is not functional. In other words, to use the term applied in similar circumstances by those who have worked with the Minoan Linear A and B scripts, the signs have "dead vowels." From this to a system in which all the vowels are "dead" and therefore non-existent would have been very simple, particularly since the resulting system had only a third of the total number of signs that were necessary to the syllabic system. Almost all of the later alphabetic signs occur already in more archaic form (usually, but not always) in the Byblos Syllabic texts.

CONCLUSION

1. With the demise of the Early Bronze urban civilizations with high population density, a migration of some magnitude took place into the region that had previously contrasted culturally and linguistically to the migration source. This contrast was primarily between the "Coastal Dialect" area that lay between the mountains and the sea coast from the border of Egypt to the Jebel Aqra, and the "Inland Dialect" area that included the fertile regions of North Syria, the Syrian Jezireh, and perhaps, to the South, Transjordan. It remains to be seen how great a contrast existed in the Early Bronze period between the North Central Syrian (i.e., Ebla region) and the Syrian Jezireh (i.e., Amorite proper) areas of high population density. It is entirely justified to posit some considerable contrast between these two regions, but it seems at present that this contrast was not nearly so great as between them and the Coastal region.

2. The Amorite migrations carried with them cultural and linguistic traits that were new to the regions of both the East and the West. To the East the linguistic innovations combined with existing spoken dialects to become rapidly Old Babylonian and Old Assyrian. To the West, this Inland Dialect superimposed upon the existing Coastal Dialect resulted in Ugaritic and other Coastal region local dialects that were quite analogous to Ugaritic. One such is the language underlying the Amarna Glosses in Palestine. The old question whether Ugaritic is "Canaanite" is a non-question that merely quibbles about labels. What is important is the similarity of the historical process that displaced an older language

in those regions where it was displaced. In the East, the older language (Old Akkadian) died out forever. In the West the older language was modified especially in vocabulary, but retained its basic linguistic structure. It is this fact that led nineteenth-century scholars to rely on Classical Arabic as the primary model for reconstructing "Primitive Semitic." Only now are we beginning to see the specific historical context and historical process underlying the Arabic model for "Primitive Semitic."

3. Language is the primary means of conveying ideological (over against technological and social organization) aspects of culture. But language never communicates in contextual vacuum. What it communicates is inextricably bound up with customs, ideas, and values. Through the language is communicated the content of legal and religious traditions, and there is good reason to identify as Amorite the myth of cosmic conflict (Marduk vs. Tiamat, and Baal vs. Yam), and also the content of the "case law" tradition that underlies both the Code of Ḫammurapi and the Covenant Code of Exodus 21–23. Both bodies are to be traced not to Amorite literary forms but to traditional Amorite customary folk tradition and no doubt folk ways of solving inner-societal disputes, based upon concepts of right and justice that enabled the society to exist at all.

4. Extremely closely connected with this is the fact that a surprisingly large body of vocabulary of primary significance to biblical theology seems clearly to be Amorite in origin. Roots that are very productive in Biblical Hebrew, such as *yṯᶜ*, *ṣdq*, *špṭ*, *ḥsd*, *nqm*, most closely associated with religious ethical concepts, seem to be Amorite in origin, and most of them continue as productive roots also in pre-Islamic Arabic. Much more work needs to be done, however, in the field of comparative lexicography before we can be confident about systemic semantic contrasts between Coastal and Inland dialects of the Early Bronze Age. It is clearly a very subtle problem that requires sophisticated methods, but the difficulties involved should not obscure the fact that lexical contrasts are just as much an index of dialect differentiation as is phonetics or morphology, and even the most important.

5. Finally, the entire field of onomastics is also involved. It is increasingly clear that the compound-sentence name type is particularly characteristic of the Inland dialect region, though it includes also Mesopotamia, of course. The Coastal dialect names seem always to have been strongly mono-verbal—one word names, though not exclusively so. Far too little evidence exists so far, but what we have points strongly in this direction. In addition, the most characteristic Amorite onomastic forms such as *sumu-ilu= šemuʾel*, and other theophoric names including kinship terms, cannot be explained at present on the basis of Coastal Dialect tradition. This Amorite onomastic tradition is attested already in the

Execration Texts from Egypt and in the dynastic royal names from Byblos during the Middle Bronze period—and most importantly, exhibiting the sibilant shift already in such forms as *šemu-abi, Yapa-šemu-abi,* and the like.

The conclusion is inescapable that the Amorite migration from Northeast and probably North Syria into Palestine, Transjordan, the Sinai and Egypt had a diverse impact upon local culture and language. In the western heartland, the Amorite language caused radical phonetic and lexical dislocation leading to quite new phonetic structures and probably even verbal forms. In the non-urban scene, it added merely new lexical items and to some extent proper names, but introduced relatively minor disturbances of the earlier phonetic and morphological structures. One of the most important bodies of evidence for this thesis still remains to be made available, and it is curiously the most ancient corpus of specifically alphabetic inscriptions that we have—the Proto-Sinaitic Inscriptions, which almost certainly now should be identified as proto-Midianite, for it is in the regions remote from the primary locus of radical linguistic and cultural change that original and very ancient linguistic systems are almost always to be found.

Mari: The View from Ebla

Piotr Michalowski

The University of Michigan

The discovery of extensive third millennium remains at a variety of archaeological sites has revitalized the study of the history of Syria and has focused new attention on the early civilizations of the Near East.[1] Among the discoveries of the last two decades, the ancient city of Ebla has attracted the most attention, and the cuneiform archives of Tell Mardikh have achieved much notoriety. Although much of the publicity that greeted the recovery of these texts was harmful and misleading, the difficult task of publication of the tablets has proceeded with admirable speed. A substantial portion of the recovered archives has already been made available to scholars, and therefore we are in a position to reexamine and redefine many of the early assumptions about the epigraphical finds from Ebla.[2] The texts published to date do not support many of the early claims about the organization of the Ebla state, but this is understandable as the study of these difficult documents progresses. At the present time, I would venture that one should posit the following working hypotheses: the archives cover only about one generation of the activities of a presently undefined organization within the city, the chief administrators of that organization, and possibly even the rulers of the city-state, who were perhaps Ebrium and Ibbi-Zikir, and there is little evidence for the rule of other individuals. The documents record only a limited sphere of activities, and the geographic horizon of the texts extends through northern Syria, the Habur region, the Euphrates corridor down to Mari, and to some cities farther east.

Author's note: A full version of this paper has been published as "Third Millennium Contacts: Observations on the Relationships Between Mari and Ebla," *Journal of the American Oriental Society* 105 (1985) 293–302 (= Michalowski [1985]). There the reader will find a more complete explanation of my current opinions on various aspects of the Ebla archives which are only summarized in the opening paragraphs of this article.

[1]No systematic overview of recent archaeological activity in Syria is currently available. For discussions of third millennium sites in that geographical area, see Weiss (1983, 1985).

[2]For a complete listing of all Ebla texts published prior to January 1, 1984, see Beld, Hallo, and Michalowski (1984).

Mari is, together with Kakmium and Manuwat, one of the three most commonly attested place names in the available Ebla texts.[3] It would be next to impossible, and in this context quite useless, to list and analyze all the available references to persons and goods coming from or going to Mari. Instead, I shall concentrate on a few central matters which must be discussed as we build the foundations for future research on the topic. There are fifty-seven presently known pre-Sargonic texts from Mari, of which only a handful have been published.[4] Recent archaeological research, moreover, has exposed impressive, well-preserved, third millennium remains in that city, and thus one can expect that our knowledge of this period will be expanded in the near future.[5]

The Ebla documentation concerning Mari is difficult to analyze. The texts preserve the names of nine individuals who, according to modern scholarship, were the rulers of Mari. Following is a list of these "kings," as proposed in a recent article by A. Archi, with their attested titles.[6] Many of these persons are mentioned in the well-known letter of Enna-Dagan to an en at Ebla.[7]

Name	*Title*
Saʾumu+	en
Ištup-šar+	lugal
Iplul-Il*	en, lugal
NI-zi	lugal
Enna-Dagan*	en, lugal
Ikun-šar	en
Igi	lugal
Ḫidaʾar	lugal
Šura	lugal (?)

[+ = mentioned *only* in the Enna-Dagan letter; * = mentioned in the Enna-Dagan letter.]

I must partly sidestep the issue of the meaning of the words en and lugal and will proceed to analyze the data without any prejudice on this matter.[8] If the Ebla material does not cover more than one generation,

[3]For Kakmium, see Röllig (1977), although one must keep in mind the fact that it is only an assumption that the Kakmium of the Ebla tablets is identical with the city by that name known from Mesopotamian documents. Manuwat has yet to be identified.

[4]On these tablets, see Charpin (1982).

[5]A preliminary report can be found in Margueron (1983).

[6]Archi (1981a) and, more recently, Pomponio (1983).

[7]This text is now fully available in Pettinato (1980b).

[8]There is at present no compelling evidence which would clearly indicate that en in the Ebla texts means 'solitary ruler'. The matter is further complicated by the fact that the terminology at Mari could have been different. For a discussion see Michalowski (1985).

then we would not expect to find nine contemporary rulers attested for Mari. The first two of these persons, marked by a plus sign on the chart, only occur in the Enna-Dagan letter and may refer to individuals who ruled before the actual period of the preserved archives. That still leaves us with seven individuals who are designated as en or lugal in the administrative documents. An analysis of these texts reveals that the matter is much more complicated than would appear from the short preliminary study provided by Archi. One suspects that either these persons ruled for a short time each, or that many, if not all, were contemporary, and that a city could have more than one en and possibly more than one lugal at a time. Important, in this context, are the texts which mention two ens of Manuwat.[9] Another tablet, only partially published, appears to record an unspecified number of ens of the city of Armi.[10] If these individuals were indeed contemporary, then it may also be true that the Enna-Dagan letter does not refer to past historical events, but to a series of contemporary expeditions by various generals of Mari. According to this hypothesis, we would have to include the first two "rulers" on the list, Saʾumu and Ištup-šar, who are documented only in the Enna-Dagan text, among the ens and lugals of Mari at that time. However, while it is tempting to conjecture that all of these officials were contemporary, there are data which complicate the matter and may indeed contradict this reconstruction.

An account published in Archi (1981a) 132–33 (TM.75.G.1953) records a series of transactions labeled níg-ba, traditionally translated 'gift', from, or to, persons connected with the city of Mari. The structure of the text consists of three sections, within each of which there is a sequence of níg-bas, from, or to, a person, the AB×ÁŠ.AB×ÁŠ of Mari, and the e-gi$_4$-maškim.e-gi$_4$-maškim of Mari.[11] The first two sections end

[9]ARET 3 271 iii 2′–3′ and 338 i 5′–6′.

[10]See, possibly, níg-ba en en ar-mi.ki, in TM.75.G.10188 obv. ix 7–11, quoted, without context, in Archi (1981a) 134.

[11]The function of the AB×ÁŠ.AB×ÁŠ in the Ebla texts is not clear. It is tempting to see these 'elders' as leaders of the main family groupings of the local elite, but the evidence available is simply too limited for speculation. The e-gi$_4$-maškim (e-gi-maškim, maškim-e-gi$_4$, maškim-e-gi) officials have been discussed by Pettinato (1980a) 45. Note that a recently published Ur III version of the "Names and Professions List" contains the entry PA.AL, to be read either as šabra, or as ugula máḫ, in place of the e-gi-maškim of the Early Dynastic version: Fales and Krispijn (1979–80) 41 line 6, and commentary on p. 44. The Ebla version of this lexical text has e-gi$_4$-maškim (Pettinato 1981b: 127; Archi 1981c: 185, see also Milano 1980: 16). The word occurs in still another Ebla lexical text, followed by ugula nagar (Pettinato 1981b: 208 line v 21). More interesting is the entry lú kas$_4$-e-gi$_4$ in "Sumerian Word List A" from Ebla (Pettinato 1981b: 137 line vi 8). Is it possible that maškim (= PA.KAS$_4$) is to be read ugula KAS$_4$ 'overseer of the KAS$_4$', and that e-gi$_{(4)}$ is a gloss to KAS$_4$? This would help to explain why it is followed by ugula nagar in another text and why the Ur III lexical text utilized šabra, probably to be understood as ugula máḫ in this case, in the place of this entry. In summary, I would, with due caution, suggest

with a clause which begins *in* UD.UD, possibly meaning 'during the time of', or simply 'when'. Schematically, the structure of the parts of the text which are of interest here may be represented thus:

A. *ip-lul-il* lugal *ma-rí*.ki	*in* UD.UD *ip-lul-il* lu[gal] *m*[*a*]-*r*[*í*.ki]
B. NI-*zi* [l]ugal [*ma-rí*.ki]	*in* UD.UD NI-*zi*
C. *en-na-da-gan*	

The evidence of this text would suggest that NI-*zi* followed Iplul-il as lugal of Mari and that Enna-Dagan was not yet lugal at the time this transaction was recorded. Accordingly, one could interpret the order of appearance and titulary of Iplul-il and Enna-Dagan in the Enna-Dagan letter as evidence for a similar interpretation; Iplul-il, then, would have been first an en, and only later a lugal, while Enna-Dagan was only en at the time the letter was composed.

There are, however, important reasons to question this reconstruction. Most important is the fact that the same officials are mentioned time and again on tablets which also include the names of ens and lugals of Mari. I have tabulated some of this data in table 1. As one can readily see, there is a great degree of overlap between the names of officials who occur in texts which mention NI-*zi*, Iplul-il, Enna-Dagan and Ḫidaʾar. Unfortunately, some texts which contain references to these rulers of Mari have only been excerpted by Archi, and therefore could not be used in this study.

Three other individuals have been identified as probable rulers of Mari: Igi, Ikun-šar, and Šura. Igi is attested only once as lugal of that city, but nothing can be said about the document since it remains unpublished.[12] The case of Ikun-šar is uncertain since there is only one passing reference to his tenure as an en.[13] The final ruler on the list, Šura, may well not have been a person at all. His name has been crucial, in fact, for the commonly accepted notion that Mari was subject to Ebla and is the motivation behind the idea that a son of Ebrium assumed the throne of Mari after it was supposedly conquered by Ebla. First, there is absolutely no indication in the published documentation of any military expedition, successful or not, from Ebla against Mari. Second, the son of Ebrium who purportedly became ruler of Mari was named Šura-Damu, and it can hardly be assumed that Šura and Šura-Damu were the same person. But, even granted these assumptions, there is reason to suspect the very

that the word is to be read egi_x or ugula egi_x and that it possibly refers to ambassadors, or chief messengers of various cities. For a recent discussion see also Krebernik (1984: 324), who cites the parallel between maškim.e-gi_4 and *dag-da-su* in two literary texts from Ebla. These two tablets are now published in Edzard (1984: nos. 1 and 3).

12TM.75.G.2235, cited by Archi (1981a) 162.

13TM.75.G.1321, also cited without context by Archi (1981a) 162.

Table 1.

Text	*Pub.*	*"Ruler"*	*Title*	*Other Officials*
TM.75.G.1299	137	Enna-Dagan	—	A L T
		NI-*zi*	—	
TM.75.G.1987	139	NI-*zi*	—	G
TM.75.G.1866	139	NI-*zi*	lugal M.	A
TM.75.G.1293	141	Enna-Dagan	lugal	I
TM.75.G.1564	142	Enna-Dagan	—	A G
TM.75.G.1368	MEE 2, 43	Enna-Dagan	—	I Gu
		Ḫidaʾar	—	
		NI-*zi*	lugal	
TM.75.G.1233	145	Enna-Dagan	—	L T G I Gu
		Ḫidaʾar	—	
TM.75.G.1657	ARET 2, 4	Iplul-il	lugal	A L T G I

Notes to the table: A = Ar-ennum, L = Ladat, T = *Ti-ti-na/nu*, G = GIBIL-*zi/za-il*, I = Ikna-Damu, Gu = *Gul-la* (the brother of Enna-Dagan: Archi 1981a: 142, TM.75.G.1271, obv. IV 4–6: *gul-la*/ŠEŠ / *en-na-*^{d}*da-gan*). Steinkeller (1984: 33–34) has suggested that *Gul-la* may be same person as *gul-la* / dumu / *kum*-BÀD / šeš lugal 'Gulla, son of *Kum*-BÀD, brother of the king', who is attested in a votive inscription from Mari (Dossin 1967b: 319 M. 2278 1–4). If this is so, then it would strengthen the case for the identification of Iplul-il of the Ebla text with the ruler of the same name who is known from the votive inscriptions from Mari. Note that Ḫidaʾar also appears in ARET 4 21 iv 1–2 in connection with Mari, but without a title. None of the aforementioned officials occurs in this text.

existence of anyone named Šura as ruler of Mari. The only evidence for this is the "year-date" diš mu šu-ra lugal *ma-rí*.ki.[14] Although the patterns of similar "year-names" suggest that šu-ra is indeed a personal name, the matter is far from certain in view of our ignorance of these formulas. It is more important, however, that the element šu-ra occurs in different contexts which suggest that it may have to be interpreted not as a proper name but as a verb or, at the most, as a verbal noun.[15]

Thus we are left with four or six persons who may have been either the sovereigns, or, more likely, simply important high officials of the independent city-state of Mari. One of these, Iplul-il, is homophonous with a person who bore the title lugal Mari and is known from statue inscriptions found in the pre-Sargonic levels of that city. He is thus the only serious candidate for the role of ruler of this city.[16]

[14]TM.74.G.101, cited by Pettinato (1975) 367, and (1979) 3, as well as Archi (1981a) 162.

[15]See, for example, ARET 2 34 ii 3 and ARET 3 1 viii 8′, as well as ten other occurrences in the latter volume; see the index, p. 389. ARET 2 34 i 8 also contains the negated form nu šu-ra.

[16]See Dossin (1967b) and n 12 above.

Recently, it has been suggested that the Sumerian King List may preserve the traces of names of kings of Mari who may be the same individuals as those who occur in the Ebla records. M. Geller (n.d.) proposes, on the basis of collations by M. Green and E. Leichty, that PBS 13 1 v 14 is to be read NÁ-*zi* dumu x x and to identify this person with the NI-*zi* of the Ebla tablets. Even if we are to accept the interpretation of the broken sign in the King List as NÁ, which is by no means certain, there would still be problems with this proposal. The main objection to this identification is that it is based on the unlikely coincidence of two unknown readings. The sign NI is used at Ebla with a variety of readings, among them *ni*, bu_4, and *ià*, and it is not presently known how to read this sign in the name NI-*zi*. Even if it should turn out that the name began with the syllable *ni*, one would still have to explain the unique use of NÁ with a syllabic value *ni* in the King List. Further, Geller reads col. v line 29 of the Weld-Blundell prism (OECT 2 1) as [x (x) *s*]*a*-*ᵓu*-*me* mu 30 *ì*-*ak* on the basis of his own collation and proposes to identify this name with Saᵓumu (*sá*-*ù*-*mu*) of the Ebla sources. With even more caution, he suggests that v 30 may preserve the end of the name of Ikun-šar. Independently, J. Cooper (1986) has noted the possibility that the names of NI-*zi* and either Ištup-šar or Ikun-šar may have been preserved in the King List. He stresses, however, that "the discrepancy between the two lists are too great either to insist on these identifications or to put very much credence in the King List's testimony."[17] Thus, the suggestions of Geller and Cooper, while proposed with due caution, can hardly be accepted without further corroboration. Indeed, it would be quite surprising if the King List, which is quite broken in the early section dealing with Mari, were to preserve the names of precisely those Early Dynastic rulers of Mari who happened to be contemporary with the accidentally preserved documentation of a short period of life in the city of Ebla.

The results of this study are only preliminary and are intended primarily to open up discussion on various basic matters before further hypotheses are built upon still shaky ground. New information will undoubtedly force drastic revisions of many of my conclusions, but it is time that we question many of the primary assumptions about the terminology of the Ebla texts, as well as of the internal chronology and structures of power which have been reconstructed largely on the basis of unquestioned general assumptions. The sheer size of the data base and the difficulties of reading and defining many seemingly transparent lexical items suggest that the answers to many of the problems raised here will only come from a thorough study of computerized data. This will allow us to use a variety of tools, from the traditional study of prosopography to more complex statistical techniques, which will allow for the intelligent utilization of the rich archaeological and epigraphic materials from third millennium Syria and Mesopotamia.

[17]Cooper (1986) 4 n 12.

LÚ*ebbum* as a Professional Title at Mari

M. DELOY PACK

Brigham Young University

INTRODUCTION

The term *ebbum* has appeared several times in the Mari correspondence, and the question has arisen whether it should be considered a title of an administrative functionary, or merely an adjective which may sometimes be used substantivally.[1]

The adjective *ebbu* occurs in the lexical lists in association with *ellu* and *namru*.[2] *Ellu* may be defined as (1) "clean," "pure," (2) "holy," "sacred," (3) "free," and "noble"; and *namru* as "bright," "shining," and "sparkling."[3] *Ebbu* should have similar meanings. It is defined in the CAD as "polished," "shining," "lustrous," "clean," "pure" (in a cultic sense), and "holy."[4] These definitions apply to objects, animals, and rites, but *ebbu* also follows the vocable LÚ, indicating that it is applicable to people.

In two lexical LÚ series, *ebbu* occurs in association with *kīnu*, *qīpu*, and *ša libba kīnu*.[5] *Kīnu* may be defined as "permanent," "true," "real," "genuine," "legitimate," "upright," "just," "trustworthy," and "honest."[6] *Qīpu* is defined as "trustworthy," "trusted (person)," or "one who has been entrusted."[7] *Ša libba kīnu* would be something like "he who is true of heart." The meanings of *ebbu* should fall within the same semantic range when it is an adjective modifying the noun LÚ, *awīlu ebbu*, hence the CAD's translations "trustworthy, proper."[8]

1This contribution is based on a section of the author's doctoral dissertation, written under the supervision of Drs. Barry Eichler and Erle Leichty, and has benefited greatly from their suggestions. See Pack (1981), and especially 204–40.

2See CAD E, lexical section s.v. *ebbu*.

3See CAD and AHw s.v. *ellu* and *nam/wru(m)*.

4CAD E 4 (a) 1.

5See Civil (1969) p. 98: 135k–m; p. 184: 28–33; CAD E 39b) 2. a) 1′ lexical section.

6See CAD and AHw s.v. *kīnu*.

7See CAD and AHw s.v. *qīpu(m)*.

8CAD E 3(b) 2.

The vocable LÚ, however, may be considered simply a determinative, indicating that *ebbu* is an occupation or office held by someone. In this case, *ebbu* would be a substantive and might not even be related to the adjective, or, if so, it might acquire meanings removed from those of the adjective.

The CAD does not recognize a substantival usage of *ebbum*. It translates all the Mari references adjectivally as "trustworthy" (person).[9] The AHw does recognize a substantival usage at Mari but retains the same definitions as given in the CAD.[10]

Generally, the translations of the ARMT series have differed significantly from these dictionary entries, and even though the most recent translation of *ebbum* in the ARMT series conforms to that of the standard dictionaries, it seems doubtful that all those who have worked on the Mari materials would be in agreement—at least with respect to certain contexts.[11] Birot was quite emphatic in his defense of the *ebbum* as an official (*fonctionnaire*), not just a trustworthy person.[12]

That *ebbum* may be a substantive, and LÚ *ebbum* an occupational title, receives support from the fact that in the plural it appears in the form *ebbū* which grammatically corresponds to a plural substantive rather than a plural adjective, which would have the form *ebbūtum*. If one were to use grammatical form as a basic criterion in translating, one could expect two terms, one adjectival, the other substantival, for these plural vocables.[13] Translation of the singular, *ebbum*, is complicated by the fact that the form is applicable to both a substantive and an adjective.

Of the four most common translations used for LÚ.MEŠ. *ebbū(tum)*, three are substantives and indicate a function. These are: "census takers" (*recenseurs*), "accountants" (*comptables*), and "controllers" (*contrôleurs*). The fourth, "trustworthy (persons)" (*fidèles*), an adjective, solely describes a character trait. Since a consensus on the meaning of LÚ

[9]CAD E 4(a) 2. a) 2′ Note that, except for ARM 7 195, all the Mari references published up to 1958 had *ebbum* following LÚ, so that it could be considered an attributive adjective. Only in later volumes did *ebbum* occur independently. The entry *ebbūt* PN (ARM 7 195) does appear in the CAD, however. No translation is given. Durand and Kupper in ARMT 21 and 22 (1983) both use "*contrôleurs*."

[10]AHw 180(b) 7, "*etwa geeignet, verlasslich . . .* b) *als Subst.*"

[11]In the most recent publications, Rouault refers to them as "*contrôleurs*" and "*inspecteurs*" in ARMT 18 (1977), whereas Dossin translates, "'*fideles,*'" in ARMT 10 (1978).

[12]ARMT 9 p. 317 n 1.

[13]See von Soden (1952) 77, section 61f and k. *Ebbū* may occur alone, or in the combinations LÚ.MEŠ *ebbū* (ARM 3 19 and *passim*), and LÚ *ebbū*.MEŠ (ARMT 13 36: 37). Kupper long ago suggested that there might be a distinction between the *ebbū* and *ebbūtum*. See Kupper (1950b) 102 n 7. Finet, on the other hand, listed both forms under one definition in ARMT 15 183, as does the CAD.

ebbum has not yet been reached, we shall review the evidence from the texts at Mari to determine in what contexts the three forms *ebbum, ebbū,* and *ebbūtum* appear, and consequently, what translation(s) to apply to each or all of them. We shall begin with the plural forms *ebbūtum* and *ebbū,* considering them separately to see if there is any difference in meaning, and conclude with the singular form.

CONTEXTS IN WHICH LÚ.(MEŠ) *ebbūtu(m)* APPEARS

There are three texts in which LÚ.(MEŠ) *ebbūtu(m)* appears (sometimes the MEŠ is left out).

In ARM 1 74 Šamši-Adad wrote to Yasmaḫ-Addu saying he had sent twenty minas of silver for the mounting of a statue (l. 4). The accounts (*nikkassū*) of the statues made in Šubat-Enlil, as well as at his location, were being prepared in the temple of Aššur (ll. 3–7). Of the lines which follow, those relevant to our discussion are:

> 15 The tablets of the accounts of the silver of that statue, the silver of the mountings, the work which is mounted on the statue . . . .
>
> Rev. 25 According to his (or its, i.e., the statue's) very tablet, those *ebbūtum* and the amount of silver of the entire work which was affixed to the statue shall be inscribed and set up in Aššur's temple (ll. 25–28).[14]
>
> . . .
>
> 31 . . . of days, those LÚ.MEŠ *ebbūtum* . . . (just) as the accounts are being prepared here [at] this time in Aššur's temple, have prepared there [in] Dagan's [tem]ple accounts of the statue. In connection with the preparing of the accounts let the LÚ.MEŠ *e[bbūtum]*, [those who] have made [t]hat sta[t]ue, reside in [Dagan's] temple. Ma[y they prepare] the ac[co]unts of your statue, (and) the report of thos[e] account[s] . . . (ll. 31–38)

The context is clearly that of accounts made with respect to silver being used for mountings of statues. The LÚ.MEŠ *ebbūtum* were also clearly involved. Both their names and the quantity of silver used were to be recorded (ll. 25–27). Were they being held responsible for the figures? Lines 31–32 are too broken to give a coherent translation, and consequently, just what the LÚ.MEŠ *ebbūtum* were doing is not clear, although the context seems to be that of preparing accounts (*nikkassū*, ll. 23–33), and Birot's conclusion that the preparation of the accounts

[14]Finet is probably correct in considering *ebbūtim šunūti* a scribal error for *ebbūtum šunu* in (1956) 185, section 66t.

with respect to the silver used in making the statue(s) was entrusted to the *ebbūtum* who carried out the work in the temples of Aššur and Dagan seems well justified.[15]

Dossin translated *ebbūtum* hesitantly with "responsables(?)," an adjective corresponding to the form of the word. "Trustworthy (ones)" would be another possible translation but not as directly relevant to the context.

The LÚ.MEŠ *ebbūtum* appear again in ARM HC B.63, dealt with first by Jean and later by Finet.[16] According to this text, Tebi-girišu had taken inventory (*upaqqidam*)[17] of a certain palace, and determined (*īmur*) that there was a shortage (of supplies or personnel), ll. 3–5. Previously, when Asqudum had inventoried the palace, he had assigned twelve men to each "plow (crew)," but this had not been sufficient.[18] Now, even though the LÚ.MEŠ *ebbūtum* had determined (*īmurū*) that the cutting to be done was great, they had only assigned ten men to a crew (through line 14).[19]

The precise function of the LÚ.MEŠ *ebbūtum* in this text is not clear. They may have determined that the yield was great simply by noting the condition of the crop and estimating on the basis of experience, or made some calculations based on samples. Whether it was they or Tebi-girišu who determined that each plow(crew) should consist of ten members is also not certain.[20] They may have "assigned" (*īsikū*) the members in the sense that they drew up lists assigning persons to specific crews. The activities of the LÚ.MEŠ *ebbūtum* which seem to be indicated by this text are simple computations and possibly registration or compiling personnel lists.

Since the plural adjective form, *ebbūtum,* is employed, the translation "trustworthy persons" is possible. The translation "and the trustworthy men have determined that the cutting (to be done) is great, now the trustworthy men have arrived and assigned ten men to a crew" does make sense, but one feels a lack of precision as well as relevance to the context. There does not seem to be any reason why their trustworthiness

[15]ARMT 9 p. 317 n 1.

[16]For ARM HC B.63, see Jean (1948b) 72–77, text no. 11, and Finet (1956) 58–60.

[17]The basic idea of *paqādum/puqqudum* in this West Semitic usage seems to be to set in order, or inspect, often involving the taking of an inventory of personnel or supplies, especially to determine if there are any shortages. See AHw 825(b) ii 4), *"mustern, überprüfen;"* 826(a), D G 2); and Gelb (1980) 28: *PQD* "to order." See also Speiser (1958) 20–23.

[18]Just what was the connection between inventorying and setting "plow(crew)" quotas is not clear to me, but the repeated juxtaposition must be more than coincidental. Perhaps *puqqudum* should be translated "supply," the plow (crews) or their rations being supplied by the central palace at Mari.

[19]Cf. Finet (1956) 61, note to lines 7–8.

[20]They may simply have been carrying out Tebi-girišu's orders. Cf. Finet (1956) 61, note to lines 7–8.

should be emphasized any more than that for any administrator or functionary.

From a contextual point of view, either "registrars" or "controllers" appear to be more suitable translations. If the LÚ.MEŠ *ebbūtum* did not actually set the size of the crews but rather assigned people to crews, "registrars" best suits their activity. If they actually set the size of the crews as well as assigning people to them, an element of regulation enters in which would justify the translation "controllers."[21]

The LÚ.MEŠ *ebbūtum* appear in a controlling or supervisory capacity in some salary or ration payment texts found at Chagar Bazar.[22] These texts list groups of scribes (DUMU.MEŠ É.DUB.BI) under the supervision (NÍG.ŠU) of certain individuals. The list is summarized as being the rations of the LÚ.MEŠ *ebbūtum* on the day of the census (SÁ.SAG LÚ.MEŠ *eb-bu-tim i-nu-ma te-bi-ib-tim*). LÚ.MEŠ *ebbūtim* could refer to both the supervisors and their scribes, but it seems more likely that it refers to the supervisors. At any rate it certainly refers to them because in *Iraq* 7 no. 978 only they are mentioned.

Although the tablets do not specifically say so, it seems reasonable to conclude that the LÚ.MEŠ *ebbūtum* were "connected with the *tebibtum*."[23] The census, then, was carried out by the LÚ.MEŠ *ebbūtum*, assisted by scribes.

Since they were connected with a census, "census takers" seems a logical translation of LÚ.MEŠ *ebbūtum* for these texts, although their specific involvement is not detailed. There is, however, another term, *mubbibū*, which appears in the Mari correspondence, clearly meaning "census takers."[24] Since taking a census is the registration of a population, perhaps the more general term "registrars" mentioned above would be applicable. "Controllers" is also a reasonable translation if taken to mean some sort of supervisory control. Although there may have been some enumerations or summations in connection with the census, a translation such as "accountants" is not very applicable. Even less so is

[21]In the *editio princeps*, Jean (1948b) translated the LÚ.MEŠ *ebbū(tum)* of ARM HC B.63: 12, 13, and 34, "*les (hommes) recrutés*," "those who had been recruited." Later, Finet (1956) changed this to "the recruiters" ("*les recruteurs*"), but there is no evidence that there was any actual recruiting taking place. In the first instance, ll. 13ff., the LÚ.MEŠ *ebbūtum* could have been dealing simply with personnel lists, assigning to each crew a certain number of people whose names would have been drawn from census lists made for just such a purpose. In the second, ll. 33ff., they simply proposed a fixed payment for the work to be done. Rather than recruiting, they were involved in distributing. So, one may set aside the translations of Jean and Finet.

[22]Chagar Bazar, a site in the upper Ḫabur triangle, was apparently under the influence, if not the actual control, of Yasmaḫ-Addu at this time. See Gadd (1940) 22–24.

[23]Gadd (1940) 54.

[24]See ARM 1 129: 26 and 87: 18; AHw 665(b), "*Musterungsbeamter*"; in contrast to CAD M/2 159(a).

the vague "trustworthy persons," even though it is adjectival, corresponding to the form *ebbūtum*.

SUMMARY: LÚ.(MEŠ) *ebbūtu(m)*

Three texts from the Mari kingdom mention the LÚ.MEŠ *ebbūtum*. In ARM 1 74 they appear to be those responsible for keeping the accounts related to precious metal mountings of statues. The adjectival translation "trustworthy persons" might be appropriate for an operation involving precious metals, but there is no particular emphasis on trustworthiness in the text other than what might be inferred from the fact that the accounts are to be prepared in a sanctuary.[25] If, on the other hand, accuracy was desired, "accountants" would be a good term for those who prepared the accounts.

In spite of its correspondence to the adjectival form *ebbūtum*, the adjective "trustworthy" seems to be even less relevant to the contexts of the other two texts in which *ebbūtum* occurs. Neither the assigning of persons to plow (crews) (ARM HC B.63 = Jean 1948b) nor the taking of a census (Gadd [1940]) would demand exceptional trustworthiness. In the first case there may be an element of regulation or control, or it may have been simply an operation of registration, preparing lists of crews—"controllers" or "registrars" are possible translations. The latter case appears to involve supervision or participation in taking a census—"supervisors" or "census takers" suits the context.

These few texts show that the LÚ.MEŠ *ebbūtum* were involved with numbers and lists. They do not offer much support for the translation "trustworthy person" for LÚ *ebbum* even though the plural form is adjectival.

CONTEXTS IN WHICH LÚ.MEŠ *ebbū* APPEARS[26]

The substantival plural of LÚ *ebbum*, LÚ.MEŠ *ebbū*, occurs at Mari more frequently than the adjectival form LÚ.MEŠ *ebbūtum*. There does not appear to be any significant difference in the contexts in which the two forms occur, as can be seen from the following presentation of texts.

1. Personnel Lists.

a. *Census lists.* Three texts published by Kupper (ARM 3 19–21) are obviously closely related, the first two probably dealing with the same activity. They may be summarized as follows:

[25]The mention of a sanctuary might suggest that the LÚ.MEŠ *ebbūtum* should be cultically pure, but this would not be so in the other contexts in which it occurs.

[26]At times either MEŠ or LÚ, or both, were omitted.

The king, Zimri-Lim, had instructed Kibri-Dagan to muster (*paqādum*) the troops of his district.[27] In order to do so he recruited[28] LÚ.MEŠ *eb-bi* in each village (*ališam*),[29] and had them take a solemn oath. They then had caused the troops to be registered. Finally the tablets which had been inscribed in each village were sent on to the king.

In the third text, ARM 3 21, a census[30] was to be taken of the villages of the Yaminites. In this case the village headmen (*sugāgū*) came to Kibri-Dagan, whereupon he appointed (*aškun*) their LÚ.MEŠ *ebbū*, who registered the troops.

These three texts clearly deal with census-taking. Those who do it are called LÚ.MEŠ *ebbū*. "Registrars" or "census takers" are obviously possible translations in this context.

"Controllers" is also a possibility, since census-taking could include the idea of supervising. ARM 3 19 states that the LÚ.MEŠ *ebbū* "caused the troops to be registered," using the Š-stem (l. 18). Others could have actually written down the names while the LÚ.MEŠ *ebbū* supervised the operation. In ARM 3 21, however, it states that the LÚ.MEŠ *ebbū* inscribed the (names of the) troops, the verb occurring in the G-stem (l. 11).[31] Consequently, the evidence is ambiguous. Nevertheless, it seems most likely that the LÚ.MEŠ *ebbū* were those who organized and carried out the census-taking operation, perhaps assisted by (unmentioned) scribes, as were the LÚ.MEŠ *ebbūtum* in the texts from Chagar Bazar cited above.[32] In any case, the LÚ.MEŠ *ebbū* were actively engaged in the registration process, at least as controllers or supervisors.

The CAD translates LÚ *ebbū* in these texts with "trustworthy persons." But lines 7–11 of ARM 3 21 would have to be translated, "their village headmen came to me, I appointed (*aškun*) their trustworthy persons and they registered the troops." "Their trustworthy persons" sounds out of place. The emphasis here is not on the personal character of the LÚ.MEŠ *ebbū*, but rather that they are to function as registrars.

[27]See n 17, above. In a context of persons, *paqādum*, "to take inventory of," becomes "to take a census of," or "to muster," according to the following definitions of the word, muster, as found in *Webster's New International Dictionary:* "v., . . . 2. to assemble, as troops, for a muster . . . n., . . . 3. an assembling or review of troops . . . ; spec., in the army . . . such an assembly for roll call."

[28]Or "appoints," "assigns." Cf. CAD E 4(a) 2′; L 87(b) k), "to give a work assignment." In ARM 3 20, *lapātum* is replaced by *šuzuzzum* in l. 13.

[29]In ARM 3 20, he appointed three LÚ.MEŠ *ebbū* in each village (ll. 12–13).

[30]The verb "to take a census," *ububbum*, is here explicitly expressed (l. 6). Cf. Kupper (1950b) 99–110, and Speiser (1958) 18ff. Contra CAD E 6(a) 3′, and AHw 181(b) D, 6.

[31]In ARM 3 20: 5 and 11, the G-stem is used in reference to Kibri-Dagan (*ašṭuru*), although it is unlikely that he personally wrote down the names. Consequently, the use of the G-stem in ARM 3 21: 11 cannot be used to insist that the LÚ.MEŠ *ebbū* themselves wrote out the census lists.

[32]We shall see other occasions when the LÚ.MEŠ *ebbū* were assisted by scribes.

Furthermore, "trustworthy" is an adjective, and if *ebbum* is being used as a modifier of LÚ.MEŠ, it should have the plural adjective form *ebbūtum* rather than the substantival form *ebbū*.

To summarize, in these three texts the LÚ.MEŠ *ebbū* were called upon to compile lists of names, possibly with occasional subtotals of groups and a final summation. "Census takers" or "registrars" fits the context best, with "controllers" or "supervisors" a distant possibility.

b. *Ration lists.* The LÚ.MEŠ *ebbū* also appear in ARM HC B.63, discussed above. In the latter part of the text, the subject of food rations as payment to the laborers comes up. The LÚ.MEŠ *ebbū* came and assigned an unsatisfactorily low payment (ll. 34–38).[33] An appeal to Tebigirišu to increase the amount was apparently unsuccessful (ll. 38–45), so Ilšu-naṣir wrote to inform his lord of the situation (ll. 45–48). The precise nature of the work of the LÚ.MEŠ *ebbū* is again not clear. Rather than being the ones who set the wages, they may have been sent to compile the ration lists that would be involved. If they had some sort of administrative authority or control, it seems to have been rather limited. They were not able to change the wages, although they were less than a previously rejected offer, nor, in the earlier instance, were they able to change the size of the plow (crews), even though they had determined (and, no doubt, been told by Ilšu-naṣir) that the crews were too small for the work. They appear to have been "controllers" with very restricted authority, simply compiling lists as they were told. "Registrars," those who compile official lists or records, seems to be a more suitable translation.

c. *Rosters*(?) *in sealed containers.* In ARM 10 12, Zimri-Lim instructed his wife, Šibtu, to send some LÚ.MEŠ *ebbū* along with Yaṣṣur-Addu to retrieve some sealed tablet containers.[34] Šibtu reported that she had done as the king ordered, sending Mukannišum, Šūbnalû, and Uthiriš-Ḫebat. After they had removed the tablets, Šibtu sealed the entrance with her own seal.[35]

Dossin has translated LÚ.MEŠ *ebbū* with *fidèles* (faithful, trustworthy (persons)). One might suggest that the king wanted trustworthy men to go because he was concerned that the tablets might be lost or altered, but since they were stored in sealed containers, alteration seems unlikely: if

[33]Note that this text uses both *ebbū* and *ebbūtum* very probably in reference to the same people. Jean added *-tum* to line 34, but this may not be necessary. On the interchangeability of *ebbū* and *ebbūtum*, see below pp. 262–63.

[34]If one may judge from the similarity of the contents of ARM 10 82 and ARMT 12 14 to ARM 10 12, the tablets retrieved in the latter by the LÚ.MEŠ *ebbu* were probably personnel lists or inventories.

[35]Perhaps this last statement should not be taken literally. Šibtu had been instructed to send (*ṭurdi*) the men, and she wrote that she sent (*aṭrud*) them.

Šibtu was, in fact, present, they were not likely to get lost. If she did not go, she could have sent some "faithful" servants rather than palace administrators.

If the king was concerned, on the other hand, that the right containers be retrieved, then the queen would need someone who could recognize, or verify, the contents of the containers before removing them. Thus, she may have considered more than just their trustworthiness in choosing Mukannišum and Šūbnalû.[36]

In their capacities as administrators and suppliers, Mukannišum and Šūbnalû would have been well acquainted with inventories, accounts, and personnel lists. According to the text, Yaṣṣur-Addu only showed them in which room (*bītum*) the containers were kept—probably having been told by Zimri-Lim, who had sent him. The door was sealed; they recognized whose seal it was. Since it was not a royal seal, they broke it and entered.[37] Then they had to select the appropriate containers; only two were taken. How did they know which ones to take? Perhaps the seals indicated their contents, contents with which not just any trustworthy person but rather a registrar, a LÚ*ebbum*, would be familiar.[38]

Since it is not possible to know the motivation behind Zimri-Lim's instructions, the translation of LÚ.MEŠ *eb-bi* in line 8 as "trustworthy men," or "*des 'fidèles,'*" cannot be ruled out.[39] "Send trustworthy men with him so that he may show them the place of the tablets" (ll. 8–9) sounds quite reasonable. Its repetition in line 22, however, sounds a little out of place after the queen had named the persons involved. Thus, if LÚ *ebbū* is taken as a general expression, "trustworthy men," lines 21–23 would read: "Yaṣṣur-Addu showed the room to the trustworthy men whom I sent with him." It would seem more natural to have said: "I sent [the following trustworthy men] with Yaṣṣur-Addu, and he showed them (or those men) the room." If LÚ *ebbū* expresses a title, the repetition appears more natural: "I sent [the following *ebbu*-officials] with Yaṣṣur-Addu, and he showed the *ebbu*-officials the room."

Although the translation "trustworthy men" is a possibility, the context and style of this text may be used to argue for a more specific

[36]On Mukannišum, see ARMT 18; on Šūbnalû, ARMT 7 p. 326. See also Sasson (1972) 60–61; ARMT 18 p. 255 n 124; and Pack (1981) 470–75, 480–81, 597–607, and 613. Little is known of the third member of the party, Utḫiriš-Ḫebat. Apart from this tablet, he appears but once, in ARM 10 106. Cf. Sasson (1972) 61.

[37]Special arrangements had to be made to retrieve objects from a room sealed with a royal seal. Cf. ARMT 13 22: 24–33, as well as 10 and 14; see also ARM 10 82. If Šibtu was with them, she may have broken the seal.

[38]On another occasion, however, the tablet room keeper pointed out the containers for Mukannišum's information (recognition?: *mu-du-ti-*): ARM 10 82: 11–12.

[39]The form *ebbū* rather than *ebbūtum* militates against it, however.

translation, "*ebbu*-officials," who would be familiar with registers and accounts.[40] A specific title would also be in accord with the grammatical form.

2. Inventories

As noted previously, Finet has suggested that the LÚ.MEŠ *ebbū(tum)* of ARM HC B.63 were working under the supervision of Tebi-girišu. Just as Asqudum had taken inventory and set the size of the work crews previously, so Tebi-girišu had done, sending the LÚ.MEŠ *ebbū(tum)* to draw up the list. In fact, judging by ARM 10 3, they may very well have helped him in taking the inventory.

This letter, from the Yasmaḫ-Addu period, was sent by Kunšimatum, who felt she was being wrongly accused of misdeeds. The part relevant to the *ebbū* reads as follows (r. 12′–15′):

> Why have they alienated me so greatly from your heart? Give your *ebbū* instructions[41] and let them inventory your house. What have I (ever) taken from your house?

Here *ebbū* is used alone, not preceded by LÚ.MEŠ. It cannot be considered an adjective modifying LÚ. It is a substantive in usage as well as form.[42] "Trustworthy" is consequently eliminated as a translation.

There is no regulation involved here—the *ebbū* are to examine or inspect (*lipqidū*, l. 14), in effect, to inventory, the palace (house) to see if anything is missing—so "controllers" would not be a suitable translation.

This is a job for the registrars, those who keep records and compile lists.

3. Volume Transactions

In ARMT 13 35, Yasīm-sūmû proposed hiring ten boats to transport barley to Mari from Imar. An investment of five minas of silver would be needed. If Zimri-Lim accepted the proposal, he was to send along with the silver two scribes and ten *ebbu*-men, ll. 32–35.

What were the LÚ.MEŠ *ebbū* going to do? It may not be coincidental that they were the same in number as the boats to be hired. Since silver for payment was to be sent, the *ebbū* might act as accountants, weighing and recording. Possibly, but would one need ten of them—in addition to the two scribes?

[40]Cf. Sasson (1972) 58–59.

[41]*Šuḫizma*—or, less likely, "incite them to action." Cf. CAD A/1 181(a) 3′, 4′.

[42]Note also that there is a possessive pronoun suffixed.

Burke attributes to the *ebbū* the role of watching or supervision (*surveillant*).[43] Each *ebbum* would have to make sure personally that the calculation of the quantity loaded was accurate. He could not be distracted from his task for even a moment during the entire lengthy period of loading, and consequently, could not watch more than one boat at a time; whereas, a scribe could pass from one boat to another during the operation.[44] Rather than just watching, however, the important aspect of the *ebbū*'s work would have been to keep an accurate accounting of the volume loaded, so that, in case of a dispute about the volume of the load, with tax collectors or others, the *ebbū* could be called upon as a professional witness.[45]

4. Weighing Computations or Accounting

In ARM 1 74 the LÚ.MEŠ *ebbūtum* are involved in compiling accounts of precious metals used in mountings for statues. In ARMT 13 16 the *ebbū* appear in a similar context. In this text the king instructed Mukannišum to notify him if a sheet (of precious metal?) for mounting(s) (*iḫzū*) was available, so that he might send the *ebbū* (no LÚ). Mukannišum replied that it was available, and requested that the *ebbū* be sent so that the mounting(s) could be affixed in their presence.

What were the *ebbū* doing here? Bottéro translates "*contrôleurs.*" Rouault also sees a controlling action—he regularly refers to the *ebbū* as "*contrôleurs*": the *ebbū* were sent by the king to check on the *quality*[46] of the mounting ("*placage*") before it was affixed; the *ebbū* were inspectors for the king; only after their inspection could the mounting be applied.[47]

On the basis of ARM 1 74 it seems more likely that the *ebbū* were needed not to inspect the quality of the mounting, but to carefully verify and record its weight before it could be affixed to the *lamassu*(?) (ll. 6–10), *balustrade*(?) (ll. 7, 12), or some other object.

[43]Burke (1964b) 85.

[44]Burke (1964b) 85. In the case of ARMT 13 96, there was only one *ebbum* for two boats, but perhaps they were not loaded simultaneously.

[45]Burke (1964b) 85, also 71 ("*dont le parole sans doute faisait foi*"), and 94. Birot attributes to the *ebbū* ("*comptables*"), in his texts and elsewhere, the role of weighing and keeping accounts ("*le rôle . . . de procéder au décompte et à la pesée du grain transporté*"), (1964b) 41.

[46]The italics are mine.

[47]See ARMT 18 pp. 200, 239, and 255. Rouault also indicates his cognizance of the etymology of the word by suggesting that they were "*hommes de confiance,*" very probably chosen from among the upper echelon of administrators comparable in rank to Mukannišum.

The *ebbū* dealt with the semiprecious metal, tin, as well as the precious metals, gold and silver. Dossin has published a text in which Meptûm informed Zimri-Lim of a caravan carrying tin, and suggested that the king send either his overseer of the merchants (UGULA D[A]M.GÀR.MEŠ), l. 17, or his *ebbū* (l. 20, *e-eb-bi-šu*) to acquire tin needed by the palace.[48] The function of the *ebbū* is not precisely given, but they would have been involved in a transaction requiring weighing and accounting skills. Whether they were to supervise the transaction, or be more actively involved in the weighing or recording, is not clear.[49]

5. Bodyguards

In ARM 10 7 the *ebbū* appear in a radically different context. The goddess Annunītum, speaking to Zimri-Lim through one of her cultic personnel, warned him of an impending rebellion and told him to be careful (ll. 5–11). She continued:

12 ARAD.MEŠ *eb-bi-ka*
ša ta-ra-am-mu
Tr. *i-ta-ti-k[a]*
15 *šu-ku-un*
Rev. *šu-zi-is-sú-nu-ti-ma*
li-iṣ-ṣu-ru-k[a]

Dossin translates: "Place at your sides your servants, the faithful (ones) (*ebbī*), whom you love. Set them on watch and may they guard you."[50]

What did the *ebbū* do according to this text? The answer depends, in part, on the translation of line 12. Dossin has treated *ebbī* as a substantive in apposition to *wardī*.[51] As a result, *wardī* and *ebbī* serve as the accusative object of *šukun*, l. 15; the *ebbū*—who are the *wardū*—are to serve as bodyguards.

A more natural translation would be "the servants of your *ebbū*," in which case the servants, not the *ebbū* would be the bodyguards, and there would be no indication as to what the *ebbū* do.

[48]ARM HC A.16. = Dossin (1970), esp. 104.

[49]Dossin (1970) 105 translates "*contrôleurs*" in l. 20.

[50]ARMT 10 p. 33: "*Place à tes côtés tes serviteurs, les 'fidéles' que tu aimes. Mets-les en faction et qu'ils te gardent.*" Here he has translated *ebbū* with '*fidèles*', "faithful (ones)," as he did in the other occurrences of *ebbū* in this volume.

[51]Dossin has, furthermore, applied the possessive pronoun, *-ka*, to *wardī*, rather than *ebbī*, to which it is suffixed. Such a transposition could occur in a noun-noun construct chain [see Finet (1956) 176, section 65 k e)]. This would give here, "your servants of the *ebbū*." But since Dossin does not consider these words to be in a construct relationship, the

If *ebbum* is considered only to be an adjective, as in the CAD, the translation will be different again—*wardī ebbūti* would be "faithful/trustworthy servants"—but we have here the form *ebbī,* not *ebbūti.* The form of the word, as well as the possessive suffix, *-ka,* on *ebbī,* shows that it must be considered a substantive.[52]

Thus, either the *ebbū* or the servants of the *ebbū* were to protect Zimri-Lim. Since the context has nothing to do with record-keeping, and there is no apparent reason why servants of registrar-accountants, in particular, should be chosen as bodyguards—although Zimri-Lim no doubt had record keepers in his entourage, and one might deduce from the extensive palace archives that he was rather fond of them—nevertheless, in view of the overall context of the letter, *ebbū* seems to represent a noun "faithful (or) trustworthy ones" rather than a specific official title.

ARM 10 7, however, is the exception to the pattern. In all the other occurrences of the plural substantive form, *ebbū,* the *ebbū* are associated with registration, accounting or supervisory activities.

CONTEXTS IN WHICH LÚ *ebbum* APPEARS

In ARMT 13 96 we are told that Idin-Itūr-Mer was the *e-bu-um* of two boats loaded with bitumen, ll. 11–12. The spelling is unusual, but since *e-pu-um* (baker) is unlikely, Burke presumes a defective writing for *ebbum,*[53] and cites for support the presence of *ebbū* in association with boats in letter no. 35 of the same volume.[54]

There is no indication of the purpose for the presence of the *ebbum,* but Burke suggests that he might serve as an official witness as to the volume of the shipment, essentially an accounting function.[55]

A LÚ *ebbum* appears in one other text in association with volume transactions. ARMT 12 712 lists large quantities of grain in connection with three cities. Following this there is a badly broken line beginning, "*iškar* LÚ." The next line reads, (*awīl*) *eb-bu Ḫ*[*u*]-*ut-ba*(?)-*nu,* which Birot translates "*comptable:* Ḫutbānu(?)." In addition to "accountant," "controller" would be a possible translation.

These are the only two occurrences so far of the singular LÚ *ebbum* in the Mari archives. In both cases the LÚ *ebbum* appears to be an accountant associated with a volume transaction.

---

shift—made, no doubt, for stylistic reasons—is less justifiable. See, however, the remark to section 65 k e).

[52]As far as I am aware, pronominal suffixes may be attached to verbs and nouns (substantives), but not to adjectives.

[53]ARMT 13 p. 167 note to 96: 11. See also CAD W 4(a) (TLB 1 43: 13).

[54]If *ebbum* is correct, it is clearly being used as a title, not as an attributive adjective.

[55]See Burke (1964b) 71 and 85.

SUBSTANTIVE OR ADJECTIVE?

Having looked at the contextual meanings of LÚ *ebbum*, LÚ.MEŠ *ebbūtum* and LÚ.MEŠ *ebbū* separately, we should now make a comparative study, by listing the occurrences of each form under the most common suitable translations.

registrar (census taker)	*accountant*	*supervisor (controller)*
ebbum	*ebbum*	*ebbum*
—	ARMT 12 712	—
ebbū	ARMT 13 96	*ebbū*
ARM 3 19, 20, 21	*ebbū*	ARMT 13 35(?)
ARM 10 3	ARMT 13 16, 35, 36(?)	ARM HC B.63: 34(?)
ARM HC B.63: 34	ARM HC A.16	*ebbūtum*
ebbūtum	*ebbūtum*	ARM HC B.63: 13(?)
ARM HC B.63: 13	ARM 1 74	*Iraq* 7 990: 21(?)
Iraq 7 990	ARM HC B.63: 12(?)	

In addition there are "*ebbu*-officials" (ARM 10 12) and "trustworthy ones" (*ebbū*) (ARM 10 7).

Kupper long ago suggested that there might be a distinction between *ebbū* and *ebbūtum*.[56] This seems reasonable, since *ebbū* is a plural noun form while *ebbūtum* is the form for a plural adjective. Nevertheless, from the above it is clear that the LÚ.MEŠ *ebbūtum* and the LÚ.MEŠ *ebbū* performed similar functions. At Chagar Bazar, the LÚ.MEŠ *ebbūtum* were involved in taking a census, as were the LÚ.MEŠ *ebbū* of ARM 3 19–21. In ARM 1 74, the LÚ.MEŠ *ebbūtum* prepared accounts related to precious metal mountings, just as the *ebbū* did in ARM 13 16. In short, whether the form is *ebbū* or *ebbūtum*, whether preceded by LÚ or not, those involved performed the functions of registrars and accountants—measuring and recording. This equality of the two terms is supported by the occurrence of both forms for (probably) the same group of officials in one text (ARM HC B.63: 12–13, 34). There appears, then, to be no distinction between the vocables *ebbū* and *ebbūtum*.

Furthermore, the occurrence of *ebbū* and *ebbum* alone, not following LÚ where they could be considered attributive adjectives, shows clearly that they are substantives, and consequently, although the adjectival form *ebbūtum* does occur, it should be considered an adjective in substantival usage, and both LÚ *ebbūtum* and LÚ *ebbū* should be

[56]Kupper (1950b) 102 n 7.

considered occupational or professional titles and hence written LÚ*ebbū* or LÚ*ebbūtum*.[57]

Apparently the substantivization of the adjective as used in the professional title LÚ*ebbum* was not yet complete, so that the two forms *ebbū* and *ebbūtum* were still in competition.[58]

SUMMARY: LÚ*ebbum*

The two vocables *ebbū* and *ebbūtum* were interchangeable in the OB period at Mari. Of the most common translations suggested for the expression LÚ.MEŠ *ebbū*(*tum*) at Mari, "accountants" is the most suitable. "Census takers" is too restricted, fitting only three texts (ARM 3 19–21).[59] Furthermore, it is not related to the D-form of the verb, *ubbubum*, which means "to take a census,"[60] and the term *mubbibū*, meaning precisely "census takers," was in use at Mari.[61] A better translation for these texts is "registrars."

"Trustworthy persons" might be considered the best translation of *ebbū* in only one text (ARM 10 7) where they may be considered potential bodyguards. But even here, as in most of the texts, the grammatical form is that of a substantive rather than an adjective. Furthermore, it is clear from the use of *ebbum* without a preceding LÚ that it is not an adjective modifying LÚ, but a substantive in its own right. Consequently, when it is preceded by LÚ, the LÚ should be considered a determinative used before the title of an occupation or profession, LÚ*ebbum*.

A further weakness is that the translation "trustworthy person" lacks the specificity required by some contexts (ARM 10 12, for example): it is too vague. All administrators or functionaries ought to be trustworthy; and so, one could replace almost any administrative title with "trustworthy person" in any context and still get some sense, but at the cost of valuable clarity.[62]

[57]*Contra* CAD E 3–4, but already recognized by Leemans (1954) 62–63, and Kraus (1968) 5 n 6a. This is further substantiated by the use of the abstract noun in the construct state, *ebbūt* PN, "computation/account(ing) of PN." See n 9, above.

[58]Rather than seeing a possible West Semitic nominal plural in *ūt* in *ebbūtum*, it should be considered an example of an adjective used substantively as an occupational, or professional title (*Berufsbezeichnung*). See von Soden (1952) 77, section 61 k, and Finet (1956) 94, section 38 a, b.

[59] . . . and some ration lists at Chagar Bazar.

[60]See Speiser (1958) 19.

[61]Speiser considered both *ebbum* and *mubbibum* to be action nouns. *Mubbibum* is obviously the participle derived directly from the verb *ubbubum*. Naturally, the *ebbū*, as registrar/accountants, might have been involved in taking a census, even though this was not the primary significance of their title.

[62]An additional weakness is that there was already an adjective meaning "trustworthy" used at Mari—*taklum*. See ARMT 15 271, and AHw 1307(b).

"Controllers" is likewise too vague. Whenever anyone does any sort of administrative work involving decision-making, there is bound to be some limiting or controlling aspect to it, but not every administrative person should be called a controller.

Some texts do indicate that the *ebbū(tum)* had limited supervisory responsibilities. In one case they assigned a certain number of workers to each plow(crew), as well as set wages.[63] ARM 3 19 and 20 say that they had the people registered, and the Chagar Bazar texts may indicate that they had scribes working for them (*Iraq* 7, p. 64). Nevertheless, in most cases, they work under the supervision or orders of a superior. In ARM 3 it was Kibri-Dagan, and in ARM HC B.63, Tebi-girišu. Control or supervision does not seem to be the major element in their activities. More frequently they were directly involved, keeping track of quantities: weighing, computing, registering.

Dealing with figures was a major element in the *ebbū*'s work. Several of the texts deal with weighing operations. These include keeping accounts of the precious metals used for mountings (ARM 1 74 and ARMT 13 16), acquiring tin (ARM HC A.16), and possibly the payment for a barley purchase (ARMT 13 35). The *ebbū* deal with keeping track of volumes in ARMT 13 35 (barley loaded on ships), ARMT 13 96 (bitumen on a ship), ARMT 12 712 (produce), and ARM HC B.63 (harvest estimate).

"Accountants" is appropriate for these texts, but some texts do not deal specifically with numbers. The census texts (ARM 3 19–21) point more to registration than to computation. The *ebbū* were probably involved in making lists for workcrews and ration distribution in ARM HC B.63: 13, 34. Those to take inventory in ARM 10 3 would have been involved with both lists and figures.

A combined professional description "registrar-accountant," a sort of ancient counterpart to a Certified Public Accountant formed by expanding "census-takers" to "registrars" and combining it with the clearly related "accountants," would seem to cover the activities of the LÚ.MEŠ*ebbū(tum)* at Mari quite well.[64]

[63]See ARM HC B.63: 14–5. In both cases, the verb is *esēkum*.

[64]For a short discussion of the use of this title outside Mari, see Pack (1981) 235–36. A comparison with Gallery (1980) will show the equivalence of the titles LÚ*ebbum* and LÚSA.TAM. Apparently in southern Babylonia the Sumerian form was employed more frequently while at Mari the Akkadian LÚ*ebbum* was more common. The occurrence of both titles in the same text (Dossin [1933] 9) suggests different levels in status or competence, such as clerk or junior accountant versus comptroller or certified public accountant. See also now the comments of Durand (1983b) 123–131.

"He Restoreth My Soul": A Biblical Expression and Its Mari Counterpart

JONATHAN D. SAFREN

Ben-Gurion University of the Negev
Beer-Sheva, Israel

The 23rd Psalm begins with the beloved metaphor of the Lord as shepherd and provider.[1] Both translators and commentators have indicated that v 3a, נפשי ישובב, which RSV translates "he restores my soul,"[2] is part and parcel of the shepherd metaphor.[3] By providing fresh fodder and water, the Lord "restores the soul," or, more in line with the vehicle of the metaphor, "revives" or "refreshes" the sheep, which has become faint from its exertions. The tenor of the metaphor can be taken to mean that the Lord provides not only for the physical, but also for the spiritual needs of the Psalmist.

The expression of v 3a is comprised of the *polel* form of the verb שוב, literally meaning "he returns, brings back," and the noun נפש, literally meaning "throat," the organ which takes in nourishment, but here to be understood in the derived connotation of "vital life-force," or "life" itself.[4] The expression שובב נפש can thus be taken to mean "bring back life," "revitalize," hence "revive" and "refresh."

This interpretation is borne out by the use of the similar expression השיב נפש, with the verb שוב in the *hiphᶜil*. In the description of the agonies brought on by the destruction of Jerusalem in Lam 1, the poet

[1]On Psalm 23 and its interpretation, see, aside from the commentaries, Morgenstern (1946) 13–34, and Koehler (1955) 217–34. Further literature is cited by H. J. Kraus (1966) 186.

[2]NEB has, "he renews life within me."

[3]RSV and NEB indicate this by punctuation. For the commentaries, see, for example, Briggs and Briggs (1906) 207, 209; Gunkel (1968) 99–100; Dahood (1966) 145; and H. J. Kraus (1966) 189. Morgenstern (1946) 21 is of the opinion that combined activities of pasturage, drinking and leading have preserved the life of the sheep, while Koehler (1956) 231 gives the reason for the need to renew the strength of the flock: it has become weakened by its daily march. Kirkpatrick (1902) 125 prefers to regard v 3a as part of the "guide" metaphor of vv 3–4, translating, "renews and sustains my life."

[4]On נפש, see KBL 626b–7b; Licht (1968) 898–904, with appended bibliography; and Wolff (1974) 10–25.

dwells twice on the suffering caused by famine. In v 11, all the people are groaning in their search for food; in v 19, the priests and elders have already perished from hunger. In both cases, the object of the vain quest for nourishment was "to revive their strength,"[5] or simply "to keep alive."[6]

In all three passages cited above, the connection between the expressions used and food and drink is evident. Nourishment restores vitality which has become drained and weakened by hunger, thirst and physical exertion. One can then justifiably treat שובב נפש and השיב נפש as two variant forms of the same expression.

Gunkel[7] has recognized the relationship between the above expression and שבה רוח, literally meaning "the wind returned," with the verb שוב in the *qal*. In Judg 15:19, Samson, feeling faint from thirst, drinks of the waters of Lechi and "his spirit returned and he revived."[8] Similarly, in 1 Sam 30:12, David's troops find an Egyptian who has neither eaten nor drunk for three days and nights. They give him food and drink and "his spirit revived."[9] The Hebrew noun רוח, here having the force "breath of life," "life-spirit," can be equated in this expression with נפש, "vital life-force."[10]

It can thus be concluded that the primary connotation of the expression השיב/שובב נפש is "to revive, restore to full strength and vitality by means of food and drink." The four remaining instances of the use of the expression can be considered as derived from this primary connotation.

Thus, in Ps 19:8[11] the Torah is described as "reviving the soul,"[12] i.e., imbuing it with new vitality. The Psalmist considers the Word of God as necessary for sustaining life as food itself, an equation also made, as Briggs has pointed out,[13] in Deut 8:3. This interpretation has even more to say for itself when one compares the expression as used here to the instances already considered.

[5]RSV thus translates להשיב נפש in v 11, and וישיבו את נפשם in v 19. NEB has, "to give them strength again," and, "to renew their strength," respectively.

[6]Among the commentators who have explained the phrase in this manner are Weiser in Ringgren and Weiser (1958) 49; H. J. Kraus (1968) 21, but cf. the commentary on p. 30: "die Lebenskraft zurückbringen;" Plöger (1969) 133–34; Hillers (1972) 2, 4; and Gordis (1974) 131–32.

[7]Gunkel (1968) 80 n 3, and especially 100. See, similarly, Wolff (1974) 33 n 4.

[8]RSV for ותשב רוחו ויחי. NEB has, "his strength returned and he revived."

[9]RSV for ותשב רוחו אליו. NEB has simply, "he revived."

[10]On רוח see KBL 877a–9b; Oppenheimer (1976) 330–36, with appended bibliography; and Wolff (1974) 32–39.

[11]The verse count of the Hebrew text is followed.

[12]RSV for משיבת נפש. NEB gives the participle verbal force: "revives the soul."

[13]Briggs and Briggs (1906) 169 n 3.

In Prov 25:13, the value of a reliable messenger to his senders is compared to the coolness of snow on a hot harvest day, for "he refreshes the spirit of his master."[14] The simile in this verse is generally considered to refer to an ice-cold drink (perhaps cooled by snow brought from Lebanon).[15] The relationship of the expression השיב נפש, as used here, to its basic connotation would then immediately become clear. One cannot, however, ignore Scott's comment that the "coolness of snow" may refer to nothing more than an unseasonably cool June day.[16] In this case, one could understand the expression in the derived, more generalized connotation of "relieve, refresh."

In Lam 1:16, the all-too-distant comforter of Zion is described as "my reviver."[17] The poet has utilized the expression in vv. 11, 19, in the primary connotation of reviving by means of food and drink. Now he may be re-using it figuratively.[18] Translators and commentators have taken differing views as to the exact intention of the expression here. Thus, Kraus, translating "der mich erquickte,"[19] goes on to explain: "Trost aber ist so notig wie der tägliche Brot damit Zion das Leben gewinnen kann."[20] Gordis, perhaps influenced by the use of the expression elsewhere in the chapter, has "who might sustain my life."[21] NEB, less literal-minded, translates, "renew my strength," while RSV prefers

[14]RSV for ונפש אדניו ישיב. NEB deletes this clause, relegating it to a textual note. Most commentators, as well as BH^3 and BHS delete this hemistich as a superficial gloss because the comparison has already been completely expressed in the preceding clauses, requiring no further elucidation, and because the hemistich does not fit in with the distich structure of the verses in this section. See, for example, Toy (1899) 464; Steuernagel (1923) 313; Gemser (1963) 90; Scott (1965) 154 (translation); and Whybray (1972) 145 n *b*. The textual evidence for this emendation is most skimpy, however (BH^3 cites one medieval Hebrew MS), and the meaning of the proverb is certainly preserved and clarified by the third hemistich. If an addition, then, it is almost certainly very ancient, and can be taken as one piece with the rest of the verse.

[15]The simile was first so construed by F. Delitzsch in his *Proverbs of Solomon* II. The edition available to me is the translation by M. G. Eaton (Grand Rapids, 1950) 160. (See Delitzsch [1873] 406, ed.). He is followed in this by Toy (1899) 464; Fritsch (1955) 929; and Whybray (1972) 148.

[16]Scott (1965) 155.

[17]משיב נפשי. NEB, translating the two participles in v 16b verbally, understands them as referring to two distinct individuals: "for any to comfort to me and renew my strength are far from me." This interpretation misconstrues the synonymous parallelism in which מנחם//משיב נפשי.

[18]It is noteworthy that Lam 1:16b and c has a high concentration of words and expressions used elsewhere in this chapter: אין/רחק מנחם, vv 2, 9, 17, 21; השיב נפש, vv 11, 19; שמם, v 13; and הגדיל/גבר אויב, v 9. These are preceded by a summarizing introduction in v 16a. Cf. Löhr (1906) 7 n.

[19]H. J. Kraus (1968) 22.

[20]H. J. Kraus (1968) 32.

[21]Gordis (1974) 132.

"revive my courage." Hillers, influenced by the preceding word מנחם, "comforter," renders "anyone to console."[22]

However, one should not overlook the possibility that the primary connotation of the expression is also intended here. One of the duties of the מנחם, the "comforter, consoler," was to supply the mourner with food and drink.[23] In doing so, he was literally reviving, restoring the strength, of the mourner, who had been weakened by fasting.[24]

In Ruth 4:15, Naomi's neighbors claim that her newborn grandson will be her "restorer of life."[25] It would appear self-evident that the meaning of the expression as used here is that Ruth's son is to comfort Naomi for the death of her own two sons.[26] Perhaps this is the reason that this phrase has so rarely been commented upon separately. It has been justified on the grounds of Naomi's special love for Ruth,[27] or treated as another example of the use of the key word שוב in Ruth.[28] Campbell, while citing the other occurrences of the expression השיב נפש, and giving the literal meaning, makes no attempt to explain its use here.[29]

It has been noted by both Campbell[30] and Rudolph[31] that the following clause, "and a nourisher of your old age,"[32] stands in a broadly parallel relationship to what precedes it, and in fact completes the first phrase by supplying a "double duty" 2 f. sg. pronominal suffix after the noun שיבה, something lacking after the noun נפש. If this parallelism is taken in a narrower sense, it can be argued that both phrases refer to the grandson's providing for Naomi's physical needs in her old age. He will "nourish" or provide for her, thus "reviving" her by means of food and drink, an activity which would normally have been performed by Naomi's sons, now deceased. Thus, the expression השיב נפש can be understood here too in its primary connotation.

In sum, it has been demonstrated that the Biblical expression השיב נפש/שובב נפש denotes "to revive, refresh, restore to full vitality (by means of food and drink)." Imparting food and drink means returning

[22]Hillers (1972) 3.

[23]2 Sam 3:35; 12:17; Jer 16:7; and Ezek 24:17, 22.

[24]2 Sam 3:35; 12:17. On the funerary banquet as a mourning ritual in the ancient world, see Pope (1977) 210–29.

[25]RSV for משיב נפש. NEB translates the participle verbally: "will give you new life."

[26]This interpretation is, in fact, given in a medieval Jewish commentary attributed to Salmon ben Yeroḥam, and cited by Beattie (1977) 89.

[27]Hertzberg (1969) 282.

[28]Campbell (1975) 164.

[29]Campbell (1975) 164.

[30]Campbell (1975) 164.

[31]Rudolph (1962) 69.

[32]RSV for ולכלכל את שיבתך. NEB has, "and cherish you in your old age."

life. Three[33] of the seven occurrences of this expression clearly have this connotation. The remaining four are either figurative uses of the expression,[34] or can in part be reinterpreted as referring to the primary connotation.[35] The conclusions presented are supported by the usage of the related expression שבה רוח.[36]

A hitherto-unrecognized Akkadian equivalent to the Hebrew expression can be shown to exist in the Mari letters. In ARM 14 5,[37] Yaqqim-Addu, governor of Sagarātum, asked permission of the king to send an overfed, prime-quality bull off to Mari by boat, along with a cook to tend to the animal on the way.[38] The pertinent passage is cited below:

1 GUD ŠE SAG *ša i-gi-se-e-em*
ma-di-iš ik-bi-ir-ma i-ḫa-aš {x x}
ŠÀ.GAL *ma-ḫa-ra-am* [*l*]*i-mu*
i-na-an-na as-sú-ur-ri
GUD *šu-ú i-ma!-qú-ut-ma ši-ir-šu i-qá-li-il*
be-lí li-iš-pu-ra-am-ma
GUD *ša-a-tu i-na* 1 GIŠ.MÁ
Rev. *lu-ša-ar-ki-ba-am-ma*
lu-ús-ki-pa-am
ù as-sú-ur-ri GUD *šu-ú*
i-na qa-ab-li-it gi-ir-ri-i[*m*]
i-ḫa-aš 1 LÚ.MU *be-lí li-iṭ-ru-dam*
aš-šum na-pí-iš-ti GUD *ša-a-tu*
ú-ta-ar-ru-ma
ši-ir-šu a-na É.GAL-*lim i-ru-bu*

Translation

(5) A fattened, prime-quality bull intended for dues[39] has become very fat and has been/is "ill."[40] It refuses to take fodder. Now,

[33]Ps 23:3 and Lam 1:11, 19.

[34]Ps 19:8; Prov 25:13; Lam 1:16; Ruth 4:15.

[35]Lam 1:16 and Ruth 4:15.

[36]Judg 15:19 and 1 Sam 30:12. It should be noted that the expression שובב/השיב נפש appears six times in poetic passages, and only once in a prose context (Ruth 4:15), which itself exhibits a certain form of parallelism. The related שבה רוח, on the other hand, occurs only in prose contexts.

[37]ARMT 14 6, addressed to Šunuḫraḫalu, a highly placed court official, and Yaqqim-Addu's friend (ll. 16–17, 29), is a companion letter to ARM 14 5, and deals with the same matter.

[38]ARM 14 5: 5–19, paralleled by ARM 14 6: 5–6, 18–28.

[39]*Igisûm* at Mari is neither a voluntary "offrande" (ARM 14 5: 5), nor a one-time "gift" (CAD I 42b). Yaqqim-Addu had been raising *igisûm*-bulls for some time (ARM 14 6: 10–11). The *igisûm*-bull of ARM 2 82: 29 was being presented by Zakira-Ḫammû, governor of Qattunān, who made it clear in his letter that the bull was *expected* by the

> lest that bull decline and lose weight, (10) let my lord write me, and I will have that bull embark on a boat and will dispatch (it). Moreover, in case that bull becomes/remains "ill" (15) during the voyage, let my lord send me a cook, so that he may revive[41] that bull, so that its flesh enter the palace.

The illness of the bull has caused it to lose its appetite. It is not clear whether the bull has remained ill, and may continue to remain ill during the voyage to Mari, or whether it has suffered an "attack" of the illness which has passed, but which may recur during the trip.[42] The example of ARMT 13 25, in which a similarly-ill bull is detained until its symptoms are either verified or disappear, would argue for the latter case: a bull would not be sent on to Mari if it were truly "ill."

In any case, it is not the death of the bull that is envisaged by Yaqqim-Addu for the near future, but its loss of weight and healthy appearance. For this reason, the speedy dispatch of the animal by boat is so urgent, requiring the good services of the governor's intermediary at court, Šunuḫraḫalu.[43] Were there any danger of the bull's imminent death, either at Sagarātum or on the way to Mari, it is questionable whether its flesh would be acceptable to the king, and there would be no need for the hasty measures taken by Yaqqim-Addu. For this reason, the rendering of ARM 14 5: 9 for *imaqqutma šīršu iqallil*, "dépérisse et . . . sa chair . . . déprécie," is unsuitable here.

It is against this background that one is to understand Yaqqim-Addu's request for a *nuḫatimmum* to accompany the bull on its way to

---

palace, and Zakira-Ḫammû must justify its not being sent. The person presenting the *igisûm*-bull in ARM 1 86: 19 was the governor of Terqa, and later Tuttul, Šamaš-ellassu. The bull of ARMT 13 25: 5, 15, which was presented by Warad-ilišu, another high official (ARMT 16/1 212), seems to fit in this category too. The *igisûm*-bulls were apparently delivered to, or kept at, the *bīt igisûm* (ARM 10 72: 12). Their fodder rations were noted (ARM 9 24 iv: 54). ARM 7 217 is a list of *igisûm* and other payments (l. 22) received in the form of silver. Several of the persons mentioned in the text can be identified as officials.

The conclusion to be drawn from this evidence is that the *igisûm* at Mari was a kind of tax paid by office-holders to the palace. Perhaps "kickback" would be a good term to describe the payment. The use of the term at Mari would then approximate its use elsewhere in the Old Babylonian period (*contra* ARMT 10 p. 265, note to 72: 12).

[40]The verb *ḫâšum* seems to indicate some sort of illness, as has been pointed out in ARMT 13 p. 163, note to 25: 8, and ARMT 14 pp. 215–16, note to 5: 6. This interpretation is perhaps supported by CT 19, Pl. 45, K 264 rev.: 21 (a list of diseases).

[41]Literally, "return the *n*."

[42]The orthography *i-ḫa-aš* of l. 6 can represent either the preterite tense *iḫāš*, or the present/future *iḫâš*. In l. 16, it is clear from the context that the latter form is intended.

[43]ARM 14 6: 16–29. For other instances of Yaqqim-Addu's use of Šunuḫraḫalu as an intermediary, see ARM 14 11, 29, and 36. In return for his help, Šunuḫraḫalu received gifts from Yaqqim-Addu (see ARM 14 36: 16–21). Šunuḫraḫalu held a high position at court. On this, see Birot (1964c) 26; Oppenheim (1965) 253–56; Sasson (1972) 57; and ARMT 18 p. 254 n 321.

Mari. The bull has been ill and has lost its appetite. Should it remain ill, or become ill again, on the boat, it will continue to refuse fodder and lose in weight and appearance. The royal cook, then, is to prepare special delicacies for the *igisûm*-bull in the hope that these will arouse the beast's appetite! If the cook is successful in his efforts, he will have "revived" the bull, and this is the meaning of the expression *napištam turrum* in ARM 14 5: 17–8 and 6: 27.

This thesis is supported by the following considerations:

1. There is no other known occurrence of *napištam turrum*, and therefore no evidence to support the suggested translations of the phrase as it occurs here: "rende le souffle,"[44] "slaughter,"[45] or "bend the neck back (for slaughtering)."[46]

2. There is no other known attestation of the *nuḫatimmum* as slaughterer or butcher. Where his duties are mentioned, they are concerned either with food preparation in general, or with baking bread in particular.[47] It is in fact in the specialized connotation of "baker" that the word came over into Mishnaic Hebrew *via* Aramaic.[48]

3. The semantic range of Akkadian *napištum* parallels that of נפש in Hebrew,[49] and thus the connotation "vital life-force" would be entirely in order in our text.

It could also be added that the cramped quarters of a boat are hardly suitable for slaughtering and butchering a bull; and even if this were conceivable (for example, if the boat put into port on the way), the flesh of the slaughtered beast might easily decompose before reaching the palace in Mari.

When taking all these considerations into account, as well as the interpretation offered of the text itself, it becomes plausible to conclude that the Akkadian expression *napištam turrum* has the same connotation as the Hebrew expression שובב/השיב נפש—"to revive, restore to full vitality (by means of food or drink)." Since the only known occurrences of the Akkadian expression are in Old Babylonian Mari letters, it is possible that the expression is a loan translation from West Semitic ("Amorite").

[44]ARMT 14 5: 18; 6: 26; and p. 216, note to 5: 17s.

[45]CAD N/2 314a, para. a.

[46]AHw 1335a, para. 15a.

[47]See the references listed in CAD N/2 314a, para. a.

[48]On *nuḫatimmum* in Aramaic and Hebrew, see Kaufman (1974) 79 and n246, and references cited therein.

[49]For *napištum*, see CAD N/1 296a–304b, and AHw 738. For נפש, see the references in n 4, above.

Bibliography

Aisleitner, J.

1967 *Wörterbuch der ugaritischen Sprache.* Berlin.

al-Aḫṭal

See Musil (1927) 86 n. 48, and Hitti (1968) 196, 220, 252.

Albright, W. F.

1925 A Babylonian Geographical Treatise on Sargon of Akkad's Empire. *Journal of the American Oriental Society* 45: 193–245.

1926 Notes on the Topography of Ancient Mesopotamia. *Journal of the American Oriental Society* 46: 220–30.

1933 Archaeological and Topographical Explorations in Palestine and Syria. *Bulletin of the American Schools of Oriental Research* 49: 23–31.

1940 New Light on the History of Western Asia in the Second Millennium B.C. *Bulletin of the American Schools of Oriental Research* 77: 20–32; 78: 23–31.

Albright, W. F., and Moran, W.

1950 Rib-Adda of Byblos and the Affairs of Tyre (EA 89). *Journal of Cuneiform Studies* 4: 163–68.

Alster, B., ed.

1980 *Death in Mesopotamia: Papers Read at the XXVIe Rencontre Assyrologique Internationale.* Mesopotamia—Copenhagen Studies in Assyriology 8. Copenhagen.

Ammianus Marcellinus

See Rolfe (1935–39).

Anbar, M.

1971 L'organisation du royaume de Šamši-Addu Ier. Ph.D. dissertation, Université de Liège.

1973 Le début du règne de Šamši-Addu Ier. *Israel Oriental Studies* 3: 1–33.

Anderson, J. G. C.

1897 The Road System of Eastern Asia Minor with the Evidence of Byzantine Campaigns. *Journal of Hellenic Studies* 17: 22–44.

Andrae, W.

1922 *Die archäischen Ischtar-Tempel in Assur.* Wissenschaftliche Veröffentlichungen der Deutschen Orient-Gesellschaft 39. Leipzig.

Archi, A.

1979 An Administrative Practice and the "Sabbatical Year" at Ebla. *Studi Eblaiti* 1: 91–95.

1980 Notes on Eblaite Geography. *Studi Eblaiti* 2: 1–16 and figs. 1a–5c.

1981a I rapporti tra Ebla e Mari. *Studi Eblaiti* 4: 129–66.

1981b Kiš nei testi di Ebla. *Studi Eblaiti* 4: 77–87.

1981c La "Lista di Nomi e Professioni" ad Ebla. *Studi Eblaiti* 4: 177–204.

Archi, A., and Biga, M. G.
1982 *Testi amministrativi di vario contenuto (archivo L.2769: TM.75. G.3000–4101).* Archivi Reali di Ebla, Testi 3. Rome.

Arø, J.
1960 Review of *Textes juridiques et administratifs,* by G. Boyer (ARM 8). *Orientalistische Literaturzeitung* 55: 260–62.
1966 Review of *Textes administratifs de la salle 5 du palais,* by M. Birot (ARMT 12). *Orientalistische Literaturzeitung* 61: 142–44.

Astour, M. C.
1971 Tell Mardīḫ and Ebla. *Ugarit-Forschungen* 3: 9–19.
1973 A North Mesopotamian Locale of the Keret Epic? *Ugarit-Forschungen* 5: 29–39.
1976 Habiru. In K. Crim, ed., *The Interpreter's Dictionary of the Bible, Supplementary Volume,* 382a–85a. Nashville.
1978 The Rabbeans: A Tribal Society on the Euphrates from Yaḫdun-Lim to Julius Caesar. *Syro-Mesopotamian Studies* 2/1: 1–12.
1979 The Arena of Tiglath-Pileser III's Campaign against Sarduri II (743 B.C.). *Assur* 2/3: 1–23 [69–91].
1981 Ugarit and the Great Powers. In G. D. Young, ed., *Ugarit in Retrospect: Fifty Years of Ugarit and Ugaritic,* 3–29. Winona Lake, Indiana.

Bardet, G., *et al.*
1984 *Archives administratives de Mari* 1. ARM 23. Paris.

Barton, G.
1914 *Haverford Library Collection of Cuneiform Tablets or Documents from the Temple Archives of Telloh* 3. Philadelphia and London.
1915 *Sumerian Business and Administrative Documents from the Earliest Times to the Dynasty of Agade.* University of Pennsylvania, the Museum, Publications of the Babylonian Section 9/1. Philadelphia.

Beattie, D. R. G.
1977 *Jewish Exegesis of the Book of Ruth.* Journal for the Study of the Old Testament Supplement Series 2. Sheffield.

Beitzel, B. J.
1978 From Ḫarran to Imar along the Old Babylonian Itinerary: The Evidence from the *Archives Royales de Mari.* In G. A. Tuttle, ed., *Biblical and Near Eastern Studies: Essays in Honor of William Sanford LaSor,* 209–19. Grand Rapids.
1984 Išme-Dagan's Military Actions in the Jezīrah: A Geographical Study. *Iraq* 46: 29–42.

Beld, S.; Hallo, W. W.; and Michalowski, P.
1984 *The Tablets of Ebla: Concordance and Bibliography.* Winona Lake, Indiana.

Bell, G. L.
1911 *Amurath to Amurath.* 2nd edition London.

Beyer, D.
1980 Notes préliminaires sur les empreintes de sceaux de Meskéné. In J.-C. Margueron, *Le Moyen Euphrate: Zone de contacts et*

d'échanges. Travaux du Centre de Recherches sur le Proche-Orient et la Grèce Antiques 5: 265–83. Strasbourg.

1983 Stratigraphie de Mari: remarques préliminaire sur les premières couches du sondage stratigraphique (chantier A). *Mari—Annales de Recherches Interdisciplinaires* 2: 37–60.

1984 Le sceau de Kabi-Addu, fils d'Asqudum. *Mari—Annales de Recherches Interdisciplinaires* 3: 255–56.

1985 Scellements de portes du palais de Mari. *Mari—Annales de Recherches Interdisciplinaires* 4: 375–84.

Biga, M. G., and Milano, L.

1984 *Testi amministrativi assegnazioni di tessuti (archivo L.2769).* Archivi reali di Ebla, Testi 4. Rome.

Biggs, R.

1967 Semitic Names in the Fara Period. *Orientalia* n.s. 36: 55–66.

1974 *Inscriptions from Tell Abu Ṣalabikh.* Oriental Institute Publications 99. Chicago.

1980 The Ebla Tablets: An Interim Perspective. *Biblical Archaeologist* 43: 76–87.

Bilgiç, E.

1945–51 Die Ortsnamen der "kappadokischen" Urkunden im Rahmen der alten Sprachen Anatoliens. *Archiv für Orientforschung* 15: 1–37.

Birot, M.

1960a *Textes administratifs de la salle 5 du palais.* ARM 9. Paris.

1960b *Textes administratifs de la salle 5 du palais.* ARMT 9. Paris.

1964a *Textes administratifs de la salle 5 du palais* 2. ARMT 12. Paris.

1964b Lettres de Iasîm-Sumû. ARMT 13: 45–79. Paris.

1964c Les lettres de Iasîm-sumû. *Syria* 41: 25–65.

1969 *Tablettes économiques et administratives d'époque babylonienne ancienne conservées au Musée d'Art et d'Histoire de Genève.* Paris.

1973 Nouvelles découvertes épigraphiques au palais de Mari (Salle 115). *Syria* 50: 1–12.

1974 *Lettres de Yaqqim-Addu gouverneur de Sagarâtum.* ARMT 14. Paris.

1976 *Lettres de Yaqqim-Addu gouverneur de Sagarâtum.* ARM 14. Paris.

1978a Données nouvelles sur la chronologie du règne de Zimri-Lim. *Syria* 55: 333–43.

1978b Review of *The Old Babylonian Tablets from Tell al-Rimah,* by S. Dalley, C. B. F. Walker, and J. D. Hawkins. *Revue d'Assyriologie et d'Archéologie Orientale* 72: 181–90.

1979 Noms de personnes. ARMT 16/1: 43–249. Paris.

1980 Fragment de Rituel de Mari Relatif au *kispum.* In B. Alster, ed., *Death in Mesopotamia,* 139–50. Copenhagen.

Birot, M.; Kupper, J.-R.; and Rouault, O.

1979 *Répertoire analytique 2: Tomes I–XIV, XVIII et textes divers hors-collections,* part 1: *noms propres.* ARMT 16/1. Paris.

Böhl, F. M. Th. de Liagre

1909 *Die Sprache der Amarnabriefe, mit besonderer Berüchsichtigung.* Leipziger semitische Studien 5/2. Leipzig.

Boissier, A.

1919 Inscription de Narâm-Sin. *Revue d'Assyriologie et d'Archéologie Orientale* 16: 157–64.

Börker-Klähm, J.

1980 Eine folgenreiche Fundbeobachtung in Mari. *Zeitschrift für Assyriologie und vorderasiatische Archäologie* 69: 221–33.

Bottéro, J.

1954a *La Problème des Ḫabiru à la 4ᵉ Rencontre Assyriologique Internationale.* Cahiers de la Société Asiatique 13. Paris.

1954b Paléographie, Syllabaire, Liste des idéogrammes et Table analytique. ARMT 15: 1–92, 285–348. Paris.

1956 *Textes administratifs de la salle 110.* ARM 7. Paris.

1957 *Textes économiques et administratifs.* ARMT 7. Paris.

1964 Lettres de Mukannišum. ARMT 13: 15–44. Paris.

Bottéro, J., and Finet, A.

1954 *Répértoire analytique des tomes I à V.* ARMT 15. Paris.

Boulanger, R.

1970 *Turkey.* Trans. J. S. Hardman. Hachette World Guides. Paris.

Boyer, G.

1957 *Textes juridiques et administratifs.* ARM 8. Paris.

1958 *Textes juridiques et administratifs.* ARMT 8. Paris.

B. R. 513 *Syria*

1944 B. R. 513 (Restricted). *Geographical Handbook Series: Syria. April 1943. Naval Intelligence Division.* Reprinted 1944 with minor corrections. Prepared under the direction of Lt.-Col. K. Mason. (No place).

Briggs, C. A., and Briggs, E. G.

1906 *A Critical and Exegetical Commentary on the Book of Psalms.* The International Critical Commentary. Edinburgh.

Broadhurst, R. J. C., ed. and trans.

1952 *The Travels of Ibn Jubair.* London.

Brooks, E. W., ed. and trans.

1923 *John of Ephesus.* Lives of the Eastern Saints, ed. and trans. E. W. Brooks. *Patrologia Orientalis* 17/1. Paris.

Buccellati, G.

1977 A Cuneiform Tablet of the Early Second Millennium B.C. *Syro-Mesopotamian Studies* 1/4.

Buccellati, G., and Biggs, R.

1969 *Cuneiform Texts from Nippur: The Eighth and Ninth Seasons.* Assyriological Studies 17. Chicago.

Burke, M. L.

1963 *Textes administratifs de la salle 111 du palais.* ARMT 11. Paris.

1964a Lettres de Numušda-naḫrâri et de trois autres correspondants à Idiniatum. ARMT 13: 81–102. Paris.

1964b Lettres de Numušda-nahrâri et de trois autres correspondants à Idiniatum. *Syria* 41: 67-103.

Cagni, L.

1981 *La lingua di Ebla.* Atti del Convegno internazionali (Napoli, 21-23 Aprile 1980). Naples.

1983 Miscellanea Neo-Sumerica, IX. *Oriens Antiquus* 22: 73-118.

Campbell, E. F., Jr.

1975 *Ruth: A New Translation with Introduction, Notes, and Commentary.* Anchor Bible 7. Garden City, New York.

Canard, M.

1951 *Histoire de la Dynastie des H'amdanides de Jezira et de Syrie* 1. Publications de la Faculté des Lettres d'Alger 2/21. Algiers.

Caquot, A.; Sznycer, M.; and Herdner, A.

1974 *Textes ougaritiques* 1: *Mythes et Légendes.* Paris.

Cassuto, U.

1975 *Biblical and Oriental Studies* 2. Bible and Ancient Oriental Texts 2. Jerusalem.

Castellino, G.

1972 *Two Shulgi Hymns.* Studi Semitici 42. Rome.

Chabot, J.-B., ed. and trans.

1899-1910 *Chronique de Michel le Syrien, patriarche jacobite d'Antioche (1166-1199).* 4 vols. Paris. (Offprint edition, Brussels, 1963.)

Charpin, D.

1980 *Archives familiales et propriété privée en Babylonie ancienne: Étude des documents de "Tell Sifr."* Centre de Recherches d'Histoire et de Philologie de la IVe Section de l'École Pratique des Hautes Études 2. Hautes Études Orientale 12. Paris and Geneva.

1982 "Mari et le calendrier d'Ebla." *Revue d'Assyriologie et d'Archéologie Orientale* 76: 1-6.

1983a Relectures d'A.R.M. VIII: compléments. *Mari—Annales de Recherches Interdisciplinaires* 2: 61-74.

1983b Un inventaire général des trésors du palais de Mari. *Mari—Annales de Recherches Interdisciplinaires* 2: 211-14.

1984 Inscriptions votives d'époque Assyrienne. *Mari—Annales de Recherches Interdisciplinaires* 3: 41-81.

1985 Les archives du devin Asqudum dans la résidence du "Chantier A." *Mari—Annales de Recherches Interdisciplinaires* 4: 453-62.

Charpin, D., and Durand, J.-M.

1983 Relectures d'A.R.M. VII. *Mari—Annales de Recherches Interdisciplinaires* 2: 75-115.

1985 La prise du pouvoir par Zimri-Lim. *Mari—Annales de Recherches Interdisciplinaires* 4: 293-343.

Civil, M.

1962 Un nouveau synchronisme Mari—IIIe dynastie d'Ur. *Revue d'Assyriologie et d'Archéologie Orientale* 56: 213.

1967 Šu-Sîn's Historical Inscriptions: Collection B. *Journal of Cuneiform Studies* 21: 24-38.

1969 *The Series LÚ = ša and Related Texts.* Materials for the Sumerian Lexicon 12. Rome.

1979 *Ea A = naqû, Aa A = naqû, with Their Forerunners and Related Texts.* Materials for the Sumerian Lexicon 14. Rome.

1982 Studies on Early Dynastic Lexicography, I. *Oriens Antiquus* 21: 1–26.

Claudius Ptolemy

See C. Müller (1884).

Clay, A. T.

1927 *Letters and Transactions from Cappadocia.* Babylonian Inscriptions in the Collection of James B. Nies 4. New Haven.

Cohen, M. E.

1976 A New Naram-Sin Date Formula. *Journal of Cuneiform Studies* 28: 227–32.

Collon, D.

1975 *The Seal Impressions from Tell Atchana/Alalakh.* Alter Orient und Altes Testament 27. Neukirchen-Vluyn.

Contenau, G.

1920 *Tablettes Cappadociennes.* Musée du Louvre—Département des Antiquités Orientales, Textes Cunéiformes 4. Paris.

Cooper, J. S.

1986 *Sumerian and Akkadian Royal Inscriptions* 1: *Presargonic Inscriptions.* New Haven.

Dahood, M.

1966 *Psalms 1–50.* Anchor Bible 16. Garden City, New York.

Dalley, S.

1968 The Tablets from Tell al-Rimah 1967: A Preliminary Report. *Iraq* 30: 87–97.

1976 Old Babylonian Trade in Textiles at Tell al-Rimah. *Iraq* 39: 155–59.

Dalley, S.; Walker, C. B. F.; and Hawkins, J. D.

1976 *The Old Babylonian Tablets from Tell al-Rimah.* Hertford, England.

de Boor, C., ed.

1887 *Theophylacti Simocattae Historiae.* Leipzig.

Deimel, A.

1914 *Pantheon babylonicum: Nomina deorum e textibus cuneiformibus excerpta et ordine alphabetico distributa.* Rome.

1922 *Schultexte aus Fara, in Umschrift herausgegeben und bearbeitet.* Wissenschaftliche Veröffentlichungen der Deutschen Orient-Gesellschaft 43. Leipzig.

Delitzsch, F.

1873 Das Salomonisches Spruchbuch. In C. F. Keil and F. Delitzsch, *Biblischer Commentar über das alte Testament* 4: *Poetische Bücher* 3. Leipzig.

1950 *Biblical Commentary on the Proverbs of Solomon,* vol. 2. Trans. M. G. Eaton. Grand Rapids, Michigan.

del Monte, G. F., and Tischler, J.
1978 *Die Orts- und Gewässernamen der hethitischen Texte.* Répertoire géographique des textes cunéiformes 6. Tübinger Atlas der Vorderen Orients, Reihe B (Geisteswissenschaften) 7/6. Wiesbaden.

Dever, W. G.
1977 The Patriarchal Traditions. In J. H. Hayes and J. M. Miller, *Israelite and Judaean History,* 70–120. Philadelphia.

Dewing, H. B., ed. and trans.
1914 *Procopius: History of the Wars.* 8 vols. Loeb Classical Library. London and New York.

Dhorme, É.
1938 La question des Ḫabiri. *Revue de l'Histoire des Religions* 118: 170–87.

Diakonoff, I. M.
1968 *Predystorija armjanskogo naroda: istorija Armjanskogo nagor'ja s 1500 po 500 g. do n. e.: xurrity, luvijcy, protoarmjane.* Erevan.

Dietrich, M.; Loretz, O.; and Sanmartín, J.
1976 *Die keilalphabetischen Texte aus Ugarit: Einschliesslich der keilalphabetischen Texte ausserhalb Ugarits* 1: *Transcription.* Alter Orient und Altes Testament 24. Neukirchen-Vluyn.

Dillemann, L.
1962 *Haute Mésopotamie orientale et pays adjacents: Contribution à la géographie historique de la region du Ve s. avant l'ère chretienne au VIe s. de cette ère.* Institut Français d'Archéologie de Beyrouth, Bibliothèque Archéologique et Historique 72. Paris.

Donald, T.
1964 *Old Akkadian Tablets in the Liverpool Museum.* Manchester Cuneiform Studies 9/1. Manchester.

Dornemann, R. H.
1978 Tell Hadidi: A Bronze Age City on the Euphrates. *Archaeology* 31/6: 20–26.
1979 Tell Hadidi: A Millennium of Bronze Age Occupation. *Annual of the American Schools of Oriental Research* 44: 113–51.
1981 The Late Bronze Age Pottery Tradition at Tell Hadidi, Syria. *Bulletin of the American Schools of Oriental Research* 241: 29–47, 59.
1982 Tell Hadidi. *Archiv für Orientforschung* 28: 218–23.

Dossin, G.
1930 Une inscription cunéiforme de haute Syrie. *Revue d'Assyriologie et d'Archéologie Orientale* 27: 85–92.
1933 *Lettres de la première dynastie babylonienne.* Musée du Louvre—Département des Antiquités Orientales, Textes Cuneiformes 17. Paris.
1938a Les archives épistolaires du palais de Mari. *Syria* 19: 106–26.
1938b Signaux lumineux au pays de Mari. *Revue d'Assyriologie et d'Archéologie Orientale* 35: 174–86.
1939a Benjaminites dans les textes de Mari. In *Mélanges Syriens offerts à Monsieur René Dussaud, secrétaire perpétuel de l'Académie des*

Inscriptions et Belles-lettres par ses amis et ses élèves. Institut Français d'Archéologie de Beyrouth, Bibliothèque Archéologique et Historique 30/2: 981–96. Paris.

1939b Iamḫad et Qatanum. *Revue d'Assyriologie et d'Archéologie Orientale* 36: 46–54.

1939c Les archives économiques du palais de Mari. *Syria* 20: 97–113.

1939d Un cas d'ordalie par le dieu Fleuve d'après une lettre de Mari. In J. Friedrich, J. G. Lautner, and J. Miles, eds., *Symbolae ad iura Orientis Antiqui pertinentis Paulo Koschaker dedicatae,* 112–18. Studia et Documenta ad Iura Orientis Antiqui Pertinentia 2. Leiden.

1939e Une mention de Hattuša dans une lettre de Mari. *Revue Hittite et Asianique* 5: 70–76.

1940 Inscriptions de fondation provenant de Mari. *Syria* 21: 152–69.

1946 *Lettres.* ARM 1. Paris.

1950a *Correspondance de Šamši-Addu et de ses fils.* ARMT 1. Paris.

1950b Le Panthéon de Mari. In A. Parrot, ed., *Studia Mariana,* 41–50. Documenta et Monumenta Orientis Antiqui 4. Leiden.

1950c Transcription, Traductions et Bref Commentaire. Contribution to A. Lods's article, Une tablette inédite de Mari, intéressante pour l'histoire ancienne du prophétisme sémitique. In H. H. Rowley, ed., *Studies in Old Testament Prophecy Presented to Professor Theodore H. Robinson,* 103–7. Edinburgh.

1951a *Lettres.* ARM 4. Paris.

1951b *Lettres.* ARM 5. Paris.

1951c *Correspondance de Šamši-Addu et de ses fils (suite).* ARMT 4. Paris.

1952a *Correspondance de Iasmaḫ-Addu.* ARMT 5. Paris.

1952b Le royaume d'Alep en le XVIIIe siècle avant notre ère d'après les 'Archives de Mari.' *Bulletin des Académie Royale de Belgique. Classe des Lettres* 38: 229–39.

1955 L'inscription de fondation de Iaḫdun-lim, Roi de Mari. *Syria* 32: 1–28.

1956 Une lettre de Iarîm-Lim, roi d'Alep à Iašûb-Iaḫad, roi de Dîr. *Syria* 33: 63–69.

1958 Deux lettres de Mari, relatives à l'ordalie. *Académie des Inscriptions et Belles-Lettres. Comptes rendus*: 387–93. Paris.

1959 Légendes des empreintes. In A. Parot, *Mission Archéologique de Mari, 2/3: Le palais: Documents et monuments,* 251–57. Paris

1961–62 La site de la ville de Kaḫat. *Les Annales Archéologique de Syrie* 11: 197–206 and pls. I–II.

1964a Tablette administrative. ARMT 13: ix–xii, 1–14. Paris.

1964b A propos de la tablette administrative de A.R.M.T., XIII, no. 1. *Syria* 41: 21–24.

1967a *La correspondance féminine.* ARM 10. Paris.

1967b Les Inscriptions des Temples de Ninni-Zaza et de (G)Ištarat. In A. Parrot, *Les temples d'Ishtarat et de Ninni-Zaza.* Mission Archéologique de Mari 3: 307–31. Paris.

1967c Un "pantheon" d'Ur III à Mari. *Revue d'Assyriologie et d'Archéologie Orientale* 61: 97–104.

1970 La route de l'étain en Mésopotamie au temps de Zimri-Lim. *Revue d'Assyriologique et d'Archéologie Orientale* 64: 97–106.

1971 Deux listes nominatives du règne de Sûmu-Iamam. *Revue d'Assyriologie et d'Archéologie Orientale* 65: 37–66.

1972a *Adaššum* et *kirḫum* dans des textes de Mari. *Revue d'Assyriologie et d'Archéologie Orientale* 66: 111–30.

1972b Le *madārum* dans les "Archives royales de Mari." In D. O. Edzard, ed., *Geselleschaftsklassen im alten Zweistromland und in den angrenzenden Gebiete: XVIII. Rencontre assyriologique internationale, München, 29. Juin bis 3. Juli 1970*, 53–63. Bayerische Akademie der Wissenschaften, Philosophisch-Historische Klasse, 75. Veröffentlichungen der Kommission zur Erschleissung von Keilschrifttexte, A/6. Munich.

1973 Une opposition familiale. In A. Finet, ed., *La voix de l'opposition en Mésopotamie: Colloque organisé par l'Institut des Hautes Études de Belgique 19 et 20 Mars 1973*, 179–88. Brussels.

1978 *Correspondance féminine.* ARMT 10. Paris.

Forthcoming *Correspondance d'Itûr-Asdu.* ARM 20 and ARMT 20. Paris.

Dossin, G.; Bottéro, J.; Birot, M.; Burke, M. L.; Kupper, J.-R.; and Finet, A.

1964 *Textes divers.* ARMT 13. Paris.

Driver, G. R.

1933 Cappadocian Texts at Oxford. *Analecta Orientalia* 6: 68–70, 8 plates.

du Mesnil du Buisson, R.

1948 *Baghouz, l'ancienne Corosôtê.* Documenta et Monumenta ad Orientis Antiqui 3. Leiden.

Durand, J.-M.

1980 À propos du "Pantheon" d'Ur III à Mari. *Revue d'Assyriologie et Archéologie Orientale* 74: 174–76.

1981a À propos de légendes des empreintes de sceaux des *Šakkanakku* de Mari. *Revue d'Assyriologie et d'Archéologie Orientale* 75: 180–81.

1981b À propos de MAM II, p. 255 (ME, 227). *Revue d'Assyriologie et d'Archéologie Orientale* 75: 188.

1982a *Textes administratifs des salles 134 et 160 du Palais de Mari.* ARM 21. Paris.

1982b Relectures d'A.R.M. VIII I: collations. *Mari—Annales de Recherches Interdisciplinaires* 1: 91–135.

1982c Sumérien et Akkadien en pays Amorite, 1: Un document juridique archaïque de Mari. *Mari—Annales de Recherches Interdisciplinaires* 1: 79–89.

1983a *Textes administratifs des salles 134 et 160 du Palais de Mari transcrites et traduits.* ARMT 21. Paris.

1983b Relectures d'A.R.M. VIII, II: le travail du métal à Mari. *Mari—Annales de Recherches Interdisciplinaires* 2: 123–39.

1983c Relecture d'A.R.M. XIII, I: lettres de Mukannišum (n° 2-24); II: lettres de Numušda-nahrârî (n° 58–101). *Mari—Annales de Recherches Interdisciplinaires* 2: 141–63.

1983d À propos des foies de Mari. *Mari—Annales de Recherches Interdisciplinaires* 2: 218.

1984a Trois études sur Mari. *Mari—Annales de Recherches Interdisciplinaires* 3: 127–80.

1984b Deux tablettes de Mari? *Mari—Annales de Recherches Interdisciplinaires* 3: 264–66.

1984c À propos du nom de nombre 10 000, à Mari. *Mari—Annales de Recherches Interdisciplinaires* 3: 278–79.

Durand, J.-M., and Kupper, J.-R., eds.

1985 *Miscellanea babylonica: Mélanges offerts à Maurice Birot.* Paris.

During Caspers, E. C. L., and Govindankutty, A.

1978 R. Thapar's Dravidian Hypothesis for the Locations of Meluḫḫa, Dilmun, and Makan: A Critical Reconsideration. *Journal of the Economic and Social History of the Orient* 21: 113–45.

Ebeling, E.

1910 Das Verbum der El-Amarna Briefe. *Beiträge zur Assyriologie und semitische Sprachwissenschaft* 8: 39–79.

Ebeling, E., and Meissner, B., *et al.*

1932– *Reallexikon der Assyriologie.* 6 vols. to date. Berlin, Leipzig, and New York.

Ebor, D., chair of joint committee

1970 *The New English Bible with the Apocraypha.* 2nd edition. Oxford.

Edzard, D. O.

1960 Sumerer und Semiten in der frühen Geschichte Mesopotamiens. *Genava* 8: 241–58.

1967 Pantheon und Kult in Mari. In J.-R. Kupper, *La Civilisation de Mari,* 51–71. Paris.

1970 *Altbabylonische Rechts- und Wirtschaftsurkunden aus Tell ed-Dēr im Iraq Museum, Baghdad.* Abhandlungen der Bayerischen Akademie der Wissenschaften, Philosophisch-Historische Klasse, 72. Munich.

1981a *Verwaltungstexte verscheidenen Inhalts (aus dem Archiv L.2769).* Archivi Reali di Ebla, Testi 2. Rome.

1981b Der Text TM.75.G.1444 aus Ebla. *Studi Eblaiti* 4: 35–59.

1981c Neue Erwägungen zum Brief des Enna-Dagan von Mari (TM.75. G.2367). *Studi Eblaiti* 4: 89–97.

1984 *Hymnen, Beschwörungen und Verwandtes (aus dem Archiv L.2769).* Archivi Reali di Ebla, Testi 5. Rome.

Edzard, D. O., and Farber, G.

1974 *Die Orts- und Gewässernamen der Zeit der 3. Dynasty von Ur.* Répertoire géographique des textes cunéiformes 1. Tübinger Atlas des Vorderen Orients, Reihe B (Geisteswissenschaften) 7/2. Wiesbaden.

Edzard, D. O.; Farber, G.; and Sollberger, E.

1977 *Die Orts- und Gewässernamen der präsargonischen und sargonischen Zeit.* Répertoire géographique des textes cunéiformes 1. Tübinger Altas des Vorderen Orients, Reihe B (Geisteswissenschaften) 7/1. Wiesbaden.

Eisen, G. A.
1940 *Ancient Oriental Cylinder and Other Seals, with a Description of the Collection of Mrs. William H. Moore.* Oriental Institute Publications 47. Chicago.

Eisser, G., and Lewy, J.
1930–35 *Die altassyrischen Rechtsurkunden vom Kültepe.* Mitteilungen der Vorderasiatisch-Aegyptischen Gesellschaft 33 (1930: parts I and II, Urkunden 1–290) and 35 (1935: parts III and IV, Urkunden 291–341, and Register zu teil I–IV). Leipzig.

Elliger, K., and Rudolph, W., eds.
1967–77 *Biblia Hebraica Stuttgartensia.* Stuttgart.

Ellis, M. deJ.
1974 The Division of Property at Tell Harmal. *Journal of Cuneiform Studies* 26: 133–53.

Erkanal-Öktü, A.
1979 Ein Rollsiegel aus der Nähe von Gercüş. *Zeitschrift für Assyriologie und vorderasiatische Archäologie* 69: 234–43.

Erman, A., and Grapow, H.
1926 *Wörterbuch der Ägyptischen Sprache.* Berlin.

Evagrius
See Migne (1857–66).

Fales, F. M.
1973 *Censimenti e catasti di epoca neo-assira.* Centro per le antichità e la storia dell'arte de vicino Oriente. Studi economici e technologici 2. Rome.
1984 An Archaic Text from Mari. *Mari—Annales de Recherches Interdisciplinaires* 3: 269–70.

Fales, F. M., and Krispijn, T. J. H.
1979–80 An Early Ur III Copy of the Abū Ṣalābikh "Names and Professions" List. *Jaarbericht van het Vooraziatisch-Egyptisch Genootschap "Ex Oriente Lux"* 26: 39–46.

Falkenstein, A.
1954 Review of *Lettres,* by G. Dossin (ARM 1); *Lettres,* by C.-F. Jean (ARM 2); and *Lettres,* by J.-R. Kupper (ARM 3). *Bibliotheca Orientalis* 11: 112–17.
1960 Review of *Textes administratifs de la salle 110,* by J. Bottéro (ARM 7); *Textes juridiques et administratifs,* by G. Boyer (ARM 8); *Textes économiques et administratifs,* by J. Bottéro (ARMT 7); and *Textes juridiques et administratifs,* by G. Boyer (ARMT 8). *Bibliotheca Orientalis* 17: 175–79.
1963 Zu den Inschriftenfunden der Grabung in Uruk-Warka 1960–1961. *Baghdader Mitteilungen* 2: 1–82.

Falkner, M.
1957–58 Studien zur Geographie des alten Mesopotamien. *Archiv für Orientforschung* 18: 1–37.

Faulkner, R. O.
1962 *A Concise Dictionary of Middle Egyptian.* Oxford.

Figulla, H. H.
1923 *Keilschrifttexte aus Boghazköi.* Wissenschaftliche Veröffentlichungen der Deutschen Orient-Gesellschaft 30/3. Leipzig.

Figulla, H. H.; Forrer, E.; and Weidner, E. F.
1923 *Keilschrifttexte aus Boghazköi.* Wissenschaftliche Veröffentlichungen der Deutschen Orient-Gesellschaft 30/1. Leipzig.

Finet, A.
1954 Liste des erreurs de scribes, Index des noms propres, and Lexique. In J. Bottéro and A. Finet, *Répértoire analytique des tomes I à V.* ARMT 15: 95–281. Paris.
1956 *L'accadien des lettres de Mari.* Académie Royale de Belgique, Classe des Lettres et des Sciences Morales et Politiques 51/1. Brussels.
1959 Une affaire de disette dans un district du royaume de Mari. *Revue d'Assyriologie et d'Archéologie Orientale* 53: 57–69.
1964a Lettres de Iawi-Ilâ. ARMT 13: 137–56. Paris.
1964b Iawi-Ilâ, roi de Talḫayûm. *Syria* 41: 117–42.
1966a Adalšenni, roi de Burundum. *Revue d'Assyriologie et d'Archéologie Orientale* 60: 17–28.
1966b La place du devin dans la société de Mari. In *La divination en Mésopotamie ancienne et dans les régions voisines,* 87–93. Rencontre Assyriologique Internationale 14. Paris.
1973 *La voix de l'opposition en Mésopotamie.* Brussels.

Fisher, R. W.
1966 A Study of the Semitic Root BŚR. Ph.D. dissertation, University of Michigan.
1974 The Herald of Good News in Second Isaiah. In J. J. Jackson and M. Kessler, eds., *Rhetorical Criticism: Essays in Honor of James Muilenburg,* 117–32. Pittsburgh Theological Monograph Series 1. Pittsburgh.

Forbes, R. J.
1950 *Metallurgy in Antiquity: A Notebook for Archaeologists and Technologists.* Leiden.
1958–64 *Studies in Ancient Technology.* 9 vols. Leiden.
1971 *Studies in Ancient Technology* 8. 2nd edition. Leiden.

Forrer, E.
1920a *Keilschrifttexte aus Boghazköi.* Wissenschaftliche Veröffentlichungen der Deutschen Orient-Gesellschaft 30/4. Leipzig.
1920b *Die Provinzeinteilung des assyrischen Reiches.* Leipzig.
1922 *Die Boghazköi-Texte in Umschrift* 2. Wissenschaftliche Veröffentlichungen der Deutschen Orient-Gesellschaft 42/1 Leipzig.
1932 Alzi. In E. Ebeling and B. Meissner *et al., Reallexikon der Assyriologie* 1: 88–89. Berlin.

Foster, B. R.
1982 An Agricultural Archive from Sargonic Akkad. *Acta Sumerologica* 4: 7–51.

Frankena, R.
1974 *Briefe aus dem Berliner Museum.* Altbabylonische Briefe 6. Leiden.

Friedrich, J.
1924–25 Ein Bruchstück des Vertrages Mattiwaza-Suppiluliuma in hethitischer Sprache? *Archiv für Orientforschung* 2: 119–24.

Friedrich, J.; Meyer, G. R.; Ungnad, A.; and Weidner, E.
1940 *Die Inschriften vom Tell Halaf: Keilschrifttexte und aramäische Urkunden aus einer assyrischen Provinzhauptstadt.* Archiv für Orientforschung Beiheft 6. Graz. Reprint, Osnabrück, 1967.

Fritsch, C. T.
1955 The Book of Proverbs: Introduction and Exegesis. In G. A. Buttrick, ed., *The Interpreter's Bible* 4: 767–957. Nashville.

Fugmann, E.
1958 *Hama: Fouilles et recherches de la fondation Carlsberg, 1931–1938. L'architecture des périodes pré-Hellénistique* 2/1. Copenhagen.

Gabriel, A.
1940 *Voyages archéologique dans le Turquie orientale, avec un recueil d'inscriptions arabes par Jean Sauvaget.* 2 vols. Paris.

Gadd, C. J.
1940 Tablets from Chagar Bazar and Tell Brak, 1937–38. *Iraq* 7: 22–61, pls. I–V.
1973 Hammurabi and the End of His Dynasty. *CAH*³ 2/1: 176–227.

Gadd, C. J.; Legrain, L.; and Smith, S.
1928 *Ur Excavation, Texts* 1: *Royal Inscriptions.* London.

Gaebelein, P. W., Jr.
1976 Graphemic Analysis of Old Babylonian Letters from Mari. Ph.D. dissertation, University of California, Los Angeles.

Gallery, M.
1980 The Office of the *Šatammu* in the Old Babylonian Period. *Archiv für Orientforschung* 27: 1–36.
1981 Review of *The Old Babylonian Tablets from Tell al Rimah,* by S. Dalley, C. B. F. Walker, and J. D. Hawkins. *Journal of Near Eastern Studies* 40: 343–49.

Gardiner, A. H.
1933 The Dakhleh Stela. *Journal of Egyptian Archaeology* 19: 19–30.

Garelli, P.
1963 *Les Assyriens en Cappadoce.* Bibliothèque archéologique et historique de l'Institut Français d'Archéologie d'Istanbul 19. Paris.
1965 Tablettes Cappadociennes de Collections Diverse 3: Tablettes du Musée d'Art et d'Histoire de Genève. *Revue d'Assyriologie et d'Archéologie Orientale* 59: 19–48.

Garstang, J.
1942 Šamuḫa and Malatia. *Journal of Near Eastern Studies* 1: 450–59.
1943 Hittite Military Roads in Asia Minor. *American Journal of Archaeology* 47: 35–62.

Gelb, I. J.
1935 *Inscriptions from Alishar and Vicinity.* Researches in Anatolia 6. Oriental Institute Publications 27. Chicago.
1938 Studies in the Topography of Western Asia. *American Journal of Semitic Languages and Literatures* 55: 66–85.

1952 *Sargonic Texts from the Diyala Region.* Materials for the Assyrian Dictionary 1. Chicago.

1953 The Double Names of the Hittite Kings. *Rocznik Orientalistyczy* 17: 146–54.

1955 *Old Akkadian Inscriptions in the Chicago Natural History Museum: Texts of Legal and Business Interest.* Fieldiana: Anthropology 44/2. Chicago.

1956 On the Recently Published Economic Texts from Mari. *Revue d'Assyriologie et d'Archéologie Orientale* 50: 1–12.

1957 *Glossary of Old Akkadian.* Materials for the Assyrian Dictionary 3. Chicago.

1960 Sumerians and Akkadians in Their Ethno-linguistic Relationship. *Genava* 8: 258–71.

1961[2] *Old Akkadian Writing and Grammar.* Materials for the Assyrian Dictionary 2. 2nd edition. Chicago. (First edition, 1952.)

1967 Approaches to the Study of Ancient Society. *Journal of the American Oriental Society* 87: 1–8.

1968 The Word for Dragoman in the Ancient Near East. *Glossa* 2: 93–104.

1969 *Sequential Reconstruction of Proto-Akkadian.* Assyriological Studies 18. Chicago.

1970a *Sargonic Texts in the Louvre Museum.* Materials for the Assyrian Dictionary 4. Chicago.

1970b *Sargonic Texts in the Ashmolean Museum, Oxford.* Materials for the Assyrian Dictionary 5. Chicago.

1975 Homo Ludens in Early Mesopotamia. *Studia Orientalia* 46: 43–76.

1977 Thoughts about Ibla: A Preliminary Evaluation, March 1977. *Syro-Mesopotamian Studies* 1: 3–30.

1980 *Computer-aided Analysis of Amorite.* Assyriological Studies 21. Chicago.

1981 Ebla and the Kish Civilization. In L. Cagni, ed., *La Lingua di Ebla,* 10–73. Naples.

Geller, M. J.

n.d. The Lugal of Mari at Ebla and the Sumerian King List. Privately circulated.

Gelzer, H.

1890 *Georgii Cyprii Descriptio Orbis Romani: Accedit Leonis Imperatoris Dia typosis, genuina ac inedita.* Leipzig.

Gemser, B.

1963 *Spruche Salomos.* 2nd edition. Handbuch zum alten Testament 16. Tübingen.

Genouillac, H. de

1922 *Textes économiques d'Oumma de l'époque d'Our.* Musée du Louvre—Département des Antiquités Orientales, Textes Cuneiformes 5. Paris.

Georgius Cyprius

See Gelzer (1890).

Gibson, J. C. L.
1978 *Canaanite Myths and Legends.* Edinburgh. (Originally edited by G. R. Driver and published in the series Old Testament Studies under the auspices of the Society for Old Testament Study.)

Gibson, M., and Biggs, R., eds.
1977 *Seals and Sealing in the Ancient Near East.* Bibliotheca Mesopotamica 6. Malibu, California.

Giorgadze, G. G.
1969 Xetty i xurrity po drevnexettskim tekstam (Hittites and Hurrians in Old Hittite Texts). *Vestnik Drevnii Istorii* 1 (107): 71–85 [English summary on p. 85].

Glaeseman, R. R.
1978 *The Practice of the King's Meal at Mari: A System of Food Distribution in the 2nd Millennium B.C.* Ph.D. diss., University of California at Los Angeles.

Goetze, A.
1940 *Kizzuwatna and the Problem of Hittite Geography.* Yale Oriental Series, Researches 22. New Haven.
1946 Review of *Hurrians and Subarians,* by I. J. Gelb. *Journal of Near Eastern Studies* 5: 165–68.
1953a An Old Babylonian Itinerary. *Journal of Cuneiform Studies* 7: 51–72.
1953b Four Ur Dynasty Tablets Mentioning Foreigners. *Journal of Cuneiform Studies* 7: 103–7.
1955 An Incantation against Diseases. *Journal of Cuneiform Studies* 9: 8–18.
1957 The Roads of Northern Cappadocia in Hittite Times. *Revue Hittite et Asianique* 15: 91–103.
1960 Review of *The Geography of the Hittite Empire,* by J. Garstang and O. R. Gurney. *Journal of Cuneiform Studies* 14: 43–48.
1964 Remarks on the Old Babylonian Itinerary. *Journal of Cuneiform Studies* 18: 114–19.

Gordis, R.
1974 *The Song of Songs and Lamentations.* 2nd edition. New York.

Gordon, C. H.
1965 *Ugaritic Textbook.* Analecta Orientalia 38. Rome.

Görg, M., ed.
1983 *Fontes atque Pontes: Eine festgabe für Hellmut Brunner.* Ägypten und Altes Testament 5. Wiesbaden.

Grayson, A. K.
1971 The Early Development of Assyrian Monarchy. *Ugarit-Forschungen* 3: 311–19.
1972–76 *Assyrian Royal Inscriptions* 1: *From the Beginning to Ashur-resha-ishi I*; 2: *From Tiglath-Pileser to Ashur-nasir-apli II.* Records of the Ancient Near East 2. Wiesbaden.

Grayson, A. K., and Sollberger, E.
1976 L'insurrection générale contre Narām-Suen. *Revue d'Assyriologie et d'Archéologie Orientale* 70: 103–28.

Gröndahl, F.
1967 *Die Personennamen der Texte aus Ugarit.* Studia Pohl 1. Rome.

Groneberg, B.
1980 *Die Orts- und Gewässernamen der altababylonischen Zeit.* Répertoire géographique des textes cunéiformes 3. Tübinger Atlas der Vorderen Orients, Reihe B (Geisteswissenschaften) 7/3. Wiesbaden.

Gunkel, H.
1968 *Die Psalmen.* 5th edition. Göttingen.

Gurney, O. R.
1973 Anatolia c. 1750–1600 B.C. *CAH*[3] 2/1: 228–55.

Güterbock, H. G.
1938 Die historische Tradition und ihre literarische Gestaltung bei Babylonien und Hethitern bis 1200. Zweiter Teil: Hethiter. *Zeitschrift für Assyriologie und verwandte Gebiete* 44: 45–149.

Güterbock, H. G., and Jacobsen, T., eds.
1965 *Studies in Honor of Benno Landsberger on His Seventy-fifth Birthday, April 21, 1965.* Assyriological Studies 16. Chicago.

Hachman, R.
1982 *Bericht über die Ergebnisse der Ausgrabungen in Kāmid el-Lōz in den Jahren 1971 bis 1974.* Saarbrücker Beiträge zur Altertumskunde 32. Bonn.

Hackman, G. G.
1958 *Sumerian and Akkadian Administrative Texts from Predynastic Times to the End of the Akkad Dynasty.* Babylonian Inscriptions in the Collection of James B. Nies 8. New Haven.

Hallo, W. W.
1953 The Ensi's of the Ur III Dynasty. M.A. Thesis, University of Chicago.
1957 *Early Mesopotamian Royal Titles.* American Oriental Series 43. New Haven.
1963 *Tabulae cuneiformes a F. M. Th. de Liagre Böhl collectae* 3. Leiden.
1964 The Road to Emar. *Journal of Cuneiform Studies* 18: 57–88.

Hamlin, C.
1971 The Ḫabur Ware Ceramic Assemblage of Northern Mesopotamia: An Analysis of Its Distribution. Ph.D. dissertation, University of Pennsylvania.

Harris, R.
1955 The Archive of the Sin Temple in Khafaje. *Journal of Cuneiform Studies* 9: 31–58, 51–105 (with an appendix by T. Jacobsen containing copies of the Khafaje tablets, 106–20).

Haury, J.
1905 *Procopii Caesariensis opera omnia,* 1: *De bellis Libri I–IV.* Leipzig.
1913 *Procopii Caesariensis opere omnia, 3/2: Peri ktismaton Libri VI sive De aedificiis. . . .* Leipzig. Reprinted with additions and corrections, 1964.

Haussig, H. W., ed.
1965 *Wörterbuch der Mythologie,* 1/1: *Die alten Kulturvölker: Götter und Mythen in vorderen Orient.* Stuttgart.

Hawkins, J. D.
1969 The Babil Stele of Assurnasirpal. *Anatolian Studies* 19: 111–20, pl. x.
1976 The Inscribed Seal Impressions. In S. Dalley, C. B. F. Walker, and J. D. Hawkins, *The Old Babylonian Tablets from Tell al Rimah*, 247–55. Hertford, England.

Hayes, J. H., and Miller, J. M., eds.
1977 *Israelite and Judaean History*. Philadelphia.

Heinrich, E., *et al.*
1971 Dritter vorläufiger Bericht über die von der Deutschen Orient-Gesellschaft mit Mitteln der Stiftung Volkswagenwerk in Ḥabūba Kabira und in Mumbaqat unternommenen archäologischen Untersuchungen (Herbstkampagne 1970). *Mitteilungen der Deutschen Orient-Gesellschaft* 103: 5–58.
1973 Vierter vorläufiger Bericht über die von der Deutschen Orient-Gesellschaft mit Mitteln der Stiftung Volkswagenwerk in Ḥabūba Kabira (Ḥabūba Kabira, Herbstkampagnen 1971 und 1972 sowie Testgrabung Früjahr 1973) und in Mumbaqat (Tall Munbaqa, Herbstkampagne 1971) unternommenen archäologischen Untersuchungen. *Mitteilungen der Deutschen Orient-Gesellschaft* 105: 5–52.

Heintz, J. G.; Marx, A.; and Millot, L.
1975 *Index documentaire des textes de Mari*. ARMT 17/1. Paris.

Helck, W.
1983 Zur Herkunft der Erzählung des sog. Astartepapyrus. In M. Görg, *Fontes atque Pontes*, 215–23. Wiesbaden.

Helck, W., and Otto, E., eds.
1980 *Lexikon der Ägyptologie*, 3 (Horhekenu–Megeb). Wiesbaden.

Hertzberg, H. W.
1959 *Die Bücher Josua, Richter, Ruth*. 2nd edition. Das Alt Testament Deutsch 9. Göttingen.

Hillers, D. R.
1972 *Lamentations: A New Translation with Introduction and Commentary*. Anchor Bible 7A. Garden City, New York.

Hirsch, H.
1952–53 Keilschrifttexte nach Kopien von T. G. Pinches. *Archiv für Orientforschung* 16: 35–46.
1963 Die Inschriften der Könige von Agade. *Archiv für Orientforschung* 20: 1–82.

Hitti, P. K.
1968 *History of the Arabs from the Earliest Times to the Present*. 9th ed. New York.

Holland, T. A.
1977 Preliminary Report on Excavations at Tell es-Sweyhat, Syria, 1975. *Levant* 9: 36–65.

Holma, H., and Salonen, A.
1940 *Some Cuneiform Tablets from the Time of the Third Ur Dynasty*. Studia Orientalia 9/1. Helsinki.

Hommel, F.
1885 *Geschichte Babyloniens und Assyriens.* Berlin.

Honigmann, E.
1930 Urfa keilschriftlich nachweisbar? *Zeitschrift für Assyriologie und verwandte Gebiete* 39: 301–2.
1935 *Die Ostgrenze des byzantisches Reiches.* Brussels (= A. A. Vasiliev, *Byzance et les Arabes* 3).

Hrouda, B.
1957 *Die bemalte Keramik des zweiten Jahrtausends in Nordmesopotamien und Nordsyrien.* Istanbuler Forschungen 19. Berlin.
1958 Waššukani, Urkiš, Šubat-Enlil: Ein Beitrag zur historischen Geographie des nördlichen Zweistromlandes. *Mitteilungen der Deutschen Orient-Gesellschaft* 90: 22–35.

Huehnergard, J.
1983 Five Tablets from the Vicinity of Emar. *Revue d'Assyriologie et d'Archéologie Orientale* 77: 11–43.

Huffmon, H. B.
1965 *Amorite Personal Names in the Mari Texts: A Structural and Lexical Study.* Baltimore.

Hunger, H.
1976–80 Kalendar. In E. Ebeling and B. Meissner *et al.*, *Reallexikon der Assyriologie* 5: 297–303. Berlin.

Jacobsen, T.
1939 *The Sumerian King List.* Assyriological Studies 11. Chicago.
1955 Autograph copies of Khafaje tablets. *Journal of Cuneiform Studies* 9: 106–20 (appendix to Harris [1955]).
1969 The Battle between Marduk and Tiamat. *Journal of the American Oriental Society* 88: 104–8.

Jean, C.-F.
1939 Excerpta de la correspondance de Mari. *Revue des Études Sémitiques* 1939: 62–69.
1941 *Lettres.* ARM 2. Paris.
1948a Arišen dans les lettres de Mari. *Semitica* 1: 17–24.
1948b Lettres de Mari (IV), transcribes et traduites. *Revue d'Assyriologie et d'Archéologie Orientale* 42: 53–78.
1950a *Lettres diverses.* ARMT 2. Paris.
1950b Les noms propres de personnes dans les lettres de Mari. In A. Parrot, ed., *Studia Mariana,* 63–98. Documenta et Monumenta Orientis Antiqui 4. Leiden.
1952 *Six campagnes de fouilles à Mari, 1933–1939: Synthèse des resultats.* Cahiers de la nouvelle revue théologique 9. Tournai–Paris.

Jestin, R. R.
1937 *Tablettes sumériennes de Šuruppak conservées au Musée de Stamboul.* Mémoires de l'Institut français d'archéologie de Stamboul 3. Paris.
1952 Textes économiques de Mari (IIIe Dynastie d'Ur). *Revue d'Assyriologie et d'Archéologie Orientale* 46: 185–202.

John of Ephesus
See Brooks (1923).

Johns, C. H. W.
1898–1923 *Assyrian Deeds and Documents Recording the Transfer of Property, Including the So-called Private Contracts, Legal Decisions, and Proclamations Preserved in the Kouyunjik Collections of the British Museum, Chiefly of the 7th Century* B.C. 4 vols. (1: 1898, 2: 1901, 3: 1901, 4: 1923). Cambridge.
1901 *An Assyrian Doomsday Book; or, Liber Censualis of the District Round Ḫarran in the Seventh Century* B.C. Copied from the Cuneiform Tablets in the British Museum. Assyriologische Bibliothek 17. Leipzig.

Jones, T. B., and Snyder, J. W.
1961 *Sumerian Economic Texts from the Third Ur Dynasty: A Catalogue and Discussion of Documents from Various Collections.* Minneapolis.

Kaiser, O.
1959 *Die Mythische Bedeutung des Meeres in Ägypten, Ugarit und Israel.* Beihefte zur Zeitschrift für die Alttestamentliche Wissenschaft 78. Berlin.

Kaufman, S. A.
1974 *The Akkadian Influence on Aramaic.* Assyriological Studies 19. Chicago.

Keiser, C. E., and Kang, S. T.
1971 *Neo-Sumerian Account Texts from Drehem.* Babylonian Inscriptions in the Collection of James B. Nies 3. New Haven.

Kelly-Buccellati, M., and Shelby, W. R.
1977 A Typology of Ceramic Vessels of the Third and Second Millennium from the First Two Seasons. *Syro-Mesopotamian Studies* 1.

Kessler, K.
1980 *Untersuchungen zur historischen Topographie Nordmesopotamiens nach keilschriftlichen Quellen des 1. Jahrtausends v. Chr.* Tübinger Atlas des Vorderen Orients B/26. Wiesbaden.

Kienast, B.
1980 Der Feldzugsbericht des Ennadagan in literar-historischer Sicht. *Oriens Antiquus* 19: 247–61.

Kiepert, H.
1883 [Map] in E. Sachau, *Reise in Syrien und Mesopotamien.* Leipzig.

King, L. W.
1898 *Cuneiform Texts from Babylonian Tablets . . . in the British Museum* 5. London.

Kirkpatrick, A. F.
1902 *The Book of Psalms with Introduction and Notes.* Cambridge.

Kittel, R.
1937 *Biblia Hebraica.* 3rd edition. Leipzig.

Klengel, H.
1965 *Geschichte Syriens im 2. Jahrtausend v. u.Z.* Deutsche Akademie der Wissenschaften zu Berlin, Institut für Orientforschung 40/1. Berlin.

Knudtzon, J. A.
1908–15 *Die El-Amarna-Tafeln.* 2 vols. Vorderasiatische Bibliothek 2/1–2. Leipzig.

Koehler, L.
1955 Psalm 23. *Zeitschrift für die Alttestamentliche Wissenschaft* 68: 227–34.

Koehler, L., and Baumgartner, W., eds.
1953 *Lexicon in veteris testamenti libros.* Leiden.

Kramer, S. N.
1956 *From the Tablets of Sumer: Twenty-Five Firsts in Man's Recorded History.* Indian Hills, Colorado. (Reprinted as *History Begins at Sumer,* Garden City, New York, 1959.)

Kraus, F. R.
1966 *Staatlichen Viehhaltung im altbabylonischen Lande Larsa.* Mededelingen der Koninklijke Nederlandse Akademie van Wetenschappen, afd. letterkunde 29/5. Amsterdam.
1968 *Briefe aus dem Archive des Šamaš-Ḫāzir.* Altbabylonische Briefe in Umschrift und übersetzung im auftrage de Königlich Niederländischen Akademie der Wissenschaften mit unterstützung der Niederländischen Organisation für Reinwissenschaftliche Forschung (Z.W.O.) 4. Leiden.

Kraus, H. J.
1966 *Psalmen.* Biblischer Kommentar, Altes Testament 15/1. Neukirchen-Vluyn.
1968 *Klagelieder (Threni).* 2nd edition. Biblischer Kommentar, Altes Testament 20. Neukirchen-Vluyn.

Krebernik, M.
1982 Zu Syllabar und Orthographie der lexikalischen Texte aus Ebla 1. *Zeitschrift für Assyriologie und vorderasiatische Archäologie* 72: 178–236.
1983 Zu Syllabar und Orthographie der lexikalischen Texte aus Ebla 2 (Glossar). *Zeitschrift für Assyriologie und vorderasiatische Archäologie* 73: 1–47.
1984 *Die Beschwörungen aus Fara und Ebla: Untersuchungen zur ältesten keilschriftlichen Beschwörungsliterature.* Hildesheim.

Küchler, F.
1904 *Beiträge zur Kenntnis der assyrisch-babylonischen Medizin.* Assyriologische Bibliothek 18. Leipzig.

Kupper, J.-R.
1948a *Lettres.* ARM 3. Paris.
1948b Nouvelles lettres de Mari relatives à Ḫammurabi de Babylone. *Revue d'Assyriologie et d'Archéologie Orientale* 42: 35–52.
1949 Uršu. *Revue d'Assyriologie et d'Archéologie Orientale* 43: 79–87.
1950a *Correspondance de Kibri-Dagan, gouverneur de Terqa.* ARMT 3. Paris.
1950b Le recensement dans les textes de Mari. In A. Parrot, ed., *Studia Mariana,* 99–110. Documenta et Monumenta Orientis Antiqui 4. Leiden.
1952 Le canal Išîm-Iaḫdunlim. *Bibliotheca Orientalis* 9: 168–69.
1953 *Lettres.* ARM 6. Paris.
1954 *Correspondance de Baḫdi-Lim préfet du palais de Mari.* ARMT 6. Paris.

1957 *Les nomades en Mésopotamie au temps des rois de Mari.* Bibliotheque de la Faculté de Philosophie et Lettres de l'Université de Liège 142. Paris.

1959 Sceaux-cylindres du temps de Zimri-Lim. *Revue d'Assyriologie et d'Archéologie Orientale* 53: 97–100.

1961 Sutéens et Ḫapiru. *Revue d'Assyriologie et d'Archéologie Orientale* 55: 197–200.

1964a Lettres de Kibri-Dagan au roi. ARMT 13: 103–36. Paris.

1964b Correspondance de Kibri-Dagan. *Syria* 41: 105–16.

1967 *La Civilisation de Mari.* XVe Rencontre Assyriologique Internationale organisée par la Groupe François Thureau-Dangin (Liège, 4–8 Juillet, 1966). Bibliothèque de la Faculté de Philosophie et Lettres de l'Université de Liege 182. Paris.

1969 Rois et *šakkanakku. Journal of Cuneiform Studies* 21: 123–25.

1971 La date des *šakkanakku* de Mari. *Revue d'Assyriologie et d'Archéologie Orientale* 65: 113–18.

1973 Northern Mesopotamia and Syria. *CAH*^{3} 2/1: 1–41.

1978 Les Hourrites à Mari. *Revue Hittite et Asianique* 36: 117–28.

1979 Noms géographiques. ARMT 16/1: 1–42. Paris.

1983 *Documents administatifs de la salle 135 du palais de Mari transcrits et traduits.* ARMT 22. Paris.

Lackenbacher, S.

1982 Nouveaux documents d'Ugarit 1: Une lettre royale. *Revue d'Assyriologie et d'Archéologie Orientale* 76: 141–56.

Lambert, M.

1970 Textes de Mari—Dix-huitième campagne—1969. *Syria* 47: 245–60.

1975 Recherches sur les réformes d'Urukagina. *Orientalia* n.s. 44: 22–51.

Lambert, W. G.

1981 The Statue Inscription of Ibbiṭ-Lim of Ebla. *Revue d'Assyriologie et d'Archéologie Orientale* 75: 95–96.

1982 The Hymn to the Queen of Nippur. In G. van Driel *et al., Zikir Šumim,* 173–218. Leiden.

1985 A List of Gods' Names Found at Mari. In J.-M. Durand and J.-R. Kupper, *Miscellanea babylonia,* 177–203. Paris.

Landsberger, B.

1924 Über die Völker Vorderasiens im dritten Jahrtausend. *Zeitschrift für Assyriologie und verwandte Gebiete* 35: 213–38.

1954 Assyrische Königsliste und "Dunkles Zeitalter." *Journal of Cuneiform Studies* 8: 31–73.

1967 *The Series ḪAR-ra = ḫubullu Tablet XV and Related Texts.* Materials for the Sumerian Lexicon 9. Rome.

Landsberger, B.; Reiner, E.; and Civil, M.

1973 *The Series ḪAR-ra = ḫubullu Tablets XX–XXIV.* Materials for the Sumerian Lexicon 11. Rome.

Langdon, S.

1923 *The Weld-Blundell Collection, 2: Historical Inscriptions, Containing Principally the Chronological Prism, W-B 444.* Oxford Editions of Cuneiform Texts 2. Oxford.

1935 *Babylonian Menologies and the Semitic Calendars.* The Schweich Lectures of the British Academy, 1933. London.

Laroche, E.

1946–47 Recherches sur le nom des dieux hittites. *Revue Hittite et Asianique* 7/46.

1971 *Catalogue des textes Hittites.* Études et Commentaires 75. Paris.

Larsen, M. T.

1967 *Old Assyrian Caravan Procedure.* Uitgaven van het Nederlands Historisch-Archaeologisch Institut te Istanbul 22. Istanbul.

1976a *The Old Assyrian City-State and Its Colonies.* Mesopotamia 4. Copenhagen.

1976b Partnerships in Old Assyrian Trade. *Rencontre Assyriologique Internationale* (University of Birmingham) 23: 119–45.

Lattimore, O.

1979 Geography and the Ancient Empires. In M. T. Larsen, ed., *Power and Propaganda: A Symposium on Ancient Empires,* 35–40. Mesopotamia 7. Copenhagen.

Lau, R. J.

1906 *Old Babylonian Temple Records.* Columbia University Oriental Studies 3. New York.

Leemans, W. F.

1954 *Legal and Economic Records from the Kingdom of Larsa.* Studia ad Tabulas Cuneiformes Collectas a F. M. Th. De Liagre Böhl Pertinentia 1 (2). Leiden.

1982 La fonction des sceaux apposés à des contrats vieux-babyloniens. In G. van Driel *et al., Zikir Šumim,* 219–44. Leiden.

Legrain, L.

1912 *Le temps des rois d'Ur, recherches sur la société antique, d'après des textes nouveaux.* Bibliothèque de l'École des Hautes Études (sciences historiques et philosophiques) 4/199. Paris.

1913 *Tablettes de comptabilité . . . de l'époque de la dynastie d'Agadê.* Mémoires de la Délégation en Perse 14. Paris.

1922 *Historical Fragments.* University of Pennsylvania, the Museum, Publications of the Babylonian Section 13. Philadelphia.

Lehmann-Haupt, C. F.

1907 *Materialen zur älteren Geschichte Armeniens und Mesopotamiens.* Abhandlung der königlichen Gesellschaft der Wissenschaften zu Göttingen, Philologisch-Historische Klasse 9/3. Berlin.

1910 *Armenien einst und jetzt* 1. Berlin.

Le Strange, G.

1905 *The Lands of the Eastern Caliphate: Mesopotamia, Persia, and Central Asia from the Moslem Conquest to the Time of Tamur.* London and Cambridge.

Lewy, H.

1956 The Historical Background of the Correspondence of Baḫdi-Lim. *Orientalia* n.s. 25: 324–52.

1958 Šubat-Šamaš and Tuttul. *Orientalia* n.s. 27: 1–18.

1959 The Synchronism Assyria-Ešnunna-Babylon. *Die Welt des Orients* 2: 438–53.

1967 The Chronology of the Mari Texts. In J.-R. Kupper, ed., *La Civilisation de Mari*, 13–28. Paris.

Lewy, J.

1926 *Die altassyrischen Texte vom Kültepe bei Kaisarija*. Keilschrifttexte in den Antiken-Museen Stamboul. Constantinople.

1935 *Tablettes Cappadociennes* 3/1. Musée du Louvre—Département des Antiquités Orientales, Textes Cunéiformes 19. Paris.

1936 *Tablettes Cappadociennes* 3/2. Musée du Louvre—Département des Antiquités Orientales, Textes Cunéiformes 20. Paris.

1937 *Tablettes Cappadociennes* 3/3. Musée du Louvre—Département des Antiquités Orientales, Textes Cunéiformes 21. Paris.

1950–51 Tabor, Tibar, Atabyros. *Hebrew Union College Annual* 23: 357–86.

1952 Studies in the Historic Geography of the Ancient Near East. *Orientalia* n.s. 21: 1–12, 265–92, 393–425.

1953 Šubat-Enlil. *Annuaire de l'Institut de Philologie et d'Histoire Orientales et Slaves* 13: 293–321.

1961 Amurritica. *Hebrew Union College Annual* 32: 31–74.

Licht, J.

1968 בפא. *Encyclopaedia Biblica* 5: 898–904 [Hebrew].

Lichtheim, M.

1976 *Ancient Egyptian Literature* 2: *The New Kingdom*. Berkeley, Los Angeles, and London.

Limet, H.

1975 Observations sur la grammaire des anciennes tablettes de Mari. *Syria* 52: 37–52.

1976a *Textes administratifs de l'époque des šakkanakku*. ARM 19. Paris.

1976b *Textes administratifs de l'époque des šakkanaku*. ARMT 19. Paris.

1976c Le panthéon de Mari à l'époque des šakkanakku. *Orientalia* n.s. 44: 87–93.

Littman, E.

1910 Wörter mit Gegensinn. In T. Nöldeke, *Neue Beiträge zur semitischen Sprachwissenschaft*, 67–108. Strassbourg.

Lloyd, S.

1938 Some Ancient Sites in the Sinjar District. *Iraq* 5: 123–42.

Loewenstamm, S. E.

1980 *Comparative Studies in Biblical and Ancient Oriental Literatures*. Alter Orient und Altes Testament 204. Neukirchen-Vluyn.

Löhr, M.

1906 *Die Klagelieder des Jeremias*. Handkommentar zum Alten Testament 3/2/2. Göttingen.

Luckenbill, D. D.

1926–27 *Ancient Records of Assyria and Babylonia*, 1: *Historical Records of Assyria from the Earliest Times to Sargon*; 2: *Historical Records of Assyria from Sargon to the End*. Chicago.

1930 *Inscriptions from Adab*. Oriental Institute Publications 14. Chicago.

Luke, J. T.

1965 Pastoralism and Politics in the Mari Period: A Re-examination of the Character and Political Significance of the Major West Semitic Tribal Groups on the Middle Euphrates, ca. 1828–1758 B.C. Ph.D. dissertation, University of Michigan.

Malamat, A.

1965 Campaigns to the Mediterranean by Iaḫdunlim and Other Early Mesopotamian Rulers. In H. G. Güterbock and T. Jacobsen, eds., *Studies in Honor of Benno Landsberger on His Seventy-Fifth Birthday*, 365–73. Assyriological Studies 16. Chicago.

1966 The Ban in Mari and the Bible. In *Biblical Essays 1966: Proceedings of the 9th Meeting "Die Ou-Testament Werkgemeenskap in Suid-Afrika,"* 40–49 (52–61). Pretoria.

1971 Syro-Palestinian Destinations in a Mari Tin Inventory. *Israel Exploration Journal* 21: 31–38.

1979 *Ummatum* in Old Babylonian Texts and Its Ugaritic and Biblical Counterparts. *Ugarit-Forschungen* 11: 527–36.

Mallowan, M. E. L.

1936 The Excavations at Tall Chagar Bazar and an Archaeological Survey of the Ḫabur Region, 1934–35. *Iraq* 3: 1–59.

1937 The Excavations at Tall Chagar Bazar and an Archaeological Survey of the Ḫabur Region: Second Campaign, 1936. *Iraq* 4: 91–154.

1946 Excavations in the Baliḫ Valley, 1938. *Iraq* 8: 111–62.

Mallowan, M. E. L., and Rose, J. C.

1947 Excavations at Brak and Chagar Bazar. *Iraq*. 9: 1–259.

Margueron, J.-C.

1980 *Le Moyen Euphrates: Zone de contacts et d'échanges.* Travaux du Centre de Recherches sur le Proche-Orient et la Grèce Antiques 5. Strasbourg.

1982 Rapport préliminaire sur la campagne de 1979. *Mari—Annales de Recherches Interdisciplinaire* 1: 9–30, pls. 1–6.

1983 Mari: rapport préliminaire sur la campagne de 1980. *Mari—Annales de Recherches Interdisciplinaires* 2: 9–35.

Matthiae, P.

1980 Two Princely Tombs at Tell Mardikh-Ebla. *Archaeology* 33/2: 8–17.

1981 *Ebla: An Empire Rediscovered.* Garden City, New York.

Meek, T. J.

1935 *Old Akkadian, Sumerian, and Cappadocian Texts from Nuzi.* Harvard Semitic Series 10. Excavations at Nuzi 3. Cambridge, Massachusetts.

Meissner, B.

1920–25 *Babylonien und Assyrien.* 2 vols. Kulturgeschichtliche Bibliothek Reihe 1 (Ethnologische Bibliothek mit einschluss der altorientalischen Kulturgeschichtliche) 3 and 4. Heidelberg.

Mellink, M. J.

1969 The Early Bronze Age in Southwest Anatolia: A Start in Lycia. *Archaeology* 22: 290–99.

1972 Archaeology in Asia Minor. *American Journal of Archaeology* 76: 165–88.

1976 Archaeology in Asia Minor. *American Journal of Archaeology* 80: 261–89.

1978 Archaeology in Asia Minor. *American Journal of Archaeology* 82: 315–38.

Mendenhall, G. E.

1985 *The Syllabic Inscriptions from Byblos.* Beirut.

Mercer, S. A. B.

1939 *The Tell el-Amarna Tablets.* 2 vols. Toronto.

Meriggi, P.

1962 Über einige hethitische Fragmente historischen Inhaltes. *Wiener Zeitschrift für die Kunde des Morgenländes* 58: 66–110.

Michael Syrus

See Chabot (1899–1910).

Michalowski, P.

1980 New Sources Concerning the Reign of Naram-Sin. *Journal of Cuneiform Studies* 32: 233–46.

1981 Königsbriefe. In E. Ebeling and B. Meissner *et al., Reallexikon der Assyriologie* 6: 51–59. Berlin.

1983 History as Charter: Some Observations on the Sumerian King List. *Journal of the American Oriental Society* 103: 237–48.

1985 Third Millennium Contacts: Observations on the Relationship between Mari and Ebla. *Journal of the American Oriental Society* 105: 293–302.

Migne, J.-P

1857–66 *Patrologiae cursum completus . . . , series graeca.* 161 vols. in 166 books. Paris.

Milano, L.

1980 Due reconditi di metalli da Ebla. *Studi Eblaiti* 3: 1–21.

Miller, K.

1916 *Itineraria Romana: Römanische Reisewege an der Hand der Tabula Peutingeriana.* Stuttgart. Reprint, Rome, 1964.

Moran, W.

1951 New Evidence on Canaanite *taqtulū(na). Journal of Cuneiform Studies* 5: 33–35.

Morgenstern, J.

1946 Psalm 23. *Journal of Biblical Literature* 65: 13–24.

Morrison, M. A.

1984 A New Anchor Axehead. *Oriens Antiquus* 23: 45–48.

Müller, C., ed.

1884 *Claudii Ptolemaei Geographia.* Books I–V, with Latin translation and atlas. (Vol. 1/2 ed. C. Th. Fischer [Paris, 1901].)

Müller, V.

1931 *En Syrie avec les bédouins.* Paris.

Musil, A.

1927 *The Middle Euphrates: A Topographical Itinerary.* American Geographical Society, Oriental Explorations and Studies 3. New York.

Nassouhi, E.
1926 Statue d'un dieu de Mari, vers 2225 av. J.-C. *Archiv für Orientforschung* 3/4: 109–14.
Nöldeke, T.
1910 *Neue Beiträge zur semitischen Sprachwissenschaft.* Strassbourg.
Nougayrol, J.
1956 *Textes accadiens des archives sud (archives internationales).* Le palais royale d'Ugarit 4. Mission de Ras Shamra 9. Paris.
1968 Pantheon d'Ugarit (RS 20.24). In J. Nougayrol *et al.*, *Ugaritica* 5: *Nouveaux textes accadiens, hourrites et ugaritique des archives et bibliothèques privées d'Ugarit,* 42–64. Mission de Ras Shamra 16. Institut Français d'Archéologie de Beyrouth, Bibliothèque Archéologique et Historique 80. Paris.
Oates, D.
1965 The Excavatons at Tell al Rimah, 1964. *Iraq* 27: 62–80.
1968 *Studies in the Ancient History of Northern Iraq.* London.
Opitz, D.
1926 Die Lage von Waššuggani. *Zeitschrift für Assyriologie und verwandte Gebiete* 37: 299–301.
Oppenheim, A. L.
1948 *Catalogue of the Cuneiform Tablets of the Wilberforce Eames Babylonian Collection in the New York Public Library: Tablets of the Time of the Third Dynasty of Ur.* American Oriental Series 32. New Haven.
1952 The Archives of the Palace of Mari: A Review Article. *Journal of Near Eastern Studies* 11: 129–39.
1956 *The Interpretation of Dreams in the Ancient Near East with a Translation of an Assyrian Dream Book.* Transactions of the American Philosophical Society 46/3. Philadelphia.
1965 A Note on the Scribes in Mesopotamia. In H. G. Güterbock and T. Jacobsen, eds., *Studies in Honor of Benno Landsberger on His Seventy-Fifth Birthday,* 253–56. Assyriological Studies 16. Chicago.
1970 The Cuneiform Texts. In A. L. Oppenheim *et al.*, eds., *Glass and Glassmaking in Ancient Mesopotamia,* 1–101. Corning, New York.
Oppenheimer, B.
1976 רשץ. *Encyclopaedia Biblica* 7: 330–36 [Hebrew].
Orlin, L. L.
1970 *Assyrian Colonies in Cappadocia.* Studies in Ancient History 1. The Hague and Paris.
Orthmann, W.
1983 *Halawa 1977 bis 1979: Vorläufiger Bericht über die 1. bis 3. Grabungskampagne.* Saarbrückner Beiträge zur Altertumskunde 31. Bonn.
Orthmann, W., and Kühne, H.
1974 Mumbaqat 1973: Vorläufiger Bericht über die von der Deutschen Orient-Gesellschaft mit Mitteln der Stiftung Volkswagenwerk unternommenen Ausgrabungen. *Mitteilungen der Deutschen Orient-Gesellschaft* 106: 53–97.

Ory, S.
1971 Ḥiṣn Kayfā. In B. Lewis *et al.*, eds., *Encyclopédie de l'Islam* (new ed.) 3: 524–26. Leiden and Paris.

Osten, H. H. von der
1930 *Explorations in Hittite Asia Minor, 1929*. Oriental Institute Communications 8. Chicago.

Otten, H.
1955 *Keilschrifturkunden aus Boghazköi* 36. Berlin.

Owen, D. I.
1975 *The John Frederick Lewis Collection: Texts from the Free Library of Philadelphia* 1. Materiali per il vocabolario neosumerico 3. Rome.

Özgüc, N.
1977 Acemhöyük saraylarinda bulunmuş olan mühür baskilari. *Belleten* 41: 357–81.
1980 Seal Impressions from the Palaces at Acemhöyük. In E. Porada, ed., *Ancient Art in Seals*, 61–99. Princeton.

Pack, D.
1981 The Administrative Structure of the Palace at Mari (ca. 1800-1750 B.C.). Ph.D. dissertation, University of Pennsylvania.

Parker, B.
1961 Administrative Tablets from the North-west Palace, Nimrud. *Iraq* 23: 15–67, pls. 9–30.

Parpola, S.
1970 *Neo-Assyrian Toponyms*. Alter Orient und Altes Testament 6. Neukirchen-Vluyn.

Parrot, A.
1935 Les fouilles de Mari: première campagne (hiver 1933–34), Rapport préliminaire. *Syria* 16: 1–28, 117–40.
1936a Les fouilles de Mari: deuxième campagne (hiver 1934–35). *Syria* 17: 1–31.
1936b *Mari, une ville perdue . . . et retrouvée par l'archéologie française*. Paris.
1938 Les fouilles de Mari: quatrième campagne (hiver 1936–37). *Syria* 19: 1–29.
1955 Les fouilles de Mari: dixième campagne (automne 1954). *Syria* 32: 185ff.
1956 *Mission Archéologique de Mari*, 1: *Le Temple d'Ishtar*. Institute d'Archéologie de Beyrouth, Bibliothèque Archéologique et Historique 65. Paris.
1958 *Mission Archéologique de Mari*, 2: *Le Palais: Peintures Murales*. Institut d'Archéologie de Beyrouth, Bibliothèque Archéologique et Historique 69. Paris.
1959 *Mission Archéologique de Mari*, 2/3: *Le palais: Documents et monuments*. Institut Français d'Archéologie de Beyrouth, Bibliothêque Archéologique et Historique 70. Paris.
1964 1934–1964: Trentième Anniversaire de la découverte de Mari. *Syria* 41: 1–20.

1965a Les fouilles de Mari: quatorzième campagne (Printemps 1964). *Syria* 42: 1-24.
1965b Les fouilles de Mari: quinzième campagne (Printemps 1965). *Syria* 42: 197-225.
1966 Une réapparition mystérieuse. *Syria* 43: 333-35.
1967 *Mission Archéologique de Mari, 3: Les temples d'Ishtarat et de Ninni-zaza.* Institut français d'archéologie de Beyrouth, Bibliothèque Archéologique et Historique 86. Paris.
1974 *Mari: capitale fabuleuse.* Bibliothèque Historique. Paris.
1975 Les fouilles de Mari: XXIe campagne des fouilles (autome 1974). *Syria* 52: 1-17.

Parrot, A., and Dossin, G.
1968 *Mission Archéologique de Mari, 4: Le "trésor" d'Ur, avec, pour l'épigraphie, la collaboration de Georges Dossin.* Paris.

Peeters, P.
1908 Le martyrologe de Rabban Sliba. *Analecta Bollandiana* 27: 129-200.

Petermann, H.
1865 *Reisen im Orient 1852-1855: Berichte und Ergebnisse einer Forschungsreise in der Levante, in Mesopotamien und in Persien.* 2 vols. Leipzig. Reprint, Amsterdam, n.d.

Pettinato, G.
1974 Carchemiš—Kār-Kamiš. Le prime attestazioni del III millenio. *Oriens Antiquus* 15: 11-15.
1974-77 Il calendario di Ebla al tempo del re Ibbi-Sipiš sulla base di TM.75.G.427. *Archiv für Orientforschung* 25: 1-36.
1975 Testi cuneiformi del 3. millenio in paleo-cananeo rinvenuti nella campagna 1974 a Tell Mardikh= Ebla. *Orientalia* n.s. 44: 361-74.
1976 The Royal Archives of Tell Mardikh-Ebla. *Biblical Archaeologist* 39: 44-52.
1977a Gli archivi reali di Tell Mardikh-Ebla: riflessioni e prospettive. *Rivista Biblica Italiana* 25: 225-43.
1977b Relations entre les royaumes d'Ebla et de Mari au troisième millénaire d'après les archives Royales de Tell Mardikh-Ebla. *Akkadica* 2: 20-28.
1977c Il calendario semitico del 3. millennio riconstruito sulla base dei Testi di Ebla. *Oriens Antiquus* 16: 257-85, pls. XI-XII.
1979a *Catalogo dei testi cuneiformi di Tell Mardikh-Ebla.* Istituto Universario Orientali di Napoli, Seminario di Studi Asiatici, Series Maior 1: Materiali Epigrafici di Ebla 1. Naples.
1979b *Ebla: Un impero inciso nell'argilla.* Milan.
1979c Culto ufficiale ad Ebla durante il regno di Ibbi-Sippiš. Con appendice di Pietro Manden. *Oriens Antiquus* 18: 85-215, pls. I-XII. (Also published as Oriens Antiquus Collectio 16. Rome.)
1980a *Testi amministrativi della bibliotheca L.2769,* part 1. Istituto Universario Orientali di Napoli, Seminario di Studi Asiatici, Series Maior 2: Materiali Epigrafici di Ebla 2. Naples.
1980b Bollettino militare della campagna di Ebla contro la città di Mari. *Oriens Antiquus* 19: 231-45.

1981a *The Archives of Ebla: An Empire Inscribed in Clay*. Garden City, New York.

1981b *Testi lessicali monolingui della bibliotheca L.2769*. Istituto Universario Orientale di Napoli, Seminario di Studi Asiatici, Series Maior 3: Materiali Epigrafici di Ebla 3. Naples.

1981c Gasur nella Documentazione Epigraphica di Ebla. In M. A. Morrison and D. I. Owen, eds., *Studies on the Civilization and Culture of Nuzi and the Hurrians in Honor of Ernest R. Lachemann on His Seventy-Fifth Birthday, April 29, 1981*, 297–304. Winona Lake, Indiana.

1982 *Testi lessicali bilingui della bibliotheca L.2769*. Istituto Universario Orientali di Napoli, Seminario si Studi Asiatici, Series Maior 4: Materiali Epigrafici di Ebla 4. Napoli.

Plöger, O.

1969 Die Klagelieder. In Handbuch zum alten Testament 18: *Die fünf Megilloth*, 127–64. Tübingen.

Pohl, A.

1934 *Neubabylonische Rechtsurkunden aus den Berlin Staatliche Museen* 2. Analecta Orientalia 9. Rome.

1935 *Vorsargonische und Sargonische Wirtschaftstexte*. Texte und Materialen der Frau Professor Hilprecht Collection of Babylonian Antiquities im Eigentum der Universität Jena 5. Leipzig.

Poidebard, A.

1927 Les routes anciennes en Haute-Djezireh. *Syria* 8: 55–65.

1934 *La trace de Rome dans le désert de Syrie: Le limes de Trajan à la conquête arabe; Recherches aériennes (1925–1932)*. 2 vols. Haut-commissariat de la République Française en Syrie et au Liban. Service des Antiquités et des Beaux-arts. Bibliothèque Archéologique et Historique 18. Paris.

Pomponio, F.

1983 Considerazioni sul rapporti tra Mari ed Ebla. *Vicino Oriente* 5: 191–203.

Pope, M. H.

1977 *Song of Songs: A New Translation with Introduction and Commentary*. Anchor Bible 7C. Garden City, New York.

Pritchard, J. B., ed.

1969 *Ancient Near Eastern Texts Relating to the Old Testament*. 3rd edition with supplement. Princeton.

Procopius

De aedificiis. See Haury (1913).

De bello Persica. See Haury (1905) and Dewing (1914).

Ptolemy, Claudius

See C. Müller (1884).

Pulgram, E.

1960 Linear B and the Greeks. *Glotta* 38: 171–81.

Rawlinson, H. C.

1863 Assyrian Discovery. *Athenaeum*, 1842: 228–29.

Reade, J. E.

1968 Tell Taya (1967): Summary Report. *Iraq* 30: 234–64.

1978 Studies in Assyrian Geography. *Revue d'Assyriologie et d'Archéologie Orientale* 72: 47–72, 157–80.

Reclus, E.

1895 *The Earth and Its Inhabitants: Asia, 4: South-Western Asia.* Trans. E. G. Ravensten and A. H. Keane. New York.

Reiner, E., and Civil, M.

1973 *The Series ḪAR-ra = ḫubullu Tablets XX–XXIV.* Materials for the Sumerian Lexicon 11. Rome.

Ringgren, H., and Weiser, A.

1958 *Das Hohe Lied, Klagelieder, Das Buch Esther.* Das Alte Testament Deutsch 16/2. Göttingen.

Rolfe, J. C., trans.

1935–39 *Ammianus Marcellinus.* 3 vols. Loeb Classical Library. Cambridge, Massachusetts.

Röllig, W.

1977 Kakmum. In E. Ebeling and B. Meissner *et al., Reallexikon der Assyriologie* 5: 289. Berlin.

Rostovtzeff, M.

1932 *Caravan Cities.* Trans. D. Rice and T. Talbot Rice. Oxford.

Rouault, O.

1970 Andariq et Atamrum. *Revue d'Assyriologie et d'Archéologie Orientale* 64: 107–18.

1976 *Mukannišum: lettres et documents administratifs.* ARM 18. Paris.

1977 *Mukannišum: l'administration et l'économie palatiales à Mari* ARMT 18. Paris.

1979 Noms divins and Noms de mois. ARMT 16/1: 251–68, 269–72. Paris.

Rudolph, W.

1962 *Das Buch Ruth.* Kommentar zum Alten Testament 17/1. Gütersloh.

Rutten, M.

1938 Trente-deux modèles de foie en argille inscrits provenant de Tell-Hariri (Mari). *Revue d'Assyriologie et d'Archéologie Orientale* 35: 36–70.

Sachau, E.

1883 *Reise in Syrien und Mesopotamien.* Leipzig.

1897 Glossen zu den historischen Inschriften Assyrischen Könige. *Zeitschrift für Assyriologie und verwandte Gebiete* 12: 42–61.

Salonen, A., *et al.*

1954 *Die Puzriš-Dagan-Texte der Istanbuler Archäologischen Museen* 1. Annales Academiae Scientarum Fennicae B/92. Helsinki.

Sarre, F., and Herzfeld, E.

1911 *Archäologische Reise in Euphrat- und Tigris-Gebiet.* Forschungen zur Islamischen Kunst 1. Berlin.

Sasson, J. M.

1969 *The Military Establishments at Mari.* Studia Pohl 3. Rome.

1972 Some Comments on Archive Keeping at Mari. *Iraq* 34: 55–67.

1973 Biographical Notices on Some Royal Ladies from Mari. *Journal of Cuneiform Studies* 25: 59–78.

1979 The Calendar and Festivals of Mari during the Reign of Zimri-Lim. In M. A. Powell and R. H. Sack, eds., *Studies in Honor of Tom B. Jones*, 119–41. Alter Orient und Altes Testament 203. Neukirchen-Vluyn.

1980 Two Recent Works on Mari. *Archiv für Orientforschung* 27: 125–35.

1983 Mari Dreams. *Journal of the American Oriental Society* 103: 283–93.

1984 Thoughts of Zimri-Lim. *Biblical Archaeologist* 47: 110–20.

Sauren, H.

1975 *Wirtschaftsurkunden des Musée d'Art et d'Histoire in Genf*. Materiali per il vocabolario neosumerico 2. Rome.

Schaeffer, C. F.-A.

1949 *Ugaritica II*. Mission de Ras Shamra 5. Institut Français d'Archéologie de Beyrouth, Bibliotheque Archéologique et Historique 64. Paris.

Scheil, V.

1900 *Textes élamites-semitiques* 1. Mémoires de la Délégation en Perse 2. Paris.

1921a Catalogue de la Collection Eugène Tisserant. *Revue d'Assyriologie et d'Archéologie Orientale* 18: 1–33.

1921b Vocabulaire Pratique: Suse, Époque d'Ur. *Revue d'Assyriologie et d'Archéologie Orientale* 18: 49–78.

1925 Passim. *Revue d'Assyriologie et d'Archéologie Orientale* 22: 141–62.

Schramm, W.

1970 Die Annalen des assyrischen Königs Tukulti-Ninurta II (890–884 v. Chr.). *Bibliotheca Orientalis* 27: 147–60.

Schroeder, O.

1920 *Keilschrifttexte aus Assur verschiedenen Inhalts*. Wissenschaftliche Veröffentlischungen der Deutschen Orient-Gesellschaft 35. Leipzig.

1922 *Keilschrifttexte aus Assur historischen Inhalts* 2. Wissenschaftliche Veröffentlichungen der Deutsche Orient-Gesellschaft 37. Leipzig.

Scott, R. B. Y.

1965 *Proverbs-Ecclesiastes*. Anchor Bible 18. Garden City, New York.

Seeck, O., ed.

1876 *Notia Dignitatum: Accedunt Notitia urbis Constantinopolitanae et Laterculi provinciarum*. Berlin.

Seux, M.-J.

1967 *Épithètes Royales Akkadiennes et Sumériennes*. Paris.

Sjøberg, A.

1965 Beiträge zum sumerischen Wörterbuch. In H. G. Güterbock and T. Jacobsen, *Studies in Honor of Benno Landsberger on His Seventy-fifth Birthday*, 63–70. Chicago.

Smith, S.

1921 *Cuneiform Texts from Cappadocian Tablets in the British Museum* 1. London.

1924 *Cuneiform Texts from Cappadocian Tablets in the British Museum* 2. London.
1927 *Cuneiform Texts from Cappadocian Tablets in the British Museum* 4. London.
1956 Ursu and Ḫaššum. *Anatolian Studies* 6: 35–43.
1957 Yarim-Lim of Yamḫad. *Rivista degli Studi Orientali* 32: 155–84.

Smith, S., and Wiseman, D. J.
1956 *Cuneiform Texts from Cappadocian Tablets in the British Museum* 5. London.

Snell, D. C.
1974 The Mari Livers and the Omen Tradition. *Journal of the Ancient Near Eastern Society of Columbia University* 6: 117–23.

Soan, E. B.
1912 *To Mesopotamia and Kurdistan in Disguise*. London.

Socin, A.
1881 Zur Geographie des Ṭūr ᶜAbdīn. *Zeitschrift der Deutschen Morgenländischen Gesellschaft* 35: 237–69.

von Soden, W.
1952 *Grundriss der Akkadischen Grammatik*. Analecta Orientalia 33. Rome.
1953 Zum akkadischen Wörterbuch. 54–60. *Orientalia* n.s. 22: 251–61.
1965–81 *Akkadisches Handwörterbuch*. 3 vols. Wiesbaden. I (1965): A–L; II (1972): M–S; III (1981): Ṣ–Z.

Sollberger, E.
1954–56 Sur la chronologie des rois d'Ur et quelques problèmes connexes. *Archiv für Orientforschung* 17: 10–48.
1956 Selected Texts from American Collections. *Journal of Cuneiform Studies* 10: 11–31.
1960 Byblos sous les rois d'Ur. *Archiv für Orientforschung* 19: 120–22.
1967 Lost Inscriptions from Mari. In J.-R. Kupper, ed., *La Civilization de Mari*, 103–7. Paris.
1969 La perle de Mari. *Revue d'Assyriologie et d'Archéologie Orientale* 63: 169–70.
1972 *Pre-Sargonic and Sargonic Economic Texts*. Cuneiform Texts from Babylonian Tablets . . . in the British Museum 50. London.
1980 The So-Called Treaty between Ebla and "Ashur." *Studi Eblaiti* 3: 129–55.

Sollberger, E., and Kupper, J.-R.
1971 *Inscriptions royales sumériennes et akkadiennes*. Paris.

Speiser, E. A.
1935 *Excavations at Tepe Gawra* 1. Philadelphia.
1958 Census and Ritual Expiation in Mari and Israel. *Bulletin of the American Schools of Oriental Research* 149: 17–25.

Spender, R. D.
1976 Irrigation at Mari. Ph.D. dissertation, Dropsie University, Philadelphia.

Stadelmann, R.
1967 *Syrisch-Palästinische Gottheiten in Ägypten*. Probleme der Ägyptologie 5. Leiden.

Starr, R. F. S.

1939 *Nuzi: Report on the Excavations at Yorgan Tepe near Kirkuk, Iraq, Conducted by Harvard University in Conjunction with the American Schools of Oriental Research and the University Museum of Philadelphia 1927–1931.* 2 vols. Philadelphia.

Steinkeller, P.

1976 Seal Practice of the Ur III Period. In M. Gibson and R. Biggs, eds., *Seals and Sealing in the Ancient Near East,* 41–53. Bibliotheca Mesopotamia 6. Malibu, California.

1984 The Eblaite Preposition *qidimay* "before." *Oriens Antiquus* 23: 33–37.

Stephens, F. J.

1944 *Old Assyrian Letters and Business Documents.* Babylonian Inscriptions in the Collection of James B. Nies 6. New Haven.

Steuernagel, C.

1923 *Die Heilige Schrift des Alten Testament* 2. Tübingen.

Stol, M.

1971 Review of *Water for Larsa,* by S. D. Walters. *Bibliotheca Orientalis* 28: 365–69.

1979 *On Trees, Mountains, and Millstones in the Ancient Near East.* Mededelingen en verhandelingen van het Vooraziatisch-Egyptisch Genootschap "Ex Oriente Lux" 21. Leiden.

Streck, M.

1898 Das Gebiet der heutigen Landschaften Armenien, Kurdistan und Westpersien nach der babylonisch-assyrischen Keilschriften. *Zeitschrift für Assyriologie und verwandte Gebiete* 13: 57–110.

1927 Ḥiṣn Kaifā. In M. T. Houtsma *et al.,* eds., *Encyclopédia de l'Islām* (1st ed.) 2: 340–41. Paris and Leiden.

1934 Ṭūr ᶜAbdīn. In M. T. Houtsma *et al.,* eds., *Encyclopédie de l'Islām* (1st ed.) 4: 915–22. Paris and Leiden.

Tadmor, H.

1958 The Campaigns of Sargon II of Assur. *Journal of Cuneiform Studies* 12: 22–42, 77–100.

Talon, P.

1980 Un nouveau panthéon de Mari. *Akkadica* 20: 12–17.

Theophylactus Simocatta

See de Boor (1887).

Thompson, R. C.

1904 *Cuneiform Texts from Babylonian Tablets . . . in the British Museum* 19. London.

Thompson, T. L.

1974 *The Historicity of the Patriarchal Narratives: The Quest for the Historical Abraham.* Beiheft zur Zeitschrift für die alttestamentliche Wissenschaft 133. Berlin.

Thureau-Dangin, F.

1903 *Recueil de tablettes chaldéennes.* Paris.

1907 *Die sumerischen und akkadischen Königsinschriften.* Vorderasiatische Bibliothek 1. Leipzig. (French edition: *Les inscriptions de Sumer et Akkad,* Paris, 1905.)

1910a *Inventaire des tablettes de Tello conservées au Musée Impérial Ottoman* 1: *Textes de l'époque d'Agadé (Fouilles d'Ernest de Sarzec en 1895).* Paris.

1910b *Lettres et contrats de l'époque de la première dynastie babylonienne.* Musée du Louvre—Département des Antiquités Orientale, Textes cunéiformes 1. Paris.

1922 La passion du dieu Lillu. *Revue d'Assyriologie et d'Archéologie Orientale* 19: 175–85.

1928 *Tablettes Cappadociennes* 2. Musée du Louvre—Département des Antiquités Orientales, Textes Cunéiformes 14. Paris.

1934 Inscriptions votives sur des statuettes de Ma'eri. *Revue d'Assyriologie et d'Archéologie Orientale* 31: 137–45.

1936 Textes de Mâri. *Revue d'Assyriologie et d'Archéologie Orientale* 33: 169–79.

1937 Inscriptions votives de Mari. *Revue d'Assyriologie et d'Archéologie Orientale* 34: 172–76.

1939 Sur des étiquettes de paniers à tablettes provenant de Mari. In J. Friedrich, J. G. Lautner, and Miles, J., eds., *Symbolae ad Iura Orientis Antiqui Pertinentis Paulo Koschaker Dedicatae,* 119–20. Studia et Documenta ad Iura Orientis Antiqui Pertinentia 2. Leiden.

Tocci, F. M.

1960 *La Siria nell'età di Mari.* Studi Semitici 3. Rome.

Toy, C. H.

1899 *A Critical and Exegetical Commentary on the Book of Proverbs.* The International Critical Commentary. Edinburgh.

Van Driel, G.; Krispijn, T.; Stol, M.; and Veenhof, K., eds.

1982 *Zikir Šumim: Assyriological Studies Presented to F. R. Kraus on the Occasion of His Seventieth Birthday.* Leiden.

Van Liere, W. J.

1957 Urkiš, centre religieux hurrite, retrouvé dans la Haute Jézireh syrienne. *Les Annales Archéologiques de Syrie* 7: 91–94.

1963 Capitals and Citadels of Bronze-Iron Age Syria in Their Relationship to Land and Water. *Les Annales Archéologiques de Syrie* 13: 109–22.

Van Liere, W. J., and Lauffray, J.

1954–55 Nouvelles prospection archéologique dans la Haute Jezireh syriennes. *Annales archéologiques de Syrie* 4/5: 129–48.

Van Seters, J.

1975 *Abraham in History and Tradition.* New Haven and London.

de Vaux, R.

1969 El et Baal: le dieu des pères et Yahweh. In *Ugaritica* 6: 501–17. Mission de Ras Shamra 17. Institut Français d'Archéologie de Beyrouth, Bibliothèque Archéologique et Historique 81. Paris.

1978 *The Early History of Israel.* Philadelphia.

Veenhof, K. R.

1972 *Aspects of Old Assyrian Trade and Its Terminology.* Studia et Documenta ad Iura Orientis Antiqui Pertinentia 10. Leiden.

Waetzoldt, H.

1972 *Untersuchungen zur neusumerischen Textilindustrie.* Studi economici e technologici 1. Rome.

Walker, C. B. F.

1970 A Foundation-Inscription from Tell al Rimah. *Iraq* 32: 27–30.

Walters, S. D.

1970 *Water for Larsa: An Old Babylonian Archive Dealing with Irrigation.* Yale Near Eastern Researches 4. New Haven and London.

War Office and Air Ministry

1962 Map, Survey D: Series 1404 (1:500,000), *s.v.* Deir ez Zor.

Weidner, E.

1921–23 Assyriologische Studien. *Rivista degli studi orientali* 9: 469–79.

1923 *Politische Dokumente aus Kleinasien: Die Staatsverträge in akkadischen Sprache aus den Archiv von Boghazköi.* Boghazköi Studien 8. Leipzig. Reprint, Hildesheim, 1970.

1924 *Keilschrifturkunden aus Boghazköi* 8. Berlin.

1928–29 Die Kämpfe Adadnarâris I. gegen Ḫanigalbat. *Archiv für Orientforschung* 5: 89–100.

1935–36 Aus der Tagen eines assyrischen Schattenkönigs. *Archiv für Orientforschung* 10: 1–48.

1959 *Die Inschriften Tukulti-Ninurtas I. und seine Nachfolger, mit einem Beitrag von Heinrich Otten.* Archiv für Orientforschung Beiheft 12. Graz. Reprint, Osnabrück, 1970.

1966 Assyrische Erlasse aus der Zeit Adadnirâris III. *Archiv für Orientforschung* 21: 35–41.

Weinfeld, M.

1973 Covenant Terminology in the Ancient Near East and Its Influence on the West. *Journal of the American Oriental Society* 93: 190–99.

Weiser, A.

1958 *Klagelieder.* In H. Ringgren and A. Weiser, *Das Hohe Lied, Klagelieder, Das Buch Esther.* Das alte Testament Deutsch 16/2. Göttingen.

Weiss, H.

1983 Excavations at Tell Leilan and the Origins of North Mesopotamian Cities in the Third Millennium B.C. *Paléorient,* 1983: 39–52.

1985 Review of *Fifty Years of Mesopotamian Discovery: The Work of the British School of Archaeology in Iraq, 1932–1982,* ed. J. Curtis. *Journal of the American Oriental Society* 105: 327–30.

Westenholz, A.

1974 Early Nippur Year Dates and the Sumerian King List. *Journal of Cuneiform Studies* 26: 154–56.

1975 *Old Sumerian and Old Akkadian Texts in Philadelphia Chiefly from Nippur,* 1: *Literary and Lexical Texts and the Earliest Administrative Documents from Nippur.* Bibliotheca Mesopotamica 1. Malibu, California.

1978 Some Notes on the Orthography and Grammar of Recently Published Texts from Mari. *Bibliotheca Orientalis* 35: 160–69.

Whiting, R. M., Jr.
1972 The Dual Personal Pronouns in Akkadian. *Journal of Near Eastern Studies* 31: 331–37.
1977 More about Dual Personal Pronouns in Akkadian. *Journal of Near Eastern Studies* 36: 209–11.
1987 *Old Babylonian Letters from Tell Asmar.* Assyriological Studies 22. Chicago.

Whybray, R. N.
1972 *The Book of Proverbs.* Cambridge.

Wilhelm, G.
1982 Die Fortsetzungstafel eines briefes aus Kāmid el-Lōz. In R. Hachman, *Bericht über die Ergebnisse der Ausgrabungen in Kāmid el-Loz,* 123–29. Bonn.

Winfield, D.
1977 The Northern Routes across Anatolia. *Anatolian Studies* 27: 151–66.

Wiseman, D. J.
1953 *The Alalakh Tablets.* London.
1975 A Gilgamesh Epic Fragment from Nimrud. *Iraq* 37: 157–61.

Wolff, H. W.
1974 *Anthropology of the Old Testament.* Philadelphia.

Woodbury, R. B.
1941 Geography and Routes in the Near East. Unpublished paper.

Woolley, C. L.
1934 *Ur Excavations II: The Royal Cemetery.* London and Philadelphia.
1955 *Alalakh: An Account of the Excavations at Tell Atchana in the Hatay, 1937–1949.* Reports of the Research Committee of the Society of Antiquaries of London 18. Oxford.

Wüstenfeld, F., ed.
1866–73 *Jacut's Geographisches Wörterbuch aus den Handschriften zu Berlin, St. Petersburg, Paris, London und Oxford, auf Kosten der Deutschen Morgenländischen Gesellschaft herausgegeben von Ferdinand Wüstenfeld.* 6 vols. Leipzig.

Yāqūt
See Wüstenfeld (1866–73).

Young, G. D., ed.
1981 *Ugarit in Retrospect: Fifty Years of Ugarit and Ugaritic.* Winona Lake, Indiana.

Zettler, R.
1977 The Sargonic Royal Seal: A Consideration of Sealing in Mesopotamia. In M. Gibson and R. Biggs, eds., *Seals and Sealing in the Ancient Near East,* 33–39. Bibliotheca Mesopotamia 6. Malibu, California.

General Index

Abraham narrative 233, 234
absolute state 181
accountant/accounting 201, 250, 254, 261, 262, 263, 264, 264n.64
accusative case 182
accusative suffixes *see* suffixes
active participle 191
Adab calendar *see* calender
adjectives 178, 191
administrative texts, from Mari 123, 126, 129–30, 150, 160–61, 165–67, 200, 201
adverbial suffixes *see* suffixes
Akkadē Empire 122
Akkadian phonology 15
Akkadians 121, 123, 124, 195, 235
Amarna glosses 239
Amarna letters 214
Ammianus Marcellinus 17 n. 86, 17 n. 88
Amnaneans 204 n. 3, 207
Amorite migrations 233–41
Amorites 195, 233–41
Ana-Sîn-taklāku, cylinder of 59 n. 2
anointing with oil 168
anthropophagy 2 n. 6
apocopation 177
Arabic 21 n. 111, 240
Aramaic phonology 9 n. 35, 10, 20 n. 105, 29 n. 152, 29 n. 155
Armenian empire 10 n. 49
asseverative 194
Assyrian interregnum 74 n. 71, 114, 116 n. 15
Assyrian Treaty (Ebla) 193
Astarte Papyrus (Egyptian) 212
ʔAwnān tribe 130

Babylonian Creation epic 215
Babylonian Dream Book 13 n. 66
Babylonians 233
barley 86
Barth-Ungnad Law 188
beer 86
Black Monolith 20 n. 108
bodyguard 260–61, 263
bowls 79, 80, 81, 82, 84, 85
bracelets 86
Broken Obelisk of Aššur-bēl-kala 7 n. 26, 20 n. 101
Bull Colossi Inscription *see* inscriptions

calendar
  Adab 138, 139
  Ebla 135–47
  Gezer 136
  Mari 135–47
  Semitic 135–47, 167, 201
Canaanite language 237
Canaanite mythology 212
Canaanites 233
caravan routes 35–57
Carbon-14 78
causative 192
census 50, 253, 254, 255, 255 n. 30, 263, 263 n. 61, 264
  Ḫarrān 38, 38 n. 17, 54
  lists 254–56, 255 n. 31
  taker 250, 253, 254, 255, 256, 262, 263, 264
certified public accountant 264n.64
Cilician ware *see* pottery
Classical Arabic 240
clerk 264n.64
Code of Ḫammurapi 240
comptroller 264n.64
construct state 181, 191
controller 250, 253, 254, 255, 256, 258, 261, 262, 264
cooking pots 80
copper *see* metals, precious
covenant 208 n. 16, 240
CRD-82 78
cups *see* pottery
cylinder seals 59–76, 151

daggers 129
dative-allative 185

dative suffixes *see* suffixes
David 266
decimal system 124, 125
deities 133–35
demonstrative pronoun *see* pronouns
determinative-relative pronoun *see* pronouns
divination 61–63
divine names 133
djed pillar 237
driving of the nail 168
dromos 221
dye-works 222

ebbu official 249–64
Ebla archive 122, 243 n. 1, 243 n. 2
Eblaic 125
Eblaic empire 125
Egyptian 212
  djed 237
  w3ḏ-wr 212
  w3ḏ-wr ʾim 212 n. 6
Elamites 157
enclitic *mem* 238
ʾEnna-Dagan Letter (Ebla) 125, 127, 130, 131, 147, 201, 244–47
Enuma Eliš 215
Evagrius 10 n. 46
Execration Texts (Egyptian) 241

fientive 189
figurines 85
funerary banquet 268 n. 24

genitive suffixes *see* suffixes
geography, of Old Assyria 36, 38, 42, 50
Georgius Cyprius 9 n. 37, 18 n. 95, 29 n. 152, 30 n. 161
Gezer calendar *see* calender
god-lists 167
gold *see* metals, precious
governor-generals, of Mari 152–60, 161, 162, 164, 195

Ḫabur ware *see* pottery
Ḫammurapi, Code of 240
Ḫapiru 23, 24, 24 n. 129
Ḫarrān census *see* census
hats 86
headdress 85–86
helmet 181
Hittite expedition against Ilānṣurā 2–5
Hittite Old Kingdom 1
horned headdress 85–86
Ḫurri 4
Hurrian
  purullu 12 n. 60
Hurrians 4, 195

Ibla 122
Ibn Ḥauqal 31 n. 163
igisûm bull 269–71, 269 n. 39
imperative 190
incantations 190
indeclinables 193–94
indefinite pronoun *see* pronouns
infinitives 178, 191–92
inscriptions 77
  Bull Colossi 20 n. 108
  Proto-Sinaitic 237, 241
  royal 123
  Syllabic 235–39
  votive 123, 125, 126, 128, 130, 135, 150, 151, 152, 163, 164, 177, 195, 196, 200, 201
interrogative pronoun *see* pronouns
intransitive 192
inventories 258
Israel/Israelites 119, 233
Ištar festival 208, 210
itineraries 43
  Old Assyrian 29 n. 150
  Old Babylonian 36, 39, 41, 45, 53
  Old Babylonian Yale 8, 8 n. 33, 28, 28 n. 144
  of Šamši-Adad I 51
  of Tukulti-Ninurta II 49, 49 n. 72
  Urbana 17 n. 87, 24 n. 132, 28 n. 144, 50

Jacobite literature 9 n. 35
jars *see* pottery
Jerusalem, destruction of 265
John of Ephesos 10 n. 43
jugs *see* pottery

Kaniš *kārum* Ib 56
King List *see* Sumerian King List
Kinunim 117
Kish
  and Mari 121–25, 200–202
  civilization 121–25, 134, 144, 197, 200–202
  tradition 123–24

Kishite 124
Kishites 123
kraters *see* pottery
kudurrus 123, 125, 130, 168
Kurdish 21 n. 111

Laḫḫum 117
language of Mari 197
legal text, at Mari 167–69
lexicon 194
Lilliatum 208
Lîm dynasty 153, 164, 165, 168, 169, 200
Linear A and B 239
literary-critical method 234
liver omina 155, 163, 164, 165, 166, 169–94, 182, 195, 200

Man-ištušu Obelisk 161, 168
Mari
  and Kish 121–25, 200–202
  excavations at 217–32
mathematics 201
measures, system of 124, 125
Mediterranean Sea, divine nature of 211–15
mem, enclitic 238
merchants 35, 42
Mesanepada pearl 127
metals, precious 129
  copper 45, 57
  gold 41, 129
  silver 129
  tin 35, 43, 45, 53, 54, 57
metonymy 153
metrology 201
Michael Syrus 10 n. 44
mimation 182, 238
Mitanni 14
month names 124, 125, 174, 175, 176, 178, 179, 180, 182, 197, 208
  Ebla 135–47
  Mari 135–47
  Ugaritic 138
mourning ritual 268 n. 24
mubassirū messengers 113–20
Muqadassi 31 n. 163
musical instruments 139

nail, driving 168
Naomi 268
necklaces 86
Neo-Syriac 21 n. 111
nīsum oath *see* oath
nomads 233
Northwest Semitic 237
nouns 177–83
numerals 178, 181
nunation 182, 238
Nuzians 114

oath 203–10
  of the gods 208 n. 17, 210
ocean, as deity 213 n. 14
oil 129
  anointing with 168
Old Akkadian 121, 124, 129, 198–99, 240
Old Assyrian 163, 198–99, 239
Old Assyrian Caravan Road 7 n. 27, 35–57
Old Assyrian geography *see* geography of Old Assyria
Old Assyrian itineraries *see* itineraries
Old Babylonian 239
Old Babylonian Itinerary *see* itineraries
Old Babylonian Larsa letter 189
Old Babylonian Yale Itinerary *see* itineraries
onomastics 194, 240

painted sherds 81
Pan-Sumerianism 122
pantheon
  Mari 61
  Ugaritic 211–15
Papyrus D'Orbiney (Egyptian) 212
participles 178, 191
passive participle 191
Pelopidai 2 n. 6
perfect tense 190
permansive 191
Persian Royal Road 45
Perso-Byzantine wars 10
Philistines 233
phonology 175–77
plaques 85–86
plow crew 252, 254, 256
postpositional-adverbial suffixes *see* suffixes
pottery 56
  Cilician ware 82
  cup, carinated 79
  cups 79, 81, 82, 84
  Ḫabur ware 56, 56 n. 110, 81, 82
  jars 79, 80, 81, 82, 83, 85, 86

pottery (cont'd.)
jugs 81
kraters 79, 82, 83
Mari 77-112
painted sherds 81
pots 80
Tell Hadidi-Azu 77-112
precious metals *see* metals, precious
precious stones *see* stones, precious
predicate state 181
prepositions 193, 194
present-future tense 190
preterit tense 190
primordial sea 215
Procopius 9 n. 36, 16 n. 84, 17 n. 85, 17 n. 86, 29 n. 152, 30 n. 160, 215 n. 21
pronominal suffixes *see* suffixes
pronouns 183-86
demonstrative 186
determinative-relative 186
indefinite 186
interrogative 186
Proto-Sinaitic 238
Proto-Sinaitic Inscriptions *see* inscriptions
Ptolemy 9 n. 35, 13 n. 64

quadriconsonantal 192

radiocarbon 78
ration lists 256
Razamā, battle of 57
reflexive-reciprocal mood 190, 192
registrar 253, 254, 255, 256, 257, 258, 261, 262, 263, 264
registrar-accountant 264
religion 125
Res Gestae, of Ḫattušiliš I 4, 4 n. 12, 5
river ordeal 26, 28, 30-31
royal inscriptions *see* inscriptions
Ruth 268

šakkanakkū 152
sale contracts 168
Šamši-Adad I, itinerary of *see* itineraries
Samson 266
Sargonic dialect 124
scribes 15, 201, 253, 255 n. 32
seal impressions 59-76, 151; *see also* Index of Texts
Semites 121, 132, 150
shawl 86
shepherd 265
sherds, painted 81
sibilants 9 n. 38, 15, 32, 134, 138, 139, 149, 175-76, 237, 241
silver *see* metals, precious
snow 267
stands 80, 82
state economy 121
stative 190
stative participle 191
stem 192-93
stones, precious 129
Subarians 157
subjunctive 190-91, 192
suffixes
accusative 183, 185
adverbial 193
dative 184, 185
genitive 183
postpositional-adverbial 193
pronominal 183-85, 190
Sumerian King List 123, 125, 126, 127, 128, 130, 131, 150, 201, 248
Sumerians 121, 123, 132, 195, 235
Sumerian Word List A (Ebla) 245 n. 11
supervisor 256
Syllabic Inscriptions *see* inscriptions
syllabic writing system 239
syntax 194
Syriac *see* Aramaic

Table of Nations 236
taboo 205-6
Tabqa Dam Project 218
"Tale of Two Brothers" (Egyptian) 212, 212 n. 7
tax collector 259
tehom 215
Tell Hadidi-Azu, pottery *see* pottery
temple economy 121
temples 128
tense 190
textiles 35, 43, 54, 129
Theophylactus Simocatta 10 n. 45, 17 n. 86, 18 n. 95
throat, touching of the 210
time of day 182
tin *see* metals, precious
Tomb of the Princess 81
touching of the throat 210
treaty 128
Treasury of Mesanepada 127
Tukulti-Ninurta Epic 203 n. 1

Tukulti-Ninurta II, itinerary of *see* itineraries
Turkish 21 n. 111
  kerh 7 n. 25
  maden 12 n. 62

Ugaritic pantheon 211–15
Ugaritic poetry 211
Urartu 5
Urbana Itinerary *see* itineraries

Valley of the Cedar 212
vases 80
vassal-suzerain relationships 207
verb 186–93
vocalic pattern 189–90
votants 130–33
votive bowl 151
votive inscriptions *see* inscriptions

W 199000 205 n. 6
Weld-Blundell prism 248
wood 129
wool 54, 54 n. 93, 130
Word List A (Ebla) 245 n. 11
writing 147, 163, 171–75
  language 195–200
  system 124, 125, 239, 123

Yahweh 119
Yaminites 23, 24, 255
Yāqūt 31 n. 163, 17 n. 89
year dates 124, 125

Zion 267

Index of Names

PERSONAL NAMES

AB+ÁŠ 130
Ab-ba 130
Abban 71 n. 58, 74 n. 74
Abdi-A.AB.BA 214
Abdi-Yamm 214
ʾAbī-ješuʾ 165
A-bir$_5$*-tum* 133, 174
Abraham 233, 234
A-bu-DÙG 160
Abum-El 65
Adad-Narāri I 17 n. 91
A-da-tum 160
Addu-dūri 73
ʾAddu-nûrī 156
A-du-ni-a-bi-ia 184
A-ga-iš 193
AG-ba-ni 160
AG-*ba-ni I-din*-AG 160
Aḫṭal 24, 24 n. 135, 25
ʿAlma 128, 130, 133, 148, 149, 150
Amaduga 65, 67, 76
AMAR-DINGIR 130, 132
A-me-ir-ʾÀ-a 158
A-me-ir-An-nu 158
A-me-ir-Gag-ga 158
A-me-ir-Ma-ma 158, 191
A-me-ir-^{d}*Nu-nu* 158, 159, 160, 165, 191
A-mi-ir-^{d}*Šul-gi* 160
ʾĀmir-Nunu 158
ʿAmmī-ditana 165
Ammi-iluna 76
Ammiṣaduqa 4 n. 12
Ammunaš 5
ʿAmmu-rāpiʾ 165
Amud-pī-El 209
A-mur-^{d}*Šul-gi* 160
A-na-aḫ-ì-lí 187
Anāku-ilumma 65
Ana-Sîn-taklāku 59 n. 2
AN.BU 126, 127
ʾAnnum-Dagan 159, 162
An-sud$_4$ (BU*gunu*) 126
ʾÀ-num-^{d}*Da-gan* 158, 160
A-pil-ki-in lugal 160
Apil-kîn 65, 132, 152, 153, 154, 155, 162, 163
Appūḫ-illassunu 71
Aqba-Aḫum 118
Aqba-ḫammû 62
A-ra-ḫé-iš 193
Ar-ennum 247
Ar-ri-a-LUM 130
Ar-si- 149
ʾArśî-ʾaḫa 130, 149
Aškur-Addu 8 n. 31, 23, 23 n. 126, 48, 48 n. 69, 62
Asqudum 60, 61–63, 66, 67, 68, 220, 252, 258
Aššurbanipal 119
Aššur-bēl-kala 7 n. 26
Aššur-īdī 54
Aššur-nādā 54, 55
Aššurnasirpal II 7, 7 n. 25, 7 n. 26, 9 n. 38, 9 n. 40, 11, 14 n. 70, 15 n. 77, 20, 20 n. 104, 20 n. 107, 21, 22, 23, 32, 215
ʾAšurum 175, 191
Atamrum 15, 18, 19, 19 n. 97, 19 n. 100
ʾAwnānim 130, 148
Azraq, ibn 29 n. 153

Baḫdi-Lim 16
BE-*bu*-BÀD 130, 132
Bēlšunu 48
Bí-bí 130
Bi-il-ti-^{d}*Da-gan* 193
Bi-in-ì-lí-ia 184
Binu-ma-Haddu 194
BÍ.RU 148
Būnu-Ištar 16
Būnuma-Addu 54
Bûr-ʾilim 132
Bûr-Sin 154, 155, 162

Choseroes 215 n. 21

Dabi'um 66
Dabrum 130, 148, 149
Daduša 63
^{d}*Da-gan-a-bi* 183
^{d}*Da-gan-ba-ni* 191
^{d}*Da-gan-nu-uṣ-ra-a* 184, 185
Da-i-ru-um 191
Da/Iš-[. . .] 154, 156, 157, 160
Da-lu-ul-tum 191
DINGIR-*a-ḫi* 161
DINGIR-*aš-ra-a* 184
DINGIR-*I-sar* 158, 160
DINGIR-*i-ti-na-šu* 183
DINGIR-*Pu* 130, 158
Du-a-ra-am-^{d}*Da-gan* 161
DUB-*la* 130, 131, 132, 150
DUMU.MAḪ.LÍL 6, 4

E-a-ma-lik 181
Eanatum 127
Ebrium 243, 246
E-la-ag-ì-lí 160
É.MES 160
ʾEnna-Dagan 125, 126, 127, 128, 130, 132, 133, 147, 148, 150, 244, 246, 247
En-na-ì-lí 150
En-ne-nu-um 159
ʾEnnin-Dagan 158, 160
En-nin$_{9}$*-Ma-ma* 159
En-ni-nu-um 159
En-nin-x-[. . .] 159
EN.TI-*il* 130, 133
Entin 236
^{d}EN.ZU-*ti-ri* 142
Erišum I 69
EŠ$_{4}$.DAR-*a-li-a* 181
EŠ$_{4}$.DAR-*dam-ga* 181
EŠ$_{4}$.DAR-*tal-e* 187
EŠ$_{4}$.DAR-*ti-da* 187
EŠ$_{4}$.DAR-*tu-ri-ia* 184
Èš-pum 130, 149

*Ga-ba-*LUM 160
GAL-*iš*-DÙG 130
GIBIL-*zi/za-il* 247
Gudea 41
Gul-la 130, 132, 150, 247
Gumli-Haddu 184

Ḫa-al-ma-tum 128
Ḫabdu-Mālik 118
Ḫammi-takim 117
Ḫammurapi of Babylon 13, 16, 57, 64, 72, 152, 165, 205, 207, 208, 209, 210, 217, 220, 240
Ḫammurapi of Kurdā 8, 13, 14, 15, 15 n. 80, 16, 18, 118
Ḫana 72
Ḫasidānum 47
Ḫatni-Addu 73, 73 n. 67, 74
Ḫatni-[. . .] 72, 73
Ḫatnu-rapi 8 n. 31, 16, 18 n. 94, 8, 23 n. 126
Ḫattušiliš I 4, 4 n. 12, 5, 31
Hattušiliš III 42
Ḫāya-abum 26 n. 140
Ḫāya-sūmû 1, 1 n. 2, 17, 18, 23, 24, 25, 26, 26 n. 141, 28, 30, 32 n. 167, 63, 63 n. 18
Ḫazip-ulme 21, 21 n. 112
Ḫi-da-ʾar 126, 131, 132, 149, 244, 246, 247
Ḫimdiya 51
Ḥinninum 159
Ḫutbānu 261

Ia-ku-un-bi-ia 184
Ia-šu-ub-Ia-ḫa-ad 174, 183
Ibal-Addu 10, 11, 55
Ibal-Pī-El 46, 63
Ibbî-Sin 153, 154, 155, 157, 160, 162, 164, 169
Ibbi-Zikir 243
I-bí-[. . .] 131
Ib-lul-Il 131, 132, 134, 148
Ibnatum 51
Ibni-Addu 61
Iddiyatum 48
*I-din-*AG 160
Idin-Itūr-Mer 261
I-dur-^{d}*Me-ir* 160
Igi 126, 131, 132, 244, 246
Igmilum 71 n. 60
Ikna-Damu 247
I-ku-Il 130
I-kùn(KUM)*-Ma-rí*^{KI} 130, 131, 134
Ikun-šar 244, 246, 248
I-ku-^{d}*Ša-ma-gan* 131
I-ku-Sar 131, 135

For names beginning with *i*, see also *j*.

Il 130
Ilā-kabkabû 69
Il-e-da-bi-bu 191
ᵓIlī 131, 149
Ili-Addu 26, 26 n. 141, 28
Ì-lí-aš-ra-ia 185
Ì-lí-^{d}*Da-gan* 160
Ì-lí-dan 161
Ì-lí-en-núm 150
Ì-lí-gu-um-li-ia 184
Ili-irîṣa 185
Ì-lí-iš-ma-ni 183
Ili-Ištar 26, 26 n. 141, 28, 28 n. 149
Ì-lí-iš-ti-gal 161
Ì-lí-i-ti-na-šu 183
Ì-lí-i-ti-šu 183
ᵓIlī-Jiddinam 168
Ì-lí-tu-ra 185
Ì-lí-tu-ra-ia 185
Ì-lí-tu-ri-ia 184
Ìl-su$_x$(BU) 127
Ilšu-naṣir 256
Iltani 62
Ì-lum-a-ḫi 161
ᵓIlum-Jiśar 158
ᵓIlum-Pu 126, 134
ᵓIlum-Pum 127
Ilušuma 69
^{d}IM-*ì-lí* 183
^{d}IM-*tu-ra-a* 184, 185
Ini-Tešub 71 n. 58
^{d}INNIN-NITA 134
^{d}INNIN-*Zar-bat* 134
^{d}INNIN-ZA.ZA 134
Iplul-Il 244, 246, 247
Ìr-ì-ba 130
Irišum I 69 n. 49
Irkabtum 74 n. 74
Irra-dalîlî 168
I-sar-Pum 131, 158
I-sar-^{d}UTU 134
Išbî-Era 169
Iš-bi-Ìr-ra 160, 161
*Iš-dub-*DINGIR 160
Iš-dub-Il 130
Iš-dub-Sar 131, 135
Iš$_x$*-gi*$_4$ 131
^{d}*Iš-ḫa-ra-gu-um-li* 184
Išḫi-Addu 113, 114, 115, 116
Iš$_x$(LAM)*-gi*$_4$*-Ma-rí* 126, 131, 134
Iš-làl-^{d}*Da-gan* 190
Iš-má-^{d}*Da-gan* 160
Iš-má-Il 130
Iš-má-ì-lum 130
Iš-ma-ni-^{d}*Nu-nu* 183
Išme-Dagan 29, 46, 48, 49, 49 n. 74, 56, 57, 115, 116, 117, 118, 155, 161, 162, 169; *see also* Jiśmaᶜ-Dagan
Ištup-šar 244, 245, 248
*I-šu-ub-Ja-*ᵓ*à-ad* 183
I-ti 130
I-ti-^{d}*Da-gan* 160
*I-ti-*DINGIR 160
I-ti-^{d}ÍD 131, 134
I-ti-Il 131, 134
*I-ti-*LUM 130
Itūr-Asdu 23
I-zi-^{d}*Da-gan* 160

Ja(WA)*-bi-sa-tum* 176
Jibbiṭ-Lîm 188, 189, 191, 196, 200
Jibbiᵓ-Zikir 145
Jiblul-ᵓIl 122, 126, 128, 148, 201
Jiddin-Dagan 157, 158
Jiddin-ᵓIl 149
Jiddin-ᵓilum 157, 158
Jiddin-Mama 168
Jikûn-Mari 126, 128, 148
Jikûn-Šamakan 126, 134, 149
Jikûn-Śamaś 149
Jikûn-Śamša 126
Jikûn-Śarr 126, 148
Jiśar-Pum 127, 134
Jiśbî-ᵓEra 154, 157, 162
Jîṣiᵓ-Dagan 158
Jiśmaᶜ-Dagan 154, 155, 156, 161
Jiśṭup-ᵓilum 154, 155, 156
Jiśṭup-Śarr 126, 128, 148
Jitûr-Mer 158
John Zimiskes 29 n. 153
Justinian 16, 17, 215 n. 21

Kabi-Addu 62
Ka-ka-tu-ri-ia 184
Kaniu 6
Kibri-Dagan 255, 255 n. 31, 264
*Ki-ma-*DINGIR 194
KIN.URI 131

For names beginning with *i*, see also *j*.

Ku-Bau 126
KUM.BÀD 131, 132, 247
Kunšimatum 258
Kur-bi-la-ag NI.NI 160
Ku-um-li-A-du 184
*Ku-um-li-*dIM 183, 184

Lá-as-ga-an 183
*Lá-da-ba-*DINGIR 181
Ladat 247
La-gi-pu-um 161
La-ṭâba-ʾIl 181, 194
Lāʾûm 209
Lawīla-Addu 24
Lîm dynasty 153, 164, 165, 168, 169, 200
Lucullus 5
Lugal-ane-mundu 126

Ma-da-en-nam 150
Ma-ma-a-li-a 181
Mamuka-tišaša 114, 115
Ma-na-áš-tu-šu 183
Man-ʾaśtuśu 186, 193
Man-ištušu 161, 168
Manna-balti-ʾEl 193
Mannu-kīma/balum-Eštar 71
Marduk-mušallim 64, 76
Masum-adal 21 n. 112
Meptûm 26, 28, 30, 260
Meśalim 125
Mesanepada 127
ME-*Ul*x*-maš* 151
Migir-Dagan 151
Mi-ka-ʾIl 149
MI-*lá-A-ga* 157, 160
Mi-māḫirśu 149
Mim-ma-ḫir-sud 131
Mukannišum 71, 71 n. 59, 256, 257, 257 n. 36, 257 n. 38, 259, 259 n. 47
MUNUx-GÁ 132, 148
*Munu*x(PAB)*-gá* NIN 131

Nabum-Malik 117
Na-ni 131
Nannī 149
Narâm-Sin 132, 151, 169
Nīmer-Sin 65
NIN-GÁ 132
Niqmepuḫ 74 n. 74
Ni-wa-ar-Me-ir 160
Niwar-Mer 158
NI-*zi* 126, 131, 132, 244, 246, 247, 248

d*Nu-nu-da-mur* 187
d*Nu-nu-da-ti* 187
d*Nu-nu-li-tí-a* 176, 183, 184
d*Nu-nu-li-tí-ja* 176, 183, 184

PAB.GÁ 132, 148
Piyyašiliš 7 n. 23
PÙ.ŠA-*Eš*4*-dar* I 160
PÙ.ŠA-*Eš*4*-dar* II 160
PÙ.ŠA-*Kag-ga* 183
PÙ.ŠA-*Ma-ma* 161
PÙ.ŠA-*ra*-dUTU 130
PÙ.ŠA-d*Sa-mu-uš* 134
Puzur ᶜEštar I 153, 154, 155, 157, 162
Puzur ᶜEštar II 154, 155, 156, 157
Puzur-Šamaš 66

Qarni-Lim 8, 8 n. 30, 15, 16, 19 n. 99, 49, 118, 209
Qurādum 151

Rí-im-sá-ì-lí 184, 185
*Rí-im-si-*d*Da-gan* 183, 184
*Ri-im-ši-*DINGIR 184
Ri-im-ši-ì-lí 184
Rîmuš 123, 141, 169
Ripʾi-Dagan 66
Rîṣa-Dagan 185
*Ri-za-*d*À-a-a* 184

Śaʾāliš 193
Śaʾāmiš 193
Sá-ba 130
Šaknu 24
Ša-la-aš-tu-ra-ia 185
Śalim 131, 149, 183
Sá-lim-ke-lí 191
Šalmaneser III 32
Salmon ben Yeroḥam 268 n. 26
Samādaḫum 206
Šamaš-ellassu 270 n. 39
Ša-maš-ì-lí 135, 175
Šamaš-šunittum 16
Sammêtar 65, 67
Śamśī 134
Šamši-Adad I 8, 11 n. 51, 19, 20, 21, 23, 25, 37, 38, 47, 49 n. 74, 51, 53, 56, 59, 60, 62, 64, 65, 67, 68, 68 n. 40, 69, 69 n. 43, 69 n. 50, 70, 70 n. 51, 74, 74 n. 71, 114, 204, 206, 206 n. 12, 208, 209, 251
Šamši-muballiṭ 117
Śamśu-ʾiluna 165

Sargon 69 n. 49, 122, 123, 124, 125, 151, 162, 168, 169, 196, 201
Šarrāya 18 n. 94
Šarriya 118
Šarrum-kīma-kalima 62 n. 10
Šarrum-Pum 127
Šattiwaza 7 n. 23, 14
Śatupān 178, 191
Sa-ú-mu 127, 131
Śa˒˒umu 126, 127, 128, 148, 149, 150, 244, 245, 248
Shalmaneser III 20, 21, 215
Sibkuna-Addu 6
Šibtu 73, 74, 74 n. 73, 256, 256 n. 35, 257, 257 n. 37
Šîbum 130
Ṣill-˒Akka 157, 160
Ṣilulu 69 n. 49
Sin-gimlanni 184
Sin-muballiṭ 65
Sin-rîṣam 185
Siyyatum 64
Šûba-˒Il 185
Šûbi-Haddu 184
Šūbnalû 66, 256, 257, 257 n. 36
Šubram 25 n. 139, 51
Šu-^{d}*Da-gan* 161
Šu-^{d}*Iš-ḫa-ra* 161
Šū-Ištar 54
Šukrum-Teššub 51
Šulgi 154, 155, 162, 169
^{d}*Šul-gi-pa-lí-il* 161
Su$_{x}$(BU)*-ma-* 127
ŠUM.U 131, 132
Śumu-˒abum 165
Sūmu-epuḫ 74, 74 n. 71, 75, 114, 115
*Šu-mu-*EŠ$_{4}$.DAR 175
Sumu-Yamam 76
Šuppiluliumaš I 5, 6, 6 n. 21, 13, 14, 31, 65, 66, 67, 70, 269 n. 37, 270, 270 n. 43
Šupram 25, 25 n. 138, 25 n. 139, 26, 26 n. 140, 26 n. 141, 28, 29 n. 150, 30
Šura 126, 131, 132, 150, 244, 246, 247
Šura-Damu 131, 246
Šu-Sin 154
Su-wa-da 131, 132, 150

Tab-ni-Ma-ma 187
Ṭāb-ṣilli-Aššur 65, 117
Tarâm-Uram 153, 163
Tebi-girišu 252, 252 n. 20, 256, 258, 264
Tiglath-pileser I 22, 32
Tiglath-pileser III 10 n. 42
Tigranus the Great 10 n. 49
Ti-ir-An-nu 158
*Ti-ir-*EŠ$_{4}$.DAR 158, 166
Ti-ir-^{d}*Nu-nu* 158, 165
Tir-Dagan 158, 160
Tiš-atal 17 n. 87
Tispatum 28 n. 149
Tiš-Ulme 72
Ti-ti-na/nu 247
Tukulti-Ninurta I 11, 12, 13
Tukulti-Ninurta II 14, 22, 32, 49, 49 n. 72
*Tu-ra-ì-lí-*MAR.TU 185
Tûram-Dagan 154, 155, 156, 157, 160, 162, 163, 184, 185

Ù.BÍ.BÍ 130
Urānum 63 n. 14
URI.KIN 131
Ur-Nammu 65, 132, 151, 152, 153, 154, 162, 164, 197
UR-^{d}NANŠE 131, 132, 134
UR-^{d}UTU-ŠA 131, 132, 134
Utḫiriš-Ḫebat 256, 257 n. 36

WA-*bi-sa-tum* 191
Warad-ilišu 270 n. 39

Yaggidlim 213
Yaḫad-maraṣ 66
Yaḫdun-Lim 83, 59, 62, 64, 70, 72 n. 65, 73, 75, 211–15
Yaḫuzanum 76
Yamama 62
Yamatti-El 64, 76
Yanṣibum 48
Yantin 236
Yaqqim-Addu 46, 49, 204 n. 3, 207, 269, 269 n. 37, 269 n. 39, 270, 270 n. 43
Yarīm-Lim I 60, 73, 74, 74 n. 71, 74 n. 72, 74 n. 73, 75, 75 n. 75, 76
Yarīm-Lim II 74 n. 74
Yarīm-Lim III 74 n. 74
Yasīm-El 48, 51
Yasīm-sūmû 258

For names beginning with *y*, see also *j*.

Yasmaḫ-Addu 19, 29, 46, 47, 53, 59, 64, 65, 67, 68, 114, 115, 116, 204, 206, 206 n. 12, 209, 251, 253, 258
Yassi-Dagan 16
Yaṣṣur-Addu 256, 257
Yašūb-Dagan 67, 68
Yašūb-Yaḫad 74 n. 73
Yatar-Ami 30 n. 157
Yataraya 73
Yawi-ilā 51, 53, 204, 207
Ym-il 214 n. 18
Ymn 214 n. 18
Ymy 214 n. 18

Za-ḫir-tum 177, 191
Zakira-Ḫammû 269 n. 39, 270 n. 39
Za-ki-ru-um 191
Za-na-r-i 139
Za-na-ru-um 139
Zaziya 16, 16 n. 81
Zimri-Lim 1, 1 n. 2, 6, 7 n. 27, 8, 8 n. 31, 11, 11 n. 51, 16, 17, 18, 18 n. 94, 23, 23 n. 126, 24, 25, 26, 26 n. 139, 28, 28 n. 149, 30 n. 157, 35, 46, 48, 49 n. 74, 51, 52, 55, 57, 59, 60, 61, 62, 64, 65, 66, 66 n. 34, 67
Zimriya 16
Zuppa 4, 4 n. 8
Zūzu 26 n. 140

X-*ba-rúm* 131
X-*ba-rúm*(BÍ.RU) 149

[. . .]-*lum* 131
[. . .]-*zi*-[. . .] 131

DIVINE NAMES

ᶜAbirtum 133, 149, 174
À-da 145, 146
Adad 66, 74, 74 n. 71, 75 n. 75
A-dam-ma 146, 150
AMA.RA 146
Ama-ušum-gal 133, 135
Anath 212
Annunītum 260
ᵓApiḫ 133
Aš-da-bi$_5$ 145, 146
Aš-dar-ra-at 133, 150
Aššur 68, 69, 69 n. 49, 70 n. 51, 251, 252
ᶜAštar 133
ᶜAštarat 133, 149, 183
Astarte 212
ᵓAṯtr 212

Baal 211, 211 n. 2, 240
BARA$_{10}$-ra 146
be-AL puḫrim (UKKIN) 157

Dagan 61, 65, 66, 69, 70 n. 51, 72, 73, 133, 135, 149, 156, 164, 165, 169, 193, 195, 204, 206, 213 n. 12, 251, 252
Dar-am-Me-ir 187
DINGIR.DINGIR 133
Dîrîtum 178

Enlil 64, 69, 70 n. 51, 73, 133
EN.TI 133
Epiḫ 133
ᵓEśamîtum 178

Ga-mi-iš 146
GIR 14 n. 67

Haddu 194
Ḥajja 184
Ḫi-ša-mi-tim 174, 178
Ḫubur 158

ÍD 133, 134
ᵓIl 134, 149, 158, 193, 211, 213 n. 12, 215 n. 24
IM 134
INANNA 20 n. 107
ᵓInnin 129, 133, 134
INNIN-GIŠ.TIR 134, 135

For names beginning with *i* or *y*, see also *j*.

INNIN-NITA 135
INNIN-Zar-bat 135
INNIN-ZA.ZA 135
I-sar 158, 183
Iš-ḫa-ra 146
IŠKUR 75 n. 75
Ištar 65, 69, 208, 210
Ištarat 128
Itūr-Mer 204, 206

Jaḥad 174, 175, 183
Jiśar 158

Kaspa 183
Kubaba 146
KUR 169, 195

Lama 71 n. 56
Lillu 4 n. 9
Lîm 135
LUGAL-Ban-ga 134
LUGAL-KALAM.MA 135, 134
LUGAL-ma-tim 135, 156

Mama 195, 169
Marduk 215, 240
Ma-rí^{KI} 134
Me-sar 183

Nahar 211
Nanše 134
Nârum 134
NIN-da-ra-at 134, 150
NIN+E-bir$_5$-tum 174
NIN+E-sá-me-tum 174
NIN-mu-ra-ra-at 181
Ninnizaza 128
NIN+Taš-ki-Ma-ma 187
Ninurta 145
Nin-zi-Wa-ra-ne^{KI} 128, 134, 135
Nunu 165, 169, 195

Ocean 213 n. 14, 214 n. 15

Pu 127, 134, 149
Pù-ra-DINGIR.DINGIR 134

Ša-ma-gan 134, 149
Śamaš 175
Šamaš 67, 75 n. 76, 175, 213
Śamša 134, 150
Śar(r) 149, 135
Śarr(u)-mâtim 135, 156
Seth 212
Sin 75 n. 75, 208, 208 n. 16, 209

tâmtum 214 n. 17
Tiamat 215, 240

UTU 134, 135, 188
UTU-ša 135, 149, 150

Yam(m) 211–15, 212, 212 n. 6, 212 n. 10, 214 n. 18, 240

Zababa 145
Za-na-ru 139

GEOGRAPHICAL NAMES

A[x x]tan 48
Aasāfīr, Tell 52
Abattum 75
ᶜAbd el-Azīz, Jebel 39, 44
Abīsamar 75
Abissa 9 n. 41
Abi-tiban 35
Abou-Kemal 218, 222
Abrum 36, 37, 39, 40, 41
Abū Marīya(h) 19, 22 n. 123
Abu Salabikh 123, 124, 125, 127, 129, 135, 137, 138, 140, 144, 166, 193, 200, 201
Abudazum 36
Acem Hüyük 11 n. 51, 68, 72 n. 65

For names beginning with *i* or *y*, see also *j*.

Adab 126, 138, 139, 140, 141, 142, 144
Adiyamān 40, 44
ᶜAfar, Tell 19
Ailoun, Tell 50 n. 78
Akbas 10
Akkadē 123, 124, 125, 132, 162, 169, 196, 201
Alalakh (Alalaḫ) 24, 74, 77, 78, 182, 183
Alaya 12, 13
Aleppo 60, 71 n. 58, 74, 74 n. 71, 75, 122, 209, 219
Alilānum 21 n. 112
a-li-ma-zu-ra-am-ma^{KI} 18
Alše 6, 12
Alzi 3, 12, 12 n. 59, 13
Amadani 13 n. 62
Amanus 214
Amarna 214, 235, 239
Amaz 18 n. 94, 36, 37, 44, 50, 51, 52, 52 n. 84
Amedi 9 n. 41, 22
Amida 3, 5 n. 15, 7 n. 28, 9 n. 41
Ammodion 17 n. 86
Ammôdios 17, 17 n. 86
ʾAmnān 132
ʾAmnānum 132
ᶜAmouda 50 n. 78
ᶜĀmūdā, Tell 17, 17 n. 87, 28, 32
Amudis 17, 17 n. 86
Amuq 81, 82, 83
Amurru 24 n. 130
ᶜĀna 19 n. 100
Anatolia 5, 11 n. 51, 56
Andariq 8, 8 n. 30, 14, 15, 18–23, 27, 44, 46–50, 51
Andivar 19 n. 98
Anduli 15
Anti-Lebanon 214
Antioch 215
ʾAparśal 128
Aphumon 9 n. 41
Apqu(m) 19, 20 n. 104, 22 n. 123, 44
Apsiyaya 15
Apum 25, 25 n. 138, 26, 26 n. 140, 29 n. 150, 35, 36, 44, 50, 52, 52 n. 84
ʾAqbā 10
Aqra, Jebel 239
Arabian Gulf *see* Persian Gulf
Arazani River 3
Arbaki 9 n. 41
ᶜArbān, Tell 39, 39 n. 29, 44
ᶜArbīd, Tell 29 n. 150
Arcania 9 n. 41
Arġanah 9 n. 41, 13 n. 62
Aribachon 9 n. 41
Armenia 2, 6 n. 21, 17, 41
Armenia Minor 13 n. 64
Armi 245
Arqania 3, 9 n. 41, 13 n. 62
Arsanias River 3, 5, 9 n. 41
ᶜArsūz 55, 55 n. 101
Arzania 9 n. 41
Asach 21 n. 111
Asaḫ 21
ᶜAšāra, Tell 20 n. 101, 37, 78, 80, 81, 165
Asiḫi 15
Ašiḫum 19, 20, 20 n. 102, 21, 23, 27, 36, 37, 39, 44
Ašima 47
Ašlakkā 11, 17 n. 91, 25 n. 138, 44, 50, 52, 55
Asmar, Tell 134, 142, 190
Ašnakki 28
Ašnakkum 17 n. 91, 24, 25 n. 138, 28, 28 n. 144, 44, 50, 50 n. 78
Asqudum 61–63
Aššur 11 n. 51, 19, 19 n. 100, 19 n. 99, 20, 37, 39, 41, 42, 44, 45, 46, 49, 52, 56, 57, 64, 65, 65 n. 23, 70, 70 n. 52, 78, 81, 114, 119 n. 25, 141, 158, 161, 162
Assyria 30 n. 157, 32, 48, 114, 121 n, 140, 141, 144
Atachas 29 n. 152
Atchana, Tell 82
Atmi 39
Atmum 36, 38, 39, 40, 41, 53
Attachas 29
ʾAwnān 132
ʾAwnānim 132, 149
ᶜAyn Dīwār 19 n. 98
Azakh 21 n. 111
Āzeḫ 21, 21 n. 111, 29
Azu *see* Hadidi, Tell
Azuḫinum 37, 39, 46, 50, 53, 53 n. 89

Babanāḫi 12
Babil 22, 22 n. 119, 22 n. 120, 22 n. 121, 23, 23 n. 124
Babylon 19 n. 97, 30, 48, 72, 208, 209, 210

Babylonia 48, 121, 121 n, 122, 123, 124, 125, 126, 132, 134, 135, 140, 141, 144, 147, 151, 153, 163, 196, 201, 202, 219
Badna 54 n. 97
Bagas 24 n. 133
Baghouz 78, 81
Balikh (Balīḫ) River 6, 36, 38, 40, 42, 44, 45, 53–54, 56, 219
Banga 134
Barri, Tell 14 n. 68, 20 n. 102
Barzanista 15
Batman River 3, 6 n. 21, 10, 11, 12
Bekes 24 n. 133
Beqaᵓ 212
Bireçik 39, 40, 41, 44, 45, 56
Bitlis Pass 10
Bīt-Zamani 22
Botan 12, 21 n. 112
Boxwood Mountain 213, 214
Brak, Tell 20 n. 102, 129, 166
Burallum 36
Burama[x] 50
Burullum 36, 38, 39, 53
Burundum 7, 11 n. 51, 40, 42, 44, 51, 52, 55
Burušḫanta 11 n. 51
Bušši 12, 12 n. 59
Byblos 188, 214, 235, 236, 238, 239, 241

Canaan 238
Cappadocia 7, 7 n. 27, 11 n. 51, 35, 45 n. 54
Carcha 7 n. 25
Carchemish 4, 11, 30, 30 n. 157, 41, 44, 54, 55, 56, 71 n. 58, 173, 174
Cedar Mountain 213, 214
Cephae 30
Ceyhan River 44
Chagar Bazar 24, 29 n. 150, 32, 33, 45, 50, 50 n. 78, 51 n. 79, 185, 253, 253 n. 22, 255, 262, 263 n. 59, 264
Charcha 7 n. 25
Chlomaron 6 n. 21, 9 n. 41
Chūēra, Tell 39 n. 29
Cilicia 56
Cizre 10, 21, 22 n. 119, 23 n. 124, 27, 29
Constantina 7 n. 28
Cudi Dağ 12

Dabiš 63 n. 14
Daghjagh River 44
Dalhīs, Tell 39 n. 29
Dar 17
Dara 16, 16 n. 83, 17, 27
Darendi 41, 44
Debenne Su 22 n. 116
Derik 7 n. 28, 16, 16 n. 83, 39, 40, 44
Divrik 56
Diyala region 135, 178, 191, 193
Diyala River 124, 134, 144, 186, 196
Diyarbakir (Diyarbekir) 5 n. 15, 6, 7, 7 n. 28, 22, 31, 41, 42, 44, 54, 54 n. 92
Djezireh Ibn Omar 21
Dunaysar 10 n. 49
Dura-Europos 218
Dūr-Yaḫdun-Lim 117, 203, 207

Ebla 42, 77, 121–202, 218, 219, 221, 223, 237, 239, 243–48
Edessa 55
Egypt 212 n. 10, 239, 241
Ekallātum 16, 19 n. 99, 44, 49, 118
Elaḫut 7 n. 27, 18 n. 94, 37, 40, 40 n. 33, 41, 44, 51, 52, 55
Elam 30 n. 157, 151, 161, 162
Elâziğ 5, 13, 44
Elazij 41
Elbistan 41, 44, 45
E-lu-ḫu-ut^{KI} 11
Emar 28, 129, 189, 258
Ergani 3, 9 n. 41, 13 n. 62
Ergani-Maden Pass 5 n. 15, 13 n. 62
Ergani Su 13, 13 n. 62
Ermen, Tell 7 n. 27
Ešnunna 18, 19 n. 97, 19 n. 100, 32, 63, 162, 219, 208
Euphrates River 4 n. 11, 5, 11, 13, 13 n. 64, 19, 19 n. 100, 20 n. 101, 25, 30, 31, 36, 37, 38, 39, 40, 40 n. 35, 41, 42 n. 46, 44, 45, 51 n. 80, 54–56, 69, 70, 77, 78, 82, 83, 84, 85, 121 n, 123, 129, 134, 152, 165, 213 n. 12, 218, 219, 221, 243

Feḫerīyeh, Tell 7 n. 23, 39
Fēš Ḫabūr 23 n. 124
Finik 29, 29 n. 155
Finiki Geli 29 n. 155
Fis 9 n. 41
Fum 9 n. 41

Ğaġġaġ River 14 n. 68, 20 n. 102, 27, 28 n. 150
Garis Ağa 29 n. 155

Gasur 140, 142, 144, 183
Gawra, Tepe 78, 81
Gaziantep 39, 44, 55
Ǧazīrāt Ibn ᶜOmar 31
Ǧebel *see under main site name*
Gercüş 21 n. 112, 24 n. 133, 24 n. 134
Ǧerībah, Ǧebel 14
Ǧerraḫri River 27
Gersüş 24
Göksü River 44
Gölcük 13
Gülharrin 17
Gurdê 14 n. 68
Gurête 14, 15
Gürün 41, 44
Guzana 21 n. 110

Habuba Kabira 83, 122
Ḫabūr River 6, 7, 7 n. 23, 11, 12, 14 n. 71, 19, 19 n. 98, 19 n. 101, 20 n. 101, 20 n. 102, 25, 30, 37, 39, 41, 44, 45, 47, 49, 51, 51 n. 80, 52, 53, 56, 57, 78, 219, 243, 253 n. 22
Ḫabūr Triangle 8 n. 31, 14, 17 n. 91, 19 n. 98, 23, 24, 25 n. 138, 32, 41, 42, 46, 50
Ḫabura 36, 38, 39
Hadhail, Tell 49, 49 n. 74
Hadidi, Tell 77–86
Ḫaḫḫaš 42
Ḫaḫḫu(m) 3, 4, 5, 6, 7 n. 27, 9 n. 41, 11, 11 n. 51, 13, 36, 40, 41, 42, 45, 54, 55, 55 n. 100, 56
Haikal 19 n. 99
Ḥalaf, Tell 21 n. 110, 53
Halawa 83, 84
Halilan 21 n. 112
Ḫalpa 4 n. 11
Hama 78, 81, 82, 83, 84
Ḫamarāni 15 n. 78
Ḥamīdī, Tell 28 n. 150, 29 n. 150
Ḫamrāni 15 n. 78
Ḥamrim, Jebel 44, 46, 133
Ḫana 72, 184
Ḫanat 19 n. 100
Ḫanaziḫ River 44
Ḫanigalbat 4, 17 n. 91, 26 n. 142
Hany 6 n. 21
Ḫaqa 36
Ḫarabisina 15 n. 78
Ḫarbē 46, 47
Ḫarbisina 15 n. 78
Ḥarīri, Tell 45, 51 n. 80, 77, 203
Harisǧa 29 n. 155
Ḫarmiš River 14 n. 70
Ḫarput 13, 41, 42, 44
Ḫarrān 4, 11, 14 n. 67, 38, 39, 41, 44, 53, 54, 208
Ḫarrusi 28
Ḫarsi 28, 28 n. 150
Hasak 21 n. 111, 23 n. 124
Ḥasakah 20 n. 102
Hasankeyf 3, 30, 30 n. 158
Ḥaseče 20 n. 102
Hasseke 42, 44, 45, 52, 53
Ḫaššu(m) 5, 36, 55
Ḫatarika 15 n. 78
Hatik 29
Ḫatka 27, 29
Ḫatna 16 n. 82
Ḫatra 39, 44, 48, 50
Ḫatrika 15 n. 78
Ḥattaḫ 29, 29 n. 153
Ḫatti 13, 32
Ḥayal, Tell 50, 50 n. 75
Hazak 21 n. 111, 21 n. 112, 23, 23 n. 124
Hazar Gölü 13
Hezek 21 n. 111
Ḫimār 129
Hini 6 n. 21
Ḫi-ša-am-ta^{KI} 174, 178
Ḥisnā de-Kīphā 30
Ḥiṣn Kayfā 10, 30
Ḥiṣn Kīfā 30
Horren 17
Ḥorrīn 17 n. 89
Ḫurarā 29
Ḫurmiš 53
Ḫurrā 17, 17 n. 91, 25 n. 138, 27, 50
Ḥurrīn 17
Ḫuršānum 18 n. 94
Huwaish, Tell 49, 49 n. 74, 50 n. 75

^{d}ÍD 134
Iātu 20
Ibla *see* Ebla
Īdamaraṣ 32

For names beginning with *i*, see also *j*.

Idamaraz 19 n. 98, 25, 25 n. 138, 32, 32 n. 167, 45, 50
Idamaraz District 50–53
Idil 21 n. 111
Ilānṣurā 1–33, 44, 47, 48, 50, 63
Imat 44
Iran 122
Iraq 81
Irrid 54
Irrite 14 n. 67
Isana 20 n. 104
Isin 132, 155, 157, 160, 167, 169
Išnun 138, 140, 141, 142, 144, 183
Ispallurê 15
Israel 189, 211
Ištarāte Pass 20
Išuwa 3, 5 n. 15, 6, 13
Iyati 19, 21, 23, 27, 36
I-za-al-tu^{KI} 8 n. 34
Izalla 22, 22 n. 118, 8 n. 34, 9 n. 41
Izalli 15, 20

Jalgandagh Mountain 44
Jarmuti 151
Jarri River 44
Jebel *see under main site name*
Jezīrah 44, 46, 47, 48, 49, 49 n. 74, 239
Jirjib River 44, 51
Jiśrô-ᵓEl 189
Judeideh, Tell 82, 83, 84

Kadmuḫi 12, 20, 23
Kaḫat 14 n. 67, 25 n. 138, 44
Kakmium 244, 244 n. 3
Kallassu 74 n. 71
Kallat River 3, 9 n. 41, , 10
Kaluzanum 36
Kalzu 15 n. 78
KÂ Me-ir^{KI} 158
Kamira, Tell 49 n. 74
Kaniš 5, 6, 11 n. 51, 35, 36, 40, 41, 44, 45, 46, 52, 54, 56
Karabegh 41
Karaca Dağ 7, 19, 44
Karanā 8 n. 31, 13, 16, 18, 18 n. 94, 19 n. 97, 23 n. 126, 38, 44, 45, 46, 47, 48, 48 n. 70, 49, 49 n. 74, 53
Karanā Corridor 46–50
Karkamiśijum 178
Karmut 24 n. 133
Kasapā 2 n. 5, 13–16, 19 n. 98
Kašiyari Mountains 3, 8 n. 34, 9 n. 38, 11, 12, 12 n. 59, 20, 22, 22 n. 118
Kašpi 15
Kastron Attachas 29 n. 152
Kastron Massarôn 18 n. 95
Kastron Rhiskêphas 30
Kawala 52
Kedabekbegh 41
Kefr Ǧōz 24 n. 133
Kemah 56
Kēphā 31 n. 162
Kerh 3, 7, 7 n. 25
Kešaf, Tell 15 n. 78
Khabur *see* Ḫabur
Khafaje 134, 168
Khazel, Tell 78
Kibaki 20, 20 n. 105, 23, 27
Kiduḫ 19 n. 97, 26, 28, 29
Kiphas 30
Kirdaḫat 25 n. 138, 50
Kish 121–202
Kīvaḫ 20, 20 n. 105, 21, 23, 29 n. 155
Kiwaḫ 20 n. 105, 29 n. 155
Kizilirmak River 10 n. 49, 44
Kiziltepe 7 n. 27
Kᶜlimar 9 n. 41
Kᶜlmar 6 n. 21
Koçhisar 10 n. 49
Kōdaḫ 29, 29 n. 155
Kôdakh 29
Korde 16, 17, 18, 23
Kotmir 3, 6 n. 21
Krmûte 24 n. 133
Kudaḫ 12, 20 n. 105
Kullimmeri 6 n. 21, 9 n. 41
Kültepe 7, 45
Kunmar 6 n. 21
Kurdā 8, 13–18, 25, 27, 44, 46, 47, 48, 49, 118
Kurḫ 7 n. 28
Kurti 12 n. 57
Kutmar 3, 6, 6 n. 21, 9 n. 41
Kuwaḫ 20 n. 105, 29 n. 155

Labadudu 15 n. 78
Labdudu 15 n. 78
Lagaš 41, 127, 138, 140, 141, 142, 144, 183

For names beginning with *i*, see also *j*.

Laḫayum 40 n. 35,
Lakušir 19, 21, 36
Larsa 189, 28
Lebanon 212, 214, 236, 267
Lechi 266
Leylān, Tell 8, 8 n. 33, 15, 28, 29 n. 150, 32, 33, 49, 51 n. 80
Lice Su 10 n. 48
Liḫšu 37
Luḫaya 37
Luḫayum 36, 37, 40, 40 n. 33, 41, 42, 55, 57
Lulliu 11
Lullû 11, 55
Lullubum 194
Lu-lu-ta 11

Maʾama 54, 55, 55 n. 99
Madani 3, 9 n. 41, 12, 13 n. 62, 13 n. 65
Madara 9 n. 40, 9 n. 41, 17, 27
Maden 3, 9 n. 41, 12, 41
Madni 13 n. 62
Magarisi 14, 14 n. 70
Majdal, Tell 52
Malatya 3, 41, 42, 44, 56
Malitiya 3
Mallan 9 n. 41, 13 n. 62
Mallani 9 n. 41, 13 n. 62
Mamma 7 n. 27
Mammagira 51
Manuwat 244, 244 n. 3, 245
Maraṣ 41, 44, 45
Mardaman 36, 38, 40, 41, 72
Mardikh, Tell 42, 78, 81, 82, 83, 84, 122, 218, 243
Mardin 8 n. 34, 9 n. 39, 10, 27, 38, 39, 41, 42, 44, 46
Mari 1, 6, 7, 16, 16 n. 80, 19, 20 n. 101, 21, 30, 30 n. 157, 32, 36, 46, 49 n. 74, 51, 51 n. 79, 76, 85, 114, 123, 124, 126, 127, 128, 129, 130, 132, 133, 135, 151, 158, 159, 160, 161, 162, 164, 183, 184, 189, 197, 200, 201, 202, 203, 209, 213, 243, 243–48, 269, 270
MAR.TU 24 n. 130
Martyropolis 10, 10 n. 48, 10 n. 49
Māṣertā 18 n. 96
Maserte 18
Massara castellum 18 n. 95
Massarôn 18
Mat(i)yati 20
Matar 9 n. 40
Maṭara 9 n. 40
Mathra 9 n. 40
Matiyati 20 n. 106, 22 n. 123, 23
Matzaron 17, 18, 18 n. 95, 27
Mayafarqin 10 n. 48
Ma-zu-ra-am-ma^{KI} 18
Mediterranean Sea 44, 55, 81, 121, 211–15, 218
Megiddo 184
Melid 5 n. 15
Melik Ḥateḫ 29 n. 153
Melitene 3, 5 n. 15, 13 n. 64
Menâkhir 38
Mersin 82
Mesopotamia 1, 4, 5, 9 n. 35, 10, 19, 20 n. 104, 23 n. 124, 35, 121 n, 129, 217, 234, 236, 240
Midyat 10, 20, 20 n. 106, 21, 21 n. 111, 22 n. 123, 23 n. 124, 24 n. 134, 29
Minos 239
Mitanni 6, 26 n. 142, 32
Mitras, Tell 14 n. 70
Mōsul 42, 44, 45
Mouazar, Tell 39 n. 29
Mozan 32
Muḥammad, Tūlūl 33
Mu-ma-a-a 12
Mumbaqat 83
Mummi 12, 12 n. 59
Murat River 3, 5, 44
Mūzān, Tell 32, 33

Nagar 25 n. 138
Naḫiri, Tell 38 n. 17
Naḫr Darwîn 51 n. 80
Naḫur 7, 7 n. 27, 17 n. 91, 23, 25 n. 138, 27, 36, 37, 38, 39, 40, 41, 44, 50, 51, 52, 52 n. 84, 55, 57
Najma, Jebel 44, 46
Naṣibina 8 n. 32, 33
Naṣipina 33
Nihan Dağ 13 n. 65
Niḫani 11, 12, 13, 13 n. 65
Niḫriyā 3, 5 n. 15, 6, 7, 7 n. 27, 27, 36, 37, 40, 41, 42, 44, 53–54, 55, 57
Nippur 123, 141, 144, 153
Niṣibīn 8 n. 32, 38, 42, 44, 50 n. 78
Nisibis 8 n. 32, 22
Nuḫašše 37, 40 n. 33, 44
Nuḫuyana 4, 11–13
Nurrugum 18, 19, 19 n. 99
Nusaybin 8, 8 n. 32, 28, 28, 29, 32, 33

Nuzi 30 n. 157, 78, 81
Nymphios River 3, 10

Okbas 10
ʾOqbā 10
Orontes River 44

Pabḫi 3, 12, 12 n. 57
Palestine 188, 189, 236, 241
Palu 6 n. 21
Papanḫi 12
Persian Gulf 121, 121 n, 122
Pheison 9 n. 41
Pitiyarik 42
Purukuzzi 12 n. 57
Purulumzi 12, 12 n. 57, 12 n. 60
Puššì 12

Qā 25 n. 138, 50
Qarab Šūk Ṭaġ 19
Qaṣaybah 14 n. 71
Qatanum 209
Qaṭarā 35, 36, 46, 49, 50, 50 n. 75, 55, 114
Qattunān 44, 269 n. 39
Qatunan 21
Qṣēbah 2 n. 5, 14, 14 n. 71, 15
Qulmēri 6 n. 21, 9 n. 41

Raṣappa 20 n. 104
Rās el-ʿAyn 7, 10 n. 49, 45, 52
Razamā 35, 38, 44, 46, 48, 50, 57, 118
Razamā ša Burama[x] 36
Razamā ša Uḫakim 36
Rhosus 37, 44
Rimāḥ, Tell er- 8 n. 31, 13, 18, 38, 45, 46, 46 n. 58, 49, 49 n. 74, 62, 71, 71 n. 56
Riskêpha 31 n. 162
Rumaylān, Tell 22 n. 123

Sa-an-ga-ra-tim^{KI} 20 n. 101
Ša-ba-si-im^{KI} 29
Saduatum 35
Sagarātum 19, 19 n. 101, 20, 20 n. 101, 21, 36, 44, 269, 270
Saḫrū 207
Salihiye 222
Salt Lake 11 n. 51
Samānum 75
Samsat 39, 42 n. 46, 44, 45, 56
Sangarite 20 n. 101
Šapanazum 51

Ṣarbat 129, 134, 150, 183
Šâriš 24, 24 n. 134
Šarmaneḫ 50
Saur 46
Ṣaur 9 n. 38, 9 n. 39
Ṣaura 9
Sauras 3, 9, 17
Savur 3, 9, 9 n. 39, 9 n. 40, 10, 15, 17, 18, 23, 24 n. 134, 25
Ṣawr 9, 25
Šéirš 24 n. 134
Sejer 51 n. 80
Şerşe 24, 24 n. 134, 25
Ṣibat 206
Šíerš 24
Siḫaratā 50
Sikani 7 n. 23
Šīlārḥā 22 n. 123
Silvan 3, 10
Sinabu 7 n. 26
Šinaḫ 17 n. 91, 50
Sinai 241
Šinamu(m) 7, 7 n. 26, 26 n. 142, 27
Sinjār, Ǧebel 14, 14 n. 73, 19 n. 98, 39, 42, 44, 45, 46, 47, 48, 49, 53
Sippar 151, 219
Širun 36, 38
Širwun 38
Siverek 44
Sophene 3, 5
Ṣōr 9, 25
Šubarijū 178
Šubartum 11, 12, 19 n. 97, 46, 51
Šubat-Enlil 8, 8 n. 33, 15, 16, 18, 19, 19 n. 98, 20, 21, 24, 25, 25 n. 139, 26 n. 142, 27, 28, 36, 37, 44, 47, 48, 49, 50, 51, 251
Šudā 3, 6–9, 10, 14 n. 67, 27, 44
Šuduḫu 25 n. 138
Sufan Çay 22, 22 n. 123
Sufan dere 21, 22
Sumer 121, 123
Šunā 25 n. 138, 26, 26 n. 140, 27, 28, 28 n. 144, 29, 32, 33
Sunê 32
Šunḫum 25–30, 33
Supnat River 22, 27
Sūra 9 n. 38
Šūra 9 n. 38
Sürgü 44, 45
Ṣuri 9 n. 38
Ṣurra 3, 6–9, 9 n. 41, 10, 15, 16–18, 25, 27

Sürüç 54 n. 97
Šurušum 23–25, 27
Susā 18 n. 94, 25, 25 n. 138, 25 n. 139, 29 n. 150, 44, 50, 51, 52
aṣ-Ṣuwar 24, 25, 25 n. 136, 25 n. 136, 25 n. 136
Ṣuwwar 25 n. 136
Sweihat, Tell 83, 84
Syria 20 n. 101, 20 n. 102, 22 n. 119, 78, 81, 83, 114, 122, 123, 124, 188, 189, 214, 217, 219, 239, 241, 243, 243 n. 1

Ta'adum 26 n. 142
Ta-al-ḫa-yi-im^KI 11
Tabite 14
Tabqa Dam 218
Tādum 26, 26 n. 142
Ta'idi 26 n. 142
Talḫayum 11 n. 51, 17 n. 91, 25 n. 138, 36, 42, 44, 50, 51, 52, 53, 55, 57
Taljun River 41
Tapura 13 n. 64
Tarakum 35, 36
Tarmani 25 n. 138, 50
Tarrum 29
Tarsus 82
Taurus Mountains 3, 5, 10, 11, 12, 43, 43 n. 53, 44
Tektek, Ğebel 44, 45
Telilâ 29 n. 155
Tell *see under main site name*
Tenēnir, Tell 14 n. 70
Tepe *see under main site name*
Tepurzi(ya) 12, 13, 13 n. 64
Terakum 37
Terqa 19 n. 100, 20 n. 101, 37, 44, 123, 165, 270 n. 39
Thapsakos 37, 44
Tharse 44
Thelailah 29 n. 155
Tigranocerta 10 n. 49
Tigris River 3, 5, 6, 7, 8, 9, 10, 11, 12, 13, 13 n. 62, 13 n. 65, 14 n. 73, 15 n. 78, 16, 17, 19, 19 n. 98, 19 n. 99, 22, 22 n. 116, 23, 23 n. 124, 24 n. 134, 26 n. 142, 27, 29, 30, 30 n. 157, 30 n. 158, 31, 37, 42, 44, 48, 48 n. 70, 49, 49 n. 74, 121 n, 124
Til-Ḫanî 15
Til-ḫarabe 6 n. 21
Tillā 18–23, 27, 36, 51, 51 n. 80
Tillê 20, 20 n. 104, 22
Tiluli 20, 20 n. 104, 22, 23
Til-Zanî 15
Timilkia 55
Ti-ni-ši-pa 4 n. 8
Transjordan 239, 241
Transtigris 15 n. 78, 16
Tschilara, Tell 22 n. 123
Tūlūl Muḥammad 33
Ṭūr ʿAbdīn 2, 7, 8, 8 n. 31, 8 n. 34, 9 n. 40, 10, 11, 12, 15, 16, 17, 18, 19, 19 n. 97, 20, 21, 21 n. 111, 21 n. 112, 22, 23, 23 n. 124, 24, 24 n. 134, 25, 25 n. 138, 27, 28, 29, 30, 31, 32, 41, 44
Turkey 22 n. 119
Turukkû 16
Tušḫa(n) 3, 7, 7 n. 25, 7 n. 26, 26 n. 142
Tušḫum 27
Tuttul 44, 75, 270 n. 39
Tuttuli 155
Tu-tu-ul^KI 156
Tüz Gölü 11 n. 51
Tzauras 9

Ugarit 77, 78, 81, 144, 191, 211, 212, 212 n. 10, 215
Uḫakim 50
Uḫuš(u)man 14 n. 67
Umma 137, 140, 144
Upi 127
Uppumu 9 n. 41
ʿUqāb, Tell al- 10 n. 49
Uqabuwa 3, 4, 6, 7, 9–11
Ur 132, 151, 153, 169
U₉-ra-na-a^KI 134
Ù-ra-nè^KI 134
U-ra-NI-im^KI 134
Urarṭu 10 n. 42
Urfa 39, 44, 45, 53, 54 n. 92, 55
Urgiš 17, 17 n. 87, 17 n. 91, 27, 28, 28 n. 144
Urkiš 32
Uršu(m) 4, 7 n. 27, 20 n. 102, 36, 37, 39, 41, 45, 54, 55, 55 n. 100, 55 n. 99, 56, 156
Uzuḫinum 36, 53
Uruk 205

Van, Lake 10, 41
Viranşehir 7, 7 n. 28, 39, 40, 44, 45, 53

Wa-a-ra-an^KI 134
Wadi Aʿwej 41, 44
Wadi Dārā 17
Wadi Jirjib 45

Wadi Radd 15 n. 75
Wadi Tharthār 44, 45, 46
Warane 134
Wa-ra-nu^KI 134
Waššukkan(n)i 7, 7 n. 23, 14 n. 67

Yabliya 19 n. 100
Yadaʾi 15
Yaḥmūm 24, 25
Yaḫmumum 23–25
Yahya, Tepe 122
Yamḫad 30, 55, 74, 75, 76
Yapturum 51, 52
Yemen 238
Yenice River 44

Za-al-ma-qí-im 11
Zab River 14 n. 73, 15 n. 78, 21 n. 112, 44, 124
Zagros mountains 11
Zalluḫān 17 n. 91, 25 n. 138, 50
Zalmaqum 6, 42, 50, 53, 54, 55
Zalpa 40, 41
Zalpaḫ 54
Zar-bat^KI 148
Zebenne Su 22 n. 116
Zergān 51
Zerqan River 44
Zu[. . .] 6
Zunnanum 8, 49
Zuramma 18
Zurrā 18

[. . .]-ar-ri-ya^KI 18

For names beginning with *y*, see also *j*.

Index of Texts

ANCIENT NEAR EASTERN TEXTS AND SEALS

AbB 6 30 13 n. 66
ADD 742 15 n. 76, 15 n. 77
ADD 950 32
Andrae 1922 158
AnOr 9 99 161
Archi 1981a 128, 130, 131, 148

ARET
2 4 247
2 34 247 n. 15
3 1 247 n. 15
3 271 245 n. 9
3 338 245 n. 9
4 21 247 note to table
5 3 188
5 6 188

ARM 1
1 55, 75
19 6, 189
24 55
26 19, 21, 36, 37, 51, 51 n. 80
28 6
30 209
37 205, 208
39 6, 113 n. 3
40 113 n. 2
43 55
45 113 n. 3
53 51
62 51 n. 82
74 251, 254, 259–60, 262, 264
77 114 n. 10
84 113 n. 3
86 270 n. 39
87 253 n. 24
91 74 n. 71

ARM 1 (cont'd.)
93 113 n. 3
97 6, 113 n. 3
103 53
105 113 n. 3
107 52
109 38
120 113 n. 4
129 253 n. 24
131 29
132 46–47

ARM 2
10 113 n. 3
13 204, 205, 206
23 46 n. 59
33 17 n. 91, 50
34 46 n. 60
35 50
37 50
38 17 n. 91, 50
39 49
41 15, 47 n. 64
43 48, 48 n. 70
45 113 n. 3
50 16 n. 82
51 204 n. 3
55 113 n. 5, 204, 205, 206
62 1 n. 2, 7 n. 29, 8 n. 31, 17–19, 47 n. 65
63 38
69 15, 16 n. 80
72 113 n. 3
77 204–5, 207, 208, 209
78 21
82 269 n. 39
98 51 n. 82

In the general index, for Proto-Sinaitic texts, see *inscriptions*; for text types, see *inscriptions, itineraries, legal texts, lexicon,* and *liver omina*; for classical and Arab historians, see under the author's name.

ARM 2 (cont'd.)
99 113 n. 5
109 18 n. 94, 25 n. 139, 51
112 52
113 52
120 19 n. 100
130 16, 47 n. 64, 49 n. 74
131 55, 56
135 24

ARM 3
19 203, 204, 250 n. 13, 254, 255, 262, 263, 264
20 254, 255 n. 28, 255 n. 29, 255 n. 31, 262, 263, 264
21 254, 255, 255 n. 31, 262, 263
44 7 n. 29
57 54

ARM 4
3 113 n. 2
5 20 n. 101
29 49
31 113 n. 3
35 52
40 17 n. 91
51 9 n. 40
74 19 n. 100
78 203
88 19 n. 100

ARM 5
15 114 n. 11
16 114, 114 n. 12, 115–16, 119
17 113, 114
18 114 n. 13
19 114 n. 13
36 49
37 50
38 113 n. 2
40 49
51 50
67 38, 47

ARM 6
21 113 n. 4
24 113 n. 4
26 48 n. 69
31 176
33 16
62 113 n. 4

ARM 7
4 118 n. 22, 118 n. 23
21 113 n. 6, 118 n. 19
40 118 n. 18
42 118 n. 20
47 118 n. 18
49 118 n. 18
75 114, 116–17, 116 n. 15
104 53
106 62
113 53
117 118
156 114, 116, 116 n. 15, 117, 118, 119
185 113 n. 4
195 250 n. 9
199 50 n. 77
217 270 n. 39
219 50, 52, 53
225 63 n. 14
226 62 n. 10, 63 n. 14
234 62 n. 10
292 63 n. 16

ARM 8
1 185, 205
11 206 n. 11
12 168
13 168
16 205, 206
17 203
52 63 n. 17
85 205

ARM 9
5 190
24 270 n. 39
43 67 n. 37
58 67 n. 36
131 113 n. 4
168 208 n. 17
213 208 n. 17
218 208 n. 17
259 8 n. 34
298 32 n. 167

ARM/ARMT 10
3 258, 262, 264
7 260, 261, 262, 263
12 71 n. 60, 256–57, 256 n. 34, 262, 263
32 47 n. 65, 113 n. 2, 203
50 156

ARM/ARMT 10 (cont'd.)
63 204
72 270 n. 39
82 256 n. 34, 257 n. 37, 257 n. 38
84 51
85 113 n. 2
98 28 n. 149
106 257 n. 36
119 73 n. 68
121 17 n. 91, 28 n. 144
133 72
151 74 n. 73, 76
165 47 n. 66, 49 n. 74
168 16
176 113 n. 2
177 210

ARM/ARMT 11
69 65 n. 23
87 65 n. 23
93 67 n. 36, 67 n. 37
198 50 n. 77

ARM/ARMT 12
14 256 n. 34
21 208, 208 n. 17
46 208 n. 17
108 67 n. 36
606 208 n. 17
712 261, 262, 264
723 67 n. 36

ARM/ARMT 13
1 62
10 257 n. 37
14 257 n. 37
16 259, 262, 264
22 71 n. 59, 257 n. 37
25 270, 270 n. 39, 270 n. 40
35 258, 262, 264
36 250 n. 13, 262
96 259 n. 44, 261, 262, 264
131 113 n. 4
139 51, 53
140 51
141 51
142 51
143 51
144 51, 52
145 51
146 51
147 204, 207, 51

ARM/ARMT 13 (cont'd.)
148 51
149 51
150 51

ARM/ARMT 14
5 269–70, 269 n. 37, 269 n. 38, 269 n. 39, 270 n. 40, 271, 271 n. 44
6 269 n. 37, 269 n. 38, 269 n. 39, 270 n. 43, 271, 271 n. 44
11 270 n. 43
29 270 n. 43
36 270 n. 43
50 19 n. 97
64 203
67 205
77 54
81 51 n. 82
89 203, 204 n. 3, 207, 209
94 18 n. 94
98 51 n. 82
106 53, 203
108 53
109 8, 47 n. 66, 49
112 51 n. 82
115 20 n. 101

ARM/ARMT 15
130 18 n. 93
136 20 n. 102
138 18 n. 93
183 250 n. 13
271 263 n. 62

ARMT 16/1
23 18 n. 93

ARMT 19 (referred to as "adm." + no.)
1 180
14 181
17 178, 180
18 179, 184, 185, 190
19 181, 182
20 180, 181, 182
23 193
32 142, 178, 180, 193
33 178, 180
34 186
35 166, 181
36 166
37 176, 180, 181, 186
38–45 173

ARMT 19 (cont'd.)
38 166, 174, 179, 187
39 166, 187
40 166, 187
41 166, 187
42 166, 187
43 166, 187
44 166, 187
45 166, 187
46 166, 187
47 166, 187
48 166, 176, 187
49 166, 187
50 166, 187
55 181, 182
57 181, 182
59 180
60 186
61 180, 181
64 191, 192
84 179
92 194
96 174, 178, 181, 186, 191
103 175, 176, 180
104 180
106 179
107 175
110 179
111 191
114 177, 192
120 192
133 179
152 179
160 175
164 180
165 187
166 179
173 191
182 179, 182
184 180
193 166
194 166, 179, 191
199 183
200 183, 184, 190
201 186
202 186
205 183, 184, 190, 191
207 179
210 166
212 177, 180, 181, 191
218 187
223 178

ARMT 19 (cont'd.)
230 186
238 166
247 180
248 173, 175, 177, 179, 180, 183, 190, 191
252 178, 179
254 186
258 166, 179, 180
260 178
266 179, 193
267 179
277 179
279 174, 176, 177, 178, 180, 183, 191
280 179, 180, 194
282 180
283 175
284 180, 186
285 183
286 180, 194
287 180, 186
288 179, 186
289 184, 185
290 180
291 179, 186
292 180
293 179
294 135, 175
295 174, 176, 180
296 179, 180
298 194
299 174
300 166, 174, 180, 186
301 180
302 180
303 179, 181, 186
304 175, 179, 180
306 178, 180
307 179
308 165, 183, 184
309 179
310 179
311 131, 179
312 131
313 179
314 174, 176, 180, 183, 186
315 173, 178
316 179, 183
319 157
321 176, 183, 184
322 184, 185
324 173, 179, 180, 187, 192

ARMT 19 (cont'd.)
324* 179
325 184, 185
326 178, 179, 187
327 179
330 173, 178
331 180
332 179
333 183
334 179
337 178
338 191
339 179, 180
341 184
342 179
347 179
351 174, 176, 179
363 174, 177, 181
364 178
365 173, 174, 177, 180
369 184, 185, 190
370 175, 191
373 165
375 193
376 181, 183, 190
377 150
378 174, 176, 181, 191
379 183
381 173, 174, 176, 178, 180, 181, 186
382 179, 187
384 180, 181, 187, 191, 191
385 150
389 166, 177, 179, 180, 181, 181, 183, 193
391 179, 185, 193
393 175, 176, 177, 180, 187, 191, 192
394 194
395 179
396 174, 178, 179
397 173, 178, 187
407 179
408 176, 183, 184
413 177, 180
418 187
424 179
427 173, 173, 179
430 133, 174
442 173, 179, 186
449 184, 185
459 177, 179
460 166, 174, 177, 179, 180, 181, 183
461 181, 183, 194

ARMT 19 (cont'd.)
462 166, 175, 176, 180, 181, 191
463 180, 186
1460 173

ARM/ARMT 21
9 157
88 63 n. 18
91 64

ARM HC
A.16 260 n. 48, 262, 264
A.49 7 n. 26, 23 n. 125
A.479 47 n. 65
A.926 50
A.929 50
A.952 51
A.1121 74 n. 71
A.1153 74 n. 71, 74 n. 72
A.1212 25 n. 138, 32 n. 167, 50 n. 77
A.1270 57
A.1314 74 n. 73, 75 n. 75
A.2145 8 n. 34
A.3093 19 n. 97, 48
A.3151 62 n. 10
A.3188 160
A.5439 161
AREP. 19 n. 99, 28 n. 144, 50, 203, 208, 209
B.63 252, 252 n. 16, 253 n. 21, 254, 256, 258, 262, 264, 264 n. 63
B.81 8 n. 31
B.308 11 n. 50, 42 n. 47, 51, 52, 55
BENJ. 203, 208 n. 16
E.20 71 n. 55
E.40 71 n. 55
E.45 71 n. 55
EXCE. 52
FOND. 203, 204
HATT. 46 n. 56
IAMḪ. 204, 209
M.1572 159
M.2802 75 n. 76, 211–15
M.5148 68
M.5151 68
M.8884 63 n. 14
M.13161 73 n. 67
M.13185 66
M.18025 73 n. 68
ORD1 30 n. 157, 54
ORD2-A 25, 25 n. 137, 26 n. 141, 28, 30

ARM HC (cont'd.)
ORD2-B 25 n. 137, 26, 30
S.115 16 n. 81, 50, 52, 65 n. 24, 68, 72 n. 66, 74 n. 73
SIGN. 17 n. 91
TEXT. 46 n. 59

AS 17 12 141
AS 23 6 190
Astarte Papyrus 212
AT 55 182
AT 56 182

BIN
3 221 161
4 124 35
4 193 35
4 219 55 n. 99
6 176 54
8 41 127

Birot 1969: 60 139
Birot 1980 169
Black Monolith 20 n. 108
Boissier 1919: 163 151
2BoTU 21 2
Broken Obelisk 7 n. 26, 20 n. 101
Bull Colossi 20 n. 108
Byblos Syllabic texts 235–39
Castellino 1972: 48 139

CCT
1 26b 36, 37, 53
1 27a 36, 37
1 42a 36
2 11a 55 n. 99
2 22 42 n. 47, 53, 54, 55
4 28b 55
4 36b 53
5 44c 36, 37, 40, 52

Civil 1962 153
Creation Epic 215

CT
5 2 128, 134, 149, 133
19 45 270 n. 40
50 70 134
50 71 151
50 72 151
50 73 151
50 74 151

Dawson no. 9 161
Deimel 1914: no. 2571 134
Deimel 1922: 1 134
DeZ 2521 26 n. 142
D'Orbiney Papyrus 212
Dossin 1930 184
Dossin 1938a 203, 208, 209
Dossin 1939a 203, 208 n. 16
Dossin 1939b 204, 209
Dossin 1940 153, 156, 158, 203, 204
Dossin 1950b 174, 178
Dossin 1955 211–15
Dossin 1967c 158, 183
Dr. Serota no. 13 156
Dream Book 13 n. 66
Durand 1980 173, 174, 175, 178, 179, 180, 181, 183, 187
Durand 1982c (referred to as "legal") 167–69, 172, 173, 174, 178, 179, 182, 183, 184, 186, 187, 188, 190, 193, 194, 195
Durand 1984b 141, 142
Durand 1984c 181, 182
EA 246 184
EA 340 214 n. 16
Edzard 1967 133
Edzard 1970: no. 117 142
EL 210a–b 53
ᵓEnna-Dagan Letter 127, 128, 130, 131, 147, 201, 244–47
Enuma Eliš 215

Gadd 1940
926 50
929 50
978 253
990 262
p. 41 185

Garelli 1965: 42 #17 53
Gelb 1955: 18 134
Gelb 1955: 19 134
Gelb 1955: 34 139
Gezer calendar 136
Goetze 1953b 160
Grayson and Sollberger 1976: 112 151
Hammurabi Law Code 30 n. 157, 240

Hirsch 1952/53
36 151
38 151
43 151
49 151

HLC 3 162 157
Holma and Salonen 1940: no. 22 155

HSS 10
5 138
41 140
63 140
82 140
96 140
125 140
144 140
166 142
170 140
184 142

HT 21 7 n. 23
IM 61406 139
ITT 1 1079 141
ITT 1 1291 140
ITT 1/1 923 127
Jacobsen 1955: 107 no. 59 168
Jean 1948b: no. 11 252 n. 16
Jestin 1937: 750 131
Johns 1901: 4 54 n. 95
Johns 1901: 8 54 n. 95
Johns 1901: 15 54 n. 95
K.264 270 n. 40
K.4384 7 n. 24
KAH 2 80 141
KAV 1 141
KAV 202 119 n. 25

KBo
1 1 13, 14 n. 67, 6 n. 17, 6 n. 21
1 3 14 n. 67
1 11 4
3 60 1 n. 1, 2, 2 n. 6, 5, 6, 6 n. 17, 9, 11
4 14 5 n. 15

KTS 7a 11 n. 53
KTS 12 33 53
KTU 1 39 212 n. 4
KTU 1 46 212 n. 4
KUB 8 80 7 n. 23
KUB 36 71 5
Küchler 1904 136
Lambert 1970 135, 173

MAD 1
102 140
109 134
153 142

MAD 1 (cont'd.)
154 141
163 142
178 182
184 141
185 182
215 134
241 134
270 136
273 140
287 142
292 140
293 142
296 140
299 140
306 140
330 140
331 142

MAD 4 10 140
MAD 4 44 142
MAD 5 51 134
MAH 16158 37
MAM 1 p. 122 128, 131
MAM 2/1 p. 12 159

MAM 2/3 (by text no.)
146 59 n. 2
156 64 n. 21
157 64 n. 21
158 64 n. 21
159 64 n. 21
160 64 n. 21
162 70 n. 53
163 70 n. 53
164 70 n. 53
165 70 n. 53
166 70 n. 53
167 70 n. 53
194 66 n. 33
241 65 n. 30
247 59 n. 2
251 64 n. 21
252 64 n. 21
253 66 n. 31, 70 n. 53
254 73 n. 68
255 73 n. 69
256 66 n. 33

MAM 2/3 (by p. no.)
3–4 156
17–18 157

MAM 2/3 (cont'd.)
81 159
146–47 158
156–57 158
157–58 158
157 157
158 157
159 159
160 159

MAM 3 (by p. no.)
309 130, 131, 134, 149
310 131
311 131, 134, 135
312 131, 131, 134
314 132, 134
315 130, 131, 134, 148, 150
316 132, 134, 150
317 131, 148, 149, 150
318 130, 131, 131, 131, 134, 147, 148
319 130, 134, 141, 147
320 130, 134, 147
322 131, 147
323 131, 131, 134
324 131, 131
325 131, 141, 147
326 134, 141, 147
327 131, 131, 134
328 131, 131, 134, 149
329 130, 131, 131, 133, 134, 147
330 131, 133, 149
331 130
332 147
336 149

MAM 4 pp. 58–58 159
Man-ištušu Obelisk 161, 168
MCS 9/1 233 137, 140

MDP
2 A 161
2 1 168
14 6 142
14 24 142
14 25 142

ME
3 71 n. 55
14 158
16 71 n. 55, 66 n. 32
18 66 n. 33
20 71 n. 55
21 71 n. 55

ME (cont'd.)
27 71 n. 55
29 71 n. 55
31 71 n. 55
35 71 n. 55
36 71 n. 55
40 71 n. 55
48 71 n. 55
49 71 n. 55
54 72 n. 64
56 157
57 158
64 158
68 157
166 70 n. 54
170 73 n. 69
189 159
193 64 n. 19
194 159
197 159
213 159
220 66 n. 32
225 64 n. 19
272 65 n. 30

MEE 1
3 129
29 129
676 166
813 129
929 166
997 129
1046 129
1095 129
1124 166
1391 129
1649 166
1706 128
1728 128
2000 128
4174 134
4175 134
4176 134
4177 134
4178 134
4179 134
4180 134
4973 184

MEE 2 43 128, 247
MEE 2 p. 134 131
MEE 2 p. 135 131

MEE 3 134 182
MEE 3 156 182
Metr. Mus. 86.11.134 151
MSL 11 121 139

MVN
2 205 185
2 238 155
3 246 138
3 384 161

Nassouhi 1926 157
ND 2618 14 n. 68
ND 2640 15 n. 78

OBTTR
1 18 n. 94
4–5 48 n. 70
4 23 n. 126
18 13 n. 66
33 23 n. 126
68 48
79 49
100 49
122 46 n. 57
145 53
196 50
197 50
198 50
200 49
202 16 n. 82, 49
213 50
215 50
216 49, 49
251 38
277 62 n. 10
278 49
281 13 n. 66
319 49

OECT 2 1 (Weld-Blundell Prism) 248

OIP
14 58 127
14 92 141
14 117 142
14 165 140
47 41 127
99 508 135, 140
99 513 138, 140

Oppenheim 1948 161
Parrot 1936a 156
Parrot 1938: 16 159
Parrot 1955 151
Parrot 1964 133, 134, 174
Parrot 1965a: 15 no. 12 148
Parrot 1965a: 15 no. 13 129
Parrot 1965b 131, 133
PBS 9 119 141
PBS 13 1 248
PBS 13 27 151
PDTI 161 160
PDTI 594 155
Pettinato 1977b: no. 2 131
Pettinato 1981a 191
Peutinger Table 9 n. 41
Res Gestae (Ḫattušiliš I) 4, 5

RTC
106 140
117 140
133 127
215 139

Rutten 1938 (referred to as "liver" + no.)
1 170, 178, 181
1b 170, 187
2 170, 183, 186, 194
3 170, 171, 174, 190
3b 186
3e 170
4 170, 178, 181, 191, 192
4a 170
5 171, 174, 190
6 170, 171, 178, 183, 186, 190, 192
7 170, 173, 175, 176, 190, 192, 193, 194
8 170, 171, 179, 190, 193, 194
9 170, 171, 186, 190, 191, 194
10 170, 171, 173, 175, 176, 178, 179, 187, 190, 192, 193, 194
11a 170, 194
11b 155, 170, 171, 179, 190, 192, 193
12 170, 176
12a 171, 193
12b 192, 194
12c 176, 187
13a 170, 171, 186
13c 193
14 174, 175, 179, 183, 187, 191, 192, 193, 194
15a 191
16 170, 187, 190, 192
17 170, 175, 178, 190

Rutten 1938 (cont'd.)
18a 170, 174, 176, 177, 178, 179, 180, 191
18b 170, 171, 174, 176, 194
19 170, 171, 175, 176, 184, 185, 188, 191, 192, 194
20 193
21 194
21a 170
22 171, 175, 177, 187, 190, 192, 193
23 170, 171, 176, 180
24a 170, 171, 174, 179, 187, 194
24b 170, 171, 187
26 176
27b 170, 171, 175, 176, 178, 179, 187, 193
28 170, 177, 178, 179, 181, 191, 192
29 170, 171, 175, 176, 187, 190, 191
30a 169, 170, 171, 174, 178, 180, 192, 194
30b 170, 177
31 191
31a 169, 170, 171, 174, 175, 176, 177, 181, 184, 185, 188, 194, 187
31b 171, 178, 180, 192, 193, 194
31c 191
31d 170, 171, 174, 177, 180, 193, 194
31e 185
32a 171, 174, 181, 193, 194
32b 170, 171, 174, 177, 181, 194
33a 169
33b 170
34a 170
35 170, 175, 176
35b 170
36 187

Scheil 1921 139, 148
Scheil 1925 142
SET 59 156
Sollberger 1956 151
Sollberger 1960 161
Sollberger 1967 130, 131, 131, 134, 147, 149, 153, 155
Sumerian King List 123, 125, 126, 127, 128, 130, 131, 150, 201, 248
T 66 129
T 67 139
T 70 129
TA 1931.326 142
TC 1 18 45, 54
TC 2 57 36
TC 3/1 24 55
TC 3/2 163 35
TCL 1 237 184
TCL 5 6036 178
Thureau-Dangin 1907 127, 139
Thureau-Dangin 1934 130, 131, 133, 134, 148, 149, 150
Thureau-Dangin 1936 158
Thureau-Dangin 1937 157
TLB 1 43 261 n. 53
TLB 3 25 161
TM.75.G.101 247 n. 14
TM.75.G.1233 247
TM.75.G.1271 247 note to table
TM.75.G.1293 247
TM.75.G.1299 247
TM.75.G.1321 246 n. 13
TM.75.G.1368 247
TM.75.G.1564 247
TM.75.G.1657 247
TM.75.G.1866 247
TM.75.G.1953 245
TM.75.G.1987 247
TM.75.G.2235 246 n. 12
TM.75.G.2268 128
TM.75.G.10188 245 n. 10
TMH 5 80 151

TRU
47 156
52 156
227 156
230 156
342 157

Tukulti-Ninurta Epic 203 n. 1

UE 2
312 127
313 127
322 127
378 127

UET 1 12 127
VAT 9260 36, 38, 53
Walters, YNER 4 no. 43 189
W[arka] 199000 205 n. 6
Weidner, *RSO* 9 (1921/23) 161
Word List A (Ebla) 245 n. 11

SCRIPTURE

Genesis
10 236

Exodus
21–23 240

Numbers
32:21 214
32:22 214

Deuteronomy
8:3 266

Judges
15:19 266, 269 n. 36

Ruth
4:15 268, 269 n. 34, 269 n. 35, 269 n. 36

1 Samuel
30:12 266, 269 n. 36

2 Samuel
3:35 268 n. 23, 268 n. 24
5:6 214
8:3 214
12:17 268 n. 23, 268 n. 24
12:29 214

2 Kings
8:3 214
8:17 214
28:11 214

Psalms
19:8 266, 269 n. 34
23:3–4 265 n. 3
23:3 269 n. 33
23:3a 265–71

Proverbs
25:13 267, 269 n. 34

Isaiah
40:9 119
41:27 119
52:7 119

Jeremiah
16:7 268 n. 23

Lamentations
1:2 267 n. 18
1:9 267 n. 18
1:11 266, 266 n. 5, 267, 267 n. 18, 269 n. 33
1:13 267 n. 18
1:16 267, 267 n. 17, 267 n. 18, 269 n. 34, 269 n. 35
1:17 267 n. 18
1:19 266, 266 n. 5, 267, 267 n. 18, 269 n. 33
1:21 267 n. 18

Ezekiel
24:17 268 n. 23
24:22 268 n. 23

Language Index

ARABIC

ʾaḍdād 137
baḫara 141
ḥiṣn 31
ḥrṯ 138, 148
ġarasa 138
ġulām 138
fa 237
karada 15 n. 74
maʿdīn 12 n. 62

ARAMAIC (INCLUDING SYRIAC)

ʾīlān 31
g^{e}*mal* 10 n. 47
guryetā 15 n. 75
ḥōrā 9 n. 35
ḥrt 138
kark 7 n. 25
kēph(ā) 9 n. 35, 30, 31
rēš 31
šunar 10 n. 47
t^{e}*lūlē* 20 n. 104

AKKADIAN (INCLUDING EBLAITE, KISHITE, AND AMORITE, PLUS SEMITIC WORDS FOUND IN CUNEIFORM SOURCES)

-a 156, 163, 185
a-a-ab-ba 214
adî 155
aḫum 70
a-ia-ba 214
ʾajjûmme 186
akālum 205–6, 210
alākum 214
a-li 18
aluzinnum 168
-am 156, 163, 170, 171, 185
a-mu-ut 170, 173
ʾana 148, 149
a-na 150, 155, 171, 193
ʾa$_{x}$(NI)*-na* 163
a-na ma-ḫar 155
ʾannijum 186
appānum 208, 208 n. 17
asakkum 205–6, 205 n. 7, 210
aššatum 73 n. 68
áš-tu 193
a-ti 155
ʾawatum 169, 170
awīlum qallum 113

baʾālum 173
bābil tuppim 113
Ba-ḫi-ir 141, 143, 144
Baḫīrum 136, 141
baḫrum 141
baḫum 136
beʿālum 170
bêlatum 129, 148
beʿlum 170, 173, 204
bērū 47, 47 n. 68
bītum 61, 257
bussurum 113, 115, 116, 119

dabābum 204
dag-da-su 246 n. 11
dannum 65
da-núm 153

See the general index for words from *Egyptian*, *Hurrian*, and *Turkish*.

/dariʾātim/ 170
daššupum 177
dātum 40–41, 42–43, 52, 56, 56 n. 106
duššupum 177, 191

ebbum 249–64
ebbūtum 249–64
ʿebdum 149
elîm 50
ellu 249
elûm 50, 55
emmum 136
endan 17 n. 87
esēkum 264 n. 63
eširtum 53

gab(a)ʾu 8 n. 31, 49
Ga-da-ad 142
gajjum 132, 151, 194
Ga-mi-iš 146
gāmirum 70
Gaśśum 138
gazāzum 138
/Gazzum/ 142
Gi-um 138
gur- 15
gūru 15 n. 75

Ḫa-bi-in-gal-ba-ti-i 4 n. 12
Ḥalîtum 138
ḫalṣum 6 n. 22, 50
Ḫa-lu(l)-ut 142
Ḫa-ni-kal-bat 4 n. 12
Ḫapiru 23–24
ḫasāsum 203, 203 n. 3
ḫâšum 270 n. 40
ḫi-bi 153
ḫimêtum 138
Ḥiriśatum 138
ḥnn 159
Ḫu-lu-mu 146
Ḫur-mu 146

-ī 149
I-ba₄-sa 139
I-ba-ša-áš 139
igisûm 269–71
ig-za 137
iG-zum 136
ikṣûm 136
iku 168
ik-zum 136
Ì-la-mu 146
ilān 31
ʾilum 158, 213 n. 12
ʾin 171
in 150, 193
ì-na 148
/ʿIrīśa/ 143
I-rí-sá 138
Ir-me 146
-iš 193
iš 150, 171, 193
iššiʾakum 69, 69 n. 49
iś(ś)um 136

jaśibum 178
jašibum 178
/Jiqṣa/ 142
Jiqṣum 136
jiśruk 147
jizziz 147
jkṣ 136

karadû 15 n. 74
kardû 15 n. 74
Karḫ 7 n. 25
/karmē/ 170
kārum 53, 54 n. 92, 56
Kaśśum 138
kaššum 53
kaṣûm 136
kazāzum 138
kīnu 249
ki-ra-ab 170
kirâdu 15 n. 74
kiṣʾum 136
Kiʾum 138
krd 15
kùr 14 n. 67
kurādu 15 n. 74

lá 194
lamassu 259
lapātum 169, 195, 204
lāsimum 113
li-im 166, 182
Lilliatum 208
liʾmum 195
liptu 204–5, 207
luliu 11 n. 53
lulû 11 n. 53
lulutu 11 n. 53

-ma 18, 141
ma 194
maḫar 141, 147
maḫ-rí 155
maḫrijum 141
maliktum 129, 148, 194
malkum 129, 148, 194
māmītu 203 n. 1
man 149, 186
mannum 149
maprās 176
marpiqatum 72, 72 n. 63
mār šiprim 113
mārum 74 n. 72
mārum qallum 113
masājum 166, 195
massû 37, 39, 40, 53 n. 89
mātum 20, 47, 55
mazāʾum 166, 195
me-at 129, 166, 182, 194, 195
mi 149
milku 170, 177
mubassirū 113–20
mubbibū 253, 263
Mu-ma-a-a 12

namru 249
napištum 204–5, 271
naptanum 208, 208 n. 17
narāmum 65, 66, 68, 69, 72, 73, 74
narpiqatum 72 n. 63
nêšum 203 n. 1
nikkassū 251
nindabûm 145
nīqum 208
nīsum 203–10
nubattū 51 n. 80
nuḫatimmum 270, 271

pāliḫum 70 n. 51
paqādu(m) 252, 252 n. 17, 255, 255 n. 27, 258
parrusum 150
pašāšum 139, 169
pum 127, 158
purrusum 150

qabûm 203
Qaśśum 138
qaṭṭurum 150
qātu 48
qīpu 249
qirbu(m) 155, 177
qiṣjum 136
Qiʾum 138

rāb 24 n. 130
rabiš 213 n. 14
rabium 213 n. 14
raḫatum 195
rākibum 113
ramāku 214, 215 n. 20
raʾšijum 139
raʾštijum 139
raʾšum 139
rí-ba-at 182
ribb 182
rimku 215 n. 20
rittum 166
rpq 72
/rubāʾum/ 170
ru-si 166

sá 170
sāmūkānum 178
sá-ni-en 166
sasqû 208, 208 n. 17
si 170
-su 157, 163
sugāgū 255

Ṣaʾattum 138, 142
ṣābu 119
ṣaḫrum 177, 181
Ṣaliltum 138
ṣalmum 147
ṣiḫum 170
ṣll 139
ṣūr 31
ṣurā 31
ṣwr 25

śakānum 170
śamś 134
śaʾnum 195
-śarr 135
śarratum 148
śarru(m) 129, 135, 148
śiṭru 177
-śu 148, 149

šaḫluqtum 192
šakānum 204

šakinte 32
šakkanakku(m) 64, 152, 161
šaknum 61, 64, 65, 66, 69, 70 n. 51, 72, 73
Ša-ni-i 142, 144
šāpiṭum 51 n. 82
šaplānu 48
šênum 166
šêrtum 182
šîbum 130, 147
šiṭir šamê 155
šiṭirti šamâmî 155
šiṭrum 155, 170
-šu 157, 163, 176
šu 170, 186
šuḫurrurum 192
šu-ut 170, 176

taklum 263 n. 62
tamûm 203
Taš-ni-tim$_x$ 142
tebibtum 253
tēru(m) 142
tiʾamtum 213
tillu 20 n. 104
Ti-ru 142
-tum 150
tuppum 208
tûra- 156
turgamanum 4 n. 12
turrum 269–71

-ū 170
ú 163, 194
ʾu 148, 172
ubbubum 263, 255 n. 30
-um 146, 147
ummatum 215 n. 24
/ʾurāṣum/ 177
uridū 71
ù-šu-rí 128

wabālum 113
wabartum 54 n. 97
wābil tuppim 113
warassu 64 n. 20
wardūm 64 n. 20, 260
warkijum 140, 141
warkum 65, 139
waṣāʾum 170
wšr 128

Za-ʾà-tum 138
zakārum 203
Za-nar 139
zannarum 139

EARLY NORTHWEST SEMITIC (INCLUDING UGARITIC AND THE LANGUAGE OF THE BYBLIAN SYLLABIC TEXTS)

iln 31
zbl 211
ḥlt 138
ḫrš 138
ym 211, 211 n. 2
krd 15 n. 74
-ma 238
mdd 211
mi 149
mn ḥlt 144
nšʾ 237
pa 237
rḥt 166
ṯpṭ nhr 211

HEBREW AND PHOENICIAN

ʾēlōn 31
ʾummah 215, 215 n. 24
ʾaf 237
hlk 214
ḥsd 240
yqṣ 136
yšʿ 240
yšr 158
layil 182
m^ebaśśēr 119
my 149
mnḥm 268
nḥm 268
npš 265–71
nqm 240
nśʾ 237

ṣdq 240
ṣō᾽n 138
ṣūr 31
qyṣ 136
qṣy 136
rwḥ 266
rḥt 166
šwb 265–71
šaḥar 182
šybh 268
šēm 240
špṭ 240
tehôm 215

SUMERIAN

a-a-ab-ba 213
A.AB.BA 214
AB+ÁŠ 147
AB×ÁŠ.AB×ÁŠ 245
AL 157
AMA 4 n. 8
AMAR 132
AN 213 n. 12
AN.BU 126

d [divine determinative] 133, 148
DAM 128, 148
DAM.A.NI 62
DINGER 204
DÙL 147
DUMU 70 n. 54, 147
DUMU LUGAL 155
DUMU.MAḪ.LÍL 4, 6
DUMU.NITA 147

egi$_x$ 246 n. 11
e-gi$_4$-maškim.e-gi$_4$-maškim 245
É.MES 161
EN 126, 127, 129, 131, 148, 244–45, 244 n. 8, 246
EN$_5$.SI.GAL 133
ERÍN 4 n. 12, 119

GAL 24 n. 130
GAL.KUD 206
GAR 32
GÉ 4 n. 9
GÌR.NITA 156, 161, 162

ḪA 128
ḪÚB.TI.LÁ 117–18

ì . . . ag 168
ÍD 134
IGI.ME 147
Ì.GUB 147
INANNA 20 n. 107
IN.PÁD.BA.DÈ.MEŠ 205
in UD.UD 246
Ì.NUN 145
ÌR-ZU 64 n. 20
ITI 143
IZI.GAR 145

kag . . . dú 168
KI [place determinative] 149
KIN.URI 131
KIŠIB 72
KUG.DÍM 129
KUR 14 n. 67

LAM 126, 131
LI 145
LÍL 4 n. 9
LÚ 155, 156, 157, 159, 160, 161, 162, 163, 164, 249–64
LUGAL 69, 126, 127, 129, 131, 147, 155, 160, 161, 162, 204, 244–45, 246, 247
lú kas$_4$-e-gi$_4$ 245 n. 11

MAḪ 128
MARTU 235
MÁŠ.ŠU.SÙ.SÙ 61
MU 147

NÁ 248
NI 170, 248
NÍG.BA 129, 245
NÌ.GUB 61
NIN 126, 129, 131, 148

PA.AL 245 n. 11
PAB.GÁ 148

SAG 139, 144
SAG.ḪÚB.DU 147
SAR 206 n. 11

SIG$_7$ 139, 144
SILÁ 4 n. 8, 168
SIMUG 62 n. 10

šabra 245 n. 11
šu-ra 247

Ú 157
UGULA 260
ugula máḫ 245 n. 11
ugula nagar 245 n. 11
URI.KIN 131
UTU 134

ZU 18

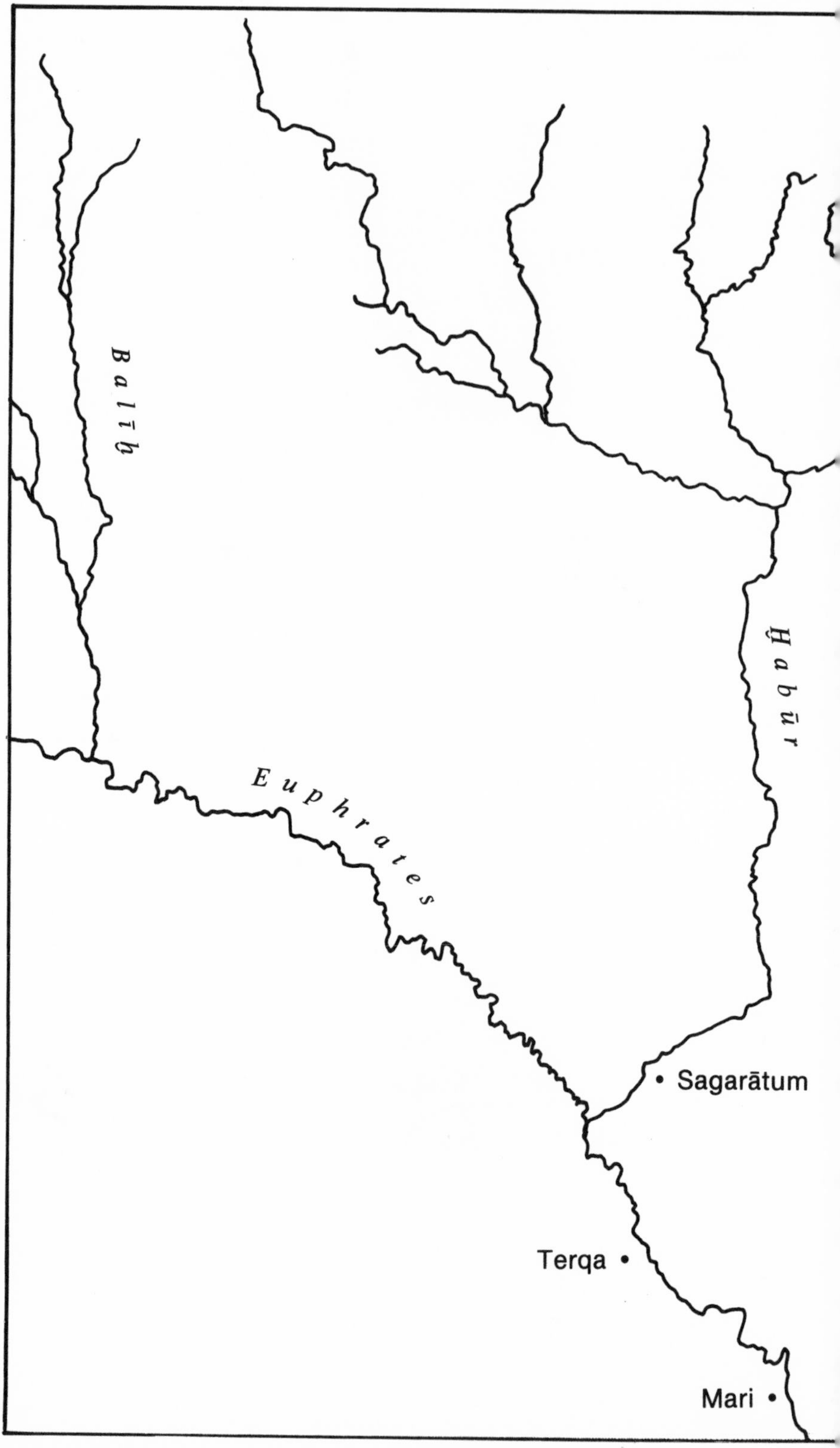
Balīḫ
Euphrates
Ḫabūr
Sagarātum
Terqa
Mari